EDUCATION ACROSS CULTURES

Second Edition

MILES V. ZINTZ
Professor of Education

The University of New Mexico
Albuquerque, New Mexico

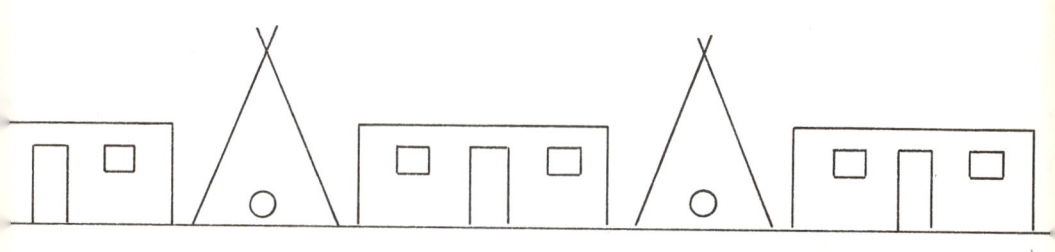

KENDALL/HUNT PUBLISHING COMPANY
DUBUQUE, IOWA

Copyright © 1963, 1969 by
Miles V. Zintz

Library of Congress Catalog Card Number: 63-22647

SBN 8403−0007−7

All rights reserved. No part of this book may be reproduced in any form or by any process without permission in writing from the copyright owner.

Printed in the United States of America

Acknowledgements

The problem of education across cultures in the Southwest has been a serious one for decades and will continue to be for some time. Only through the combined efforts of many educators will progress be made.

I am indebted to Dr. Loyd Tireman for introducing me to the many educational problems in New Mexico and for initiating the research proposal which led to many of the studies reported here. His thirty-two years of service which terminated with his death in 1959, included reading testing programs, the San Jose Experimental School, and the Nambe Community School. I am also indebted to Dr. Frank Angel, whose professional career has been devoted to the alleviation of the problems rooted in the culture, language, and experience barriers for minority group children.

Many graduate students have shaped my thinking and have evaluated the ideas embodied in this text. Their efforts are appreciated. A few must be mentioned personally: Dr. Horacio Ulibarri, Dr. Le Roy Condie, Dr. Hitoshi Ikeda, Dr. Carol Charles, Dr. Jean Luse Legant, Dr. Joyce Morris, Edward Marinsek, Sophie Thompson, Maryanne Danfelser, Charles Sanchez, and Kathryn Polacca. My greatest indebtedness is undoubtedly to Mrs. Arlene Cameron who helped edit the manuscript and worked indefatigably to complete the typing.

Miles V. Zintz
July, 1969

Table of Contents

Chapter		Page
	List of Tables and Figures	vii

PART ONE

1.	Educating Minority Groups: An Introduction	3
2.	Foundations for Educating Minority Groups	35
3.	The Background of the Middle-Class Teacher	79
4.	Social Institutions Across Cultures and the Acculturation Process	106
5.	Bicultural Problems in Relation to School Achievement	131

PART TWO

6.	Foundations for Educating Navajo Children	165
7.	Foundations for Educating Pueblo Indian Children	187
8.	Foundations for Education of Spanish American Children	220

PART THREE

9.	Teaching English as a Second Language	253
10.	The Problem of Vocabulary	297
11.	Counseling the Indian Student	347
12.	Adjusting the Curriculum	359
13.	Unsolved Problems	388

Appendices			Page
	PART FOUR		
A	An Autobiography		413
B	A Spanish Culture in Transition		430
C	Ways of Working With the Navajos Who Have Not Learned the White Man's Ways		445
D	Reading List for Retarded Readers		462
E	Tests		471
	1. A Reading Test		473
	2. Multiple Meanings Test		485
Bibliography			490
Author Index			531
Subject Index			537

Tables and Figures

Table		Page
I.	Barriers to Successful School Achievement for Bilingual-Bicultural Children.	27
II.	Foundations for Judging Pupil Behavior in the Classroom.	71
III.	Scale of Acculturation: Spanish American to Anglo	114
IV.	Leading Causes of Death Among Navajos and Comparative U. S. General Population Rates, 1954	117
V.	"L" County Rural Schools Survey	134
VI.	Age-Grade Distributions, Albuquerque Area, 1951: Indian Children in Federal Schools and Public Schools in Grade 5	135
VII.	Mean Chronological Ages and Reading Grade-Placement Scores by Ethnic Groups, April, 1960: Gates Reading Survey Test	136
VIII.	Grade Placement Scores and Ratings by Schools: Gilmore Oral Reading Test, Form A, Spring, 1959	138
IX.	Summary by Ethnic Groups, Gilmore Oral Reading Test, Form A, Spring, 1959	139
X.	Median Raw Scores and Percentile Ranks, New Standard Vocabulary Test, Form A, November, 1958	140
XI.	Percentile Ratings of 326 Eleventh-Grade Students in Multi-Cultural Classrooms: Diagnostic Reading Test, Survey Section, Spring, 1960	141

Table		Page
XII.	Percentile Ratings of 232 Twelfth-Grade Students in Multi-Cultural Classrooms: Diagnostic Reading Test, Survey Section, Spring, 1960	141
XIII.	Anglo-Pueblo Cultural Values in Conflict	210
XIV.	Diagnostic Test for Students of English as a Second Language: Performance of 53 Mescalero Apache Students--Grades 7-12, February, 1958	304
XV.	Diagnostic Test for Students of English as a Second Language Performance of 33 Practical Nursing Students: April, 1958	304
XVI.	Results of Diagnostic Test for Students of English as a Second Language, University of New Mexico, June, 1960	305
XVII.	Mean and Median Scores and Standard Deviations by Grades on the Idioms Test, Spring, 1959	307
XVIII.	Statistical Differences Between Ethnic Groups and Norming Group on the Idioms Test, Spring, 1959	307
XIX.	Percentile Norms for the Yandell-Zintz Idioms Test of 90 Items. Based on Raw Scores Earned by 237 Sixth Grade Students in Albuquerque, 1959	309
XX.	Results of the Zintz-Yandell Idioms Test of 90 Items, Gallup-McKinley County Grade, May, 1967, Percentile Ranks By Ethnic Groups	310
XXI.	Performance of Gallup-McKinley County Sixth Grade on an Idioms Test in May, 1967	311
XXII.	Comparison of Average Scores on the Multiple Meanings Test by Ethnic Groups of Sixth Grade Students	314
XXIII.	Antonyms Used in Elementary School Textbooks	333
XXIV.	Homonyms Used in Elementary School Textbooks	335
XXV.	Prepositions in the English Language	339

Figure

1.	The class structure in middle-sized communities.	85
2.	Behavior in Society	109
3.	Navajo Reservation and Peripheral Area	166
4.	Grade Achievement Level of Population 25 Yrs. and Over.	182
5.	Indian Pueblos of New Mexico.	188
6.	Language Patterns among the Pueblo Indians	192
7.	Instructional Aids for teaching English language concepts to Indian children	317
8.	Twenty prepositions that have to do with position or direction in space	338
9.	Time expenditure schedule for Alfred Begay.	353
10.	Relationship of local community to world community.	373
11.	Social interaction in a tri-cultural fifth-grade classroom	392

Oh, our mother, the earth, oh, our father, the sky,
Your children are we, with tired backs
We bring you the gifts that you love.
Then weave for us a garment of brightness,
May the warp be of the white light of morning,
May the weft be of the red light of evening,
May the fringes be the falling rain,
May the border be the standing rainbow.
Thus weave for us a garment of brightness.
That we may walk fittingly where birds sing,
That we may walk fittingly where grass is green,
Oh, our mother, the earth, our father, the sky.

from the Jicarilla Apache.

Part One

CHAPTER 1

Educating Minority Groups: An Introduction

A NEW TEACHER IS TROUBLED

Mary crossed the plaza between the two wings of the elementary school and went down the newly finished street to her efficiency apartment. It was five o'clock and Mary was exhausted. Usually, she would have been running over in her mind what she might have for dinner that she could get together without too much work. Besides, this was Tuesday so she needed to do her hair before she went to bed. None of these things was uppermost in Mary's mind tonight. Only six days of school had gone by this September, but to Mary it had seemed interminably long. Was she or wasn't she a fourth-grade teacher? Upon arriving at the apartment, she lay down on the davenport and let her mind relive a decisive bit of the past.

Last February in southern Iowa where Mary was finishing her third year of teaching in the fourth grade in the county seat, she had decided that she needed a change. Yes, she had been very successful according to both her own evaluation and that of her supervising principal. She had worked hard and really enjoyed teaching. Change was what she needed, however. And now that she had had her degree for three years, maybe she should go to summer school. The teacher's college had not done badly getting her ready for that fourth, but it certainly had not said anything about this one!

Mary could have gotten an overseas job teaching American dependent children. France, Spain, Japan, Germany? Her aunt in Phoenix had written about teaching in the Indian Service in Arizona. Mary had heard, too, that the ratio of men to women was higher in the west, and she was twenty-four. So she completed Form 57 and sent it to the Branch of Education of the Office of Indian Affairs. Her appointment was mailed to her early in June, and her assignment was to teach fourth grade in a Bureau School in the Rio Grande Valley in New Mexico. She was sent information about the Indian Service and was told to report early in August for an orientation program in order to get ready to teach on September 1.

Mary wondered if there weren't something she should have studied in summer school that would have been of more help to her now. In her first summer in graduate school, she had taken Research Methods in Education, Elementary School Curriculum, and History of Education.

The orientation program which was planned by the Indian Service seemed somehow small and remote now that she had tried for six days to teach the fourth grade the way she had always done it in Iowa. One lecturer had talked at length about the cultural differences. Mary felt that she understood what he was talking about pretty well. There were strange people in southern Iowa who certainly had behavior patterns different from those of her family. Even while that anthropologist had been talking, her mind wandered off to some of the strange expressions in English she had heard in Iowa. In her own home town there was a lady who used funny expressions like "He was as addled as a goose in a hailstorm." And one day when one little boy wanted to do something with the bigger ones, she had said, "Why, he's no bigger than a pound of soap after a week's wash." Mary wondered if the Indian children would say things like these. Until now, she had not supposed that they would not say anything at all!

One of the speakers had mentioned pediculosis as being apt to make its appearance in the classroom. This was the health educator from the United States Public Health Service. Mary knew that this was a fancy name for having lice, and lice had never been part of her own personal background of experience. She did remember teachers back home who were assigned to teach across the railroad tracks, and they had learned to comb the nits out of children's hair and wash it with kerosene. But then, in a lighter vein, Mary remembered a rousing round they used to sing at Methodist Youth Camp that went like this:

"There may be cooties on some of you beauties
But there ain't no cooties on us.

"There may be bugs on some of you mugs
But there ain't no bugs on us."

By then the speaker had gone on to say something about the possibility that these children might need to be taught not to spit on the floor. This explained cultural differences, and anyway, hadn't everybody had a three-semester hour course in Principles of Sociology? Mary's puzzlement, at this point, suggested that she needed additional orientation.

One of the supervisors had reminded the teachers that they might find a different set of moral standards among the people in the villages from those they had known at home. But Mary had known some girls in southern Iowa who had "gotten into trouble," and one family right in her neighborhood had six children, three of whom were married less than the usual time before their first children were born. Anyway, the way Mary felt tonight, she could not see of what great importance that had in relation to her work.

The principal of the school had shown her all the standard texts and closets of supplies that were available to her. There certainly was no shortage of fourth-grade textbooks, workbooks, and teaching materials ordered for her use. She quickly had counted many copies of six different fourth-grade readers in the cupboard where they were neatly shelved.

Then the children had come. Mary had struggled through roll call and had had some difficulty understanding their names (Aguilar, Calabaza, Armijo, Jaramillo) even when they said them quickly in their staccato, chopped speech. She noticed immediately that when she asked any child a question, she got a short, chopped-off "Yes," and invariably that ended the conversation.

She had, of course, tried "Sharing Time," since all her little midwestern Anglos had acted as though they not only enjoyed talking, but also as if they could talk all day without running out of things to tell. But when no one here had anything to share, she had asked her neighbor-teacher of some years experience what she did about that. But the teacher had just said, "They won't talk. Anyway, they wouldn't want to let you in on the village secrets." So Mary had decided to let "Sharing Time" drop for a while, at least until she got to know the children better.

She had discussed the group intelligence test scores of the children with the principal and had been told that, while these scores were low, the tests were culturally biased, so that they probably had more ability than the test showed. The average IQ of 83 bothered Mary somewhat because that meant that they were almost all dull normal and some were really retarded. What could one possibly teach a child with an IQ of 67 in a regular room? Where she came from, they had special rooms for such children.

Mary was not sure what "culturally biased" meant, either, but she did know that performance on any test required some background of experience that would make concepts meaningful before one could check right answers. Anyway, Mary decided, it did not help much to know that tests were culturally biased if they were given anyway, and then no one knew what to do about the biases.

The readers in her room were quite familiar to her so she thought that a "Quick Class Survey"[1] would be easy to get the group broken down into those who could read the reader and those who could not. When she asked each child to read a sentence or two around the circle, after she had given them a synopsis of the story, only two girls could really pronounce the words to her satisfaction. Then, they were so shy, so withdrawn, so unwilling to hold their heads up and look at her, that Mary was not sure that they even did as well as they otherwise might have.

Mary's disappointment grew when she asked them to write sentences using some of the words that had been in the story and which they had talked about together. Some of the sentences they wrote were:

"The bird will make a <u>honest</u>." (nest)
"I <u>guilty</u> wash the dishes, then I watch TV." (quickly)
"I just had an <u>examining</u>." (examination)
"The <u>ashamed</u> means trouble of our self." (to feel shame?)

When Mary tried to talk to the class about their work for the coming year, she had not been able to get any response either. Once she had had a suspicion that the girls thought it would be wrong for them to talk first, that the boys should do that. Then she felt once that most of the boys looked to Antonio before they shared anything with her. Maybe he was their leader. He was older and the biggest boy in the room.

The children talked "Indian" a great deal on the playground. Mary had not known quite what to say about that. Since the boys and girls seemed so distant and cool toward her, she was sure that if she scolded them for not talking English, that would only make matters worse. She had tried a few times to "require answers in complete sentences," as she had been instructed to do. But this only meant greater avoidance of situations requiring language.

By now, Mary was not sure, but she felt that the other teachers were not being much more successful than she. They were just "putting up with it." The other fourth-grade teacher had even gone ahead the second day of school and issued each child a full set of fourth-grade textbooks to keep in his desk. Mary was sure now that at least half of her children had fairly good basic sight vocabularies, but that they could read reasonably well from only the second reader.

At least Mary knows that she is in trouble. She had learned where her children are, and is willing to start there. She had not yet resigned herself merely to "putting up with" her charges. But Mary does need help.

She has never had to face the fact before that her outlook on life, all the things she believes in as the "right" things, the "best" things, the "good" things, may not be valued exactly this way by others. She has never faced the fact before that what is "success" for her will not necessarily be "success" for other people. She must realize, too, that there are many people who may not want someone like a conscientious school teacher to come along with a missionary zeal to give them all the "good things" in life.

Mary is naive, too, about the fact that these Indian children have parents or grandparents who may suspect that what she really wants to do is take away their language, their values, their age-old customs and to make the children over into "little school teachers!"

As she rose to get some supper in response to subconscious twinges of hunger, Mary wondered in what areas lay the answers to her dilemma? It is more psychology, or more sociology, or anthropology? The speaker at the orientation had been introduced as a cultural anthropologist. There really must be answers.

WHO ARE THE MINORITY GROUPS?

Brophy and Aberle report a 1960 census total of 523,591 Indians in the United States.[2] The states of California, Arizona, New Mexico, Colorado, Utah, and Nevada, which also have large populations of Spanish-speaking people, have a total Indian population of 196,586 or 38% of the total. When Oklahoma is included with these states of the Southwest, about half of the American Indian population is accounted for.

Spanish-Americans in the Rio Grande Valley of New Mexico and the San Luis Valley of Colorado are the direct descendants of the Spanish conquistadores who followed Coronado. Large numbers of these people still live in this region. They constitute between 30% and 40% of the total population of the state of New Mexico. In perhaps a half-dozen counties in northern New Mexico, these Spanish surname families constitute more than 90% of the population there.

Their ancestors came from Spain via Mexico City into the Rio Grande Valley and established San Gabriel as the capitol of Nuevo Mejico in 1598. The capital of the territory was moved to Santa Fe in 1609. So far removed from Mexico City, they maintained little direct contact either politically or religiously, and this little enclave existed for some 150 years as a separate, self-sufficient, agrarian culture.

The 1960 census showed that 2,793,000 Mexican aliens were admitted to the United States as agricultural workers.[3] These workers migrate to many states during the crop seasons but the majority have until recent times, spent the winters in California, Arizona, and Texas. A map showing the travel patterns of seasonal migratory agricultural workers is shown in this section.

Annual School Census Report of Indian Children for Administrative Areas of the Bureau of Indian Affairs, Fiscal Year 1966.*

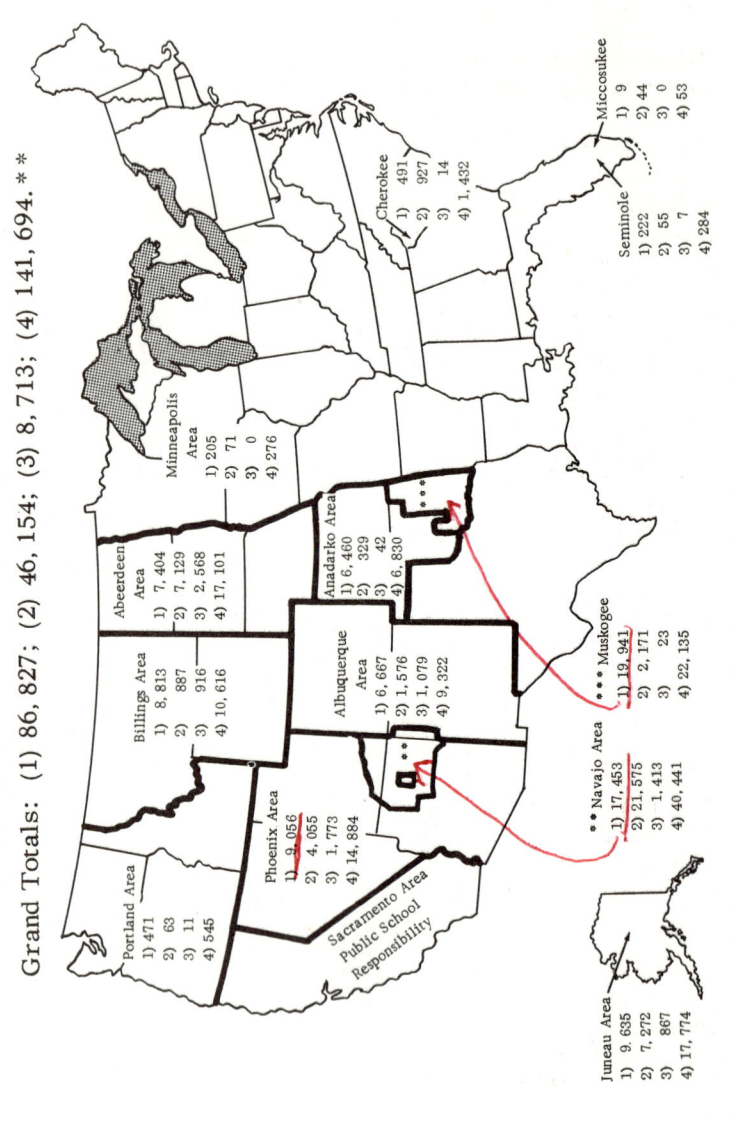

Grand Totals: (1) 86,827; (2) 46,154; (3) 8,713; (4) 141,694.**

Portland Area
1) 471
2) 63
3) 11
4) 545

Billings Area
1) 8,813
2) 887
3) 916
4) 10,616

Aberdeen Area
1) 7,404
2) 7,129
3) 2,568
4) 17,101

Minneapolis Area
1) 205
2) 71
3) 0
4) 276

Anadarko Area
1) 6,460
2) 329
3) 42
4) 6,830

Albuquerque Area
1) 6,667
2) 1,576
3) 1,079
4) 9,322

Phoenix Area
1) 9,056
2) 4,055
3) 1,773
4) 14,884

***Navajo Area
1) 17,453
2) 21,575
3) 1,413
4) 40,441

****Muskogee
1) 19,941
2) 2,171
3) 23
4) 22,135

Cherokee
1) 491
2) 927
3) 14
4) 1,432

Seminole
1) 222
2) 55
3) 7
4) 284

Miccosukee
1) 9
2) 44
3) 0
4) 53

Sacramento Area Public School Responsibility

Juneau Area
1) 9,635
2) 7,272
3) 867
4) 17,774

*Division of Education, Bureau of Indian Affairs, Fiscal Year 1966, Statistics Concerning Indian Education, (Lawrence, Kansas: Haskell Institute, 1966).
**(1) Public School Enrollment; (2) Federal School Enrollment; (3) Mission School Enrollment; (4) Total Enrollment All Schools.

Scholes says,

> the most important group within our seasonal agricultural labor force has been the Spanish-speaking persons.[4]

He continues:

> These are the people who have been a backbone of the seasonal agricultural labor force in the Southwest for over sixty years.[5]

Scholes reports that approximately 182,000 migrants, based on records of the Texas Employment Commission or the Bureau of Labor Statistics, migrated to thirty-seven other states from Texas in 1964.[6]

Day and Edshammar report:

> Idaho is an eddy into which some of the nation's 400,000 migrant workers spill from two of the three great migratory routes. One leads from Southern California up the Pacific Coast into Oregon and Washington, following the path of the ripening crops. Another goes up the spine of the Rockies from New Mexico into Montana. The third goes from Florida through the Middle Atlantic and Midwestern states into New England.[7]

TRAVEL PATTERNS OF SEASONAL MIGRATORY AGRICULTURAL WORKERS

This map shows the major directions of the northward migratory movement of domestic agricultural workers. The movement is reversed as the crop season ends in the northern States and the workers drift back to their home-base areas--for many of them, southern California, Texas and Florida.

Southern Negroes predominate among the agricultural migrants in the East Coast States and U. S. citizens of Mexican ancestry in the other States. In addition, low-income southern white families, Puerto Ricans, and Indians are found in the domestic agricultural migrant population.

Domestic Agricultural Migrants in the United States, (U. S. Government Printing Office: Public Health Service Publication No. 540, Revised August, 1966.)

The Anglo-American, referred to as the Anglo, came to the Southwest in large numbers after the Civil War. All the various nationalities of immigrants who came to America rather quickly freed themselves from their previous national and language backgrounds, and fitted into the social class structure that is Anglo-America. They hastened to master English as the language of the land and to meld into the great American melting pot. Many of these people refused to allow their children to learn the mother tongue so that they would more quickly be assimilated into the great, new country to which they had come.

The Spanish Americans and the Indians were satisfied with their languages and cultures, and they felt the intrusion of the Anglos was aggressive and insulting. They largely rejected both the new behavior and the new language, and did not accept the new way of life that began settling about them in the 1870's.

When one considers the problems of formal education, the children of these Southwest minority groups present themselves geographically as (1) completely stable people in permanent villages, (2) isolated rural people who must be housed in dormitories throughout the school year, and (3) migrant, nomadic people who move into town and stay a few weeks or, at most, a few months and then move again. A whole set of alien cultural values, a foreign language from the point of view of the public school, and educational retardation that is unacceptable in the rigid grade placement patterns of public school procedures, create problems for which the school system has made inadequate provision.

P.L. 815, making available federal money for building schools in areas of "Federal Impact," was first used in the Southwest in the early 1950's. With amendments to P.L. 815 in 1953, it was directed toward a great deal of school building construction for Indian children. P.L. 874 provided for local districts to be reimbursed with federal money for educating Indians in public schools. As these laws became operative, public school authorities began to make public school facilities available for all Indian children and youth in their districts. This need had been recognized because evidence accumulated through the years showed that Indian children demonstrated serious educational retardation on tests of academic achievement.[8] Further, Indian children in public schools performed significantly better than did Indian children in schools operated by the Bureau of Indian Affairs, or in schools operated by various religious missions. Also, segregation of Indian children in schools for Indians only became less and less acceptable as a means of giving all children equal opportunity for self-realization in the larger society.

While the Spanish-speaking people have always been accommodated in the public schools, test data indicates that, on the average, they have not achieved as well as their potential suggests. They also need special educational services to counteract barriers in their cultural background, language differences, and lack of experiences common to Anglo children if they are to succeed in school.

According to Pei, when the population of the United States was about 175,000,000 in 1955, there were 22,000,000 people in the country for whom English was, at best, a second language.[9] Many of these people knew very little English. In other words, about 12 1/2 per cent of the population is handicapped in the fluent use of the language of the land in which they live. The minority groups of the Southwest constitute a sizable proportion of this 12 1/2 per cent. Lack of fluency in the dominant tongue is one basic factor underlying educational retardation.

ACCEPTING CULTURAL DIFFERENCES

Prejudices toward the American Indian have existed in the thinking of the Anglo throughout American history.[10] Anglos labeled the Indian in terms of their relationships with him. When the colonists came to New England and needed the help and support of the Indian who befriended them, who taught them to plant and who loaned them food from their storehouses, the settlers named these kind people "Noble Savages." Later, in the settling of this country, Anglos wanted the lands of the first Americans. Because the Indians felt called upon to defend their own homelands, they became known as "Treacherous Savages." When the Anglos dominated the entire country, the Indians were confined to reservations. As they became dependent upon Anglo care and as they submitted to Anglo decision-making, they were more than once referred to as "Filthy Savages."

The Indian people are now at the threshold of achieving for themselves desirable economic and social status in the American society. Will the Anglos fear them as competitors and hail them as "Incompetent Savages," or will they face realistically the unjust and improper status accorded the Indian population in times of stress and tension in the past, making sure that every Indian is afforded his individual opportunity to win status in the dominant culture?

The Anglo, generally, has only poorly understood the place of the American Indian in national history. He has grown up with many prejudices that influence him to believe that the Indians were savage, treacherous, and deceitful. The American Indian has been rigidly stereotyped by many of his fellow citizens. The raiding done by a small number of Apaches in the eighteenth and nineteenth centuries in the Southwest has provided a tremendous amount of melodrama for the motion picture and television industries. The history lessons learned by many Anglos have included the notion that "the only good Indian was a dead Indian." The negative attitude that prevailed in colonial times persisted through the years, as is indicated in the report of J. Madison Cutts to the United States Army about 1850 in which he says of the Apache Indians:

> Every Apache is a born robber and murderer. Extermination, whether in war or under the form of reservations and legal justice, is their certain fate; and the quickest way is the most merciful.[11]

Recent authors have used a more reasonable tone to point out philosophical differences between the Indian and the Anglo. Reifel, in his analysis of cultural factors in social adjustment, had summarized four main differences between the American way of life and the traditional pattern of the Plains Indians.

1. In the American way of life, those of us who are carried along in its social stream are future-oriented. We think in terms of what is ahead. In contrast, those whose lives are governed by the values of the Indian life are oriented to the present; they are prone to live in the present -- the "Exultation of the now." The non-Indian life is one of "conquest over nature" as against the Indian way of "harmony in nature." Another way of comparing them is to describe the former as existing in a state of anticipation, while the latter finds nothing to look forward to and feels that the essence of living is to be found in the present timelessness.

2. Time, in the sense of measuring duration by clocks and days-of-the-week calendars as we do, is not important to the person caught in the Indian way of life.

3. Saving as a means to achieve economic development has not been a part of the economic life of the Indian in his nomadic state where he lived largely by hunting and food gathering (direct appropriation).

4. Habituation to hard work, including drudgery for over a period of years, if necessary to earn a living, was not in the Indian system, particularly for the men.[12]

Adair and Deuschle describe some of the problems of the inexperienced physician who has not come to know the cultural practices of the Navajo Indians: [13]

> The doctor may be baffled by the refusal of a patient's relatives to donate blood for indicated surgery or the treatment of anemia. He may not realize that the concepts of sympathetic and contagious magic are still strongly believed in by most of the Navajos. In this instance, if the patient were to die, then the donor of the blood might also sicken and die.

. . . The harried physician may be chagrined to discover that the hours of precious time he spent convincing the husband of one of his patients to continue hospital treatment had been completely wasted. The family member who really wielded the power of decision in this matter -- the patient's grandmother -- had been directed to the waiting room to sit while the parley had taken place.

He may fail to understand the "request for medical leave" from the sanatorium by a patient who wants to go home for a "sing," which is a Navajo healing ceremony.[14]

. . .

He may ask the ward orderly to take care of a corpse, and get an outright refusal; or if the order is carried out, the orderly may request the following day off so that the correct ritual may be performed to cleanse the body of the evil that comes from close associations with the dead.[15]

The Navajos do not have the same concept of time as we have in our society. Thus a sick Navajo living in the bottom of a canyon may decide to saddle his horse and ride to the nearest field clinic to obtain some medicine late Friday afternoon. When he finally arrives at the clinic on Friday night, he finds the clinic doors locked and the doctor away for the weekend. The Navajo patient cannot understand why he does not get medical service after his arduous trip to the clinic.[16]

These observations are cited because the experiences of classroom teachers in understanding the behavior of children are analogous to experiences of doctors in dealing with their patients. Adair and Deuschle state that, currently, each physician must find out much of this information for himself. They feel that a handbook revealing relevant cultural materials would be most helpful. Since the Navajo Indians have been subjects of intensive study by anthropologists for years, much of this information could be synthesized from the abundant literature. Classroom teachers also need to have readily available the knowledge of cultural differences and practices that would help them understand the children with whom they work.

Information about the cultural values of her pupils would be helpful to Mary, the fourth-grade teacher described at the beginning of this chapter. Without concrete information about the students she teaches, it will not be possible to set up the long-range objectives of education. The philosophical foundation for such long-range objectives is discussed in the following section.

THE NATURE OF THE PROBLEM

With respect to Indian children and the failure to achieve commensurate with Anglo children, many people have expressed their views:[17]

(1) I suspect that our schools are not beginning to tackle adequately the basic difficulties of language .... I suspect that this failure to comprehend on the part of the Indian child accounts in large measure for the lessening of interest and enthusiasm for school which I am told begins for Indian children along about the fourth grade.

The big advantage of our Indian children attending off-reservation public schools is the fact that here their youngsters are forced to use the English language on the playground because that is the only way they can make themselves understood . . . In their associations with non-Indians, they learn how to accommodate themselves to another culture and to learn how white children behave. This acquaintance is a two-way procedure in that the non-Indian child also comes to understand Indian behavior in the same way. Thus, both groups make compromises, change and adjust to each other's values in a natural, open, relaxed relationship.

(2) In order to understand why Indian communities remain isolated from the main stream, we must remember that as white settlements spread to the interior, the Indian societies were like people caught in a flooding valley moving to higher ground as the invading waters encroached upon them, until in time they were completely surrounded. Segregation was an act of self-preservation, the motivation being to keep what they had. This motivation persists. We may consider it unreasonable and self-limiting, but it is questionable whether human action is ever entirely rational and logical. Nor is it likely that human conduct can be changed merely by pointing out its irrationalities.

(3) In connection with the establishment of school districts on Indian Reservations, the Bureau must make a greater effort to involve Indian parents in school planning. The Task Force is not satisfied that simply encouraging tribes to form educational committees is sufficient. The parents of youngsters attending schools must be allowed to participate in the formulation of school programs. Wherever parent-teacher groups have not been formed, they should be established as rapidly as possible. When parents understand what the schools are trying to accomplish, they are more likely to give their support to the educational effort that when they do not. If our goal is the ultimate transfer of educational responsibility to local school districts, then the Bureau must do everything it can now to help Indian parents learn of their rights and duties with respect to schools. The time to begin providing them such assistance is not after the transfer, but before.

In a study finished in March, 1967, Anderson and Safar[18] found an almost unanimous feeling on the part of school personnel that Spanish-American and Indian students are less capable of achieving desirable goals and ultimately becoming productive members of society than are their Anglo contemporaries. School personnel seem to perceive this as lack of innate ability rather than the fault of an inadequate school system. This attitude exists even though the school program attempts in no way to compensate for the educational disadvantage of these children, many of whom can barely speak English when they enter the schools. This suggests that schools may be perpetuating the stereotype that these minorities are little interested in education, come from families that value education little, come from homes that do little to assist or support children's school efforts, and that the parents are content to live as wards of the government.

A worse value being learned may be that of the internalizing of a feeling of being inferior among the minority group youngsters, creating an insidious negative climate for these children. Do the adults in that child's life lack confidence in his ability (italics mine) to achieve the same goals as his Anglo classmates?

The absence of middle class values is too often equated at the child level with a verdict of being lazy, stupid, troublemakers, etc., by teachers and administrators, yet, the very absence of these values makes immediate and tangible rewards necessary.

Another misconception noted is that children from different ethnic groups are incapable of learning. The child will tend to live up to the expectation of the teacher, and this means that an attitude change on the part of teachers is necessary for success.

Education in our country is supposed to help people become able, economically self-sufficient, responsible citizens. Education is a state function: the state's primary objectives are to:

1. Transmit the cultural heritage - hopefully, the heritage of all the children in the respective schools.

2. Achieve economic efficiency for all its citizens - to enjoy a livelihood that enables them to pay the necessary taxes to support all the institutions of the government.

3. Enable each individual to participate in the democratic process. This requires proficiency in oral English; evaluative skills in silent reading; judgmental values commensurate with living in our society to exercise the freedoms and privileges with their corresponding responsibilities.

How these objectives are met should be flexibly determined according to what experiences meet a child's need and have personal meaning for him. One of the things needed is more reading materials of broad coverage about children who live in divergent cultural settings. It is imperative, of course, that these be depicted without stereotypes. The Owl in the Cedar Tree,[19] Navajo Sister,[20] and A Luminario for Antonio[21] are just three examples. David Gast has an encouraging article in the January, 1967 Elementary English in which he reports that minority group characters are quite honestly described in much of the recent children's literature.[22] Transmitting the cultural heritage must be flexible and to achieve the desirable objectives across the whole country must provide for teaching cultural pluralism as an affective value.

The significant problems of integrating the affective life of the child, his feelings, emotions, and attitudes, with his cognitive development - all his academic learning - are crucially dependent upon the particular classroom teacher he chances to work with in his classroom. It must be added that the school is only one institution of many operating to develop the totally integrated individual - the family, religious instruction, health practices, welfare services and economic pressures are also at work.

> Perhaps the dangers for most classroom teachers are covert. He may not tell the Indian child that he is superstitious or primitive but in the way that the teacher emphasizes that his way is superior, he teaches the child subtly to feel his own inferiority.
>
> Teachers manage very early in the child's school life to build an attitude about the way "people" build gabled-roofed bungalows with windows with curtains and a chimney with smoke. Before the child leaves first grade, he has usually learned about this completely stereotyped kind of line drawing expected during his reading work period.
>
> One must eat green leafy vegetables all winter, a bed is better than a sheepskin, and "we" all brush our teeth after meals. If the teacher unconsciously emphasizes that his way is the "right and proper" way, then the child has twelve long years to realize that the teacher feels his life is inadequate, inferior, and rejected or he early rejects the white man's way and value.[23]

Kelley[24] recently expounded the philosphy of the fully developing personality. This philosophy is generally accepted by teachers as representing the successful personality for our times. It is particularly interesting because it presents the opposite of what Pueblo Indians traditionally would consider an ideal concept of the "good man":

The fully functioning self . . . sees himself as a part of a world in movement--in process of becoming. When one looks outward rather than inward, the idea of change--in self, in others, in things--becomes apparent. The acceptance of change as a universal phenomenon brings about modification of personality . . . he will not search for the firm foundation on which he can stand for the rest of his life. He will realize that the only things he knows for sure about is that tomorrow will be different from today and that he can anticipate this difference with hopeful expectation. Optimism is the natural outcome of an accepting view of self and hence of others. Such a person is a doer, a mobile person, one who relates himself in an active way with others. Such activity would be meaningless unless the person had hopes for improvement. As has been stated, today has no meaning except in relation to an expected tomorrow. This is the basis for hope, without which no one can thrive.

The fully functioning personality, having accepted the ongoing nature of life and the dynamic of change, sees the value of mistakes. He knows he will be treading new paths at all times, and that, therefore, he cannot always be right. The fully functioning personality will not only see that mistakes are inevitable in constantly breaking new ground, but will come to see that these unprofitable paths show the way to better ones. The effective person cannot afford to have his spirit of adventure hampered. He knows that the only way to find out is to go forward and to profit from experience . . .[25]

To a culture, such as the Pueblo, whose energy has been traditionally directed toward preserving the status quo, the idea that change is natural and good is strange. To present-oriented people who tend to live and work for the present, and who do not plan far into the future, the idea that today has no meaning except in relation to some vague tomorrow is not acceptable. To state that this is the only basis for hope and necessary if people are to thrive is obviously egocentric. Many of the cultures of the Southwest have survived quite happily with the opposite orientation. If we blandly assume that we can apply our value systems in the education of Indian children, without explicitly teaching toward this end, then we will continue to see older Indian school graduates who have little understanding of the larger culture in which they must compete on an economic basis. Educators must teach attitudes toward work, time schedules, future planning, and other of the attitudes that we take for granted in a work situation, because the majority of Indians will not have these attitudes and may fail for these reasons as well as lack of basic educational skills.

Morris says of Pueblo Indian children:

> What they worship most is a . . . harmony in their universe. Man is the center of the universe in which all fragments are interrelated. This is not an egocentric view, for this is not a position of strength but rather one of concern. Any imbalance in this system could be detrimental to man. Physically, the Pueblos saw themselves as weak; a few families gathered together in the vast expanse of a dangerous government. He doesn't see himself as the "lord and master" of all he surveys, but rather as a small part of the whole. Many Pueblo Rituals and Prayers are aimed at preserving this balance and avoiding any change because change can be detrimental as well as beneficial to man's precarious state.
>
> The great gods don't interfere with the affairs of man except to preserve the status quo - the normal way of life. Most prayers ask just that all things continue in their normal way, and abundance or excesses are not asked. Anything out of the ordinary must be corrected by appealing to the gods to restore the natural order. Violence and warfare are recognized, and the Pueblos will fight, but this is seen as a disturbance of the natural course of life and not as a glorious adventure.
>
> Religion pervaded all phases of life. The native government was theocratic, with the head religious man controlling the legal and executive functions of government. A number of religious societies were responsible for curing and for weather control.[26]

The religious beliefs of the Indians present a serious problem in the teaching of scientific methods in the Anglo classroom. Dutton says that there can be no understanding of Pueblo life apart from its religious beliefs and practices. With the Keresans, clans and medicine societies are important. The dual kiva system is intimately concerned with the Katchina organization, the spirit rainmakers. Participation in ceremonials is a communal duty and privilege for all of the Pueblo people. Individuals are trained to take part in the dances from early childhood. Some of the most colorful and effective dances are performed by children exclusively, as, for example, Christmastime and Easter cermonies at Santo Domingo.[27]

Brophy and Aberle also describe a different view of the world held by the Indian.

> The spiritual attachment to nature, an essential aspect of many pre-Columbian cultures, has brought the Indian into an intimate accord with the elements. That harmony appears strikingly in his feeling for the earth. Indians have traditionally regarded land as part of a benevolent Mother and, like her, indispensable

to life. It was not considered a merchantable property but one that the users had an innate right to enjoy. This sentiment still tends to persist.[28]

Wax and Thomas chide the Anglo for his inability to understand cultural differences:

> In every human relationship there is some element of influence, interference, or downright compulsion. The white man has been and is torn between two ideals: on the one hand, he believes in freedom, in minding his own business, and in the right of people to make up their minds for themselves; but, on the other hand, he believes that he should be his brother's keeper and not abstain from advice, or even action, when his brother is speeding down the road toward perdition, death, or social isolation due to halitosis. The Indian society is unequivocal; interference of any form is forbidden, regardless of the folly, irresponsibility, or ignorance of your brother.
>
> Consequently, when the white man is motivated as his brother's keeper, which is most of the time when he is dealing with Indians, he rarely says or does anything that does not sound rude or even hostile to the latter. The white, imbued with a sense of righteousness in "helping the downtrodden and backward," does not realize the nature of his conduct, and the Indian cannot tell him, for that, in itself, would be "interference" with the white's freedom to act as he sees fit.[29]
>
> From childhood, white people and Indians are brought up to react to strange and dangerous situations in quite different ways. The white man who finds himself in an unstructured, anxiety-producing situation is trained to react with a great deal of activity. He will begin action after action until he either structures the situation, or escapes from it, or simply collapses. But the Indian, put in the same place, is brought up to remain motionless and watch. Outwardly, he appears to freeze. Inwardly, he is using all of his senses to discover what is expected of him - what activities are proper, seemly, safe. One might put it this way: in an unfamiliar situation a white man is taught to react by aggressive experimentation - he keeps moving until he finds a satisfactory pattern. His motto is "try and try again." But the Indian puts his faith in observation. He waits and watches until the other actors show him the correct pattern.[30]

Teacher-pupil conflicts are described by Wax:[31]

On the Pine Ridge Reservation in South Dakota, "country" Indians speak the Dakota language and are very poor.

. . . . teachers who teach them see them as inadequately prepared, uncultured offspring of alien and ignorant folk.

These students who leave school are . . . . "really "pushouts" or "kickouts," rather than dropouts.

By the time he reaches the eighth grade, the rural Indian boy has many fine qualities,

. . . . zest for life, curiosity, pride, physical courage, sensibility to human relationships, experience with the elemental facts of life, and intense group loyalty and integrity.

. . . . he lives in a barrack-type dormitory where competitive study is impossible . . . . . his English is inadequate for high school work.

Salisbury describes the plight of the Eskimo child who, by age seven, had internalized the cultural and language pattern of his Eskimo parents and must now adjust to the completely foreign-western classroom situation:

His teacher is likely to be a Causasian, who knows little or nothing about his cultural background. He is taught to read the Dick and Jane series. Many things confuse him: Dick and Jane are two gussuk (white) children who play together. Yet, he knows that boys and girls do not play together and do not share toys. They have a dog named Spot who comes indoors and does not work. They have a father who leaves for some mysterious place called "office" each day and never brings any food home with him. He drives a machine called an automobile on a hard covered road called a street which has a policeman on each corner. These policemen always smile, wear funny clothing and spend their time helping children to cross the street. Why do these children need this help? Dick and Jane's mother spends a lot of time in the kitchen cooking a strange food called "cookies" on a stove which has no flame in it.

But the most bewildering part is yet to come. One day they drive out to the country which is a place where Dick and Jane's grandparents are kept. They do not live with the family and they are so glad to see Dick and Jane that one is certain that they have been ostracized from the rest of the family for some terrible reason. The old people live on something called a "farm," which is a place where many strange animals are kept - a peculiar beast called a "cow," some odd looking birds called "chickens," and a "horse" which looks like a deformed moose . . . . The native child continues to learn this new language which is of no earthly use to him at home and which seems completely unrelated to the world of sky, birds, snow ice, and tundra which he sees around him.[32]

Educators in a Navajo Reservation School contrast the beliefs and values presented in the basal reading program with those already learned by young Navajo Children:

Beliefs and Values of the Scott-Foresman Basic Reading Series Contrasted with Beliefs and Values of the Navajo Children*

Middle-Class, Urban	Navajo
Pets have human-like personalities.	Pets are distinct from human personality.
Life is pictured as child-centered.	Life is adult centered.
Adults participate in children's activities.	Children participate in adult activities.
Germ-theory is implicitly expressed.	Good health results from harmony with nature.
Children and parents are masters of their environment.	Children accept their environment and live with it.
Children are energetic, outgoing, obviously happy.	Children are passive and unexpressive.
Many toys and much clothing is an accepted value.	Children can only hope for much clothing and toys.
Life is easy, safe, and bland.	Life is hard and dangerous.

* Evvard, Evelyn and George C. Mitchell, "Sally, Dick and Jane at Lukachukai," Journal of American Indian Education, 5:5, No. 3, May, 1966.

The need for parent involvement is re-emphasized:

> Now what about the place of adult education in this? The education of native children and native adults, including the parents of the children, must go together.

> It is pointed out that children cannot be educated successfully out of context with the understandings, expectations, and aspirations of their parents for them. For many years those of us in the BIA have told native parents that they should send their children to school and keep them there until they finish, but we have not done a very good job of telling them why . . . Often native parents have kept their children in school for no better reason than that they have wanted to please us. That is not a good enough reason. <u>We must start spelling out to native parents and other adults in specific terms the real concrete reasons for the increasing need for education.</u>[33]

BASIC PURPOSES OF EDUCATION OF MINORITY GROUPS

The methodology to be applied in teaching minority groups in the Southwest must, necessarily, be based upon a set of objectives. Many school systems have either set down their own statement of philosophy or carry on a routine school activity based upon the generally accepted pattern of what constitutes a good school. If such a statement of objectives had been worked out, and if it meets the expectations of the community where it applies, it is safe to generalize that it will implement the major values of American culture in general. In this text, these major values will be described as middle-class values. Among other things, these values place a great deal of importance on external conformity, acceptance of change, and a pragmatic approach to living.

Without further attention to the teacher's personal philsophy of life, it becomes clear that the objectives of education for the minority groups in the Southwest must be arrived at before they can be expected to profit from the type of education they are given. Ask yourself the following questions:

1. Is our ultimate educational objective with regard to Indians, Spanish Americans, and Mexican Americans to make "typical" Americans of them?

2. When fundamental Anglo values are in conflict with the indigenous values of a minority group, should the schools inculcate the values of the majority culture?

3. If the Navajo Indian, for example, wishes to return to the reservation to perpetuate his traditional way of life, should our school program be designed to make him a better citizen in that society?

4. Are the educational goals of economic efficiency, civic responsibility, self-realization, and human relationships equally as applicable to Spanish-speaking and Indian peoples as to Anglos?

5. Is it inevitable that, when a sub-culture (for example, a Rio Grande Pueblo) begins its assimilation into the dominant culture, it must be ascribed lower class status (socio-economically speaking) within the dominant group?

6. Reservations have served to insulate Indians from the mainstream of American life. Is the best way to facilitate cultural diffusion, and amalgamation of the two cultures, then, to abolish reservations?

7. Considering the culture, language, and experience barriers, can Indian children be taught more effectively in segregated classrooms?

8. <u>Can a person have two sets of cultural values,</u> i.e., Pueblo and Anglo, and be able to operate efficiently in either one?

9. Within Indian reservations, rapid population increases are putting great strains on the limited resources. <u>Should one of our primary objectives be, then, to teach Indians vocational skills which are marketable in Anglo society?</u>

10. The rate of juvenile delinquency and alcoholism is higher for minority groups in marginal status than for the dominant social group. Is this an <u>inevitable</u> price that people in cultural transition must pay?

11. Do educators presume to know what is <u>best</u> for the Indian or for the first generation Mexican <u>American</u> in our schools? Are we committed to the task of making him over into a middle-class Anglo before he graduates?

Answers for these questions are not easy. Nevertheless, answers must be sought before we can establish our purposes in education. We cannot know how to proceed until we know what we are trying to do. Do most adults, including teachers, have well-defined life goals thought through for themselves?

The answers to these questions must come from many different people. The learning of new behavior patterns and a new language will be necessary for adequate interaction with Anglos in the dominant culture. This effort can be aided by the cultural anthropologist who has analyzed cultural change and the behavior spheres of different societies, by the linguist who analyzes the likenesses and differences in the phonemes and structures of different languages, and by the specialist who has learned how to teach English as a second language.

The changing of the economic system of the social group, from subsistence farming, for example, to the dollar economy will be necessary if each family is to enjoy the artifacts of the dominant culture which they most desire, such as the pickup truck, the new refrigerator, or the TV set.

The improved health practices which the United States Public Health Services bring to people who heretofore accepted the <u>curandero</u>, the <u>partera</u>, or the medicine man demonstrate the superiority of <u>scientific</u> medicine in lowering mortality rates.

The questions, of accepting the dominant culture as the norm, assume a certain inevitability for the answers. Change, per se, is inevitable. In what order behaviors will be changed and over what period of time this will occur remain undetermined.

The educator has faced other problems in other areas of the curriculum and has looked elsewhere for help in their solution. The educational psychologist has investigated problems in learning, motivation, levels of aspiration, transfer, and rewards and punishment. The educational sociologist has investigated the problems of social class, child rearing patterns in different life styles, and behavior problems in society. The cultural anthropologist has studied many problems of social groups whose patterns of life are different from our own. An educational anthropologist can provide help in the problems of education across cultures. Considerable effort has been expended in this field.

The services of all these social scientists are needed in studying social interaction where cultural values are in conflict, and the alleviation of differences is dependent upon mutual empathy, trust, and understanding.

EDUCATION OF EXCEPTIONAL CHILDREN: A POINT OF VIEW

The usual pattern of American education is that a child lives at home with his parents through a pre-school period of five or six years. Then, with a great deal of experience in the English language in listening, speaking, reacting, evaluating, and making judgments in the language, he enters public school. With a listening vocabulary of perhaps 8,000 to 10,000 English words, a speaking vocabulary of 5,000 to 7,000 English words, and several years of continuous practice habituating literally thousands of sentences in the English language, the "typical" unilingual six-year-old presents his teacher relatively little difficulty in the readiness-for-reading program.

Even in this frame of reference, teachers of beginners work diligently to help children make a satisfactory adjustment to school. They deliberate over overt behavior, confer with anxious mothers, and write anecdotal records for cumulative folders. Their efforts may be described graphically something like this:

Pre-School Experience	Transition to School	Successful First Grade
Evidences mental maturity.	Gains independence from mother.	Demonstrates all the abilities in previous columns.
Develops linguistic maturity.	Becomes confident in large group of peers.	Learns basic sight words.
Shows interest in books.	Enters into competitive play.	Learns phonetic and structural analysis.
Continually broadens background of experience.	Follows directions.	Reads well orally.
Makes social and emotional adjustments.	Sits still.	Interprets stories.
Sees and hears well.	Listens well.	Expands vocabulary concepts.
Improves physical coordination and manual dexterity.	Conforms.	

The American public school system has universally been based upon the principle that all of the children of all of the people from many different ethnic backgrounds with many different degrees of motivation are to be accommodated. Actually, this principle has been operating in parts of the Southwest only very recently. Spanish American rural communities in complete isolation remained homogeneously Spanish American in cultural effect. It is only very recently that the Bureau of Indian Affairs has been transferring Indian pupils to the public schools in the communities near which they live. It is only now, then, that non-Anglos are really moving into a state of cultural transition educationally. There is every reason to believe, if the educators adopt suitable practices, that there is readiness for bringing about intergroup understanding more effectively than we have done in the past. 34

The course of study in public schools has universally been a "standard" one used throughout the country and based entirely upon a rigid, inflexible value system held by the average middle-class Anglo. For New Mexico in 1912, when statehood was established, this course of study in no way provided for the value patterns of the minority ethnic values of the Spanish American people, nor did it provide for the fact that the only language these people could speak was Spanish. The public schools in New Mexico merely provided that all the regulation subjects should be taught and that the language to be used in their teaching must be English and only English. There were no bilingual Spanish American teachers who might have helped to bridge the language and cultural gaps between where the children were and what the "foreign" course of study was detailed to accomplish. Kluckhohn emphasizes this problem in Atrisco, where she made a detailed study of a Spanish American community. 35

Tireman and Watson recognized the problem in New Mexico and demonstrated the place of the community school in the Spanish-speaking village as a way of adapting the course of study to the cultural background and immediate economic needs of the people. 36

The child who enters the public school from a minority ethnic background, where another language has been predominantly used, faces problems undreamed of by the child who is merely making the transition from pre-school experiences in English language to a specialized segment of his society that uses the same language and emphasizes, at least for the middle-class child, the same set of values.

The minority group child may be said to face two additional obstacles: he is attempting to bridge a wide chasm of cultural values and patterns that have in varying degrees emphasized different behavior spheres in his experience background, and he is immediately confronted with an entirely new language, English, that makes him completely inarticulate if he must express himself in that language from the beginning.

This predicament has been very effectively illustrated by a rather incredible story which may or may not be true. A dormitory principal is reported to have met a bus load of Indian students at his school in the fall of the year, asked them to group themselves around him so that he might say a word to them, and then made the following announcement: "The first thing I want you to do here is to forget that you are a Navajo, and the second thing I want to tell you is that we speak only English around here."

The language and culture areas of difference to be bridged by the child are illustrated in Table I.

> The term exceptional children is used to refer to those who deviate from what is supposed to be average in physical, mental, emotional, or social characteristics to such an extent that they require special educational services in order to develop to their maximum capacity. [37]

Thus, it is seen that most children of minority groups in the Southwest are exceptional children when enrolled in the public schools. Because of a cultural difference, and the language and experience barriers which this cultural difference perpetuates, they are in a very real sense exceptional children.

"Exceptional" includes all the many types of physically handicapped, mentally retarded, and intellectually gifted. It includes all the emotional scars that result from having either retardation or crippling as a handicap. It includes those children who have personal problems that prevent them from living with peers with confidence and happiness. These are the ones with too much fear, too much shyness, too much aggression, too much hate. The "too muchness" is what causes them to be exceptional -- outside the range of normality.

It is a universally accepted practice in American education to provide special educational facilities for the child who is blind, or for the child who is profoundly hard of hearing. This provision is based upon the definition already cited, that in order for such a child to achieve self-realization of his innate capacities, he must have services of special personnel that will make it possible for him to achieve on a par with non-handicapped peers of like intelligence. The same principle, also universally practiced, applies to children of subnormal intelligence. Special educationists have provided school administrators with fairly rigidly defined categories for school placement of children with below average intelligence. These special provisions, in any case, may involve segregation in institutions, segregation in school units within a school system, special classes in regular schools, assignment to regular

TABLE I

Barriers to Successful School Achievement for Bilingual-Bicultural Children

I The child before he comes to school.	II Cultural conflicts between child and teacher.	III Learning English as a second language.	IV Successful adjustment to first grade.
Birth to age 6, 7, or 8 years. Habituation of a sound system which is the language of his parents. Develops fluency in this sound system. This system meets all his linguistic needs. All his experiences are described, categorized, and evaluated in the vocabulary of that specific sound system.	School is middle-class oriented institution. Child's home was oriented to a different set of values: Time orientation; man-nature; relational values with other people. Mistrust of those who have quite different values and appearance. Social practices. Common courtesies. Manner of dress. Foods at home vs. foods in hot lunch program and talked about in health lessons.	Child must learn a new sound system. He must habituate a new sound pattern. Develop auditory discrimination of new phonemes. Internalize rhythm and stress and intonation in a new language. Memorize a whole set of common speech utterances. Develop and continually expand vocabulary concepts.	Teacher will check each child for acquisition of generally accepted reading readiness abilities: mental maturity, background of experience, ability to work with others, conversation, etc. Child exposed to a basic sight vocabulary. Child taught phonetic and structural analysis skills. Pre-patterned course of study followed.

27

classes with special class teachers assigned to tutoring for short periods, or assignment to regular classes where regular class teachers are expected to administer special educational services in the course of their teaching.

Obviously, there are other children who are categorized as exceptional children needing special services. The intellectually gifted, the emotionally disturbed, the orthopedically handicapped are only a few types. The recognition of exceptionality in children will be dependent upon the degree to which the exceptionality exists. The degree is difficult to define since many types of exceptionality are not observable to the casual observer. Diabetes, epilepsy, post-rheumatic fever, or dull-normal mentality may not be identified at all by the classroom teacher.

The child whose cultural heritage is different from that of the value system perpetuated by the school is also an exceptional child. There is evidence that failure to recognize and provide special educational services for the cultural difference has resulted in lack of achievement in school and in slow acculturation of minority groups in the Southwest, both in use of the English language and in economic adjustment. In order for such children enrolled in the public school systems and taught by teachers strongly oriented to middle-class values to achieve at the same level as Anglo children, a philosophy of special educational services is needed.

Each child coming to the public schools is expected to become oriented to certain values emphasized in the dominant culture. Some of these values are as follows: [38]

1. He must place a value on competitive achievement and climbing the ladder of success.

2. He must learn time orientation that will be precise to the hour and minute, and he must also learn to place high value on looking to the future.

3. He must accept the teachers' reiteration that there is scientific explanation for all natural phenomena.

4. He must become accustomed to change and must anticipate change. (The dominant culture teaches that "change," in and of itself, is good and desirable!)

5. He must "trade" his shy, quiet, reserved, and anonymous behavior for socially approved aggressive, competitive behavior.

6. He must somehow be brought to understand that he can, with some independence, shape his own destiny, as opposed to the tradition of remaining an anonymous member of his society.

Too many teachers are inadequately prepared to understand or accept the dissimilar cultural values. Teachers come from homes where the drive for achievement and success causes parents to "push" their children to climb the ladder of success, where "work for work's sake" is rewarded, and where time and energy are spent building for the future.

Therefore, the Indian child comes to the classroom with a set of values and a background of experience radically different from that of the average American child. To teach the Indian child successfully, the teacher must be cognizant of these differences and must above all else seek to understand, without disparagement, those ideas, values, and practices different from his own.

The need for cross-cultural understanding rests on the observations of teachers who teach these children. Some of these teachers have said, "He does real well for a Navajo " This statement, in itself, expresses a difference to be reckoned with in teaching. Other teachers have said, "I treat them just like all the rest. Indians are just like everybody else." This response would be fine if the achievement of the children met the level of the national norms. Since the educational retardation of minority group children is so great, and since it increases as they progress from grade to grade, this response must be overlooking something. Other teachers have said that these children do not have trouble with English as a language, but test results exploring the knowledge of facets of English indicate that there is little depth or breadth in their knowledge of the English language. One of the special education services these children need is attention to their bilingual abilities. If teachers recognize stages or levels of bilingualism, they will not be deceived in thinking that a child who says "Good morning," and "Yes" and "No" has a working knowledge of English.

Finally, the Education Committee of the Navajo Tribal Council has recognized the special education need of Navajo children and has taken very aggressive action in investigating this need and in seeking solutions to the problems through the annual Navajo Education Conference which it has sponsored the past six years.[39]

The school is the principal avenue by which these people can achieve an "equal" place in the dominant culture. Finding motivational techniques and providing remedial education to meet currently existing problems are means to this end. The teacher's first responsibility, then, is to acquaint himself with the unique cultural background of his students. The crucial teacher-pupil relationships in the multicultural classroom has been detailed by Tireman with reference to Spanish-speaking children.[40] An appreciation is required on the teacher's part of the contribution which the child's culture has made in the past and its significance to his people in the present -- in language, music, folklore, customs, religious and spiritual life, foods, architecture, crafts -- the whole cultural heritage.

THE INDIAN EDUCATION RESEARCH PROJECT

The Bureau of Indian Affairs has expended much effort toward helping classroom teachers in their problems of educating Indian children. Collier, director of the Bureau from 1932 until 1945, secured funds for the Indian Education Research Project, which was a joint activity of the United States Office of Indian Affairs and the Committee on Human Development of the University of Chicago. It was undertaken in 1941 to study personality development of Indians in their native environments. The hope was that an interdisciplinary approach, utilizing anthropology, psychology, linguistics, and education might prognosticate directions towards more effective Bureau of Indian Affairs administration. Several very valuable publications resulted from this research, including:

Warriors Without Weapons, A Study of the Society and Personality Development of the Pine Ridge Sioux, by Gordon MacGregor, 1946.

The Hopi Way, by Laura Thompson and Alice Joseph, 1944.

The Children of the People (Navajo), by Dorothea Leighton and Clyde Kluckhohn, 1948.

The Desert People, A Study of the Papago Indians, by Alice Joseph, Rosamond Spicer, and Jane Chesky, 1949.

These publications, as well as many others, could be most helpful if classroom teachers and administrators apprized themselves of the pertinent information which they embody.

OVERVIEW OF THE TEXT

Some of the problems in the education of minority ethnic groups have been introduced. Questions concerning the objectives of education have been raised, and a need for special educational services to encompass the cultural barrier and the language needs have been discussed. The educators role in this total problem has four aspects. These will be expanded in this part, as well as in Parts II and III of the text.

1. Obtaining background information about the people in the community will help the teacher to understand them. Anthropological literature is available to help teachers understand the life values, the cultural beliefs, and the experiential backgrounds of children from minority groups. Differences that exist in the behavior spheres of teachers and students include not only overt behavior in dress, cus-

toms, attitudes, and language, but also, more difficult to assess, covert behavior in beliefs, knowledges, and ideals. These cultural differences need to be described in terms of social institutions in the different groups: the family, the church, the economy, politics, health, education, and recreation.

2. Each teacher needs an appreciation of his own role in middle-class American culture. Before one can adequately understand another culture and its idiosyncracies, he needs to take an objective look at his own.

3. The language differences that the teacher and child must reconcile will be erased more easily if the teacher has some understanding of the comparative likenesses and differences between English and the child's vernacular. It will not be possible for the teacher, in many cases, to have much knowledge of the child's language. However, the teacher can know something of the differences in the phonemes of the two languages, the structural differences, the sentence patterning. And, of course, the classroom teacher in this situation must know how to teach English as a second language. In those areas where large populations of students have a language other than English as their first language, the schools must recognize that the teaching of English as a second language is an area of specialization for its teachers. Morrison recommended at the conclusion of the Puerto Rican Study that teachers in the New York City Schools who were assigned to teach Puerto Rican students be encouraged to plan a fifth year of preparation specializing in teaching English as a second language. [41]

4. Beyond the understanding of the cultural differences, their effect on the behaviors of children in the classrooms, and the effective teaching of English, the schools must provide an effective program of remedial instruction. Substantial evidence shows that, through the years, there has existed a general tendency for pupils to become more and more educationally retarded as they progress through the schools, with many of these students either dropping out or becoming hopelessly lost in the high school. Since children with normal intelligence are expected to move through the public school grades on a homogeneous age-in-grade scale, this educational retardation is a real challenge to present-day educators.

FOOTNOTES

[1] E. W. Dolch, "How to Diagnose Children's Reading Difficulties by Informal Classroom Techniques," The Reading Teacher, 6: 10-14, January, 1953.

[2] William A. Brophy and Sophie D. Aberle, The Indian, America's Unfinished Business, (Norman: University of Oklahoma Press, 1966), p. 217.

[3] United States Bureau of the Census, Statistical Abstract of the United States, 1962, Eighty-third Edition (Washington: U. S. Government Printing Office, 1962), p. 101.

[4] Scholes, William E., "The Migrant Worker," in Julian Samora, La Raza: Forgotten Americans, (Notre Dame: University of Notre Dame Press, 1966), p. 65.

[5] Scholes Ibid. p. 65.

[6] Ibid., p. 68.

[7] Day, Sam and Claes Edshammar, "The Migrants," The Idaho Observer, July 29, 1967, pp. 5 - 8.

[8] L. Madison Coombs, et al., The Indian Child Goes to School (Washington: Government Printing Office, 1958); Kenneth E. Anderson, et al., The Educational Achievement of Indian Children (Washington: Government Printing Office, 1953); Shailer Peterson, How Well Are Indian Children Educated? (Washington: Government Printing Office, 1948); Lewis Meriam, The Problem of Indian Administration (Baltimore: John Hopkins Press, 1928).

[9] Mario Pei, Language for Everybody: What It Is and How to Master It (New York: The Devin-Adair Company, 1956).

[10] Wilcomb E. Washburn, "A Moral History of Indian-White Relations: Needs and Opportunities for Study," Ethnohistory, 4:47-61, Winter, 1957.

[11] Robert M. Young, The Navajo Yearbook (Window Rock, Arizona: Navajo Agency, 1958), p. 235.

[12] Ben Reifel, "Cultural Factors in Social Adjustment," Indian Education, No. 298, April 15, 1957, p. 3.

[13] John Adair and Kurt Deuschle, "Some Problems of the Physicians on the Navajo Reservation," Human Organization, 16:19-23, Winter, 1958.

[14] Ibid., p. 21.

[15] Ibid., p. 22.

[16] Ibid., p. 23.

[17] (1) Wesley, Clarence, "An Approach to the Mind of the Young Indian," Journal of American Indian Education, 1:4-7, No. 1, June, 1961; (2) McNickle, D'Arcy, "How to Help Indians Help Themselves," American Indians, Walter Daniels, Editor, (New York: H. H. Wilson Co., 1957), p. 188; (3) The Report of the Task Force on Indian Affairs, Chicago, Illinois, 1961, p. 25.

[18] Anderson, James G. and Dwight Safar, "The Influence of Differential Community Perceptions on the Provision of Equal Educational Opportunities," Research Center, New Mexico State University, March, 1967.

[19] Natachee Scott Momaday, "The Owl in the Cedar Tree, (Boston: Ginn and Company, 1965).

[20] Evelyn Lampman, Navajo Sister, (New York: Doubleday and Co., Inc., 1956).

[21] Flora Hood, A Luminaria for Antonio, (Pittman, 1966).

[22] David K. Gast, "Minority Americans in Children's Literature," Elementary English, 44:12-23, January, 1967.

[23] See also, Conklin, Paul, "A Good Day at Rough Rock," American Education, (reprint) February, 1967. (unnumbered pages.)

[24] Earl Kelley, "The Fully Functioning Self," Perceiving, Behaving, Becoming, Association for Supervision and Curriculum Development Yearbook, 1962, pp. 9-21.

[25] Ibid.

[26] Joyce Morris, "A Brief Survey of the Changing Values of the Southwestern Pueblos," from a class lecture on June 15, 1965.

[27] Dutton, Bertha, "Pueblos," Pocket Handbook of New Mexico Indians and their Arizona Neighbors, (Santa Fe: The Rydal Press, 1955), pp. 9 - 10.

[28] The Indian: America's Unfinished Business, William A. Brophy and Sophie D. Aberle, (Norman: University of Oklahoma Press, 1966), pp. 4 - 5.

[29] Wax, Rosalie H. and Robert K. Thomas, "American Indians and White People," Phylon, 22:305-317, Winter, 1961.

[30] Wax, Rosalie, and Robert Thomas, "American Indians and White People," Phylon, XXII:305-317, No. 4, Winter, 1961.

[31] Wax, Rosalie, H., "The Warrior Dropouts," Transaction, Washington University, St. Louis, May, 1967, pp. 40 - 46.

[32] Salisbury, Lee H., "Teaching English to Alaska Natives," Journal of American Indian Education, 6:5, No. 2, January, 1967.

[33] Bennett, Robert L. and L. Madison Coombs, "Effective Education to Meet Special Needs of Native Children," Journal of American Indian Education, 3:25, No. 3, May, 1964.

[34] Florence Kluckhohn and Fred L. Strodtbeck, Variations in Value Orientations (Evanston: Row, Peterson and Company, 1961), p. 70

[35] Ibid., p. 246

[36] Loyd Tireman and Mary Watson, The Community School in a Spanish-Speaking Village (Albuquerque: University of New Mexico Press, 1943).

[37] Nelson B. Henry (editor), The Education of Exceptional Children, "Basic Facts and Principles Underlying Special Education," Forty-ninth Yearbook of the National Society for the Study of Education, Part II (Chicago: The National Society for the Study of Education, 1950), p. 3.

[38] Miles V. Zintz, "Indian Children Are Different," The New Mexico School Review, 40:26-27, October, 1960.

[39] See, for example, "Teaching of English to Navajo Children," Final Report of the Fourth Annual Conference on Navajo Education, Miles V. Zintz, editor (Unpublished monograph, The Navajo Tribe, Window Rock, Arizona, 1961).

[40] Loyd Tireman, Teaching Spanish-Speaking Children (Albuquerque: The University of New Mexico Press, 1951).

[41] J. Cayce Morrison, The Puerto Rican Study, 1953-1957 (New York: The Board of Education of the City of New York, 1958), p. 225.

CHAPTER 2

Foundations for Educating Minority Groups

INTRODUCTION

An eight-year-old girl who had spent her life with governesses and private tutors, was once asked to write a composition about a poor family. She wrote the following paragraph: 1.

The Poor Family

Once upon a time there was a poor family. The father was poor. The mother was poor. The children were poor. The butler was poor. The chauffeur was poor. The gardener was poor. The cook was poor. Even all four maids were poor. In fact, every person in this poor family was poor.

The End.

It is comforting to note that this passage is the work of an eight-year-old child. The tragedy for too many adults in American society, however, is that they have never seen any other stream of life than their own narrow one. To them, "Do not criticize the other fellow until you have walked a mile in his moccasins" may be a familiar saying, but it has never been experienced. Wagner uses the above story to emphasize children's need to grow in empathy -- the ability to put oneself in the other fellow's shoes. 2

A discussion of culture and cultural change, with some statements of anthropologists, sociologists, and psychologists relative to the significance of this problem, is presented in this chapter. Generalizations from anthropology and sociology in the school curriculum are pointed out in relation to research studies which were made to help understand the personality of the out-group child and in relation to the planning of social studies in the school course of study.

Until a few years ago, the literature emphasized that the difference in the learning abilities of Anglo children and minority group children (e.g., Negro, Spanish American, Indian) was genuinely one of innate capacity. As late as 1924, one author stated that the extent to which a child from one of these minority groups would be able to achieve well in comparison with Anglo children would depend upon the amount of Anglo blood which flowed in his veins.[3] More recent research has dispelled the fallacious logic in this writing. The differences that exist between cultural groups can no longer be attributed to innate intelligence. The differences are believed to lie in the cultural values and beliefs of each respective group. One anthropologist writes that:

> It is imperative that teachers understand motivations of child behavior in terms of varying cultural norms. A knowledge of anthropology can help eliminate ethnocentrism in teachers and pupils, can help teachers to overcome in their own experience many of the obstacles that impede intercultural understanding, and can lead both teachers and pupils toward a spirit of intracultural cooperation and trust.[4]

THE CONCEPT OF CULTURE

What is culture?

By culture, we mean all the ways of life that have been evolved by men in society.

By a particular culture, we mean the total shared way of life of a given people, comprising their modes of thinking, acting, and feeling, which are expressed in religion, law, language, art, and custom, as well as in material products, such as houses, clothes, and tools.

Our culture is the way we eat and sleep, the way we wash and dress and go to work. It is the actions we perform at home and on the job. It is the language we speak and the values and beliefs we hold. It is the goods and services we buy and the way we buy them. It is the way we meet friends and strangers, the way we control our children and the way they respond. It is the transportation we use and the entertainment we enjoy.[5]

Culture pervades our waking lives.

A modern American would find it hard to sleep on a mat spread on the ground or in a slatted hammock, yet people accustomed to a mat or hammock find springs and mattresses just as uncomfortable. When European and American missionaries installed Western style beds in their first hospitals in the interior of Central Africa, they found that many patients, disconcerted by the high beds with their soft mattresses and elastic springs, preferred to sleep on the floor between them.[6]

Culture is the learned behavior of a social group. The habit patterns formed by a single social group in whatever process they organize their daily and seasonal living to best maintain their existence, then, constitutes a cultural heritage. All of the ways by which groups obtain food, find adequate shelter, protect themselves from enemies or danger require planned interaction of the group. Not only weapons, tools, goods, and processes, but also attitudes, beliefs, social practices, and kinds of moral judgments--all these make up the culture. Each new generation is born into, lives in, and is controlled by the cultural framework of its previous generations. Culture is learned. No part of one's cultural heritage is inborn. The use of language, for example, is common to all social groups. However, there are literally several thousand languages. This means that your larynx, vocal cords, and all the musculature actually evolved for other purposes than speech, will be conditioned to learn whatever language the parent uses as the infant grows into childhood. Benedict says that a newborn Chinese boy or girl, introduced into a typical middle-class American family at birth will just naturally grow up into a middle-class American child--speaking only English and thinking only the culturally-framed thoughts of a middle-class American child. It has been said that in one short span of sixteen years, young pre-literate men in Ehtiopia have become skilled aviation mechanics, modern pilots, and the country of Ethiopia is able to operate an extremely safe modern air transportation system.

Custom:

Custom dictates almost all of our simple, daily behavior. It tells us approximately when to rise, when and how often to eat, and even basically of what each meal should consist. It tells us how to dress, what is proper and improper to say and to think. It tells us how and when to laugh, even when it is right or wrong to cry. We acquire these patterns as a matter of course.[7]

There is a socializing nature to the concept of culture. Only men---human beings--- possess human culture--the utilization of habits, interests, and ideas, for the solution of problems. The transmission of culture is inherent in the daily lives of the new generation as it grows up in the environment of its parent generation, learning the rules, all the mores, customs, taboos, and folkways, as they are obeyed within the social group.

Folkways are the routine ways of doing things developed through trial and error as peoples struggle to meet the needs of life.

Mores are those folkways identified with group welfare and group surival. They are compulsory. Mores can make anything wrong or anything right.

Taboos are mores dealing with forbidden acts.[8]

Laws are the mores that have been formalized and statutory. "Respect for the law" is a part of the mores; yet, if a law goes counter to the mores, many people will seek to obstruct the law. In time, the law will probably win, but only through a slow, gradual change of the mores.

Customs are, in the broadest sense, all of man's social patterns; practices of the group which have come down from the past.[9]

HOW CULTURE DEFINES HUMAN LIBERTIES[10]

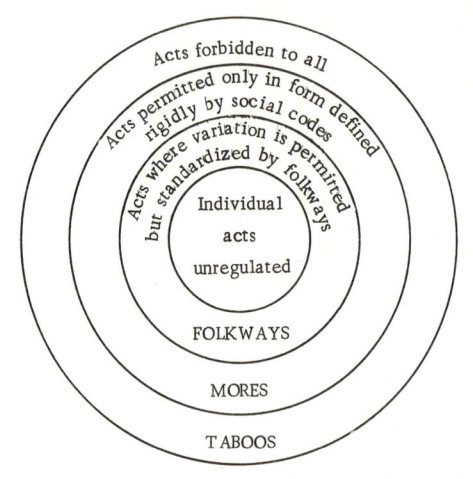

- Acts forbidden to all
- Acts permitted only in form defined rigidly by social codes
- Acts where variation is permitted but standardized by folkways
- Individual acts unregulated

FOLKWAYS
MORES
TABOOS

HOW FOLKWAYS AND MORES REGULATE THE INDIVIDUAL - You behave according to the customs and rules of your culture. Some acts are forbidden entirely by the mores. They are the taboos.

Children growing up within a society tend to learn that its particular behavior patterns, folkways, and institutions represent the "right" values and that those of other societies are "wrong" values.[11]

This socializing nature is enhanced in human life because of the ability to communicate. The cumulative aspect of culture, which clearly and completely differentiates man from the lower animals, is made possible by language. This is expressed succinctly by Strickland:

Communication through spoken and written language belongs to man and to him alone. It is the most important influence in his upward climb through the centuries. This ability to communicate has permitted each generation to rise on the shoulders of the thinkers and achievers who have gone before, to profit from their gains, to avoid their mistakes, and to pursue their dreams and aspirations and make some of them realities.[12]

Henry makes clear the contradiction which human behavior imposes on the freedom to use this communication ability in opening up new vistas and accepting new ideas:

> So it is that though language has been an instrument with which man might cleave open the universe and peer within, it has also been an iron matrix that bound his brain to ancient modes of thought. And thus it is that though man has poured what he knows into his culture patterns, they have also frozen round him and held him fast.[13]

There is extreme cultural diversity from one group to another. The mode of life for one group becomes established within fairly inflexible lines so that thought and custom and what is not tolerable, become "set" for each social group. The basic institutions---family, religion, economy---can be uniformly labeled for all social groups but the way they are practiced will vary greatly from group to group.

It is only natural that a great deal of misunderstanding or lack of understanding will prevail between groups that interpret belief in a supernatural, morality in human interaction, and right and wrong in behavior in the light of their own past experience and knowledge accumulated in their way of life. The foods that people should eat will likely depend on what foods they have eaten since infancy; the ways in which wars are waged and heroes are selected will likely depend upon how one has observed this custom from early childhood; the acceptance of universal need for compulsory formal education for all of the children of all of the people will depend upon the system of education the individual experienced as a child. Ethno-centrism is at work here, too.

Ethnocentrism:

The feeling that one's own culture is the best and only significant one is cultural ethnocentrism; the feeling that one's race is the best is racial ethnocentrism.

A woman tourist watched from a train window a group of dark-skinned men at work on the railroad. She remarked to her companion, "They ought to be giving these jobs to some of our American boys rather than to these foreigners." The "foreigners" were Navajo Indians! The woman spoke with a remnant of an accent, for her own parents were immigrants to the

United States one generation before. The Indians have been on this continent for, some scientists say, ten to twenty thousand years![14]

This is particularly meaningful to New Mexicans since both the Folsom man and the Sandia man have been found in our state and the artifacts of Pueblo Indian culture have left very concrete evidence of life here for many, many centuries.

But this conversation about who is American points up for us all the personal and emotional attachment to my country, my language, my customs and mores.

> These emotional valuations acquired in the process of learning a personality create at once stability and unity within a culture and a problem of ethnocentricity in intercultural relations. Socialization into one culture inevitably creates barriers to understanding the values of another culture. Because individuals are conditioned to the behavior, values, and norms of a given society, their capacity to understand and to appreciate that which is different from their own culture is limited. In addition to the difficulty of seeing the "other," there is the culturally conditioned incapacity to see members of other cultures in terms of that culture's values and standards. A person of one culture responds to a foreign culture in terms of the values and norms of his own culture--that is to say, ethnocentrically. Procrastination becomes laziness in the eyes of a person reared in a work-worshipping culture. A gadget-admiring American regards as inferior anyone who chooses to spend his money on a vacation instead of a refrigerator.[15]

Cultural pluralism has a special appeal for people committed to the ideals of democracy and tolerance. Cultural pluralism implies cooperation between majority and minority--appreciation and acceptance of the cultural heritages of minorities and their preservation rather than their repression. Contrariwise, any society must have a considerable agreement among its members as to basic ideals, goals, values, mores, folkways, and beliefs. Pluralism is an ideal toward which its advocates hope that race relations might move.

Responsibility of the citizen to the total society is made clear in the following statement:

> A good citizen of this country may retain a measure of loyalty to the racial, religious, ethnic, or socioeconomic group in which he enjoys membership........Should the bonds eventuate in a chauvinistic temper of the group, as they may if a policy of cultural pluralism is carried to the extreme, then there is the clearest evidence that a privilege of in-group nurture is being overworked to the neglect of out-group obligation. The

individual's pleasure in sharing one of the multiple group cultures needs to be balanced by his assumption of responsibility to keep his primary allegience to the people of the United States of America soundly enlisted. National cultural unity must not be jeopardized by an exaggerated development of the forces of cultural diversity.[16]

Cultural pluralism as an idea is not always accepted in practice. The Indian is still regarded on occasion as an exotic bit of local fauna. There is less tolerance now than in the Old Southwest for any minority group that might want to retain a substantial degree of cultural difference. The existence of Indian reservations is regarded by many government agencies, some congressmen, regional Anglo leaders, and the general public, as an anachronism that ought to be ended as soon as possible.

The Indians of the Southwest have not as yet been very active in determining what their role should be in the new Southwest.

One of the aspects of the Indian Reorganization Act of 1930's was the principle of cultural pluralism. Schusky says:

Indians were expected to develop their own talents and to govern themselves as much as possible in their own ways. Not only were Indians expected to profit, but American society would be richer with a diversity of ways. The value of heterogeneity vs. homogeneity or cultural pluralism vs. assimilation has been much debated in America. It appears that there are highly ambivalent feelings toward the issue.[17]

The Maintainence of the Culture. As will be seen in the study of this book, cultures of the groups being studied have persisted through long periods of time. One of the characteristics of cultures, as they are established, is their persistence. The habits learned early in life seem to act very inflexibly in controlling the lives of the people from generation to generation.

The Hopi villages have been referred to as the oldest, continuously inhabited villages in the New World.

The Content of Culture. The content of culture may be thought of as material aspects, the artifacts - utensils, tools, and weapons; and the non-material aspects in human attitudes and values. However, the separation is a superficial one since it is the human attitudes and values that manipulate and use the artifacts and the tools are not important when separated from the ideas, thought-processes, and problem-solving that they make possible.

Factors that determine culture may be classified into the following: Communication through language; artifacts to provide food, shelter and clothing; mythology and legends; religious rites;

family organization (a kinship system); property rites; and government and politics.

"Culture Shock" is the trauma experienced by members of one culture who take up residence for whatever reason in another, usually quite different, culture.

Nostalgia for home, actual physical illnesses, and overt rejection of the host culture are common symptoms of culture shock. The person experiencing this difficulty may isolate himself in his environment, avoid the people living in the host culture, develop hostility or aggression toward the inhabitants of the host culture, or return home.

Those who understand the reasons for the feelings one goes through, and have an interest in working through these feelings to an objective rationale, make the adjustment and find the positive, desirable values of the new culture.

Cultural Change. The negative factors that resist cultural change are (1) the overlapping of the generations; (2) cultural inertia; (3) vested interests; and (4) the degree of isolation.[18] The pace of change is slow, but continuous. Sources of change are borrowing, invention, or discovery. Sometimes the change is the result of accident rather than intent. For example, the germ theory of disease has caused revolutionary changes in primitive medicine. The discovery of the miracle drugs has saved lives and changed the course of living in many under-developed countries.

Generalizations about culture:

1. Every society has a culture which provides for a way for most of its members to satisfy their needs.

2. Cultural influences on human behavior are so great and cultural differences so pronounced that one cannot generalize about human nature from the study of any one culture.

3. Cultural differences are not biologically transmitted.

4. Each society has a certain amount of ethnocentrism. It tends to think of its culture as superior.

5. In the past, isolation made it possible for social groups to tolerate each other without very much communication. Today, interchange around the world is rapid and constant. It is mandatory to accept differences.

6. The United States has inherited from England the English language, English jurisprudence, English values and customs, and these persist as the foundation stones of the culture pattern of our country. This needs to adapt if we hope to achieve the "one-world" concept for all peoples.

Contrasting Values in Processes of Cultural Change	

Culture is overt in:
  behavior,
  artifacts,
  art,
  speech, as communication.
	Culture is covert in:
	  attitudes toward nature,
	  attitudes toward the
	    spirit world,
	  interpretations of absence
	    of overt response.

Culture is explicit in:
  modes of behavior,
    activities of work,
    activities of leisure,
    activities of government,
    activities of education,
    activities of health.
	Culture is implicit in:
	  folkways,
	  mores,
	  taboos,
	  language habits.*

Culture is ideal in:
  how one "ought to" behave
    is clearly defined.
  a vague belief in an
    after-life.
	Culture is practical in:
	  how one behaves is not the
	    same as the defined "ideal."
	  poor preparation for an
	    after-life.

Culture is stable.
  reliving the "old ways"
    gives security and comfort.
  cultural inertia,
  vested interests,
  isolation.
	Culture is always changing.
	  flexible enough to make
	    slow, continual adjustments.
	  borrowing,
	  invention,
	  discovery,
	  diffusion.

*Language is habit. All people in a given social group speak the same language without necessarily knowing anything about the grammar of that language.

7. In theory, the United States is committed to a belief in cultural pluralism: the several racial, ethnic, and religious groups can live side by side, maintain their diverse ways of living, and thus make life richer for everybody.[19]

Culture as an Influence on Society

1. The culture under which a person matures exerts a powerful influence on him throughout his life.

2. Since the culture of a society has such an impact upon an individual's personality, he feels, thinks, and acts in accord with its imperatives, not only to be accepted by his fellows, but also to maintain his self-respect and confidence. The world into which every individual must fit is defined by his culture.

3. Language is an essential, effective, and exclusively human tool for the invention and transmission of culture. Art, music, and other symbolic and aesthetic expressions are also effective means of transmitting culture.

4. Culture, the creation of human activities, may be altered by them. Norms of culture are derived historically but are dynamic and thus may be subjected to planned change.

5. All cultures provide for the essential needs of human group life but differ, sometimes markedly, in the means by which they fulfill these needs. Different cultures result in different modes of thought and action. People generally prefer the culture of their own society but should recognize that they would probably prefer another culture if they had been subject to its influences to the same degree.

6. Anthropologists have been unable to discover a scientific basis for evaluating cultures as absolutely inferior or superior.

7. A major problem in the modern world is to discover ways in which social groups and nations with divergent cultures can cooperate for the welfare of mankind and yet maintain as much respect for one another's cultural patterns as possible.[20]

PROCESSES OF CULTURAL CHANGE

Culture is transmitted socially, that is, by communication, and gradually embodies in a group tradition of which the vehicle is language. This culture in a group is a matter of habits of thought and action acquired or "learned" by interaction with other members of the group. Culture includes all of man's acquired power of control over nature and himself. It includes, therefore, on the one hand, the whole of man's material civilization, tools, weapons, clothing, shelter, machines, and even systems of industry; and, on the other, all of non-material or spiritual civilization such as language, literature, art, religion, morality, law and government.[5]

Culture is acquired, not biologically inherited. Culture is our social inheritance; it defines and limits the general patterns to which individual practices in behavior will probably conform.

Culture is one of the important factors which permits us to live together in an organized society, giving ready-made solutions to our problems, helping us to predict the behavior of others, and permitting others to know what to expect of us.[6]

All of the ways of thinking, believing, and behaving are rooted in the cultural milieu. Brown has analyzed culture as cumulative, constantly changing, and gradually diffused.[23] Cultural diffusion may be thought of as the acceptance of patterns of behavior from another culture and integrating them into one's own. The spread of Christianity around the world is an example. Diffusion happens at the more or less superficial level as well as at the more fundamental level.

In the American Southwest, there is much talk about cultural diffusion. It has been suggested that the traditional cultures of the Indian and the Spanish American have much to offer. The truth of this statement is not contested. Nevertheless, it is difficult to imagine the typical middle-class Anglo internalizing values of life based on the economy, the education, the religion, or the health practices of a traditional minority group. The diffusion usually talked about is the more obvious, observable, and superficial type: eating green chili mutton stew on feast days in a Pueblo with friends, wearing fiesta dresses with ostentatious jewelry, owning a ring with a large turquoise set or an attractive squash blossom necklace, or decorating a room in one's house with Navajo rugs and an assortment of Pueblo Indian pottery. It is highly questionable whether many people would change basic thinking patterns or would be willing to give up their two-bathroom houses and thermostat-controlled central heat!

Minority cultures undergoing change resist that change.[24] The ethnocentrism of any group may be expected to keep these factors operating.

Ellis emphasizes that understanding of the processes of cultural change are essential for all those who seek to help the Indian toward a new way of life.

> Fundamental to all the other problems of the Indian, the problem behind problems is that of the very different basic personalities of individuals raised in different cultures. This problem is the cause of the mutual lack of understanding, of the sometimes exasperating resistance to change even when that change appears to its proponents to be so convincingly beneficial.[25]

The Indian Health Education Project, developed through the School of Public Health of the University of North Carolina, and the Division of Indian Health, United States Public Health Service, recognized the need for research across cultures. An anthropological orientation has a real place in developing among the staff workers a self-awareness of their own cultural background and characteristics, as well as increasing the staff's respect for the known similarities and cultural differences, particularly in the area of value systems. It is necessary to see the concept of culture as an integrated concept of patterned living, rather than a conglomeration of separate traits. Of this, Simpkins says:

> One of the greatest blocks to the successful utilization of cultural information in cross-cultural situations is the lack of understanding, on the part of the persons in the dominant group, of their own cultural background and its tremendous effect on such situations. Americans in general tend to take their culture for granted, assuming that their way of seeing and doing things is based on science and hence is right, whereas the culture of the other group is based on ignorance and superstition and hence is wrong. The picture is further complicated by the fact that Americans are so individualistically oriented that it is difficult for the average person to perceive of a group or community as being anything other than a collection of individuals. [26]

As evidence of the utility of this cultural understanding, Simpkins goes on to say:

> As more knowledge is accumulated about a particular community and staff members come to understand the essential bases of the culture of the Indian group they are better able to respect the attitudes and ways of life. Thus the staff develops deeper insight into the differences between the Anglo culture and the Indian cultures in such areas as orientation toward time, work, material possessions, self-assertiveness, and competition. [27]

Simpkins also emphasizes that some of the behaviors observed are really similarities across cultures if we understand our own culture. [28] Some of the behaviors of Pueblo peoples, for example, are not attributable to their "Indianness" as much as to their living in a rural environment, in isolation, in being farmers, or in being a minority ethnic group.

Brown says that:

> . . . To understand the person, it is necessary first to know and to appreciate the culture into which he is born, which exercises its inexorable influence throughout the span of life and which determines the place and ceremonial of his burial rites. [29]

The psychologist cautions against criticism of behavior which is strange or unfamiliar:

> Ideas of beauty vary from one culture to another. In some, fat women are preferred to all others. Deformation of the body, beauty scars, artificially elongated necks, enlarged

46

lips, and pointed teeth are well known, to say nothing of the effects produced by head-flattening and also by the modern girdle. In our less critical moments we are likely to think that there are a lot of people in the world who do not know how to act like human beings. In our more serious reflections we must realize that anything is human that typifies the behavior of human beings. There are no other standards of humanity. In any event we cannot understand the behavior of peoples of different cultures in terms of our own system of values, but must seek explanations in their own cultural histories. [30]

The educator who studies bilingual problems of children recognizes that a child's reading, his vocabulary, and his linguistic ability are rooted in a whole set of cultural values.

> The reading problems of most bilingual children arise, generally, from the home situation. The economic status, the education of the parents, the general cultural level, the emotional pattern, the health standards, mobility, rural or urban residence, and the attitude toward the English language are interlocking factors. The product of all these factors is the child with whom you work.

> A foreign cultural background does not mean inferiority; it means difference: difference in attitude of the parents toward the significance and value of education; difference in the belief in general education; in the extent of personal sacrifices needed to send children to school; in willingness to deprive oneself of the income he might receive if the child left school and went to work. These items bear directly on the matter of regularity of attendance and the age of dropping out of school and consequently on the child's reading ability. [31]

The interdependence of the language of the child and his cultural background is well stated by Davies:

> To change a child's medium of instruction is surely to change his culture; is not culture bound up with language? And if the language should disappear, can the culture remain? Everyone must have his own orientation to life, and language provides the most natural means of reacting to life. In the deepest things of the heart, a man or woman turns naturally to the mother tongue; and in a child's formative stages, his confidence in that tongue must never be impaired. [32]

The problem of integration of local cultures is described by Hemsing:

> New Mexico has a fabulously rich but neglected storehouse of experience for society in the unique history of this state. The

last century, particularly, constitutes a remarkably condensed summary of the social development from the Stone Age to the Atomic Age. One finds here man's most vexing and persistent problems.[33]

Lee states that:

> Careful study of a culture is needed; this must include a consideration of motivations, values, the symbolic significance of even seemingly unimportant acts, and a consideration also of all of the dangers inherent in the disturbances of the delicate balance between a culture and its local environment. Such study can result in the introduction of technological improvement which neither destroys the culture it is designed to improve nor opens up a Pandora's box of dangerous secondary results.[34]

> . . . it is reported that the Girl Scout manuals which were recently sent from the United States to a school in Indonesia were thrown away unused. The people to whom they were sent are Mohammedans, and they explained that as Moslems they found it abominable to have human beings equated with bears, beavers, and wolves, and to have girls urged to name themselves after animals.[35]

Teachers who work with Indian children in the Southwest need to remember that primitive education (all pre-literate education) was a community project in which many of the elders participated. This made "the child's education a constant challenge to the elders to review, analyze, dramatize, and defend their cultural heritage."[36] Because of this attitude, Indian leaders today may wish to have an active part in programming in the public schools which enroll their children. Teachers should react constructively to this interest on the part of tribal leaders.

Mead reminds us that the teacher is one of the key people in shaping the thinking of the immigrant child. That in making an immigrant child into an "American," the teacher may be forcing him to give up all of his past, his traditions, his language, his parentage. Of immigrant children, Mead writes:

> They are not only poor, but they are foreign; they have unpronounceable names and eat strange things for breakfast; their mothers come with shawls over their heads to weep and argue and threaten a teacher who is overworked, whose nerves are frayed by the constant battle with the polyglot youngsters who surge through her classroom.[37]

> They must be taught, not the constancies of their parents' immediate past. . . but they must be taught to reject, and usually despise, their parents' values. They must learn those

things which, to the extent that they make them Americans, will alienate them forever from their parents, making them ancestorless, children of the future, cut off from their past.[38]

The typical teacher of today is mobile upward, moving from lower class to lower middle class or from lower middle class to a better middle-class position. She is someone who must transcend her own past and so in a sense is the better prepared to help her pupils repudiate theirs and become mobile also.[39]

Pettitt found instances in the anthropological literature where Pueblos, Navajos, and Apaches all utilize the mother's brother as disciplinarian and teacher.[40] This characteristic disciplinary-procedure relegates the act of administering discipline to someone outside the immediate parent-child group. Perhaps parents do not wish to gain the child's ill will. Or, perhaps the practice is related to the matri-local residence where, in the past, the consanguine brother-sister relationship was more dependable than the husband-wife conjugal relationship.

In some pueblos, Katchinas, masked gods, serve as disciplinarians. If a child has been obstreperous, the parents may secretly inform the person who soon appears wearing his mask. He threatens and frightens the child, and in the end, the parent usually intercedes for the child and says he will be "good."

Teachers cannot become anthropologists, per se, anymore than they can become psychologists, sociologists, or human geographers in addition to the adequate preparation which they must have in child growth and development and methodology in teaching prescribed subject matter. Their idealism and their long-range life goals can, however, encompass a vision of the scope of human nature as a continually changing process that can eventually make possible all men living harmoniously together on this planet. Such an idealism must be rooted in some knowledge of, and appreciation for, the work of the cultural anthropologist who may eventually help man to understand himself and others so that life goals for all societies will be compatible. If all the cultural groups are sufficiently investigated and understood, a set of general working principles directed toward the common good might be worked out.

The anthropologist's purpose in studying a pre-literate culture is to find out how the basic institutions in society work for that particular group. He accepts the basic tenet that they do have a culture which they value. They have a patterned way of life that regulates operations of religion, family, economics, education, health practices, government, and recreation. The anthropologist attempts to be completely unbiased in respecting the people and respecting their culture. This respect means that he believes that each social group is struggling to find ways for human beings to live together, and he respects their efforts.[41]

In the transmission of American culture, that which is transmitted need not be quite so narrow a perspective as is generally common today. If the peoples of the world are ever going to understand each other's language well enough, accept each other's feelings extensively enough, and compromise differences in cultural practices graciously enough to approach a world view across all the cultures, societies like ours will have to place great faith in their teachers to understand and promote this cause.

Even within the local community of each classroom teacher as it exists today, there really are much wider horizons than most people admit or promote. Although education has long accepted and compromised the cultural lag in the acceptance of new ideas and practices and their adoption in the school curricula, still there is a corresponding responsibility for educators to diminish the cultural lag when and where possible. The one element that would be most helpful to teachers everywhere is that of vision, the knowledge about issues so that they might reason logically with school patrons to help them lift their sights and broaden their horizons. In this sense, the anthropologist has a body of knowledge available to the teacher in this specific area of educating across cultures. Education deals with children in culture, and serves the ends of a culture.

Individuals learn from their own culture their system of values, emotional patterns, and behavior standards, by internalizing the culture into their personalities so that they want to act as they have to act. The school reflects but a part of American culture, namely, the middle class. It enforces the values of the middle class, shapes its program to promote ways of thinking that are middle-class oriented, and is culturally biased in both the measurement and cultivation of intelligence.[42] Taba states that:

> . . . the American Society produces a character which emphasizes uncritical conformity, other-orientation, publicly attuned adjustment, and which essentially denies the importance of inner life, autonomy and individuality, spontaneous and private in personality development.[43]

As a study of man across the cultures of the world, anthropology has been recognized as having a major contribution to make to the course of study in the social sciences. For example, one recent course of study lists the following generalization from anthropology which teachers are expected to integrate into their classroom teaching:

1. The understanding of the concept of culture is basic to an appreciation of the communities around the world and to the world community.

2. The evolution of human life on the earth is knowable and understandable.

3. Culture is a product of man's exclusive capacity to comprehend and communicate symbolically (e.g., via language).

4. A written record of the past enables each new generation to profit from all that has been accumulated through the ages and to begin at the frontier of human endeavor to solve new problems.

5. The culture under which a person is reared exerts a powerful influence on him throughout his life.

6. Human beings, regardless of their racial or ethnic backgrounds, are nearly all capable of participating in and making contributions to any culture.[44]

In the problem of education across cultures, the whole concept of a causal approach to behavior is rooted in understanding the background out of which the individual emerged.

James' recommendation is that geography and history be taught by grouping all the countries of the world into seven major culture areas. Each of the seven possesses distinctive characteristics related to the world-wide processes of change (European, American, North African-Southwest Asian, Oriental, Soviet, African, and Pacific).[45]

Socio-cultural differences include differences in dress, customs, attitudes, beliefs, knowledges, and ideals. These cultural differences need to be understood in terms of basic social institutions. Anthropologists have considered much of the Southwest as a "goldmine" for decades, and field studies have been going on in the area since 1920. However, there is still largely an unmet need for educators to incapsulate the specific body of knowledge that would help classroom teachers appreciate the two worlds in which the teacher and his Indian pupils live.

THE PSYCHOLOGICAL ROLE OF THE TEACHER IN THE CLASSROOM

The emotional climate of the classroom is determined by the interaction of the teacher and the children he teaches. The teacher's responses to the overt behavior manifested in his classroom forces him into many psychological roles during the school day. Some of the psychological roles discussed by Redl and Wattenberg are summarized below.[46]

1. As representatives of society, teachers attempt to inculcate in children the values of the community. These include moral attitudes, thinking patterns, and life goals.

2. Teachers act as judgers and screeners in their marking systems, report cards, promotion schemes, and the day-to-day work of conducting class sessions and correcting papers.

3. As a source of knowledge, teachers are expected to be living textbooks from which one can get information.

4. Teachers are helpers in the learning process where there is difficulty. They ask leading questions, go over problems step-by-step, and conduct discussions.

5. As a referee, every teacher is expected to be a Solomon. He is judged by his ability to be fair and to help children reconcile their differences.

6. Psychologically, some children may use the teacher as a respected person with whom they identify themselves.

7. The teacher is a temporizer of anxiety. Confidence, competence, and humor can help to reduce anxiety in children. Stern threats, rigid severity, fear of failure, and disapproval can increase anxiety.

8. The teacher will be an ego-supporter for many children when he helps them muster their courage and gives them reassurance.

9. As a group leader, the teacher sets the tone of the class, and helps the group function harmoniously in reaching group goals.

Some of these roles can be more adequately met by teachers of minority groups if they understand the cultural backgrounds of the children in their classes. There may be serious conflicts between values held by parents and a teacher. While a teacher may teach children certain values which their parents do not hold, he should not teach young children that their parents have wrong values. For example, from the teacher's point of view, the Indian's religion may not be rational, scientific, or philosophically sound. Indian mythology, unlike its Christian counterpart, is accepted literally rather than allegorically. The teacher's belief that there is a scientific explanation for all natural phenomena is juxtaposed to the unscientific ritualism of Indian cultures where witches, not germs, bring sickness.

A teacher may find that discipline patterns in a child's home differ from those of his own childhood. Shame and fear are often effective controls within the family. The bogey-man is a reality for the Indian child, but not the hickory stick. Coming from a culture where conformity and anonymity are primary values, children are apt not to seek to be different or individual. Few Indian children may wish to demonstrate that they are the best readers or spellers in the class.

Teachers report that children from Spanish speaking and Anglo homes watch closely when a dispute involves one Anglo child and one Spanish speaking child to see if the teacher is completely fair in making a settlement. The teacher is apt to be accepted in relation to the degree of fairness which the group feels he exercises.

The understanding teacher will see many opportunites in school to nurture ego-needs of children. Specific ways of doing this for Indian children or Spanish speaking children will not always follow the patterns the teacher himself experienced. The Indian child who never lets his eyes meet his teacher's when responding to him, but hangs his head shyly, must learn that this is a custom unfamiliar to many of his teachers. The way in which attempts are made to change children's behavior will determine, to a great extent, the teacher's success. Children who come to school from homes where authoritarian practices are in vogue will need more security in learning to operate in a free classroom atmosphere where children plan with the teacher, where children's suggestions can be important, and where children may even disagree with the teacher in acceptable ways. Perhaps a new system of motivations is indicated.

PRINCIPLES OF CHILD GROWTH AND DEVELOPMENT

The role of the psychologist in defining principles or generalizations in growth and development of children may appropriately be summarized. Child growth, as evaluated by the psychologist, must be viewed in the role expectations of the individual in his particular cultural heritage.

Child growth and development is generally studied in five broad aspects: Physical, mental, social, emotional, moral and spiritual. General principles that relate to physical growth, mental growth, and social growth, also relate to emotional growth and moral and spiritual development.

The human being is an organism obeying several principles of maturation. These principles have been derived from the observation of certain characteristics of people as biological organisms. These characteristics include:

1. Stability: the organism has stability in such physical conditions as permanent body temperature and regulated bodily systems (respiration, circulation, metabolism, etc.).

2. Sensitivity: the organism has a highly developed central nervous system and specialized senses.

3. Activity: the organism develops curiosity and movement.

4. Organization: the organism is intricately well organized and the coordination of its total operation improves with physical maturity.

5. Development and change: the organism is continuously developing, growing toward maturity. This change has continuity and increasing complexity.

The process of growth and development in all five of the areas indicated above can be described as following general principles of growth and development. In other words, these principles have predictive value for the alert teacher who can relate them to normal growth and development.

1. The first principle is that behavior develops from generalized to specific responses. This is illustrated in the gross, over-all movements of infancy that develop eventually into the refined, differentiated specific movements of the well-coordinated adult. This sequence is clearly seen in the uncontrolled, over-all activity of a tiny baby in response to a desired stimuli and in his later well-controlled reaching and grasping. This differentiation proceeds from the general to the specific, from the simple to the complex, and from the homogeneous to the heterogeneous. As regards both structure and activity, the development is in the direction of complexity and variety. Growing refinement and discrimination characterize all aspects of development.

2. The second principle is that over the long run, development is forward and continuous. Physical development, for example, is continuous throughout the life of the individual. In general, all individuals follow the same pattern. Babies progress from lifting their heads, to sitting up, to standing, and finally to walking unaided.

   For normal children, reasonably well-loved and secure individuals, there is a natural pull toward growing up in the expected pattern. All the rewards are on the side of growing toward adulthood. All the satisfactions of experiencing greater and greater independence and freedom are on the side of growing up "normally."

3. The third principle is that, over short periods, growth may appear irregular. The two-year-old, whom mother believes is toilet trained, has accidents. The eight-year-old, who has been mother's little helper, forgets, dawdles, or rebels. This has been termed asynchronous growth, meaning out of harmony. Adolescence is probably the most noticeable period of life to exhibit asynchrony, as, for instance, when the adolescent boy becomes "all arms and legs."

   One fourteen-year-old boy, for example, went to a junior high Christmas party and proudly exercised his privilege of meeting girls under the mistletoe. A few days later he cried real tears after he got home from a university band concert, explaining to his mother that he would never be able to play his trumpet as the college players did.

4. The fourth principle is that various aspects of growth are interrelated. Tall children tend to reach puberty first; bright children tend to be slightly above average in weight and other measures of growth. Olson averaged several "ages" such as reading, mental, grip, dentition, height, and weight, and termed this the "organismic age."[47] This has come to be recognized as the best single measure of the child's degree of maturity. Olson[48] and Olson and Hughes[49] illustrate two important generalizations: (a) growth tends to be unified, and (b) achievement is a function of total growth.

5. The fifth general principle is that the growing child resists displacement from his basic growth pattern. If a child does miss school, or suffers a short illness, or for any other reason seems to fall behind his age group, usually he is able to make adjustment for it and continue with his age group. This resistance to displacement is strongly evidenced in the value placed on conforming in a group.

It might be said in this frame of reference that conformity is an over-valued commodity in middle-class Anglo culture. All children are assigned to first grade public school classes at age six; all children are expected to get promoted each year; all nine-year-olds in the fourth grade are expected to learn the multiplication tables. Peer group pressures force children either to conform or to develop feelings of guilt, disapproval, or inadequacy if they are unsuccessful.

6. The sixth general principle is that growth patterns are individual and unique. Most adults accept at the verbal level that no two children are alike. Yet this principle is lost sight of in the great emphasis on conformity. When all six-year-olds are placed in formal reading situations, individual growth patterns are being ignored. Some sixes are good readers already; many sixes are ready to begin reading; and some sixes still lack maturity, physically, socially, mentally, and emotionally, for the complex process of reading.

7. The seventh general principle is that the sequence of development is dependable and predictable but the exact timing is not. With individual children, timing may be erratic, and intervening steps of development may sometimes be omitted. The sequence of happenings in growth and development may be expected to follow a dependable pattern. In physical growth, the child first crawls, then creeps, then walks, then runs. In the language arts, children first understand when they listen to others, then they learn to talk, then they learn to read, and last in the heirarchy, they learn to write.

8. Finally, there is a need for understanding what is normal. Normality must be seen merely as a measure of statistical expectation. In this frame of reference, no one child could be described as the specific norm, but most children fit in a so-called normal range. When the normal range is seen as a distribution on a long continuum, most children are normal.

There are great individual variations in the ways in which children mature. Girls are apt to develop a normal speech pattern earlier than boys. Girls usually enter their pre-adolescent growth spurt two years before boys do. As for mental development of both sexes, teachers consider all ten-year-olds with mental ages from nine to eleven to be "normal" in intelligence. Consider the implications of this two-year range in what is termed normal ability of all the children in a fifth grade class for achievement in all the tasks of the school. Again, with respect to physical development of girls, the menarche may begin with considerable regularity before the eleventh birthday, or it may not begin before the sixteenth birthday. This extreme range in "normal" girls has many ramifications in their social and psychological development.

These examples should not confuse the issue of what is normal. It is hoped that they help to emphasize the uniqueness of each individual and to show that each person must arrive at his own level of maturity in his own good time.

Within the framework of these generalizations, behavior, either overt or covert, is the conduct of the individual. The responses of each individual register his ways of coping with the problems of life. Responses to frustration, for example, may vary in many ways: ignoring or overlooking important facts, trying to escape or evade unpleasantness, attempting to shift or substitute responses to escape, and straightforward facing of the facts. Individuals have all degrees of success-failure responses to needs, feelings, emotions, attitudes, frustrations, and aspirations. The personality of the individual encompasses his total experience in learned ways of behaving.

CONCEPT OF LIFE-SPACE

When the Spanish American or Indian child comes to public school in New Mexico, he is apt to have a meager background of experience which will make it difficult for him to participate meaningfully in the formal work of the classroom. Havighurst and Neugarten use the concept of life-space in delineating the total environment in which the child lives.[50] The concept of life-space "involves at least three different elements: physical space, the objects contained within that space, and the people who inhabit that space. All three elements are socially defined or socially determined."[51]

There are extreme differences in the experiences of middle-class Anglo children. This has been clearly demonstrated, for example, in classrooms when various individuals describe the range of travel experiences of their families.[52] Some children in any teacher's classroom will have had most meager out-of-school experiences. It is difficult for the teacher to make reading experiences equally meaningful for the two children at opposite extremes of the wide range of first-hand experiences.

> The school needs to perform the dual function of enlarging the child's life-space and of helping him feel secure in that life-space. To do this, the school must provide a rich curriculum and a psychological atmosphere that lends itself to cultivating happiness and security within the child. . . . It is important for the teacher at least to know that the life-space does have different meanings for different children and to know something of the nature of these meanings.[53]

The life-space of the child is one of the most significant factors determining the school's success in teaching him the values which he must acquire. The meager background of experience, the lack of familiarity with artifacts in Anglo culture, the use of a second language in his life outside the school, the complete absence of books, magazines, and newspapers in the child's home and in the experience of his elders create many problems in the administration of a school. Teachers must attempt to overcome these problems and at the same time transmit the heritage of the people from both cultures.

ENVIRONMENTAL FACTORS AND MOTIVATION

A study by Deutsch, relative to the influence of environmental factors on motivation for learning in school, and on the child's ego status concerning his own possibilities, is significant in its application to the education of minority groups everywhere.[54] Deutsch's study is important because there is evident need for comparable research studies to analyze the social distance between the child and his environment, on the one hand, and the teacher and the middle-class orientation of the school on the other. If the findings of Deutsch regarding Negro children in a northern metropolis apply across cultures to minority groups in the Southwest, as this writer believes, there exists an urgent need for understanding of the conflicts that exist and for developing some techniques to alleviate them.

The purposes of Deutsch's study were to investigate the existence of special problems in minority group education, and to provide increased understanding into social and behaviorial factors as they relate to the perception of the self, frustration, tolerance, group membership, and the rate of learning.[55] The study attempted to determine how social stress affects motivation, personal aspiration, concepts of self, and how it differentiates the minority group child from the majority group child of similar background.

The Negro children in Deutsch's study came from an impoverished area where social rejection, high rates of family breakdown, chronic economic anxiety, and low aspiration level were prevalent. A family atmosphere index comparing Negro and White (control) groups showed that the Negroes came from more unfavorable backgrounds and also regarded their home environment less favorably than did their White counterparts.

According to Deutsch:

> . . . there is a general absence of persistence on the part of these children when they find a task to be difficult.
>
> . . . there seems to be a complete absence of preparation for the school experience. It is not that the parents are "anti-school," but that the rewards of schooling are foreign to their experience.
>
> . . . a negative self-image is seen to relate strongly to being Negro. . . . In completing the sentence, "If someone makes fun of me. . . . ," 47 per cent of the whites, but only 6 per cent of the Negroes, suggested counteraction . . . he senses that the larger society views him as inferior and expects inferior performance from him.[56]

. . . . . .

In addition to this special handicap of the Negro boy -- i.e., lack of a strong male with whom to identify -- there is a particularly dismal aspect of his future relative to competition for jobs. In our culture a man is expected to achieve, to provide, to compete, and this necessarily involves more contact with the larger society. Whatever handicaps the Negro boy starts with are likely to be increased by his contact with the majority group as a minority group member with consequent lower status.

We really cannot calculate the full extent of the deleterious effects on personality development of the continual reaffirmation of inferior status, segregation and quasi-segregation, and discrimination. These realities are especially met with in the job areas, where in our upward mobile society the Negro is most often forced to remain stationary.[57]

. . . . . .

The participating teachers were middle-class and the majority were Negroes; the children they taught were lower-class Negroes. For the most part, the teachers felt alien to the community within which they worked. . . .[58]

. . . . . .

Observers keeping diaries during the study recorded that teachers often directed derogatory remarks toward individual children. The most frequent such remark was to call a child "stupid," and as a result, the teacher, and, through the teacher, the school played a role in reinforcing the negative self-image of the child, and contributed a negative reason for learning.[59]

According to Deutsch, the teacher is an essential part of the learning process, but when he is made to feel extraneous in matters of policy and curriculum and in evaluation of teaching problems, he also loses his initiative and interest in evaluating his own role.[60] For the children, their expectations, reinforced by the anxiety of their middle-class teachers, were that the larger white world would fundamentally be rejecting and critical. The ones who most need the socializing experience of the school may well be those who are least amenable to it because of their previous narrow range of experience.[61]

Deutsch emphasizes over and over the role of the social scientist in the study of these racial-class problems; he feels that the social psychologist or the cultural anthropologist should study extensively the dynamic relationships between environmental and social circumstances and between personality and intellectual performance. He states that:

> The lower-class child, and especially the lower-class minority group child, lives in an environment which fosters self-doubt and social confusion, which in turn serves substantially to lower motivation and makes it difficult to structure experience into cognitively meaningful activity and aspirations.[62]

The extent to which Deutsch's study points up the fact that Negro children cannot be taught under present conditions, reveals the need for understanding of class and ethnic cultural determinants in removing obstacles to successful achievement.

CULTURAL ANTHROPOLOGY AND THE CLASSROOM TEACHER

According to Elam:

> Upon entering school, the bilingual child experiences a "cultural shock." In this new environment the foundations of his security are shaken. A sudden change or interruption of culture may cause learning to cease. He must cling to the traditions of his culture and lag behind in acquisition of a second language, or discard his traditions and acquire a "foreign" tongue. Either choice results in emotional upheaval which may result in maladjustment toward school or his home environment.[63]

Knowing his language limitations and fearing failure, the bilingual child reasons that it is better not to try. He absolves himself of the responsibility; therefore, he reasons, he has not failed.

Warner, Havighurst, and Loeb point out that one of the hard facts in our social system is that children are not born equal.

> We know that children are not created equal socially. Every individual is born into a set of social positions. A child is born into a social status by sex. From the day of its birth a boy child is treated in a different manner from a girl child. A child is born into a status by his birth order in the family. The first-born will receive different treatment from those who come later. The last child will get a special kind of treatment. A child is born into a status by his family's position in the social structure. The child of the house "on the hill" will have nurses, servants, tutors. He will grow accustomed to having people treat him with deference. He will develop manners and speech that mark him as having grown up "on the hill." The child of the house by the railroad tracks will grow up with entirely different manners and attitudes and expectations in life. A child is born into a status by his nationality or race. If he is Jewish, Italian, Irish, German, Chinese, Hindu, Negro, he will undergo the treatment accorded to people of his group, treatment which varies from one part of the world to another and from one time to another.[64]

When children come to the public school from these diverse backgrounds of experience, it is obvious that equality of opportunity for education does not mean identity of opportunity.

Allport discusses in a concise way the way prejudice is apt to work for the naive citizen:

> One reason why categories are tenaciously held and often used is that they provide a convenient formula for living. Think of the insuperable difficulty of individualizing two and one half billion mortals on earth. It is too difficult even to individualize the people we come in contact with in our daily round. . . .
>
> Take the way that Citizen Sam's mind might work. Sam is an average, hypothetical citizen who confronts this problem of adjusting to the many people in his environment. He finds they are just too many for him. He therefore evolves the following formula: Foreigners: "All alike! Keep 'em out of the country." That bit of categorizing gets rid of most of the human race. Negroes: "All alike! They're treacherous, dirty, and so I don't want anything to do with them; they have to be kept where they belong." That gets rid of 13 million more. Jews: "As a group, they're completely untrustworthy." Good.

Cleveland Press

"*He just ain't civilized enough yet to be our equal*"

From Jet, June 8, 1961.

Acculturation is slowed down when people react emotionally (affectively) rather than remaining affectively neutral. The paradox in the cartoon above, obviously, is that the unacceptable Negro reacts with passive non-violent behavior while the in-groups of acceptable whites overpower him by sheer numbers and weapons of violence.

That gets rid of four million more. Democrats and Labor: "They're all just alike, just one big hulk -- get rid of them. As for the professors and intellectuals, they can be rejected along with all the other Communists." Soon there isn't anything left to worry about or have to deal with. The only remnants are Citizen Sam's few neighbors on Suburban Heights -- and he can get rid of them one by one through gossip! When one can get rid of these big chunks of humanity through prejudice, life seems much easier and more manageable.65

Teachers of Indian children have reported several facets of prejudice, possibly unsuspected by newly arrived teachers in the Southwest.66

. . . .

Working with an instructional aid is very helpful, they help each teacher to understand the Navajo child's background, problems, ideas, behavior and language difficulties. They helped to try to prevent any student from having an "unwanted feeling" toward teachers and advisers. A Navajo child can be hurt very easily by such things as tone of voice or facial expressions.

. . . .

A Santo Domingo Indian boy, temporarily a resident of the Bernalillo County Detention Home for fighting with a Navajo at the Albuquerque Indian School, remarked: "The supervisors at the school cater to the Navajo because of all their money."

. . . .

A Santo Domingo Indian, envious of the uranium and oil on the vast Navajo Reservation, remarked to me, "I remember when they used to work for us for an ear of corn a day.

. . . .

The people of Canyoncito are referred to as the "Anayah Dinéh," which means "informers for enemy people." They gained this reputation by aiding Kit Carson and helping him when he rounded up the Navajo to go to Bosque Redondo. The term is used by the other Navajos in a very derogatory way, and is the beginning of many fights among Navajo boys.

. . . .

While filling out an information sheet, one of the sixth grade pupils asked how to spell the word "Navajo." The teacher explained that the word in the English language would be spelled "Navaho." The most commonly used spelling "Navajo" is the spelling in the Spanish used when they came to this country long ago and found the Indians. Both spellings are used by different writers who have had their books published. Both are considered correct. After that brief discussion, the teacher told the pupils that they might use whichever spelling of the word they preferred. When the papers were collected, the teacher noted that each of the sixteen Navajos in a school room with twenty-one Anglos chose the spelling "Navaho." The Navajo has a deep sense of pride in his own group. To him the word "Navaho," although of the second language which he is learning, seems more a part of him than "Navajo" which was influenced by the Spanish.

. . . .

The greatest prejudice against the Navajo children that I have encountered in everyday doings has been from Indian or Spanish sources. I showed a Pueblo Indian friend the hole where new dormitories are to go up at the Indian school, and told him that 1,000 children were already going to school there. In tones of great scorn, he said, "All for Navajos, too." Obviously, a great waste so far as he was concerned.

. . . .

Bunker and Adair have reported an experimental seminar in cross-cultural relations designed to help in the preparation of technical consultants who undertake jobs in their professions in so-called underdeveloped areas. This study was concerned with techniques for establishing empathy between representatives of the traditional cultures and the consultants who bring ideas for technological change. Further, it emphasized the need for more ways for the various disciplines to pool their knowledges and insights in an inter-disciplinary approach to total problems. The basic concept dealt with was that of the cultural whole: the interrelationship of man's methods, beliefs, and behavior, the idea that a change in one aspect of culture often affects the entire culture.[67]

The generalizations emphasized by Bunker and Adair are applicable to teachers who are assigned to teach children who live in a culture alien to their own. These generalizations include:

1. Lack of cummunication is the greatest problem between members of different cultures.

2. An inter-disciplinary approach to problems is best.

3. Consultants from the dominant culture must learn to work through the existing social organization of the sub-culture.

4. Empathy is a prerequisite to adequate communication.

Bunker and Adair have written in their concluding chapter that "Culture can be a tyrant. Our own set of ways of looking at what we may consider the set ways of strangers may prevent us from really seeing the peoples we encounter."[68]

The concept of formal education in our public schools as representing only one small, narrow, and inflexible sector of the total of American life -- the middle-class orientation -- discussed by Davis[69] is analyzed in considerable detail by Henry.[70] Based on several previous studies in public schools, Henry's findings are collated in a cross-cultural outline for educators.

American teachers have experienced the desire for upward mobility in the social structure, the adherence to a rigid set of values by which they judge the behaviors of all children, and a vague allegiance to what may be termed the Protestant Ethic. This has caused teaching as a method of cultural transmission to be a continuous narrowing of the learners' perceptual field with respect to values and the processes of cultural change. This narrowing of the learners' concept of what values, beliefs, and attitudes are right, proper, and acceptable is directly opposed to the world view and to the concept of broadening a child's appreciations of the interactions of man in a world community!

It becomes apparent that processes of social change and broadening of outlook can happen only when the rigid pattern of the school is unsuccessful. The future of this dilemma rests on the shoulders of the teachers in the classrooms of America. Educators must recognize and clearly teach that there are wider horizons and that they can be understood and internalized in the culture if they will idealistically grope for attainment of basic objectives. Moehlman said that we must be ideal in outlook and dynamic in practice.[71] Moehlman goes on to say:

> Extreme care must be taken constantly to recognize the inevitability of change, to guard against a too narrow concept of educational activity, and to avoid the inculcation of concepts of social stratification and cultural inflexibility growing out of individual narrowness and inflexibility.[72]

Henry's observers in the schools reported:

> . . . teachers are usually teaching values by implication regardless of the immediate subject matter . . . one difficulty is that a teacher's own unconscious behavior may contradict the values he is attempting to teach . . . the school system may attempt to emphasize contradictory values. . . . Thinking would seem to involve an analytical process of some kind and also a process of synthesis. Almost none of this takes place in the elementary school. . . the pupil is limited in what he may learn from his teacher by the fact that the teacher often rushes through the lesson, lacks adequate equipment, teaches about things that are often remote from him and from the pupil either in space or time or both, and teaches subjects in which he himself is weak in knowledge. Irrelevant

interruptions and misleading explanations limit the child, too, in what he can possibly learn. 73

Attitudes toward education as a process, the immediacy with which the learner perceives the need for what he is learning, the way the teacher feels about the child and the way the child feels about the teacher, the techniques of rewards and punishments, and the application of the pain-pleasure principle, all these and many other facets determine the learner's attitude -- and how he participates -- in the learning process.

Henry says that man is continually pulled forward to new vistas by his curiosity, but pulled backward by his inherent fear that if he learns too much he will be rejecting parts of his culture. Language is the instrument by which man exercises both of these desires.

So it is that though language has been an instrument with which man might cleave open the universe and peer within, it has also been an iron matrix that bound his brain to ancient modes of thought. And thus it is that though man has poured what he knows into his culture patterns, they have also frozen around him and held him fast. 74

In another article, Henry describes a number of specific situations in which values actually being taught in classrooms are at considerable odds with that which the philosophy of the school expects to be taught. Such negative situations include destructive criticism of others, feelings of vulnerability, fear of internal hostility, confession of evil deeds, and boredom. Henry describes activities in a good citizenship club in which children reported to the teacher on good and bad behavior of their peers. He found intra-group aggression, docility in conforming to external pressure of the group and to teacher authority, feelings of vulnerability and fear of detection, and the value of spying and confession were activated and encouraged and, therefore, transmitted. 75

Henry concludes by saying that teachers, like parents, are gratifying their own unconscious needs in their overt responses to children. The constructive approach to this dilemma is not to condemn teachers, but to give them insights into how they project their personal problems into the classroom situation. 76

CONJUGAL VERSUS CONSANGUINAL RELATIONSHIPS IN FAMILY ORGANIZATION

Another area in which patterns may vary cross-culturally is that of family organization. Perpetuation of the family in society requires the contracting of marriage partners and procreation. The ramifications of daily living, ownership of worldly goods, and disciplining of the children are many and varied. Basically, family organization may follow either a relationship based primarily on the conjugal system or a relationship based primarily on the consanguinal system. In the first case, the love relationship in marriage brings together man and wife to start anew a family pattern. Decision-making is strongly severed from family ties. The blood relationship, termed consanguinal, is the typical pattern of matrilineal societies wherein the mother's brother accepts the responsibility for disciplining the children and helping his sister manage her family problems. Linton differentiates these two relationships as follows:

> In societies organized upon the conjugal basis we can picture the authentic functional family as consisting of a nucleus of spouses and their offspring surrounded by a fringe of relatives. In those organized on the consanguine basis we can picture the authentic family as the nucleus of blood relatives surrounded by a fringe of spouses.[77]

The matrilineal pattern of control of property fits the pattern of consanguine relationships. The gratification of sex needs and procreation are fulfilled by giving a non-relative a kind of marginal status with the family. However, the extended family pattern of the mother and her daughters owning the houses, the livestock, the gardens, and the children makes it possible for the consanguine group to perform the functions of the family very successfully.

The conjugal relationship, based on courtship, love, and marriage, carries with it greater emotional satisfaction. Jealousy and monogamy fit this pattern.

It has been said that the Pueblo Indian woman may divorce her husband by putting his boots and his ceremonial garb outside the door while he is away. If she does this, he knows when he returns that he should not go inside his wife's house, but should take his belongings and return to his mother's house. This point of view also explains the very accepting attitude toward illegitimate children among matrilineal groups. The expression sometimes used about a young man who causes a young girl to have a child out of wedlock is "He stole a child from her." This might be said without indicating blame or need for retribution.

In passing, it should be indicated that most societies have some degree of both of these relationships. While overt behavior in the American culture gives heavy emphasis to the conjugal basis for establishing the family unit, there are also many evidences of kinship ties. A commonly heard expression is "Blood is thicker than water."

THE MATRILINEAL VERSUS THE PATRILINEAL SOCIETY

The matrilineal society is one that reckons descent, inheritance, or succession exclusively or preferentially through females. This matrilineal organization exists in many less complex societies. Women, in matrilineal societies, own the houses, rear the children with help from maternal uncles more than from the father figure, and exercise control over the provision of the necessities of life for the family. According to Adair, "matrilineal clans and matrilocal residence are still basic to the social organization of the Zuni pueblo, and have been instrumental in the perpetuation of the Zuni culture."[78] Women control a considerable share of the wealth, they have a stronger economic position in the pueblo than they had twenty to thirty years ago, and they operate in the trade of the community independent of the men.[79]

This existence of a matrilineal society presents a real barrier to the acculturation of the Indian toward middle-class Anglo lifestyle. In middle-class Anglo culture, each man hopes eventually to own his own house and to acquire other worldly possessions. As already mentioned, money is a highly prized middle-class value. The matrilineal society does not include this within its province. Traditionally, a man was easily sent back to his mother's household by his present wife. Thus, Zuni men, for example, are apt to covet possessions only with respect to their life values of order, balance, and harmony with the cosmos. Some possessions have great value in participation in religious rites and ceremonials and in the acquiring of social status and prestige. But, possessions are not apt to be selfishly coveted in the economic sense of the Anglo. A Zuni man, for example, may work extra hard with his crops, or save his money carefully for a period of time in preparation of sponsoring a Shalako ceremony.

The extent to which families adhere to the traditional matrilineal family organization varies from one family to another within each Indian group. It is probably safe to say that members of many Indian families do share the responsibility for family decisions. In this sense, while Anglo society is legally a patrilineal one, the arriving at decisions within the family today may be much the same for Indians or Anglos.

It needs to be emphasized that while much day-to-day living in Anglo society suggests that the mother in the family has assumed much responsibility for important decision-making, the father is still legally the head of the house. One writer has recently suggested that "the American family is losing, has lost, its patriarchal pattern, and is becoming matriarchoid in character."[80] Yet in the courts, it is recognized that family possessions are owned by the husband. As a specific example, in some states if a husband dies without a will and the bank account of the family is in his name, the wife is unable to obtain any of the money until the estate is settled. Many families who did not know this have undergone inconveniences.

Failure of Anglo workers to recognize different patterns of family organization, can cause well-laid plans to go awry. When Navajos were resettled on irrigated farmland, the arrangements went counter to their established groupings. They were established as individual families of parents of children, far from their relatives, despite the fact that they had been used to working their fields cooperatively in larger units, along extended kinship lines. For reasons such as this, the project did not prosper.[81]

EXTENDED AND NUCLEAR FAMILIES

Important differences exist between the extended family and the nuclear family. Traditionally, in both the Spanish American and Indian cultures, the extended family has been dominant. An extended family consists of the several related individual families, especially those of a man and his sons or of a woman and her daughters, residing in a single large dwelling or a cluster of smaller ones. This is typically found in some Indian and Spanish families in which the grandmother or grandfather acts as the matriarch or patriarch, and the children and all the grandchildren live either with the grandparents or nearby. This is illustrated in the Spanish American family where the old patriarch lives in his house in one section of the city and his several children all live in a cluster of houses around him. Every morning, each one comes by and drinks a bit of coffee and wishes him well. He no longer is gainfully employed, but his children are delighted to see that he is provided for as well as they are able. All the grandchildren grace his doorstep, and these numerous progeny contribute to the happiness he sees in his immortality.

Concerning the Spanish American family in isolated rural communities today, Maestas says that:

> For the most part, the family is a closely knit social unit which extends beyond father, mother, and children. It includes grandparents, uncles, and sometimes cousins. There is, however, evidence that the size of the family is shrinking and family ties are weakening. There is strong parental control over children, and one seldom hears about juvenile delinquency. Even after the youth have married and have established their own homes, family loyalty and solidarity are still strong.[82]

Some of the advantages of the extended family organization can be readily seen in the mutual helpfulness of various members of related families in time of any need. Sharing of food with those sub-groups whose supply is exhausted, sharing of the work of the total family during the seasons of the year when all labor efficiently together, and sharing problems related to health and well-being are examples of this mutual helpfulness.

Reichard illustrates the practice among the Navajo of sharing with those in need.

> Perhaps when the work on American Indian ethics is written, it will be necessary to dissociate food and sustenance from wealth subject to barter, and perhaps kinship will have to be substituted for material exchange, since relatives may pay in service and kindness rather than in materials. Whatever the classification, the Navajo deplores refusal to share food -- it is the greatest sin, the offense that reduces a person to the lowest rung of the ladder in the eyes of his fellowmen.
>
> During the winter of 1932-33 I saw three apparently respectable persons collapse on the street in the more complaisant residential districts of New York City. Subsequent newspaper notices reported the deaths as due to starvation. The next summer, to emphasize the severity of the depression, I mentioned these cases to my friend, Marie. Indignantly she asked, "But there were people who had food, weren't there?" And throughout the summer, trying to comprehend the circumstances, she repeatedly reverted to our talk. "I can't see why those women died, if there were people who had enough to eat." When this question can be answered satisfactorily more souls will be saved.[83]

The advantage of the extended family is further observed in their mutual helpfulness in meeting problems of exceptionality within the group. Institutions for the mentally retarded, for the aged, and for the mentally ill were neither founded or acceptable as long as the extended family could provide care for all these individuals. An aunt, a grandmother, an older sister, or some other member of the group was available to care for the atypical.

In writing of the Mexican population of Sal si Puedes, Clark says:

> Barrio residents criticize young people who do not provide homes for their aged parents. Mexican-American people are generally horrified at the common American practice of sending aged relatives to sanitariums or nursing homes when they become ill or senile. Teresa advanced the theory that "When a person gets very old and has to have someone to take care of him, it is better for him to be at home with his family than in a hospital among strangers. When someone gets old, he may act a little crazy, and he needs his family with him to understand him and help him. In a hospital or a sanitarium he

would only feel worse because he would think that everybody had deserted him."

Elvira worked for several months as a practical nurse at a private nursing home for the aged. She reported, "Almost all the patients are old American ladies who are a little crazy. There are about twenty of them there, and only three or four have regular visitors. Others are visited by their families only once a week or even less. I think that is just terrible. They are such nice old people and they are completely neglected by their families. Their relatives just stick them in the hospital and forget about them. They could be taken care of at home just as well and would be much happier with their children and grandchildren. A few are too sick to be at home, but the least their relatives could do is to visit them regularly; someone should come every day.[85]

It is recognized that the extended family existed to a considerable degree during previous decades in other parts of the country. The middle-class values of striving for achievement and success, planning for the future, and the belief that one shapes his own destiny tend to de-emphasize the community family welfare. Further, the mobility of families, the scattering of immediate families to all parts of the country, the specialization of work, and the mechanization of daily living foster the efficiency-apartment existence of the nuclear family.

The importance of and the values inherent in the extended family need to be appreciated by the Anglo American who has known only the nuclear family in his own experience. The extended family as an institution tempers one's attitudes toward illegitimacy, toward the care of the mentally and physically handicapped in the family, and toward the need for social welfare as a government agency.

JUDGING PUPIL BEHAVIOR IN THE CLASSROOM: A SYNTHESIS

Children's overt behavior must be continually judged, evaluated, and responded to by the teacher. His ability to interact with the individuals in his classroom will be dependent upon his ability to evaluate situations quickly; to know the subtleties of both overt and covert antecedents of the observable behaviors; and to direct the people involved toward more desirable behavior in the classroom. The synthesis of judgments based on approaches oriented in anthropology, sociology, and psychology is depicted in Table II.

The individual in society is first caught in a cultural milieu which circumscribes his behavior, determines, within limits, his level of aspiration, and defines his life goals. Within this framework of a total culture, he assumes certain clearly defined roles

TABLE II

Foundations for Judging Pupil Behavior in the Classroom

```
              ┌─────────────────────┐
              │ Observable Behavior │
              └─────────────────────┘
```

Teachers' judgments based on anthropological approach.	Teachers' judgments based on sociological approach.	Teachers' judgments based on psychological approach.
Behavior rooted in culture of the social group.	Behavior determined by role the individual plays in the social group.	Behavior is individual's responses in coping with all his problems.
The culture establishes modes of living, manners, customs, and peculiarities.	Roles determine ways of responding within the basic institutions in society; family, religion, education, health, recreation, economy, government.	Individual responses are patterned in mental, physical, social, emotional, and moral and spiritual growth and development.
Specific cultural practices in everyday life establish and reinforce behavioral patterns which in turn establish institutions which teach values which are directed toward overall goals in life.	Institutions establish inflexible roles based on rank in hierarchy, class-status, etc.	Growth patterns are organized, predictable, continuous, and interrelated within normal expectancy.
	Individuals have multiple roles, all clearly defined, to play.	Individuals have all degrees of success-failure in coping with needs, feelings, attitudes, aspirations.
Culture produces a set of values that is adhered to by the entire group.	Social roles exert pressure to conform to specifically defined expectations.	Personality of the individual encompasses the total experience of the individual in learned ways of behaving.

From the intermeshing of these three approaches, there results:
agreement; agreement-conflict; or conflict

Understanding of the observed behavior.

Guidance toward the desired behavior in the classroom.

within the social group. He has a class-status role, a role in the family unit, a role as a wage earner, a role as a leader in ever widening circles from the immediate environment. Leadership roles may manifest themselves in religious or health practices, recreation, or politics. Within the framework of one's roles in a social group, the individual copes with all his problems and responds to all his opportunities through learned ways of behaving. The individual's total life experience as he has responded mentally, physically, socially, emotionally, or morally or spiritually has evolved ways of behaving to gratify his needs, overcome his fears, anxieties, and frustrations, build attitudes toward others and himself, and set his levels of aspirations as an individual.

The child learns his individual responses to fulfill his social roles within a cultural heritage from infancy as he imitates, responds to, and comes to understand his parents, his siblings, the extended family and later, those outside the family with whom he comes in contact. Thus, he very gradually learns and accepts ways of behaving and maturing within a particular social group, resolving its conflicts and gaining confidence in its agreements.

The teacher, whose total pattern of learned ways of behaving and maturing may be culturally different, has accepted a responsibility for guiding this child's behavior in school so that it will be possible for him to achieve realization of his ultimate potential both in the social group whence he came and in the larger society into which he unavoidably moves.

BRINGING ABOUT UNDERSTANDING AND ACCEPTANCE

Rasey has written that "enlightened self-interest alone dictates that each of us go about this highly crucial teacher business, a more important business than we have realized."[85] Rasey also says that we probably "do not teach"; rather, "we cause to learn."[86] Developing an enlightened self-interest may be the most important task of the teacher in achieving maturity, both as a teacher and as a participating citizen.

Most teachers everywhere come in contact with some children who have had an upbringing very different from their own. These differences may stem from social class, cultural background, or living habits of the parents. It is a part of enlightened self-interest to attempt to understand and accept differences. This can be done without surrendering one's own values. "Differences in moral codes, different standards of cleanliness, and different social customs may be troublesome to many fine people."[87]

Some suggestions for bringing about understanding and acceptance follow.

1. Teachers can develop greater "self-awareness." The better an understanding an individual has of himself, the better

he is able to be objective about his own problems -- to know which ones he can solve, which ones he cannot, and where he can get further help. In a trailer school, the teacher listened while the writer explained the purpose in defining the cultural differences and the need for greater appreciation for and acceptance of cultural differences. This teacher said, "You can call it cultural differences if you want to, but I've taught here for eight years, and I can tell you they act darn funny!" It would seem that in eight years, the teacher might have evidenced some curiosity about why the people acted the way they did, and then might have tried to find some answers.

2. Teachers can pursue any one of many avenues to adult education or supplementary interests. One way to accomplish this is to enroll at a university for courses that will help in meeting problems in teaching. Another way to accomplish this need is by wise selection of a reading program without such university enrollment. A third approach to adult education is to develop interests in courses such as ceramics, jewelry making, woodworking, typing, bridge, piano playing, golf, or any other avocational interest. A fourth approach is to plan carefully for and to use free vacation periods for educational travel, for working at some job unrelated to teaching, or for cultivating friends in other kinds of work.

3. Teachers can become more objective in evaluating their work. This includes evaluating dissatisfactions, seeking help with specific problems, talking out situations with confidants who are good listeners, recognizing possibilities in working toward advancement in the profession, and accepting the role of the teacher in the community as one of setting an example.

4. Teachers can demonstrate their acceptance of what fellow citizens hold valuable. Rapport with community leaders is important. However, conformity need not mean abandonment of one's individuality.

5. Teachers need not allow themselves to be "taken in" by the dichotomy of "either-or-ness" in such statements as "I teach children, not textbooks," or "I have and expect to uphold subject-matter standards." Teachers who have their thinking fixed on rigid subject-matter standards are sure to be frustrated by children who do not achieve to those expectations. In a teaching situation in which the culture, language, and experience barriers cause many children to be ill-prepared for work offered at fixed grade placement, they have to be taught at whatever level of academic achievement they are able to function successfully. This

does not mean that teachers teach children, not textbooks. It should mean that they use materials of instruction to teach children the knowledges and skills that are appropriate for them.

FOOTNOTES

[1] Guy Wagner, "Toward Democratic Teacher Leadership," Midland Schools 71:11, September, 1956.

[2] Ibid.

[3] Rudolf Pinter, Intelligence Testing (New York: Henry Holt and Company, 1924), p. 395. See also Thomas R. Garth and James E. Garrett, "A Comparative Study of the Intelligence of Indians in U. S. Indian Schools and in the Public or Common Schools," School and Society, 27:178-184, February 11, 1928.

[4] Annette Rosentheil, "Anthropology and Childhood Education," School and Society, 87:482-483, November 21, 1959.

[5] Kneller, George F., Educational Anthropology, (Wiley, 1965), p. 4.

[6] Brown, Ina C., Understanding Other Cultures, (Prentice-Hall, Englewood Cliffs, New Jersey, 1963), p. 81.

[7] Landis, Paul H., Sociology, (Boston: Ginn and Co., 1964), p. 56.

[8] Ibid., pp. 38-40.

[9] Ibid., p. 494.

[10] Landis, Paul H., Sociology, (Boston: Ginn and Co., 1964), p. 39.

[11] Michaelis, John U. and A. Montgomery Johnston, editors, The Social Sciences: Foundations of the Social Studies, (Boston: Allyn and Bacon, 1965), p. 335.

[12] Strickland, Ruth, The Language Arts in the Elementary School, (Boston: D.C. Heath and Co., 1951), p. 3.

[13] Henry, Jules, "A Cross-Cultural Outline of Education," "Current Anthropology," July, 1960, Volume 1, No. 4, p. 304.

[14] Dexter, Earle F., Doors Toward the Sunrise, p. 88.

[15] Taba, Hilda, Curriculum Development: Theory and Practice, (New York: Harcourt, Brace, and World, Inc., 1962), p. 52.

[16] Brown, Francis J. and Joseph Slabey Roucek, One America, (New York: Prentice Hall, Inc., 1945), p. 564, cited in Brewton Berry, Race and Ethnic Relations, (Boston: Houghton Mifflin Co., 1965), p. 224.

[17] Schusky, Ernest L., The Right to Be Indian, (Board of Missions of the United Presbyterian Church and the Institute of Indian Studies, State University of South Dakota, 1965), p. 23.

[18] Brown, Francis J., Educational Sociology, (New York: Prentice-Hall, 1948), p. 81.

[19] Quilllen, I. James and Lavone A. Hanna, Education for Social Competence, (Chicago: Scott, Foreman and Co., 1948), pp. 450-451, citing, William E. Vickery and Stewart G. Cole, Intercultural Education in American Schools, (New York: Harper and Brothers, 1943), pp. 154-155.

[20] "Generalizations from the Social Sciences," State Curriculum Commission California State Department of Education, reprinted in John U. Michaelis, and A. Montgomery Johnston, editors, The Social Sciences, Foundations of the Social Studies, (Boston: Allyn and Bacon, Inc., 1965), pp. 327-328.

[21] Charles A. Ellwood, Cultural Evolution (New York: D Appleton-Century Co., 1927), p. 9.

[22] Clyde Kluckhohn, Mirror for Man (New York: McGraw-Hill Book Company, 1949), p. 26.

[23] Francis J. Brown, Educational Sociology (New York: Prentice-Hall, Inc., 1947), pp. 68-83.

[24] Ibid., p. 81.

[25] Florence Hawley Ellis, The Indian Problem in New Mexico (Albuquerque: Department of Government, University of New Mexico, 1948), pp. 4-5.

[26] O. Norman Simpkins, "Identification and Use of Cultural Patterns by Public Health Workers," Education for Indian Health, Progress Report, 1955-1960 (Washington: Division of Indian Health, June, 1960), p. 16.

[27] Ibid., p. 17.

[28] Ibid., p. 16.

[29] Brown, op. cit., pp. 60-61.

[30] James B. Stroud, Psychology in Education (New York: Longmans, Green and Co., Inc., 1946), p. 234.

[31] Loyd S. Tireman, "The Bilingual Child and His Reading Vocabulary," Elementary English, 32: 33, January, 1955.

[32] R. E. Davies, Bilingualism in Wales (Capetown, South Africa: Juta and Co., Ltd., 1954), p. 14.

[33] William Moyer Hemsing, "History and Trends of Indian Education in New Mexico under the Administration of Federal and State Governments" (unpublished Master's thesis, University of New Mexico, Albuquerque, 1953), p. 209.

[34] Dorothy Lee, "The Cultural Curtain," The Annals of American Academy of Political and Social Science, 323: 120, May, 1959. (An abstract prepared by the editor.)

[35] Ibid., p. 121.

[36] George A. Pettitt, Primitive Education in North America (Berkeley: University of California Press, 1946), p. 3.

[37] Margaret Mead, The School in American Culture (Cambridge: Harvard University Press, 1951), p. 10.

[38] Ibid., p. 11.

[39] Ibid., p. 28.

[40] George A. Pettitt, Primitive Education in North America (Berkeley: University of California Press, 1946).

[41] Margaret Mead, People and Places (Cleveland: The World Publishing Company, 1959), p. 76.

[42] Hilda Taba, "Educational Implications in the Concepts of Culture and Personality," Educational Leadership, 15: 183-186, December, 1957.

[43] Ibid., p. 185.

[44] California State Department of Education, Generalizations Relating to Anthropology, Report of the State Central Committee on Social Studies (Sacramento: California State Department of Education, 1959), pp. 53-60. (Mimeographed.) See also Harold B. Hoffenbacher, Putting Concepts from Anthropology into the Secondary School Program (Dearborn: The Author, 5757 Neckel Ave., Dearborn, Michigan, 1959). (Mimeographed.)

[45] Preston E. James, "The Use of Culture Areas as a Frame of Organization for the Social Studies," New Viewpoints in Geography, The Twenty-Ninth Yearbook of the National Council for the Social Studies (Washington: National Education Association, 1959).

[46] Fritz Redl and William W. Wattenberg, Mental Hygiene in Teaching, Second Edition (New York: Harcourt, Brace and Co., 1959), pp. 299-302.

[47] Willard C. Olson, Child Development (Boston: D. C. Heath, 1949).

[48] Ibid.

[49] W. C. Olson and B. O. Hughes, "Growth Patterns of Exceptional Children," The Education of Exceptional Children, Forty-ninth Yearbook of the National Society for the Study of Education, Part II (Chicago: University of Chicago Press, 1950).

[50] Robert J. Havighurst and Bernice L. Neugarten, Society and Education (Boston: Allyn and Bacon, Inc., 1957), p. 158.

[51] Ibid., p. 159.

[52] Glenn O. Blough and Allan L. Dodd discuss the extensive first-hand travel experiences of an urban sixth-grade class in their article, "Children Are Their Own Resources," Childhood Education, 34: 21-24, Sept., 1957.

[53] Havighurst and Neugarten, op. cit., pp. 172-173.

[54] Martin Deutsch, Minority Group and Class Status as Related to Social and Personality Factors in Scholastic Achievement, Monograph No. 2 (Ithaca: The Society for Applied Anthropology, Cornell University, 1960).

[55] Ibid., p. 2.

[56] Ibid., p. 9.

[57] Ibid., pp. 12-13.

[58] Ibid., p. 25.

[59] Ibid., p. 26.

[60] Ibid., p. 26.

[61] Ibid., p. 27.

[62] Ibid., p. 29.

[63] Sophie L. Elam, "Acculturation and Learning Problems of Puerto Rican Children," Teacher's College Record, pp. 258-264, February, 1960.

[64] W. Lloyd Warner, Robert J. Havighurst, and Martin B. Loeb, Who Shall Be Educated? The Challenge of Unequal Opportunities (New York: Harper and Brothers Publishers, 1944), p. 149.

[65] Gordon W. Allport, "Reading the Nature of Prejudice," Seventeenth Yearbook, Claremont College Reading Conference, Claremont, California, 1952, pp. 51-64. See also The Nature of Prejudice (Cambridge: Addison-Wesley, 1954).

[66] Teachers enrolled in a bicultural workshop at the University of New Mexico during the 1959-60 summer sessions contributed these anecdotes and others used throughout the text.

[67] Robert Bunker and John Adair, The First Look at Strangers (New Brunswick: Rutgers University Press, 1959).

[68] Ibid., p. 150

[69] Allison Davis, Social Class Influences on Learning (Cambridge: Harvard University Press, 1952).

[70] Jules Henry, "A Cross-Cultural Outline of Education," Current Anthropology, 1: 267-305.

[71] Arthur B. Moehlman, School Administration (Boston: Houghton Mifflin Company, 1940), p. 126.

[72] Ibid.

[73] Henry, op. cit., pp. 273-305.

[74] Ibid., p. 304.

[75] Jules Henry, "Attitude Organization in Elementary School Classrooms," American Journal of Orthopsychiatry, 27: 117-133, January, 1957.

[76] Ibid., pp. 132-133.

[77] Ralph Linton, "The Essentials of Family Life," in Exploring the Ways of Mankind, Walter Goldschmidt, editor (New York: Holt, Rinehart, and Winston, Inc., 1960), p. 232.

[78] John J. Adair, "A Study of Culture Resistance: The Veterans of World War II at Zuni Pueblo" (Unpublished Doctoral dissertation, The University of New Mexico, Albuquerque, 1948), p. 163.

[79] Ibid.

[80] Lago Gladston, "The American Family in Crisis," Mental Hygiene, 42: 230, April, 1958.

[81] Lee, op. cit., pp. 97-111, citing Tom Sasaki and John Adair.

[82] Sigfredo Maestas, "Life Styles of Lower-Class People and Their Motivational Structure" (Unpublished graduate paper, The University of New Mexico, Albuquerque, 1958).

[83] Gladys Reichard, "The Navajo and Christianity," The American Anthropologist, 51: 69, January-March, 1949.

[84] Margaret Clark, Health in the Mexican-American Culture: A Community Study (Berkeley: University of California Press, 1959), pp. 145-146.

[85] Marie I. Rasey, editor, The Nature of Being Human (Detroit: The Wayne University Press, 1958), p. 107.

[86] Ibid.

[87] Redl and Wattenberg, op. cit., p. 491.

CHAPTER 3

The Background of the Middle-Class Teacher

Sun Chief from Old Oraibi says in his autobiography that he decided when he was about 40 that whites were like Hopis. You had to judge each one separately -- there were the missionaries for whom Sun Chief did not particularly care, there were curious tourists who came clad in almost no clothes at all and talked about the primitive savage Indians, and there were people who called themselves anthropologists who did not offend -- did not try to convince you of anything or change your ways.[1]

INTRODUCTION

Teachers in classrooms enrolling children from different cultural backgrounds must look with maturity upon the attitudes and beliefs of their students. The ability to do this is strongly dependent upon one's ability to see one's own beliefs, values, and ideals in perspective. The purpose of this chapter is to present the following four aspects of this broad problem of helping the teacher to look objectively at his own value system:

1. A brief description of some of the common conflicts in everyday life will be presented first. While these conflicts may seem to leave the individual in a state of confusion, Du Bois, an anthropologist, presents a rationale for the opposing practices of values in everyday behavior.

2. The social class orientation of school teachers with its strong emphasis on middle-class values will be discussed.

3. The impact of Judeo-Christian dogma on teacher attitudes and the resulting inflexibility on thinking patterns will be discussed then.

4. Finally, in the last section of this chapter, a recent research study will be reported. It was hypothesized in that study that the educational retardation prevalent among minority group children may be caused, in part, because teachers are unaware of the cultural orientations of the children, the value configurations held by them, and their limited understanding of the English language. The research to be discussed consists of two parts. First,

teachers' awareness of socio-cultural differences was assessed; then, their increased awareness was measured after a planned course of study of socio-cultural differences.

CONFLICTS WITHIN THE BELIEFS AND PRACTICES OF THE DOMINANT CULTURE

Anglo society is extremely complex and embraces many conflicting values.

Students of our culture cite the ruthless competition of the market place and the social climb, the disintegration of the family, the prevalence of prejudice and discrimination, war, and moral confusion as symptoms of the social chaos which now prevails.[2]

In our society the child is taught from infancy what he must and must not do. These teachings constitute the framework of his conscience. . . . A child is taught to tell the truth, but early in life he must learn to distinguish between "black" lies and "white" lies. He must learn that telling the truth is subject to infinite variations.[3]

In our society, people are constantly conforming to the accepted practices of the larger group. These behaviors are usually called mores. Actually many of these are "taboos" in the same sense that taboos exist in the behavior of minority ethnic groups. Taboos are negative -- they are specific practices which people do not do. Conformity results from habit without the individual giving any thought at the moment as to why he behaves in such a way.

Horney, in her book The Neurotic Personality of Our Time, discusses the conflicts in our values and goals:

The first contradiction to be mentioned is that between competition and success on the one hand, and brotherly love and humility on the other. On the one hand, everything is done to spur us toward success, which means that we must be not only assertive but aggressive, able to push others out of the way. On the other hand, we are deeply imbued with Christian ideals which declare that it is selfish to want anything for ourselves, that we should be humble, turn the other cheek, be yielding. . . . .

The second contradiction is that between the stimulation of our needs and our actual frustrations in satisfying them. For economic reasons needs are constantly being stimulated in our culture by such means as advertisements, "conspicuous consumption," the ideal of "keeping up with the Joneses." For the great majority, however, the actual fulfillment of these needs is closely restricted. . . . .

Another contradiction exists between the alleged freedom of the individual and his factual limitations. The individual is told by society that he is free, independent, can decide his life according to his own free will; "The great game of life" is open to him, and he can get what he wants if he is efficient and energetic. In actual fact, for the majority of people all these possibilities are limited.[4]

Spindler has noted the many ways in which our behavior in middle-class society is in constant conflict with the declared values. He says:

> . . . We appear to believe in the value of thrift, but believe even more strongly in the value of keeping up good appearances that depend upon mortgages and installment buying that strain our budgets. We believe in deferring satisfactions to the future but want the benefits of deferments now. We believe that success is to be won by hard work, but emphasize personality and social contacts as alternative techniques. We laud honesty as a virtue but acknowledge the need for pragmatic expediency in real life. We are egalitarian in ideal and in much of our practice but indulge in wide-ranging expressions of invidious prejudices. We deny sexuality but are titillated by sex in our mass media, dress, and imagery.[5]

Many of the conflicts in behavior are subtle and the individual is unconscious of them. Such expressions as "Do as I say, not as I do" have evolved in people's attempts to rationalize their own behavior.

Any Anglo parent is sure to subscribe to the axiom that honesty is the best policy. Yet, many mothers, upon seeing a caller on the front step, have asked their child to answer the door and say, "I'm sorry, my mother isn't home now." The mother can easily rationalize this little "white lie" if she must hurry to get ready to go somewhere, if it is a salesman, or if it is a neighbor who talks too long or too much.

To specify what Horney and Spindler have said, we might consider the following examples:

1. On the one hand, people accept the admonition "Love thy neighbor as thyself'; yet the drive for early achievement and success for material well-being may prevent this. Even though for some it may be without conscious effort, people compete, they are constantly alert to getting a "fair break" in professional advancement, and have internalized the necessity to climb the ladder of success. On the contrary, love of neighbor implies mutual sharing, cooperation, empathy, and equality. These sentiments are expressed in tithes and offerings at church, in Red Cross and United Fund drives, and in the office collections when

a colleague has an unexpected misfortune. This sharing is dominated, however, by a need to "try to get ahead," "to save for a rainy day," or to "keep up with the Joneses."

2. On the one hand, lip-service is given to the idea that people are free and equal under the law; yet persons in many situations experience continual anxiety and insecurity. Workers are afraid of losing their jobs, failing to please the foreman who "rates" them. The profit motive in industry causes business to be autocratic in nature. Such expressions as "boot-licking" and "apple-polishing" are commonly understood. Teachers are often anxious about how they will be evaluated, whether they will get promotions, whether their immediate supervisor has eccentricities that may cause him to evaluate someone else more advantageously than they.

3. On the one hand, Christianity teaches that sex practices are restricted to continence before marriage and monogamy in marriage. Punishment for violations of these mores is sure to generate feelings of guilt and anxiety. Yet, the potential of the sex drive is maximized in advertising, the motion picture industry, television, and popular music.

Finally Fisher emphasizes the difficulty as parents inculcate these conflicting values in the lives of their children:

> Any success-driven culture such as ours, which contains within itself the dramatic contradiction of the urge for power and the idea of cooperation and love-your-neighbor-as-yourself, inevitably produces personalities which have the basic conflict incorporated at least to some extent within themselves. Any society which says to its growing children, on the one hand, "You will be secure, if you are successful. Get to the top. Dominate before you are dominated. Use people before you get used," and on the other hand, "Be pleasant and polite or people won't like you. Learn to get along with people or they will hurt you. Selfishness is wrong. Love your neighbor as yourself," produces confused individuals who will find it hard to become consistently free and responsible and truly democratic . . . . Many of us accept the conflict as inevitable, discount its importance, and only question the costliness. . . . Those of us who have the greatest difficulty in reconciling or solving the conflict, or who resolve it at too great a cost to our personalities, become what Karen Horney calls in her book, The Neurotic Personality of Our Time, the stepchildren of our culture.[6]

Education belongs to the general process known as enculturation, by which the growing person is initiated into the way of life of his society. But education as an institution is only one of many enculturating agencies. Although the educator may want to cultivate certain qualities in the child, such as clear thinking and independent judgment, he is limited in his ability to do so by the fact that other agencies may be molding the child differently. Television is only one example of such an agency.

This conflict has been described dramatically by Margaret Mead:

> In small societies children learn by imitating their parents, relatives, and neighbors. In our huge society we use our mass entertainments to instruct our children on how they should express their emotions and what values they should have.... We are showing our youngsters exactly the opposite of what we want them to imitate. We are showing them men who brutally attack others when angry. We show people who murder because of hatred and expediency. We show that love is expressed only by hunger for another's body. And we show them little else.[7]

Du Bois proposes a kind of reconciliation of opposites in these conflicts.[8] On the one hand, we prize change itself, expressed in effort, struggle and progress. On the other hand, we compromise. The way we arrive at an understanding of our values is by an analysis of how man looks at the world, how he sees himself in relation to it, and how he sees himself in relation to other men.

The American middle-class believes: (1) The universe is mechanistically conceived; (2) man is its master; (3) men are equal; and (4) men are perfectible.[9]

These premises lead to three major values: (1) Material well-being that derives from the premise that man is master of a mechanistic universe; (2) Conformity that derives from the premise of man's equality; and (3) Effort-optimism that derives from the premise of man's perfectibility. These three values are more or less consistently interlocked. Change, and change takes place slowly in all value systems, results from the strain for consistency between the accepted values and the situational factors that arise.[10]

The goals of life of any individual are, then, based on several different facets of social interrelationships. Meeting the pressures of the moment is largely an economic need. Having an adequate life insurance plan for the family if the husband dies, or even just buying a new car as often as one's neighbor does, these tend to keep people basically materialistic in their behavior. In contrast, those values that would project beyond oneself, that would help make choices that are rooted in love for and service to one's fellowmen, might be termed in any social group as ethical values. From these values have come the ideals expressed in "Love thy neighbor. . . ," "Do unto others. . . ," and "Blessed are the meek."

While people work out their compromises between these opposing values, may they remember that, through centuries, other cultural groups have had their own ways of meeting their needs in their economy, their health practices, their ways of educating their children, and their religion. They must have had a fairly good perspective in arriving at their cultural practices since their societies persisted through centuries. Specifically, for example, it has been recorded in the literature that both Acoma and Old Oraibi, Indian villages in the Southwest, are the oldest, continuously inhabited communities in the United States.

SOCIAL CLASS ORIENTATION OF TEACHERS

One of the outstanding features of Anglo society is social stratification which results in a hierarchical arrangement of social levels called "social classes."[11] Mulligan gives a definition of social class:

> The culture theory of class conceives of social classes as selective cultural grouping which give to their members a similar stock of ideas, values, feelings, attitudes and forms of behavior. It recognizes the fact that people live, work, play and think on different class levels. The differences between classes are not merely financial or external standards of living, but encompass the entire range of social behavior: occupation, vocation, manner of speaking, social and sexual attitudes, musical and literary tastes, and philosophy of life.[12]

A commonly used grouping divides society into six social classes: the upper-upper, the lower-upper, the upper-middle, the lower-middle, the upper-lower and the lower-lower.

Warner and Srole describe the social classes as six social strata of the community in their study of ethnic groups in a representative American town which they called Yankee City. These strata are of importance in evaluating the behavior of the people of a community.

> The top level, or upper-upper class, consists of members of "old families" who are born to their position; their family genealogies show them to be products of several generations of upper-class living. This old aristocracy is the keystone in the Yankee City status system. Below this level are the "new" families or newly rich (lower-upper) who are busy transform-

ing their money into acceptable behavior through participation with those who preceded them to the top level. On the step below them are the "pillars of society," the successful men and women, who are the powerful upper-middle class who do things and see that things are done in Yankee City. These three classes, comprising no more than 15 per cent of the total, are "the big people" who are above the common run of men.

Below them, but at the top of "the little people," are the members of the lower-middle class, the small tradesmen, the skilled workers, and the white-collar workers who cling to the virtues of the "protestant ethic," despite the fact that many are members of other religions. Beneath them are the poor and respectable workers, who hope and strive to do better than they are doing, but who worry for fear of falling into the class below them, the lowest in society, where the "shiftless Yankees" and the "ignorant immigrants" are found.[13]

Warner and Srole give the percentages of the total population in each of the six social classes in Yankee City as follows: Upper-upper, 1.45 per cent; lower-upper, 1.57 per cent; upper-middle, 10.30 per cent; lower-middle, 28.36 per cent; upper-lower, 32.88 per cent; and lower-lower, 25.44 per cent.[14]

Havighurst and Neugarten graphically show the per cent of the population expected in any given area to belong to the different social classes (see Figure 1).[15]

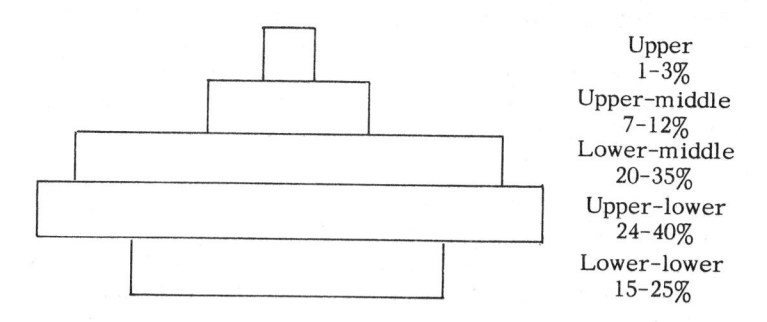

Upper
1-3%
Upper-middle
7-12%
Lower-middle
20-35%
Upper-lower
24-40%
Lower-lower
15-25%

Figure 1. The class structure in middle-sized communities. (Percentage ranges show how a given class varies in size. Ranges reported here come from studies in communities with populations from 5,000 to 100,000.)

LOOK NED HILTON

From Look, 23:38, August 18, 1959.

*"Are we in the uppermost upper part
of the lower middle class, or the mid-lower part
of the upper middle class?"*

It is evident from Figure 1 that the upper classes do not constitute any large proportion of the total population.[16] It is well recognized, too, that they tend to send their children to private schools. Thus, this group is not an active concern of public education.

Middle-class groups make a virtue of self-control, foresight, individual achievement, and responsibility. By punishments and rewards, they implant these values in their children from the first year of life.

Upward mobility in the social class strata is a driving force in middle-class America. "Mobility in the social classes requires drive and purpose, and willingness to sacrifice immediate pleasures for a greater future gain."[17]

The middle class is made up largely of active, ambitious people. Work is important just because it is work. Parents teach their children to work hard. Successful and early attainment of goals is important. Parents often exercise their demands on a child to the point that any failure is sure to bring disapproval, guilt feelings, and fear of rejection on his part.

It is this drive which a generation ago caused many middle-class mothers to make early, harsh demands on very young children in child-rearing practices. The attempt to "toilet-train" the infant before he was a year old in spite of the pediatrician's knowledge that the child did not attain sphincter control until several months later is a specific example.

In middle-class life, education is extremely important. Upper-middle class parents feel that almost all their children must attend college. The lower-middle class also values education for the ways in which it encourages social mobility to the next social class. About a third of the lower middle-class children are likely to go to college.[18] This class sees its opportunity to improve its status and to acquire more and more of the middle-class value patterns through hard work, climbing the ladder of success, and obtaining formal education. The lower-middle class provides the majority of teachers in the public school system. There is a trend to recruit more teachers from the upper-lower class.[19]

Values, beliefs, and outlook on life for all groups of people center around one's orientation to the world about him. The problems are not solved in the same manner by all ethnic groups, however. The right or wrong and the good or bad of a situation are functions of the value system held by an individual. Williams defines the term value as "any aspect of a situation, event, or object that is invested with a preferential interest as being 'good,' 'bad,' 'desirable,' and the like."[20]

The major drives of the middle-class teacher are:
1. Achievement and early success.
2. Work for "work's sake." It is "good" to work hard.
3. Getting educated.
4. Being responsible. This incorporates self-discipline, self-control, foresight as conservatively conceived in a pre-destined, divine plan.
5. Shaping one's own destiny.

Lower classes do not view education as middle classes do. Lower-class parents tend to believe that their children are impertinent or obtuse if they try to achieve education in order to climb the ladder of class difference. They are apt to think that quitting school early and earning money through hard work is superior to education and placement in white-collar or sedentary jobs.

Lower-lower class children, with many conflicting values between them and middle-class teachers, give evidence of much educational retardation and are apt to be in need of much remedial teaching. The parents are often disinterested in school, and the home is able to afford little stimulation toward home study or opportunities for vicarious reading experiences. The background of experience, or life-space, of these children is inclined to be severely limited.

Teachers must remember that in many schools the majority of the children come from the lower-lower and upper-lower classes. Each class has a set of value orientations which corresponds to its everyday practices or life style. Schools must face conflict situations arising from value patterns of the middle-class teacher and the lower-class child. The schools have presented only a limited aspect of American culture as the sum total of the curriculum. Davis says:

> The present curricula are stereotyped and arbitrary selections from a narrow area of middle-class structure. Academic culture is one of the most conservative and ritualized aspects of human culture. . . . For untold generations, we have been unable to think of anything to put into the curriculum which will be more helpful in guiding the basic mental development of children than vocabulary building, reading, spelling, and routine arithmetical memorizing.[21]

Warner and Havighurst point out that the teacher's value system is likely to be middle-class oriented. Unless a teacher is aware of this bias, and can understand and appreciate other value systems, he will find only frustration and dissatisfaction in teaching children whose backgrounds and outlooks are unlike his own.

"Oh—this old status symbol?"

Reprinted by special permission of The Saturday Evening Post. Copyright 1961, The Curtis Publishing Company.

It is incumbent upon all teachers to know something about the values that guide the lives of their students.

> . . . The American school and college system is the greatest agency we have for equalizing opportunity and for promoting the rise of able young people.
>
> Through it we maintain a degree of social mobility probably greater than that to be found in any other country. 22
>
> While . . . it should be remembered that social class is only one of several significant factors in a teacher's personality, middle-class teachers will do better if they learn to look on the values of their own social class as less than God-given. . . Prospective teachers (drawn mostly from the lower middle-class in our society) should be taught to distinguish the basic democratic values of our society from the host of lesser class-bound values which are not a necessary part of a public educational program. 23

Drawing teachers from the middle class is not bad in itself, but it would help if they appreciated the cultural differences between themselves and their pupils, and if they did not tend to feel that they must always be right in their moralizing about good and bad, and about right and wrong.

Teachers must thoroughly understand the social class structure in which they live as well as their goals of drive, achievement, self-control and responsibility, so as not to antagonize those whose goals differ or conflict. If they avoid antagonism or conflict, then perhaps they leave open the path for more and more of the young people to achieve high status -- to realize more nearly their true potential through education and experience.

The teacher is the key person in the transmission of American culture. Unless he is aware of his own cultural perspective, what is actually transmitted to children by either accident or intent may not be consistent with the teacher's declared purpose and intent. In a case study of teacher-child interpersonal relationships in a heterogenous fifth-grade class, Spindler found that: 24

1. When the teacher listed the best socially adjusted students in his class, six of the seven were from homes of middle-class status and the seventh possessed strong status-achievement drive.

2. When the teacher listed the least well-adjusted students, six of the seven were from families of lower-class status.

3. When the teacher listed the children with whom he had the most effective working relationship, five of the eight listed were from middle-class families.

4. When the teacher listed the children with whom he had the least effective working relationship, seven of the eight were from lower-class families.

5. When the teacher listed the children who were most popular and most accepted by their classmates, only one of the eight listed came from families in lower-class status.

6. When the children selected those most popular and most accepted by sociometric techniques, children identified only three of the eight identified by the teacher.

7. In response to oral reports by children, the teacher's responses -- gestures, facial expression, bodily postures, comments and silences -- were all patterned in the framework of the same selective bias indicated above.

According to Spindler, the teacher "communicated lack of interest, or suppressed distaste, for what the children of lower-class origins said, how they said it, and of what they were reading."[25]

Spindler concludes that this teacher interacted effectively with only that minority segment of his class which matched his own aspirations and values. For those children whose values and aspirations did not match his, and they constituted a majority, he was, in effect, closing doors to what he himself calls opportunity.[26]

JUDEO-CHRISTIAN INFLUENCES AND BIASES IN TEACHER'S ATTITUDES

The religious values of American society are based on Judeo-Christian doctrine. While it is not inherent in the doctrine, many people look upon Christianity as the "right" way, the "best" way, the "superior" way. Since the American people face many problems within the "Christian" dogmas of their own churches, it is not surprising that there is much difficulty in reconciling different religious beliefs as divergent as Hinduism, Buddhism, or preliterate religious rites of the American Indian.

Teachers in the Southwest must face this problem in their daily contact with both the children they teach and the parents with whom they confer. Therefore, this section will present some of the tenets of the Christian religion and will point out some of the difficulties which some minority groups may have in their acceptance. The need for acceptance of the ideas of others and tolerance for their beliefs is a basic tenet of American democracy.

A teacher need not necessarily change his personal beliefs. However, an honest searching of one's present attitudes and beliefs will lead toward greater maturity on the part of the individual teacher. Such maturity demands that each group be allowed to interpret its religion in such a way as to enable its members to find the most satisfying way of life. Before discussing certain tenets of the Christian faith, some examples of how other thinkers have tried to resolve the specific beliefs of individual groups are presented.

> Mahatma Gandhi tells about his religion: "I do not want my house to be walled in on all sides and my windows to be stuffed. I want the culture of all lands to be blown about my house as freely as possible, but I refuse to be blown off my feet by any of them. Mine is not a religion of the prison house. It has room for the least among God's creatures, but is proof against insolent pride of race, religion, or color."

> Mahatma Gandhi's teaching is: "A Hindu has only to be a better Hindu, a Christian a better Christian, a Moslem a better Moslem. God is neither Hindu, nor a Moslem, nor a Christian. Neither should his children be any one of these exclusively, but all of them cumulatively. Man has a right to inherit the full and broad stream of revelation that has flowed through several channels." [27]

When an old cacique in one of the Indian Pueblos was asked how it was that the Indians had accepted the Catholic religion from the Spanish Friars and yet had kept their own original religion, he responded in this way:

> We know that there are many ways of appeasing the Great Spirits. Many people can do this in many ways. We know that it is the ambition of all these people to satisfy these spirits whom they will meet in the Spirit World when they have finished the long trail of life. We know that there are many roads that lead to the Spirit World. Some of the roads are rough and rocky and some are smooth and easy with beautiful flowers growing along the way. Those who have not pleased the gods may have obstacles to overcome -- they may meet bears along the way; they may wear out many moccasins; they may be waylaid by witches and detained.

> We know that we will all arrive in the Spirit World. It just takes longer for some. We will need to satisfy all the gods in order to keep harmony.

> The priests told us that there was only one way. We knew better than this, but we supposed their way might be good for them, and because they wanted us to, we were glad to share it with them. Yet, we felt sorry for them that they thought their one language and their one way was the only way. We know that the Gods understand many languages and that they do not care in what language you talk to them.

> We helped the priests build their church and we go to their service one hour on Sunday, but we have much time left to pray to our gods and to practice our own religion. [28]

Consideration will now be given to five of the basic tenets of Judeo-Christian teachings. The total behavior of the majority of Judeo-Christian people is strongly influenced by these tenets whether or not they subscribe to a specific sect. These five tenets are: (1) The doctrine of original sin; (2) A "blind faith" in a heaven after death which will win anyone a reward for his life on this earth; (3) The invitation to "Go ye into all the world and preach the gospel"; (4) The belief that Jesus died for our sins; and (5) The command to "Remember the Sabbath Day to keep it Holy." [29]

The Doctrine of Original Sin

From the Horn Book, children for generations have learned

> By Adam's fall
> We sinned all.

The tenet is that a child is born in sin and, therefore, from the beginning has "to be saved." This doctrine, because of the way Adam and Eve sinned, creates a great deal of prudery, adjudication, and censure concerning sex. The commandments forbidding fornication and adultery are basic and mandatory. Nathaniel Hawthorne's classic, The Scarlet Letter, illustrates the way these mores have been perpetuated. From the standpoint of good mental hygiene, it is necessary for the teacher to see this value broadly in order to incorporate the point of view of other cultures.

In Judeo-Christian communities, inflexible mores control the activities of individual members. This means that many members of the society violate the mores, and, as a result, have severe guilt feelings and may be ostracized by the fellow members of the group. The Judeo-Christian concept dictates that people will not have sexual intercourse before marriage (fornication) and that men and women will not have intercourse with other than marital partners (adultery). Nevertheless, there is adequate documentary evidence to show that these commandments are violated by many Judeo-Christian people. [30]

> Among the social upheavals of our time, we must count a drastic revolution in sexual morals, if not so much in what people do, at least in a recognition of what they do. . . . It is obvious that official morality is widely at variance with actual practice, while psychological principles and personal morals drift uncertainly in between. [31]

Especially for the female, this violation of mores is apt to bring feelings of guilt and anxieties lest she be "found out," and in the event of pregnancy, suffer harsh rejection and severe censure by society. Cultures which place no stigma on illegitimacy and impute no guilt to extra-marital relations are, from the mental hygiene point of view, allowing their people to be much healthier.

Men and women in other societies who have not internalized these prohibitions will not have the same qualms of conscience about these acts toward which Western society exercises strong censure.

> The Navajo believes that reproduction is the ultimate human and supernatural purpose -- a man cannot therefore be conceived in sin.[32]

In one small high school enrolling approximately 150 Indian students during a recent school year, seventeen babies were born to high school girls. Some of the girls married the young men who were fathers of their children; others did not.[33]

Faith in Heaven After Death

Although the admonition is that "faith without works is dead," sometimes little emphasis is placed on the "work," and one might well believe that only the "faith of a grain of mustard seed" will win eternal life. Many people continue making immature responses to difficult situations, yet expect a reward in the hereafter without prejudice as to how maturely they faced their problems in the here and now.

A "blind faith" is perhaps best illustrated by the traditional Spanish American culture in which the small community was predominantly Catholic in faith and led by the priest. In many of these communities, the priest was the only one who had acquired formal learning and reading and writing skills. It was a part of the "blind faith" of these people that they did not need to acquire an education, or wealth, or any particular status since they believed that they would all go, with equal status, to an eternal afterlife.

Modern American society is not without its examples of stubborn adherence to outmoded dogma. The Mormons deny full fellowship to the Negro in the belief that his skin color brands him as one who was "disloyal" to the Son of God in a pre-existent world. Members of certain other sects refuse medical attention, even though diagnosis indicates their lives could surely be saved by modern medicines or surgery.

"Go ye into all the world and preach the gospel"

While there are many possible interpretations of this mandate, it has often meant to Christian missionaries that Christianity must be accepted by all peoples everywhere. Non-Christians have been viewed as having no religion at all; consequently, they must embrace Christianity. Because some of these other groups have felt that they have an adequate and satisfying religion of their own, the efforts of these missionaries have often been misunderstood and not accepted.

One of the chief purposes of the chapter on Navajo religion in the 1957 Navajo Yearbook is to emphasize to all the readers that the Navajos, as a people, have always had a religion that satisfactorily explains the origin of man, the relationship between man and his maker, the relationship between man and his brother, and the immortality of man.[34] Certainly, in all Indian religions, there is a maximum use of prayer in communicating with the Great Spirit. If the literature is accurate in any degree, Indians pray a great deal more, and more often, than their non-Indian neighbors. Reichard says of the Navajo:

> Proselytism is not so much offensive as incomprehensible to him. Believing that his way of life is invaluable and right, he thinks it should not be dissipated by "taking it out of the tribe." He would not try to convert a neighboring Indian or a white man to his religion; he cannot understand why anyone should try to persuade him to abandon his birthright. Nor can he see why anyone should be willing to give away that which he has gained only by great exertion. His reasonable conclusion is, "Of course your religion is good for you, ours for us. Why should either of us change?" With this rhetorical question he continues on his way without even curiosity about a strange religion from which he is not allowed to select.[35]

Clyde Kluckhohn reports one young Navajo woman's experience with Christianity:

> "I went to the Mission School when I was a little over five and I went away when I was fourteen. Later I was married. I was a Christian. I told everyone they had better be Christians or they would be lost when they died. When I think how I talked to my people I am ashamed. My father said I had better stop that talk, why did I want to go with white people after I died and leave my people? Then my baby about two years old got sick. I took her to the hospital at that Mission and they couldn't make her well. She got worse so I brought her home and they had a four-night sing. In two days she was well. Then my sister died when she was having a child and a couple of days later I was walking to a hogan in the moonlight and I saw her. She was on horseback and she rode right by me. She was just two yards away. I was so scared I didn't know anything. . . . After that I don't believe all that stuff the Christians talk about. They say after you die you go to heaven or you go down and get punished. I don't believe that. I believe after we die we live right here. We go around just the same. Some Navajos believe we go back to the world we came from."[36]

"Jesus died for our sins"

> The son of man must be delivered into the hands of sinful men, and be crucified, and the third day rise again.
>
> (St. Luke, 24:7)

This idea represents another major conflict. Most Navajos and Apaches are, to this day, uneasy in the presence of death, the dead, and the place in which any person dies. In the past, they abandoned the hogan or wickiup in which the person died, and built another one. The dead were hastily buried by a few people who were then ritually cleansed of the evil spirit of the dead person before they rejoined their own families. Further, with the coming of the non-Indians, if the burial of the dead could be left to them, the Indians were very happy to do just that.

Navajos have believed that the dead may return as ghosts to plague those who are living. Young writes about the Navajo belief:

> At death the essence of spirit of life, his breath, and "that which stands within him" leaves his body to blend with the cosmos and lose their identity, while the evil side of his personality remains as an unassimilated residue contaminating his corpse, the dwelling place in which he died, his possessions, and the place where he is buried. This evil remains as a ch'indii, potentially dangerous to the health, welfare and even the lives of those who come in contact with it. If he dies within his hogan, the dwelling becomes uninhabitable, and even its timbers become unusable.[37]

These people were not anxious to accept a new religion, particularly one based upon a philosophy so objectionable to them. Instead, they were intent upon maintaining their ancient harmony-with-nature philosophy.

> He believes that the present good universe was transformed from an evil one so that men could properly fit into it and enjoy it -- man is therefore the greatest thing in the universal scheme; he has no reason to abase himself because even the gods exist for his benefit. Instead of humiliating himself, the Navajo seeks through ceremonial to identify himself with deity. He cannot understand the ideals sought through mortification, penance or sacrifice.[38]

Remember the Sabbath Day to Keep It Holy

Indians have been quick to point out that non-Indians observe their religion one hour on Sunday. However, in many cases, the Anglo's unseemly behavior all the rest of the week is difficult to reconcile in terms of professed beliefs. In contrast, the Indian feels that he is living his religion every hour every day, consistent with professed beliefs.

Dozier explains the difficulty that most missionaries have in understanding the philosophy of life of the Hopi or the Tewa:

> Most of the missionaries who visit the Hopi or who have missions on the Hopi reservation disapprove of the Hopi and Tewa ceremonies. Some of the sects vehemently denounce the traditional customs and instruct their Hopi and Tewa adherents to abandon them. The Indians attend church services or Bible readings primarily to receive the gifts and nonreligious instruction which are offered as inducements to come to the missions. One woman said she had learned to sew and to can fruit by attending the services of one sect and valued this knowledge. It is obvious that few of the Hopi or Tewa have found spiritual satisfaction in their exposure to Christian teaching. Pueblo Indians are concerned about the problems of daily living and seek to find relief from illness, crop failure, and difficulties with Indian and white neighbors. Their own religion is organized to minimize the fears and anxieties of day to day existence. They cannot understand a religion that emphasizes the spiritual world. Sin and "being saved" are concepts that are simply not a part of their thinking. They do not believe that their ancestors wronged anyone and hence they have no "guilt," in the sense that whites have it. But they do have apprehensions about the contemporary world and are seeking relief from them. Hopi and Tewa ceremonies, particularly those of the Hopi, are mass magical rites with an emphasis on beauty of movement and costuming. They are designed and executed to induce the universe to pour forth the good things of life. Horticulture, the economic base of life, receives the full concentration of Hopi religious devotion and ritual. In an environment where the success or failure of the subsistence economy is always fraught with uncertainty, the religious orientation of the longer term residents like the Hopi highlights "weather control." Lean and bountiful years are explained in terms of faulty or successful observance of religious retreats and rituals.[39]

A Tewa woman living in Hano expressed the typical attitude toward missionaries in this way:

> It is best to be polite to missionaries, let them come in and preach. We will go on with what we are doing. It is not good to drive anyone away; we must be nice to people no matter who they are. But we feel that no one should disturb what we want to do. If they urge us to listen, we say nothing. Sometimes they talk a long time telling us that our dances are evil and that

we must stop them. They say unless we go the "Christian Road" we will not be saved. But we just keep quiet and they get tired after a while and leave us alone.[40]

TEACHER UNDERSTANDING OF SOCIO-CULTURAL DIFFERENCES IN CHILDREN

It has been hypothesized that the educational retardation found in minority group children was caused in part, because the curriculum of the school fails to consider sufficiently the cultural orientations of the children, the value configurations, and the language barrier.

In the spring of 1959, a questionnaire study was made which specifically attempted to measure teacher awareness of socio-cultural differences in classrooms enrolling children with different ethnic backgrounds. During the 1959 summer session at the University of New Mexico, the same questionnaire was applied to a workshop group of teachers who were enrolled in a graduate seminar concerned with bicultural education. Both of these studies are reported in this section.[37]

Teacher Awareness of Socio-cultural Differences in Multi-Cultural Classrooms

The purpose of Ulibarri's study was to determine the extent to which selected teachers are aware of socio-cultural differences as they affect the education of Spanish-speaking and Indian children in New Mexico. A major premise of the study was that the ineffectiveness of the public schools in the education of minority groups, such as the Spanish American and the Indian in New Mexico, was due in large measure to the failure to consider sufficiently the cultural difference and the behavior arising therefrom, in the development of the curricula. It was hypothesized that teachers, in general, were not aware of these cultural differences.

A twenty-item questionnaire was prepared which asked teachers to rate items on a five-point scale for each ethnic group: Indian, Anglo, and Spanish American. The types of items evaluated included:

1. Meeting psychological needs of children;
2. Emphasis on "competition" as a value;
3. Time orientation;
4. Scientific explanation of natural phenomena;
5. Attitudes toward economic efficiency;
6. Experiences of children rooted in their life space;
7. Attitudes toward education and the school curriculum;

8. Range of abilities within the class;

9. Differences in intelligence in ethnic groups.

The questionnaire was scaled from 1 to 5, with the following ratings:

1 = very little

2 = below average

3 = average

4 = above average

5 = very much

Teachers were asked to circle the number which most appropriately indicated their opinion regarding each item. Sample items follow.

4. Most school curricula are primarily oriented to the future. They emphasize hard work in the present in order to be rewarded in the future.

   To what extent do you believe the following children are able to see this future-orientation and to adjust to working hard in the present in order to be rewarded in the future?

Indian	1	2	3	4	5
Spanish American	1	2	3	4	5
Anglo	1	2	3	4	5

5. In the operation of the school, great emphasis is placed upon competition.

   To what extent do you believe the home environment of the following children develops the value of competition?
   (Scale repeated here)

   . . . .

6. Society today places much emphasis on scientific interpretation of natural phenomena.

   To what extent do you believe the following children are receptive to scientific interpretation of natural phenomena?
   (Scale repeated here)

   . . . .

17. Most curricula are geared to middle-class Anglo culture. Thus, it seems that middle-class Anglo children should be the most proficient in school work. This, however, does

not exclude children from other cultures or social classes from achieving up to par as far as grade levels are concerned.

To what extent do you believe the following children are achieving at grade level in school?
(Scale repeated here)

. . . .

19. In general, the Indian children talk in their native tongue with one another and at home; the same generally holds true for the Spanish American children.

To what extent do you believe the following children are proficient in oral expression in the English language?
(Scale repeated here)

Generally, the teachers agreed to a significant degree in assigning ranks to the three ethnic groups. That is, there was close agreement of all teachers in the sample that Indian children, for example, rated "1" or "very little" concerning their proficiency in oral expression as evaluated by Item 19.

The twenty items used were based upon available literature in anthropology, sociology, educational psychology, and education. Research investigation, then, indicated that there are, academically speaking, correct answers for the ratings in the questionnaire. Using Item 19 to illustrate further, one might expect teachers to agree that proficiency in oral English expression, on a five-point scale, might rate Indians "1," Spanish Americans "3," and Anglos "5."

In this study, it was found that teachers, in general, are not sensitive to socio-cultural differences of Indian, Spanish American, and Anglo children. On only three of the twenty items did this sensitivity show statistical significance. While teachers were aware of some rather obvious differences in language, customs, and experience backgrounds, they did not recognize underlying value conflicts. The principal implication to be drawn from this study was that equal educational opportunity is denied minority group children because the curriculum is geared to teachers' middle-class, Anglo values. The seriousness of the implication can be better appreciated if one considers the fact that these children, in general, come from homes which have very limited understanding of the Anglo culture, much less the narrow segment of middle-class life style emphasized by the public school.

Growth in Awareness of Socio-Cultural Difference Through a Planned Course of Study

A four-week workshop in bicultural education in New Mexico was offered by the College of Education at the University of New Mexico during the summer session, 1959. The main objective of the workshop was to sensitize the participants to socio-cultural differences as these differences affect the education of Indian, Spanish American, and Anglo children. This workshop grew out of two years of intensive research into the problems encountered by non-English-speaking children in the public schools in New Mexico. It was hoped that through direct instruction teachers would become more aware of socio-cultural difference among Indian, Spanish American, and Anglo children. Moreover, it was hoped that teachers would become more adept in interpreting implications for classroom behavior rooted in the cultural difference.

The scope of the workshop included academic lectures with group discussion concerning: (1) the effect of cultural difference on the education of Apache, Pueblo, Navajo, and Spanish American children; (2) cultural diffusion; (3) meaning of social class stratification; (4) the continuum of acculturation; and (5) classroom problems of educational retardation and problems with the English language.

An extensive field trip of 1200 miles was completed to permit first hand observation of the life-space of these children. Visited were the Navajo-Cornell Medical Clinic at Manyfarms, Arizona, in the interior of the Navajo Reservation, the Anaconda Uranium works which mills uranium from the Laguna Reservation, the ancient home of the Acoma Indians, Walpi on First Mesa of Hopiland, and the traditional Spanish-American villages of Penasco, Trampas, Truchas, and Chimayo in the Sangre de Cristo Mountains.

Throughout the workshop discussions, emphasis was given to understanding of the conflicts in values between ethnic groups. The major conflicts in societal values between the Indian and the Spanish American children and the middle-class Anglo teacher were studied and discussed. Many of these same conflicting values have been taught in the traditional family situation to Navajo, Apache, Pueblo, and Spanish American children in New Mexico. The greatest present need is not that teachers should change either their beliefs or the children's, but rather, that they be completely aware of and accept the differences. Accepting and facing the differences realistically will be the first step in helping the child resolve his conflicts and ultimately grow into a truly bicultural adult.

The questionnaire of twenty items, developed for Ulibarri's study, was given to the group of thirty teachers on the first day and again on the last day of the four-week workshop. The same statistical analysis was applied to the answers of the workshop group as was applied in Ulibarri's study. The first application of the questionnaire showed a higher degree of sensitivity to sociocultural differences among the teachers enrolled for the workshop than for Ulibarri's sample (eight items of twenty). Perhaps this sensitivity reflected these teachers' reasons for enrolling for the workshop. The last application of the questionnaire to the workshop sample indicated a substantial growth in sensitivity in almost all areas. Only three items showed significant sensitivity in Ulibarri's sample; eight items showed this sensitivity at the first administration in the workshop; and sixteen items of the twenty measured sensitivity at the end of the workshop. The items in which there were regressions may be explained in terms of lack of instruction in the workshop or inadequacy of wording of the items in the questionnaire. Generally, it can be concluded that conscious, directed effort to sensitize teachers to socio-cultural differences in the education of minority group children produces substantial, positive results. Whether this knowledge on the part of the teachers will be applied in the classroom serving more than one cultural group remains to be seen.

This study has special significance in the Southwest because of its rapidly growing population with respect to both the minority and Anglo groups. This rapid growth has necessitated, and will continue to necessitate, importing hundreds of teachers from other parts of the country who may not be familiar with the cultural differences present in minority group populations.

SUMMARY

Some of the conflicts in beliefs and practices of members of the dominant culture, social class orientations, and Judeo-Christian influences and biases have been explored. A research study indicating that teachers selected at random demonstrate little sensitivity to the socio-cultural differences that exist between themselves and the children they teach has been reported. The question might now be raised, in view of this report, of how will teachers go about correcting the situation.

As noted in Chapter 2, Rasey appealed to the openmindedness of teachers and their need for greater self-realization in searching for ways to meet these problems. Mead pointed out to teachers the need to learn ways to state new problems so that problem-solving approaches will be evolved for new problems not yet stated. There is certainly need for the social scientist to learn completely new ways for meeting some of the age-old problems that we have not yet worked through effectively.

FOOTNOTES

[1] Leo Simmons, Sun Chief, An Autobiography of a Hopi Indian (New Haven: Yale University Press, 1942).

[2] W. F. Vaughan, Personal and Social Adjustment (New York: The Odyssey Press, 1952), pp. 168-173.

[3] Ibid., pp. 219-221.

[4] Karen Horney, The Neurotic Personality of Our Time (New York: W. W. Norton and Co., Inc., 1937), pp. 288-289.

[5] George D. Spindler, The Transmission of American Culture, The Burton Lecture, 1957 (Cambridge: Harvard University Press, 1959), pp. 2-3.

[6] Fisher, Mary Shattuck, "Children in the World Today," in Linton, Fisher, and Ryan, Culture and Personality, American Council on Education, Washington, D. C., 1953, pp. 21-22.

[7] Margaret Mead, "The Educative Environment, "The News Letter, Bureau of Educational Research and Service, Ohio State University, Columbus, (Edgar Dale and Hazel Gibbony, editors,) 26:2, No. 8, May, 1961.

[8] Cora A. Du Bois, "The Dominant Value Profile of American Culture," American Anthropologist, 57: 1232-1239, December, 1955.

[9] Ibid., p. 1233.

[10] Ibid., pp. 1233-1234.

[11] W. Lloyd Warner and Leo Srole, The Social Systems of American Ethnic Groups, Vol. III (New Haven: Yale University Press, 1945), p. 2.

[12] Raymond A. Mulligan, "Socio-Economic Background and College Enrollment," American Sociological Review, 116: 188-189, April, 1951.

[13] Warner and Srole, op. cit., p. 2.

[14] Ibid., p. 71.

[15] Robert J. Havighurst and Bernice L. Neugarten, Society and Education (Boston: Allyn and Bacon, Inc., 1957), p. 18.

[16] Sociologists believe that the upper-upper class is negligible in present-day society.

[17] Havighurst and Neugarten, op. cit., p. 48.

[18] Ibid., p. 22.

[19] Ibid., p. 359.

[20] Robin M. Williams, American Society (New York: Alfred A. Knopf, 1951), p. 374. The major values in American culture according to Williams, are achievement and success, activity and work, moral orientation, humanitarian mores, efficiency and practicality, material comfort, progress, equality, freedom, external conformity, science and secular rationality, nationalism-patriotism, democracy, active mastery, interest in worldly goods, and emphasis on change. (Pp. 382-385.)

[21] Allison Davis, Social Class Influences on Learning (Cambridge: Harvard University Press, 1952), pp. 97-98.

[22] W. Lloyd Warner, Robert J. Havighurst, and Martin B. Loeb, Who Shall Be Educated? (New York: Harper and Brothers, 1944), p. 157.

[23] Ibid., pp. 170-171.

[24] Spindler, op. cit., pp. 32-35.

[25] Ibid., 36.

[26] Ibid., p. 37.

[27] Prem Nath Sahai, 2400 Years' History of Science in India (Delhi, India: Sahai Shiksha Prasar Kosh, 1958), p. 48.

[28] This story is based on reports of three informants from three different Pueblos.

[29] Gladys Reichard, "The Navajo and Christianity," The American Anthropologist, 51: 66-71, January-March, 1949. This article contains an excellent and concise discussion of this problem and includes all five points mentioned here.

[30] A. C. Kinsey, et al., Sexual Behavior in the Human Female (Philadelphia: Saunders, 1953); A. C. Kinsey, et al., Sexual Behavior in the Human Male (Philadelphia: Saunders, 1948); Wayland F. Vaughan, "Sex vs. Conscience," Personal and Social Adjustment (New York: The Odyssey Press, 1952), pp. 246-254.

[31] L. Joseph Stone and Joseph Church, Childhood and Adolescence (New York: Random House, Inc., 1957), pp. 312-313.

[32] Reichard, op. cit., p. 67.

[33] Observation related by a teacher informant, during the 1958-59 school year.

[34] Personal conversation with Robert Young, Assistant General Superintendent, Navajo Agency, Window Rock, Arizona, on June 13, 1959. Robert Young is author of The Navajo Yearbook (Window Rock: Arizona, The Navajo Agency, 1958).

[35] Reichard, op. cit., p. 70.

[36] Clyde Kluckhohn and Dorothea Leighton, The Navajo (Cambridge: Harvard University Press, 1946; 1956), p. 85.

[37] Young, op. cit., p. 250.

[38] Reichard, op. cit., pp. 67-68.

[39] Dozier, Edward P., Hano: A Tewa Indian Community in Arizona, (New York: Holt, Rinehart and Winston, 1966), pp. 32-33.

[40] Dozier, Edward P., Hano: A Tewa Indian Community in Arizona, (New York: Holt, Rinehart and Winston, 1966), p. 34.

[41] Section V is based entirely upon the following two studies: Horacio Ulibarri, "Teacher Awareness of Socio-Cultural Differences in Multi-Cultural Classrooms" (unpublished Doctoral dissertation, The University of New Mexico, Albuquerque, 1959); and Horacio Ulibarri and Miles V. Zintz, "Growth in Teacher Awareness of Socio-Cultural Differences in Multi-Cultural Classrooms" (unpublished monograph, College of Education, the University of New Mexico, Albuquerque, 1960). (Mimeographed). Mr. Ulibarri served as Coordinator of the Indian Research Study from 1957 to 1959. See also, Ulibarri, Horacio, "Teacher Awareness of Socio-Cultural Differences in Multi-Cultural Classrooms, "Sociology and Social Research, 45:49-55. October, 1960.

CHAPTER 4

Social Institutions Across Cultures and the Acculturation Process

INTRODUCTION

A story recorded by the Leightons in The Navajo Door has been frequently retold. Even when hearing the story, however, many Anglos fail to understand the basis which keeps it from being a funny story to a Navajo.

> ....An Indian approached a trading post riding on a horse while his wife trudged behind on foot. The trader went up to the man and asked rebukingly, "Why is your wife walking?" The Navajo replied, "Because she ain't got a horse." To the trader this was an amusing example of Indian indifference, but in terms of Navajo custom it was a sensible reply. Since, as a woman, she probably owned most of the family property, it was her own lookout if she did not choose to convert some of it into a horse.[1]

As has been emphasized, most teachers in the public schools possess and have internalized middle-class values. That is, teachers come from homes where individual successes are highly rewarded and parents emphasize "climbing the ladder of success." Value is imputed to hard work and to meticulous planning for the future. Children learn many axioms about life in general as they grow up, such as: "If at first you don't succeed, try, try again," "The elevator to success is not running, climb the stairs," "Never put off until tomorrow what you can do today," "Success is won by hard work."

The Indian child comes to the classroom with a set of values and a background of experience radically different from those of his teacher. The teacher needs to be cognizant of these differences, to attempt to understand them, and, perhaps most important of all, to respect ideas, values, and practices which are different from his own.

How does one get the values he lives by? There are certain generic problems common to all human groups. They center about one's orientation to himself, his orientation to other people, and his orientation to the world about him.² Situational factors have caused varying value patterns to emerge.

Kluckhohn illustrates man's relation to nature in three ethnic groups in the Southwest.

> Spanish-American culture in the American Southwest or Mexican culture for that matter, gives us an example of a very definite first order Subjugation-to-Nature orientation. The typical Spanish-American sheep herder, in a time as recent as twenty-five years ago, believed firmly that there was little or nothing a man could do to save or protect either land or flocks when damaging storms descended upon them. He simply accepted the inevitable. In Spanish-American attitudes toward illness and death, one finds the same fatalism. "If it is the Lord's will that I die, I shall die," is the way they express it, and many a Spanish-American has been known to refuse the services of a doctor because of this attitude.³
>
> If the dominant conceptualization of the man-nature relationship is that of Harmony-with-Nature, there is no real separation between man, nature, and supernature. One is simply an extension of the other and the conception of wholeness derives from their unity. This orientation seems to have been the dominant one in many periods of Chinese history, and it is strongly evident in Japanese culture at the present time, as well as historically. It is also the orientation attributed to the Navajo Indians by Clyde Kluckhohn.
>
> . . . . . .
>
> The Mastery-over-Nature position is the first order one [sic] of most middle-class Americans. Natural forces of all kinds are to be overcome and put to the use of human beings. Rivers everywhere are spanned with bridges; mountains have roads put through and around them; new lakes are built, sometimes in the heart of deserts; old lakes get partially filled in when additional land is needed for building sites, roads, or airports; the belief in man-made medical care for the control of illness and the lengthening of life is strong to the extreme; and all are told early in life that "the Lord helps those who help themselves." The view in general is that it is a part of man's duty to overcome obstacles, hence great emphasis upon technology.⁴

While the Anglo believes that nature will destroy him unless he prevents it from doing so, the Navajo believes that nature will take care of him if he behaves as he should and does as she directs.⁵

The Anglo is apt to believe that "nature is a malignant force with useful aspects that must be harnessed, and useless, harmful ones that must be shorn of their power."⁶ When the Bureau of Indian affairs officials initiated a stock reduction program in the

1930's to combat serious over-grazing the Navajo believed "if anything is wrong these days, it is because The People are forgetting their ways and their stories, so of course anyone would know that there would be hard times. It has nothing to do with too many sheep."[7]

The family is probably the most important institution in every culture. Through this unit, each individual learns all of the behaviors normally expected in the community. He also learns any subtle orientations that are peculiar to his individual pattern. Teachers in American schools might profitably consider the basis on which family life rests. The difference between consanguine and conjugal relationships, the contrast between matrilocal and patrilocal residence, and the contrasting values derived from extended or nuclear family structure are important concepts to be understood.

BASIC INSTITUTIONS IN SOCIETY

There are certain basic institutions in all societies. These institutions are: (1) religion, (2) the family, (3) education, (4) economics, (5) health, (6) government and politics, and (7) recreation. These institutions evolve and have permanence in a society because its members adhere to certain goals in life. Children are taught specific practices to insure that they will achieve these goals. These institutions become fixed because certain behavioral patterns establish and reinforce themselves in the social expectations of the total group. The institutions reflect, then, the values of the total society. These values, in turn, through sanction and rejection, keep the total group oriented toward the life goals of the group. This is depicted in Figure 2.

Behavior in society is observable only in individual behavior. However, individual behavior incorporates specific practices of a culture which each individual selects for himself. Unless he conforms to the dictates of the group, he will be a "non-conformist." Pressures to conform cause most people to align themselves with the social expectations of the total group.

The action framework depicted in Figure 2 consists of the institutions in any society together with its normative values and actual practices in the achievement of its goals. Taking the institution of religion for a focal point, one finds the institution teaching certain values to the members of society in order that they may achieve the life goal. These value orientations tend to make the people behave in a certain manner. On the individual level, one is selective and may conform to the dictates of the culture or deviate from the conforming pattern. There are definite limits set for deviation, and beyond these limits society places strong social sanctions against extreme social behavior. Within these limits, however, the individual or individuals may start behaving at one or the other extreme. If enough of the people begin to behave at one

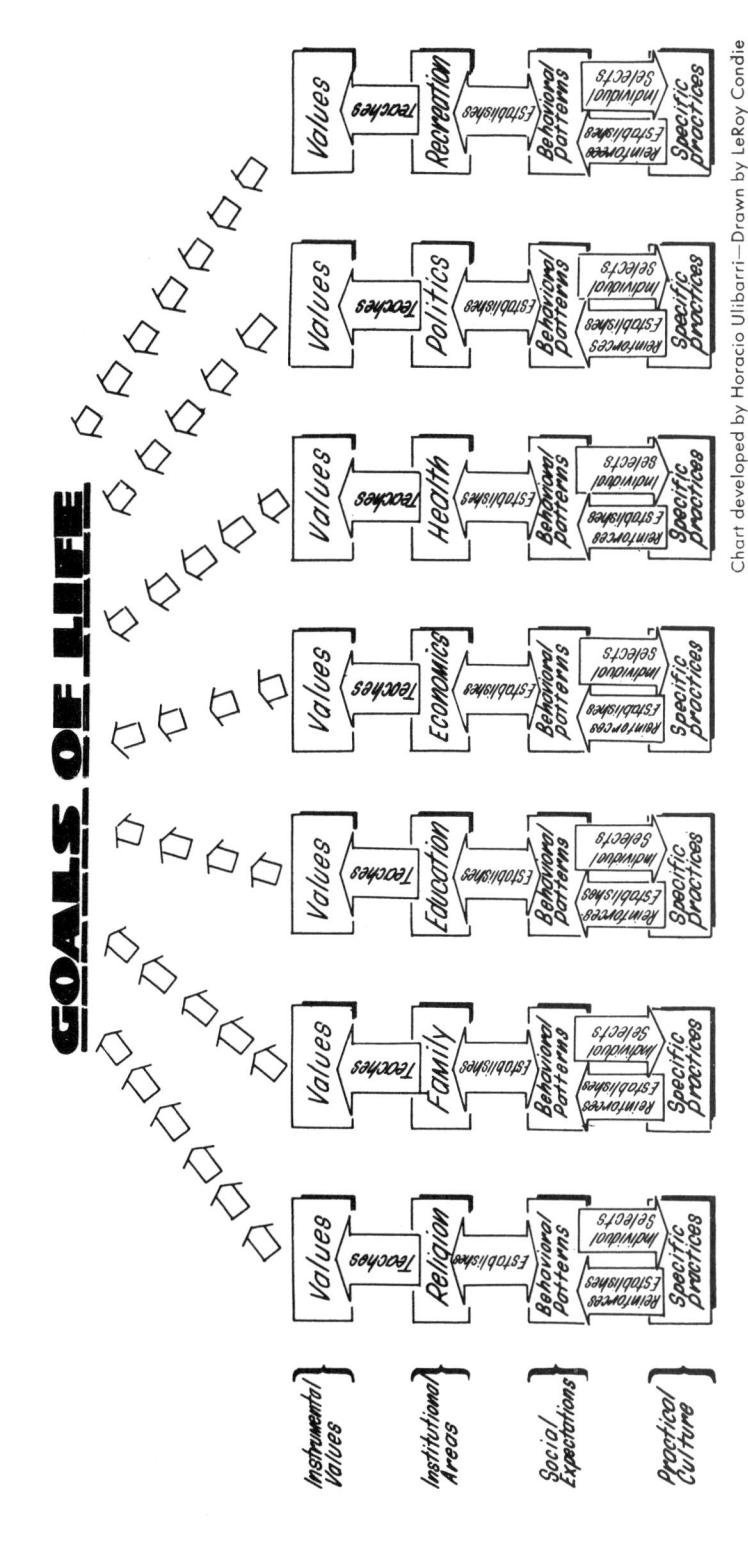

GOALS OF LIFE

| Religion | Family | Education | Economics | Health | Politics | Recreation |

Instrumental Values: Values — Teaches
Institutional Areas: Religion / Family / Education / Economics / Health / Politics / Recreation — Establishes
Social Expectations: Behavioral Patterns — Reinforces / Individual Selects
Practical Culture: Specific Practices

Chart developed by Horacio Ulibarri—Drawn by LeRoy Condie

Figure 2. Behavior in Society. This chart is to be read as follows (beginning at the bottom): Specific practice refers to individual behavior. When many individuals adopt a specific practice, a group behavior pattern emerges. It will be noted that there is a reciprocal relationship between specific practices and behavior patterns. While specific practices combine to create behavior patterns, the behavior patterns, in turn, are followed selectively by the individual. He may choose to practice some kinds of behavior, reject others. In time behavior patterns assume a permanent quality. They then become institutions. Institutions reflect the group's values. The values -- what is valued -- orient the group, and the individual, toward the goals of life.

109

end of the extreme, the middle road, or mean, moves to a new place and the limits of deviation are redefined. When enough people accept this mode of behavior, a new behavioral pattern is set and the value configurations are modified or changed, and over a long period of time the actual life goals may be changed. Thus, we see that culture is ever-changing.

This goal-of-life pattern may be easily illustrated by certain social expectations within the institution of religion. Judeo-Christian teaching has given the dominant American society specific dogma in order to achieve the life goal -- eternal life. Most people, even though they may not participate in the specific practice of regular church attendance, do reinforce the established behavior patterns of the Judeo-Christian religion.

The psychiatrist reminds us that the failure to establish this life goal based on some religious philosophy is apt to create mental illness. Jung says:

> Among all my patients in the second half of life -- that is to say, over thirty-five -- there has not been one whose problem in the last resort was not that of finding a religious outlook on life. It is safe to say that every one of them fell ill because he had lost that which the living religions of every age have given to their followers, and none of them has been really healed who did not regain his religious outlook. This, of course, has nothing to do with a particular creed or membership in a church.[8]

Most people are familiar with segments of American culture in which many specific practices are considered to be extremely conservative or puritanical. "Card playing is sinful," or "It is wrong to play ball on Sunday" are examples. The majority of people conformed to these values at one time. If what has happened to some of these practices is considered, it is seen that culture is a slowly-changing entity. Some individuals began to question the social norm and deviated from the accepted specific practices by doing what they really wanted to do. Thirty-to-forty years ago when young women began wearing short hair, it was a bit forward, perhaps, but they did it anyway. After most women accepted the practice of having their hair cut short, it was considered appropriate to do so. Thus, it is evident that as more and more people become liberal with respect to a specific practice, the liberal, instead of the original, practice becomes the norm. This evolutionary change goes on constantly in our society. The Anglo American culture changes so rapidly that each older generation feels that the younger is too revolutionary. This perhaps gives rise to such trite sayings as "the younger generation is going to the dogs."

The social behavior of a group may be studied, then, by observing the individual practices in the basic institutions. People are apt to believe that their practices and beliefs are right and, so, the practices and beliefs of the other person are wrong. People tend to deprecate the practices of others. It is "bad" to fail to do that which is "good." Stereotypes are created in this way. People with limited sophistication in social practices of others tend to say that all people of a given society behave in the same way. A few stereotypes might be mentioned. Many teachers say "All Indians are good artists," "Spanish Americans and Indians are lazy," or "He is getting along very well for a Navajo."

Teachers should be aware of stereotyping. Knowing as we do that people of any ethnic group will find their aptitudes and abilities spread along a long continuum from excellent ability to average ability to poor ability, it seems only logical that the range of ability to do art work in a large group of Indians, for example, will fall on the same continuum. It is no more logical to believe that all Indians are creative artists than to believe that all blind persons have aptitude in music.[9]

It is recognized that whole classes of Indian boys and girls who lack language ability and reading skills may perform in art class better on the average than whole classes of non-Indian boys and girls. They may compensate for their lack of certain skills in the classroom by developing others. They may also have developed keener powers of observation and be able to portray what they have seen in pictures instead of in the English language.

Surely no one who has visited the large mission churches in the Southwest or, more specifically, the beautiful church at Acoma, has concluded that Spanish Americans or Indians were, by nature, lazy. Their survival in the arid Southwest with an agrarian economy further attests to industry and hard work.

If one expects just to accept the statement that a student does "very well for a Navajo," this is an upsetting generalization. If it means that his language, culture, and experience barriers are recognized as they exist while one works diligently to overcome them, this is probably acceptance of reality. No longer is performance of a Navajo adequate until he does well as an American citizen in the larger society. To accept him as "just a Navajo" is both condescending and unfair.

The cultural difference may also be illustrated by the contrast in the homes of the Indian and the Anglo. The Anglo likes his house to have many rooms. There is undoubtedly a direct parallel between the high and low economic status of families and the number of rooms in their houses. Anglos like to have many separate rooms for food preparation, eating, resting, and sleeping. Not so the Southwest Indian. He likes a closely knit, harmonious group about him. He sees no need for putting each one in his separate room. To indicate the persistence of this cultural trait, one might cite the instances in which families have been pressured into accepting

Anglicized frame houses, but used them for storehouses and built themselves their traditional home nearby. This is further illustrated in the relocation program where the nuclear family is relocated in an apartment or house of four or five rooms in a distant city. Members of the extended family may move in with the relocated family because there is plenty of room. However, the neighbors and landlord are apt to register complaints. The Indian may not understand the complaint at all since "his way" is the way he prefers his living arrangement.[10]

Lee explains:

> To me, a room of my own means coveted privacy and convenience, as well as prestige. If my employer gives me a desk in an office shared with several others, I shall probably feel my own lack of importance. I should hardly expect to share a guest bedroom with a stranger or with my friend's children.[11]

To the Navajo, however, the "togetherness" of one big, happy family in one room has an entirely different cultural connotation. An isolated room of one's own could be interpreted as rejection.

The cultural difference as it exists in the Indian groups will be apparent also in the attitude of the child toward the figure of authority. A child who comes to school from a home that tends to be autocratic will be unable to participate easily in a classroom that tends to be democratic. Even after he begins to understand the process, he is still in conflict because of the basic difference in trying, on the one hand, to be an independent thinking individual, and trying, on the other hand, to be obedient to authority. The nature of the government of a pueblo group, for example, is theocratic, tending more toward autocracy than democracy. Theocracy is the government of a state by the immediate direction of God.[12] The priests, who represent the Deity, govern.

THE ACCULTURATION PROCESS

Why Acculturate?

The interaction of cultural groups of unequal strength, one dominant, one subordinate, leads inevitably toward more and more people in the minority groups taking their places in the social and economic life of the dominant one. The dominant group controls the economic base, the public health program, and the educational program. These institutions offer to the minority groups opportunities for acquiring desired artifacts for present-day living. The problem involves the adaptation of many individuals to new types of living.

The pressures toward progress and toward the ability to function in a highly technological age make necessary the transition of minority groups to an economy where they can participate in the American way of life. For example, in order to compete successfully in the labor market, these individuals must not only have acquired the technical skills needed in order to function on a job, but they must also speak the language of their co-workers and practice the social amenities of middle-class culture. Only in this way can they participate in all the activities of the people with whom they work. People are as apt to lose their jobs because they do not know the language and the social practices as they are because they do not know the skills required on the job.

A Scale of Acculturation

The interaction of two social groups in the course of time necessitates a certain amount of exchange of ideas, attitudes, and practices. To the degree which the exchange causes either group to accept and internalize attitudes and practices of the other, cultural diffusion is said to take place. Mutual readiness [13] for integration in the public schools indicates that both cultures have values to contribute to this amalgamation.

However, the acculturation process that is taking place is predominantly one of movement of minority ethnic groups into the dominant middle-class Anglo culture. For Indian groups and the Spanish-speaking people, this represents a significant evolutionary cultural change from a traditionally agrarian life.

That no definite statement can be made about any total group in transition needs to be emphasized. Within each group one finds a few who are entirely bicultural and who live equally at home in one culture as in another; there are a few who have rejected their traditional culture and who attempt to live entirely within the framework of Anglo values; there are those in transition who attempt to live confidently in the traditional culture but who are accepting many of the artifacts and the need for the money economy of the dominant culture; and there are those who continue to reject the intruding Anglo culture and retain the "old ways."

Table III is a scale of acculturation for the Spanish American culture of the middle Rio Grande Valley, depicting levels of traditional, low, medium, high, and complete acculturation for each of the seven social institutions. While the scale of acculturation as presented in Table III details the Spanish American situation, it serves to illustrate the process for other minority groups as well.

Economy

The unhappy truth is that the economy is the controlling element in present-day social interaction. In order to coordinate the total pattern of living for the welfare of the total society, the other basic institutions have to modify their operation to fit with the economy.

TABLE III

Scale of Acculturation: Spanish American to Anglo

	TRADITIONAL	LOW	MEDIUM	HIGH	FULL
Religion	Usually Catholic; Life Hereafter (Blind faith)	Usually Catholic; Life Hereafter (Blind faith)	Catholic, some Protestant; Life Hereafter (More enlightened faith)	Catholic or Protestant Rational faith or weak church goers	Catholic or Protestant; Rational faith
Family	Extended family concept; large families; autocratic	Extended family; medium-sized; autocratic	Little extension to family; medium-sized; less autocratic	Little extension to family; medium-sized; paternalistic	No extension to family concept; small or medium; paternalistic or democratic
Education	Barely literate or illiterate; ruling class refined and polished	Speak English brokenly; elementary school; blind faith in education	Both parents speak English; elementary & probably high school; some value in education	Parent(s) college education; professional; middle-class value to education	Has lost contact with Spanish culture, per se
Economics	Agrarian; subsistence level; welfare	Own plot of land; unskilled labor; subsistence level of income; welfare	Farm; semi-skilled labor; teacher; low average income	Professional; average or above average income; rise to middle class	Has lost contact with Spanish culture, per se
Health	Folkway; herb medicine; superstition	Folkway; patent medicines; little professional medical attention	Some folkway; more professional medicine and attention; hospitalization	Medical attention; hospitalization; modern sanitary facilities	Has lost contact with Spanish culture, per se
Politics	Lower class: uninterested or recreational Middle class: nonexistent Upper class: sharp politicians	Lower: uninterested or local (recreation) Middle: nonexistent Upper: sharp politician (political boss)	Lower: uninterested Middle: value in franchise; local political boss Upper: state political boss	Lower: uninterested Middle: value in franchise; local political boss Upper: state political boss	Indifferent
Recreation	Family recreation; communal; noncommercial	Family recreation; communal; some commercial	Little family recreation; noncommunal; commercial	Very little family recreation; noncommunal; mostly commercial	Has lost contact with Spanish culture

Evolved by the Staff of the Indian Research Study, Horacio Ulibarri, Coordinator.

"Maybe fish not bite because gods angry you pay me only one buck-fifty an hour."

Drawing J. Mirachi. Copyright 1961 by
The New Yorker Magazine, Inc.

Much of the transition to the wage economy has already taken place for the Indian guide in the cartoon from the New Yorker!

One specific example is the change effected in pueblo life by the extension of opportunities to minority groups to earn wages which has brought about a complete revolution within some of the villages near cities. There is a trend, in some pueblos, for all the able-bodied members of a family to leave their young children with grandparents from early morning until late at night so that they can commute to a near-by city to perform menial jobs for a daily wage. An informant indicates that in one pueblo almost all of the employable adults are doing this. There is concern that this will increase social disorganization within families with concomitant neglect and abandonment of children, which would lead to an increase in juvenile delinquency.

The Indians have been accustomed to a quite different economic base. On tax-free land, with homes rent-free, they have been able to provide the necessities of life with irrigated gardens and small trade in pottery, jewelry, and tourist trinkets. They had always contented themselves with an existence in which money had little value. The change has brought automobiles to the pueblos, better roads, electricity, running water, longer shopping trips, and television. Once people assimilate these artifacts in their daily lives, they are unwilling to give them up.

In order for the individual members to have more of the artifacts of the dominant Anglo culture, the Pueblo, the Apache, the Navajo, the Spanish American, or the Mexican American must adjust to the economic base -- with its weekly wages and installment buying -- that the enterprising business world extends to him. The survival of the sub-cultures probably hinges on their acceptance of the new economy. Other institutions within the sub-cultures will, of necessity, adjust to the economic change. Accepting modern health practices and the education of the young children are closely allied with the economic base of the people.

Many people recognize values in the traditional practices of the sub-cultures and feel strongly nostalgic about preserving such practices as the extended family with its congenial care of the aged and the handicapped, the security of agrarian self-sufficiency, the absence of ulcers and heart attacks among people with a slower tempo of living, and the festivals that preserve the folkways and the music, art, and dance of the social group.

Health

Bringing better health practices to the rural Indian is essential to the acculturation process. There is increasing acceptance among the Indian population of the best available medical practices. As a matter of principle, as long as scientific knowledge is available to reduce death, information and guidance must be made available to all people to make it possible for them, through enlightened self-interest, to seek the best medical care. The establishment of hospitals throughout Indian country and the development of clinics accessible to individual families make medical services directly available to the people.

> Great strides have been made in improving Indian Health. Life expectancy has increased by 15 years since 1955, and the death rate per 1,000 live births has dropped from 94 in 1954 to 49 in 1960 - a decrease of nearly fifty per cent. Among the Navajos, the death rate from tuberculosis has declined about 55 per cent during the past ten years. Marked improvements have been made in water and sanitation facilities, with more than 8,000 Navajo homes receiving some type of sanitation equipment since 1956.[14]

Adair cites statistics of the United States Public Health Service in Table IV to show the high mortality rates among the Navajo Indians.

In a discussion of changing health practices of Indians of the Southwest, the Navajo-Cornell University Field Health Project at Manyfarms, Arizona, should be mentioned. The purposes of the project, established in 1955, were to survey the health needs of a rural, isolated community and to study the means by which these health needs could be met in a form acceptable to the Navajo people. As reported in Science, January, 1960, patterns of disease of special significance to teachers are cited.[15]

In the three-year period, 1956-1958, the project reports an infant mortality rate (deaths during the first year of life per 1000 live births) of 73.1 [U.S. average: 26].[16]

The average annual birth rate over a three-year period was 48.7 per 1000 persons. This extraordinarily high birth rate was associated with a high fertility rate -- that is, the number of live births per 1000 women aged 14-55.[17]

TABLE IV

Leading Causes of Death among Navajos and Comparative U.S. General Population Rates, 1954[18]

Causes	Rates per 100,000 Navajos	Rates per 100,000 U.S. General	Per cent of total deaths Navajos	Per cent of total deaths U.S. General
Pneumonia	123.5	23.7	16.2	2.6
Gastritis, Duodenitis, Enteritis Colitis	110.2	5.3	14.5	.6
Diseases of early infancy	102.3	39.4	13.4	4.3
Tuberculosis	53.0	10.5	7.0	1.1

In this community of approximately 2,000 persons, the net gain in population (excess of births over deaths) is a three-year period was 239 persons. This represents a population expansion of "explosive" proportions.[19] [This is almost twice as many births as a fast-growing, non-white population in New York City.]

A viral disease [such as measles] widely prevalent in our society and virtually inescapable in youth is not too serious under present-day general living conditions of the United States but becomes a considerably more serious medical problem in young children living in the hogans.[20]

An examination of 270 children aged six to ten in the project area revealed that 16 per cent of this group of children showed some significant loss in hearing. When a partial loss of hearing is added to the problem of attempting to receive an education in an alien language, the implications of these streptococcal infections are very great.[21] [National non-Indian incidence of hearing loss may be estimated at 3 per cent.]

While active tracoma was found in only 2.9 per cent of school-age children under ten, inactive trachoma was found in 16.8 per cent, and 40 per cent of the persons more than 25 years of age showed evidence of previous disease.[22]

Congenital dislocation of the hip was found in a ratio of 1,090 persons afflicted per 100,000 population while a study in New York City revealed only a ratio of 3.8 per 100,000 population.[23]

Thus far relationships between the medicine men in the community and members of the project staff have been excellent. Every effort is made to accord the medicine men the respect they deserve as the spiritual leaders of the community.[24]

The medicine men believe they can distinguish between the type of "illness" most likely to be benefited by their procedures and the type that is better managed by the project staff.[25]

Many health problems of New Mexico's people are closely related to their economic situation. There are many sub-standard houses with inadequate sanitary facilities. Not only may water be very scarce, but it may be coming from contaminated sources. Modern health practices for controlling rodents and disease-carrying insects are often not carried out.

> The policy of the federal government, through the Bureau of Indian Affairs and the Public Health Service, is to help the Indian in every way possible to achieve the same degree of independence as other ethnic groups which make up our population. This policy looks far into the future toward "the termination, at the appropriate time, of federal supervision and services special to Indians." Until that day arrives, the Public Health Service will do its best to fill the needs for community hospital, local health department, and family doctor to many thousands of our Indians.[26]

Marsh writes of plans to overcome some of these problems:

> To counteract the unfavorable environment in which the Indians live, the Public Health Service has developed a sanitation program which provides instruction in the proper methods of storing and handling water, insect control, and privy construction. Indian sanitarian aids, trained by the service, return to their native home and villages with newly acquired knowledge and teach their people correct sanitary procedures.

Today's high food costs and a growing preference for the white man's processed foods are resulting in an excessive consumption of fats and carbohydrates. Acculturation is not an unmixed blessing for these Indians. 27

The <u>1958 Annual Report on Indian Health</u> indicates the seriousness of the problem.

> The health problems of the Indians . . . and the difficulties in reaching them with health services are unique. Nearly a fifth of all deaths among these groups result from infections diseases which long have been under control in the general population. Their deaths from such preventable disease as tuberculosis, gastroenteritis, influenza, and pneumonia are 3 to 6 times higher than in the population as a whole. Life expectancy among Indians . . . is 10 years shorter than the 70-year life span which prevails generally. Whereas the average age at time of death in the general population is 62, among the Indians it is only 40. This early average age at death results largely from the excessive infant death rate among Indians. Twenty-two per cent of all Indian deaths occur among infants, compared with a national average of only 7 per cent.

> During 1957, examinations in the field disclosed that trachoma, a virulent eye disease, was recurring among Indians in the Northwest and the Southwest. Inasmuch as this disease is relatively rare in the general population, very little in the way of professional literature was available for guidance of physicians who must diagnose and treat the condition among Indians.

> The excessively high death rate among Indian children remains one of the most serious problems facing the Service's Division of Indian Health. Of every 1,000 Indian infants born alive in 1956 -- the latest year for which figures were available -- 56 died within the first year. In the general population, only 26 out of each 1,000 infants born alive fail to survive beyond the first year. 28

<u>Health Services for American Indians</u> is a detailed study of the present status of Indian health and the health needs required to bring their standards in line with those for the country as a whole. 29

Medical personnel in the Public Health Service are cognizant of the need for understanding cultural differences as was pointed out in the Navajo-Cornell University Field Health Project at Manyfarms, Arizona. (See Chapter 1, page 9.) Shaw illustrates the necessity for respecting traditional Navajo beliefs in administering a hospital on the reservation.

Last summer an Indian medicine man, flown from a distant reservation by the Public Health Service, conducted mystical rites in the setting of a modern laboratory of a tuberculosis sanatorium housing 70 Indian patients. A public address system carried his chants into every room in the hospital. The medicine man had come to the hospital in response to urgent appeals by medical officials, who called him in after two patients had fled the hospital and others were preparing to leave. Lightning, which some Indians believe is a cause of illness, twice had struck a tree on the hospital grounds. The hospital and its patients had to be blessed; the spirits concerned had to be placated. When this was done, the patients settled back with confidence that danger had been warded off. The white man's medicine had been reinforced by Indian religious concepts.[30]

Marsh also illustrates how health workers have met the cultural difference and adjusted their methods to accommodate Indian customs.

... one hospital experienced little success in getting Indian women to come there to have their babies delivered. It is part of a ritual among the women in that area to drink cedar tea after delivery. Cedar tea was not served at the hospital, and as a result, prospective mothers felt they could not use its services. Once cedar tea was provided for the new mothers, acceptance of service was assured.[31]

The high infant mortality rate, the excessive number of deaths caused by preventable infectious diseases, and the inadequate sanitation facilities constitute pressing problems for the Public Health Service. Both the alleviation of these problems and the development of a health consciousness that emphasizes prevention are prerequisities to the ultimate future goal of termination of special services for Indians.

Traditional health practices among the Spanish-speaking were those that could evolve in any isolated, rural, agrarian group. There were the curanderas, who were general practitioners for certain ailments, the sobadores, who were more apt to massage, knead, or set bones, perhaps the equivalent of early chiropractors, and the parteras, who were midwives who learned their trade from helping other midwives and from their own experience. If the efforts of the curandera or the sobador did not help, the illness was often diagnosed as being due to bewitchment. Further help was needed in cases of sorcery if such cases were not accepted as punishment from God.

If a retarded child was born into a family, the explanation might be that the mother did not observe some avoidance or taboo during pregnancy or that it was punishment from God. One teacher reports a mother's explanation of her daughter's epilepsy in this way:

> In the Spanish American communities I have taught in, I was surprised at their beliefs in witchcraft. They believed that human beings could transfer themselves into balls of fire and travel along the ground. Sometimes these witches would acquire the forms of owls or coyotes, the most common animal figures in Spanish American witchcraft. One little girl I had in my room had epilepsy, and her mother always told me that if she could find out who disliked them, or find out what they had done to cause someone to have bewitched the girl, they would like to make it right with them so that the girl could be well again.

Mal ojo, the evil eye, is still much feared in some places. If an infant is going to be admired and fondled by an adult visitor, the adult must first make a cross on the child's forehead. If he doesn't, the child may become ill or even die. One teacher reports her experience with mal ojo:

> It is hard to reconcile oneself to some customs that Spanish-speaking people have. The fact that admiration of a new baby for the first time would cause "ojo" unless the admirer would put her thumb in her mouth and then make the sign of the cross on the baby's forehead has always caused me much concern, and one that I could not cope with unless I hurt the people who did this in sincere belief that they were doing what was best.
>
> As best as I could determine, "ojo" meant that the baby on being admired thus without the blessing, would find himself with maladies which were explained to me as ranging from simple stomach disorders to a type of palsy.

Finally, it was quite common for people to make special prayers to designated saints for different kinds of diseases, or to promise to make pilgrimages after recovery. These "promises" to make pilgrimages might be made under other circumstances than the usual illnesses. One informant tells that many young men in the war, in the face of possible grave danger, made promises to make pilgrimages if they were spared. El Sanctuario, in Chimayo, New Mexico, is one place to which many of these pilgrimages have been made.

The following episode concerning intercession by the saints and promises made has been reported by a teacher:

> Along with human efforts to bring health back to sick members, help was sought by intercession through the saints. This is still practiced in this particular community. A specific case

was one in which polio struck down a child in one of the leading families. The father of this family was far from acceptable from my point of view, and from many points of comparison. When this child of his became a victim of polio, he did as the children say, "I made a promise." He promised that if the child lived he would make a pilgrimage to Mexico and this he did.

Brujeria might be only manifestations of the dark, fancies of people, something one just senses; yet, they were "known" also to turn into balls of fire rolling across the plain or up the narrow valley. La Farge describes an incident concerning brujeria and an illness:

> Snow was on the ground when Policarpio Lobato was bothered one day by a fox that skulked with unusual daring around his outbuildings and chicken run. Near sundown, when he went to get firewood, the animal just stood and looked at him from a slight distance. He had a strange feeling that he knew the creature, and that it knew him by name and was mocking him. He signed himself, and then threw a billet of stove wood at it, striking it on the left shoulder hard enough to knock it over. It ran off limping. Within a day, everyone had heard that an old man who lived in Raton Canyon, and about whom there was a good deal of suspicion, had been laid up with a sudden violent attack of arthritis in the left shoulder. No one could ask for clearer evidence of brujeria.[32]

The Mexican American is likely to have the same feelings as the Spanish American toward the Anglo general practitioner who comes into the home to doctor the sick. The lack of attention to formalities, the speedy examination, the impersonal prescription to be filled at the drugstore, and the hasty departure is contrasted with the curandera by Clark:

> The doctor didn't do anything -- he just saw me for a couple of minutes and gave me some pills. Folk curers, on the other hand, usually give a lengthy and impressive performance; they sometimes work with a sick person an hour or more at a time.[33]

The story is told of a physician who was called in the middle of the night to see a very ill child.

> When the doctor arrived . . . the mother insisted that they first have a cup of tea. With the unconscious child in the adjoining room, parents and doctor sat in the kitchen and drank their tea. "The conversation was obviously forced -- yet . . . one never rushes precipitately into the middle of things; there

must be tea and talk before it is proper to examine even a patient as precious as this one. The thoughts of the mother were undoubtedly with the sick one, too, as she studied the visitor . . . she was not an indifferent mother. But if the doctor was not simpatico, how then could she possibly cure the child?" After these preliminaries, the doctor, "trying not to move with a too indecorous haste," was escorted into the next room to examine the unconscious child. The doctor had proved herself a kind and congenial person -- the parents knew they could trust her to do the right thing for their child.[34]

Many of the folk health beliefs, such as mal ojo, susto, and empacho are believed in so strongly that if the health worker denies their existence, he is sure to lose the respect of the people he is trying to help.

With the Mexican-American child, the gap between the traditional culture and the middle-class orientation of the Anglo may not be nearly so wide as the gap for the Pueblo Indian. The greatest differences probably lie in the distance between a rural, agricultural society and a highly industrialized, technological one. Isolation within the new culture exists, too, because of language and differences in custom. Tuck suggests that Mexican-American life in the United States is a sub-culture of our own civilization, not a Mexican sub-culture.[35]

MARGINALITY

The minority groups in New Mexico constitute marginal groups with respect to their status economically, socially, or professionally. By definition:

> A marginal group is an incompletely assimilated group; one which has partially relinquished its former culture and which has not yet won full acceptance in the new culture within which it is living. A term used in connection with immigrant groups in which there has been considerable mixture of different cultures, so that attitudes and values and resultant behavior patterns are characteristic of neither; the group occupying a sort of social no-man's land. Where overt characteristics make identification easy, this stage in the assimilation process may be occupied for decades, as in the case of Orientals and Latin-speaking peoples in the United States, and such groups may evolve a fairly well integrated culture of their own containing elements drawn from both the social orders concerned.[36]

Within any society one must never lose sight of the fact that there are great individual differences in the extent to which the individual members are acculturated, from the most conservative to the most anglicized. Moore gives the following definition of the marginal man:

> The marginal man, in the broadest sense, is a person who is not a fully participating member of a social group. Most marginal persons are marginal to two or more groups, as is true of partially assimilated immigrants.[37]

Antonovsky characterizes marginality in social systems by the following criteria:[38]

> 1. "Two cultures, or sub-cultures, are in lasting contact."

This suggests that they retain their identity as separate societies, and one is not diffused or in a state of dislocation and being assimilated by the other. The lasting contact indicates that they both continue to exist over a long period of time.

> 2. "One is dominant in terms of power and reward potential. Of the two, this is the non-marginal culture. Its members are not particularly attracted to, or influenced by, the marginal culture."

This clearly represents the status in New Mexico with respect to the Anglo American dominant culture and the marginal cultures among the Pueblo, Apache, Navajo, and Spanish American peoples. This causes much of the difficulty of the acculturating process. The lack of interest of the Anglos in the minority cultures is interpreted as an attitude of competitive and aggressive superiority and causes animosity within the marginal groups toward the Anglo American -- toward both his culture collectively and him as an individual.

> 3. "The boundaries between the two are sufficiently permeable for the members of the marginal culture to internalize the patterns of the dominant culture as well as their own."

This is illustrated in New Mexico by the many individual members of the marginal cultures who have availed themselves of opportunities to achieve status in the dominant culture educationally, socially, economically, and politically.

> 4. "The patterns of values between the divergent cultures cannot, in their entirety, be easily harmonized."

Opposing values of the different ethnic groups make conflicts inevitable in any attempt to reconcile values held by Anglo Americans with extremely different, contradictory values held by Indians or Spanish Americans.

> 5. "Having acquired some of the goals of the dominant culture, members of the marginal group are pulled by the promise of greater rewards offered."

124

Once the Pueblo Indian, for example, acquires a car or a television set, and finds how much these enlarge his horizons (life-space), two things are apt to follow logically. First, he must continue to function in a money economy somewhat equivalent to the Anglo American in order to afford the costs of operating them. Second, these artifacts extend his horizons so that he is continually introduced to additional desires which cause him to move, subtly at first, closer toward the anglicized life-style.

6. "The barriers between the two tend to be hardened by discrimination from the one side, and by pressure against 'betrayal' from the other side."

Minority groups are apt to be discriminated against in competition with the dominant culture. This discrimination will appear either in clearly recognizable form or in unconscious ways not easily recognized by members of the dominant culture. In the event that individuals in minority groups make the effort to compete and take the best place they can within the dominant culture, they sacrifice much of the "in-group" status they might have had with their own minority group. The Indian who acquires an education and accepts a job in state government or under civil service in his attempt to help his own people may find that his people have not accepted the dichotomy of his status. They may feel that he cannot have their best interests at heart and still place his primary allegiance with the state or the nation.

7. "Marginality acquires particular intensity when the clash persists through more than one generation."

In the Southwest, the problem has existed for centuries. Anglo Americans were the last Americans. The American Indian feels in a very real sense that he was the first. Through the years, the Indian and the Spanish American cultures apparently learned to live side by side and to maintain their social systems in lasting contact. Their life values, their family structure, their attitudes toward work, time, and saving had much in common, but were not compatible with the aggression of the Anglo American who entered the Southwest in large numbers in the middle of the nineteenth century.

With respect to marginality, then, the intensity of feeling among Indian groups today is caused by many factors. First, the economic base of the people is undergoing drastic change. All of the artifacts that provide modern living among Anglo Americans are being introduced into Indian homes. This requires a money economy, causing the adults in a family to leave the pueblo to drive to the city for work. Second, the plan to transfer the Indian children into public school classrooms has been effected rapidly and with little consideration of the time needed by the Indians to study, to discuss, and to understand the ramifications of the plan. This transfer confronts Indian elders with many philosophical problems about the future of their cultural heritage. Interaction with non-Indians may facilitate learning the English language, acquiring skills for competing economically in the labor market, and attaining a middle-class standard of living. However, the elders must face the possibility that their children will not learn their mother tongue, the nature lore, the moral values, the ceremonial rites, and the prayers of their people, and to them, these are more important.

Third, the Indians may have considerable anxiety that the transfer of children to public schools, the move toward a money economy, and the conversion from extended to nuclear family living, are all steps toward the termination of services heretofore provided through the Bureau of Indian Affairs. They have also witnessed the transfer of health services from the Bureau of Indian Affairs to the United States Public Health Service, and they have recently been urged to exercise the voting privilege.

The culture barrier, the language barrier and the experience barrier can best be met in the classroom if the teacher understands the feelings and attitudes of the people and knows that their anxieties are real and logical to them. One must "start where people are" in order to work out these problems with mutual patience, tolerance, and tact. When people understand the motives and purposes of the school and when teachers are able to empathize adequately with them in their difficulties to see a problem through, cultural differences and basic differences in beliefs will be respected, and the school will be more successful in reaching its goals.

In the acculturation of a minority group, there is apt to be a problem of social disorganization. This dislocation of members within the marginal culture has often resulted in increase in juvenile delinquency, increase in alcoholism, and increase in marital and family disharmony. It should be one major goal of the school to minimize social disorganization in the acculturation process. By bringing to bear their best efforts in educating children, in guiding and counseling parents, and in affording parents sources of help they need in working out their problems, social agencies can help to minimize the problem of transition.

As Indian children are transferred in greater numbers to public schools, evidence of their personal and social adjustment to the integrated school situation will be sought. Classroom teachers must rely on group testing instruments that are relatively easy to administer. An unpublished study by Legant is pertinent here.[39]

Legant administered the California Test of Personality, Elementary Level, Form AA, to fifty-three sixth-grade Navajo boys and girls enrolled in the Albuquerque public schools. These Navajo students lived in the Border Town Dormitory and were given twenty-four hour a day care by the Bureau of Indian Affairs. Legant compared the personal and social adjustment of these students with that of ninety-one fifth-grade children in a fairly homogeneous middle-class Anglo neighborhood in Albuquerque and with that of fifty-three fifth-grade children in a mixed racial-ethnic group lower-class neighborhood. She also compared the scores made by Navajo boys with those made by Navajo girls on the test.

The ninety-one middle-class children scored significantly higher at the one per cent level of confidence on all tests except those of personal worth and freedom from anti-social tendencies where no significant difference existed, and on the test for family relations where the significance was at the five per cent level of confidence. The fifty-three children in the mixed racial-ethnic lower-class group scored significantly higher at the one per cent level of confidence on tests of self-reliance, social standards, community relations, total social adjustment, and total adjustment; at the five per cent level on tests for total personal adjustment, freedom from anti-social tendencies, and family relations. The Navajo girls scored significantly higher than the Navajo boys on the tests of personal worth and personal freedom at the one per cent level of confidence and on the test for social standards at the five per cent level. This latter finding may be significant in terms of Deutsch's findings, reported in Chapter II, revealing that Negro girls had higher school achievement, greater sense of personal worth, and less social maladjustment than Negro boys.

When life in two social groups is juxtaposed, what will be the end result? Two cultures of approximately equal strength may live side by side for generations. When dominant and marginal cultures live side by side, the mainstream of life tends to assimilate the minority group. It is necessary to query here, however, whether the basic institutions of the sub-culture, which are the foundation stones on which it rests, can persist. Can the traditional economy of the Pueblo Indians, for example, stand side by side with the Anglo economy in New Mexico and Arizona? Their former agrarian economy based on well-cared-for gardens of beans, squash, chili, and corn will no longer cover their efforts to secure the artifacts of the dominant culture. Moreover, the ditches no longer always provide water for the gardens. TV's, pick-up trucks, refrigerators, and deep freezes must be paid for with dollars out of weekly pay checks. Economy is probably the key pivot on which our social structure turns.

What is to be said of health practices? We must continue to lower infant mortality rates, deaths due to enteric diseases, and to improve sanitation where water is scarce, but flies are not. Curing with penicillin and the surgeon's knife not only destroy the health practices of a preliterate society, but they make serious inroads into religious curing rites. The work of the medicine man is affected, and over a period of time, the basic institution of religion is changed. There is a very close interdependence between health and religion for these people.

What of education as an institution in the culture? The Indian people themselves have recognized the values of the Anglo's education. With time, the practices of following in the ways of the old people and remaining an anonymous member of a preliterate group will be superceded by an education that teaches scientific principles and the will to shape one's own destiny.

In summary, it is postulated here that the basic institutions of health, economy, and education must of necessity undergo drastic change. These are the ones in which teachers must be conscious of the change. The way in which the basic institutions of the family, religion, and recreation may be continued may be left to the people to decide. The basic institutions are not autonomous, but are rather interdependent in contributing to a social whole; consequently, it is logical to anticipate that with drastic changes in any one of the social institutions, there will be many changes in all of them.

FOOTNOTES

[1] Alexander H. Leighton and Dorothea C. Leighton. The Navajo Door: An Introduction to Navajo Life (Cambridge: Harvard University Press, 1944), pp. 19-20.

[2] Florence Rockwood Kluckholn, "A Method of Eliciting Value Orientations," Anthropological Linguistics, 2:4, February, 1960; and Cora A. Du Bois, "The Dominant Value Profile of American Culture," American Anthropologist, 57:1232-1239, December, 1955.

[3] Kluckhohn, Ibid., p. 4.

[4] Ibid., p. 5.

[5] Clyde Kluckhohn and Dorothea Leighton, The Navajo. (Cambridge: Harvard University Press, 1946), pp. 227-228.

[6] Ibid., p. 227.

[7] Ibid., p. 228.

[8] Carl G. Jung, Modern Man in Search of a Soul. (New York: Harcourt, Brace, and Co., 1939), p. 224.

[9] This is a stereotype that has existed in the past. All blind boys in state schools were believed to be potential piano tuners, and many piano practice rooms were made available to the enrollees in such institutions.

[10] Robert Young, Lectures to Teachers, June 13, 1958.

[11] Dorothy Lee, "The Cultural Curtain," The Annals, 323:121-128, May, 1959.

[12] Webster's New Collegiate Dictionary (Springfield, Mass.: G.C. Merriam Co., 1953), p. 881.

[13] This term was suggested by Dr. Vernon Beggs, formerly Director of Schools, United Pueblos Agency, Albuquerque, New Mexico.

[14] Bureau of Indian Affairs, Indians of New Mexico, (Washington, D. C. 20402: U. S. Government Printing Office, 1966). p. 16.

[15] Walsh McDermott, et al., "Introducing Modern Medicine in a Navajo Community," Science, 131:197-205, 280-287, January 22 and 29, 1960.

[16] Ibid., p. 201.

[17] Ibid., p. 200.

[18] John Adair, et al., "Patterns of Health and Disease Among the Navajos," The Annals of the American Academy of Political and Social Science: American Indians and American Life, 211:89, May, 1957.

[19] Ibid., p. 202.

[20] Ibid., p. 203.

[20] Ibid., p. 204.

[22] Ibid., p. 205.

[23] Ibid., p. 280.

[24] Ibid., p. 286.

[25] Ibid., p. 286.

[26] James R. Shaw, "Guarding the Health of our Indian Citizens," Hospitals, Journal of the American Hospital Association, April 16, 1957, p. 8, reprinted by the Public Health Service.

[27] Lucille J. Marsh, "Health Services for Indian Mothers and Children," Children, November-December, 1957, reprint, unpaged.

[28] Public Health Service, U.S. Department of Health, Education and Welfare, Annual Report on Indian Health, 1958, unpaged.

[29] Public Health Service, Health Services for American Indians (Washington: United States Government Printing Office, 1957).

[30] Shaw, op. cit., p. 8.

[31] Marsh, loc. cit.

[32] Oliver La Farge, Behind the Mountains (Boston: Houghton Mifflin Company, 1956), p. 159.

[33] Margaret Clark, Health in the Mexican-American Culture: A Community Study (Berkeley: University of California Press, 1959), p. 216.

[34] Ibid., pp. 216-217.

[35] Ruth D. Tuck, Not With the Fist (New York: Harcourt, Brace, and Co., 1946).

[36] Harry Estill Moore, in Dictionary of Sociology, Henry Pratt Fairchild, editor (Ames, Iowa: Littlefield, Adams and Co., 1957), p. 134.

[37] Ibid., p. 182.

[38] Aaron Antonovsky, "Toward a Refinement of the Marginal Man Concept," Social Forces, 35:57, October, 1956.

[39] Jean Legant, "A Comparison of Scores Made by Navajo Sixth Graders, a Valley School Fifth Graders, and a Heights School Fifth Graders on the California Test of Personality, Elementary Level," (Unpublished research paper submitted to the Department of Psychology, University of New Mexico, 1962).

CHAPTER 5

Bicultural Problems in Relation to School Achievement

INTRODUCTION

The problem of poor academic achievement has been continually underscored for both the Indian and the Spanish-speaking people. Chapter 5 reviews this educational retardation and the problem of over-ageness in grade, both in historical perspective and as found in current research. A brief review of intelligence testing of Indians is presented first.

Causal factors are explored in two final sections of this chapter: first, the relationship of language to culture, and second, the factors influencing the learning of a second language.

TESTING INTELLIGENCE OF INDIAN CHILDREN

Early investigations of the intelligence of Indian children were conducted using the standard "paper-and-pencil" tests. During the decade from the early 1920's to the early 1930's, many studies were reported in the literature. They generally concluded that Indians were inferior to whites, but approached white norms more closely in cases where there was white blood in Indian veins. It was felt that full-blooded Indians were unable to rise above mediocrity as measured by the culturally biased standards of the dominant group, and, further, that this inability was due not to test-related factors, but to a lower mental ability in the Indian.[1]

Some investigators who were dissatisfied with the above conclusions, soon began searching for explanations other than innate differences in mental ability in order to justify the poor showing of Indian students on group intelligence tests. Such non-racial factors as language, school experience, socio-economic factors, rapport, and motivation were suggested.[2]

The Indian Education Research Project undertaken jointly by the United States Office of Indian Affairs and the Committee on Human Development of the University of Chicago, beginning in 1941, was designed to investigate the personality development of a large number of Indian children from different tribes. This research made possible the individual mental testing of large numbers of Indian children. The tests selected for this project, after consideration was given to the cultural factors that would interfere with performance, were the Grace Arthur Point Performance Scale[3] and the Goodenough Draw-A-Man Test.[4] Thompson and Joseph reported mean I.Q. scores on the Arthur Point Performance Scale of 115 and 110.7; and scores of 110.5 and 115.1 on the Goodenough Draw-A-Man test for Hopi children.[5] MacGregor reported mean I.Q. scores of 102 and 113.6 on the Goodenough for Sioux Indians on the Pine Ridge Reservation.[6]

Leighton and Kluckhohn reported mean I.Q.'s of 102.5 for Navajos with some schooling and 79.8 for those with no schooling, using these same tests.[7] Joseph, Rosamond, and Chesky reported mean scores of 99.4 for Eastern and 86.9 for Western Papago children on the Arthur; mean score of 108.5 and 103.6 on the Goodenough.[8]

The research of the Indian Education Research Project points out that the racial factor is not pertinent; a wide range of scores are obtained and "above-average" mean scores are derived when large numbers of these children are tested.

The following statement by Havighurst best summarizes current thinking by social scientists about Indian intelligence:

> The conclusion which is drawn by most social scientists from the data on Indian cultures and Indian intelligence is that the American Indians of today have about the same innate equipment for learning as have the white children of America. But in those Indian tribes which have preserved their traditional cultures to some extent, there is a limited motivation of children for a high level performance in schools and colleges.[9]

HISTORICAL EVIDENCE OF EDUCATIONAL RETARDATION

Educational retardation may be defined as the extent to which students fail to achieve academically according to their capacity for such achievement. Children of normal intelligence are expected to move through the public school grades on an extremely homogeneous age-in-grade scale. Academic performance at grade-placement for children in the normal range of intelligence indicates achievement that is neither retarded nor accelerated. With minority groups, two problems are readily apparent. The first is that many children are over-age in grade. The second problem is that a general tendency has existed for a long time, and is still prevalent, for pupils to become more and more educationally retarded as they progress through school, with many of these students becoming hopelessly lost in high school.

In terms of having failed to make the necessary distinction between teaching English to native speakers of English and teaching English to speakers of other languages, a study by B. F. Haught[10] reported in the literature is worthy of review.

Haught compared the school achievement of Spanish-American and Anglo-American children testing the hypothesis that, in the beginning, language might be a handicap but that the longer the children stayed in school the less the differences in achievement could be attributed to language.

Haught said, in effect: "It seems reasonable to assume that a language handicap encountered in taking an intelligence test should decrease as the children become older, progress through the grades, and thus become better acquainted with the English language.

He found that the IQ scores actually dropped, and the drop was marked at age ten; the older students were handicapped as much as the younger. Therefore Haught eliminated language as the handicap, and reported the average Spanish-American child had an IQ of only 79 compared to the 100 for the average Anglo. He did add that some Spanish American children were as bright as the bright Anglos.

Haught's study was selected from several because of the specific hypothesis he chose. The naive statement that students would gain language sophistication merely by attending school and that they would develop all the necessary academic vocabulary for "keeping up" in subject matter may be excused in 1930, but it can hardly be condoned today. Yet, when administrators do not establish a curriculum that will systematically and consciously develop such a language sophistication along with an understanding of the cultural chasms that exist, the same naive hypothesis is being perpetuated.[11]

Retardation within Grades

The problem of being over-age in grade has been detailed by Tireman in his book, Teaching Spanish-Speaking Children.[12] Tireman revealed in 1936 the problem of classes of Spanish American children becoming more and more retarded in achievement. His findings are presented in Table V.

Coombs and his associates reported the same problem for Indian children. Testing children in six geographical areas, including the Albuquerque area, they reported that:

> . . . whereas the mean scores of the area groups were close to the published norms of the California Achievement Tests at grades four and five, they tended to fall progressively farther

TABLE V[13]

"L" County Rural Schools Survey

Grade	Number of Pupils	Language Group	Reading	Vocabulary	Average Reading	Norm
7	35	Spanish	5.6	5.4	5.5	7.8
6	41	Spanish	5.1	4.8	5.0	6.8
5	62	Spanish	4.9	4.6	4.7	5.8
4	70	Spanish	4.1	4.0	4.1	4.8
3	60	Spanish	3.3	2.8	3.1	3.8
2	82	Spanish	2.6	2.2	2.3	2.8
1	75	Spanish	2.1	1.9	1.9	1.8

Metropolitan Achievement Tests--Reading--April, May, 1936. Median Achievement.

below the "national" norms as the higher grades were reached. This phenomenon has characterized the scores of every area group in this study.[14]

The sampling of the Coombs report included 13,686 Indian school children.[15] Test results were analyzed for Indian children in public schools, Federal schools, and mission schools. A clear-cut general advantage was found in favor of the Indian children in public schools.[16] The writers emphasized the middle-class orientation of the curriculum of the school and the serious cultural conflicts that will probably cause Indian children to learn school subjects less well than white children.

More recently, Boyce writes:

> ... that achievement medians of Indian children, regardless of language handicap, tend to be up to norm by the end of second grade. Thereafter, more and more Indian children fall below published norms. By the end of the sixth grade, Indian achievement medians in the three R's tend to be two or more grades below published norms.[17]

Age-Grade Status

Sanchez reported in 1932 that 41 per cent of the elementary rural children in New Mexico were over-age for their grade placement.[18] The mean over-ageness was 2.2 years. Sininger's findings substantiated the report of Sanchez.[19]

Coombs reports age-grade distributions for all grades from fourth through twelfth in his report. The age-grade distribution for 293 fifth-grade Indian children in the Albuquerque area in 1951 is shown in Table VI. The mean over-ageness for the large group of these children was 2.1 years in 1951. However, too few fifth-grade children in public schools were tested in order to generalize.

TABLE VI [20]

Age-Grade Distributions, Albuquerque Area, 1951
Indian Children in Federal Schools and Public Schools in Grade 5

Age	Federal	Public
17		
16	1	
15	4	
14	16	
13	40	1
12	82	5
11	101	4
10	36	2
9	1	
Number	281	12
Median Age	12.0	12.0
Non-Indian Age Expectancy	10.5	10.5
Mean Years Overage	2.1	1.67
Median Years Overage	1.5	1.5

One of the major problems in the field of Navajo education is that of educational retardation. This educational retardation became strongly apparent with the transfer of Indian children to public schools. Public school personnel were concerned that Navajo children accepted for enrollment be "up to grade." Of 9,751 children whose records were analyzed in December, 1957, only 6 per cent were "up to grade," 40 per cent were retarded at least one year, and 54 per cent were retarded two or more years. [21]

The mean chronological ages and reading grade-placement scores for various ethnic groups in a public school fifth-grade sample, April, 1960, show the average over-ageness of Apache, Pueblo and Spanish-American children to be about one year (see Table VII). The Navajo children were over-age in grade about two and one-half years. The retardation in reading achievement, however, as measured by the Gates Reading Survey Test, [22] was one and one-half to two years, in spite of the over-age in grade status.

TABLE VII [23]

Mean Chronological Ages and Reading Grade-Placement Scores
by Ethnic Groups, April, 1960
Gates Reading Survey Test

	Age-Grade Expectancy	Rural Anglo (N=31)	Apache (N=52)	Navajo (N=40)	Pueblo (N=82)	Spanish American (N=40)
Chronological Age	11-0	11-0	12-0	13-7	12-2	12-1
Reading Grade Placement	5.8	5.7	4.2	3.7	3.9	4.0

It is apparent from data obtained in 1960 that there continues to be one full year of over-ageness for all minority ethnic groups. This is not as significant, however, as the indication that even though the sample children were over-age in grade, they were an additional one and one-half to two years retarded in achievement as measured by the Gates Reading Survey Test. Over-ageness and retardation must be combined to determine the full extent of educational retardation.

EDUCATIONAL RETARDATION AS MEASURED BY TEST DATA OF THE INDIAN RESEARCH STUDY

In the course of a research study conducted at the University of New Mexico, data were gathered measuring achievement of elementary, junior high, and senior high school students; and college success of Indian students enrolled at the University was analyzed.[24] The severity of educational retardation follows the pattern recognized by Sanchez, Tireman, and Sininger three decades previously.

The Gilmore Oral Reading Test was administered in the elementary schools; the Standard Vocabulary Test was administered to junior high school students; and the Diagnostic Reading Test, Survey Section, was administered to students in eleventh and twelfth grades in senior high school. A report of the test results follows.

The Gilmore Oral Reading Test [25]

The Gilmore Oral Reading Test was administered to 843 children in grades three through six in seven selected rural New Mexico schools. The Gilmore test is an individually administered oral reading test with comprehension questions. Twelve to fifteen minutes are required for the completion of one test. In an evaluation of this test, Harris says:

> The Gilmore Oral Reading Test is a quite satisfactory standardized oral reading test. There are two forms, each consisting of ten paragraphs ranging in difficulty from first grade to high school. Even in the very easy paragraphs the language is not babyish, and the paragraphs form a continuing story. The pupil reads from a spiral-bound heavy cardboard booklet, with one paragraph on each page. The examiner records errors, time in seconds, and answers to comprehension questions in a separate record booklet. [26]
>
> Norms are provided for accuracy, comprehension, and rate, and directions are provided in a twenty-six page manual. Although the norms at first-grade level are too severe, this test will probably remain popular for quite a while. [27]

A summary of this test administration by classes is given in Table VIII. The summary by ethnic groups is given in Table IX. The results of the Gilmore test presented in Table VIII show that total class groups are failing to achieve satisfactory class median scores.

Table IX shows that, while Anglo children achieved approximately at grade level, Spanish American children were about one year educationally retarded in fifth and sixth grades. Indian children showed one and one-half years of retardation in third grade, two years in fourth and fifth grades, and three years in sixth grade. There is little difference in the median scores for accuracy and comprehension, indicating that remedial reading must include both the mechanics of reading and the comprehension of ideas.

The New Standard Vocabulary Test [28]

The New Standard Vocabulary Test was administered to 143 seventh and eighth grade students in six pilot schools. A summary of performance of these pupils is presented in Table X. Median raw scores and percentiles are given.

These results give further evidence of the limited vocabularies in the English language by many of these students. Because of the low percentile scores for total classes, a break-down by ethnic groups is unnecessary to show the severity of educational retardation, although 15 to 20 per cent of these students were Anglos.

The Diagnostic Reading Tests -- Survey Section [29]

The Survey Section of the Diagnostic Reading Test was administered by Townsend to 558 eleventh and twelfth graders in four selected high schools in New Mexico where large numbers of Indian and Spanish American students are enrolled. [30] The results, pre-

TABLE VIII

Grade Placement Scores and Ratings by Schools
Gilmore Oral Reading Test, Form A

Spring, 1959

School	Grade*	Number of Students	ACCURACY Grade Equiv.	ACCURACY Rating	COMPREHENSION Grade Equiv.	COMPREHENSION Rating	RATE WPM	RATE Rating
A	3	39	2.1	Below Average	2.8	Average	72	Slow
A	4	27	3.3	Average	4.5	Average	84	Average
A	5	28	3.5	Below Average	4.3	Average	96	Slow
A	6	30	5.2	Below Average	5.6	Below Average	108	Slow
B	3	28	3.3	Average	4.0	Average	105	Average
B	4	24	3.4	Average	4.5	Average	108	Average
B	5	9	4.9	Average	6.8	Above Average	132	Average
C	3	29	2.8	Below Average	3.6	Average	81	Average
C	4	25	3.6	Below Average	3.9	Average	102	Average
C	5	27	3.4	Inferior	4.1	Below Average	108	Slow
C	6	25	4.7	Below Average	5.3	Below Average	120	Slow
D	3	28	2.8	Below Average	3.1	Average	78	Average
D	4	34	3.1	Below Average	3.2	Below Average	90	Slow
D	5	16	3.5	Inferior	4.5	Below Average	102	Slow
E	3	82	2.2	Below Average	1.9	Below Average	84	Average
E	4	73	2.8	Inferior	2.2	Inferior	96	Slow
E	5	73	3.6	Inferior	2.6	Inferior	108	Slow
E	6	55	3.4	Inferior	2.6	Inferior	108	Slow
F	3	12	2.9	Average	4.0	Average	78	Average
F	4	18	3.9	Below Average	4.5	Average	111	Average
F	5	20	3.4	Inferior	4.4	Below Average	99	Slow
F	6	11	5.4	Below Average	5.3	Below Average	120	Slow
G	3	32	1.6	Below Average	1.9	Below Average	54	Slow
G	4	30	2.8	Inferior	3.0	Below Average	90	Slow
G	5	29	4.4	Below Average	3.9	Below Average	90	Slow
G	6	28	4.0	Below Average	4.5	Below Average	90	Slow

*Since this test was administered in February, March, and April, the accurate grade placement in each class would be 3.6, 3.7, 3.8; 4.6, 4.7, 4.8; 5.6, 5.7, 5.8; or 6.6, 6.7, 6.8.

TABLE IX

Summary by Ethnic Groups
Gilmore Oral Reading Test, Form A

Spring, 1959

Ethnic Group	Grade	Number Tested	National Median	Testing Program Median Scores Accuracy	Comprehension
Anglo	3	34	3.5	3.2	3.7
	4	44	4.5	4.0	5.1
	5	24	5.5	5.4	5.7
	6	28	6.5	5.6	6.3
Spanish American	3	40	3.5	3.1	3.5
	4	32	4.5	3.5	4.1
	5	24	5.5	3.8	4.5
	6	28	6.5	5.4	5.7
Indian	3	181	3.5	2.3	1.9
	4	164	4.5	2.8	2.6
	5	127	5.5	3.6	3.2
	6	117	6.5	3.8	3.3

sented in Tables XI and XII, afford incontestable evidence that there are serious problems of educational retardation presisting in these schools which are not being satisfactorily researched or corrected.

In reading Table XI, one can see that 72 students, or 22 per cent of the junior classes, are below the 10th percentile, and in Table XII, it can be seen that 71 students, or 30 per cent of the senior classes, are achieving below the 10th percentile.

In schools H and K, more than half of the juniors achieved below the 10th percentile. In school H, 66 per cent of the senior class achieved below the 10th percentile. It is the opinion of the writer that many of these students are non-readers of English as far as making intelligent use of printed material is concerned; yet they were graduated from the secondary school!

One must point out that while the total performance in classes in school J is above the national average in Table XI and almost equal to it in Table XII, the majority of students there are Anglo American. When Indian and Spanish American students were isolated, they were found to be the poorest performers in the classes. 31

Once the analysis is made, two remedial measures are obvious. The minority group students need systematic, organized instruction in learning to speak, understand, read, and write Eng-

TABLE X

Median Raw Scores and Percentile Ranks
New Standard Vocabulary Test, Form A

November, 1958

SEVENTH GRADE

School	Number of Students	Median Raw Score	Median Percentile Rank
B	29	33	17
C	28	30.5	13
D	11	42	34
E	48	27	9
F	15	39	27
G	21	36	20

EIGHTH GRADE

B	30	36	11
D	17	38	13
E	12	31	6
F	6	38	13
G	13	45	20

TABLE XI

Percentile Ratings of 326 Eleventh-grade Students in
Multi-cultural Classrooms
Diagnostic Reading Test, Survey Section, Spring, 1960

Percentile	School H N=65	School I N=37	School J N=160	School K N=64	Total N=326
90-99	2	0	3	1	6
80-89	0	0	15	4	19
70-79	2	1	36	2	41
60-69	2	6	35	0	43
50-59	5	5	19	2	31
40-49	2	5	26	6	39
30-39	2	10	15	6	33
20-29	3	8	11	5	27
10-19	8	2	0	5	15
0-9	39	0	0	33	72

TABLE XII

Percentile Ratings of 232 Twelfth-grade Students in
Multi-cultural Classrooms
Diagnostic Reading Test, Survey Section, Spring, 1960

Percentile	School H N=47	School I N=29	School J N=99	School K N=57	Total N=232
90-99	0	0	5	0	5
80-89	0	3	10	3	16
70-79	0	4	12	1	17
60-69	0	1	12	2	15
50-59	0	10	5	5	20
40-49	0	4	9	3	16
30-39	1	4	6	3	14
20-29	4	3	14	9	30
10-19	11	0	9	8	28
0-9	31	0	17	23	71

lish as a second language, and then they need remedial instruction in all functional reading skills throughout all their formal course work.

Navajo Area Study: 1964-1965

In a Navajo Area Study in 1964-65, Navajo second grade children were found to have a mean reading score of 2.5 as compared to a national norm of 2.8; Navajo 8th grade students had a mean reading score of 5.8 as compared to a national norm of

8. 8. Not only are the Navajo achievement means behind that of the comparable National means, but the Navajo grade-populations are consistently and markedly older than the comparable Anglo grade-populations. The mean age of the second grades on the Navajo were 9.0 as compared to a National mean age of 7.8; that of the eighth grades on the Navajo was 15.6 as compared to the National mean of 13.8 years.[32]

Brophy and Aberle also report devastating statistics on both attrition and educational retardation.[33]

English Is Their Second Language

This section makes clear that both public and bureau schools have failed to help children from the minority ethnic groups overcome the educational retardation that has existed for decades. Without thorough understanding of the sound system of the English language, acquiring the English language concepts of the textbooks, and developing an expanding vocabulary as long as the student progresses through the school grades, academic achievement is impossible. A complete dedication to the task of teaching English as a second language, with the understanding that a person does not learn his second language in the same way that he learned his first one, is expounded in Chapter Nine.

Success of Indian Students Matriculating at the University of New Mexico

Practically all adolescent and young adult Indians in New Mexico are seriously handicapped in academic pursuits today because of the culture barrier which they must face in transition from their reservation life to campus life in the dominant culture. The value system which gives directions to living and determines life goals for Indians has not established the kinds of motivations, aspirations, and thought patterns necessary for success in college.

This cultural barrier underlies two much more obvious problems. These are the language barrier and educational retardation. Few Indians are competent in the use of English. Some are urged strongly (perhaps coercively) in the home to know the mother tongue well so that they can talk with the old people. Educational retardation to a severe degree is a natural result. Statistics which will substantiate the problem further are given:

1. The records of 100 Southwest Indians enrolled at the University of New Mexico between 1954 and 1958 were studied. The students in 1954 were of both freshman and upper-class status. The records of these 100 students showed that 70 per cent dropped school with low grades; 20 per cent were currently enrolled; and 10 per cent obtained de-

grees. Significantly, of the 30 per cent who remained in school or obtained degrees, the majority were at some time placed on probation for inadequate scholarship.

2. The records of thirty-one New Mexico Indians enrolled in the University of New Mexico during the fall of 1958 showed the following disposition with respect to grades earned at the end of the first semester: six left school before the end of the first semester; twelve were placed on probation by the University College (grade-point average below 0.6); eight earned grade-point averages between 0.6 and 1.0, acceptable in the University College only; and five earned grade-point averages of 1.0 or better (C = 1 grade point), which is acceptable in the degree-granting colleges. Thus, <u>84 per cent did not finish the first semester with a "C" average.</u>

The attrition rates given above for Indians can be compared with the overall attrition rate of 49 per cent for college freshmen at the University of New Mexico. This 49 per cent includes all those who leave the University or fail to re-register the second semester for any reason.

Public school personnel further attest that there are Indian (and Spanish American) students graduating from high school each spring who have sufficient learning ability to profit from higher education, and yet who do not continue their education. They are handicapped in the language arts skills, so that their level of use of the English language, their ability to think in the English language, and their assimilation of the developmental reading skills are inadequate for college success. This problem is discussed further in the chapter on counseling the Indian Student.

Summary

The results of the testing program reinforce the previous findings that as minority ethnic group children progress through the school grades, their achievement falls farther and farther behind. Not only are these students from one to two years over-age for their grades, on the average, but they are also educationally retarded an additional one to two years in achievement on standardized tests. In two of four selected high schools, half of the eleventh and twelfth grade students were in the bottom decile when compared to national norms on a survey reading test.

The testing program showed that groups of Anglo children scored from approximate grade placement to one-half year of retardation in achievement. Spanish American students were, on the average, one year educationally retarded in fifth and sixth grade, but they were an additional year over-age in grade. Indian children tended to be two to three years retarded in reading ability in sixth grade and were one to two years over-age in grade.

Since social scientists have adequately established the fact that intelligence fits a normal distribution in all ethnic groups and is comparable from group to group, differences in intelligence cannot explain the failure of the schools to teach minority group children. With large numbers of unselected children in the test samples, a normal range of intelligence is expected. The logical assumption follows that only about 20 per cent of Indian children or Spanish American children have intelligence levels below the normal range (I.Q. of 90-110), and that only approximately 3 per cent may be designated as mentally retarded (I.Q. of 70 or below). As in the Anglo population, most children have adequate intelligence to perform at grade level.

Any solution to the problem necessitates, on the part of the teacher: (1) an understanding of the significance of the cultural differences; (2) proficiency in the teaching of English as a second language; and (3) ability to use remedial teaching methods appropriate to the level of functioning of the groups taught.

RELATIONSHIP OF LANGUAGE TO CULTURE

Bilingualism

Bilingualism is defined differently by different people. Tireman wrote that the word bilingualism has a "range in meaning from equal facility in two or more languages to the very simple use of a few phrases in another tongue for asking directions or ordering a meal."[34] Malherbe defined bilingualism as varying degrees of understanding of two languages, and he wrote that bilingualism should not be considered synonymous with equilingualism.[35] He delineates six stages or steps that correspond to the social or professional demands in using a second language.[36]

Stage I: Able to follow intelligently an ordinary conversation, speech or sermon in the second language, both in its written and spoken forms.

Stage II: Able to converse intelligibly and with a fair amount of fluency in the second language.

Stage III: Able to write the second language correctly.

Stage IV: Able to function as a bilingual teacher. Correct, convincing, and fluent in both writing and speaking; and both accent and idiom must be appropriate for children to imitate.

Stage V: Able to use and is a student of both languages. Is more competent than 90 per cent of those who use either language as their mother tongue.

Stage IV: Theoretically able to approach 100 per cent proficiency in both languages.

People are bilingual in varying degrees. A tourist in a foreign country may be able to say "good morning" in two or three languages, but his guide will deliver complete lectures in several languages.

The problem of language in New Mexico has not been the same problem which is faced in other parts of the United States where many different foreign groups have migrated, diffused into the American "melting pot," and in two generations or so, become users of the common language. The Indian and the Spanish American settled in the Southwest centuries before the Anglo came. Both Oraibi and Acoma are cited by sociologists as being the oldest continuously inhabited villages in the United States and are believed to be 900 to 1000 years old. Civilization that persists for so long a time develops a cultural heritage in which there is pride and allegiance. It is no wonder that these people have resisted absorption into the Anglo culture.

The Word "Father" in Two Cultures

The way in which the language of the child is deeply rooted in his cultural heritage is easily illustrated with the word father. The word father is generally recognized in all societies and would be considered a directly translatable word. However, consider the meaning of the word father in the Zuni language and in Anglo American English. To the Zuni child, the word father will suggest the father in a consanguinal, matrilineal, extended family; to the Anglo child, the same word suggests the father in a conjugal, patrilineal, nuclear family. In a consanguinal relationship, the basic ties are those of "blood"; while in a conjugal relationship, the basic tie is the love relationship. The Zuni child's father may not discipline the child at all since this is the duty of the mother's brother. The mother's brother is the person to whom the mother looks for any discussion of economic problems in the family or in the business of running the household. The father only "enjoys" his children and "owns" nothing in the family estate except his ceremonial garb. It has been said that, traditionally, all the Zuni mother needed to do to divorce her husband was to put his few possessions outside the door while he was away and he would know that he need not re-enter the house on his return; he should merely take his possessions and return to his mother's house.

The Anglo child's outlook would be in some measure conditioned by the admonition in the New Testament on marriage: "For this cause shall a man leave his father and mother, and shall cleave to his wife; and the twain shall be one flesh." (Matthew 19:5)

The extended family of the Zuni child includes many adults in his everyday living -- all the aunts and uncles of the maternal family and the grandparents -- so that not only does the father figure play such an insignificant part in the parental tie of the Indian

145

child, but also all the ramifications of inheritance, discipline, and the goals of life that will prescribe his level of aspiration will likely be learned from his maternal uncles. Further, the teaching of respect for his elders in the total family places a different "duty" on the growing child to do the bidding of his elders in the extended family without question.

This cultural difference in the way children look on the father as a disciplinarian in the family was clearly illustrated by a Pueblo Indian college student who recorded this anecdote:

> It would sure help if the teacher knew who was directly responsible at home for the boy's behavior. I have heard the teacher say to a student, "If you don't do so-and-so, I'll tell your father." The Indian boy thought this was a big joke because he knew his real father would never lay a hand on him.

Kaulfers writes of the relation of culture to language:

> How translation can defeat its own ends if words are merely transverbalized without regard for their pleasant or unpleasant associations is illustrated by the difficulties missionaries have sometimes had in trying to convert remote populations to Christianity. Most Eskimos, for example, eat no bread. Few like it, because to them it has no taste or smell. Consequently, early missionaries found it difficult to explain the phrase "Give us this day our daily bread." To win the natives, they had to substitute walrus, polar bear, and deer. This illustration is but one of many that could be cited to show how an expert command of a second language always requires a thorough understanding of the attitudes, likes, dislikes, customs, and standards of values of the people.[37]

The interdependence of language and culture has been a subject of considerable concern. Culture is the accumulated experience of a social group through time. The only way accumulated experience can be re-created or interpreted is through language. Without language there would be no way of reviewing past experiences and communicating them to others.

It is believed by many that, since thought itself requires some kind of symbolization, thinking is, in a sense, a way of talking things over with oneself.

The cumulative aspect of culture, which clearly and completely differentiates man from lower animals, is made possible by language. This is expressed succinctly by Strickland:

> Communication through spoken and written language belongs to man and to him alone. It is the most important influence in his upward climb through the centuries. This ability to com-

municate has permitted each generation to rise on the shoulders of the thinkers and achievers who have gone before, to profit from their gains, to avoid their mistakes, and to pursue their dreams and aspirations and make some of them realities.[38]

Language is an integral part of a people's culture. It is the means by which the attitudes and feelings of the group are made known. Anthropologists and linguists have stated this interdependence of culture and language. The selected quotations which follow show how the relationship of language to culture has been viewed by linguists through the past fifty years.

Boas states that:

. . . linguistic inquiry is part and parcel of a thorough investigation of the psychology of the peoples of the world.[39]

Sapir's feeling is that:

. . . language powerfully conditions all our thinking about social problems and processes. Human beings . . . are very much at the mercy of the particular language which has become the medium of expression for their society.[40]

According to Whorf:

. . . the linguistic system (in other words, the grammar) of each language is not merely a reproducing instrument for voicing ideas but rather is itself the shaper of ideas, the program and guide for the individual's mental activity, for his analysis of impressions, for his synthesis of his mental stock in trade.[41]

Greenberg writes:

Since natural language is not devised by philosophers but develops as a living instrument of a community in its adjustment to a variety of changing needs, one would not expect and, in my experience, at least, one does not find any underlying semantic patterns such as would be required for the semantic system of a language to reflect some over-all world view of a metaphysical nature.[42]

According to Goldschmidt:

Language is a crucial attribute of culture because:
(1) It is a notative system by which the world and its affairs are organized for the speaker.

(2) It carries vicarious experiences so that the hearer and speaker "experience" to some extent that to which the verbalization refers.

(3) Persons first perceive many of their experiences through the medium of language.

Thus the world, as it comes to be perceived by each individual is in large part filtered through the medium of his mother tongue. [43]

Languages are socially determined. Their uses, form and content mirror physical setting, historical events, contacts, cultural level, mental climate, and cultural history. The language of a group is an index of most of its characteristics. Conversely, cultural and social structures are affected by the language system. Inadequate command of language retards cultural development and acquisition. The language system and socio-cultural context of a society cannot be separated -- each is both the cause and effect of the other. [44]

An individual builds his repertoire of thought and action based on the cultural behavior of which he is a part. New ideas must be interpreted in the minds that are to assimilate them. The means by which this is accomplished is language, but language is strictly relative to the culture of its users, intermeshing to the point that one can be understood fully only in the light of the other. [45]

It is of concern to teachers that the transmission of the cultural heritage is made through language.

> The complete vocabulary of a language may indeed be looked upon as a complex inventory of all the ideas, interests and occupations that take up the attention of a community, and were such a complete thesaurus of the language of a given tribe at our disposal, we might to a large extent infer the character of the physical environment and the characteristics of the culture of the people making use of it. [46]

Saunders refers to aspects of language differences in his report of Spanish-speaking people and the acceptance of modern medical care. He reminds us that what a person sees, what meaning it has for him, and how it is related to other phenomena are determined by the concepts he has, and these, in turn, are learned from the social group into which he is born and in which he lives. Concepts are represented by verbal symbols, but the verbal symbols are conditioned by the culture. In English, the clock runs; in Spanish, it walks. In English, one says he missed the bus; in Spanish, he says the bus left him. If dishes break by falling away from people, and if objects lose themselves, the way language says something may be revealing the way people in a culture view such a value as responsibility. [47]

Special problems arise in an effort to develop a new set of language patterns against a background of somewhat conflicting native language habits.

One of the chief difficulties is that a child has learned not only to attend to certain stimuli but also to ignore all those features which do not have a function in his own language. These blind spots may be exactly those features which do have signalling value in the second language. [48]

In terms of minority ethnic groups in the Southwest, languages which are most like English will be those most easily learned. Certain common elements in the language already known and the one to be learned will make the new learning easier. In this regard, Spanish has more in common with English than do the many Indian tongues.

It becomes apparent, in this context, why the old Pueblo Indian will insist that his children or grandchildren must know the mother tongue well since this is the very instrument by which his culture will be continued.

FACTORS INFLUENCING THE LEARNING OF ENGLISH AS A SECOND LANGUAGE

The cultural difference, the relationship of language to culture, and the serious degree of educational retardation have been discussed as they relate to the education of Indian and Spanish American children in New Mexico. If these children are to succeed academically in the public schools, they must develop a greater mastery of English for communication than they have done in the past. Probably the greatest need in New Mexico's schools is that all these minority groups become more articulate in English. Many different factors influence the child's learning of English as a second language. Some of these are: desire, amount of exposure, socio-economic status, influence of leaders, schools, educational adjuncts, and elements common to the two languages under consideration. [49]

Desire

Of first importance is the desire with which the learner approaches the learning. This is dependent upon the individual's receptivity to change or his ability to adopt new thinking patterns. He will succeed in some degree, too, as socio-economic pressures reward him for doing so. Immediate reinforcement offers the greatest incentive for the individual to want to learn the new language. This is illustrated by the many families who have been brought to small communities by church groups from displaced persons' camps in Europe. These families often acquire the English language very readily because they are immediately

Magellan was the first man to drive his "sheeps" all the way around the world.

   The difficulty which the elementary school child may have in understanding all the concepts presented by the teacher is illustrated by the child who, having difficulty with the long sound of "e" and the short sound of "i" in words, wrote for his teacher: "Magellan was the first man to drive his sheeps all the way around the world."*

General Washington takes command of the United States Army.

   A high school teacher of American history was lecturing to his class about the Revolutionary War. He explained that General George Washington became commander-in-chief of the United States Army. A student in the back of the room was observed drawing his idea of buffalo dancer, in all his regalia, as being his interpretation of the leadership choice as commander-in-chief.*

---

*Reported by Dr. Clara Gonzales, Reservation Principal, Zuni Indian Agency, 1960.

rewarded by satisfaction of all their life needs in the new language. This desire is more aptly illustrated negatively in New Mexico. When the people resisted the dominant Anglo culture, they also resisted the mastery of English. This desire is also negatively illustrated in Hawaii where a complex mixture of many languages allowed a kind of prostitution of the dominant languages into pidgin.

Amount of Exposure

Another factor is the amount of exposure to the second language. In some communities the language of the store, the church, and the plaza is the mother tongue. The people hear and use the second language infrequently and, consequently, the rate of acquiring it is slow. This situation still predominates among all minority ethnic groups in New Mexico.

Socio-Economic Status

Studies of emigrant groups in this country show that a foreign-speaking person rises in the economic scale as his ability to speak English increases. One may not be a direct cause of the other; they may happen concomitantly. In some types of employment, increased language facility extends job opportunities and financial rewards. When a man earns more money and eats and dresses better, he will tend to keep his children in school longer, and their mastery of English will be extended.

Influence of Leaders

This factor is well illustrated by the action of the Education Committee of the Navajo Tribal Council. In establishing a large scholarship fund, the Council has demonstrated to all the members of the tribe that the leaders place great value on education. Such positive action should influence many persons on the reservation who have little understanding of, or concern for, education. It follows that to acquire formal education, one must learn English well.

School

English is the language of the school. For this portion of the day, all the child's work will be done in English. And until recently, the school was often the child's only exposure to the English language. Whatever facility the child had with the language was acquired in the classroom. There are many homes where this condition still exists. From the time children leave school in the afternoon until they return the next day, they hear, converse in, and think only their mother tongue, albeit Spanish, Keresan, Navajo, or Zuni.

Educational Adjuncts

Closely allied to organized education are the numerous influential educational adjuncts, such as radio, television, newspapers, and books. These aids facilitate the learning of a second language.

At this point it can only be postulated that the presence of television in the Indian pueblos in New Mexico will give much impetus to fluency in speaking English as the young Indian children watch Mickey Mouse and Zorro. One small pueblo, in which practically all the citizens are handicapped in their use of English, was reported in 1958 to have nine television sets among a total population of forty-eight families.

Common Elements

The learning of a second language is affected by the presence or lack of certain common elements in the language already known and in the one to be learned. Among these factors are the phonology and structure of the language, sentence patterning, and problems in vocabulary development. It is easier for a native Spanish-speaking person to learn English than to learn Chinese. The letters on the printed page are alike in both language, and many of the words in both languages are derived from Latin. In Chinese, the printed characters are entirely different, and one reads vertically, instead of horizontally, and from right to left instead of left to right.

DIFFICULTIES IN TRANSLATION

When we become aware of the subtleties involved in word meanings, the difficulties of making English intelligible to those with widely different cultural backgrounds seem almost insurmountable. The only way we have to describe the connotations of words is by the use of other words. Inevitably, the meanings of meanings will, at times, compound our confusion. Kluckhohn poignantly illustrates this point.

> I asked a Japanese with a fair knowledge of English to translate back from the Japanese that phrase in the new Japanese constitution that represents our "life, liberty, and the pursuit of happiness." He rendered, "License to commit lustful pleasure."[50]

Pei writes that:

Translating and interpreting require a perfect command of two languages, and most of us do not command even one. Dictionaries are of limited help, because most words in one language have a dozen possible translations in another, which means that to use a dictionary properly, you must first have command of the two languages, in which case you are not too likely to need the dictionary.[51]

Pei further points out:[52]

1. There are many "untranslatable" words.

2. Technical, commercial, or literary translations require that the translator have a special knowledge of the unique area of knowledge being translated. For example, when the Coca-Cola concern hired a staff of linguists to translate "Have a Coke" into fifty foreign languages, all they got was a series of national forms of greeting; the literal rendering of "Have a Coke" would simply have made no sense.

3. Slang and colloquialisms lose their racy flavor by translating them into either correct terms or equivalent colloquialisms in the foreign tongue. When George Gershwin's "Ain't Misbehavin' " was beamed to Russia, it was very unimaginatively rendered by "I don't do anything bad" -- proper and correct, but hardly flavorful.

4. Proper word combinations in translations must be appreciated.

   In English you "take an examination," but in Italian, you "give" it; in French, you "undergo" it; and in Spanish, you "suffer" it.

5. Idiomatic expressions, being idiomatic, are untranslatable.

   The Russian "How much to you of summers?" or the Spanish "How many years have you?" impress us as peculiar renderings of "How old are you?" On the other hand, "The child is two years old" sounds quite funny to Romance or Slavic speakers; how can a child of two be old?

6. Cognates, words that sound or look alike, may likewise be pitfalls.

   Gift in English is also a German word, but means poison. Burro is donkey in Spanish, but butter in Italian. Sale in English is also an Italian word that means salt.

7. Translating from one language to another may even require the creation of new words to cover meanings.

   The Chinese had to coin over one thousand new words at the San Francisco conference alone.

   The UN finally had to establish a program of linguistic research to devise dictionaries of exactly equivalent words and phrases in its five official languages.

8. The time for competent translating is extremely long as measured in man-hours of work.

It takes on the average, three translators eighteen man-hours to get an English speech into Russian, and one translator thirty man-hours to put it into Chinese.

The advantage of a single world language to be used and understood in the conduct of world affairs is readily apparent.

SUMMARY

The seriousness of the problem of educational retardation has been discussed in some detail. The inter-dependence of language and culture and the many factors influencing learning English as a second language have also been presented. While the problem of poor achievement has persisted through the years, the schools have not, as yet, either adapted the curriculum to the immediate, environmental needs of the students or taught English as a second, instead of a first, language.

FOOTNOTES

[1] J. A. Fitzgerald and W. W. Ludeman, "The Intelligence of Indian Children," Journal of Comparative Psychology, 6: 319-328, June, 1926; Thomas R. Garth, "The Intelligence of Mixed Blood Indians," Journal of Applied Psychology, 11: 268-275, 1927; Thomas R. Garth and James E. Garrett, "A Comparative Study of the Intelligence of Indians in U. S. Indian Schools and in the Public or Common Schools," School and Society, 27: 178-184, February 11, 1928; Thomas R. Garth, Hale W. Smith, and Wendell Abell, "A Study of the Intelligence and Achievement of Full-Blood Indians," Journal of Applied Psychology, 12: 511-516, 1928; B. F. Haught, "Mental Growth of the Southwestern Indian," Journal of Applied Psychology, 18: 137-142, 1934; W. S. Hunter and E. Sommermier, "The Relations of Degree of Indian Blood to Scores on the Otis Intelligence Test," Journal of Comparative Psychology, 2: 257-275, October, 1922; Elmer Jamison and Peter Sandiford, "The Mental Capacity of Southern Ontario Indians," Journal of Educational Psychology, 19: 313-328, May, 1928, Franklin C. Paschal and Louis R. Sullivan, "Racial Influences in the Mental and Physical Development of Mexican Children, "Comparative Psychology Monographs, 3: 1-76, October, 1925; Edward B. Reuter, Race Mixture (New York: McGraw-Hill Book Company, 1931).

[2] Ada Hart Arlitt, "On the Need for Caution in Establishing Race Norms," Journal of Applied Psychology, 5: 188-195, April, 1921; Forrest Clements, "Notes on the Construction of Mental Tests for American Indians," Journal of Social Psychology, 1: 542-548, November, 1930; Phillip A. Cowen, "Testing Indian School Pupils in the State of New York," Mental Hygiene, 27: 80-82, January, 1943; Thomas R. Garth, "The Intelligence and Achievement of Mixed-Blood Indians, Journal of Social Psychology, 4: 134-137,

February, 1933; Thomas R. Garth and Owen D. Smith, "The Performance of Full-Blood Indians on Language and Non-Language Intelligence Tests," Journal of Abnormal and Social Psychology, 32: 376-381, October, 1937; Otto Klineberg, "An Experimental Study of Speed and Other Factors in 'Racial' Differences," Archives of Psychology, 92: 109, November, 1930; C. W. Telford, "Test Performance of Full and Mixed-Blood North Dakota Indians," Journal of Comparative Psychology, 14: 123-145, August, 1932.

[3] Arthur Point Scale of Performance Tests (Chicago: C. H. Stoelting Co., 424 North Homan Ave.)

[4] Florence L. Goodenough, Draw-A-Man Test, Measurement of Intelligence by Drawing (New York: World Book Co., 1926).

[5] Laura Thompson and Alice Joseph, The Hopi Way (Chicago: The University of Chicago Press, 1944), pp. 1-101.

[6] Gordon MacGregor, Warriors Without Weapons: A Study of the Society and Personality Development of the Pine Ridge Sioux (Chicago: The University of Chicago Press, 1945), pp. 1-87.

[7] Dorothea C. Leighton and Clyde Kluckhohn, Children of the People (Cambridge: Harvard University Press, 1947), pp. 1-152.

[8] Alice Joseph, B. Rosamond, and Jane Chesky, The Desert People: A Study of the Papago Indians (Chicago: University of Chicago Press, 1949) pp. 1-281.

[9] Robert J. Havighurst, "Education Among American Indians: Individual and Cultural Aspects," Annals of the American Academy of Political and Social Science, 311: 113, May, 1957.

[10] Haught, B. F., "The Language Difficulty of Spanish-American Children," The Journal of Applied Psychology, 15:92-95, February, 1931.

[11] Zintz, Miles V., "Reading Success of High School Students Who are Speakers of Other Languages," Reading and Inquiry, J. Allen Figurel, Editor, Proceedings of the Tenth Annual Convention, International Reading Association, Newark, Delaware, 1965, pp. 277-278.

[12] Loyd S. Tireman, Teaching Spanish-Speaking Children (Albuquerque: University of New Mexico Press, 1948), pp. 45-50.

[13] Ibid., p. 52.

[14] L. Madison Coombs, et al., The Indian Child Goes to School (Washington: U. S. Department of the Interior, Bureau of Indian Affairs, 1958), p. 3.

[15] Ibid., p. 18.

[16] Ibid., p. 4.

[17] George Boyce, "Why Do Indians Quit School?" Indian Education, No. 344, May 1, 1960, p. 5.

[18] George I. Sanchez, The Age-Grade Status of the Rural Child in New Mexico Public Elementary Schools, 1931-1932, Educational Research Bulletin, Vol. I (Santa Fe: Department of Education, State of New Mexico, November, 1932).

[19] Harlan Sininger, "An Age-Grade Study of the San Jose Training School and Its Two Control Schools," San Jose Training School, University of New Mexico Bulletin, School Series, Vol. 1, No. 2 (Albuquerque: University of New Mexico Press, 1931), pp. 3-10.

[20] Coombs, op. cit., p. 109.

[21] Robert Young, The Navajo Yearbook, 1958 (Window Rock, Arizona: Navajo Agency, 1958), p. 8.

[22] Arthur I. Gates, Gates Reading Survey, Form 3 (New York: Teachers College, Columbia University, 1958).

[23] Carol Charles, "The Indian Child's Status in New Mexico's Public Elementary School Science Programs" (unpublished Doctoral dissertation, The University of New Mexico, Albuquerque, 1961).

[24] "Adjustment of Indian and Non-Indian Children in Public Elementary Schools in New Mexico," Miles V. Zintz, Director. Sponsored under grant-in-aid from the U.S. Office of Education, at the University of New Mexico, College of Education, 1957-1960.

[25] John V. Gilmore, Gilmore Oral Reading Test, Form A (Yonkers-on Hudson: World Book Company, 1952).

[26] Albert J. Harris, How To Increase Reading Ability (New York: Longmans Green And Co., 1956), p. 198.

[27] Ibid., p. 201.

[28] Miriam M. Bryan and Janet G. Afflerbach, New Standard Vocabulary Test, Form A, prepared under direction of Herbert A. Landry (New York: Educational Measurement Service, 1955).

[29] Frances O. Triggs, Chairman, Diagnostic Reading Tests, Survey Section (New York: The Committee on Diagnostic Reading Tests, Inc., 1952).

[30] Irving D. Townsend, "The Reading Achievement of Eleventh and Twelfth Grade Indian Students and A Survey of Curricular Changes Indicated for the Improved Teaching of Reading in the Public High Schools of New Mexico," (Unpublished Doctoral dissertation, the University of New Mexico, Albuquerque, 1961).

[31] Ibid., pp. 100-108.

[32] "Navajo Area Study of Stanford Achievement Tests Scores 1964-65," William J. Benham, Director, Branch of Education, Navajo Area, Window Rock, Arizona, 1965.

[33] Brophy, William A. and Sophie D. Aberle, The Indian, America's Unfinished Business, (Norman: University of Oklahoma Press, 1966), pp. 139-141.

[34] Tireman, op. cit., p. 8.

[35] E. G. Malherbe, The Bilingual School (New York: Longmans, Green and Co., 1946), pp. 17-29.

[36] Ibid., pp. 19-26.

[37] Walter V. Kaulfers, "Gift of Tongues or Tower of Babel?" The Educational Forum, November, 1954, p. 82.

[38] Ruth Strickland, The Language Arts in the Elementary School (Boston: D. C. Health and Company, 1951), p. 3.

[39] Harry Hoijer (editor), Language in Culture, Vol. 56, No. 6, Part 2, Memoir No. 79 (Chicago: University of Chicago Press, The American Anthropological Association, December, 1954), p. 92, citing Franz Boas, "Introduction," Handbook of American Indian Languages Part I (Washington, D. C.: 1911), p. 93.

[40] Ibid., p. 92, citing Edward Sapir, "Conceptual Categories in Primitive Languages," Science, 74: 578, 1931.

[41] Ibid., p. 94, citing Benjamin J. Whorf, Collected Papers on Metalinguistics (Washington: Department of State, Foreign Service Institute, 1952), p. 5.

[42] Ibid., pp. 3-19, citing Joseph H. Greenberg, "Concerning Inferences from Linguistic to Nonlinguistic Data."

[43] Walter Goldschmidt, "Language and Culture: A Reply," Quarterly Journal of Speech, 41: 279-283, October, 1955.

[44] J. O. Hertzler, "Toward a Sociology of Language," Social Forces, 32: 109-119, December, 1953.

[45] Douglas G. Haring, "Cultural Context of Thought and Communication," Quarterly Journal of Speech, 37: 161-172, April, 1951.

[46] Edward Sapir, "Language and Environment," American Anthropologist, 14: 242, April, 1912.

[47] Lyle Saunders, Cultural Differences and Medical Care: The Case of the Spanish-Speaking People of the Southwest (New York: Russell Sage Foundation, 1934), pp. 113-122.

[48] Robert Lado, Linguistics Across Cultures (Ann Arbor: University of Michigan Press, 1958), p. v., citing Charles C. Fries.

[49] Loyd S. Tireman and Miles V. Zintz, "Factors Influencing the Learning of a Second Language," Education, 81: 310-313, January, 1961.

[50] Clyde Kluckhohn, Mirror for Man (New York: McGraw-Hill Book Co., Inc., 1949), p. 154.

[51] Mario Pei, The Story of Language (New York: The New American Library, 1960), p. 369.

[52] Ibid., pp. 370-371.

Part Two

The previous chapters have provided abundant evidence that the children from minority ethnic groups in the Southwest are educationally retarded in school. This evidence has also asserted that the problems do not stem from lack of general learning ability or low intelligence.

It has been suggested that the personal values of teachers are apt to be inflexible American middle-class values which are not compatible with the traditional values of the Indian or Spanish-speaking child in the classroom. The teacher's allegiance to what the sociologist has termed the Protestant ethic may cause him to fail to show respect for the child with his heritage of fears, superstitions, and taboos, his ideas, rights and aspirations.

It has been suggested, further, that the teacher might profitably understand the psychological, sociological, and anthropological roles of individuals in the social group in which they interact. Principles of child growth and development apply to all children, but the way in which teachers respond to overt behavior in children may be dependent upon an understanding of the child's motives in this behavior. These motives are culturally learned.

Before considering, then, ways of overcoming educational retardation in classrooms through efficient teaching of English as a second language and by methods of remedial teaching, a further look at the cultural backgrounds of specific children is necessary. For this purpose, the three groups selected are (1) the Navajo Indian; (2) the Pueblo Indian; and (3) the Spanish-speaking people of the Southwest.

Spanish-speaking people in the Southwest include both (1) those Spanish American people who emigrated in the seventeenth and eighteenth centuries into the middle Rio Grande Valley and who have lived here for several generations, and (2) the emigrant first or second generation Mexican American who has moved north of the Mexican border in large numbers. These not only constitute large populations in California, Arizona, New Mexico, and Texas but also have supplied workers in migrant labor forces in many parts of the United States.

Many readers may think of Indians as a singular stereotype. It is hoped that this discussion will make clear that real differences in values, in goals, and in ways of doing things exist between them. Some of the observable differences between Pueblos and Navajos have been pointed out by Bunker and Adair. The tight, complex social fabric of the Pueblo villages may be contrasted with the individualistic nature of the Navajo who lives apart in his isolated hogan on the reservation. The Pueblo Indian's age-old sufficiency and resistance to change may be contrasted with the cultural borrowings, adaptability, and willingness to change when it is advantageous as observed in the Navajo. The Pueblo Indian might appear to have adopted many non-Indian ways without even sensing any inroads into his religious beliefs and practices, while, in contrast, the Navajo, more like his Anglo neighbor, may hinge his total interaction of social institutions on the economy which he is rapidly copying from the Anglo.[1] The teacher must realize that one Indian is not necessarily all Indians.

Educational programs have been provided for Indian youth by the Bureau of Indian Affairs for many years. The objectives of these programs, outlined for teachers in the Bureau schools, have been concisely stated by Beatty:

1. To give students an understanding and appreciation of their own tribal lore. . . .

2. To teach students . . . to become constructive citizens of their communities.

3. To aid students in analyzing the economic resources of their reservation and in planning more effective ways of utilizing these resources for the improvement of standards of living.

4. To teach . . . intelligent conservation of natural resources.

5. To give students vocational skills . . . needed to earn a livelihood in the region.

6. To develop better health habits, improved sanitation, and higher standards of diet with a view to prevention of trachoma, tuberculosis, and infant diseases.

7. To give students an understanding of the social and economic world immediately about them and to aid them in achieving some mastery over their environment.

8. To serve as a community center in meeting the social and economic needs of the community.

9. To provide the training necessary to obtain and hold a job away from the reservation area for those students who desire or need such training.[2]

These are commendable objectives of education for any group. Adequately interpreted, two major goals will be pursued. The first is that, if most of these objectives are to be met by Anglo American standards, the student must learn a completely new orientation to life, a new value system, a re-formulation of personality -- he must become a bicultural individual. The second is that for his education to be successful, he must learn how to state and solve problems. Since he can never hope to learn "already made" lessons to meet his future responsibilities, the method of solving the problems becomes all important. He needs to learn a way of thinking, to internalize an attitude of knowing that there are not answers to all the problems to be faced. Mead expresses this need in this way:

> We need from the teacher . . . a totally new kind of teaching, a teaching of a readiness to use unknown ways to solve unknown problems. We need to teach our children how to think, when you don't know what method to use, about a problem which is not yet formulated.[3]

Without interpretation, these objectives could be construed to mean that the objectives of the school encompass only teaching certain facts, developing certain habits, and perpetuating the tradition of looking to the past for adequate solution of problems.

Nash has analyzed the problems impending cultural change especially with respect to relocation from reservation to urban living. Reservation life (the social system) is being modified by the impact of technology, changing social structure, and the changing ideologies. However, the impact of technology, social structure and ideology on metropolitan social systems is much more complex, impersonal, and abstract. The diagram below presents many areas in which the reservation Indian will find himself in conflict if he is rather suddenly relocated in a metropolitan area. The reader is referred to the discussion of basic institutions in society and their perpetuation beginning on page 84.

Problems Impeding Cultural Change
(Especially evident in Problems of Relocation from reservation to urban living)*

Institutions Effecting Change	RESERVATION Life	METROPOLITAN Life
Technology	Resources underdeveloped	Resources highly developed
	Dependent on public assistance	Skilled workers - high hourly wage
	Idleness much of year	Factory technology
	Minimum communication	Maximum communication
Social Structure	Kinship	Nuclear family
	Weak tribal government	National representative government
	Factions	Institutional relationships elaborate division of labor and specialization
Ideology	Sharing	Being enterprising owning property
	Compensatory religions	More universal ethical values
	Hostility	Education
	Lack of time-sense	Exact time-sense

*Nash, Philleo, Paper read at a BIA Education Conference, January 8, 1963.

Chapters 6 and 7 will further discuss the backgrounds of Indian children and the differences between their cultures and that of the dominant Anglo society. Chapter 8 is a discussion of the cultural background of Spanish-speaking children.

FOOTNOTES

[1] Robert Bunker and John Adair, The First Look at Strangers (New Brunswick: Rutgers University Press, 1959), pp. 138-139.

[2] Willard W. Beatty, Education for Cultural Change (Chilocco, Oklahoma: Chilocco Indian Agricultural School, 1953), p. 13.

[3] Margaret Mead, The School in American Culture (Cambridge: Harvard University Press, 1951), p. 31.

CHAPTER 6

Foundations for Educating Navajo Children[1]

INTRODUCTION

In the American Southwest, encompassing an area of approximately sixteen million acres in Arizona, New Mexico, and small areas in Utah and Colorado, lies the Navajo Reservation. The Navajo tribe has a population estimated at approximately 100,000 people[2] and a birth rate higher than any other group of people in the United States. There are some 30,000 school-age children, and it has been estimated that half of the Navajo population is under 18 years of age, a highly significant fact in future plans for the education of these people.

A sketch of the geographical setting of the reservation is presented on the following page. The peripheral area, designated as a checkerboard area, refers to land where individual Indians own farms and live side by side, off reservation, with non-Indian neighbors. Condie has described Navajoland:

> Much of the country is indeed dramatic and beautiful. Certainly one does not have to argue the Beauty of the Painted Desert, the symmetrical red mesas of the Wingate Formations, the exquisite Canyon de Chelly, the alpine meadows of the Lukachukai mountains or the mysterious vistas of Monument Valley.[3]

HISTORICAL BACKGROUND

It is generally believed that the Navajo people migrated to the North American continent by way of the Bering Strait from Asia. One of the reasons for this belief is the similarity of languages between Navajos and Orientals. The Navajos speak the Athabascan tongue, a dialect related to languages spoken along the route they may have traveled in coming to the Southwest.

The Migration from Alaska, Canada, and northern United States required many years. In the beginning, the Navajos may have had few, if any, of the living habits they possessed when the white man intruded into their homeland. However, they had their

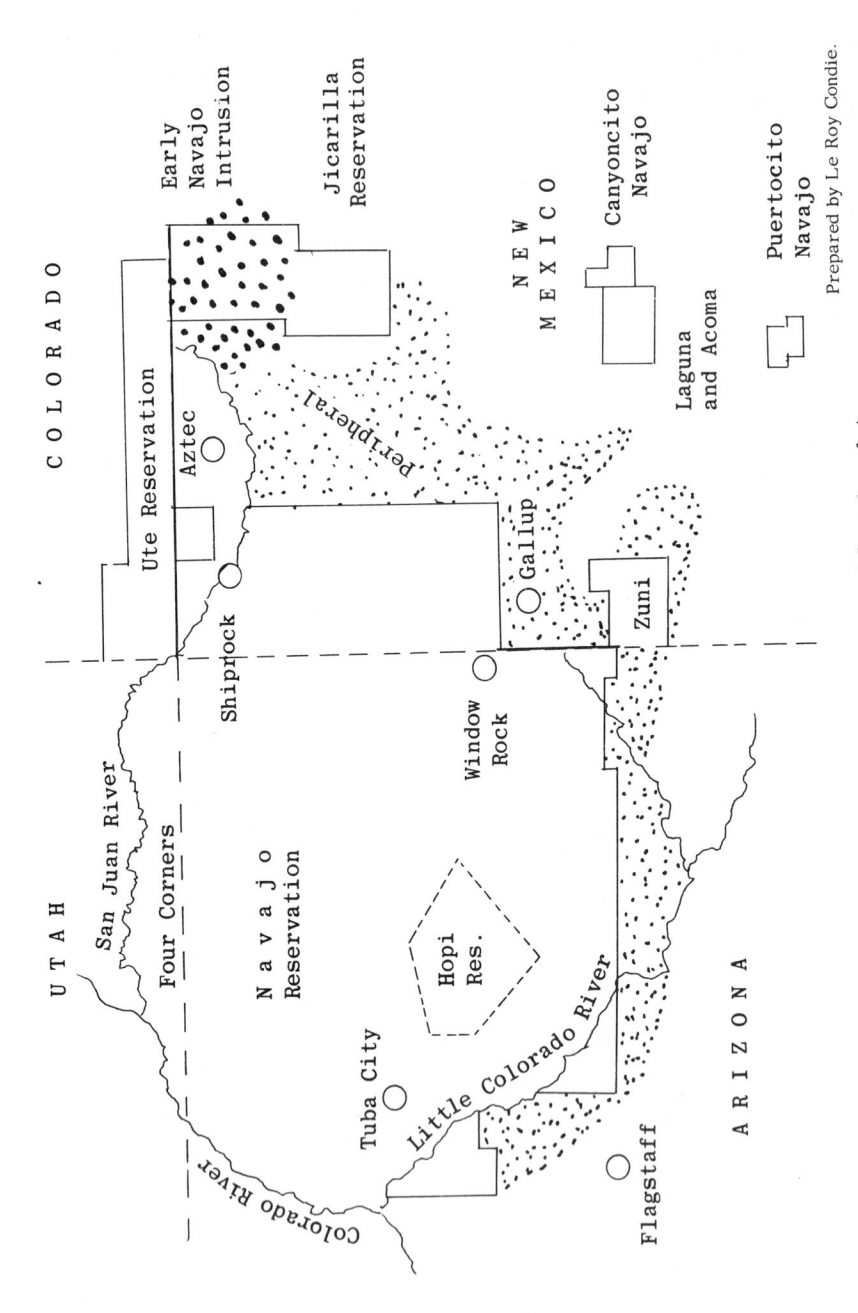

Figure 3. Navajo Reservation and Peripheral Area.

language even then. Their migration may have been encouraged through the generations either by their search for a land of milder winters or by their meeting with other tribes that had already laid claim to the territories through which they passed. Eventually they arrived in the Southwest, to live in fairly close proximity with the Pueblo Indians already here and the Spanish Americans soon to arrive.

> When and how the Navajo arrived in the Southwest are still matters of speculation. The date may be as early as about A. D. 1000; it may be later, or even earlier. The earliest hogan site to be dated by the tree ring method indicates that the Navajo were definitely living in north central New Mexico by 1540. [4]

This is not the story the Navajo people have traditionally taught their children about their origin. They have passed from generation to generation, by the story-telling method, a creation myth that explains the beginning of life for their people. Emerging from an underworld is a common theme in the stories of creation among the Indians. Young relates the Navajos' story of creation.

> It was then that First Man and First Woman picked up Sierra Blanca Peak. They picked up Mount Taylor, San Francisco Peak, La Plata Mountain, Huerfano, and Gobernador Knob. They gathered up all the seeds of the plants. In a certain place there was a mountain, and all the creatures climbed to its summit. Then the mountain began to absorb the water and dissolve itself into mud with them on it. At this point they became desperate, and planted a tree to ascend by, a fir tree, they say, but it only grew to the present height of such trees. They were in desperation, and while they were in the treetop two people (men) of some kind arrived there nearby. [5]

Older Navajos say "We have always been here." Between the four mountains is their world. When one Navajo woman was questioned about the fact that Navajos did not build churches, her reply was that anywhere between the four mountains is a sacred place.

The earliest recorded encounter of the Navajo with the Spanish is 1626

> . . . the first known reference to . . . (the Navajo) in a European document occurred in 1626. From this time until the United States took possession . . . in 1846 there is a long record of Navajo raids and Spanish reprisals. It should be noted, however, that the Navajos were primarily raiders, rather than fighters. They were interested chiefly in taking food, women, horses, or other booty... . [6]

The Navajos learned many things from the Spanish. They acquired animal husbandry in sheep and horses, silversmithing, and firearms from the Spanish. Of the domestic animals, Young observes:

> It was no doubt some time in the 16th or early 17th century that the introduction of the horse and the sheep into Navajo culture set in motion the trend of events that revolutionized Navajo life. The horse not only provided mobility, but greatly expanded opportunities for hunting, raiding, and food gathering.[7]

The horse served as a beast of burden, of great significance to women in emancipating them from that position, and as a way of travel much more desirable than on foot. The sheep provided food that could be relied on, mattresses for sleeping that were warm, dry, and comfortable, and raw materials for making rugs.

In passing, it is interesting to note the "slave trade" that once existed among Navajos, Spanish, and northern Indians. All groups kidnapped and held victims captive. Sometimes they assimilated these "slaves" into their own groups; sometimes they traded them back to regain their own people. The Navajo Yearbook in 1957 records historical entries in government documents that indicate the "slave traffic" was extensive.

> There are in the territory a large number of Indians, principally females (women and children) who have been taken by force, or stealth, or purchases. . . .[8]

> I think the number of captive Navajo Indians held as slaves to be underestimated. I think there are from five to six thousand. I know of no family which can raise one hundred and fifty dollars but what purchases a Navajo slave, and many families own four or five.[9]

In addition to the mixing of the different groups through intermarriage, Spanish women probably taught domestic arts of their experience to the Navajos. Beyond weaving and silversmithing, methods of cooking food were no doubt diffused. The "fry bread" staple of the Navajos is probably a borrowed food from the Spanish, the Indian version of sopapillas.

From the Pueblo neighbors, the Navajos borrowed skill in agriculture. The Pueblo Indians were cultivating gardens of corn, beans, melons, squashes, and chili when the Navajos came. In spite of recorded raiding against the Pueblos, there is evidence that there were periods of cooperative endeavor. The Pueblos may have had help from the Navajos during the 1680 revolt and they shared camps with them in time of danger.[10]

Amsden believes that the Navajos were not directly involved in the war between the Spanish and the Pueblos. He believes that the Navajos raided both the retreating Spanish and the Pueblo communities without their warriors. They increased their flocks and their herds of horses. And, in the period following 1692, when the Spanish returned, if the Pueblos camped in the remote canyons of northern New Mexico with them for periods of time, the Navajos could have mastered the weaving craft.[11]

Through the generations, then, they became more or less stable farmers. A fixed home, or perhaps a summer and a winter home to accommodate the grazing pattern, growing crops, weaving, and making silver jewelry -- these lent stability to living.[12]

Following the treaty of Guadalupe Hidalgo in 1848, more and more Anglo Americans penetrated, passed through, and stopped among "The People." Forts were built and army troops came and went.

The Long Walk [13]

The Navajos began to feel the presence of American troops in military outposts in the Southwest. Amsden indicates that the Navajo apparently was not greatly concerned about this in the 1850's.

> A great believer in talk he (the American) seemed to be; treaties were his solution for every trouble, with much big talk about peace and friendship. That was probably because his soldiers obviously did not know much about the country, or about Indian fighting, or because Big Chief Washington was afraid to lead his own war parties against the powerful, swift-riding Navajo.[14]

When many of the American troops were transferred eastward during the Civil War, however, raiding parties against pioneer settlers increased, and the United States Army was assigned the task of completely subduing the Navajos. Kit Carson and his forces, in 1864, corralled about 8,000 Navajos and marched them 300 miles from northeastern Arizona to Bosque Redondo, near Fort Sumner, New Mexico, on the Pecos River.

An attempt was made to convert the Navajo men into quiet farmers. After five years without successful crops, the Navajos were released and returned to northeastern Arizona and northwestern New Mexico. Amsden describes the terms and evaluates the situation:

> So, on June 1, 1863, another Navajo treaty took its place in the long series. . . . . It was drawn to encourage farming (for the men must be kept busy at something besides raiding), with free implements and seeds, a tract of land (not over 160 acres)

to each head of a family wanting it, and a small clothing allowance yearly for ten years. It provided schools as needed, one for every thirty prospective pupils. Fifteen thousand sheep and goats were to be bought for the tribe (in fact, thirty thousand were bought). . . . The conquered Navajo set forth from the Bosque on June 18, 1868, and on November 1 of that year Agent Dodd at Fort Wingate formally assumed charge of 7, 111 Navajo Indians. . . . The Navajo were home again, a sadder and wiser tribe. [15]

The "long walk" emphasizes the demoralization of the Navajo from the care-free, free-living individual he had believed himself to be into the defeated, broken-in-spirit person he was in 1868.

The Stock Reduction Program

In the 1930's, the Navajo population was increasing rapidly. Numbers of sheep, goats, and horses were increasing also. The limited grazing which was possible on the desert and semi-desert rangeland was being completely destroyed by over-grazing. The Bureau of Indian Affairs recognized the necessity to upgrade the poor quality of livestock and to decrease the number of livestock on the range. This they proceeded to do. The program was explained to the Navajos by Anglo agents. The fact that fewer animals could yield greater return than the present numbers if better breeding stock was introduced was also explained.

It is probably true that most Navajos did not really understand the program. In the first place, it seemed to the Navajo that his economy was being destroyed -- literally taken away from him. While it was being done peacefully, it was reminiscent of Kit Carson's conquest seventy-five years before. In the second place, it was contrary to the Navajo's philosophy of life. As the flocks increased, if man were living in harmony with nature, so did the rains, and thus the grass and forage would also increase. Reducing the stock was, in effect, doubting the powers of the supernatural. This was basically wrong from the point of view of the Navajo.

Because of the economic poverty of the Navajo people and because of inadequate communication with them, the stock reduction program left a resentment and bitterness that will be remembered for a long time by the older people.

BELIEFS AND VALUES

Several contrasting values from the Navajo were made apparent in Chapter 3 when the teacher was asked to take an objective look at some of the basic tenets of Christianity. In pursuing further the way a Navajo is apt to look at life, this contrast will continue to be in evidence.

Present-day missionaries sometimes say that they are not primarily seeking converts. Nevertheless, the motivation that causes one to become a missionary in the first place is apt to arise from a feeling that one's religion is better than that of the person to be helped. The possible error in such subjective judgment that merely because a society is technologically complex and diversified it is better than one that is preliterate has already been mentioned. Cultural practices in any society evolve to meet recognized needs. If they have lasted through centuries of time they must, to some degree, be meeting the needs of the people who live by them.

The Navajo believes that he evolved from the underworlds. His "next world" will be one in which he will retain his present form and go on in much the same type of life he has here with the people who have died before him.

His primary goal is harmony with the cosmos. The basic purpose of his religion is to keep in harmony -- with himself, with his people, with all living things, with his gods.

> The myths, songs, and rituals are in effect manuals of instruction for the conduct of relations of men with each other, with natural forces, and with the supernaturals who have charge of the flow of benefits and dangers. [16]

Should illness strike, or the crops need rain, or some other misfortune come, the Navajo becomes fearful and anxious about his relationship with his gods. Either he is out of harmony because of his own behavior or he is being bewitched. Religious rituals can cleanse him if it is the former and can break the spell if it is the latter. Albert says:

> Men are assumed to be a mixture of good and bad. Natural biological impulses are not considered evil. On the other hand, the ghosts of even the best men are bad. At birth one of the "four winds" enters the body and determines what sort of personality will develop. If it is the Good Wind, a man will be honest, have good thoughts, and do what is right. The Happy Wind makes people cheerful, good-natured, and in all respects good. Should the Bad Wind enter, life will be a series of blunders, accidents and petty misfortunes. The Mad Wind is especially dreaded for its effect is to produce a mean man, the worst of all possible types. [17]

The idea of good and evil in the same being is to be contrasted with the Anglo's conception of God as good and the devil as evil. Young says that this concept permits the Navajos to conceive of their gods as sharing the same characteristics as man himself -- both good and evil, both chaste and lustful, both kind and cruel. [18]

Anglos might remember that this was also the view of the ancient Greeks.

This makes understandable the numerous reports of teachers that among these children stealing and lying are bad only if caught, and behavior with strangers is classified differently than with clansmen. Albert says:

> Certain kinds of actions such as lying or stealing are discouraged on principle, but these are not bad "in themselves." If, however, the lie or the theft are discovered, hostility will be expressed by the offended person, and group harmony will be disturbed. But unethical treatment of strangers may result in benefits to the in-group (as, in earlier days, the theft of horses, slaves, and goods from the Spanish), and will, therefore, be approved behavior.[19]

Leighton and Leighton write:

> Religion enters every phase of Navajo life. It is scarcely ever out of their minds from the time they are old enough to understand anything about it. Every Navajo man and woman knows and performs some rituals, prayers, songs, and legends. All through life each may collect new items and add to his store. These personal rites are used in planting, trading, housebuilding, care of stock, treating illness, warding off danger, and for general good hope; nearly all are expected to work by creating or maintaining harmonious living of man with the forces of the universe. Some of this lore is common knowledge, but much of it is secret. One person learns a bit from another and after he can perform it perfectly, he pays for it to make it his own. Navajos buy songs and prayers from each other as they do jewelry.[20]

There is real danger that the uninformed will believe that any preliterate people are heathen or atheistic. Analysis of the time devoted to appeasing the gods, placating the gods, and absolving oneself of possible guilts, emphasizes the fallacy of this. The Leightons provide further evidence concerning this.

> In one area, records kept over a period of time by Dr. Kluckhohn showed that the men spent approximately one-fourth to one-third of their productive hours in religious activity, and women one-sixth to one-fifth. This does not mean that all this goes on while they are sitting in the hogan, while they chant, but includes time used going to and from ceremonials, gathering medicinal herbs, and other necessary apparatus, hauling wood and water, preparing food, and doing all the various things required for a ceremonial. On the average, twenty per cent of the family income is devoted to religion.[21]

There are thirty five principal Navajo ceremonials . . . The time required for performance ranges from two to nine days and nights. . . . Thirty-two animals are supposed to bring illness, and of these the commonest are the bear, deer, coyote, porcupine, snake, and eagle. . . Dreams are always taken seriously as sources of harbingers of disaster. Lightning, wind, and, to a certain extent, the earth itself may cause illness . . . Any ceremonial may infect a person if he commits improper behavior in relation to or during the cermonial . . . . Spirits of the dead are especially dangerous. . . Night and darkness are related dreads because then the spirits are thought to be abroad.

Witchcraft is a particularly important source of sickness . . . As with other cultures, the witches run counter to all the religious and moral laws. They murder their own nearest, and dearest, practice incest, handle corpes freely. . . . deliberately cause illness to others.[22]

The Blessing Way . . (is) . . a rite whose legends, songs and prayers are chiefly concerned with the creation and placement of the earth and sky, sun and moon, sacred mountains, and vegetation, the inner forms of these natural phenomena, the control of the he- and she-rains, dark clouds and mist, the inner forms of the cardinal points and life phenomena that may be considered the harbingers of blessing and happiness.

The Blessing Way is performed specifically for girls at puberty, for pregnant women, for a returned travler who has lived for a time with non-Navajos, for a family after a death, and in general when the need is felt for "Good Hope."[23]

The Singers practice and direct the ceremonials. These esoteric matters are believed to have been handed down in an unbroken chain from the time when the gods gave the ceremonials to the first Navajos, in a manner similar to the Apostolic succession. . . . the amount of detailed and exact knowledge required is staggering. . . . He must learn hundreds and hundreds of songs full of archaic words. . . . and an enormous number of rules about sequence that are almost obsessive in their complexity and thoroughness. . . . He knows all the legends concerned in the origin of the ceremonials, how to find and prepare the herbs concerned, how to make the fetishes and paraphernalia, how to make the sandpainting, direct the dances, and finally all the acts and procedures of the ceremonial.[24]

Another type of Navajo religious practitioner is the Diagnostician. The function of the Diagnostician is to discover the cause and proper cure of sickness as well as to find lost property and point out witches. As the Diagnostician offers a prayer to the Gila Monster Spirit, he extends one hand which begins to tremble and makes many involuntary motions which help the Diagnostician discover the cause of the difficulty. When all the desired information has been gathered, the hand stops trembling and the Diagnostician opens his eyes and reveals what he has found. Many women do Hand Trembling but are almost never Singers. . . . Hand Trembling sometimes comes when a person is alone, especially after sleeping.[25]

What has been said about Navajo religion must be interpreted as traditional values recorded through the years. They do not represent values of any specific individual, nor do they necessarily describe majority opinion in 1969. Young cautions:

Today the code of ethics and the cultural values of traditional Navajo society, like the religion, are undergoing rapid change under the . . . impact of non-Navajo society and institutions. The framework remains, but it is rapidly disintegrating in the face of the new order and a new way of life, and the traditional pattern is no longer as valid as a generalization as it was even twenty years ago.[26]

There will be those who will say that "none of this is true anymore." They are wrong. Culture changes slowly and even when people learn new values after they originally internalized others, they resort to the original ones in times of stress. Non-scientific beliefs learned in childhood and practiced by one's elders with conviction, return to haunt the "converted" new generation.

Further, the reader is apt to think of the few acculturated Navajos he has met and believe that these values do not apply to them. In this case, it is the degree to which they apply that is important. For some, the degree may be considerable. Beyond this, the teacher will teach children who have come to school from the remotest sections of the reservation. For at least one more generation, these cultural beliefs and practices will have almost complete acceptance by their parents.

The effort of the school must be directed toward understanding the contrasting values in the two cultures. The child must be able to retain the stabilizing values in the old culture while he is learning values in the new. If the child is encouraged to reject the traditional controls of his heritage and if he fails to internalize those of the dominant society, he is apt to become demoralized and part of society's problem of the "lost generation." It is hoped that, with understanding of the cultural differences, with specific teaching to bridge the language barrier, and adequate preparation in both social and academic skills in the dominant culture, the transition from one culture to another will be smoother and freer of "lost generation" casualties.

The following paragraphs, written by a young Navajo, discuss change in the lives of the Navajos.

1. Events of Modern Times:

    None of the previous historical events have caused nearly so much havoc as have the impacts of World War II, the Korean War, and the discovery of oil and uranium on the Navajo Reservation. These have caused such radical and rapid changes that the Navajo is in a turmoil as he has tried to keep up with them.

2. Rejection of Taboos:

    Traveling with the Armed Forces showed the Navajo youths a new facet to life, a facet that made them question the infallibility of the old people. For where, off the reservation, was any of the rest of the world concerned with not offending witches; why didn't the men in the rest of the world avoid their mothers-in-law; and why didn't they become blind when they looked at each other's genitals as the old ones said they would; and where was the chindi, the greatly feared evil spirit of the dead? During battles, Navajos saw many dead, and even at times took refuge behind their bodies without evil results - a disconcerting thing for a traditional Navajo to find out.[27]

3. Concerning the Language, the Customs, the Mores, and Folkways:

    Because of long absences from the reservation, some Navajo youths have forgotten the Navajo terms for different objects. Some of their pronunciations of Navajo words has become faulty. It is evident that if some of the Navajo tongue has been forgotten, that certainly some of the parts of the Navajo culture will have been forgotten. This latter forgotten material will include the mores, folkways, ceremonial behavior, "squaw dance" songs, as well as the myths and legends.[28]

4. About Religion:

    The religion of the old Navajos has been one that aims in keeping equilibrium between man and the gods. According to the old ones, everything in the world is a part of it and important in its relation to the rest of the world. This belief teaches that the world is run by certain rules, and that man is assured of peaceful, long living only if he learns the rules and lives by them, thus making sure of his harmony with the gods. A Navajo is concerned in securing harmony in human, natural, and supernatural relationships. This will make positive a long life for himself and for members of his family. The Navajos have taught of no hereafter with treasures stored up in Heaven, of no Hell with its punishments for sins and transgressions; they have taught only that one lives today and is punished by the gods with some misfortune or illness when he gets out of step with the laws of the Holy People.

Consequently, when one becomes ill, his family engages a man with a knowledge of hand-quaking who uses his wisdom to recommend which medicine man or which sing should be utilized in reestablishing the healing equilibrium. The faith-healing of the medicine man has long been predominant in the Navajo culture.[29]

5. Learning to Trust the White Man:

Personal aggression is a trait hitherto foreign to the Navajo culture for on the reservation children are taught to work for the honor of ones family and clan instead of for ones own personal advancement. Taught at home to trust only his own family or clan members, the Navajo will have to learn to trust, at least in part, those in the Non-Indian population with which he comes into close contact. Trusting in a genuine sense may develop slowly since Indian elders tell and re-tell their succeeding generations such historical facts as:

> . . . . . . since 1789, our government officials in Washington have ratified 389 treaties with eighty-nine tribes, but has broken 379 or 97.4% of all of them; or, Washington took eighty-seven years to start to work seriously on keeping the promise of the treaty of 1868 regarding a school room for every thirty Navajo children; or, that as late as 1950, Washington officials sold without Indian consent, land belonging to the San Ildefonso Pueblo.[30]

Of course, all three of these "historical facts" has more than one explanation. The important thing to remember, however, is that if parents tell these incidents over and over as "historical facts" the children are already prejudiced about them when they come to the "white man's" school.

THE PEOPLE: THE FAMILY PATTERN

The traditional Navajo family accepted the father as the formal head, but the mother with her matrilineal descent, had as much, or more, influence in managing the family as her husband. The family remained in the mother's extended family group, the tangible goods belonged largely to her, and her brothers contributed greatly to the teaching and discipline chores of the children.

The father in the family had obligations to both his wife and to his mother's family. In a situation like this, if the marriage dissolved, the wife was in the better position of the two because her home life stayed stable because of the nature of her consanguine relationship to her family. The husband, in the traditional family, then, experienced greater family dislocation and financial loss.

The transition in family organization which may be taking place at the present time will have far-reaching effects on the children in school. As the livelihood of the family converts more and more to the wage economy, it is the man who does the work and earns the pay check. Since he earned it and it belongs to him, he may not share it with his wife. He will be away from home more if the work is off reservation. Anyway, if he works for someone else, he no longer is investing any part of himself in his wife's farming enterprise. As money becomes more important and the woman has less of it, her position in the family changes. She becomes dependent upon her husband now. As families move to new places to work for wages, the extended family is broken up. If women find wage work, they are usually less well paid than the men.

Agricultural and herding occupations have been less profitable, and the cost of the necessities has greatly risen.

When the extended matrilineal family is broken up on the reservation, the following effects are apt to occur:

1. Women lack the company and support of the other members of the family;

2. They have continuous care of children, not now shared by grandmother, sisters, aunts.

3. Women no longer have continuous advice from elders, brothers, or others for child-training and discipline.

4. Middle-aged women traditionally could hope to be fairly well off in the Navajo sense as they gained status in an extended family; as nuclear families emerge, and the male provider may not be so good, they may be worse off.[31]

Dutton suggests that the Navajo woman today has had her family role altered in three important ways: (1) her function within the family has lost significance; (2) her economic position has been undermined; and (3) her security and bargaining power in family interaction has been greatly reduced. She also says that "While the men are adopting the life and culture of the white man, the Navajo women are being left stranded on the reservation."[32]

Work for the non-Indian generally requires (1) school-learned skills; (2) fluent use of the English language; and (3) social

177

amenities practiced easily by the dominant group. Work for the acculturating Indian will require the same skills.

Of the Navajo people, it may be said that they have many qualities similar to the middle-class Anglo, whose culture and values they are now accepting.

The Navajos have always considered themselves a separate, dignified, important people. They did not name themselves Navajo; they called themselves Diné, or Dinéh. Diné means "The People"; to the Navajo, it means The People. This implies a strong degree of ethnocentrism easily observable, also, in the Anglo. The Navajos have always been an adaptable people. Consider their abilities in learning their economy from the Spanish and the Pueblos; their ability to eke out their existence on the dry mesas of their reservation.

Ruth Underhill emphasizes the adaptability of the Navajos in her book as she narrates historically, the four beginnings of the Navajo. First, they moved into the area where the Pueblos lived and settled down to grow gardens of corn, beans, and squash as the Pueblos did; second, the Spanish arrived and horses and sheep were taken in raids. As noted earlier, the acquisition of horses and sheep drastically changed the living habits of the people. The third beginning dates from their release at Fort Sumner and the establishment of reservation boundaries within which they were to be settled farmers. The fourth major adjustment has been that resulting from the tremendous change in outlook evident at the end of the world war in 1945 and the passage of the Long Range Rehabilitation Program in 1950, exhibiting itself in a Navajo Tribal Council of 74 members who sit in session and plan the spending of the tribal income of some thirty million dollars accumulating largely from oil and uranium leases and bonuses.[33]

> Adaptability and change is exemplified in the Navajo Forest Products Industries at Navajo, New Mexico. Since 1960, the tribe has built a new eight and one half million dollar sawmill, which can produce about fifty million board feet of lumber a year, employ 450 Navajos, and provide an annual payroll of one and one half million dollars. The tribe practices a sustained yield policy in cutting in its 458,457 acres of Ponderosa Pine. From open country, the town of Navajo anticipates a stable population of some five thousand inhabitants and a twelve-grade school.[34]

> . . . . today's Navajo has mastered relatively sophisticated power machine-tools. . . . the Navajo has demonstrated an adaptability and capability in working as a team at laying welded rail. . . . power saws, gang-drills, spike drivers, tie adzers, ballast cribbers, and other similar machines are oper-

ated by Navajos. . . . A follow up to the steel force is that of the welders.[35]

The New Mexico State University Extension Service reminds us of the adaptability and technology of the modern Navajo:

> The Navajo Indians are in the midst of an agricultural revolution. . . . Today hundreds of Navajos are working in fields of cucumbers, onions, potatoes, tomatoes, and other vegetables. . . . The Council sponsors a crops show at the annual Navajo Window Rock Fair that has grown to about twenty-five times the size of the crops show to be seen at the New Mexico State Fair. . . . the Navajos have worked hard on the development of pickling cucumber crops. During a three-month season an average of 1,000 persons have been employed on about 550 acres of cucumbers which required only about 1100 acre feet of the Navajos' water resources.[36]

> In spite of the enormous problems confronting the Navajo, observers who know them best feel that this tribe will eventually make the transition from the old culture to the modern world more successfully than any other Indian group. For one thing, their history has shown them able to adopt the traits of other people and to integrate them into Navajo culture. An example of this ability is shown in their taking many items of religious culture from the neighboring pubelos and recasting them into a religion which is specifically Navajo. Also, in the field of material culture, they learned weaving from the pueblos and sheep herding from the Spanish; and in each case the new traits were integrated into Navajo culture and became something quite different from what they had been in the originating cultures. Perhaps the best example of this quality of the Navajo is the adoption and rapid development of representative government and the evolution of a tribal, even nationalistic feeling, in a very few years.[37]

In their way, Navajos have been a very moral people. They teach:

> Look after your property. Don't gamble or waste it, or you will get poor and your family might be ashamed.

> Think about things so you can do everything right and make pretty things. Then people will respect you and ask you to help them.

> Get along well with everyone.

> Do what your family want you to do, so you will get along well and nobody will have to scold you.

If you have lots of property, even though you worked hard for it, help your relatives. Then you won't have too much. People (witches) won't take it away from you or make you sick.

Diné Sání At Gallup Ceremonial

"I WISH THAT I HAD MY CAMERA. SIGHTS LIKE THAT MIGHT VANISH SOMEDAY."

From Navajo Times, August 4, 1960

The Navajo Evaluation of Anglo customs in dress must not be much different from Anglo evaluations if the native's view of the tourist on the reservation, depicted above, is reliable.

If you do something wrong and people find out, make friends with them again. Give back what you took away, or pay them with property.

Be careful about dealing with strangers, or in exposing yourself to unfamiliar or disorderly situations.

In the presence of danger, or in a frustrating situation, do nothing or escape.[38]

The Navajos are moving in many directions to make their adjustment in today's world. Many families follow the traditional economy of sheepherding, gardening, and piñon harvesting. Many families have found careers with the Bureau of Indian Affairs, both on and off reservation. Many have found work with the railroads so that the wage from work was the basis for their livelihood even if their families continued to live on the reservation.

Many have found expression in rug weaving, silversmithing, and painting, although the economic value of these crafts is not great. Many have taken advantage of the Bureau's relocation program and are enjoying urban living in such cities as Phoenix, Denver, and Los Angeles.

EDUCATION IS THE LADDER

My Grandchild,
The Whites have many things which we Navajos need.
But we cannot get them.
It is as though the Whites were in a grassy canyon,
And there they have wagons, plows, and plenty of food.
We Navajos are up on the dry mesa.
We hear them talking, but we cannot get to them.
My Grandchild, Education is the ladder.
Tell our people to take it.[39]

Manuelito was one of the first Navajos to express this acceptance of white man's education. Since World War II, the general attitude of the Navajos has been one of complete acceptance of and urgent requesting of formal education.

Condie reports one Navajo father's logic for keeping his son at home to do the work only one short generation ago:

I was about nine years old then. My father and I were on horses, just riding along. It was almost time for school to start at Ganado. I told him I wanted to go to school. He said, "let us think about this. Think of those sheep. Who will take care of the sheep? You are the one who knows how to find the grass. You are the one to take them to water. If you go to school, there will be just Small Girl to herd the sheep. Maybe they will grow thin. Maybe she will lose some of them. Some of these are your sheep. Later I will give you some more. If you go to school for many years you will have no sheep when you get back." That was a strong argument my father made, but I went to school anyway.[40]

The median educational level in the United States for people twenty-five years old or older is eleventh grade; the median level achieved for the total United States Indian population the same age is fifth or sixth grade; the median for the Navajos in the 1950 census was less than first grade. It is higher now, but still below the level of most other Indian groups. This means that there is a large population of adults, still young and not yet in their potentially most productive years, who are, for all practical purposes illiterate. Thompson, speaking at the Fourth Annual Navajo Education Conference, illustrated this educational status as shown in Figure 4.[41]

TO CATCH UP EDUCATIONALLY

POPULATION: GENERAL INDIAN NAVAJO

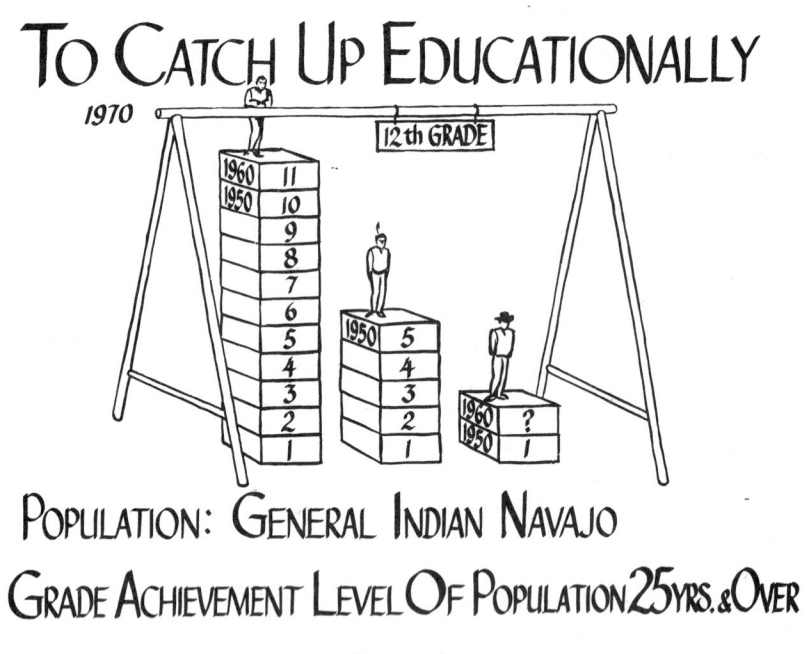

GRADE ACHIEVEMENT LEVEL OF POPULATION 25 YRS. & OVER

Figure 4.

Magazine articles sometimes end on the very optimistic note that now all Navajos are suddenly wealthy from the royalties earned by the tribe on timber, oil, gas, and uranium. This is, for some, a misleading statement. The tribe, itself, has realized a very enviable annual income from this source during the past few years. However, the tribe has used the money entirely as a tribal income, and planned its use for the benefit of all the Navajos with long-range plans being their prime considerations. So, it should be clearly understood that there has been no per capita payments and no individual has shared directly in the revenues paid to the tribal treasury. While his tribe is relatively wealthy, the annual family incomes across the reservation are extremely low.

DIFFERENCES IN VALUES: A SUMMARY

The American public school teaches:

1. Mastery over nature. Man must harness and cause the forces of nature to work for him.
2. Future time orientation.
3. Strict adherence to time schedules.
4. Scientific explanation for natural phenomena. Nothing happens contrary to natural law. There is a scientific explanation for everything.
5. Saving. Everybody should save for the future.
6. Society is based on a patrilineal, conjugal, nuclear family organization.
7. Everyone should try to climb the ladder of success.

The traditional Navajo family learned:

1. Harmony with nature. Nature will provide for man if he will behave as he should and obey nature's laws.
2. Present time orientation.
3. Unhurried inexactness results from using sun time and having no clocks.
4. Non-scientific explanation for natural phenomena. Mythology, fear of the supernatural, witches, and sorcery may be used to explain behavior.
5. Don't have too much. People (witches) won't take it away from you or make you sick. You might be thought of as selfish or stingy.
6. Society is based on a matrilineal, consanguinal, extended family organization.
7. Success rests more in being a good person than in acquiring things.

Fonaroff, after discussing at length the problems of Navajo economy and the confusion of being lost between two cultures, poses the question: "How do you get him to want what he needs?"[42]

The school is the basic institution for effecting change. Teachers must be able to prepare the child psychologically for the changing of his values, and this requires understanding. Before teachers can succeed in their attempts to transmit the skills of the three R's, they must recognize basic differences in ways of thinking and acting. Then, conflict will be replaced with understanding; condemnation will be replaced with encouragement; and hostility will be replaced with friendliness.

Annie Wauneka, a Navajo leader herself, has been working for a number of years to help her people understand how to overcome health and sanitation problems on the reservation. Writing about tuberculosis, she says:

> There is no word for "germ" in our language. This makes it hard for the Navajo people to understand sickness, particularly tuberculosis.
>
> I asked the medicine men what they thought caused the lungs to be destroyed; what caused the coughing and the spitting up of blood. According to the stories learned from their ancestors, tuberculosis is caused by lightning. If lightning struck a tree and a person used that tree for firewood or anything, it would make him sick, cause blisters to develop in his throat and abscesses in his lungs.[43]

The reading list in the bibliography provides a variety of suggestions for further study. The teacher who expects to teach in schools enrolling Navajos should read extensively to develop understanding of and insight into the way of life of the Navajo people. Included are the writings of anthropologists, journalists, and fiction writers.

Appendix A is an autobiography of a young Navajo girl who faced the cultural barriers described here and has, if the values expressed at the end of the story are interpreted correctly, learned to synthesize the values of both cultures and plan constructively for her future.

Appendix C is an article expressing beliefs and feelings of the Navajo about the white men who come to work on the reservation.[44]

FOOTNOTES

[1] This chapter discusses (1) historical background, (2) beliefs and values, (3) the family, and (4) education as the ladder to successful transition.

[2] Robert Young, The Navajo Yearbook, VIII, A Decade of Progress, 1951-1961, includes a statistical estimate of 94,000 Navajos in 1961.

[3] Le Roy Condie, "The Effect of Cultural Difference in the Education of Navajo Children" (Unpublished monograph, College of Education, The University of New Mexico, 1958), p. 3. (Mimeographed)

[4] Leonard McCombe, Evon Z. Vogt, and Clyde Kluckhohn, Navajo Means People (Cambridge: Harvard University Press, 1951), p. 131.

[5] Robert Young, The Navajo Yearbook (Window Rock, Arizona: The Navajo Agency, 1957), p. 189.

[6] McCombe, Vogt, and Kluckhohn, op. cit., p. 132.

[7] Young, op. cit., pp. 215-216.

[8] Ibid., citing Chief Justice Kirby Benedict, p. 216.

[9] Ibid., citing Dr. Louis Kennon, c. 1865, p. 217.

[10] Paul S. Martin, George Quimby, and Donald Collier, Indians Before Columbus (Chicago: University of Chicago Press, 1949), p. 158.

[11] Charles Avery Amsden, Navajo Weaving: Its Technic and History (Santa Ana, California: The Fine Arts Press, 1934), p. 129.

[12] Ibid.

[13] Adapted from Condie, op. cit., pp. 28-34.

[14] Amsden, op. cit., p. 154

[15] Ibid., pp. 167-168.

[16] Ethel M. Albert, "The Classification of Values: A Method and Illustration," American Anthropologist, 58: 228, April, 1956.

[17] Ibid., p. 291.

[18] Young, op. cit., p. 196.

[19] Albert, op. cit., p. 235.

[20] Alexander H. Leighton and Dorothea C. Leighton, The Navajo Door (Cambridge: Harvard University Press, 1944), p. 24.

[21] Ibid., p. 30.

[22] Leighton Alexander, and Dorothea Leighton, "Therapeutic Values in Navajo Religion," Arizona Highways, 43:2, No. 8, August, 1967.

[23] Leighton, Alexander and Dorothea Leighton, "Therapeutic Values in Navajo Religion," Arizona Highways, 43:3, No. 8, August, 1967.

[24] Leighton, Alexander and Dorothea Leighton, "Therapeutic Values of Navajo Religion," Arizona Highways, 43:4, No. 8, August, 1967.

[25] Leighton, Alexander and Dorothea Leighton, "Therapeutic Values of Navajo Religion, Arizona, Highways, 43:8, No. 8, August, 1967.

[26] Young, op. cit., p. 210.

[27] Patrick, Kenneth, "The Changing Navajo Culture," unpublished paper, University of New Mexico, 1958, p. 3.

[28] Patrick, Kenneth, "The Changing Navajo Culture," unpublished paper, University of New Mexico, 1958, p. 7.

[29] Patrick, Kenneth, "The Changing Navajo Culture," unpublished paper, University of New Mexico, pp. 8-9.

[30] Patrick, Kenneth, "The Changing Navajo Culture," unpublished paper, University of New Mexico, 1958, p. 11.

[31] Bertha Dutton, address given at the Third Annual Dorothy Canfield Fisher Library Award, Gallup Public Library, April 16, 1961, n. p.

[32] Ibid.

[33] Ruth Underhill, The Navajos (Norman: University of Oklahoma Press, 1956).

[34] Knifke, John J., editor, "'Horned Moon' Navajo Lumber Products," Santa Fe Magazine, 60:4-7, March, 1967.

[35] Knifke, John J., "Navajo 'Know-How' Lays the Rail," Santa Fe Magazine, 59:4-6, October, 1966.

[36] White, John M., editor, "Navajos Revolt!" New Mexico Extension News, 46:6-7, Fall, 1966.

[37] Smith, Anne M., New Mexico Indians: Economic, Educational, and Social Problems, (Santa Fe: Museum of New Mexico, 1966), p. 61.

[38] Albert, op. cit., pp. 236-238.

[39] Manuelito, famous Navajo war chief, to Chee Dodge, interpreter.

[40] Condie, op. cit., p. 103.

[41] Hildegard Thompson, "Teaching English to Indian Children," Fourth Annual Conference on Navajo Education (Window Rock, Arizona: The Navajo Tribe, January, 1961). (Mimeographed.) p. 9.

[42] Leonard S. Fonaroff, "The Trouble With the Navajo," The John Hopkins Magazine, 13: 14-18, 30 ff., December, 1961.

[43] Annie D. Wauneka, "Helping a People to Understand," The American Journal of Nursing, 62: 88-90, July, 1962.

[44] Kathryn Polacca, "Ways of Working With the Navajos Who Have Not Learned the White Man's Ways," Journal of American Indian Education, November, 1962, (College of Education, University Of Arizona, Tempe, Arizona).

CHAPTER 7

Foundations for Educating Pueblo Indian Children

INTRODUCTION

More than 20,000 Indians living in more than twenty separate small villages in New Mexico and Arizona are designated collectively as the Pueblo Indians. They have a long and continuous history in the Southwest dating back to about the time of Christ. They learned to build and to live harmoniously together in multi-storied dwellings termed by Underhill as America's first apartment houses.[1] Pueblo Bonito, in Chaco Canyon in northern New Mexico, was a tremendous structure containing about 800 adjacent rooms. The geographical location of these pueblos in New Mexico and Arizona is shown in the sketch on the following page. These individual pueblos developed their own in-groups feelings and may be said to possess the same ethnocentrism typical of any group somewhat enamored of its own self-worth.

This chapter will present a brief discussion of the history of the Pueblo Indians in the Southwest, something of their beliefs and values as traditionally practiced, the family pattern of living with some of its complications arising in cultural change, and the outlook for education in the classroom as it is based on these observations.

An elementary teacher recorded in 1960 a series of anecdotes that point up Pueblo Indian-Anglo cultural differences:

> I moved from a mid-western city to an Indian Pueblo when I was in the fourth grade. I remember incidents happening at that time, many of which have become understandable to me since I have been a teacher.
>
> One day my brother and I killed a rattlesnake and we felt quite proud of our prowess until our Indian friends frowned on us and refused to play with us.
>
> We soon learned that the Indian children had a different sense of humor. Many times my hurt was increased when my Indian companions laughed if I fell.

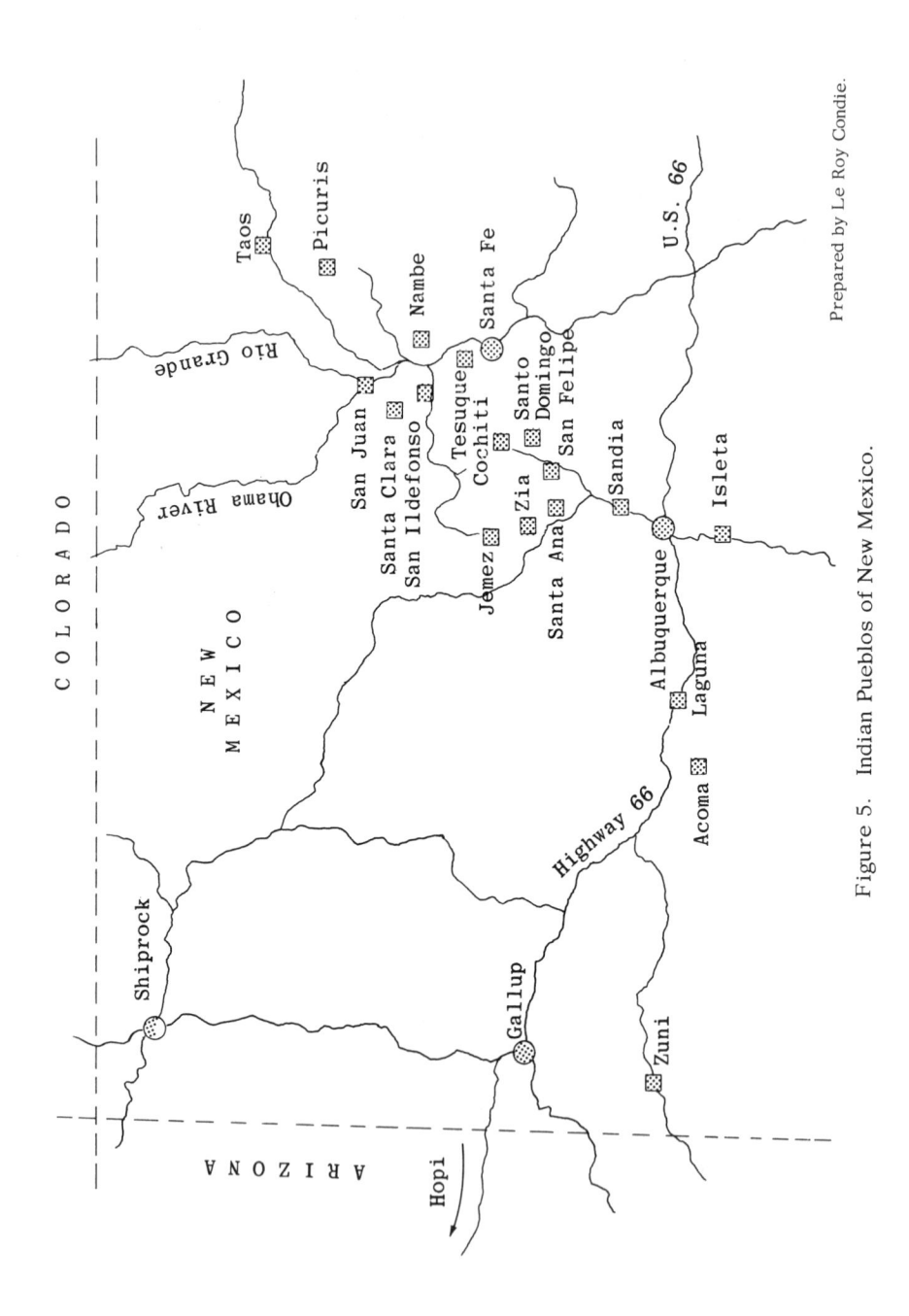

Figure 5. Indian Pueblos of New Mexico.

I noticed that Pueblo children can be very cruel to a kitten or a puppy, and get great amusement watching them struggle when tied with a rope or wire.

Being punctual at school or meetings is not important. Of course, the children are beginning to respond to pressure in school, but tribal gatherings usually begin whenever the people get there and often last many hours. No speaker is brief, and each one is allowed to ramble on as long as he wants to. Many times children come to school breakfastless because no one was up to cook a meal.

More and more noticeable as children grow older is the reluctance to excel in anything. Any pupil who puts forth an effort to stand out soon finds himself in disfavor among his fellows.

The belief that witches cause misfortune is strong. For years an old Pueblo man was known to be a witch, and one day when a student fell and skinned his elbow quite badly, he said it was because that witch looked at him. Witches are blamed for robberies, too. For a year or two some one broke into my apartment in the school building with revolting regularity.

When I enlisted the help of the governor in stopping this, I was told that nothing could stop it -- a witch was responsible for it. The governor told me that his own tools had been taken in the same way.

Mothers apparently accept the philosophy that children must be allowed to do what they want to do. A parent of a child who had had infectious hepatitis was told to keep the child at home until the doctor gave permission for his return to school. As soon as the boy felt better, his mother sent him to school with a note saying that the child wanted to come to school so she couldn't keep him home anymore. Sometimes this makes it hard for Jimmy to see why he should write numbers when he wants to play with clay or color.

Along with this tendency to let children do what pleases them goes the idea that the school should discipline the child for wrong things he does at home. Recently, I received a note asking me to "do something" to a boy who had shot another boy with a slingshot.

When a child is angry at another child, instead of saying something mean about the child himself, he will make a disparaging remark about a near relative, usually the mother. George comes to me in anger because Tom said his mother was too fat or had big ears or something equally belittling. Perhaps this only corresponds with the boast made by Anglo boys: "My dad can lick your dad any time."

HISTORICAL BACKGROUND

The fact that the pueblos have been here for centuries makes difficult any definite statement about where the people came from. They have their own creation myth, generally consistent from tribe to tribe, but told in its own way by each. It is a story of an emergence from an underworld; the people came up from a dark, multi-leveled underworld, climbing out of a less desirable environment. Parsons records the story of creation this way:

> The story of creation is a story of emerging from the underworld. There is no query about how the earth was made or about the first people, that is, prior to those who emerged. The Emergence is a satisfactory starting point, that drama of finding an opening into the sunny upperworld and the climb by tree or reed. Similarly, the most precious things about the people today, the "mothers," the "old ones," as well as the societies and ceremonies, the war gods who are leaders or watchmen, sometimes the katchina, all are accounted for as coming up with the People, all just as they are today. To secure a sense of authenticity or validity for fetish, spirit or institution, the Pueblo has but to say, "It came up with us."[2]

The mythology of a people gives credence and authenticity to the customs, ceremonies, and rituals that they support. Reasons for doing culturally enforced behavior are rooted in the vague, tradition-bound explanation, "We've always done it this way." This is a common experience in many Anglo church doctrines. They are not explained logically; they are derived superficially in the shadow of "It's tradition."

With respect to both the emergence and departure, A Hopi informant explained the belief of his people as: "They say we came up over there. Somewhere in the Grand Canyon. We came up from down under the ground. They say we will go back there, too." His explanation about going back carried the notion that all would go back, but those whose lives here left much to be desired would have to work much harder to get there. He explained that the effort for them to get back might be compared to every time one took a step forward, he might slip back almost all of it.[3]

Anthropologists have divided the development of Pueblo culture into four pre-historical eras:

Basketmaker Period from sometime B. C. until A. D. 450.

A sedentary, farming pattern of living superceded the nomadic hunting and gathering. They grew corn and squash which they stored in stonelined bins. They wove fine baskets, hence, the name. They used spears, spear throwers called atlatls, and clubs for hunting and defense.

Modified Basketmaker Period 450 A. D. - 700 A. D.

During this period, they developed the art of pottery making. Began to live in pithouses instead of cave or rock shelters. Began using the bow and arrow.

Developmental Pueblo Period 700 A. D. - 1100 A. D.

Began building adobe or stone buildings above ground. Pithouses were modified into the first kivas, ceremonial chambers. Began to cultivate cotton and weave textiles.

Great Pueblo Period 1100 A. D. - 1300 A. D.

Buildings, pottery, and other crafts reached peak in Pueblo development. Multi-storied apartment houses were built - Aztec, Mesa Verde, Chaco Canyon.

End of this great period may have been caused by a long drought (1276 - 1299), friction within or without, or just an urge to move to new locations.

Regressive-Renaissance Pueblo Period 1300 A. D. - 1540 A. D.

Historical Period 1540 to the present.[4]

The historical period dates from 1540 as written records are available from that date.

The Golden Age of Pueblo culture designated as Pueblo III, was chronologically 200 or 300 years before Coronado came to the Tiguex Pueblo in 1540. This classic period may have been destroyed by the prolonged drouth in the Mesa Verde area. The dates of this long drouth have been established through tree rings as 1276-1299.

Pueblo Indians migrated from Mesa Verde to several areas in New Mexico and Arizona. It is not known for sure whether they migrated directly to sites of present-day pueblos. It is believed that the present Hopi villages have been inhabited since the year 1000. The village of Acoma, atop the high mesa and called Sky City, is also believed to have been inhabited since about that time. These inhabitants may have migrated directly from the Mesa Verde (Four Corners) area.[5]

The migration into the Rio Grande River Valley gave them permanent home sites where it was not too difficult to make an adequate subsistence living for centuries. They brought corn with them and they developed ingenious systems of irrigating the gardens from the Rio Grande River.

Obviously, all the inhabitants of more than a score of pueblos did not come from the same starting point. This is apparent from the languages they speak. Their languages have been determined

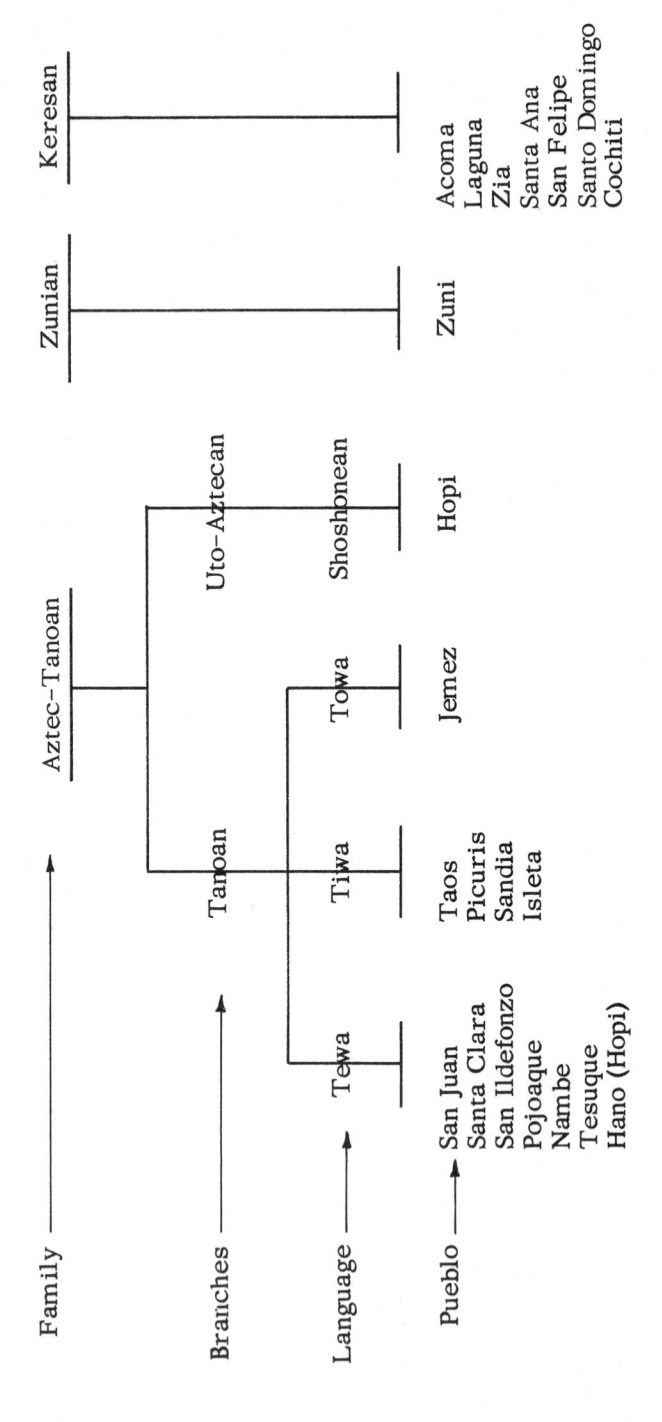

Figure 6. Language patterns among the Pueblo Indians.

to belong to four major linguistic families: Tanoan, Keresan, Zunian, and Uto-Aztecan. The language chart on the preceding page illustrates this graphically. As one would expect, there is greater similarity in the lives of Pueblo Indians speaking the same language.

The early Spanish Conquistadores, looking for the seven cities of gold and hoping to claim land for Spain, found the Pueblo Indians living in highly organized villages. They gave the name pueblo to these villages, which has since become the means of referring to them.

The number of pueblos was probably about the same when Coronado came in 1540 as it is today. Laguna is newer than the first explorations of the Spanish, but several other villages have completely died out. As late as 1838, the last remaining Pecos Indians joined the Jemez Pueblo, people with whom they had a common language, Towa.

It is apparent, then, that the Pueblo Indians had had a very long history in the Southwest before the Spaniards came.

Spanish Rule

From the earliest immigration of Spanish colonists to the Rio Grande Valley in the seventeenth century, a concentrated effort was made to convert all the Indians to Catholicism. Dozier describes the policy of the Spanish in their attempts to establish Catholicism in the villages.

> Seventeenth-century records are replete with instances of attempts to eradicate native ceremonies by force. Kivas were raided periodically and masks and ceremonial paraphernalia of all kinds were burned and destroyed. Those Indian leaders who persisted in conducting ceremonies were executed or punished in a variety of ways. The encomienda system in New Mexico aggravated conditions by exacting tribute from the Indians, while the missionary program vied with the encomienda system in forcing the Indians to abandon their native practices and was equally coercive and brutal. To supplant native ceremonial patterns and beliefs, missionaries baptized Indians, forced attendance at Mass, and made instruction in Catholic doctrine compulsory in missionary establishments.[6]

The Pueblo personality was of such a passive nature that the Spanish could dominate, legally, at least, for a hundred and fifty years, making their demands as they would. Yet, an ingenious organizational ability of the many pueblos may explain the means by which all the separate pueblos on a designated day in 1680 revolted, killed many of the Spanish priests and soldiers in the area, and forced every living Spaniard to retreat below the Mexican border. This suggests that an all-pueblo council functioned in 1680 much as the All-Pueblo Council functions today for the existing nineteen pueblos. Then, in 1692, when the Spanish soldiers came back with sufficient forces to overpower the pueblos one by one, the Indians continued to live side by side with their Spanish neighbors.

Nevertheless, the Spanish policy, all through their period of domination, was directed deliberately to the eradication of Indian beliefs and practices. The Indians, especially those on the Rio Grande River in close proximity with the Spaniards, took their religious practices underground.

Although the Pueblo Revolt occurred 280 years ago, the details of its happening have been passed from generation to generation through very effective retelling. Many of the older people in the pueblos today react to the events of the revolt almost as if they had personally experienced it.

In the exercise of many of their religious ceremonies, the significance of the revolt is still exhibited in adult behavior. Outsiders, including school teachers in pueblo schools, are asked to leave when these secret ceremonies are to be held. On occasion when an Indian is married to a non-Indian in the pueblo, the non-Indian is asked to leave during the performance of such rites. When the Shalako ceremony at Zuni is held each year, some Zunis hope that the Spanish Americans will not come to watch.

The Pueblo and Spanish American cultures existed through nearly three centuries of time in mutual co-existence, with each maintaining much of the same basic solidarity it had in the beginning.

The passing of the Mexican Territory from Spanish rule to Mexican rule to United States rule brought the Anglo in greater and greater numbers to the Southwest. The American Indian policy had always been one of pushing the "savages" back from their homelands to an ever-receding frontier. Even when the possibilities of new frontiers were gone, the aggrandizement continued. Even though Indians were given certain "reservation" areas, the Anglo's greed for "good" land caused the Indians to be deprived of their desirable farming and timber lands. By 1848, when New Mexico became a United States Territory, hundreds of non-Indians had already claimed ownership of lands in the Pueblo land grants. This usurping of land was not stopped until 1924 when the Pueblo Lands Act was passed in Congress.

Probably worse than the pressures to take Pueblo lands, at least psychologically, was the unrelenting insistence that the Indians were heathen and "savage," and must give up their life ways of past centuries. The primary goal of Indian Bureau officials and missionaries was the complete eradication of the traditional culture.

The forced recruitment of Indian children to be enrolled in boarding schools at considerable distances from reservations was designed to wean Indian youngsters away from their traditional culture. In the schools the use of the Indian language and all other "Indian" ways were prohibited. Infractions were dealt with brutally through a variety of physical punishments. During the early 1900's investigators were sent to the Pueblos to study reported immoral and anti-Christian practices of the Indians. These investigators brought back reports of customs which violated Anglo-American standards of decency and morality. Under the Religious Crimes Code, Indian Service officials were instructed to stop ceremonial practices of the Indians which might be contrary to accepted Christian standards.[7]

The Indian Reorganization Act of 1934 delineated the relationship between the United States and the Indian tribes. It restored dignity to the Indian as a human being with rights; it gave him authority for local self-government. It prohibited alloting land to non-Indians, restored land to the tribes, provided economic assistance on a loan basis to individuals or groups within a tribe; and recognized the importance of education.[8]

Much confusion existed through the years concerning the status of Indians. To be "wards" of the government indicated some kind of "second class" citizenship. Cohen says that the Pueblo Indians became citizens with the signing of the Treaty of Guadalupe Hidalgo:

> . . . it would appear that the historical evidence supports the claim that the Pueblo Indians did enjoy citizenship under Mexican and under United States rule. It seems clear, in any event, that as Mexicans they were protected by Section 9 of the Treaty of Guadalupe Hidalgo which promised, eventually, "all the rights of citizens of the United States," and immediately "free enjoyment of their liberty and property."[9]

Voting is a privilege delegated to the control of the various states. Some states require high enough literacy ability so that many of their citizens are denied the franchise. Currently, these barriers are being eliminated.

RELIGIOUS PRACTICES

Every aspect of the Pueblo Indian's daily life is permeated by his religion. His social life, his economic duties, and his attention to health and recreation are all integral parts of a deeply religious life. Dutton says:

With the Pueblo Indians, their religion transcends all else. It is the very core of their existence. All aspects of Pueblo life -- the arts, crafts, and industries, social structure and religion -- are inextricably woven, thoroughly integrated.[10]

Religious rites are performed at planting time in the spring to insure germination and maturation of the crop; dances and prayers for rain go on in the summer; and harvest dances are performed in the fall. There are dances at the winter and summer solstices, animal dances to obtain the proper permission to kill game, and the rites of the curing societies. Marinsek describes the theme of Pueblo religion:

> If Pueblo religion has a theme it is that of fertility. Fertility is intimately bound with rain and corn. One has but to reflect momentarily on the environmental forces present in the Southwest to realize the significance of fertility to the Pueblos. In this arid region of the United States, a sedentary people such as the Pueblos depended on life-giving corn for existence. The sacredness of corn is everywhere evident. Corn meal is a significant part of all ritual; perfect ears of corn are favorite fetishes. The production of corn depends on rain or other sources of water ultimately dependent on rain. Water and fertility mean corn, and corn is synonymous with life.[11]

Bunzel states the religious theme this way:

> If they are asked the purpose of any religious observance, they have a ready answer. It is for rain. This is of course a more or less conventional answer. But it reflects a deep-seated Zuni attitude. Fertility is above all else the blessing within the bestowal of the gods, and in the desert country of the Zuni plateau, rain is the prime requisite for the growth of crops. The retreats of the priests, the dances of the masked gods, even many of the activities of the medicine societies are judged by whether or not there has been rain.[12]

Animism is a part of most preliterate religions. The Pueblos are no exception. Animism is the attributing of a living soul to natural phenomena and inanimate objects.

> To the Zuni, the whole world appears animate. Not only are night and day, wind, clouds and trees possessed of personality, but even articles of human manufacture such as houses, pots, and clothing are alive and sentient. All matter has its spiritual essence.[13]

These animistic spirits have abilities to act, with feeling and reason, like living people. The sun is recognized and revered in this animistic pattern. The ceremonial calendar is regulated by the sun's behavior. The sun is traditionally greeted at dawn with a prayer and a sprinkling of corn meal.

Animism is extended to the birds and animals. The water serpent, the bear and the badger are associated with curing. Animals may also cause sickness; they may cause fright which will cause sickness. Parsons mentions other animals that figure prominently in rites, beliefs, and mythology, including snakes, ants, lice, beetles, locusts, spiders, coyotes, and buffaloes.[14]

For the Dakota Indian, man's relationship to the spiritual world is expressed in his concept of animism:

> The world and everything in it possessed a living, dynamic force for good and/or evil. Man and every species of plants and animals, mountains, lakes and rivers, celestial bodies, thunder and lightning, sun and earth, and the four winds possessed this mysterious force which waxes and waned at special seasons and for certain events and which was predictable in some cases and promiscuous in others. The world of spirits completed and imitated the circles of nature and kinship.[15]

Naquima's father illustrates the meaning of animism in the daily life of the people when he tells Naquima:

> We must not kill any more than we need. And we must ask the animal people to forgive us and not be too angry, because we kill only to live. Just the same as you and your mother asked the plant people to forgive you when you picked weeds for weaving.[16]

Talayesva describes one of his experiences with the snake which he believed had supernatural power:

> One day, while I was working in the field, it rained. Since it was nearly noon, I went to my father's field house and lay down to eat my lunch. Glancing to my left I saw a snake coiled with raised head. He looked straight into my eyes and stuck out his tongue several times. I remained very still, thinking hard and prayerfully. When it stopped raining, the snake crawled to me, touched the toe of my shoe, and drew back. He returned, touched my ankle, came up to my knee, and drew back again. He seemed to think for a moment, came a third time, crawled up along my side to my chin, and licked my face and nose. I was frightened and sweating, but tried not to tremble. I spoke to the snake very quietly and in a pleasant voice: 'My Father, I am the son of the snake and the lizard. You have come to examine my heart and learn what kind of

man I am. I am only a common man and not very good or wise. Please do me no harm.' Then the snake coiled partly around my neck and lay still for a moment. I thought to myself, "If this sacred snake wants to harm me, what can I do?' Finally he moved away as if satisfied with me. I was glad that he had come to me, for if my heart had been evil, he would never have been so gentle. I felt that this was the work of my Guardian Spirit, and that I was safe in his hands. I remembered how I had once raised a stone to kill a snake that almost choked me, and now I knew that it was my Spirit Guide that changed my mind just in time. I could also remember how when I dug a hole to die in, I was saved at the very edge of my grave. And, of course, I could never forget how the snakes dropped their heads when they saw me on the death journey and how my Guardian Spirit restored me to life and promised to protect me. All these things were proof to me that the ancestral spirits approved of my conduct and wanted me to stay on the Hopi Sun Trail."[17]

Kachinas are masked gods. The Pueblo dancers who wear the masks to impersonate the gods are believed by some to become the gods while they are wearing the masks. The kachina masks have special rain-making powers; they are very sacred, and prayer sticks are set in obeisance to them. The most widely known of the kachina dances open to non-Indians is the Shalako at Zuni, which takes place at the time of the annual winter solstice. It is a fertility ceremony at which new houses constructed during the year are blessed. Masked impersonators dance in the Shalako houses throughout the night.

A fetish is any material object, stone, or prayer stick believed to be the abode of a spirit, and to give its possessor power over the deity. Hence, it is an object to be highly revered. Fetishism among the Pueblos is described by Marinsek.

> Fetishism is an inevitable ingredient of magic. Fetishism is the use of powers believed to be inherent in certain inanimate objects. Fetishes are receptacles of supernatural power used in connection with ritual which may be used to induce the gods and spirits to reward the supplications of man. Almost any object may become a fetish -- a stone, an old arrowhead, a piece of ancient pottery or a perfect ear of corn.

> Fetishes are the most sacrosanct objects in the care of man. Possession of a valuable fetish, not material wealth, is the mark of a wealthy family among the Pueblos. Fetishes must be reverently cared for and fed daily. They are removed only on ceremonial occasions, for such objects are of great power which can be dangerous if mishandled.[18]

The sacred medicine bundle of the priesthood at Zuni is of "indescribable sanctity."[19]

The medicine man, known as the shaman, is a religious practitioner who performs curing rites. His performance would appear to non-Indian as a bag of magic tricks. He can suck out intruded objects causing illness; he can perform sleight of hand, or other types of magic.

Priests are religious practitioners; they gain their status by the knowledge of prayers, chants and long rituals.

Acts of purification, rites of exorcism, and avoidance of taboos all have a part in the Pueblo religious life.

When the Spanish came with the Catholic religion, the Pueblo Indians outwardly seemed to adopt it. They publicly participated in the observance of mass and the administration of the sacraments. However, the final sacrament of Holy Orders -- becoming a member of the clergy -- was never embraced by any Pueblo Indian. This is noteworthy, since it is the policy of the Church to develop native clergy wherever it spreads its doctrine.

Marinsek believes that Indians took great care to see that Catholicism did not penetrate the core of their native religion. (See the statement of the cacique, page 92.)

> The Catholic faith did not replace native Pueblo religion, but merely augmented it. Saints' day celebrations, most notably, were added to the ceremonial calendar. The Spanish Patron Saint was added to the pantheon and in a few cases, Jesus was included as a minor figure. All Souls Day, Christmas, and the Holy Week are duly celebrated. Yet, Catholic practices never made any serious inroads into the core of the native belief. This core of belief is kept scrupulously free of Euro-American influences. Even though the Eastern Pueblo once spoke Spanish fluently, he carefully avoided adaptations of this foreign idiom into his native language. Ritual and ceremony are purged of non-Indian elements of language, custom, etc. On the other hand, Catholic-derived practices are associated with the Spanish language, customs, and even with the system of Spanish-derived officials, the governor and his associates, e.g., fiscal mayor.
>
> Catholic prayers are usually said in Spanish, and use of holy water is restricted to Catholic practices. Typically Spanish fruits, such as watermelons and apples, are appropriate refreshments for neighbors invited in for Catholic prayers. The sowing of wheat, a Spanish-introduced grain, is accompanied by Christian rites, while corn meal offerings are used only in purely native rites. The Spanish-derived celebrations, such as saints' days and All Souls Day, are under the direction of

the once Spanish-imposed officers of the village, the governor and his assistants, while the native ceremonies are under the direction of traditional Pueblo religious leaders. Such compartmentalization has served to preserve the indigenous beliefs through long centuries of outside pressures.[20]

When Waters has Martiniano in his novel speak of the Catholic church in his community, Martiano does so in a derogatory manner:

> On his way to the trading post, Martiniano had passed the little Catholic church in the pueblo. . . . It was merely an empty form by which the Indians were dutifully baptized and buried, though they lived by their own. A tall pointed steeple with a cross, the phallic symbol of the male lustful to conquer. Everywhere this was the white's form of faith.[21]

Some cultural practices of Pueblo Indians have been described by teachers.

Religious Practices

A boy I taught in high school graduated, attended college, and went to work for the Santa Fe Railroad. After he married and had a baby, my wife and I visited him at the pueblo, where he was living with an older sister who had raised him.

His baby was lying in a nice bassinet, strapped to a cradle board. His sister also had a small baby, and it was lying on the bed covered by a baby blanket. When the mother took the blanket off for us to see the baby, we saw several ears of corn beside the child. The Indian belief is that if an evil spirit should come near the baby, it would see the corn and not harm the baby.

Burial Practices

Joe's wife Mary died suddenly from a heart attack while her husband was away in the potato fields. Joe wept unrestrainedly, not only for his loss but because he had been unable to see her again as it is the custom to bury the dead within twenty-four hours (as the sun rises in the morning).

Fear of Witchcraft

Pueblo Indians, not of Taos extraction, are taught never to look a Taos Indian in the eye. It is believed that the Taos Indians, because of their old traditions and way of life, possess a bewitching power in their eyes.

This may account for the social rejection of Taos Indian students by students from other pueblos. I do not know the time range or age of this superstition, but I do know that it is in practice currently.

Witchcraft, Sorcery

When men, women or children have their hair cut, they do not throw the clippings away in the fashion of the Anglo. The hair clippings must be burned. If they are left around or thrown out with the refuse, someone (a devil) may pick them up and take them with him to the underworld where spells will be cast upon them, and sometime soon after, the person to whom the hair belonged will be bewitched. They may become ill, suffer a catastrophe, or in some cases become bald.

FAMILY LIFE

The extended family is the most important social unit among the Pueblo people. Lineage is traced through the mother. The consanguine (blood) relationship is important, while the conjugal (love) relationship is less so. While husbands provide economic support, brothers and fathers provide ritual help. On important religious occasions, married men may return to the homes of their mothers or sisters to participate. [22]

For the woman there is no conflict. Her allegiance is undivided and her position in terms of economic security and social orientation is strong. The man, however, is divided in his allegiance between his mother and sisters on the one hand and his wife on the other. Benedict says:

> For women there is no conflict. They have no allegiance of any kind to their husbands' groups. But for all men there is double allegiance. They are husbands in one group and brothers in another. Certainly in more important families, in those which care for permanent fetishes, a man's allegiance as brother has more social weight than his allegiance as husband. In all families a man's position derives, not, as with us, from his position as breadwinner, but from his role in relation to the sacred objects of the household. The husband, with no such relationship to the ceremonial possessions of his wife's house to trade upon, only gradually attains to position in the household as his children grow to maturity. It is as their father, not as provider or as their mother's husband, that he finally attains some authority in the household where he may have lived for twenty years. [23]

Man's status, and he does acquire status, derives from his preoccupation with rituals, fetishes, religious objects, and participation in ceremonies. These are most important; more mundane affairs can be handled by the women.

Children are loved and fondled by all the members of the extended family. All observers are in agreement that permissiveness of adults to infants exists to a noticeable degree. Weaning and toilet training are relaxed and unhurried. Frustrations are minimized. The child has no fixed or imposed schedules for eating or sleeping. Schroeder recently found in one Pueblo that there is a change in childrearing practices among those mothers who had attended secondary schools outside the Pueblo. The change is toward making greater demands on the children to conform to the practices in the dominant culture.[24]

A teacher reports:

Zuni parents never strike their children. When children misbehave, they are threatened with the "boogie-man," who is especially assigned by the tribe for this task.

As the child grows older, he is constantly reminded to conform to pueblo ideals. Shame and fear become his primary agents in this educational process. The bogey man who lives on the mesa, the owl that can pick out his eyes, snakes that can bite or strangle, or just Navajos who might catch him -- all these can persuade a young child to conform.

Pettitt describes the bogey man who appears periodically in the Zuni village to frighten children and to assure them that their behavior is being constantly evaluated.

The A'doshle have bulging eyes, protruding teeth, and a mat of tangled hair. The husband of each pair carries a huge knife with which to cut off heads, and the wife bears a huge basket in which to carry off the children and a large crooked stick with which to catch them. At the time of the annual ceremony they make a perfunctuary dance and then begin to search for bad children, of whom they have, presumably, been notified in advance. The parents of the bad children make apparently herculean efforts to repel the terrible A'doshle. They barricade the door of the house, and beat drums and pans. In recent years they have carried the mummery to the point of firing guns over the heads of the A'doshle. But all of this is of no avail. The A'doshle are supernaturals. They break through the barricade -- thereby demonstrating to the children that punishment for misbehavior is as inevitable as the rising of the sun. The old woman with the crooked stick puts it around the bad girls and drags them over to a metate to grind them up. The old man whirls his knife in the face of bad boys. There is a threat in reserve that they will eat up bad children. They go so far as to bite the child in the neck. The elders of the family add to the dramatic effect by evincing great fear themselves. To demonstrate further that this discipline comes from the outside, the A'dishle frequently lecture to parents, sometimes seriously if one happens to be lazy or otherwise remiss. Only when the visiting disciplinarians have been bought off with presents of meat and meal will they consent to forego more drastic punishment. Meanwhile the shouting has been listened to by neighboring children from the darkest corners of their respective homes.[25]

Another teacher reports:

We happened into Cochiti Pueblo one recent Sunday morning as the River Men Ritual was coming to a close. This is the annual disciplining of the children who have been naughty, which seemed to include all of them under the age of five. Six men in black raincoats and rough gunny-sack masks, carrying whips, had been scouring the village, in and out of all the houses, all morning, and wide-eyed small children scurried around corners to avoid them. When they caught a child, they snatched him up screaming and ran away. At his first shriek, his mother and perhaps a grandmother or aunt, had burst from his house like antelopes and they quickly ran down the River Men and rescued the child. One little unfortunate was apparently too far from home for his mother to keep up with events, for nobody ran after him. Upon grasping this circumstance, the River Men set him down and sternly encircled him while he did a little dance, quakingly, then released him.

This is one Indian ritual I had felt I would not choose to witness, shrinking, like most of my kind, from the thought of frightening children with bogymen. However, although the fright of the children is real, the whole occasion is less abhorrent than it sounds because of the great good-natured and kindly atmosphere accompanying it -- a spirit of "This will soon be over and you will be better for it." This is not to say I approve, but I do not consider myself so great a success in parental discipline as to say it is entirely wrong to have the punishing come from outside.

Naquima recalls the time he was not "good" and the Katchinas found out. His father comes as a Katchina with a heavy, menacing voice and an ugly mask. The Katchina says in Naquima's hearing: "We always eat the bad Hopi children." After frightening the child considerably, the mother says:

> Please, Katchina, he will be good. I promise you. His Uncle will see that he is. He didn't mean to be a bad boy, and he won't be any more. Take this food, and leave Naquima with us, please![26]

Dozier reports the memories of an adult Tewa living in Hano about the Hopi bogeyman, Soyoku, who comes to punish all the bad children:

> When I was a little boy I wished that our house would be the first one to be visited by the Sokoyu. But this never happened, for we lived almost at the other end of the village. As I heard the Sokoyu coming nearer and nearer, the perspiration would start running all over me. Some children cried, but I just tightened up and felt like I was going to die. My aunt (kiyu, father's sisters) always came to tell me that the Sokoyu would not carry me away, but my mother would say that I was very bad and that she didn't care if the Soyoku took me. When the Sokoyu arrived, my aunts would fight with them to keep them away from me. My mother would bring corn meal and meat to give to the Sokoyu, and she would say to me: "See how bad you've been, I have to give them all the food we have so they won't take you." That would make me feel very bad, for I felt that I was responsible for my mother giving all the food away. I would then run to my mother and grasp her dress crying: "Don't let them take me; I will be a good boy; I will work hard and get back all the food you've given to the Sokoyu." Even after I was initiated and knew that the Sokoyu were just ordinary people I would get frightened when I heard the noises they made.[27]

> I dreaded to take the part of the Giant Nataska to frighten my nieces, nephews, and other children to make them behave. But Ira and I were requested to do this because we were the tallest men in Oraibi. The frightful mask was so large that my whole face would fit into the long bill with its jagged teeth. I painted my face black so that no child would be able to recognize me, and when we came into the village, I was very careful not to touch anyone in reaching for his gifts of meat and other food. As I leaped at one little boy and grabbed his piece of meat, I peeped through the teeth of my mask, saw him trembling with fear, and felt tears running down my own cheeks.[28]

Attitudes toward sex is one of the problems which teachers may find difficult to rationalize. Bunzel has said that the only sphere in which the individual acts individually rather than as a member of the group is in that of sex, and, interestingly enough, this sphere of life is of but passing importance to the group-minded Pueblo Indian.[29]

The facts of sexual intercourse are apparently understood from very early ages. The young children observe the sex act done by animals and discuss it freely. One non-Indian observer reported that two children only five or six were observed in attempting the sex act. Premarital sex experience is common in all Indian villages. Smith and Roberts state that it is so generally engaged in that it seems to be a normal element of the courtship period.[30] Teachers report the following incidents:

> My gardener, Joe, is from San Felipe. He has two daughters. The younger, although unmarried, has a charming baby girl. However, when she was ready to come home from the County-Indian Hospital, the boy's parents and sister came after her because it was their grandchild. The christening festivities were very impressive and in time the girl may marry the boy. Her sister had her first two children before she married her husband.
>
> . . . . .
>
> To Indians, every individual is important. Occasionally, a high school girl becomes pregnant. She is out of school a short time, during delivery, but returns and continues as usual. In fact, the other Indians are very protective at this time. A husband is found for this girl. It is usually the father of the child, but if he is not available, it will be someone else.
>
> . . . . .
>
> Among the Zunis, pornography and vulgar language is very common, even among third graders. Since this is accepted by the culture, it is difficult for the teacher to teach otherwise.
>
> . . . . .

In the Anglo way of thinking, there are many "illegitimate" births. Illegitimacy is not understood in Pueblo culture, however, as it is in Anglo society. It has been said that the Indians have no word, no concept, in their language for illegitimacy. Children, once born into extended families are loved and cherished and there is no stigma. As reported in Chapter 3, the bastard child is considered to be stolen from his father's people -- quite the opposite attitude from Anglo-oriented persons.[31] While no guilt results from either illicit sex experiences or from illegitimate children, they do present problems of an economic nature.

Anthropologists report many practices from other cultures that may surprise conservative American teachers:

> In Samoa, sex is considered natural and pleasurable. The young Samoan may experiment freely with different sexual practices, only incest being prohibited. Indeed, the Samoan girl often postpones marriage in order to prolong the sexual freedom of adolescence. Sexual deviations, which lead in this country to neuroses because of the moral and social stigma they carry, in Samoa carry no appreciable stigma whatever.[32]

The attitude toward twins is reported by one teacher:

> The village where I was teaching was one of the largest Pueblo villages. The following incident brought to my attention the fact that we had only one set of twins in all our school records.
>
> Ruth, an Indian lady about forty years of age, was a very good friend of mine. I knew she was expecting a baby, so of course, I asked one of her sons who was in my classroom if mama had had her baby yet. Readily he answered "No," until the time of the event. Then he became very evasive and unwilling to answer. So, I decided to go see Ruth, thinking perhaps the child had died. However, I found that Ruth had given birth to twin sons, but she hastened to assure me that only one baby was for her and her husband; the other child was intended for Joe's sister who had had only one child and could have no more. At less than one month, the second son went to live with Joe's sister, who became his mother. His recorded name was Joe's sister's name, and to this day the children are referred to as separate children -- never as twins. They are now six years old and are cousins -- not brothers. It is a curse to have twins, according to old cultural belief here.

. . . . .

There are many references to the occasion of multiple births in the literature. It is often stated that the father of twins believes that this can happen only if the wife is unfaithful, and that two men would be necessary to father two children. Discussion with several informants concerning the birth of twins indicates that this belief is no longer held by most people, and this writer is of the opinion that Indians look with favor upon twins.

Coolidge recorded, in 1930, among the Navajo:

"Twins are regarded as a gift of the gods."[33]

STATUS AND PRESTIGE

The most important individual in the pueblo is the cacique. He holds office for life; he is honored and respected as the spiritual head of the village. He presides over all the important ceremonies.

While industry and thrift are culturally desirable, too much accumulation of goods or hoarding is despised. Little emphasis is placed on acquisition. The sponsoring of a Shalako house at the annual ceremony is a method of re-distributing the wealth of an individual family. The sponsor of the Shalako house undertakes the whole responsibility without personal recognition.

Aggressive behavior toward acquiring tribal office is disparaged. If a person were openly to seek such power, he would likely be charged with witchcraft. Modesty is a Pueblo virtue. Respect and veneration of the old is a cultivated value. Children are taught early to show deference and respect.

The Pueblo Indians look reverently to the past. They believe that the "good things" are those that have been tried and proved; these do not need to change. Keeping old men in power, who look to the past for making judgments, their roots in the traditions, leads to ultra-conservatism. This conservatism helps to insure conformity and is preserved to the extent that the people insist on unanimity.

Following in the ways of the old people becomes a primary value. Teachers report the following:

> John was a very dirty little boy -- very slow, even to the stage of being called "lazy" -- but with beautiful, expressive eyes and such a winning smile, when he did smile. John was over-age and educationally retarded, even in second grade. His attendance pattern was terrible -- absent a half day, or would arrive an hour or more late. Many home visits did not improve the situation and discreet inquiry in the village gave no clue as to why this was occurring. John's father talked good English and assured me he wanted John to have an education.
>
> After about five months, a serious accident resulted in my being called to the village by the medicine man (the messenger said). I went, and the medicine man was John's father. After this, I learned why John's attendance was as it was. He was gathering herbs -- they must be gathered at the right time. When it is time for a ceremony, and many come up unexpectedly, John had to be there. Through much talking, and much more silent sitting, the situation was improved, but not cured.

. . . . .

The Pueblo Indians hold crops and supplies of food in a common storehouse. It is expected of each man in the Pueblo to do his proportionate share of the work in the preparation and raising of the crops grown on the land. It is required that each Indian that is employed off the Pueblo do his share of the work in cleaning ditches. Many want to hire others to do their share, but this is frowned upon by the Tribal Council, and oftimes it is demanded that the one employing another to do his work is fined for not doing it himself. By requiring each one to return to the Pueblo and do his required tasks, he is kept in closer contact with the Pueblo and its traditions.

. . . . .

Even little children know better than to tell the "white man" about anything that is happening in the village. They do not reveal any advance information about dancing, and, should they be so inclined to tell, the school Indian custodian is always around to see that they do not do so. However, one day little Serafin, a very pert, lively youngster who was often absent, came early in the morning and followed me around in my room and finally stood by my desk when I sat down. "Do you want something special, Serafin," I asked. After much squirming, he finally whispered, "Today we dance. I am going to be an Indian." Can you imagine how surprised I was at this statement? "May I come, Serafin?" I asked, and he whispered, "Yes." Sure enough, at one o'clock, the Governor came to tell us that we would have no children -- they were dancing -- and we could come and observe. I could hardly wait to see what part Serafin would be as an Indian.

Some of the dancers carried the usual branches; some were deer or hunters, or other animals. Serafin was in the group of singers; he was an Indian!

. . . . .

Anonymity is the preferred trait; carrying one's individuality too far is scrupulously avoided. Life is rigidly routinized, formal, and ritualistic. The ideal man is the one who adheres most meticulously to the traditional pattern. Hill says of conformity:

> . . . conformity represented a summation of all values and all desirable personality traits. A conformist was one who conducted life's activities according to the traditional pattern and implemented them by expressions of personality which fall within the approved boundaries of the culture. To say a man was a conformist was in the Santa Clara sense to say he had integrity. The stress placed upon this concept elevates it to the position of the most all-pervading theme in Santa Clara culture.[34]

The Pueblo Indians seek consensus. "Let us move evenly together" expresses the cultural ideal of unanimity. The ideal is that of complete agreement. Tranquility, industry, generosity, and courtesy are values esteemed in the Pueblo culture.

Teachers report:

> Indians do not usually admire too much forwardness or aggressiveness, especially in public or before the public. Some years ago, several Hopi girls were talking about another Hopi girl who was usually very active in school life -- more so than many of the others. One girl said to the others, "She has too much vitamin I."

. . . . .

Difficulties are encountered in organization. When dues are set by a majority vote, those not voting feel no obligation to pay because it was not unanimous.

THE TASK OF EDUCATION

The adults of many of the villages are shifting rapidly to a wage economy. The overt manifestation of this change appears in the material possessions. Cars and pick-up trucks are everywhere in evidence; TV antennae are readily observable; electrification of villages has occurred; even the advantages of modern plumbing may be found in individual homes.

One reservation has yielded great deposits of uranium, and the ore is being developed under contract with the tribe. The royalties are amassing millions of dollars for the tribal treasury and affording employment for many of the men. This pueblo has shifted almost exclusively to a wage economy.

Over half of the adult employable population in several of the villages are commuting to urban areas daily to work, usually at unskilled jobs. The old people react to this by saying: "Those young people don't want to work in the fields. We have talked to them. They don't listen to the old people anymore."

Should this be interpreted to mean that Pueblo people are ready to give up their language, eradicate their customs, and prepare to move into the mainstream of urban American life? The answer is that most Pueblo Indians are probably toying with both cultures and wish to choose the economic advantages of the Anglo and to keep the traditional past.

The acquiring of the artifacts of the dominant culture has, up to now, been of little consequence in measuring "inner feelings" of the Indian. Rapid cultural change should not be adjuged to be taking place.

Vogt says:

> . . . . it is now clear that just because Zuni Indians, for example, build more modern type houses with running water and electric lights, invest in radios and refrigerators, and drive new automobiles, it does not mean that they necessarily abandon their kinship obligations or give up dancing in Katchina dances. Indeed it has been startling to many of us to observe how completely the inventories of material culture in Indian households are composed of items derived from white American culture, and, yet, how relatively slow the rate of change is in social organization and religion in the same community.[35]

The greatest need for teachers of Indian children is an understanding of the background out of which the child comes to the school. The teachings of the family, the school, and the church in the American culture have not prepared most teachers for these Indian children. The social distance between the Indian pupil and his middle-class teacher is an immense one. It may be difficult not to make invidious comparisons between the child's "normal" behavior pattern and the expected practice in the teacher's childhood. A blaming kind of attitude toward a pregnant Pueblo school girl, for example, may not be helpful if the pregnancy is already a fact and the parents accept it without alarm.

A principal of an elementary school enrolling non-Pueblo Indians called on the father of a thirteen-year-old girl who was pregnant. The principal explained that the girl should stop coming to school until after the baby came. In his search for how the Indian father might feel about the situation, all he learned was that the parents of the girl felt they needed do nothing even though they knew which boy fathered the child. They expressed only surprise that the children were old enough that they could have a baby!

The contrast between the child and the teacher's backgrounds is summarized in Table XIII.

TABLE XIII

Anglo-Pueblo Cultural Values in Conflict

Traditional Pueblo Culture Places Great Value on:	Middle-Class Anglo Teacher Is Sure to Place Great Value on:
Harmony with nature.	Mastery over nature. "I am the master of my fate, I am the conqueror of my soul."
Present time orientation.	Future time orientation.
Explanation of natural phenomena: Mythology, fear of supernatural, witches, sorcerers.	There has to be a scientific explanation for everything. Nothing happens contrary to natural law.
Level of aspiration: Follow in the ways of the old people.	Climb the ladder of success. Each man is expected to achieve at a level higher than his father achieved.
Cooperation.	Competition.
Anonymity.	Individuality.
Submissiveness.	Aggression (socially acceptable).
Work to satisfy present need.	Work to "get ahead."
Sharing wealth.	Saving for the future.
"Time is always with us" (Indian time)	"Clock watching." "Time lost can never be regained."
Humility.	Win first prize if at all possible.
Win once; let others win.	Win all the time.

The problem of the young Indian faced with choosing between the two cultures - that of his family and that of the modern school, has been ably described by both Indians and Non-Indian writers.

The experience of Tulto (Sun Elk), a young Taos Indian who went to the Carlisle Indian School, is recorded by Embree in Indians of the Americas.[36] Tulto describes his happy childhood: riding horses, herding the cattle, playing the usual boys games, and learning to hunt rabbits, and deer.

In seven years at Carlisle, Tulto learned to be a type setter in a print shop. He was taught that Indian ways were bad and that he must get civilized. Back at the Pueblo after seven years, he was very happy to be reunited with his family. But the old chiefs were not happy to have him come back. They told Tulto's father:

> Your son who calls himself Rafael has lived with the white men. He has been far away from the pueblo. He has not lived in the kiva nor learned the things that Indian boys should learn. He has no hair. He has no blankets. He cannot even speak our language and he has a strange smell. He is not one of us.[37]

Tulto left the pueblo and worked for a time as a printer, then in blacksmith shops and on farms. But he was not very happy so he returned to Taos. His father shared his land with him and he built himself a house outside the pueblo. He married a Taos girl.

> When we were married I became an Indian again. I let my hair grow, I put on blankets, and I cut the seat out of my pants.[38]

Polingaysi Qoyawayma is a Hopi woman who has recorded many of the conflicts in her attemps at a bicultural adjustment in her autobiography No Turning Back.[39] Her curiosity to learn more about the white man's world, to participate in that world, and to combine the best of the two cultures made her life as a teacher in government schools a continual struggle. She wanted to reject the simple artifacts and symbolism of her Hopi religion and in return she endured rejection from both her own people and from many of the non-Indians to whom she looked for understanding and acceptance. She could not dismiss the teachings of her elders which had given her the dignity, and the values that were her whole life:

> A true Hopi is a part of the universe and must keep himself in balance, she had been told. All things, animate and inanimate, have life and being. A true Hopi tries to be aware of the deep spiritual essence that is at the heart of all things. All things have inner meaning and form and power. The Hopi must reach into nature and help it to move forward in

its cycles, harmoniously and beautifully.

She had been taught to be helpful and generous. She knew the Hopi idea of responsibility to oneself. One's family, clan, community, and race. To be in harmony with the true Hopi way would help all people, she had learned early in life.

> When you make your morning prayers, breathe a wish that your life will be good. Those who have something good to live by want to live a long life. Those who are happy sing. Sing as you run to your gardens at dawn. Sing as you work in the sunshine. Do not allow anger to poison you. Thoughts of anger toward another open ways into the angry one's life through which bad influences find their way.

It was a beautiful way of thinking . . . .

Martiniano in The Man Who Killed the Deer[40] returns from his years at the white man's school and is angered by his people when he is asked to cut the heels off his shoes and to cut the seat out of his trousers. He lives outside the pueblo, refuses for a time to participate in the dances, and marries a girl whom he met at the boarding school. Yet, when he and Flowers Playing do have a son, Martiniano realizes that he must be permitted to join the kiva and really be an integral part of his people.

> One must not forget one's beginning, thought Martiniano. And that was why he had consented to the adoption of his son into a kiva, with Palemon for the boy's godfather, his preceptor. Times were changing, and his son should know something of the old before he was confronted with the new.

CASE STUDY REPORT[41]

Educators of ethnic groups must have an adequate background and understanding of the particular ethnic group with which they are dealing, so that judgment and discretion may be exercised when directing cultural change.

In order to illustrate some of the problems which directed culture change (education-acculturation) have produced, by overlooking one or two of the interdependent facets, when the culture change was aimed solely in one direction, a questionnaire was given to a sixteen-year-old Pueblo Indian girl. This girl has attended the Pueblo day school, a public school in a nearby town, and a Catholic boarding school in Santa Fe. This fall she will enter the tenth grade at a school which, at present, is undetermined. It is strongly felt that this girl is a representative example of her peer group in her Pueblo. She will be called Lilly in this report.

Lilly's parents received their education in government schools. Her mother has a sixth-grade education. Lilly's father, a veteran of World War II, is a high school graduate. He is employed by the county public schools and does maintenance work. The family lives in a home on the periphery of the village; however, they also own a home within the village which they occupy only on weekends and on ceremonial occasions. There are seven children in the family, three girls and four boys. Lilly, who is sixteen, is the oldest. The youngest child is eighteen months old.

Lilly's parents practice both Catholicism and the traditional Pueblo religion. Their behavior indicates that their Catholicism is well compartmentalized, and that their true beliefs and values are founded in the native religion of their village which they learned when they were youngsters. They are attempting to instill in their children the same systems of behavior, belief, and value which they believe they possess.

It is difficult to assess the degree of their awareness of the part which they are playing in the continual state of culture change. Nevertheless, the fact remains that even though they now live on the periphery of the village and take part in the wage-economy, they still retain their traditional beliefs and values despite the alteration of some behavior patterns.

The following questions and answers included in the questionnaire serve well to illustrate how a change in belief has caused a change in behavior patterns and values.

Question:

List as many things as you can, that you have been taught in school, which you think are O.K. or acceptable to you, but which your parents have found fault, or do not agree, with. State whether your parents disagree because these things you have learned are against their old traditions, and if so, what their traditions are.

Answer:

In school, I learned that we can't have two gods. Our old traditions tell us that we have to believe in our false gods or "rain gods." Our Catholic religion forbids us to believe in false gods. I think it is much better if you don't have too many gods to believe in. So I would tell my parents that our old tradition of believing in the "rain gods" is not real, but just a superstition among us Indians. When I tell them this, they always raise a fuss with me and say that the "gods" will come and punish me. I don't believe in the "rain gods." I would rather die and be a martyr, and die for my faith in the real God. I would much rather choose my own religion which I learn in school, rather than the "fake" religion I'm taught to believe in at home.

Analysis: Belief-directed change. Lilly's answer points out the conflicts which developed between the child and the parents in regard to religion. Not only does a conflict in religion result, but an antagonism between the parents and the child regarding other relationships in the home environment. Values are affected in that the child no longer has regard or esteem for the old customs and traditions of the Pueblo, which the parents hold in high regard. Behavior is influenced or affected because the child no longer feels the need to adhere to parental direction, or a need to respect the beliefs of the parents. The child stops participating in ceremonies and dances. This is also shown in the following statement made by Lilly:

> When I am away from my parents or grownups, and with my friends, we like to go for rides with boys. Sometimes, if the boys have money, they treat us to beer and cigarettes. Then we have all kinds of fun.
>
> When I came home once after drinking and smoking, my parents took me to see the governor. He really talked to me. But I don't care because he is just a silly man. He scolded me for not dancing anymore and said I was doing wrong things against the gods. I think that my God is better because he forgives me for doing wrong things. I can drink and smoke as much as I want because it always turns out O.K. I don't get talked to in front of everybody either.
>
> When I am at home I get in trouble with my parents because of the darn old traditions. Some of my friends go out on dates at an earlier age. Our tradition tells us that young girls are not supposed to be out on dates because our ancestors weren't wild like today's youngsters. If they see you talking to a boy, they get crazy ideas in their stupid minds and think awful things about you.

The effect that a change in value has had upon belief and behavior patterns is illustrated in the following question and answer.

Question:

If you had a chance to choose between the following, which would you choose: Living in the Pueblo or in a city like Albuquerque or Santa Fe; give the reasons for your choice.

Answer:

I would rather live in a city so that I could have all the modern equipment and a nice house. Our governor does not allow us to have certain things. Since this is a free country, I can just choose what I want to be and what I want to do.

Analysis: Value-directed change. Lilly, as illustrated in her remark, values independence, whereas the traditional Pueblo culture is based on dependence. This change in value has influenced her behavior in that she prefers the city and would rather live outside the Pueblo. She shows a marked lack of respect for authority.

Education of ethnic minorities (Indians) includes a process of directed behavior change. One purpose of this process is to alter the introvert characteristic of the minority group, in this case the Pueblo Indian, and replace it with outgoing, aggressive behavior. It is essential to produce this change in order to equip these individuals with a behavior pattern which will fit into the Anglo scheme of things. The need for this will be readily seen upon consideration of the following comparisons: The Pueblo Indian strives to follow in the ways of the old people; the Anglo strives to climb the ladder of success. The Pueblo Indian wins once, and then lets the others win; the Anglo wins all the time he can. The Pueblo Indian prefers to remain in the background (anonymity); the Anglo strives for individuality.

Through personal contact and by direct observation of Lilly, over the past seven years, the following changes in behavior patterns have been observed.

1952-1953

First contact was made when Lilly was nine years old and was attending school in the village. She was very shy, and her behavior was that of the classic pueblo type. After six visits to her home, over a period of four months, she began to accept me as a friend.

1955

Lilly was twelve years old. After attending public school in the nearby town for four months, there was a marked change in her behavior. Lilly was now openly looking for recognition. She no longer hid her face or appeared embarrassed, and she seemed to enjoy telling me about her experiences at school. She was reluctant to discuss "boyfriends" and would giggle at the mere mention of boys. She took great pleasure in displaying and wearing the turquoise and silver jewelry that her father had made for her.

1957

Lilly had just become fourteen and was preparing to leave the Pueblo to attend boarding school in Santa Fe. She confessed that she did not want to go and that she would rather stay at home with her parents, who were still living in the village. The knowledge that five other girls her age were also starting to the same school in Santa Fe was some consolation to her.

Before leaving for school, she voluntarily participated in the August Corn Dance.

1960

Lilly is now sixteen years old. She will enter the tenth grade this September. Her parents will not allow her to return to the Catholic boarding school in Santa Fe due to conflicts involving Lilly's violations of old traditions. At present, a new school has not been chosen. In the last two years, she has danced in the village only once, at which time, her parents paid her the sum of $3.00 for participating. She no longer wears or displays her Indian jewelry. She prefers to wear "dog-chains" and "ID bracelets." She proudly displays a "broken-heart" necklace which she won for her dancing ability in a "rock-n-roll" contest on a local television program.

When in the company of fellow Indian students, who are members of her peer group, her behavior is overt, and at times she displays many aggressive tendencies. She makes friends quickly with Anglo youngsters of her own age group, and, at the earliest conversational opportunity, in a blasé manner, tells stories which point out how "fake" and "meaningless" the traditions of the Pueblo peoples appear to her.

She expresses her desires to attend Anglo social functions or gatherings; however, once she finds herself in the middle of such gatherings, she becomes shy and retiring and prefers to leave the room or go off in a corner by herself. She admits that at times she is stricken with strong guilt feelings. She has also admitted that she just doesn't seem to fit in anywhere.

For any given culture, an individual's behavior and sense of value is based upon his traditions, customs, and world view.

> World view may be used to include the forms of thought and attitudes toward life. . . . But if there is an emphasized meaning in the phrase "world view," I think it is in the suggestion it carries of the structure of things as man is aware of them. It is in the way we see ourselves in relation to all else. Every world view is a stage set. On that stage, myself is an important character; in every world view there is an "I" from which the view is taken. On the stage the other people, toward whom the view is directed. And man, as a collective character, is upon the stage; he may speak his lines very loudly, or he may be seen as having but a minor part among other parts.[42]

Having given up old behavior patterns, which are functions of the old, traditional world view, the individual must adopt the behavior patterns of the new culture. Correspondingly, he must adopt the world view of the new culture. The new behavior patterns are learned and adopted more readily than the new world view. Hence, due to the time lag between adoption of the new behavior patterns and the new world view, there is a period during which the individual has no world view upon which his sense of values or his beliefs may be based. Therefore, it becomes necessary for him to seek an adjustment of his own. This adjustment may or may not be acceptable to either culture group.

> If a man does away with his traditional way of living and throws away his good customs, he had better first make certain that he has something of value to replace them.[43]

FOOTNOTES

[1] Ruth Underhill, First Penthouse Dwellers of America, Second Edition (Santa Fe, New Mexico: Laboratory of Anthropology, 1945), p. 110.

[2] Elsie Clews Parsons, Hopi and Zuni Ceremonialism, (Menasha, Wisconsin: The American Anthropological Association, 1933), p. 210.

[3] A Hopi informant, 1959.

[4] National Park Service, The Trail to Frijoles Ruins, (Box 1562, Gila Pueblo, Globe, Arizona 85501: Southwestern Monuments Association, 1966), pp. 11-16.

[5] Four Corners is the point at which the four states, Arizona, New Mexico, Colorado, and Utah meet. Mesa Verde National Monument is located near this point.

[6] Edward P. Dozier, "Rio Grande Pubelos," in Perspectives in American Indian Culture Change, Edward H. Spicer, editor (Chicago: University of Chicago Press, 1961), pp. 94-95.

[7] Ibid., p. 96.

[8] The reader is directed to Felix S. Cohen, Handbook of Federal Law (Washington: Government Printing Office, 1942), for reading in detail about legal relationships between Indians and the Government.

[9] Ibid., p. 393.

[10] Bertha P. Dutton, Pocket Handbook of New Mexico Indians (Santa Fe, New Mexico: New Mexico Association on Indian Affairs, 1955), p. 3.

[11] Edward Marinsek, "The Effect of Cultural Difference in the Education of Pueblo Indian Children," (Unpublished monograph, College of Education, The University of New Mexico, Albuquerque, 1958), p. 18. (Mimeographed.)

[12] Ruth Benedict, Patterns of Culture (Boston: Houghton, Mifflin and Co., 1934), p. 58, citing Ruth Bunzel.

[13] Ruth Bunzel, "Introduction to Zuni Ceremonialism," Forty-Seventh Annual Report of the Bureau of American Ethnology (Washington: Government Printing Office, 1932), p. 483.

[14] Parsons, op. cit., p. 194.

[15] Malan, Vernon D., "The Value System of the Dakota Indians," Journal of American Indian Education, 3:24, No. 1, October, 1963.

[16] Walter Goldschmidt, editor, Ways of Mankind (Boston: The Beacon Press, 1954, p. 58. "Desert Soliloquy" written by Len Peterson.

[17] Simmons, Leo W., Sun Chief, the Autobiography of a Hopi Indian, (New Haven: Yale University Press, 1942), pp. 206-207.

[18] Marinsek, op. cit., p. 25.

[19] Bunzel, op. cit., pp. 473-554.

[20] Marinsek, op. cit., pp. 34-35, summarizing from Edward H. Spicer, "Spanish-Indian Acculturation in the Southwest," American Anthropologist, 56:681, 1954; and from E. L. Hewitt and B. P. Dutton, Pueblo Indian World (Albuquerque: University of New Mexico Press, 1945), p. 99.

[21] Frank Waters, The Man Who Killed the Deer (Denver: Alan Swallow, 1942), p. 79.

[22] Fred Eggan, Social Organization of the Western Pueblos (Chicago: University of Chicago Press, 1950), p. 298.

[23] Benedict, op. cit., pp. 69-70.

[24] Florence Margaret Schroeder, "An Exploratory Study of Beliefs and Practices of Jemez Pueblo Indians of New Mexico Pertaining to Child Rearing in the Pre-School Years in Relation to the Educational Status of the Mother," (Unpublished doctoral dissertation, New York University, New York City, 1960).

[25] George A. Pettitt, Primitive Education in North America (Berkeley: University of California Press, 1946), p. 34.

[26] Peterson, Len, "Desert Soliloquy," in Ways of Mankind, Walter Goldschmidt, editor, (Boston: The Beacon Press, 1954), pp. 56-57.

[27] Dozier, Edward P., Hano: A Tewa Indian Community in Arizona, (New York: Holt, Rinehart and Winston, 1966), p. 69.

[28] Simmons, Leo W., Sun Chief, the Autobiography of a Hopi Indian, (New Haven: Yale University Press, 1942), p. 295.

[29] Bunzel, op. cit., p. 476.

[30] Watson Smith and John M. Roberts, Zuni Law: A Field of Values (Cambridge: Peabody Museum Papers), 43:64, No. 1, 1954.

[31] Parsons, op. cit., p. 43.

[32] Kneller, George F., Educational Anthropology, An Introduction, (New York: John Wiley and Sons, 1965), pp. 100-101.

[33] Coolidge, Dane, and Mary Roberts Coolidge, The Navajo Indians, (Boston: Houghton Mifflin Company, 1930), p. 54.

[34] W. W. Hill, "Santa Clara Pueblo" (Unpublished manuscript, University of New Mexico, Albuquerque), p. 323.

[35] Evon S. Vogt "The Accultrration of American Indians," The Annuals of the American Academy of Political and Social Science, May, 1957, p. 138.

[36] Embree, Edwin R., Indians of the Americas, (Boston: Houghton Mifflin Co., 1939), pp. 223-234.

[37] Ibid., pp. 229-230.

[38] Ibid., p. 231.

[39] Qoyawayma, Polingaysi (Elizabeth Q. White) as told to Vada F. Carlson, No Turning Back, (Albuquerque: University of New Mexico Press, 1964), pp. 128-129.

[40] Waters, Frank, The Man Who Killed the Deer, (2679 So. York St., Denver 10, Colorado: Alan Swallow, 1942), pp. 309-310.

[41] This case study report of a sixteen-year-old Pueblo Indian girl in acculturation-education conflict was reported by Maryanne Atherton Danfelser, July, 1960.

[42] Robert Redfield, The Primitive World and Its Transformations (Ithaca: Cornell University Press, 1953), p. 86.

[43] Robert Ruark, Something of Value (New York: Doubleday and Company, Inc., 1955), p. ix.

CHAPTER 8

Foundations for Education of Spanish American Children

INTRODUCTION

Writing in 1940, Sanchez summarized the status of formal education among the Spanish Americans in New Mexico with these facts: of almost 60,000 Spanish-speaking children enrolled in school, more than half were in the first three grades; over one-third of this school enrollment was found in the first grade; in every grade beyond the first, more than 55 per cent of the children were more than two years overage in grade; while the Spanish-speaking children constituted half of the public school enrollment, they made up less than one-fifth of the enrollment in the twelfth grade.[1]

It will be difficult for today's teachers to appreciate fully the extent to which large segments of this total population were illiterate in English as recently as three or four decades ago. Tireman and Sanchez worked as pioneers in the attempt to alleviate this crisis in educational level of the state. The San José and Nambe experiments showed children in the schools to be severely handicapped in adjusting to the narrow, inflexible middle-class life style of the public school.[2,3] These barriers, manifested in basic cultural differences, are overtly most apparent in language and experience differences.

Sanchez explains causal factors from the point of view of the traditional culture of the people in this way:

> In this frontier situation there was little need for formal education. The priests and parents drilled children in Church doctrine. Sometimes the local scribe or priest was employed by a family or two to give instruction in reading, writing and counting to the children for a few weeks a year. Literacy was the exception rather than the rule. There was little to read, only an occasional agreement to sign, communications were by word of mouth, and letters were rare. The counting that was needed could be carried by tallies. Weights and measurements were approximate as there was no need for arithmetic refinement. Though, in rare instances, a leading family

might send a son to school in far-off Mexico, the priesthood offered the only career in which such training was warranted. The duties of public office required but little more education than was needed in ordinary affairs. It is understandable, then, that the people should have little interest in education and should place no great importance on book learning. Formal schooling did not fit into the culture and economy of the colony.[4]

This situation does not prevail today. Nevertheless, the processes of cultural change evolve slowly, and no situation as grave as this can be overlooked in attempting to put present-day problems in historical perspective.

Loomis, when he returned to El Cerrito in 1956 after having made a thorough study of contemporary life in a rural, agrarian Spanish American village in 1940, found only minor changes had taken place in the thinking of the people who still resided in El Cerrito.[5]

The Indian Research Study revealed that school achievement results, during the period 1957-1960, continue to show that educational retardation among Spanish American children still exists.[6]

At an urban secondary school in 1959, when college personnel were invited to talk with senior classes about college opportunities, one university dean made this observation. The population was approximately half Anglo and half Spanish American in ethnic origin; yet the ratio of students who appeared to discuss college possibilities with him was approximately five to one. This shows, for reasons which will be discussed presently, there is still in the public schools a great lack of equality of educational opportunity.

It will not be easy for teachers to determine what specific situations do prevail where they teach. Some explanation of the historical background of the Spanish-speaking people, some understanding of the cultural values and practices of these people, and some comparison of their attitudes, practices, and ideals with the American middle-class teacher will be of value to teachers facing these problems in the classroom.

This chapter will be presented in four sections: (1) Historical background; (2) beliefs and values of the traditional Spanish-speaking people; (3) behavioral problems in antagonisms, conflicts, and misunderstandings in communication; and (4) the task of education. The short section on teachers' reports will be continued in this chapter to record useful anecdotes of contemporary situations. While taken singly, these are isolated details, they may alert teachers to types of experiences they may meet in today's schools in the Southwest.

HISTORICAL BACKGROUND

The Movement of Spaniards into New Mexico

Coronado made his expedition into the Rio Grande Valley in 1540. For two years, he and his men trekked up and down the valley and into the eastern plains seeking the fabulous cities of gold that previous adventuring Spaniards had reported finding there. He returned to Mexico City without success.

It was 1598 when Oñate came into New Mexico to colonize. Oñate's colony of 400 people, 62 lumbering oxcarts, 1000 head of cattle, 4000 head of sheep, 1000 goats, 100 black cattle, 150 colts, and 150 mares arrived to establish a permanent colony in north central New Mexico, near the San Juan Pueblo.[7] (This was nine years before the settlement of the first permanent English colony at Jamestown, Virginia, in 1607.) From this time on, the Spanish officials, soldiers and their families, and the Franciscan padres, came and went, teaching the Indians and holding the land for Spain.

There was the short interval from 1680 to 1692 when the Pueblos revolted and drove the Spanish south beyond El Paso. It was from there that de Vargas and his men came in 1692, found little resistance from the individual pueblos of Indians, and re-established Spain's claim to the area.

During the eighteenth century, while English colonies were being founded on the east coast of the United States, Spanish settlements were being established up and down the Rio Grande Valley, and trade was being carried on over the Chihuahua Trail. Spain was also establishing missions and military posts in Texas and California.

The colonies in the Rio Grande Valley were so far removed from Mexico City that there was little exchange for more than two centuries. As a result, New Mexico has preserved folk lore, customs and manners, and a language little modified by forces from the outside.[8]

In 1789, when the thirteen colonies won their independence as the United States of America, the capital of Northern New Spain had been in existence in Santa Fe for 179 years, since 1610. The Spanish patrons, controlling tiny self-sufficient, independent villages with little outside contact except for the Indians who lived nearby, carried on the Spanish traditions for generations.

With the Mexican revolt, Spain's control ended in 1820. Very soon trade lines were established from the expanding frontier of the United States; the Santa Fe Trail and the southern route to California were soon being used. By the middle of the nineteenth century, the United States had annexed the Mexican Territory, and its soldiers, traders, and more daring settlers moved into the region.

When the two-class structure was challenged -- or more accurately, destroyed -- by the intrusion of the Anglo culture, the Spanish American population emerged, largely, as members of the lower class, socio-economically speaking.

Through the efforts of those few Spanish Americans who made the transition successfully and maintained respected positions in the Anglo-dominated culture, many young Spanish Americans were helped and given encouragement to seek places in the professions and in the government. Also, many young people were able to combine working for a living with furthering their formal education so that they, too, were able to climb the ladder of success. School teachers are an excellent example. They were able to obtain teachers' certificates to teach with little formal education. Then, through summer school attendance, or by saving their money for taking time off to go to school, they were able to complete university educations or broaden their scope of knowledge through other types of experiences.

There is now, to be sure, a sizeable population of Spanish American people in the American middle class. These were the people who, basically, believed that they, too, could climb the ladder of success. Pressures are increasing within this population for more and more of their ethnic group to internalize middle-class values. The challenges of formal education are more accessible.

Too, as Spanish American families acquire the artifacts of the middle class -- new cars for which monthly payments must be made, television sets, the convenience of bathrooms -- the desire to have and to keep these artifacts places the individual in a position where he must extend himself more and more into the dominant culture.

The traditional Spanish American culture had existed in a two-class society. The few, a very small per cent of the total group, constituted the patron class. The patrones, comparable in American society to the upper-middle-class, had values in time orientation, planning for the future, efficient management, and aggressive competition. The peon, comparable in some measure to the lower class in American society, was generally lacking in values of saving for the future or working to get ahead. It is probably true that the patrones and the priests, who together represented the leadership in the little communities, did not insist on higher levels of achievement or any changes in values. An uneducated, illiterate peon class was more subservient to their existing leadership. Further, a religion that taught them that this life was a kind of way-station on the road to their eternal reward, that the uneducated had the same chance at the reward of eternal life as the educated, and that whatever happens is just God's will, was conducive to the perpetuation of values in the peon class equivalent to the values of the lower class in American society.

This picture of a two-class society, the existence of only patrones and peons, does not exhibit the most significant sector of the general American society, the existence of a middle class. One of the apparent developmental processes in the United States is the expansion of a greater and greater middle-class group. It is this middle class that establishes and perpetuates the rigid, inflexible standards described in Chapter 3 in explaining the background of the American school teacher.

The subsistence, agrarian economy of the Spanish American crumbled with the rather sudden intrusion of the Anglo about the middle of the nineteenth century. The Anglo brought big business, large-scale stock raising, and a new legal system that was totally strange to the local people.

The new legal system proved to be of primary significance. The old Spanish Jurisprudence System had worked very well for centuries in dealing with the Indian neighbors, but the exactness of the English system was completely demoralizing for the Spanish Americans. Generally, the Spanish system of laws had ruled that any agreement that could be reached and adhered to through the years was legal. Establishing water rights by mutual consent and recognizing natural landmarks as controls had worked for nearly two hundred years. Land grants from the King of Spain, with only such general descriptions of the area included, had been held for generations.

The new system brought in by the Anglo Americans contested rightful ownership of land, required exact proof of boundaries, and carried with it lawful authority to evict people who could not prove in the new system what their rights were. The Anglo Americans, recognizing the confusion and defeat felt by the residents, were able to obtain their own ends, even if it required exercising greed and deceit.

> With the Anglo Americans came ruthless politicians and merchants. They acquired the water rights and land of the people. The New Mexican, who had built his folkways and mores on the good will of his neighbor, found himself being exploited by the Anglo. He failed, completely, to understand the bitter, competitive nature of this immigrant. The exploitation caused him to fear, resent and hate the intruder. Yet, the new order did little or nothing to bridge the cleavage between the two cultures. No effort was made to bring the Spanish American, who was a foreigner in culture, into the American fold. Before 1890 there were virtually no public schools in New Mexico and the only education available was that provided in private or parochial schools.[9]

In the early years of Anglo settlement in New Mexico the unsuspicious and naive Spanish Americans were victimized on every hand. When the men from the states came out west to dispossess the poor natives of their lands, they used many subterfuges. One was to offer the owner of the land a handful of silver coins for the small service of making a mark on a paper. The mark was a cross which was acceptable as a signature and by which the unsuspecting natives deeded away their lands. By this means, many a poor family was robbed of all its possessions.[10]

The account of the Santa Fe Ring is documented by this New Mexico Historian, on page 150:

From the Land Grant Ring grew others, as the opportunities for speculation and plunder were developed. Cattle Rings, Public Land Stealing Rings, Mining Rings, Treasury Rings and Rings of almost every description grew up, until the affairs of the territory came to be run almost exclusively in the interest and for the benefit of combinations organized and headed by a few longheaded ambitious and unscrupulous Americans.[11]

The Spanish settlers were able to acquire private ownership of land tracts through the "land grants" bestowed by the Spanish government. Most of these grants were community grants in which a rural farming community was settled by ten or more families living in a little village. Accepting the grant prescribed the selecting of a site, drawing lots for houses to be situated around a central plaza, developing an irrigation system, assigning irrigable farming plots, and building a Catholic church. Around the village site was an extensive ejido, or community grazing land. The ejido also provided wood and space for hunting. The boundaries of the grant were determined loosely by the use of familiar landmarks or other markers. (page 2), citing, Perrigo, Lynn I., *Texas and Our Spanish Southwest*, (Dallas: Banks Upshaw and Co., 1960), pp. 79-80.[12]

By the end of the 1920's the majority of the Spanish-American villages had been dispossessed of most of their ejido land. The village grazing lands were gone. What remained had suffered badly from overgrazing. The Spanish-Americans became a society of stockmen without a range. Every aspect of their culture was impoverished, deprived of meat, the inhabitants began to suffer from malnutrition. Anxiety and fear began to grow. The village population, however, struggled to maintain its traditional way of life. More men were forced to leave the villages as migrant workers, but they usually returned to their villages in the fall. Irrigated farming land was utilized to the fullest extent permitted by archaic farming methods. Men unable to provide for their families found support in their extended family networks. There was still little migration from the villages, and the Spanish-Americans did what they could to adjust to the changing economic situation.[13]

The federal government did establish a Court of Private Land Claims to hear cases originating in titles to Spanish land grants in New Mexico and southern Colorado. The judges were from other sections of the U. S. who knew little of the Spanish law under which the people had operated and knew nothing of Spanish-American land owning customs. Rigid adherence to Anglo legal precepts maintained. Keleher reports that two-thirds of all Spanish-American land claims coming before the court were rejected.[14]

For New Mexico, the destruction of the traditional Spanish-American village life, destroyed by chronic land loss, has created a large distressed area covering most of the northern part of the State. Northern New Mexico is scarred by poverty, malnutrition, cultural disorganization, family breakdown, rising indexes of juvenile delinquency, and formidable rates of disease and infant mortality that are among the highest in the United States. The area survives on high rates of unemployment and welfare payments.

The Spanish-American inhabitants of northern New Mexico have been caught in a harsh cycle of cultural shock, resentment, hostility, bitterness, apathy, and even self-hatred, which has paralyzed their ability to deal effectively with their own problems.[15]

A small Spanish-American subsistence farmer living in the villages was singularly unprepared to adjust to a fixed land-tax system. Cultivating his land to feed his family, he seldom ever possessed enough actual cash to pay taxes requiring money payments. Frequently, he was not even aware of the existence of the land tax until the sheriff came out to dispossess him from his land for nonpayment.

Probably no other Anglo-American measure has had a harsher impact upon Spanish-American property than the fixed land tax.

The inability to pay land taxes is still probably the most important cause of continued loss of land among the Spanish-American rural population of New Mexico.[16]

Tireman found that the U. S. Government showed an appalling lack of understanding.

> Political rights peculiar to a democratic people were conferred upon a people conditioned to aristocratic institutions. . . . By a stroke of the pen it was expected that a whole population would suddenly change its ways of living and thinking.
>
> This statement could be documented in countless ways. The system of landholdings was suddenly changed from royal, tax-free grants to one requiring annual taxes. A social system founded upon caste was discarded overnight for a social system built upon freedom and equality. A monarchial government of kings and viceroys was replaced by an electoral system.[17]

Tireman points out that, in other territories acquired by the United States, efforts have been made to acquaint the people by education in the schools with the new American institutions. No such effort was made in New Mexico.

The Spanish American people had no tradition of competition, of aggression in business, or of Anglo American democracy, with its resulting individualistic nature. Theirs had been one of communal activity, the primary concern being the well-being of the community. Their way of life had persisted through generations of isolation and of wresting a living from a rather hostile environment.

Generally, these people produced only what they needed for subsistence; to do a great deal more might have been thought greedy or gluttonous. This was not much of a money economy. Men exchanged "days of work," and the ditch association demanded communal support, fairly distributed to each family, to keep the irrigation ditches in good repair.

The Anglo merchant, establishing himself in a community, found many legal, but shrewd, ways to deal with the people. Bartering for seed crops, wool from the sheep, and other produce worked while the people could bring things to the store to barter. Beyond this, long-term credit accounts were established. It was not long until the merchant was "carrying" the Spanish American family on account all through the year and taking the farmer's season's produce at low prices. When farmers paid profit-making prices for their merchandise, and then sold their crops at ridiculously low prices when they were marketable, it is little wonder that many of them never finished "settling their accounts."

The Spanish American did not share the attitudes of the Anglo American toward work, avoiding poverty, and shaping one's own destiny. The Anglo came indoctrinated in a value system that taught that work for work's sake has its own reward and is the way to climb the ladder of success; that poverty is to be avoided, that is, overcome; and that in this great democracy, it is possible to exercise mastery over nature and to shape one's destiny -- to become what one wishes if one is willing to work hard enough.

The Spanish American was not engrossed with the idea of getting too much ahead, and through the years had accepted a much slower-paced approach to living -- "Work a little; rest a little." While he did not want to live in poverty, he had been taught that it was as easy for a poor man to enter the Kingdom of Heaven as for a rich one -- easier, in fact, since he had heard the admonition that "it is easier for a camel to go through the eye of a needle than it is for a rich man to enter the Kingdom of Heaven." Further, the Spanish American did not share at all the Anglo's notion that he was "the master of his fate, the conqueror of his soul."[18] Rather, he believed, as pointed out in Chapter 4, that he was completely dependent upon God's will. This subjugation-to-nature orientation is directly opposed to the mastery-over-nature position of the Anglo.

> The culture . . . of the Spanish-American . . . is the culture of an enclave. The Spanish-Americans constituted the population of the state of New Mexico when this was annexed by the United States. In the face of a differing dominant culture, of rapid technological change around them, they maintained the values, the concepts, the attitudes of their fathers, not through ignorance of another way of life, but by choice. They accepted a few traits from the "Anglo" culture, plucked them out of context and gave them their own background. They took electricity for their houses, but in general they rejected running water and plumbing, because these were manipulations of nature, with which they were familiar and intimate. They play basketball, and light a candle to the saint for aid in winning. They accepted schooling, but not the "Anglo" motivations for education, the higher standard of living, the better job. When the latest technology came to them in the form of atomic explosions at the New Mexico testing grounds, many of them had never seen a train or a steamboat. When they become urbanized, they reproduce their village community, and buy a piece of land to till. They choose and reject according to their system of values.[19]

From the time Anglo Americans first appeared in New Mexico, they were called "Gringos," a term of contempt referring to them as foreigners or intruders, a group unlearned in the ways of the country.

The Family

The family is the moving force in the total Spanish American culture. All the other institutions, religion, communal economy, transmission of the culture through education, all these were dependent upon the family as an institution. Mead says, "To be Spanish is to belong to a <u>familia</u>."[20] "<u>La familia</u> means more than parents and their children -- it includes grandparents, brothers, sisters, uncles, aunts, cousins, of the third and fourth degrees."[21]

Angel illustrates the nature of the extended family:

> Next to me lives an old man, Don Pablo Ortiz, about seventy, and his wife. This morning as I left for school I noticed a usual practice that is characteristic of the traditional Spanish American culture. The neighboring pieces of property, which are subdivisions of the original property, are occupied by homes built by his sons and daughters. Every morning, rather early in the morning, all the sons and daughters, who are now married with families of their own, come to bid the old folks good morning and eat a little breakfast or have some coffee. This extended family practice is a traditional one.[22]

<u>Respect for elders</u> is a deeply-entrenched value among the Spanish American people. Note the following teachers' reports:

Respect for Elders

> All elders to the Spanish American youth are Don and Doña, Mr. and Mrs., not just "Hey, you." If an elder is to speak or address a younger boy or girl, man or woman, their response should be "Senor" or "Senora," not just "Que?" or "What?" or "Yes?" If we should respond in the latter, said elder would be in the right to slap us, with a good getting-after from our own parents besides. Should we be on our way to run an errand for our parents, and some elderly person stopped us and asked us to run an errand for him or her, we must set our parent's errand aside and do as the elder requested and after having done so, then go about making our errand for our parents.
>
> . . . . .
>
> Should any elder request a favor of us and upon doing that favor for him, we are to stand before the elder with our arms crossed before him until such time as he should see fit to dismiss us.
>
> . . . . .
>
> Should we greet an elder, we must say, "Good morning to you," and not just "Good morning"; if so, he would reply, "Good morning to the Devil," or "Good morning <u>las del Payaso</u>," or "Good morning to the Clown."
>
> . . . . .
>
> In the Spanish American culture, there has existed the practice that the young person must obey the older person. If a

father sends his son on an errand, the boy goes pronto to execute the command. However, if on the way to carry out the command, another older person sees the boy and asks him to run an errand for him, the boy interrupts his father's errand and does first the errand for the older person. He then continues with his father's command. If the errand has delayed him too much, the boy is in trouble. His father may punish him for being late. However, if the boy had refused to do the errand for the older man, then the older man could have reported to the father that the boy refused to comply with his request, and the father would then give him a "sound thrashing" for not showing respect for his elders.

. . . . .

The Spanish American child is taught to have great respect for his elders. If an older person was visiting and asked for a drink of water, the child was sent to get one for him. The child brought the drink and stood before that person, crossed his arms and waited until that person was through drinking. Only then could he go away. If the elder decided to take a drink, then carry on with the conversation, and kept doing this, the child had to wait for as long as it took for that person to finish the drink. If the child as much as turned around or showed any signs of impatience, he was reprimanded as soon as the company left.

. . . . .

The children talked much about grandfathers and grandmothers and old age -- ninety or upwards. Old age is revered by the children. The same reverence for godparents was shown. The children themselves were treated as if they were sons or daughters of the padrinos and, in turn, the godchildren showed obedience and respect to them as if they were parents.

The changing status of the Spanish American woman is significant. Traditionally, her place was in the home. While her role of motherhood was highly respected, even revered, she was in all other respects completely dominated by her husband. World War II forced her to act more independently and lent support toward her emancipation from her traditional role. If the husband left home to go to military service, she had financial support, but was forced to care for her family and make many decisions women had never traditionally made in the family. If the husband was not in military service, but obtained defense work, moving the family into Anglo society enlightened the women to new vistas to feminine conduct. If it were possible to do so, many women went to work and earned paychecks of their own. When the war ended, the women were unwilling to revert to the pre-war practices. Of course, this has a serious impact on family harmony if the wife assumes independence in work and action, and the father, without formal education or salable skills, finds his security in the family completely undermined. This destroys his traditional authoritative place in the disciplining of the children, too, if their efforts at formal education have failed to build respect for the traditional culture from which they came. This has, in many urban areas, led to greater percentages of juvenile delinquency than found in the dominant culture. [23]

The traditional Spanish American people were Roman Catholic in their religious faith, and completely devoted in their religious practice. They were a humble people, praying often, lighting candles, and making novenas. Contradictory as it may be, there also existed a substantial folklore on witchcraft. Being largely an uneducated people, in a formal sense, they probably did not understand the basis for much of their religion nor logically analyzed conflicts in their behavior where religion was concerned. Witchcraft was manifested in sundry types of experiences. Human beings could transform themselves into balls of fire and roll across the land at high speeds; witches could take the form of owls and coyotes; noises at night were significant; and premonitions of future happenings were prevalent.

> This belief in witchcraft is overtly exhibited today only among the least acculturated. Some village teachers may still have a hard time getting students to accept scientific facts because these facts contradict the old beliefs taught at home by the parents. [24]

EDUCATION

The movement of Mexican families into the Southwest across the Rio Grande River and the southern borders of New Mexico, Arizona, and California, has created a problem for the schools in these states for many years. This problem has been given much study by several scholars for decades. Sanchez and Tireman are not completely agreed on methods of meeting the problem. Sanchez has resisted the practice of segregating the children even for the first year in school in order for them to learn English as a second language. [25] Tireman, as a result of his extensive reading testing program in New Mexico schools in the late 1920's and his San Jose Experiment, concluded that a pre-first grade year was necessary for these children to acquire a minimum vocabulary in English in order to do satisfactory work in the first grade during their second year in school. Tireman did recommend that these children have their pre-first year experience when they were five years old so that they might begin first grade at the same chronological age as their Anglo peers. [26]

Manuel spent decades at the University of Texas developing measuring instruments, both for intelligence and achievement, to inventory more adequately the abilities and the school progress of Mexican American children in the Southwest and Spanish-speaking children universally.[27]

The California State Department of Education has also worked with the problems associated with integrating Spanish-speaking children into the schools for decades. Meriam did a study in English language teaching for Mexican children at Placentia, California, in 1937.[28] Dispensing with traditional subjects, the children in grades pre-first through eight were taught four types of activities: enjoyment of stories, engaging in wholesome play, handwork in useful construction, and social studies derived from the children's enlarging environment.[29]

No specifically organized English class was taught. Meriam was able to demonstrate that these children could do as well or better on standard tests as the other children in southern California. Other facets of school organization, the increased parent interest and cooperation and decrease of absenteeism, were evidences of success. At the end of the experiment, Meriam concluded:

> The best way to teach English is not to teach English in the form of reading, writing, language, spelling, etc., but to proceed vigorously to read for enjoyment or for needed information; to write with great care when there is a real occasion for doing so; to speak . . . when such oral expression definitely functions. English is of value . . . as it functions. Bilingual children acquire English incidentally.[30]

A research study sponsored by the United States Office of Education and conducted at Arizona State University, 1958-1960, was entitled "Investigation of Mental Retardation and Pseudo Mental Retardation in Relation to Bilingual and Sub-Cultural Factors." The research consisted of two parts. The first was an extensive review of related literature concerning bilingualism and education of minority groups. A bibliography of 1440 items was compiled, and 151 studies judged to be related to the basic problem of pseudo mental retardation and bilingualism and sub-cultural factors were annotated. The two conclusions drawn from this massive review were:

> (1) Most of the findings were inconsistent and inconclusive in showing the effects of bilingualism on the education of the children; and (2) most of the studies stressed implementation and details of methods and materials rather than diagnosis and identification of behavior outcomes related to socio-economic and educational influences.[31]

In the second phase of the study, 120 primary school Mexican-American children in the Phoenix, Arizona, area were studied. Individual case studies were developed for 35 of these children. Some of the findings reported were:

1. The median number of siblings per family was approximately twice the national average.
2. Almost ten per cent of the fathers had no schooling; only four per cent had completed high school.
3. The median family income was in the lowest quartile nationally.
4. Bilingual children showed median performances on tests of mental ability at roughly one standard deviation below national norms.
5. Reading achievement measured on standard tests showed the median child in grade two to be .15 below the norm; in grade three, .60 below the norm; and in grade four, 1.5 below the norm.
6. When the parents interviewed were categorized as "positive," "resignation" or "negative," on the basis of attitude toward school and level of aspiration for their children, the children in the "positive" category scored higher than the other two groups on the intelligence test, obtaining a median score slightly above 100.
7. The children with the highest socio-economic rating in the group studied earned the highest I.Q. scores.[32]

Some ideas suggested by consultants but not developed in this research are listed here since they certainly suggest areas for further research in this field.

> The importance of kindergartens, especially for the underprivileged; the dangers in arbitrary assignments of bilingual children to two or three years in first grade; recognition of the idea that no special teaching "formula" is required for these children; the flexibility of I.Q.'s depending on age, maturity, the teacher, the psychometrist, the specific test used, and many other factors; the place of television in learning another language; assimilation versus acculturation; the need for developing pride in one's origins; family attitudes as they influence motivation of children. . . . [33]

> The G. I. Bill, in effect in 1945 when veterans returned from the second World War, was one of the most important events in the history of the Spanish-American and Mexican American. For the first time, the doors of colleges and universities

opened wide to them. Hundreds were able to secure a college education and move into the professions, government service, and private business on a white collar and managerial level. Thousands of others acquired the technical skills through on-the-job training to open small businesses and to find employment as skilled and semi-skilled workers. The housing provisions of the bill permitted a large number of veterans to escape from the slum neighborhoods. Some moved into existing lower class and middle class Anglo American neighborhoods, and others developed Spanish American and Mexican American businessmen and professions found many economic opportunities during and after the war to enter real estate, expand their businesses, and to make money. They created a newly rich group anxious to be accepted by their Anglo-American peers.[34]

Language and School Success

All children have difficulty with the English language. Woods points out the inconsistencies of the English language that one foreign student found difficult to reconcile.

> When you say you are going to dress a chicken, you mean that you are going to undress it. A cow may be said to have a pretty skin, but a woman may never be said to have a pretty hide. The plural of foot is feet, but the plural of boot is not beet. The plural of this is these, but the plural of kiss is not keese.[35]

Woods also believes that we can tell much about a culture by its language. She says:

> Language gives clues to the understanding of behavior. While the English clock "runs," the Spanish clock "walks"; hence, the English-speaking person must hurry to make use of time before it runs away, but the Spanish-speaking person may take a more leisurely attitude. The English-speaking person who arrives late for work tends to say, "I missed the bus," making himself the active agent and accepting responsibility for his tardiness. The Spanish-speaking person, however, is more apt to say that the bus left him, that the dishes fell out of his hands and broke, or that diseases are manifestations of God's will. Language, then, is a good guide to the way a person perceives events and objects in the world about him.[36]

Clark presents a case study of Frank that raises many questions which school personnel must answer before such failures as his will be successes. If he could have understood the language from the beginning of school, if his teacher had been alert to both his experiences of everyday living in Mexico and his dearth of associative experiences to which to tie the myriad of happenings at school, if teacher-parent contacts had been maintained through the years, and if a school social worker had helped to interpret the school to the parents and to establish a level of aspiration for Frank more in keeping with the dominant cultural expectancy, then the gap in cultural transition might have been lessened.

Frank was discouraged by his failure to pass from the first to the second grade, but equally disheartening was his difficulty in understanding the things the teacher talked about and the things he read about in books. Things and people and stories that Anglo children had learned about before they started to school, Frank knew nothing about. It was a long time before he could figure out what a jack-o-lantern was and what it had to do with the Feast of All Saints. . . . . Although Frank had heard his parents and grandparents discuss many times the way in which the holiday was celebrated in Mexico, with all the people carrying food and paper decorations to the cemetery to adorn the graves, never once had anyone mentioned a pumpkin cut to resemble a face. He always felt a little at a loss when things that he did not understand were mentioned: how could he know about valentines or prairie schooners or Mother Goose or crossword puzzles? The American cultural tradition was so much a part of life for Frank's Anglo teacher and fellow students that they scarcely thought of it, but it was a vast store of knowledge which Frank had to learn slowly and by inference.

Gradually Frank discovered that he was getting further and further behind in his studies. Because his grades were poor, he was constantly afraid that he would have to repeat another grade and fall another year behind his agemates. But somehow he completed junior high school and entered James Lick High. Many of his friends had become discouraged in school and dropped out. Some of them picked up odd jobs and always had a little money in their pockets and better clothes than Frank's parents could buy him. In high school, Frank discovered for the first time what it meant to be a Mexican-American boy in a school society dominated by Anglo students and teachers. Anglo students of his age often drove cars, wore good clothes, had spending money, and were usually a year or two ahead of him in school. Sometimes they made remarks in his presence about "dumb Mexicans." Now sixteen, and in his first year of high school, Frank wants nothing so much as to quit school and go to work. He sees no future for him in school, does not want to wait until he is twenty years old to go to work and begin making money for himself, and is not convinced that graduation from high school will help him to get a better job. Frank has not dropped out of school before only because his parents will not let him; they keep reminding him that this is his only chance to get an education and prepare himself for something besides day labor. To Frank, at sixteen, the wages of even an unskilled laborer seem a veritable fortune, and continuance in school seems a painful and unrewarding chore. More and more he fails to attend classes, preferring to go to a movie or just loaf around the streets with some of his friends. Sometimes his father discovers that Frank has not been to school and becomes angry and threatens him with a beating. On these occasions Frank feels that even his own family is against him, and sometimes runs away from home for a day or two, spending the night with a friend in another part of town. It seems likely that this will be Frank's last year of formal schooling. [37]

MIGRANT CHILDREN

Many of the millions of migrant workers in the United States are of Mexican ancestry. Because these children attend school irregularly and leave school young, they become adults who relive their parents' lives uneducated, practically non-English speaking, and culturally isolated.

In addition to being culturally isolated and leading an unstable existence, most Americans know or seem to care little about their plight. There is little continuity to efforts made to help them -- no coordination among the respective states through which they will migrate in one season. Some separate states and individual school systems have attempted to devise special school programs to accommodate these children. [38]

Thomas and Steuber point out that the migrant Mexican-American child is squarely our responsibility. His parents are reasonably predictable in their annual migrations through the crops, often groups appearing on schedule to do contract jobs. The cultural isolation can be met if schools, instead of insisting on the narrowing, inflexible middle-class American values exclusively, can attack the problem more broadly as cultural diffusion, language learning, and overcoming education retardation.[39] Teachers have reported the following incidents:

> In my school there is a family of children who came from Mexico to the United States to live. They moved here four years ago.
>
> One day last summer, I had employed the older boy, who was a sixth-grade pupil, to help me do some work. When lunch time arrived, he had not finished, so I invited him to have lunch with us. At first he was very reluctant to do so without his parents' consent, but finally agreed. When we were ready to eat, food was passed to him first as guest, as is customary in our society. He declined to accept food until all adults present had served themselves. According to his home training, children were not to be served until all adults had been served.
>
> . . . . .

We have a family in our school who moved from Mexico four years ago. After the oldest boy had been in school for two years, his youngest brother started to school. On the first day, he took the six-year-old to the primary teacher, and told her that if his little brother didn't do just as he should, she was to let him know so that he could see to it that his brother behaved. This illustrates that older siblings in Mexico are expected to help in the training of younger brothers and sisters.

. . . . .

The most noticeable difference, aside from the skin color, between the Spanish-speaking people of southern New Mexico and the English-speaking people, lies in the language. The Spanish language is almost exclusively spoken in the homes of the Mexican-American children, especially by the parents. Some of the parents do not know enough English to converse with teachers or any Anglos.

. . . . .

As soon as the "Spanish" children leave the classroom, they congregate in little groups and speak Spanish, or the form of it commonly spoken in this vicinity. This sets them apart from the Anglo students who have not yet learned enough Spanish.

These upper-grade students who arrive at the age of fifteen or sixteen, and who speak only halting English, will always be set apart from the dominant group of the United States.

. . . . .

The most important group within our seasonal agricultural labor force has been Spanish-speaking persons. They have been the backbone of the seasonal agricultural labor force in the Southwest for more than 60 years (page 65).

School attendance is often difficult, irregular, and most sadly, unplanned for by the school that receives the students for short terms.

The greatest problem is the use of the English language. Teachers are prepared only to teach English as it is taught to native speakers of the language, never to teach English as a second language.

Special summer schools - either head start programs for young children, or "catch up" schools for older ones - will help to reduce the extent of retardation but the problem can never be solved until teachers are prepared to teach English as a new language.

Scholes recommends special summer schools, urging parents to stay at home base for as much of the school year as possible, hiring retired teachers or young mothers on part time bases to give more individual instruction, and making sure that Spanish-speaking children of agricultural workers are participating in the best integrated educational opportunities.[40]

Minorities are subgroups within a culture which are distinguishable from the dominant group by reason of differences in physiognomy, language, customs or culture patterns (including any combination of these factors). Such subgroups are regarded as inherently different and not belonging to the dominant group; for this reason they are consicously or unconsciously excluded from full participation in the life of the culture.[41]

Spanish-speaking people represent the second largest disadvantaged minority in the U. S. About four and one half million people belonged to this minority group in 1960.

Mexicans have experienced, and continue to experience, extreme economic and social deprivation.

Many of these workers have already been displaced by machines. Farm managers have adopted use of cotton-picking machinery, machines that shake fruit trees, and other machines that pick tomatoes.

There are few lawyers, doctors, professors, and trained public servants with Spanish surnames.

Buying on credit has kept many Mexicans in economic bondage.[42]

The enormous language gap between teacher and pupil severely hampers effective communication. Teachers, counselors and principals who cannot establish rapport with parents or children inadvertently perpetuate social institutions that induce hostility and social alienation.

Immigration from Mexico, both legal and illegal, is an inescapable fact of life for this southwestern region of the country.

There is evidence of a growing militancy and an increasing awareness of an ethnic identity.

Few young Mexicans in the urban areas know Mexican culture. Fewer still can speak Spanish fluently.

A search for cultural identity is in evidence.

The fear of government, of the police, of the social worker, the educator, and of other officials is a direct product of the social distance that obtains between government and the people.[43]

In 1955, Idaho used a peak labor force of 26,816 to harvest 169,700 acres of potatoes. Ten years later, it harvested 282,000 acres of potatoes with a labor force of 9,165. The bigger farm units and the new harvesting machines made the difference.[44]

. . . . in the raising of sugar beets . . . . the mono-germ beet seed has virtually eliminated the need for thinning and cultivation, and in the fruit industry . . . . the field work force has been reduced by 40 per cent in the last decade by the use of sprays, pruning, dwarf trees, controlled atmosphere storage and the bulk handling of fruit.[45]

Contrast of Phonemes in the Languages

There are certain basic errors which Spanish-speaking children are likely to make in the pronunciation of English words. Many of these errors are directly traceable to basic differences in Spanish and English. The Spanish-speaking teacher will probably be able to understand why these errors are made, but he must be very careful that he does not make some of them himself. A teacher reports:

One of these common errors is the tendency to put an "e" before words starting with an "s." This leads to such words as "estop" for "stop." Another is the tendency to reverse the sounds of "sh" and "ch." This gives such pronunciations as "shicken" for "chicken," or "share" for "chair." In Spanish, the word "en" is equivalent to the English "in" or "on." This leads to confusion between these two words. The short sound of "i" in the English language is often confused with the long sound of "e." It leads to the use of such words as "ship" for "sheep," or the reverse. The Spanish-speaking children often become confused with the gender of pronouns. They may use "she" in referring to their brothers.

Teachers have also reported the following:

Adherence to tradition

Sombreros, or big straw hats, are an institution in Mexico, and with the descendants of the Spanish-speaking people who were "born and bred" in Mexico. The same is true of the colorful shawls, rugs, blankets, and fiesta dresses. These things are always used in the public schools of the southern counties of New Mexico at fiesta celebrations, to make the occasion purely Mexican.

. . . . .

The five teenaged Spanish-speaking children in my special education class always included in their pictures, during "free drawing" periods, sleepy-looking people with sombreros, a red reboso thrown around their shoulders. These things were never in the pictures of the Anglo children, bringing out a cultural difference.

Social Status

At a University of Texas (Austin, Texas) function for foreign dignitaries, a group of female foreign students, as well as regular American-born students, were requested to help the hostesses "serve" the refreshments to the foreign dignitaries. The wife of one was highly vocal in her criticism. She turned to me and said, "You North Americans reduce our student daughters to the position of servants to serve you." My reply was as tactfully worded as possible, and I endeavored to point out the fact that North American students, were "serving". . . that in our North American culture, our university "helpers" were chosen carefully because they were honor students, not servants.

Following in the way of one's parents

There was one small boy whom I had in seventh grade who was very irregular in his attendance at school. He would come one day and be absent two or three days. His father and mother wanted him to get an education, but had little success in getting him to school. When I questioned him as to why he didn't want to come to school, he said, "I don't need an education to be a ditch-digger."

His father was a ditch-tender, keeping the ditch free of weeds and debris that would block the flow of water into the ditch. This Spanish American boy had the idea that the only job he would be able to hold was that of a ditch-digger or some similar job. He did not have a desire to try to better himself over the life lived by his parents. "What is good enough for them is good enough for me."

The differences which the Anglo teacher needs to understand include:

1. The language barrier: the Spanish-speaking is apt to have had no formal preparation for participating in the American school where innumerable subtle understandings of concepts expressed in English are taken for granted.

2. The life style of the family, beyond the handicap of language, has incorporated many cultural practices and beliefs unfamiliar to the typical school teacher: limited lifespace, absence of books in any language in the home, belief

in the supernatural to solve those questions where information is lacking, reverence for the old, and acceptance of family ties rooted in a foreign culture and language.

3. The life style of the family, beyond both the language and culture barriers, is immediately closely identified with the values of the lower-lower class when fitted into the American culture. Such a milieu includes continual presence of poverty, immediate needs unmet (someone has said that bread must come before language learning), ignorance in problem-solving because of dearth of factual knowledge possessed, often the victims of shrewd middle-class business dealers who are motivated by their ability to sell rather than by reason, low level of aspiration because of both immediate needs and because of ignorance of wider horizons that might be accessible.

SUMMARY

The major differences between the value systems of the two cultures are summarized below.[46]

American school teachers are sure to place great value on these practices.	Children from traditional Spanish-speaking families may be said to have accepted these general patterns.
Language. The language of the school is English; almost all teachers are unilingual.	Language. The language of the people is Spanish, and is rooted strongly in the whole syndrome of beliefs, values, and practices. Sometimes an expression does lose its significance in the translation. Sometimes there is no word in the second language that means exactly the same thing.
Mastery over Nature. Man must harness and cause the forces of nature to work for him.	Subjugation to Nature. An often observed reaction in the traditional Spanish American was, "If it's God's will."
Future Time Orientation. All living in our society is future oriented.	Present Time Orientation. For the traditional Spanish American family, the only important goal of life was going to heaven after death. One only passed through this temporal life to receive his "reward" in the next.

Status and Prestige. One acquires status for what he does. The value is on climbing the ladder of success.

A Universalistic Approach. Do what is best for the common good, without regard to one specific individual.

Affectively neutral. The doctor looks at himself first as a doctor and secondly as a friend of the patient.

Level of Aspiration. Climb the ladder of success. Success is measured by a wide range of superlatives: first, the most, the best.

Work. Success will be achieved by hard work.

Saving. Everybody should save for the future. "A penny saved is a penny earned." "Put something away for a rainy day." "Take care of the pennies and the dollars will take care of themselves."

One Had Status for Who He Was. This assigning status on ascription was dependent upon family lineage.

A Particularistic Perspective. A businessman looks first at himself as a brother to the man who is asking for credit; secondly, as a businessman who is dealing with a customer.

Emotional Response Is Involved. The curanderas and sobadores visited with the family, drank tea, and consulted with the family before diagnosing symptoms. This friendly warmth made the impersonal nature of Anglo doctors unacceptable to the families.

Level of Aspiration. "To work a little, rest a little." Follow in one's father's footsteps. Be satisfied with the present.

Work. Work to satisfy present need. The Spanish American was particularistic in nature. He operated on emotional response rather than subordinating the individual to the societal institution.

Sharing. Traditional pattern included sharing with the extended family group. In cultural transition, Spanish Americans suffered considerable economic poverty. Those established in the dominant culture accepted Anglo values in sharing.

Adherence to Time Schedules. "Take care of the minutes and the hours will take care of themselves." In practice, we have become so enslaved to time schedules, we might be termed "clock watchers."

Acceptance of Change. Change, in and of itself, is accepted as modal behavior.

Scientific Explanation for All Behavior. Noting happens contrary to natural law. There is a scientific explanation for everything.

Competition. Aggression. One competes to win. Winning first prize all the time is a coveted goal.

Individuality. Each individual shapes his own destiny. Self-realization for each person is limited only by his capacities to achieve.

Adherence to Time Schedules. The expression for the "clock runs" translated from Spanish is "the clock walks." It has been said that this explains the "manana" attitude which Anglos have observed in Spanish Americans.

Reaction to Change. We may follow in the old ways with confidence.

Non-scientific Explanation for Natural Phenomena. Witches, fears, and non-scientific medical practices could be used to explain behavior.

Humility. Acceptance of the status quo. Submission, might categorize behavior.

Obedience. The Catholic Church kept life routinized, placed emphasis on obedience to the will of God.

Jones concluded that these characteristics of the Spanish American people in her community are still considerably different from the Anglo American.

1. The home has remained a more closely-knit institution than the Anglo home.
2. There is more parental dominance on the part of the Spanish American.
3. The Spanish American father has a more authoritarian position in the home.
4. The Spanish American mother holds a very different position in the home.
5. Relationships are more of the "extended family" nature in the Spanish American home.
6. Adolescent females are overly protected in the Spanish American home.
7. Courtship and marriage customs continue to be quite different from Anglo customs.

8. The trait of personal courtesy is most important to Spanish American people.[47]

In his monograph, "The Effect of Cultural Difference in the Education of Spanish American Children," Ulibarri writes:

Spanish American children, in general, are in need of a new orientation to:

1. Acquisiton of the Anglo value of achievement and success.

2. Time orientation that will be precise according to the hour and minute, but also placing great emphasis on planning for a definite future in this "temporal life."

3. Scientific interpretation of natural phenomena.

4. Acceptance of change and a zeal in looking forward to change.

5. Social relationships, whereby their "docility" and "timidity" will evolve into a desirable degree of aggression.

6. Economic efficiency, whereby they will learn the value of money and acquire the ability to spend it wisely.

7. A more universalistic outlook on life so that they will see the total picture instead of ascribing importance to the separate details.

8. Acceptance of scientific medical practice.[48]

These children besides needing to learn the regular skills and processes, also need to learn a new language and a new culture. In describing school problems of Nambe, Tireman wrote that the public school was so foreign to the type of thinking of a Spanish American, that it become an island and the children attended school irregularly or dropped out quickly.[49]

The school should take concerted steps to show the way, take leadership to improve situations under which people live. The school should provide opportunity for development of thoughtful leadership to these Spanish American citizens who have for so long followed unthinkingly other individuals.

Saunders summarizes one of his addresses concerning the history of the Spanish American in this way:

The Spanish-speaking people of the Southwest, like all the rest of us, have come a long way in the past hundred years. The changes they have undergone can be dramatically symbolized in terms of contrasts: the thatch-roofed hut and the skyscraper; the horse-drawn wagon and the stratocruiser; the wooden hoe and the mechanical cotton picker; the corrido singer and the juke box; the open fireplace and the atomic pile. The social distance they have traversed is greater than that between the most isolated village in New Mexico and the heart of downtown San Antonio. They have not all moved at the same rate, nor are they at the same point now. But they are all upon the same road and moving in the same direction. And there will be no turning back.[50]

THE PRESENT DAY SPANISH SURNAME POPULATION OF THE SOUTHWEST

Many readers, themselves part of the rapidly changing Spanish surname ethnic group, are apt to think that there is little in the description of Saunders and Parsons (pages 241-243) that accurately describes the present day Spanish or Mexican of the Southwest. The value system described by Parsons in 1951 and by Saunders in 1954 has, of course, been changing through the past twenty years.

However, the reader is reminded of previous discussion in this text: (1) all the factors influencing the learning of a second language have been operative for a long time. (See pp. 149ff.) And there has been, at the same time, rejection of the language and the culture of the settlers from the East. (2) In the scale of acculturation, no definite statement can be made about a total group in transtion. Ulibarri (see p. 114) has depicted the range all the way from the traditional way of life through low, medium, high, and full acculturation stages. These stages were met by the parents of many readers of this book. For these, few vestiges of the previous culture remain. (3) The text, page 223, further amplifies the movement of the Spanish surname people into the middle class, largely through the advantage of formal education. As a result of the G. I. bill, following the second World War, many of the present generation moved into the professions and established themselves in middle class society. (4) Appendix B describes one young man's personal experience in the cultural transition of his family - from a traditional way of life in the Rio Grande Valley - through four generations. He indicates that it was his father who moved farthest in making the transition. He emphasizes, too, the extent that language creates a barrier between the generations. The great-grandmother cannot understand English and the little children learn only that they must "be quiet" in her presence.

The Spanish surname teacher may have had parents who were highly acculturated to the middle class society. For this teacher, the traditional values may no longer be applicable.

A few educators are raising questions today about whether the differences discussed in this chapter are really cultural differences or only economic differences. This is to say, given the economic advantage of the middle class, all cultural differences would disappear. Simpkins posed this problem in sorting out which values were based on the rural, isolated, agrarian economy and which were cultural among the Pueblo Indians. (See p. 46).

One basic tenet of this book is that the teacher can better understand others when he more completely understands himself. This chapter has described some of the cultural beginnings of the Spanish-speaking people of the Southwest. The traditional culture will continue to be significant in the education of the boys and girls for some time. Spanish surname children, on the average, are not achieving commensurate with their potential. Teachers must continue to search for the reasons why this is so.

FOOTNOTES

[1] George I. Sanchez, Forgotten People (Albuquerque: University of New Mexico Press, 1940), pp. 28-35.

[2] Harlan Sininger, San Jose Training School, School Series Bulletin, Vol. 1, No. 2 (Albuquerque: University of New Mexico Press, 1931).

[3] Loyd Tireman and Mary Watson, A Community School in a Spanish-Speaking Village (Albuquerque: University of New Mexico Press, 1948).

[4] Sanchez, op. cit., p. 8.

[5] Charles Loomis, et al., Culture of a Contemporary Community, El Cerrito, New Mexico, Rural Life Studies, No. 1 (Washington: Government Printing Office, 1941); Charles Loomis, "El Cerrito, New Mexico: A Changing Village," New Mexico Historical Review, 33: 53-75, January, 1958.

[6] A research study entitled "The Adjustment of Indian and Non-Indian Children in Public Elementary Schools in New Mexico," sponsored by the U.S. Office of Education and the University of New Mexico, College of Education, Miles V. Zintz, Director, 1957-1960.

[7] Ruth Underhill, The Navajos (Norman: The University of Oklahoma Press, 1956), p. 34, citing George P. Hammond and Agapito Rey, Gallegos Relation of the Rodriguez Expedition to New Mexico (Albuquerque: Historical Society of New Mexico, 1927), p. 19.

[8] Dorothy Woodward, "Historical Backgrounds," Preface in Horacio Ulibarri, "Effect of Cultural Difference in the Education of Spanish-American Children" (unpublished monograph, the College of Education, University of New Mexico, Albuquerque, 1958), p. viii.

[9] Horacio Ulibarri, "The Effect of Cultural Difference in the Education of Spanish American Children" (Unpublished monograph, College of Education, The University of New Mexico, 1958), p. 38. (Mimeographed.)

[10] Sister Blandina Segale, AT THE END OF THE SANTA FE TRAIL, (Milwaukee: The Bruce Publishing Co., 1949), pp. 194-195.

[11] Lamar, Howard Roberts, THE FAR SOUTHWEST, 1846-1912, (New Haven: Yale University Press, 1966), pp. 136-170.

[12] Knowlton, Clark S., "Land Grant Problems Among the State's Spanish-Americans," New Mexico Business, 20:1-13, No. 6, June, 1967.

[13] Knowlton, Clark S., "Land Grant Problems Among the State's Spanish-Americans," New Mexico Business, 20:1-13, No. 6, June, 1967.

[14] Keleher, William A., The Fabulous Frontier, (Santa Fe: The Rydal Press, 1945), pp. 86-87.

[15] Knowlton, Clark S., "Land Grant Problems Among the State's Spanish-Americans," New Mexico Business, (Bureau of Business Research, UNM), June, 1967. Page 11.

[16] Knowlton, Clark S., "Land Grant Problems Among the State's Spanish-Americans," New Mexico Business, 20:7, No. 6, June, 1967.

[17] Loyd Tireman and Mary Watson, A Community School in a Spanish-Speaking Village (Albuquerque: University of New Mexico Press, 1943), pp. 16-17.

[18] "Invictus" by William Ernest Henley.

[19] Margaret Mead, editor, Cultural Patterns and Technical Change (New York: The New American Library of World Literature, Inc., 1955), p. 151.

[20] Ibid., p. 153.

[21] Charles P. Loomis, Informal Groupings in a Spanish American Village (Washington: U.S. Bureau of Agriculture Economics, 1940), p. 5.

[22] Personal conversation with Dr. Frank Angel, University of New Mexico, 1961.

[23] Lawrence Weiss, "Kids with the Odds Against Them," Denver Post, November 29, 1959.

[24] Ulibarri, op. cit., p. 23.

[25] George I. Sanchez, "The Crux of the Dual Language Handicap," New Mexico School Review, 33: 13-15, 38, March, 1954.

[26] Loyd S. Tireman, Teaching Spanish-Speaking Children (Albuquerque: The University of New Mexico Press, 1948), p. 65.

[27] H. T. Manuel, Inter-American Tests (Princeton, New Jersey: Educational Testing Service, 1951).

[28] J. L. Meriam, Learning English Incidentally: A Study of Bilingual Children (Washington: Government Printing Office, 1938.

[29] Ibid., p. 27.

[30] Ibid., p. 99.

[31] Willard Abraham, Coordinator, "Investigation of Mental Retardation and Pseudo Mental Retardation in Relation to Bilingual and Sub-Cultural Factors" (Tempe: College of Education, Arizona State University, 1960), p. 189.

[32] Ibid., pp. 193-197.

[33] Ibid., pp. 192-193.

[34] Knowlton, Clark S., "Spanish Speaking People of the Southwest," unpublished paper, March 31, 1967.

[35] Sister Frances Jerome Woods, Cultural Values of American Ethnic Groups (New York: Harper and Brothers, 1956), p. 34.

[36] Ibid., p. 35.

[37] Margaret Clark, Health in the Mexican-American Culture: A Community Study (Berkeley: University of California Press, 1959), pp. 66-67.

[38] Donald R. Thomas and Ralph K. Stueber, "No Desk for Carmen," Teacher's College Record, 61: 143-150, December, 1959.

[39] Ibid.

[40] Scholes, William E., "The Migrant Worker" in Julian Samora, editor, La Raza: Forgotten Americans, (Notre Dame: University of Notre Dame Press, 1966), pp. 79-80.

[41] Schermerhorn, R. A., These Our People, (Boston: D. C. Heath and Co., 1949), page 5.

[42] Guzman, Ralph, "The Mexican People - An Introspective View," UCLA, Mexican-American Study Project, 1966.

[43] Guzman, Ralph, "The Mexican People - An Introspective View," UCLA, Mexican-American Study Project, 1966.

[44] Day, Sam and Claes Edshammar, "The Migrants," The Idaho Observer, July 29, 1967, pages 5-8.

[45] Day, Sam, and Claes Edshammar, "The Migrants," The Idaho Observer, July 29, 1967, pp. 5-8.

[46] This summary is based upon the following two works: Talcott Parsons, The Social System (Glencoe: The Free Press, 1951), pp. 198-199; and Lyle Saunders, Cultural Differences and Medical Care (New York: Russell Sage Foundation, 1954), pp. 111-140.

[47] Ann Jones, "The Application of School Administrator Competencies in a Spanish-American Community" (unpublished research paper, College of Education, University of New Mexico, Albuquerque, 1958), pp. 71-72.

[48] Ulibarri, op. cit., p. 97.

[49] Tireman and Watson, op. cit., p. 225.

[50] Lyle Saunders, "The Social History of Spanish-Speaking People in Southwestern United States Since 1846," Proceedings of the First Congress of Historians from Mexico and the United States Assembled in Monterrey, Nuevo Leon, Mexico, September 4-9, 1949 (Mexico City: Editorial Culture, T.G., S.A., 1950), p. 165.

Part Three

The text, thus far, has emphasized the need for an understanding of the school child in his role in the community with his family. This includes his development of a value system, establishing a basis for his attitudes toward school success when he encounters his first teachers, and being aware of the many conflicts that arise in interaction across cultures.

Part Three has two major emphases. The first is that the child whose first language has not been English must first learn English as a second language. Mastery of the listening and speaking aspects of communication must be realized before the child can profit from the usual techniques of remedial teaching which classroom teachers can effect. Remedial teaching, in a language understood by the student, can overcome retardation in academic achievement. The second necessary emphasis is that the student cannot get these helps in many school classrooms unless adjustments are made in the school curriculum to accommodate him. Consequently, Chapter 11 contains an evaluation of the place of the course of study in a teacher's daily work with students, the need for and accessibility of appropriate teaching materials, and the need to structure the child's working day at school as flexibly as possible so he can study what he can learn.

CHAPTER 9

Teaching English as a Second Language

INTRODUCTION

A teacher of primary-grade children made the following anecdotal records of difficulties with right choice of words in free conversation:

> The children in my second-grade language class were taking turns telling what they had seen in a picture after glancing at it and then closing the books. When Hosteen, an eight-year-old Navajo, was asked what he had seen, he immediately responded, "I saw a <u>time</u>." He meant that he had seen a <u>clock</u>.

> John, a seven-year-old Anglo, was proudly showing a tooth which his mother had pulled only that morning. He explained he expected to find a quarter under his pillow the next morning. Kenneth, my only Indian child, contributed with interest, "Once I had a tooth under my pillow, and I found a <u>money</u>." He had found a <u>penny</u>.

> A teacher reported a third-grade Indian child complained, "Joe's <u>coughing me</u>." Finally, the teacher observed that Joe was <u>copying</u> the other student's work.

> An Indian girl entered a trading post in the pueblo and asked for a black <u>eraser</u>. The trader's wife asked her to repeat what she wanted. "Oh, you know, a black eraser to comb my hair." What she wanted was a black, fine-toothed <u>comb</u>.

A psychometrist who worked in a city school system enrolling large numbers of Spanish-American children reported the following:

> A little Spanish-American girl who did not really learn to speak English until the fourth grade was her teacher's prize, as she seemed to blossom out linguistically about midyear. One morning she came in crying because she had been scolded by her Spanish-speaking grandmother with whom she lived for "forgetting her Spanish and speaking English all the time."

253

Several counselors have mentioned, and I have had the same experience, having a Spanish-American child misinterpret the question on the Wechsler Intelligence Scale for Children, "How many ears do you have?" The child translates literally in Spanish what you are saying and thinks that you have asked, "How many years do you have?" (How old are you?) He will answer "seven," "eight," or "nine," as the case may be.

These examples, and the others that will follow, indicate several problems that confront teachers when Indian and Spanish-speaking children come to school. We have already noted factors influencing the learning of a second language. The student must have a desire to learn it; otherwise, the teacher's attempts at motivation may be unsuccessful. The amount of out-of-school exposure to the language, the attitude toward the second language of the parents and community leaders, the need for the language in improving socioeconomic status, the presence of radios, television, and current reading materials in the home -- all influence the child's assimilation of the language of the school.

The examples also suggest that weakness in vocabulary, inadequate understanding and differentiation of related words (time, clock; money, penny), and the patterning of sentences in English (How many ears-years do you have?), after the patterning used in the vernacular, are problems of immediate concern to the teacher.

THE AURAL-ORAL APPROACH

The aural-oral method of learning a language is a method of instruction that places emphasis, especially in the beginning stages, on hearing and speaking the new language rather than on learning grammatical structure, translation, reading and writing. The emphasis is entirely upon hearing and speaking the language first. When this method is strictly followed, the learner says only what he has heard, reads what he has said, and writes what he has heard, said, and read.[1] As specified in this definition, second language teaching will emphasize, in its elementary form, pronunciation and sentence patterning.

Pronunciation may be understood to incorporate the pronunciation of the phonemes in the language; intonation and stress as differentiated in statements, questions and commands, and in producing the emotional overtones in surprise, delight, anger, or disgust, and in rhythm. Pronunciation of the phonemes may generally be said to include initial consonants, consonant blend sounds, digraphs, all the variant sounds of the English vowels, and vowel-consonant teams.

Intonation and stress vary with native speakers. Teachers need to be cognizant of the dimensions of rhythm, intonation and stress in clear, understandable English; and they must realize that slurring, phrasing, and contractions are much used in "normal" speech. For example, the variation of stress is pointed out in the following question (the reader is to stress the underlined word in each case): What do you do? What do you do? What do you do? A great deal of practice on master tapes for older students using the language laboratory and continuous review drills will be necessary to give the student a pattern of speech approaching the vernacular.

The aural-oral method of teaching English as a second language has been generally accepted for the beginning stages of the learner. That is, hearing and speaking are emphasized in the beginning to the total exclusion of grammatical structure, translation, reading or writing.

Agard and Dunkel compared the achievements of high school and college classes where those learning by aural-oral methods were classified as experimental and those learning by the reading-grammar approach were the controls.[2] Their findings are interesting. They suggest that the bottom 50 per cent in class achievement in either group are not apt to attain a high degree of mastery. "These students languish in the limbo of those who cannot read nor speak nor comprehend.[3] The notion that aural-oral competence automatically creates reading ability and that reading, per se, need not be specifically taught, was not supported in this investigation. "Oral-aural skills and reading proficiency constitute separate, independent skills which do not develop one from the other, but rather only from direct training in each separately, ... Over a period of time, oral-aural drills tended not to be drilled to the point of overlearning needed, memorization held too much superficial mimicry, and boredom set in."[4]

This study is helpful in stressing the genuine concern teachers must have for both aspects of English teaching: (1) the absolute necessity for the fundamental drills in speech patterns and the development of native-sounding conversational abilities; and (2) as initial learning is consolidated, the equivalent necessity to teach reading skills, vocabulary, grammatical structures, and writing fluency.

TEACHING OF ENGLISH TO SPEAKERS OF SPANISH OR NAVAJO

Phonology

Phonology, or phonetics, is the study of the sound system of a language. Phoneme refers to the separate phonetic elements in the composition of a word. Phonology encompasses the understanding of, and the ability to hear and produce the phonemes in a language. While most single-letter symbols constitute a phoneme in English, this is not a consistent relationship. In the word sing, for example, "s" and "i" are single-letter phonemes, but "ng" is a double-letter phoneme.

In the teaching of English as a second language, the teacher must be aware that the learners have mastered all the sound symbols of another language in infancy. By the time they are three years old, most children have mastered the sound symbols of their vernacular. Through endless repetition they have memorized all of the separate sounds as they are used in myriad combinations in daily speech utterances. Although two languages may be similar, there will be a few sounds not common to both. There are few entirely different phonemes in Spanish-English comparisons, but there are many in Navajo-English.

Teachers illustrate difficulties which Spanish-American children often have with English pronunciation. Note the following list of words given in English with a commonly used pronunciation by Spanish-American children.

English	Mispronunciation
vote	bote
think	sink
they	dey
shoe	chew
yellow	jello
sing	sin
view	few
teeth	teef
chin	gin
who	woo
you	jew

The Spanish alphabet does not incorporate the following underlined sounds: v<u>i</u>ne, <u>z</u>oo, b<u>i</u>t, b<u>a</u>t, b<u>u</u>t, f<u>oo</u>t, and b<u>oa</u>t. In contrast, three sounds in the Spanish alphabet that do not appear in the English one are: caba<u>ll</u>ero, pe<u>rr</u>o, and peque<u>ñ</u>o. A table showing the comparative phonology of Spanish and English is shown below:

Vowels:

Spanish has only <u>five</u> vowel <u>sounds</u>. English has many.

A few difficult contrasts in pronouncing English vowels are:

saying "bit" for "beat"
"bet" for "bate"
"Dan" for "Don" for "done"
"boat" for "but" for "bought"
"full" for "fool"
"put" for "putt"

256

Consonants:

The consonants not pronounced in Spanish as in English are:

"v"	in "vein"	pronounced "bein"	or "vote"	as "boat"
"z"	in "zoo"	"sue"		
"th"	in "think"	"sink"		
"sh"	in "shin"			
"z"	in "azure"			
"ng"	in "sing"	"sin"		
"ch"	in "chew"	"shoe"		
"y"	in "you"	"Jew"	or "yellow"	as "jello"
"wh"	in "What"			
"W"	in "woo"	"who"	or "w"	as "h"

Phonology -- Navajo

Many phonemes in the Navajo language do not appear in the English language and vice versa. Because of many new sounds and a totally different sentence patterning, Navajo children will have more trouble learning English than will Spanish-American children. Teachers need to remind themselves continually that it is harder for a Navajo to learn English than it is for an Anglo to learn an European language. In learning English, Navajo children may transfer phonemes from their language to English, whether they are closely related or not. Once a faulty pronunciation habit becomes established this way, it is difficult to break. As a specific example, the ('), glottal stop, designated with the apostrophe, is a phoneme occurring frequently in Navajo. The child is most likely to carry its use over into English as to make his speech sound "choppy." "Drill designated to call attention of the learner to the fact that English and Navajo differ in this respect would help in overcoming this aspect of non-standard usage."[5]

> A good basic knowledge of the phonology of both English and Navajo could be of inestimable value to teachers concerned with teaching English to Navajo children and adults.[6]

With respect to the specific phoneme comparison, the table showing comparative phonology of the consonants in Navajo and English is presented on the following page. It will be noted that the English phonemes -- v, gl, d, g, p, f, and ng -- have no corresponding sounds in Navajo, except for the partial equivalents for d, g, and b. The Navajo has to learn to aspirate and voice the b, g, and d, and the sound of p is entirely new to him. He is likely to use his unaspirated b for the English b and p; his unaspirated d for English d and t; and his unaspirated g for English g and k. Navajos learning English frequently use the glottal stop in place of g, d, b, p, t, and k at the ends of words, and this error should be pointed out to them. Specific drill should be directed to correct such faulty pronunciations.

257

COMPARATIVE PHONOLOGY*
Consonants -- Navajo-English
(Simplified)

	LABIAL		DENTAL		ALVEOLO-PALATAL		PALATO-VELAR		GLOTTAL	
	English	Navajo	English	Navajo	English	Navajo	English	Navajo	English	Navajo
1. STOPS a. Voiced	b	--			d	--	g	--		
b. Unvoiced Unaspirated	--	b			--	d	--	g		
c. Aspirated	p	--			t	tx	k, kw	k, kw		
d. Glottal					--	t'	--	k'		
2. AFFRICATES a. Voiced					j	--				
b. Unvoiced Unaspirated					--	dz, dl, j				
c. Aspirated					ch	ts, tl, ch				
d. Glottal					--	ts', tl', ch'				
3. SPIRANTS a. Voiced	v	--	dh	--	z, zh	z, zh	--	gh, ghw		
b. Unvoiced	f	--	th	--	s, sh	s, sh	--	x, xw	h	h
4. LATERALS a. Voiced					l	l				
b. Unvoiced					--	--				
5. NASALS	m	m			n	n	ng	--		
6. INVERTED					--					
7. SEMIVOWELS	w	(ghw)		r			y	y		

*From: THE NAVAJO LANGUAGE by Robert W. Young.

Other consonant sounds appearing in Navajo which are not found in English include dz, dl, ts', tl', ch'. There are also vowel sound differences between the two languages. While in English, long and short vowels are distinguished with different sounds, in Navajo, long and short are used to refer to duration in time in pronouncing the vowel.

Unlike the English speaker, the Navajo distinguishes meaning by changing the pitch of a vowel, by lengthening or shortening the duration of the vowel sound, or by denasalizing the vowel.

Morphology

In the context used here, morphology refers to inflections and derivations in the structure of language. Inflections and derivations are changes in word forms. Inflected forms are those that retain the same root but otherwise add prefixes, suffixes, or change to the plural; derived forms are those that change the meaning of the root word when suffixes or prefixes are added. Inflected forms include: talks, talked, talking, from the base word talk. However, crosses, crossed, and crossing are inflected forms of cross; and uncross, double-cross, crosswise, crisscross, and cross section are derived forms of the word cross. Learning all of the irregular forms of verbs is necessary in learning the proper structure of English. Even for the young child for whom English is the vernacular, such forms as "I threw the ball," instead of, "I throwed the ball," must be taught.

A few statements about the morphology of Navajo will help to emphasize the extreme differences between its usage and English. Young states:

> ..... each syllabic element that composes Navajo words has an inherent pitch or tone which can be altered only in conformity with morphophonemic laws governing such alteration. ..... although Navajo is not spoken without varying pitch for emphasis, for the connotation of anger, surprise, etc., the inherent highness or lowness of syllable tones must be carefully distinguished since tone differentiates meaning. The fact that Navajo employs tone to distinguish meaning in this manner places certain restrictions on the use of sentence and word pitch as a medium through which to express such overtones of meaning as surprise, incredulity, disgust, interrogation, exclamation, etc.[7]

Contrast Between English and Navajo

Young and Morgan state:

> . . . the pattern of thought varies so greatly from our English pattern that we have no small difficulty in learning to

think like, and subsequently to express ourselves like the Navajo.[8]

There are two basic assumptions concerning which English and Navajo differ: first, English is a thing oriented language, which leads to a tremendous accumulation of nouns, while Navajo is action oriented, which leads to a complicated system of verbs. The second assumption is that in English, man is seen as the actor who performs actions on things. In contrast to our view of man as the supreme doer who acts on nature, Navajo sees nature as the agent who acts on man. English says, "I am hungry." or "I am drowning." Navajo says, "The spirit of hunger sits beside me." and "Water is killing me." Thus, there can be seen a philosphical difference in Anglo and Navajo views of nature that is reflected in the linguistic systems.[9]

There is a great difference in the way thought patterns are expressed in the two languages -- English and Navajo. While Navajo is a verb language, English is a noun-adjective language.[10] The verb is the most important part of speech in Navajo grammar. To turn a sentence from English into Navajo or from Navajo into English involves a great deal more than choosing the proper word for word equivalents from a dictionary.

Navajo is more precise or literal in meaning than English. For example, when a Navajo wants to say he went somewhere, he never fails to specify whether he went by foot, on horseback, by train, wagon, auto, or airplane.[11]

Since the Navajo use of pitch to differentiate meaning is unlike the English, he will have to be taught something about the way subtle changes in emotional rather than literal meaning take place as a result of inflection of the voice.

Navajo nouns have no gender, and most have the same forms for both singular and plural.[12]

For the teacher of Navajo children, the following are two excellent sources for reading nontechnical information about the Navajo language:

> Clyde Kluckhohn and Dorothea Leighton, The Navajo (Cambridge: Harvard University Press, 1956), Chapter 8: "The Tongue of the People," pp. 182-215.

> Robert Young, "The Navajo Language," The Navajo Yearbook, Vol. VIII, A Decade of Progress, 1951-1961 (Window Rock: The Navajo Agency, 1962), pp. 429-509.

Syntax

Syntax is that part of grammar which teaches the proper construction and arrangement of words in a sentence. English order in the sentence is adjective, noun, and verb. This order will need to be learned. Misplaced modifiers, dangling participles, and run-on sentences cause trouble for native speakers; they must be bases for greater confusion for second language speakers.

OBSERVATIONS CONCERNING SECOND LANGUAGE TEACHING

Some of the miscellaneous principles that teachers may wish to consider in second language teaching are these:

1. Is it necessary for the child always to answer in complete sentences? While the teacher should wish to encourage answering in complete ideas, it would be unwise to require the child always to answer in complete sentences. In answer to the question, "Where do you live?" the child may be required to say "I live in Albuquerque, New Mexico." This teaches the pattern of the complete idea. It is much more natural in usual conversation, however, to answer, "In Albuquerque, New Mexico." Other examples where complete answers may be required at the beginning to enable children to practice the pattern are:

Question	Answer
What is your name?	My name is George.
When will it be time to go?	It will be time to go at 9:30.

The short answers, "George," and "at 9:30," are the usually expected conversational replies.

2. A related problem that will be of concern to teachers of Indian children is the question requiring only "Yes" or "No" for answer. It seems advisable to ask these children always to give a more complete answer than just "Yes" or "No" since they overtly avoid further communication by giving the clipped one-word answer. The following question and answer pattern will illustrate:

Question	Answer
Are you in the second grade?	Yes, I am, or No, I am not.
Do you like to eat apples?	Yes, I do, or No, I don't.
Have you been to the zoo?	Yes, I have, or No, I haven't.
Can you spell the words?	Yes, I can, or No, I can't.

Question	Answer
Is it time to go?	Yes, it is, or No, it isn't.
Are the buttons missing?	Yes, they are, or No, they're not.

3. Also, slurring or running words together is the expected pattern in conversational English. One does not say, "My name is Tom"; rather, he says, "My name's Tom." "What are you doing?" more nearly approximates "Whater ya doing?"

4. When children are learning to use the second language, one of their primary needs is to learn to ask all the questions himself. As the Language Guide for Grade II suggests, the class may be divided in half, and, by turns, half the class ask the questions while the other half answers.[13] Formulating questions with who, what, which, when, where, and how, as these words are taught, with continuous review when it is functional, will help to develop this skill. An exercise which may be helpful in changing statements to questions is given below. Students need help to see that they only reverse the positions of the subjects and the verbs and they have made a question:

Listen to the sentence below as it is said to you. Change the sentence to a question. The first one is done for you.

1. There are three girls in my class. Are there three girls in my class?
2. There are four books on the table.
3. There are two cars in the driveway.
4. There are two reasons why I cannot go.
5. There are some people here to see you.
6. There are apples in the refrigerator.
7. There are bananas in the cupboard.
8. There are smiles on their faces.
9. There are fifty problems in the lesson.
10. There are several coats to choose from.

5. It will be well to select one way of expressing an idea for repeated practice until that pattern is clearly understood. Then variant ways of expressing the same idea should be learned.

6. The general principles of second language teaching are based on the knowledge that the communication arts develop in children in this order: listening, speaking, reading, and writing. Reading and writing will not be attempted until some skill in understanding and speaking have been established. Once a sufficient vocabulary has been mastered,

sentence patterns of a meaningful and interesting nature should be practiced. Drill on sentence patterns until their use is correct and automatic is basic. This overlearning of commonly expected responses, phrases, and leading questions is completely logical when one realizes the innumerable times in a child's life experience in learning his own tongue that he has heard, responded to, and uttered the limited core of speech utterances that constitute the majority of casual talk. This overlearning of patterns is stressed by O'Connor and Haden in teaching Spanish as a foreign language:

Learning a foreign language is not primarily acquiring vocabulary, necessary as this is. It is much more important for the student to focus his attention upon the structure of the foreign language and to engage in practice which will most quickly form habits of articulation, of stress, of intonation, and of word order. The sooner these matters become habit, and not choice, the sooner he will achieve mastery of the language.[14]

LINGUISTIC PRINCIPLES AND TEACHING ENGLISH SENTENCE STRUCTURE

There are several linguistic principles that impinge directly on the work of the classroom teacher. Many teachers are undoubtedly aware of these; others may need to study them carefully and reflect upon their meanings.

1. Language is oral. It is speech before it is reading or writing. Spoken language is the "natural" expression commonly used by the native speaker with its contractions, idiomatic and slang expressions, and one word answers. "How are you?" may be spoken as if it were only one word and "It is a book" is sure to be spoken "Itza book."

2. Language is habit. It is learned behavior. Native speakers are not conscious of each sound or word they say nor of the sequence of the sounds of words. They are primarily concious of the ideas or thoughts they are trying to convey. The stringing together of sounds in certain positions is an unconscious act. The language habit is automatic for children by the time they start to first grade. Because language is learned behavior, it is learned through the repetition of producing it. When children learn the first language in a free, relaxed, trial-and-error atmosphere, there is time for error, correction, and repetition without conscious effort. When any language is super-imposed as a second language, there is much interference between the two sound patterns and much guided repetition, correction, and drill are indicated.

3. Language is arbitrary. It has a specific, prescribed structure. There are only a few basic sentence patterns in the English language that are used frequently. The teachers models, expands, amplified, and reinforces, always hoping that the language is related to concepts, to teach this arbitrary structure. In second language learning, the student should not be permitted to practice an incorrect pattern and reinforce it since it will have to later be unlearned.

4. Language is personal. Language relfects the individual's self-image and is his only avenue to expressing all that he is, all that he has as a heritage, and all that he aspires to be. Just how personal is perhaps well illustrated in the way in which the Paraguayan people have for centuries now had Spanish as the official language of business and government, but have to this day retained Guarani, a pre-literate Indian dialect, as the language of the home and family in which they express their most personal thoughts. It is said that Paraguay is our most bilingual country.

5. The language of a given group of people is neither "good" nor "bad"; it is communication. Reference to dialects of English other than "standard" English are best referred to as "non-standard" rather than "sub-standard."

6. Language is more than words. This is evidenced by the fact that the spoken language can reveal more meanings than the written language. The suprasegmentals of pitch, stress, and juncture as well as facial expression, gesture, and bodily movement add a great deal to meaning and interpretation of language.

7. Language is culturally transmitted; it is complicated; and it is always slowly changing.

METHODOLOGY

Teaching English as a second language is not at all like teaching English to English speakers although teacher preparation in most colleges of education ignores this very important fact. Most teachers find themselves totally unprepared when they go to teach in areas where large percentages of children enrolled in school are learners of English as a new language. On the other hand, the fact remains that no one can help himself in our English-speaking society anywhere until he can speak the language of his peers fluently and spontaneously. The audio-lingual approach to second language learning can prepare boys and girls for much more profitable formal school experiences. For several years, these specific methods of second language teaching have been getting efficient results in bi-national centers all over the world.

First Language Learning vs. Second Language Learning:

The learning of English by the native speaker may be contrasted with learning English as a second language in several ways:

When learning English as a native language:

1. Time is not a factor. The CHILD has six pre-school years to master the sound system of the language of his mother.

2. Infants are usually richly rewarded for each imitative effort. Trial-and-error works very well - with much time - in a friendly, supportive, informal atmosphere.

3. Parents and friends are very patient and expect to repeat, reward, and reinforce.

4. The child grows up in an environment where he enjoys a maximum opportunity to repeat and to remember everything he hears.

5. What the child doesn't remember today, or whatever mistakes he keeps making today, he can unlearn to relearn in the weeks or months in the future.

When learning English as a second language:

1. Time is a crucial factor. One may have eight weeks in the summer; an intensive course; or one must continue an academic course of study in English while learning English.

2. The student must "Listen, repeat, and memorize."

3. The student is "expected" to speak the language of the school. He must have a course of study that is organized, sequential, and efficient. Those who have the patterns internalized are often impatient with older students. Teachers must repeat, reward and reinforce.

4. The classroom situation is conducive to much forgetting. What one learns during one hour, he has all day, all weekend, all vacation periods to forget. One tends to forget almost all of what he studies in a "formal" manner.

5. Drills cannot be avoided. Students must have many repetitions, and carefully spaced reviews on all patterns they need to learn to use automatically.

Learning a foreign language is not primarily acquiring a vocabulary in that language. It is much more important for the student to focus his attention on the structure of expression, sentences, or patterns in that language and to engage in practice which will most quickly form habits of articulation, of stress, of intonation, and of word order. The sooner these matters become habit, and not choice, the sooner the student will achieve mastery of the language.

Language is learned behavior. Native speakers of the language are not conscious of each sound or word they say or of the sequence of the sounds or words. They are primarily conscious of the ideas or thought they are trying to convey. The stringing together of sounds in certain positions is generally unconscious. It is a habit which is automatic by the time children start first grade. Since the spoken language is primary, the sounds of the language, "the stream of speech," should take precedence in our teaching.

Language learning means acquiring the ability to ask and answer questions; to make statements; and to produce the normal expressions used by the native speakers of the language. Answering in complete ideas does not require that one always answer in complete sentences. For example, to the question, "When will it be time to go?" "at 9:30" is a complete answer.

Finally, students must acquire the vocabulary of the language: the nouns, the prepositions, the verbs, the descriptive words, the figures of speech. However, as already emphasized, in the early stages, vocabulary must be subordinated to the sounds and the structures of the language. Vocabulary can be accumulated fairly rapidly and to meet the needs for it after the basic sound structure in the language is mastered. The student learning to speak English must learn communication skills in the hierarchial order of listening, speaking, reading and then writing.

PRINCIPLES OF LANGUAGE ACQUISITION
SUGGESTIONS TO TEACHERS

1. The learner acquires the ability to use the language communication skills of English in the order of listening, speaking, reading, and writing. First, he hears with understanding; second, he reproduces the language he has heard--trying to imitate a "good" model; third, he is then ready to learn that part of the language he has heard and spoken; and fourth, he can then learn to spell and write the language he needs to use, but only after he has heard, spoken, and read it.

2. The learner learns the "sound system" of the language. "The stream of speech," or the words running together rapidly, is the way the spoken language sounds and takes precedence over everything else in learning a new language.

Acquiring a vocabulary of many words <u>is not the important thing</u> at first. Patterns, intonation, and stress are the elements for the student to focus attention on.

3. The language must be learned through <u>repetition</u> in producing it. Guided repetition, correction, and <u>drill</u> are indicated. Drills must be lively, interesting, and not too long, but they cannot be avoided.

4. Three types of language exercises most used are:

   a. Question and answer; changing statement to question; negative, positive, and qualified answers to questions.

   b. Short conversations - dialogs - memorized and practiced over and over.

   c. Substitution drills; expansion drills; paraphrasing ideas in new sentences.

The pressure to move children into formal reading groups before they have learned listening and speaking habits in the language is one of the gravest errors which we continue to make with young children who must learn English as a second language.

Gertrude Hilderth observed Cuban children in Florida schools a few years ago and wrote:

> . . . few could express their ideas well in oral English. All were trying to read material that was too difficult and none were familiar with the life portrayed in the textbooks. The pupils could recognize few words at sight and none of them could use phonics to work out new words. To instruct these children in reading and written work before they speak English is sheer waste of teaching effort.[15]

Some adaptation of the language experience approach to teaching reading could utilize all the advantages in helping second-language students relate the written form of language to the limited spoken language they have learned. Experience charts written in the language of the learned will make reading useful for remembering things; will make reading rewarding in preserving one's own ideas; and will give him good practice in all the skills he needs later for more formal reading.

Experience units of work teaching concepts in social studies and elementary science can be developed with the teacher doing what little writing needs to be done, and the students having much opportunity to talk about the experiences, to evaluate the problems involved, and to discuss freely what is going on in each learning situation.

Roach Van Allen, author of new material now being published by Britannica, says "Children who write, read! They have to read!" He continues emphasizing the "writing way to reading" in this way:

> To children who have experienced authorship many times, reading is not lessons, worksheets, practice exercises, or a time each day in a time schedule (perhaps to dread). It is the continuous discovery of stepping-stones to a lifetime of enjoyment of books. It results in the conceptualizations:
>
> What I can think about I can say.
>
> What I can say, I can write.
>
> What I can write, I can read.
>
> I can read what I can write and what other people have written for me to read.[16]

Contrastive Analysis of Spanish and English

Any teacher who has taught Spanish-speaking children has heard these expressions:

1. Mary is no here;
2. We went through the rooms bigs;
3. Mary is wear a dress red;
4. He no go to school;
5. Yesterday, your brother I saw;
6. I am ready for to read;
7. I see you later;
8. Is Tuesday;
9. This apple is more big than that one;
10. I have twenty years old;
11. He works? Works this man?;
12. The boy is here, no?;
13. The head hurts me;
14. She is nurse;
15. I get myself up early.

The following English-Spanish contrasts are given in the following lists:[17]

ENGLISH	SPANISH
The use of <u>not</u> with verb forms: "Mary is not here."	Usually replaced by <u>no</u>: "Mary is no here."
The use of <u>s</u> for most plural nouns: "boys, pencils."	A silent <u>s</u> is more usual in the Carribean countries. The tendency is therefore to say: "My two girl are big."
The use of "s" in our simple present: "The boy eats."	Verbs are fully inflected. Learning our comparatively uninflected English the student tends to drop even the inflections which persist, to say: "The boy eat."
Negatives with <u>do</u>, <u>does</u>, <u>did</u>: "He did not go to school."	No auxiliaries exist. The tendency is to say: "He no go/went to school."
English adjectives usually preced the noun: "the red dress."	Adjectives usually follow the noun: "The dress red."
Non-agreement of adjective with nominal in either number or gender: "The big rooms."	Agreement of adjective. Tendency is to say: "The rooms bigs."
Adverbs of time appear only at the beginning or end of sentence, usually at the end: "I saw your brother yesterday."	Tendency is to place adverbs of time at the beginning of sentence only: "Yesterday, I saw your brother."
The <u>ed</u> past ending for regular verbs: "wanted."	For a comparatively uninflected form, the tendency is to say: "The baby want milk yesterday."
Use of the gerund: "I am ready for reading."	Tend to replace the gerund with the infinitive: "I am ready for to read."
<u>Going to</u> to express future time: "I am going to sing."	Tendency is to substitute the simple present: "I go to sing."
The auxiliary <u>will</u> in our future: "I will see you later."	Tendency is to carry over the inflection and to say: "I see you later."
The use of <u>it</u> to start a sentence: "It is Tuesday."	Tendency to make the ethnic omission of <u>it</u> and to say: "Is Tuesday."
Comparison of most adjectives with <u>er</u> and <u>est</u>: "tall, taller, tallest."	Spanish uses only <u>more</u> and <u>most</u>: Tendency is to say: "more big," "most big."

Use of <u>to be</u> to express age: "I'm twenty years old."	<u>To have</u> is used: "I have twenty years."
Use of <u>to be</u> to express hunger, thirst, etc.: "I am thirsty."	To have is the more common usage; to be expresses an extreme: "I am hungry" means "I am famished."
Our negative imperative: "don't run!"	Replaced by <u>no</u>: "No run!"
Questions with <u>do</u>, <u>does</u> or <u>did</u>: "Does this man work?"	No auxiliaries exist in Spanish. Tendency is to say: "This man works?" or "Works this man?"
Inversion of subject and verb for question: "Is the boy here?"	Tendency is to use rising intonation rather than inversion: "The boy is here?"
Use of continuous present: "I am working now."	Tendency is to use simple present for all forms of the present: "I work now."
Verbs in indirect discourse: Use the same tense in each clause: "He said that he was sick."	<u>That</u> is followed by the present: "He said that he is sick."
The use of pronouns as subjects: "She can go."	Spanish uses verbal inflection to indicate person and number. Tendency is therefore to omit the pronoun to say "Can go."
Verbal contractions: "<u>I'm</u>, we<u>'ll</u>."	No contractions exist in Spanish, causing ensuing difficulties in English.
Possessive adjective for parts of the body and clothing.	Spanish uses the definite article. Tendency is to say: "The head hurts me."
No definite articles before titles: "I see Dr. Fox."	Definite articles always appear before titles, leading to uses such as "I see the Dr. Fox."
Indefinite article in usual prenominal position with words identifying occupation: "She is a nurse."	Indefinite article not required in such usages; tendency is therefore to say "She is nurse."
Non-separation of compound verbs: "I get up early in the morning."	Same as in English except for the greater use of the reflexive: "I get myself up early in the morning."[17]

Methodology

1. <u>Using selected picture cards</u> from PICTURE CARDS FOR PHONETIC KEY TO READING (P. O. Box 25308, 1901 North Walnut, Oklahoma City, Oklahoma 73125: The Economy Company, 1966), one can practice some very elementary patterns. (The picture cards are part of a set of 200 cards about 7" and 9" in color which are designed to be a part of the beginning phonics program of the Economy program in reading in the first grade. They are excellent for promoting desired oral English with adults in a TESL program.) The following cards which show nouns also included in the test Rapid Test: Vocabulary Game:[18]

a spoon	a bed	a clock	a horse	a shirt
a boy	a light bulb	a house	a cup	some fruit
a chair	a telephone	a cat	a tree	a book
a newspaper	a watch	some books	a stove	a cow
<u>an</u> apple	a fish	a pipe	some apples	a boat
a car	a ruler	a loaf of bread	a stool	a plate
a knife	a hat	a bird	a doll	a rake

Using these pictures, practice:

What's this?	It's a chair.
What's this?	It's a telephone.
What's this?	It's an apple.
What's this?	It's a <u>loaf of</u> bread.
What are these?	These are books.
Is this a book?	Yes, it is.
Is this an apple?	Yes, it is.
Is this a ruler?	Yes, it is.
Are these apples?	Yes, they are.
Are these books?	Yes, they are.
Is this an orange? (holding apple)	No, it isn't. It's not an orange. It's an apple.
Is this a cow? (holding up horse)	No, it isn't. It's not a cow. It's a horse.

What's this?•	It's a bird. It's a red bird. It's a beautiful, red bird.
Is it a beautiful, <u>blue</u> bird?	No, it isn't. It's not a <u>blue</u> bird. It's a beautiful, <u>red</u> bird.
Is it a brown horse?	Yes, it is.
What color is the horse?	It's brown.
What color is the cow?	It's black and white.
Is it a <u>small</u> house?	No, it isn't. It's not a <u>small</u> house. It's a <u>large</u> house.

All of these questions and answers must be repeated by most of the members of the class individually. Beginning classes seem animated and actively involved in lessons such as this one. Other sources of good pictures are:

- a. PHONICS PICTURES FOR THE FIRST THREE PRE-PRIMERS, Detroit City Schools Reading Program, Follett Publishing Company, 1010 West Washington Boulevard, Chicago, Illinois 60607.

- b. PICTURE AND KEY CARDS, The Reading Readiness Program, McKee and Harrison, Houghton Mifflin Company, 110 Tremont Street, Boston, Massachusetts, 02107. 220 cards 9" by 12" - 4 colors used.

- c. The Ideal Reading Readiness Charts, Tagboard, 23" by 36", in color. Developing rhyming words, Selecting rhyming words, Pictures alike and different, Missing parts in pictures, Shapes alike and different, Recognition of size, Lower case letter identification, Action pictures, Name words. Order number 270, nine charts, with manual $4.00. Available from University Book Store - Allied School Supply Co., P. O. Box 1568, Albuquerque, New Mexico.

2. <u>Substitution Drill</u>:

<u>Learners must be taught the structure system in our language</u>. They must <u>drill on</u> other words within word classes that can be substituted for each of words in a pattern:

Did <u>he</u> go to the store this morning?

Did <u>she</u> go to the store this morning?

Did <u>Jack</u> go to the store this morning?

Did <u>father</u> go to the store this morning?
Did father <u>ride</u> to the store this morning?
Did father <u>walk</u> to the store this morning?
Did father <u>drive</u> to the store this morning?
Did father drive to the <u>office</u> this morning?
Did father drive to the <u>airport</u> this morning?
Did father drive to the <u>station</u> this morning?
Did father drive to the <u>farm</u> this morning?
Did father drive to the farm this <u>afternoon</u>?
Did father drive to the farm this <u>evening</u>?

3. Language learning means acquiring the ability to ask and answer questions; to make statements, and to produce the normal expressions used by native speakers of English. Answering in <u>complete ideas</u> does not require that one always answer in <u>complete sentences</u>. In answer to the question, "Where do you live?" the expected answer is "In Albuquerque," or to the question, "When will it be time to go?" the expected answer is "At 9:30," not "It will be time to go at 9:30."

There are only a few basic sentence structures in the English language that are used frequently. Teachers must <u>model</u> the basic structures and make sure that the student learns how to repeat them accurately. The teacher needs to be a good model to imitate. The teacher tells the student exactly what to say and repeats it until the student can imitate correctly.

1. Repeat, repeat, and repeat. One cannot habituate spoken language without a great deal of practice. Guided repetition, correction, and drill. Teachers should always use six or eight repetitions on a pattern in substitution drills before leaving it.

2. Break up utterances into short units, if necessary, for the student to imitate. For example:

Model: The zookeeper was feeding the animals in the zoo.
in the zoo.
the animals in the zoo.
feeding the animals in the zoo.
The zookeeper was feeding the animals in the zoo.

Starting with the end phrase is called "<u>the backward buildup</u>" and is very helpful for those who have trouble remembering the whole sentence. The teacher should allow several students to repeat each phrase before adding more of the sentence to it.

3. <u>Memorize short conversations</u>. Ask students, in pairs, to practice the character parts.

   A six line dialog:

Student:	Can you please tell me where the Post Office is?
Man (on street):	Yes, I can. Are you walking or riding?
Student:	I'm walking.
Man:	It is two blocks straight ahead and one block to the left. It's on a one way street.
Student:	Thank you very much.
Man:	You're welcome.

   A ten line dialog: In a Clothing Store

Clerk:	May I help you?
Customer:	Yes, thank you. I'd like to buy a shirt.
Clerk:	Here are our sport shirts. What size do you wear?
Customer:	I wear medium size.
Clerk:	What color would you like?
Customer:	I want a blue one.
Clerk:	Do you like these?
Customer:	How much do they cost?
Clerk:	These are on sale for $3.49.
Customer:	I'll take this one.

4. Practice changing <u>statements</u> to <u>questions</u>. Also, practice using <u>negatives</u>. Changing sentences to questions:

   There are four chairs in the room. Are there four chairs in the room?

   You will get the paper on the desk. Will you get the paper on the desk?

   There are apples in the refrigerator. Are there apples in the refrigerator?

   <u>Can</u> he come? No, he <u>can't</u>.

   Is it a book? No, it <u>isn't</u>.

5. Provide a great deal of word substitution drill practice. In the frame-work below, any one of the subjects, adverbs, verbs, and prepositional phrases will constitute a good sentence:

Subject	Adverb	Verb	Prepositional Phrase
I	often	work	on Saturday nights.
My sister	usually	works	after dinner.
Jack	sometimes	stays	after school.
My father	never	studies	during the weekend

6. Expansion drills.

    Model: He can read the lesson at home tomorrow.

                    He can read.

        What?   He can read the lesson.

        Where?   He can read the lesson at home.

        When?   He can read the lesson at home tomorrow.

    Model: The American boy in my class lives there in that house on the corner.

        He lives there.

        The boy lives there.

        The boy lives there in that house.

        The boy lives there in that house on the corner.

        The American boy lives there in that house on the corner.

        The American boy in my class lives there in that house on the corner.

    Model: He went to the store to buy a new shirt to wear to the school dance in the gymnasium on Saturday night.

        He went to the store.

        He went to the store to buy a new shirt.

        He went to the store to buy a new shirt to wear to the school dance.

        He went to the store to buy a new shirt to wear to the school dance in the gymnasium.

        He went to the store to buy a new shirt to wear to the school dance in the gymnasium on Saturday night.

Basic Sentence Structures in English

1. Subject-Verb

    I am going   We can drive   He studies

2. Subject-Verb-Object or Predicate noun or adjective.

    John shot a deer.

    He studied his lesson.

    He is class president.

    Her dress is blue.

3. Subject-Verb-Prepositional phrase
   It is on the table.
   He is in the house.
   Mary went to the store.
4. Use of it, this, that, these, there, they're to begin sentences.
   It's a book.   These are mine.   These're mine.
   They're here.   That's a good example.
5. Use of negatives:
   Example: Do you work on Sunday?
   No, I don't work on Sunday.
   Do you like to study English?
   No, I don't like to study English.
   Is it a book?
   No, it isn't. It isn't a book. It's a briefcase.
   Is it a sweater?
   No, it isn't. It isn't a sweater. It's a jacket.
6. Changing simple statements to questions and vice versa.
   The coat is blue. Is the coat blue?
   Is that man an engineer? That man is an engineer.
   (No words added. Only rearranging of the same words.)
   Do they wear cotton clothes in summer?
   They wear cotton clothes in summer.
   (Do must be "added" to ask the question.)
7. Choosing an answer when "or" is used:
   Is the dress green or blue? (Not, "yes, it is") It's blue.
   Is the stop sign red or green? (Not, "Yes, it is") It's red.
8. Learning how to ask questions using What, When, Where, Why, Who, How.
9. Learning past, present, and future:
   I go to work. I went to work yesterday. I will go to work tomorrow.
   I understand the lesson. I understood the lesson yesterday. I will understand when you tell me.

10. Prepositions:

in, into, on, of, to, after, before, up, at.

The book is on the table.

The book is in the desk.

We went into the room.

I live in Albuquerque.

I live on Marble Avenue.

I live at 3028 Marble Avenue, N. E.

11. Tag-on questions:

He can do the work, can't he?

He does his work well, doesn't he?

He did study his lesson, didn't he?

12. If, whether, however, in spite of.

I will come if it doesn't rain.

Mary will marry him whether her father likes it or not.

He drove through the mountains is spite of the fact that it snowed all day.

13. Special words:

A. Begin early drilling on correct use of "a" and "an," a book, an apple, a map, an egg, a knife, an umbrella.

B. Drill on countable and uncountable nouns.

a ball	some sand	some milk
three balls	some bread	some paint
a map	some money	some medicine
two maps	some coffee	some wood
an umbrella	some sugar	some meat
six umbrellas		

English-Spanish Phonemic Sound Differences

1. English uses the sound feature of voicing (voiced vs. voiceless sounds) which distinguishes (s) from (z) as the sole contrasting item that separates meanings of words. Example: race - raise; lacy - lazy; niece - knees; seal - zeal; price - prize. This is never the sole feature to separate meanings in Spanish.

2. English uses the sound difference between (n) and (ng) as a means of distinguishing meanings while the Spanish Language does not. Example: ran - rang; sin - sing; kin - king; thin - thing; fan - fang; ban - bang.

3. The Spanish speaker learning English must learn many new consonant blend sounds. "Sh" in shine; "Wh" in when; or the short "a" in man.

   English contains a great many consonant clusters in initial and final positions which are not found in Spanish. These are often difficult for the student to discriminate and reproduce. Fries writes that there are thirty-nine such consonant clusters in English compared to only twelve in Spanish.

4. While Spanish uses only five vowel sounds, English uses many more to distinguish meanings. Practice must be given to develop auditory discrimination of these pairs of vowels: heat - hit; met - mate; tap - tape; look - luck; pin - pine; hat - hot; sheep - ship; mit - meet; eat - it; late - let; bed - bad; fool - full; coat - caught; caught - cut.

5. Consonant sounds can cause trouble too: pig - big; pig - pick; thank - sank; then - den; place - plays.

   Also, clusters like "ts" in hats; "lpt" in helped; "lkt" in talked.

6. Minimal pairs. The phonene is the minimum feature of the expression system of a spoken language by which one thing that may be said is distinguished from any other thing which might have been said. Thus, bill and pill differ in only one phoneme. They are, then, a minimal pair. (See page 282.)

7. Modifiers do not follow the noun in English:

   The blue sky, not the sky blue.

   The juicy apples, not the apples juicy.

   also,

   "The bus station" is not the same as "the station bus."

   "The pocket watch" is not the same as "the watch pocket."

8. Word order in sentences has more flexibility in Spanish than in English. Example: "I came yesterday here." "Throw the cow over the fence some hay."

9. The irregularity of some verbs causes much difficulty after children learn to generalize from regular forms:

   "I teared the paper." "I throwed the ball." "I dood it." The irregularity of singular-plural forms of nouns, also: mouse - mice; man - men; goose - geese; sheep - sheep; child - children.

10. Intonation and stress are very important in conveying meanings:

Which book did you buy?   Are you going back to school this fall?

Which book did you buy?   Are you going back to school this fall?

Which book did you buy?   Are you going back to school this fall?

Cautions for the Teacher

1. Do not introduce a new vocabulary item at the same time that you are introducing a new structure pattern. Rather, teach new vocabulary in old sentence patterns; and teach new sentence patterns with old vocabulary items.

2. Do not teach two items that might be confusing during the same class period. For example, children need a few prepositions. Crymes suggests concentrating on these nine: at, on, in, of, for, from, by, with, and to. However, they must be taught one at a time, not all at once.

    Also, Allen suggests not teaching word opposites as new concepts during the same class period. In the pairs, large-small, old-young, up-down, teach one of the pairs in one lesson and the other member of the pair after the first is understood. If the child tries to learn both at once, he may confuse the two completely.

3. Young children need words that are required for the use of fundamental grammatical patterns such as the names of the days of the week, months of the year, numbers to ten, and common adjectives. We should not try to teach all the days of the week in one lesson, or all the months of the year, or all the numbers from one to ten. If you try to teach these as lists, the student will remember them as lists. Then when he needs just one of them, he will have to go mentally through the whole list before arriving at the day, or month, or number that he needs. Start with one day that has special significance - perhaps the five school days as they fall in rotation, or with Sunday if it is a special day. After all seven days of the week have been taught, in several separate lessons - then give the whole list and provide lots of review.

    Don't try to teach beginners all the words that pertain to clothing, shelter, food, or transportation: only the items that are important to the learners in their environment should be taught at this time.

    At this point, the mastery of structure and sounds is most important; the size of vocabulary load must be subordinated to this mastery.

4. Do not spend drill class time talking to the class about what they need to be learning. Do not present long lists of isolated vocabulary to work on, for example. Rather, strive for as much of the time for class participation as possible. Work on patterns, with zest, with variations, and keep the responses changing. Plan many substitution drills, expansion drills, changing sentence order drills, and as soon as children are "comfortable" in group responses, move to smaller group and individual responses. For beginning groups many words can be taught through objects and pictures, through demonstration - pointing to objects, pointing to small models of furniture, pointing to articles belonging to the students.[19]

The six component parts of a school program of teaching English as a second language are:

1. Experiences. The teacher needs to capitalize on or to create experiences in which the need for speaking English is present. The child's acquaintance with the concept through firsthand and concrete experience should help to insure understanding of the idea and integration of the concept into his total background of experience.

Morris reminds us that learning cannot take place in a vacuum. Too often this is what we are expecting when children are asked to deal with facts and concepts of an urban, industrialized society in terms of their own rural, non-industrial cultural experiences.

Morris goes on to say:

A survey of commonly used social studies and science textbooks in the primary grades shows that they emphasize units dealing with cities, urban activities, and with the artifacts of a modern, industrial society. The large city fire department, factories, newspaper and telephone offices, machines and modern sources of power.

Morris attempted to meet this problem of vocabulary development by providing a series of fifteen field trips for first and second graders with language patterns planned for oral-aural practice both before and after the excursion.[20]

2. Vocabulary. The teacher needs to develop systematically a vocabulary for expressing oneself. Acquiring a knowledge of words, practicing precise use of prepositions, idioms, synonyms, pronouns and verb tenses, is a never-ending task in language. The problem of meaningful concepts in vocabulary will be expanded in Chapter 10.

3. Sentence Patterns. The teacher needs systematically to develop automatic control and fluency in the use of natural

and accurate English language patterns. Children must habituate the commonest speech utterances and be able to use them with ease. Approximately 300 common English expressions constitute a large percentage of the language used in casual conversation in greetings, passing the time of day, and obtaining or giving information for satisfying one's needs. These were first developed in detailed lesson plans for teachers in the <u>Language Guides of the Puerto Rican Study</u>, the Teachers' Guides for Teaching English prepared by the Philippine Center for Language Study, the <u>Fries American</u> English Series, and Hornby's <u>Teaching of Structural Words and Sentence Patterns.</u>

4. Imitation of a good speech model in the vernacular. The teacher needs to help the learner understand and produce precise sounds, rhythm, and intonation. This will be accomplished by imitation of a native speaker, or competent speaker, whose inflection, emphasis, stress, and pitch characterize a "normal form" of English speech. It will be helpful, at times, if the teacher knows the student's vernacular so that he will be aware of differences in the two languages in rising and falling inflections, words stressed in sentences, and whether the tone of voice affects meaning.

5. Reading and writing. The learner will not be expected to read and write language he has not heard and come to understand in oral usage. This means that reading and writing will be delayed until the learner has mastered a sizeable speaking vocabulary. When the learner demonstrates sufficient readiness, the teacher needs to teach all the developmental skills in reading. Continual emphasis must be given to understanding concepts and testing the child's ability to paraphrase meanings of concepts presented. Only when the child has reached this level of competency in the use of the language is he ready to develop writing as a useful skill.

6. Contrasting English with the child's vernacular. The teacher will function with greater confidence if he knows something of the phonology, morphology, and sentence patterning in the child's language.

Speakers of English as a second language need lots of help with minimal pairs. Minimal pairs are words that sound almost alike but have one phoneme that is not the same, and that one sound makes the two words entirely different in meaning. For example: live and leave; bit, bet and beat; mit and meet; He's living here - He's leaving here; chop and shop; share and chair; chip and ship; chin and shin; shoes and chews; shock and chock. A long list of minimal pairs follows:

MINIMAL PAIRS - contrasting phonemes in English for speakers learning English as a new language:

leave	leaf	suit	soot	tree	three
life	live	soon	sun	boat	both
few	view	noon	nun	tent	tenth
safe	save	fool	full	toot	tooth
proof	prove	spoon	spun	true	through
feel	veal	tube	tub	team	theme
		pool	pull	brought	broth
mat	met	booze	buzz	nutting	nothing
mass	mess				
dad	dead	sowed	sawed	seat	seed
sad	said	phone	fawn	bet	bed
bat	bet	choke	chalk	tent	dent
ran	wren	coat	caught	feet	feed
pan	pen	coal	colt	sat	sad
sand	send	oat	ought	heart	hard
		load	lawn	bleat	bleed
robber	rubber	boat	bought	set	said
cop	cup	cold	called	bolt	bold
lock	luck				
shot	shut	rip	rib	late	let
doll	dull	pit	bit	taste	test
hot	hut	pie	buy	age	edge
cot	cut	pack	back	pain	pen
model	muddle	mop	mob	braid	bread
not	nut	staple	stable	rake	wreck
		rope	robe	gate	get
tuck	tug				
bake	beg	boat	vote	live	leave
ache	egg	curb	curve	sin	seen
pick	pig	bent	vent	mitt	meat
peck	peg	berry	very	chip	cheap
cold	gold	best	vest	bit	beat
back	bag	covered	cupboard	dip	deep
weather	whether	thought	taught	threw	true
watt	what	Sue	zoo	thinker	tinker
witch	which	place	plays	wreath	reef
wear	where	price	prize	thorn	torn
clash	class	laugh	lath	death	deaf
leash	lease	sink	zinc	with	whiff
shale	sale	loss	laws		
		dice	dies		
		lacy	lazy		
		rice	rise		

They also need help with noun plus noun combinations--where to put the stress: Christmas tree; wrist watch; watch pocket and pocket watch; shoe box.

Drill must be made as meaningful as possible. Mechanical drill is necessary, but teachers must always seek ways to move from mechanical to more creative types of drills.

What is important is that the student talk, whether or not he makes mistakes. If he does make mistake, the teacher should repeat the item as it should be but with no scolding or explanation. If the students are making too many mistakes, the teacher should look to his teaching. If the child does not talk, there is no language to try to improve.

As a result of an experiment carried out during the 1963-64 School Year, Talley recommended a special enriched language arts program, including the teaching or oral English as a second language, and study of idiomatic English expressions and the multiple meanings of words, be implemented in the school system for all children who hear and/or speak a language in their home situations which is not the one in which they are required to function at school. After six months of working with experimental groups in fourth and sixth grades, the experimental groups made significantly greater gains on reading tests than control groups, but what seems more significant, their mean I.Q. scores on alternate forms of the California Test of Mental Maturity increased ten points while the control groups increased only three points.[21]

Teachers need techniques for interesting and varied pattern practice, habituating the signals in the sound system which convey meaning.

Materials for Teachers for Teaching English as a Second Language

I. Selected materials for teachers to use with students in classes.

Since the teachers will be learning how to use the techniques of teaching the audio-lingual approach, they must have a set of materials which they can follow quite closely until they establish confidence in what they are trying to do.

They will find textbooks like the English 900 paperback textbooks useful. These books are prepared by English Language Services, Inc., and published by The Macmillan Company, 866 Third Avenue, New York, New York, 10022. 1965 editions. Six books in the series each contain 150 sentence patterns. Intonation exercises, question and answer exercises, conversations are developed around pattern in units.

Teachers need supplementary practice like that given in PRACTICING AMERICAN ENGLISH, Pattern Drills for Oral Practice

(330 West 42nd St., New York, New York 10036: The McGraw-Hill Book Company, 1962). This book presents over 500 pattern drills to facilitate the student in learning the audio-lingual approach. Models, without explanation, for both excellent oral and written exercises, are given.

National Council of Teachers of English, English for Today, Books 1-6, (New York: McGraw-Hill, 1962). Teacher's edition for each text. Oriented toward the oral-direct teaching method. Vocabulary is controlled and the patterns are sequenced. Emphasizes oral drills to give understanding of the structure and grammar.

In the last twenty years, a near-revolution in second-language teaching has been effected by the application of some of the insights of descriptive linguistics to the preparation of second-language teaching materials, and to the use of such materials.

. . . . Only with the ability to hear and to speak a language effectively can students ever hope to read and write it with anything like near-native proficiency.

. . . . What is needed is a systematic and pattern-sequential language program which attempts, inasfar as is possible, to keep capability in spoken English ahead of the demands of written English.[22]

Holm encourages teachers:

TESOL, then, for us, might be said to be the selection and teaching of useful English sentences of certain basic types in a manner that will enable Navajo pupils to make habitual not so much the content of these sentences as the rules of their formation and transformation. Only if children truly learn these rules and learn them so well that they too are largely unaware of them will they ever be able to form, transform, and realize their own sentences in English; that is, to speak English rather than just some English.[23]

It is clear . . . that there is a strong emotional element involved in the learning of a foreign language, just as there is in the learning of a native language. The small child needs the security and encouragement of a warm and loving atomsphere in order to develop verbal fluency, and the student of the foreign language needs to feel at ease with his teacher if he is to be able to imitate and assimilate the language adequately. (This is, incidentally, an element which is completely lacking in a language laboratory booth, unless it is supplied by the supervising teacher.)[24]

"SITUATIONAL" AND "STRUCTURED" PATTERNS IN THE LANGUAGE PROGRAM

There are two kinds of learning of English going on in every teacher's classroom when he is following a planned TESL course of study.

One kind of language learning is that which has been used and enriched in the past to teach the child all the language he needs to use "now" to meet his present needs. Most traditional programs for pre-first grades were planned around supplying the child with what he needs to know first. This is the really vital and dynamic part of the language program from the child's point of view the first year. To completely and easily understand all the expressions giving directions and making announcements is very important to the security and well-being of the child. "Tell us about it." "It is time for lunch now." "Get your black crayon." "Write your name on your paper." These are only a few of those common uses of English that make teaching English incidentally or teaching situational English an absolute must.

In this communication, the only expectation in terms of goals is to communicate now in a meaningful way. There is not expectation that children will learn sentence structure and to generalize about it.

This teaching of the situational language is not the same as the planned, sequential development of spoken language; emphasizing that language is structured; or that language will be habituated through repetition, substitution, and drill.

This part of the language program meets the immediate needs of the present.

The other kind of language learning should be the specifically planned, organized, sequenced development of automatic control on the part of the child of the commonest sentence patterns in the English language. The basic objective is to obtain mastery of the basic structure of the English sentence patterns. The program moves from the simple to the more complex in graduated lessons in which new vocabulary or structure is introduced in terms of what English the student has already mastered. Obviously, the teacher need not think of the two parts of the language program as opposing each other. It is hoped that they will complement each other. As the child learns to use basic sentence structures which include expressions already taught for their cruciality, the teacher can take advantage of this learning and fit that known language into the sequenced plan for learning the structure of English.

The distinction between "Situational English" and "Structured English as a Second Language" is delineated for teachers on the Navajo in this way:

> One, the short-range need, is to be able to "function" or to "communicate" in English with a non-Navajo speaking teacher who must of necessity teach from English language texts; the other, the long-range need, is to develop the ability to "Make one's own sentences in English," i.e., to develop mastery of the structure of English. The Area ESL Program, then, is a dual one: a "situational" program intended to help the child cope with specific situations and a "structural-sequential" program intended to help the child develop progressive mastery of English structure.[25]

In Teaching English as a second language teachers emphasize:

There are a few little connecting words in English that are required in speech but in which all the stress is omitted. Helping the learner of the language to understand what is happening when he uses these unstressed little words, may facilitate his understanding of spoken messages. Some of these words are "to", "for", "of", "the".

We pronounce "to" as "tu" most of the time; "for" as "fer"; "of" as "uv"; and "the" as "tha".

"I am going to the store" is rendered as "I'm going tu tha store."

"What did you come for?" is rendered as "What'd ya cumfer?"

"I've lots of time." is rendered as "I've lots uv time."

METHODS FOR EFFECTING CHANGE IN SCHOOL ACHIEVEMENT

An analogous problem was analyzed for Negro students by Jones[26] in the Saturday Review. He stated that the lack of success could be solved by the following four steps: (1) Measure the degree and extent of unreadiness; (2) Admit it; (3) Determine the whys; and (4) Do what needs to be done to remove the unreadiness.

We have been measuring the extent of the problem for a long time. Some have accepted the problem and probed for kinds of solutions. The solutions are not easy--encompassing the anthropological, as well as the sociological and phychological, nature of cultural heritage, understanding the interdependence of language and culture, learning the elementary linguistics involved in contrasting the sound systems of the two languages, and developing some sophistication in the teaching of English as a second language may be a great deal to ask of a classroom teacher--but teachers of this caliber are the ones who will help students overcome their language, experience and cultural barriers. Administrators and supervisors who plan the curriculum and purchase the materials of instruction must also acquire these skills.

School administrators need to:

1. Try again to define "where we are" in the earnest attempt to "start where we are" with respect to both students and faculty. But if we "start where the students are" in school, we'll begin with an understanding of their values and modes of life and thought--and help them to understand contrasting or conflicting values of the middleclass Anglo school.

   By and large, we've never started where they were. We've largely ignored the cultural difference or actively opposed it--which largely defeats our purpose.

   Then we've blindly ignored the communication barrier and started teaching formal reading in English before we habituated any flow of spoken English.

2. Tool up for intensive teaching of English as a second language. This is not basic English as traditionally taught to undereducated adolescents and adults whose native language was English. For some, basic English would mean teaching the grammatical structure of the language, and in TESL, we will teach and habituate selected patterns without teaching formal grammar except as it is needed.

3. Administer tests of achievement for a purpose--when they reveal weaknesses, teachers must teach diagnostically to correct weaknesses. This means competent remedial reading for bilinguals and competent remedial reading where needed for culturally disadvantaged.

4. Help all our students establish realistic educational goals. They need not go to trade schools if they have greater innate potential, but all university lectures will be given at a rapid rate in the English language if they enroll there.

5. Teach reading and writing skills at whatever level students can function successfully. But reading and writing skills will not likely improve very much if we have not first made sure that the student understands well what he hears and that he commands an ample oral vocabulary.

TESTING INSTRUMENTS FOR MEASURING
LEVEL OF UNDERSTANDING ENGLISH

Obviously, if a teacher has some native speakers of English in his class, some students who have advanced to an intermediate stage in learning English, and some students who know practically no English, he must have some way of measuring this language power so that he can establish sub-groups within the room and assign material that is sufficiently challenging but not too difficult.

One method of operating in such a situation will be to identify those tests that are available that meet specific purposes and try to select those that might be appropriate for some of the second language learners in a given class.

I. Tests for those with practically no knowledge of English:

   A. Rapid Test: Vocabulary Game, For students of foreign languages, (Lincolnwood, Illinois: National Textbook Corporation, 1963). This test contains one-hundred small pictures of common nouns to be identified. The student may write the name on the space provided or he may merely name the picture and the teacher record his response. Teachers could utilize this test to get a "beginning" score for a student who had no English-speaking ability and, after teaching the language for a while, re-test to demonstrate the growth made. This is the "naming" level for students who do not yet understand the sound pattern of the language.

   B. The Common Concepts Foreign Language Test, (Del Monte Research Park, Monterrey, California: California Test Bureau, 1963). In this test, the teacher reads a simple sentence in English and the student selects the appropriate picture in a series of four as a multiple choice response. For students in fourth grade and above, the student marks his answers on a separate answer sheet. If administered to younger children, the system of marking answers will have to be adapted to his level of ability. This test has been successfully administered individually to kindergarten children with the person administering the test marking the answer sheet as the child indicates which picture is correct.[27] This test measures the ability to understand the spoken language at a very elementary level. All of the eighty sentences in any one of the forms are simple sentences. Half of the complete test, or forty items, could be administered individually in about ten minutes. This test could also be used as a pre-test and a post-test to measure progress.

   C. Adult Basic Learning Examination, Level I, Form A. (New York: Harcourt, Brace and World, Inc., 1967). While this test contains several parts and includes reading, spelling and arithmetic computation, it has two sections that are listening tests. These test the understanding level of spoken English. One sub-test is a fifty-item test, multiple-choice vocabulary items, which is read aloud to the subject and he indicates which choice is correct. The other test is an arthmetic test of story problems for which the child selects correct multiple-choice answers. While the testing of understanding of oral English among elementary school children was not the purpose for which the test was designed, these two sub-tests could be useful for this purpose.

D. A teacher can easily test the ability of a student to understand context reading by selecting a passage with an identified grade-level of difficulty, reading it to the student, and then asking him either to answer comprehension questions about the passage or to retell the sequence of ideas contained in the passage. Such short passages as those contained in the New Practice Readers should serve this purpose. The average length of passages and the level of reading difficulty of each of the books in the series are shown below:

New Practice Readers, Clarence Stone, et. al., (St. Louis: Webster Division, McGraw-Hill Book Co., 1960-1961).		
Book	Average Number of Words per Article	Grade Level of Difficulty*
A	110	2.5
B	130	3.2
C	155	4.5
D	175	5.1
E	195	5.7
F	199	6.2
G	220	6.8

* Levels A and B rated on Spache Readability Formula; Books C through G rated on the Dale-Chall Formula for Predicting Readability.

After listening to the teacher read a passage, the student must be able to answer at least 75% of the questions asked to show that he understands the ideas, or he must be able to retell the story with the ideas in proper sequence in his own words and in the retelling show that he is not merely verbalizing but knows the meanings contained in the words.

II. Tests for those students able to read and write some English:

A. Diagnostic Test for Students of English as a Second Language, A. L. Davis Educational Services, 1730 Eye Street, N. W., Washington 6, D. C., 1953. This is a 150-item multiple-choice test of English usage. Part I tests proper use of pronouns, nouns, adjectives, adverbs, ellipses, prepositions, word order. Part II tests verb models and modes, verb tenses and voice, and verbals. Test III is idiomatic vocabulary. The answer sheet is so designed that it shows diagnostically in which of these areas the student makes the most errors. When administered to a sample of fifth and sixth grade English-speaking students, it was found that they made average scores of 130 - 135. The American Language Center found that University students from foreign countries could do satisfactory college work if they earned scores of 125 or above on this test. (See page 303.)

B. An English Reading Test, for Students of English as a Foreign Language, Harold King and R. Campbell, English Language Services, Washington, D. C., 1964. It was designed as a screening device for foreign students who wish to attend American universities. It contains fifty items of increasing difficulty. Not a speed test, the thirty-minute time limit does insure comparable results from student to student. Tentative norms indicate that 70% correct is the minimum score usually acceptable for recommendation to university work.

C. The Michigan Test of English Language Proficiency, The English Language Institute, The University of Michigan, 1962. Is used to determine academic qualifications of students in the English language. Tests grammar, vocabulary, and reading comprehension. A minimum score indicates sufficient knowledge of English to enroll for full-time college work.

D. Test of Aural Comprehension, Robert Lado, English Language Institute, University of Michigan, 1957, Forms A, B, and C. This is a forty-minute test to measure understanding of spoken English by persons whose native language is not English. The test is objective and the student marks a multiple choice answer on a separate answer sheet. On the sixty-item test, a score of 80% or better indicates sufficient understanding of spoken English to attempt university work.

E. Informal tests. The fifty-item revised Yandell-Zintz reading test of common idiomatic expressions and the 100-item Cox Multiple Meanings Test can be used and interpreted using the limited norming data now available. (See Appendix.)

III. Other Tests.

A. Speech Improvement Cards, Brying Bryngelson and Esther Glaspey, (Chicago: Scott Foresman and Co., 1951). By completing the speech record blank for initial, medial, and final sounds, the teacher can attempt to determine which of the consonant sounds and the non-native English speaker is distorting, substituting, or omitting. <u>The Speech Improvement Cards</u> will provide sets of pictures for practice on those sounds giving difficulty.

B. <u>The Durrell Reading Capacity Test</u>, Donald D. Durrell and H. B. Sullivan, (World Book Co., Yonkers-on-Hudson, 1937). This is a test in which the examiner does all the reading and the student marks his multiple choice answer by selecting one of three pictures that answers the question read by the examiner. For second language students, the results would be some indication of the extent to which they understand spoken English. This test is now old enough and the black and white pictures are so small that the results need to be interpreted with caution.

C. <u>Phonics Survey, Reading Laboratory I</u>, Don H. Parker and Genevieve Scannell, (259 Erie Street, Chicago 11, Illinois: Science Research Associates, Inc., 1962). For older students already attempting formal reading, this test might serve excellent diagnostic purposes in locating gaps in the student's learning of phonetic and structural analysis skills. The twenty-one sub-tests cover initial and final consonants, digraphs, blends, long and short vowels, phonograms, endings, compound words, vowel digraphs, the magic "r", and prefixes and suffixes. If students above third grade are having trouble in any of these areas, the teacher may better direct his teaching to the point of error if this diagnosis is made.

D. <u>Silent Reading Diagnostic Test, Form D-A</u>, Guy Bond, Cyril Hoyt, and Theodore Clymer, (Chicago: Lyons and Carnahan, 1955). This test measures: ability to recognize words in isolation, words in context, and reversible words; ability to locate word elements; ability to divide words in syllables and locate root words; and ability to synthesize words when divided at the end of the line. The test is diagnostic in that it reveals initial, middle, and final errors, knowledge of word elements, beginning and ending sounds, and rhyming words. For any student above the third grade, the completed profile of this test reveals specific areas where corrective teaching is needed.

Selected Materials for Teaching English
to Speakers of Other Languages

I. Professional Reading for the teacher:

1. Allen, Harold B., Editor, TEACHING ENGLISH AS A SECOND LANGUAGE, A BOOK OF READINGS, (New York: McGraw-Hill, 1965).

2. Brooks, Nelson, LANGUAGE AND LANGUAGE LEARNING, (New York: Harcourt, Brace and World, 1964).

3. Bumpass, Faye L., TEACHING YOUNG STUDENTS ENGLISH AS A FOREIGN LANGUAGE, (New York: American Book Company, 1963).

4. Dacanay, F. R., and Donald Bowen, TECHNIQUES AND PROCEDURES IN SECOND LANGUAGE TEACHING, (Dobbs Ferry, New York 10522: Oceana Publications, Inc., 1963).

5. Finocchiaro, Mary, ENGLISH AS A SECOND LANGUAGE: FROM THEORY TO PRACTICE, (New York: Regents Publishing Co., 1964).

6. Fires, C. C., TEACHING AND LEARNING ENGLISH AS A FOREIGN LANGUAGE, (Ann Arbor: University of Michigan Press, 1947).

7. Lancaster, Louise, INTRODUCING ENGLISH: AN ORAL PRE-READING PROGRAM FOR SPANISH-SPEAKING PRIMARY PUPILS, (Boston: Houghton Mifflin, 1966).

II. Materials for use in teaching English as a second language:

1. Boggs, Ralph S., and Robert J. Dixson, English Step by Step With Pictures, (200 Park Avenue South, New York, New York 10003: Regents Publishing Co., 1956).

2. Bumpass, Faye L., We Learn English With Pepe and Bing, (New York: American Book Company, 1955). A six-book series for elementary school.

3. Dixson, Robert J., Complete Course in English, Book I and II, (200 Park Avenue South, New York, New York 10003: Regents Publishing Co., 1955).

4. Dorry, Gertrude Nye, Games for Second Language Learning, (New York: McGraw-Hill Book Company, 1966).

5. English Language Services, Inc., English This Way, A twelve-book series for teaching English from the beginning level, (New York: The Macmillan Company, 1963). Two teachers manuals are available for the series.

6. English Language Services, Inc., English 900, A six-book series containing 900 sentence patterns for using practical English. (New York: The Macmillan Company, 1964). Teacher's guide available.

7. Finocchiaro, Mary, Learning to Use English, Books I and II, (200 Park Avenue, South, New York, New York 10003), 1968.

8. Hall, Eugene J., Practical Conversation in English for Advanced Students, (200 Park Avenue South, New York, New York 10003, Regents Publishing Co., 1967).

9. The Institute of Modern Languages, Inc., <u>Contemporary Spoken English</u>, A six-book series, prepared by John Kane and Mary Kirkland, (New York: Thomas Y. Crowell Co., 1967-1968).

10. The Institute of Modern Languages, Inc., <u>Contemporary Review Exercises</u>, A two-book series, prepared by B. Kirk Rankin III and John Kane, (New York: Thomas Y. Crowell Co., 1967).

11. Keelty, Gladys S., <u>Building American Sentences, Elementary Level</u>, and <u>Building American Sentences, Advanced Level</u>, (2526 Grove Street, Berkeley, California 94704: McCutchan Publishing Corporation, 1966).

12. National Council of Teachers of English, <u>English for Today</u>, A six-book series, (New York: The McGraw-Hill Book Company, Inc., 1962-1966). Project Director and General Editor: William R. Slager. Teacher's Edition available for each text.

    Book I: <u>At Home and At School</u>, 1962.
    Book II: <u>The World We Live In</u>, 1962.
    Book III: <u>The Way We Live</u>, 1964.
    Book IV: <u>Our Changing World</u>, 1966.
    Book V: Life In English Speaking Countries, 1964.
    Book VI: Literature in English, 1964.

13. Lado, Robert and Fries, C. C., <u>An Intensive Course in English</u>, (Ann Arbor: University of Michigan Press, 1954). <u>English Pronunciation, Exercises in Sound Segments, Intonation, and Rhythm</u>; <u>English Sentence Patterns, Understanding and Producing English Grammatical Structures: An Oral Approach</u>; <u>English Pattern Practices, Establishing the Patterns as Habits</u>, revised 1958; <u>Lessons in Vocabulary</u>.

14. Philippine Center for Language Study, <u>Teacher's Guides for English in Grade I</u>, <u>English in Grade II</u>, and <u>English in Grade III</u>, (Manila, Philippines: Philippine Center for Language Study and Bureau of Public Schools, 1961).

15. Phillips, Nina, <u>Conversational English for the Non-English Speaking Child</u>, (New York, New York: Teachers College Press, Teachers College, Columbia University, 1968).

16. Rojas, Pauline, et. al., <u>Fries American English Series</u>, Books I through Book VI with Teacher's Guides, (Boston: D. C. Heath, 1952-1957).

17. Rojas, Pauline, editor, American English Series Revised, available through Book III, (Boston: D. C. Heath, 1968).

18. Slager, William R., English for Today, see National Council for Teachers of English.

19. Taylor, Grant, Consulting Editor, Saxon Series in English as a Second Language, (New York: McGraw-Hill, Inc., 1956). Learning American English, Mastering American English, Practicing American English, Advanced English Exercise, Modern Spoken English, Mastering Spoken English.

20. Thomas, Hadley A., and Harold B. Allen, Oral English, Learning a Second Language, Book I, and Teacher's Edition Oral English, Learning A Second Language, (Oklahoma City, Oklahoma: The Economy Company, 1968).

21. Wheeler, González, Let's Speak English, Books I through VI, (New York: McGraw-Hill Book Co., 1967).

22. Wright, Audrey L., Practice Your English, All English Edition, Second Edition, (New York: American Book Company, 1960).

23. Wright, Audrey L., and James H. McGillivray, Let's Learn English, Beginning Course, Third Edition, (New York: American Book Company, 1966).

Other Sources

Other systematic approaches to sequential drills in sentence patterning are provided by Hornby, Lado and Fries, and The Electronic Teaching Laboratories. The Teaching of Structural Words and Sentence Patterns, Stages I and II, by Hornby, provides approximately 125 patterns with variations in use of pronouns, verb forms, and prepositional phrases.[28] Lado and Fries have planned lessons in sentence patterns and in vocabulary.[29] The Electronic Teaching Laboratories has prepared an intensive course of study on magnetic tapes for use in the language laboratory.[30] There are 150 tapes presenting lessons of increasing difficulty.

An excellent series of educational motion pictures has been prepared to point out to teachers the application of modern principles of second language teaching. Each film is black and white, and is approximately thirty-two minutes in length. (They are available from Teaching Film Custodians, Inc., 25 West 43rd Street, New York, 36.) Titles include the following:

Film 1: The Nature of Language and How It Is Learned

Film 2: The Sounds of Language

Film 3: The Organization of Language

Film 4: Words and Their Meanings

Film 5: Modern Techniques in Language Teaching

FOOTNOTES

[1] James S. Holton, et al., Sound Language Teaching (New York: University Publishers, 1961), p. 240.

[2] Frederick B. Agard, and Harold B. Dunkel, An Investigation of Second Language Teaching (Boston: Ginn and Company, 1948).

[3] Ibid., p. 295.

[4] Ibid., p. 292.

[5] Robert Young, The Navajo Yearbook, 1958 (Window Rock, Arizona: The Navajo Agency, 1958), pp. 159-60.

[6] Ibid., p. 165.

[7] Ibid., p. 171.

[8] Kluckhohn, Clyde and Dorothea Leighton, The Navajo, (New York: Anchor Books, Doubleday and Co., 1946), p. 255.

[9] Morris, Joyce, An Investigation into Language-Concept Development of Primary School Pueblo Indian Children," Unpublished doctoral dissertation, Graduate School, University of New Mexico 1966), p. 111.

[10] Clyde Kluckhohn and Dorethea Leighton, The Navajo (Cambridge: Harvard University Press, 1956), Chapter 8: The Tongue of the People," p. 199.

[11] Ibid., p. 199.

[12] Ibid., p. 189.

[13] Philippine Center for Language Study, op. cit., p. 10.

[14] Patricia O'Connor and Ernest F. Haden, Oral Drill in Spanish (Boston: Houghton Mifflin Company, 1957), p. 9.

[15] Gertrude Hildreth, Teaching Reading (New York: Henry Holt, Rinehart, and Winston, Inc., 1958), p. 564.

[16] Roach Van Allen and Claryce Allen, An Introduction to a Language Experience Program, Level I (425 North Michigan Avenue, Chicago: Encyclopedia Britannica Press, 1966), p. 21.

[17] Board of Education of the City of New York, Teaching English as a New Language to Adults, Curriculum Bulletin No. 5, 1963-1964 series. (Board of Education of the City of New York, Publication Sales Office, 110 Livingston Street, Brooklyn 1, New York, $1.50), pp. 7-9.

[18] National Textbook Corporation, Lincolnwood, Illinois, 1963. See Test Instruments in Chapter IV.

[19] Dr. Virginia French Allen, Teachers College, Columbia University, prepared for Western States Small Schools Project,

Workshop, Flagstaff, Arizona, June 7-11, 1965, Teaching English as a Second Language.

[20] Joyce Morris, "Teaching English as a Second Language to Second Grade Children at Santo Domingo School," Research in Progress, University of New Mexico, College of Education, 1966.

[21] Kathryn S. Talley, "Effects of a Program of Special Language Instruction," unpublished Ph. D. Dissertation, University of New Mexico, 1965, pp. 114-121.

[22] Holm, Wayne, "Let It Never Be Said," Indian Education, No. 416, March 15, 1965, p. 5.

[23] Holm, Wayne, "TESOL: The Nature of the Venture," Indian Education, No. 437, October 1, 1966, p. 3.

[24] Rivers, Wilma G., The Psychologist and the Foreign-language Teacher, (Chicago: University of Chicago Press, 1964).

[25] "Narrative of the Pl 89-10 Navajo Area ESL Project," William J. Benham, Director, Branch of Education, Navajo Area, Window Rock, Arizona, March, 1967, p. 12.

[26] Jones, Lewis Wade. "The Social Unreadiness of Negro Youth," The Saturday Review, September 20, 1962, pp. 81 ff.

[27] Rohn, Ramona, "Improvement of Oral English in the First Grade in the Santo Domingo School," Unpublished Masters Thesis, Graduate School, University of New Mexico, 1963, and Joyce Morris, "An Investigation into Language-Concept Development of Primary School Pueblo Indian Children," Unpublished Doctoral Dissertation, Graduate School, University of New Mexico, 1966.

[28] Hornby, loc. cit.

[29] Robert Lado and C. C. Fries, Monographs for Teaching English as a Second Language: English Pattern Practices; English Pronunciation; Lessons in Vocabulary; English Sentence Patterns (Ann Arbor: The University of Michigan Press).

[30] Electronic Teaching Laboratories, Everyday American English; A Modern Intensive Course of Study Employing Pre-recorded Magnetic Tutorial Tapes Expressly Prepared for Use in the Language Laboratory (Washington: Electronic Teaching Laboratories, 5034 Wisconsin Ave., N. W., 1954).

CHAPTER 10

The Problem of Vocabulary

INTRODUCTION

Many children from different ethnic groups enter school with very little or no experience in speaking or understanding the English language. Most of the personnel who teach these children have had no previous experience in the teaching of English as a foreign language. This combination may not end in an impasse, but it is sure to be an extremely difficult situation at best. It may also be a traumatic experience for the child. Sometimes teachers, by trial and error, evolve methods that work well for them, and their accumulated experience through the years enables them to work successfully. Conversely, however, many teachers remain in one post too short a time to evolve any kind of a plan for coping with the situation. The frustration, helplessness, and naiveté experienced by new teachers are apt also to be experienced by the child in the class. Such a child realizes that he understands nothing, yet knows that he must if he is to gain anything from his attendance at the school.

Teachers report revealing anecdotes from children in their classes that emphasize over and over again the necessity for a systematic approach to the learning of English as a second language.

> I have always found catalogs to be the most wonderful textbooks for teaching a language. Once at Cañoncito I was using a seed catalog and teaching the children the names of foods. We came to the picture of an onion and one little girl dabbed her finger down on that and looked up at me with shining eyes. I could see she thought she knew my word for that, and with real glee, she said, "cebolla!" Yes, she knew one white man's word for it -- but it was the Spanish word. I wanted her to say "onion."
>
> In that same school, I soon learned that the Spanish man who ran the trading post was very angry with me. I had no idea why. The Indian bus driver told me that the trader did not want catalogs on the reservation. (I had had the children send for Sears Roebuck and Montgomery Ward catalogs for English

exercises. At that time, I had not even thought about educating them about standard prices as well.)

. . .

We read many articles on misconception of words in arithmetic which make arithmetic hard for children to understand. It is indeed shocking to find out how many children do not understand common words as borrow and carry which are used in arithmetic. Some teachers assume that most of the terms in arithmetic are learned in connection with other school subjects, but if they are learned, they have different grammatical meanings. Several other words learned with nonarithmetical meanings may include words like count, both, enough, and each.

. . .

I find when I substitute teach that on the whole, these youngsters are very bright and eager to learn. When they understand, they are excellent students -- when they understand. Unfortunately, too frequently, the language passes them by completely, even in high school. They can spell the words perfectly, but often they have no idea what the words mean. This is unfair really. It bothers me to see one white child in a group of Pueblos answer every question immediately when it is asked. Nine times out of ten, even if the child does know the answer, he or she is too shy to answer or too unsure of his words, or too afraid that the rest of them will make fun of him. Pueblos are notorious for making fun of others, and this causes great hurt to them if they are the ones being ridiculed. They have great pride, like the Navajos.

. . .

A group of children were scanning through a music book. One page contained the picture of a spotted horse. The title of the song contained the word "Pinto." One child spoke up saying, "Why do they have to put beans in this song?"

. . .

Even though these children can pronounce correctly many of the words they read, they do not attach meanings. As an example, one day a small group of fifth-graders read aloud for me with no difficulty. But when I asked them to write sentences containing some of the words, they had much trouble. For the word honest, one little girl wrote: "The bird will make a honest." For the word guilty, another girl wrote: "I guilty wash the dishes, then watch TV."

. . .

A fifth-grade Spanish-American child, Magdalene, was one of my brightest pupils. She was severely handicapped in her use of the English language, however. I knew she was one of eight sisters, so I asked other teachers of her sisters if they had the same difficulty. They assured me that they did not. Upon further questioning, I found that Grandmother, who knows no English, lived next door, and Magdalene had been more or less given to her to help her.

I tried to explain to Magdalene that she must work hard on her English or she never would be able to achieve the college education that her father wants them all to have. Next day, she told me she had told her father what I had said. He had tested her and said there was nothing wrong with her knowledge of the English language. I questioned her as to how he had tested her. He had pointed to objects in the room and she had told him <u>chair</u>, <u>table</u>, <u>window</u>, etc.

. . .

My third-grade group had finished an extensive study about milk in a unit on foods. They had seen films and film strips about dairy farms, dairies, and creameries. We had made many charts with pictures and stories showing cows being milked by hand and machine. The charts also showed how the milk was handled so that it would stay clean; how it was strained, cooled, pasteurized, bottled, capped, and delivered to the stores and homes. The children were discussing these things very freely, when a little boy, on the front seat, raised his hand and said, "But the milk we get from the cafeteria doesn't come from a cow." Wondering what he could be thinking, I asked him where it does come from. Raphael replied, "It comes from the welfare."

. . .

Navajo children have difficulty in learning the use of the singular and plural forms of words, especially verbs. One may say, "He go." Recently, one hot afternoon on the playground, a small boy remarked, "My feets is hurt." Difficulty is experienced in understanding the difference in gender and in how to express family relationships. This makes a problem for the teacher when trying to get information for a pupil's record. Male relatives may be spoken of as brothers when they are actually uncles or cousins. Female relatives may be reported as sisters, but are actually aunts or cousins. A Navajo boy, age seven, partially solved the gender problem when he said, "My brothers are boys, all of them." Personal pronouns confuse the Navajo child. One may say, "He's my grandmother," or "She's my grandfather."

. . .

During a word analysis and discussion period, the teacher pointed to the word <u>appealing</u>. An eager, bright-eyed

Spanish-American boy waved his arm into the air. When the teacher called on this third-grade youngster, he said: "It means that if you take a knife and peel an apple, you say, 'I'm appealing the apple.'"

. . .

High school students who make these errors in writing original sentences need much help with elementary vocabulary:

Sentence as written:	Probably means:
He was a <u>fatherless</u> father to his girls.	He was not a good father to his girls.
She is very <u>curtsey</u>.	She is very courteous.
She made a <u>noble</u> last year.	She did something noble last year.
His mother <u>scowled</u> him because he did wrong.	His mother scolded him because he did wrong.
The woman <u>intruder</u> in the conversation.	The woman interrupted the conversation.
My sisters are very <u>barren</u>.	(No translation)
He was special as an <u>intruder</u> for the company.	He was a special inspector for the company.
She was <u>grudge</u> in her past year.	She carried a grudge against someone during the past year.

MEASURING KNOWLEDGE OF ENGLISH

Vocabulary Load of Textbooks

Rojas made startingly clear that the number of words in a primary child's book does not represent the vocabulary burden of that book for him if he is learning English as a second language.[1] The number of different words does not at all correspond to the number of <u>vocabulary items</u> which he must know in order to be able to read the book with understanding. For example, the <u>miss</u> in <u>Miss</u> <u>Hill</u> and the <u>miss</u> in <u>We</u> <u>miss</u> <u>you</u> are two entirely different vocabulary items with respect to meaning. Rojas illustrates how difficult verbs may be for the beginner in analyzing the use of the word <u>get</u> in one first-grade reading vocabulary list.

> The verb <u>get</u>, for example, when combined with <u>up</u> becomes <u>levantarse</u> in Spanish; <u>get</u> <u>out</u> (of the house) becomes <u>salir</u>; <u>get</u> <u>out</u> (of the bus) becomes <u>apearse</u>; <u>get</u> <u>on</u> (a pony), <u>montar</u>; <u>get</u> (fat) <u>ponerse</u> (gordo); <u>get</u> (here), <u>llegar</u>; <u>get</u> <u>dinner</u>, <u>hacer</u> <u>comida</u>; <u>go</u> <u>to</u> <u>get</u> <u>a</u> <u>person</u>, <u>procurar</u>; and <u>go</u> <u>to</u> <u>get</u> <u>something</u>, <u>traer</u> or <u>buscar</u>.[2]

When Rojas delineated the total number of vocabulary items a child would need to read the different words in the first-grade reading program of three reading series, she found that the Curriculum Foundation Readers contained 332 different words, but 1,483 different vocabulary items; the Children's Own Readers series contained 356 different words, but 848 different vocabulary items; and the Happy Road to Reading series, 209 different words, but 568 different vocabulary items.[3]

Rojas further points out that the English-speaking child is entirely familiar with all the concepts used in the readers, and he needs only to learn to recognize the graphic symbols which stand for these concepts. On the other hand, the Puerto Rican child has no meanings to bring to the words pronounced for him. For these reasons, Rojas concludes that such reading series are unsuitable for use in Puerto Rico and should be discarded. Planned lessons, based on the science of foreign language teaching, should be substituted.[4]

Measuring Reading Readiness

Condie completed a field study in which selected pre-first and kindergarten teachers attempted to improve the ability of the children to perform on a standard reading readiness test as an indication of readiness for formal school instruction in the first grade.[5] In all of these kindergartens and pre-first grades, almost all of the children entered school with an extremely limited knowledge of English or with no usable knowledge at all. The study had a twofold purpose of testing ways of enriching kindergarten curricula directed toward language teaching and of evaluating the professional qualifications of kindergarten teachers. He tested the children completing kindergarten or pre-first grade in May, 1959, and used them as a control measure; then, he encouraged teachers to incorporate into their programs during the 1959-1960 school year those aids and techniques intended to facilitate the learning of English and readiness for reading. He tested the children in the kindergarten and pre-first grade classes again in May, 1960.

Aids and techniques incorporated into the program included a teacher in-service workshop held every third Saturday through the school year, a visit to each classroom during the month intervening between workshops, the administration of an unstandardized test of "Knowledge of English for Children for Whom English is a Second Language," in September and January, an enlarged vocabulary word list consisting of 2,053 selected words, three-dimensional objects, picture files, a tape recorder, filmstrip library, books, flannel boards, record players, blocks, and collections of finger plays.

The comparison of results of the Metropolitan Reading Readiness Test show mean percentiles advanced for School A from 49.8

in May, 1959, to 72.69 in May, 1960; for School B, from 15.1 to 55.32; for School D, from 3.26 to 16.195; and for School E, from 15.05 to 18.0. The critical ratios show the results to be significant at the one percent level of confidence for Schools A, B, and D, while little gain was measured in School E. Since the difference did not seem to be in the teacher variable, it was pointed out that the Pueblo Indian children in School E knew the least amount of English when they came in September (as measured on the nonstandard test administered by Condie). They live in a conservative pueblo where a high value is placed on knowing the mother tongue well, and little English is spoken there by the adults. Condie concluded that readiness for school tasks can be upgraded as measured by a standardized test when supervision, and abundance of techniques and material aids, and in-service workshops are provided.

Testing Knowledge of English

Approximately 90 percent of the activity that goes on in elementary schools during the formal school day is estimated to be reading and writing activity. This activity is pursued, of course, in the English language. For approximately half of the pupils in public schools in New Mexico, English is, in reality, a second language. In their attempts to perform in this bilingual situation, these children labor under a considerable handicap.

The relationship and interdependence of language and culture are well understood. The language of a people reflects the ways in which the values of the culture are practiced; therefore, the way of thinking of an Indian child may be quite different from the way of thinking of his non-Indian teacher. With language structures as different as English and Indian tongues, the language patterning presents obstacles with which the child needs help. These school children vary all the way along a continuum from very little knowledge of English to considerable knowledge. In families where the father and mother belong to different Indian tribes, or where one parent is Indian and the other is not, the children may speak only English -- and it may or may not be limited in scope.

New instruments for measuring understanding of verbal concepts in English are needed. Tests constructed to measure the understanding of idiomatic expressions, multiple meanings of common English words, simple analogies, and opposites will be described, and the results of administering them will be reported.

DIAGNOSTIC TEST FOR STUDENTS OF ENGLISH AS A SECOND LANGUAGE

A search was made for possible tests of knowledge of English as a second language which could be used for elementary pupils. The Diagnostic Test for Students of English as a Second Language[6] was obtained and used experimentally. This test is designed to test college students from foreign countries who wish to attend colleges or universities in the United States. It is a test of English usage, and measures understanding of general grammar, parts of speech, ellipses, word order in sentence patterning, and idiomatic vocabulary.

The test is diagnostic in nature. The answer sheet is so constructed that errors in any one of the categories tested are grouped for easy identification. An instructor can readily determine, then, if errors predominate in identifying a particular part of speech, in word order, or in idioms. There is a possible score of 150, and the manual of directions provides tentative norms which were established at the American University's Language Center. The norms are:

Score	Recommendations
125 and above	Satisfactorily prepared for college work in the United States, although students may need additional oral-aural training.
100-125	Students need considerable extra help, possibly six weeks of intensive training.
40-80	Students need to take full-time instruction in English, often as much as a semester of intensive work.

This test was administered in 1958 on an experimental basis to two small groups of Indian students in New Mexico. The first group included fifty-three Mescalero Apache Indians enrolled in a Bureau of Indian Affairs school and a public school in grades seven through twelve.[7] Results of this administration are given in Table XIV. The mean score of 108.64 indicates that the group needs considerable help with English usage.

The second group included thirty-three students enrolled in a one-year practical nursing course.[8] Most of these students were high school graduates. Table XV presents raw scores and first languages of individual students. It should be noted that twenty-one of the thirty-three students scored above 125 (124-1/2), which would indicate satisfactory preparation for college work. The mean score of 127.4 is above the minimum score indicated for success in college work. Of the seven Navajos in this group, all scored lower than 125, their median score being 109-1/2.

TABLE XIV

Diagnostic Test for Students of English as a Second Language
Performance of 53 Mescalero Apache Students -- Grades 7-12
February, 1958

Raw Score Intervals	Frequency	Raw Score Intervals	Frequency	Raw Score Intervals	Frequency
146-150	1	96-100	0	46-50	1
141-145	3	91-95	2	41-45	0
136-140	2	86-90	1	36-40	0
131-135	7	81-85	2	31-35	0
126-130	3	76-80	0	26-30	1
121-125	7	71-75	2	21-25	0
116-120	7	66-70	2	16-20	0
111-115	4	61-65	1	11-15	0
106-110	2	56-60	1	6-10	0
101-105	3	51-55	0	1-5	1

Mean = 108.64 S. D. = 30.2

TABLE XV

Diagnostic Test for Students of English as a Second Language
Performance of 33 Practical Nursing Students
April, 1958

Language Spoken	Raw Score	Language Spoken	Raw Score
Laguna	148-1/2	Apache	132
Laguna*	145-1/2	Apache	127-1/2
Laguna	145-1/2	Zuni	124-1/2
Sioux	145-1/2	Creek	124-1/2
Acoma	144-1/2	Alabama Coushatta	121-1/2
Acoma	144	Choctaw	118-1/2
Taos	144	Navajo	118-1/2
Zuni	144	Navajo	115-1/2
Acoma	141	Navajo	115-1/2
Blackfeet	141	Navajo	109-1/2
Arapahoe	139-1/2	Navajo	109-1/2
Crow	138	Apache	102
Crow	138	Apache	102
Tewa	138	Sioux	99
Tewa	135	Navajo	97-1/2
Zuni	133-1/2	Navajo	96
Zuni	133-1/2		

Mean = 127.4 S.D. = 18.6

Kluckhohn administered the Davis test to thirty-three Navajo high school graduates enrolled in a four-week orientation-to-college program.[9] The results are presented in Table XVI.

TABLE XVI

Results of Diagnostic Test for Students of English as a Second Language, University of New Mexico, June, 1960

Range of Scores	Frequency
145-150	8
140-144	12
136-139	8
130-135	3
125-129	0
120-124	2

This test was analyzed to find the most common errors in grammar. However, the minimum score of 125, measuring language ability for success in college, was earned by all but two students and those two earned scores above 120. The test did not, however, reflect the students' ability to write an original essay nor did it account for the serious barriers in cultural background.

Examination of the results of performance on this test shows that, by the raw score alone, many of these students were able to perform satisfactorily. However, the <u>ability to function in the language</u> was not as satisfactory as this test indicated. It is hypothesized that the test bridges less cultural difference when used with college students from European countries than it does with Indians of the Southwest.[10] The experience background, the cultural heritage, and the basic thinking patterns of the foreign students may fit the middle-class Anglo life style more closely than do the background, heritage, and thinking of the Indians tested. The standard score acceptable for the foreign student would not necessarily be acceptable for the Indian student. In addition, even though the Indian makes a satisfactory score on this diagnostic test, it is possible that he lacks orientation to Anglo conceptualization in thinking and that he has not acquired the habit of demanding meaning when he uses English vocabulary either in reading or listening.

THE IDIOMS TEST

On the Navajo Reservation, a foreman came upon one of his Navajo workers. When he found him relaxed and resting, he said, "You're getting away with murder." To this, the Navajo replied, "Oh, no, I would <u>never</u> kill anybody." It can be assumed by his answer that <u>murder</u> has, for him, only its literal definition.

When a student presents a project to the teacher for his evaluation of the student's progress, how may the student interpret what the teacher says if he uses expressions like: "You haven't scratched the surface yet," or "You haven't even made a dent in it."

A Navajo had taken a job off the reservation. He was told that he had been assigned to the graveyard shift. With only the literal meaning for the word graveyard, and his rejection of all activity associated with death, the man left, without a word of explanation, and went home.[11]

Idiomatic expressions, as they occur in elementary school readers, are one of the facets of the English language troublesome to language learners. When bilingual children encounter idioms, they need to know the colloquial meanings. Even though idioms do not translate literally, people who have limited knowledge of English tend to give them an exact literal translation. Since the reading textbooks used by Indian and Spanish-American children contain many English idioms, a study was designed to reveal difficulties which they have in understanding these expressions.[12] It was felt that such a study would furnish useful information for teachers of reading and language. McPherson says that idioms lead to wrong understandings until explained. She urges teachers to take nothing for granted, to see that every means possible is employed to explain idioms and to emphasize concrete experiences for children to help illustrate idiomatic meanings.[13]

Preparation of the Idioms Test

A multiple-choice idioms test of ninety items was prepared using selected idiomatic expressions found in commonly used elementary reading texts.[14] Textbooks used included fourth, fifth, and sixth-grade readers of the Ginn,[15] Row, Peterson,[16] and Scott, Foresman[17] series. Sample items follow.[18]

"Saved by a hair! Just by a hair!" yelled Tom.

    a. by using his head
    b. just barely made it
    c. safe and secure
    d. by sticking his head out.

"I leave it to you to break him in."

    a. break his habits
    b. to get him inside
    c. to hurt him
    d. get him used to things.

A 90-item idioms test appears in Appendix E.

Administration and Results of Testing in 1959

The Idioms Test was administered to 1,290 pupils in fourth, fifth, and sixth grades. These pupils, all children for whom English was a first language, were from Waterloo, Iowa; Albuquerque, New Mexico; and Gallup, New Mexico. When means and standard deviations were computed, there was an apparent upward trend in achievement from fourth to sixth grade. These results are given in Table XVII. Means of 54.38, 60.91, and 67.12 were obtained for fourth, fifth, and sixth grades, respectively.

TABLE XVII

Mean and Median Scores and Standard Deviations
By Grades on the Idioms Test
Spring, 1959

Grade	Number	Median Score	Mean Score	Standard Deviation
4	376	58.90	54.38	15.00
5	356	64.00	60.91	14.34
6	558	70.00	67.12	11.05

After establishing norms, the Idioms Test was administered to the minority ethnic groups in selected schools in New Mexico. Yandell tested 164 Anglo, 224 Navajo, 52 Zuni Pueblo, and 76 Spanish-American sixth graders in Gallup-McKinley County.[19] The test was later administered to 38 sixth-grade Jicarilla and Mescalero Apache children.[20] The performance on this test by ethnic groups is reported in Table XVIII.

TABLE XVIII

Statistical Differences Between Ethnic Groups and
Norming Group on the Idioms Test
Spring, 1959

Group	Number	Median	Mean	SD	SE_d	CR	Confidence Level
Sixth Grade Norming	558	70.00	67.12	11.05			
Anglo	164	68.00	63.88	13.62	1.14	2.84	.01
Spanish-American	76	49.00	46.33	15.25	1.81	11.48	.01
Apache	38	34.00	36.58	15.74	2.59	10.26	.01
Navajo	224	30.00	31.23	13.23	.995	36.08	.01
Pueblo	52	39.00	37.38	15.27	2.18	16.46	.01

The significant differences between the mean scores of each minority group and the norming group indicate the extreme degree to which these children are having difficulty with idioms in the English language. This table shows dramatically that Spanish-American, Navajo, Apache, and Pueblo sixth graders have a very poor understanding of the common idioms in school readers when compared to the norming group.

Yandell reported that the median score earned by the Spanish-American group ranked at only the fifth percentile in the distribution of scores in the Waterloo, Iowa, sample. The median score earned by the Pueblo sixth graders ranked at the second percentile in the distribution of scores in the Waterloo sample; the median score earned by the Navajo sixth graders ranked at the first percentile.[21] The raw score of 65 fell at the 20th percentile in the distribution of scores in the Waterloo sample. However, in the Spanish-American sample, 65 fell above the 80th percentile; in the Pueblo sample, 65 fell above the 90th percentile; and in the Navajo sample, 65 fell at the 99th percentile.[22]

When Yandell computed the coefficient of correlation between the reading ability and the raw scores on the Idioms Test for seventy-seven Navajo sixth graders, they obtained a result of .941. This indicated an almost perfect relationship between the ability to read English as measured in the standard test and the ability to interpret idiomatic expressions as measured in the Idioms Test.

Interpretation of the Idioms Tests Results
Gallup-McKinley County Public Schools Sixth Grade

The 1967 test results permit four very important generalizations:

1. There is a noticeable "drop" in scores earned by the unilingual Anglo students. This may be an indication that the teachers work so hard to teach English to students in minority groups that they do not give attention to vocabulary development and work study to those who already know English. One of the inherent dangers in teaching heterogenous groups, including other-language speakers and native speakers of English, is that the teacher does not effectively "teach" the complete range of differences all at the same time.

2. The Spanish-American and Zuni children have shown consistent growth at all decile levels since the first testing. The median score for the Zuni children moved from the second percentile to the ninth percentile on the norming group distribution; the median score for the Spanish-American children moved from the seventh percentile to the tenth percentile. The school system needs to evaluate whether

TABLE XIX

Percentile Norms for the Yandell-Zintz Idioms Test of 90 Items Based on Raw Scores Earned by 237 Sixth Grade Students in Albuquerque, 1959.

Percentile Rank	Raw Score	Percentile Rank	Raw Score
99	84	15	59
92	79	14	58
90	78	13	57
85	77	11	56
80	76	10	55
75	75	09	54
70	74	09	53
65	73	08	52
60	72	08	51
50	71	07	50
45	70	07	49
40	69	06	48
37	68	06	47
33	67	05	46
30	66	05	45
25	65	04	44
23	64	04	43
22	63	03	42
20	62	03	41
18	61	02	40
17	60	02	39
		01	38

or not the change to teaching English as a second language accounts for this progress, and if so, to re-double its efforts. Percentile ranks do not show the real progress clearly, however. This is because the native speakers upon whose scores norms are based naturally "pile up" in a normal distrubtion. The entire quartile range, from the 25th precentile to the 75th percentile, encompasses only ten raw score points. It is more revealing to point out that the Zuni median score increased from 39 to 53, or 14 raw score points, the Spanish-American from 49 to 55, or six raw score points.

3. The effect of any teaching of English as a second language program has not yet produced any measurable effect with the Navajo students. While a few Navajo students earned higher scores, the median raised only from 30 to 31. Administratively, this group constitutes a very serious problem because they are extremely deficient in English and are now ready for the junior high school. They must be taught Eng-

TABLE XX

Results of the Zintz-Yandell Idioms Test of 90 Items, Gallup-McKinley County Sixth Grade, May, 1967, Percentile Ranks By Ethnic Groups

Percentile Rank	Norming Group: 1959 N = 237	Anglo Group N = 209	Spanish-American Group N = 104	Zuni Group N = 76	Navajo Group N = 266	Other Indians* N = 21
99	84	83	76	80	73	
90	78	76	67	66	59	
80	76	73	63	63	48	64
75	75	71	62	60	46	
70	74	70	61	58	41	
60	72	68	58	56	35	
50	71	65	55	53	31	58
40	69	60	51	48	27	
30	66	56	46	40	24	
25	65	53	44	33	23	48
20	62	50	42	29	22	
10	55	42	34	23	19	
05	45	34	30	20	16	
02	39	22	25	16	15	
01	38	17	24	13	14	

* Other Indians = all other Indians living in Gallup, including seven Zunis who attend school outside the Zuni Pueblo.

TABLE XXI

Performance of Gallup-McKinley County Sixth Grade on an Idioms Test in May, 1967

Raw Scores	Anglo	Other Indians	Spanish American	Zuni	Navajo
83-84	1				
81-82	11				
79-80	11111 11111 11				
77-78	11111 11111 1111				
75-76	11111 11111 11111		1		
73-74	11111 11111 11111				
71-72	11111 11111 11111 1111		111	1	11
69-70	11111 11111 11111	1			1
67-68	11111 11111 11111	11	11111 1	111	11
65-66	11111 11111 111	11	111	111	11
63-64	11111 1111	111	11111 111	11111	111
61-62	11111	1	11111 11111 11	11111	11
59-60	11111 111		11111 1	11111	11111 1
57-58	11111 11111 111	1111	11111 11	11111 111	1111
55-56	11111 11		1111		11111 11
53-54	11111 1	11	11111 111	11111	11111 11
51-52	11111	1	11111	111	11111 11111
49-50	11111 1111		11111	11	11111 11111 1
47-48	1	11	1	111	111
45-46	11111 111		11	11	11111 11111
43-44	1111	1	11111 1	111	11
41-42	1111		11111	111	1111
39-40	1	1	11111		11111 1
37-38	11111 1		1111	1	111
35-36	11		11	111	11111 11111 1111
33-34	1		111	11	11111 11111 111
31-32	1		111	111	11111 11111 11111
29-30			1		11111 11111 11111 111
27-28	111		1	1	11111 11111 11111 1111
25-26			1	111	11111 11111 11111 1111
23-24		1			11111 11111 11111 111
21-22	11			1	11111 11111 11111 111
19-20	1			11	11111 11111 11111
17-18	1			11111	11111 1111
15-16	1				11111 11111
13-14				1	111

311

lish as a second language on a systematically planned basis before they can profit from any other kind of academic education. One may conclude that this problem is equally severe in all grades seven through twelve.

4. While primary teachers are continuing the emphasis on teaching English as a second language with all primary students entering school, there is a ten-year gap between this program and the students who are now seniors in high school. Every student who has not internalized the sound system of English as the language of the school, must be grouped at whatever grade level he now is, and taught English as a second language. Every teacher must learn the ways in which teaching English as a second language is not at all the same as teaching English to native speakers. Then, the only salvation for many of these students in junior and senior high school is to group them for special second language learning in all subjects areas. Subject matter teachers with TESL consultation can do this very well. There are excellent texts on the market to guide teachers in teaching English to speakers of other languages.

UNDERSTANDING MULTIPLE MEANINGS, ANALOGIES, AND OPPOSITES IN THE ENGLISH LANGUAGE

In addition to idiomatic expressions, some of the facets of the language that can be isolated are multiple meanings, analogies, and antonyms. Three individual studies were undertaken in the same elementary schools to investigate the performance of different ethnic group children with multiple meanings, opposites, and analogies.[23,24,25] The purpose of these studies was to compare the efficiency of Indian and Spanish-American children in public school fourth and sixth grades with the performance of a norming group of selected fourth-grade Anglo pupils.

The same procedure was followed in the three separate studies. This procedure included:

1. Objective tests were prepared based upon English expressions found in reading textbooks which were no more difficult than fourth-grade level. The multiple meanings and analogies tests were of the multiple-choice type. One part of the test on antonyms was column matching, while another part used completion statements in which the opposite needed was determined by context in sentences. Sample items of each test are given below.

Analogies. (Directions: Select the right answer.)

Water is to drink as bread is to   eat   bake   butter

312

Arm is to hand as leg is to   toes <u>foot</u> pants
Chair is to sit as floor is to   <u>stand</u> carpet sleep

<u>Multiple Meanings</u>. (Directions: Which one is not correct.)

1. a. It came in a <u>plain</u> package.
   b. The answer is <u>plain</u> to everyone.
   ⓒ The <u>plain</u> wore off his new coat.
   d. The house was built on a high <u>plain</u>.

2. a. Don't <u>hold</u> me.
   b. Look in the <u>hold</u> of the ship.
   c. The cup can <u>hold</u> water.
   ⓓ Your clothes are full of <u>hold</u>.

3. a. He hurt my <u>left</u> hand.
   b. There is nothing <u>left</u>.
   ⓒ We put <u>left</u> in the pan.
   d. We <u>left</u> the city.

<u>Antonyms</u>

A. Directions: Draw a line from the word in Column I to the word in Column II that means the opposite.

    wide   enemy
    friend   dark
    light   narrow

B. Directions: Select and underline the word in each row that means the opposite of the first word.

    there   place   open   <u>here</u>
    kind   <u>mean</u>   good   woman

2. The tests were administered by classroom teachers to a selected sample of ninety-five fourth-grade children in an urban, typical, middle-class Anglo neighborhood where English is the vernacular. These children constituted the norming group.

3. The tests were administered by classroom teachers to fourth and sixth-grade classes in selected public schools where Navajo, Apache, Pueblo, Spanish-American, and Anglo children were enrolled in integrated groups.

4. The performance of these fourth and sixth-grade children was compared with the norming group to determine the extent to which Indian and Spanish-American children, as bilinguals, understand multiple meanings, analogies, and opposites in the English language.

5. Recommendations based on this performance were presented for teachers of reading.

In all three of these studies the results were the same. The fourth-grade norming group performed statistically significantly better than all of the fourth and sixth grades in the minority ethnic groups. This empirical evidence emphasizes the need in the schools enrolling these children for a systematic approach to learning the English language well.

Cox[26] prepared a 100-item test of multiple meanings of common words and administered it to sixth grade students from all the minorities with the same results. Repeated administration of this test in unilingual, English-speaking, middle-class neighborhoods shows an average class median for middle-class Anglo children of 87 raw-score points while Spanish-American sixth graders with second language interference achieved a median score of 58. The mean scores for the three Indian groups were: Apache, 62; Navajo, after direct teaching, 58; and Pueblo, 44.

The following is a sample item from the multiple meanings test developed by Cox:

1. a. place where liquor is sold b. fasten c. ale
   d. barrier e. the court

   _____ 1. Don't <u>bar</u> the door.
   _____ 2. The men had a drink in the <u>bar</u>.
   _____ 3. The class constructed a sand <u>bar</u>.
   _____ 4. The lawyer pleaded the man's case at the <u>bar</u>.

The complete test will be found in Appendix E.

TABLE XXII

Comparson of Average Scores on the Multiple Meanings Test by Ethnic Groups of Sixth Grade Students

Sixth Grade	Average Score*	Number of Pupils
Anglo	87	84
Apache Indian	62	17
Spanish-American	58	81
Navajo Indian	58**	61
Pueblo Indian	44	31

* Mrs. Cox reported Mean Scores for the three Indian groups; the Anglo and Spanish-American are Median Scores.

** The score for the Navajo group was determined after Mrs. Cox had planned special units of work for teaching multiple meanings of words.

TEACHING AIDS

In order to provide activities through which oral language can be encouraged, the following materials and teaching aids can be utilized: flannel graph with cutouts (the teacher can make additional cutouts), large building blocks, a low work table for arranging dioramas, toys of all kinds, dolls, puppets, growing plants and animals, an extensive vertical picture file, record player with unbreakable records, film projectors, and pictured library books. Materials have also been developed by special groups to help teach English and are described below.

Vertical Picture File

The Branch of Education, Bureau of Indian Affairs, has made available to teachers of beginning Navajo children a picture card file designed to facilitate the teaching of the words in the Minimum Word List for Beginners. One hundred seventy-five picture cards were prepared to teach some 315 words in the pre-first grade list. As nearly as possible, the cards were drawn with one idea for the center of the picture. No background detail was included that might prevent easy recognition. The cards were numbered and cross-referenced. On the back of each card was a suggested lesson plan. (See example on following page.)

It is important to point out that a picture of a girl combing her hair in front of a mirror can be used to elicit many naming words as well as a few short sentences. It is intended, of course, that the children will _first_ experience these words and concepts by watching a _real child_ look in a mirror, comb his hair, and identify the artifacts in sentences. After the concrete experience, the semiconcrete two-dimensional picture serves an excellent purpose for repetition and review. It also can be used to good advantage to relate this experience, by cross-reference filing of the cards, to other experiences related to grooming, personal cleanliness and neatness, or household objects.

Constructed Devices

While there are many teaching aids available commercially for teachers, they may not be suited specifically to the environment of the minority ethnic group child. Three teaching aids developed by Condie, and found to be useful in his work, are described in the following pages to illustrate different aspects of vocabulary teaching. A sketch of these devices is included.

1. Carton with dividers. This is extremely easy to make. A good-sized carton should be obtained from the supermarket with the bottle dividers still intact; the dividers then are disassembled for easier painting. The inside and the dividers of the box should be painted one color, and the outside another color. The box is then reassembled, placed on

Word(s):

    caught

Suggested conversation for teacher:

    This is a teacher.
    This is a girl.
    They are playing.
    They are playing ball.
    The girl **caught** the ball.

Numbers of related pictures:

    B-72 get (the ball)

Level: Beginners

Refers to: Minimum Essential Goal 11

Additional ways of teaching vocabulary and concepts:

Play "catch" with a group of children. When one child **catches** the ball, have him say, "I caught the ball." The rest of the group might say, "John caught the ball," etc. Give each child several opportunities to catch the ball and repeat the sentence.

Play the game "Cat and Mouse". When the cat has **caught** the mouse have the cat say, "I caught John," etc.

Developed by Dr. Le Roy Condie, Language Consultant, State Department of Education, Santa Fe, New Mexico.

Figure 7.

edge, and it is ready to teach, "top row," "second row," "bottom row," etc., as follows:

Teacher: Who can put the ball in the second box in the top row?

Pupil: (As he performs) I'll put the ball in the second box in the top row.

The device is more useful if a middle row and/or column is provided. Grocery cartons do not usually come with a middle row, but one can sometimes be worked out by stapling two boxes together. The teacher must remember that the rows in the carton, and in arithmetic, run horizontally; the row of seats in the classroom are usually thought of as vertical to the pupils and to the teacher. An explanation may be in order.

2. Hollow log. A 10 x 12 x 8-inch carton is resealed, then cut to receive a 16-inch length of cardboard tube, the latter four or five inches in diameter. A story about the little skunk (or chipmunk or whatever it may be) can be told. The skunk lives in the den, comes out to play, strays far away, is called back to play near home, jumps up on the log, goes in the log, through the log, jumps over the log, and runs around the rock. The children should put him through the same antics, and they can perform similar actions themselves.

3. Horse cutouts. Horses are dear to the heart of every Navajo child, and the water hole with its windmill (well) is a familiar sight in Navajoland. The horses and water hole scene are cut out of wallboard or oak tag.

At beginning level, the arrangement may be used to elicit such expressions as, "That's the windmill," "That's a tree," "That's a red horse," "That's a white horse," etc. More talkative students can tell such sequences as, "The red horse is first," "The black horse is second," "The white horse is third," "The little colt is last." This can be related to the lunch time line-up: "Jose is first, Jackson is second, Paul is third. . . and Rita is last."

Booklets Developing Elementary Reading Concepts

The Branch of Education, Bureau of Indian Affairs, has recently published booklets that will be of much value to teachers whether in Federal Indian Schools or in any public school. It is hoped that the variety of booklets will continue with additional suggestions to help classroom teachers. Three of these are described on the following pages:

1. <u>Billy Black Lamb</u> by Caroline H. Breedlove (Lawrence, Kansas: The Haskell Institute, 1959).

   In a well-illustrated story of the antics of Billy Black Lamb, seven concepts are taught: <u>around</u>, <u>beside</u>, <u>behind</u>, <u>in front of</u>, <u>into</u>, <u>over</u>, and <u>under</u>. The text on pages six and seven reads:

   > "First I will run," he said.
   > "I will run around things."
   > So he ran around the hogan.
   > He ran around the wagon.
   > He ran around the big tree.
   > And he ran around Sleepy Old Horse.

2. <u>Coyote and His Name</u>, a tale retold by Wayne Holm (Lawrence, Kansas: The Haskell Institute, 1960).

   A tale is simply told of two coyotes, using 60 different words. When people saw them, they said, "There goes a coyote. And there goes another one." The coyote who didn't want the same label as his brother coyote decided his name was "Another One."

3. <u>Our Family</u> by Virginia Jackson (Lawrence, Kansas: The Haskell Institute, 1960).

   Using only fourteen words, the story presents the members of the nuclear family.

Free and Inexpensive Materials

Carefully selected free materials will be useful. The National Dairy Council, Chicago, is only one example. The Dairy Council provides food models in color. On twelve large cards are 171 different food models: dairy products, vegetables, fruits, eggs, meat, fish, legumes, cereals, bread and other foods. These food models can promote conversation both for reporting meals eaten and for planning appropriate menus. Local dairy council offices are equipped to provide excellent teaching materials to teachers; pictures, films, and experiments in healthful living may be secured.

A selected list of addresses where teachers may write for free or inexpensive materials is given on the following pages.

1. American Dental Association
   Bureau of Dental Health Education
   222 East Superior Street
   Chicago 11, Illinois

   "Frank Visits the Dentist" is the story of Frank's visit to the dentist. The children in all grades will enjoy reading this story and will learn the importance of proper dental health at the same time. Nineteen pages. Single copies.

2. American Institute of Baking
   400 E. Ontario Street
   Chicago 11, Illinois

   "Bread in the Making" is a unit for intermediate grades. It is adaptable to all grades. This teaching kit includes a fifteen-page illustrated reader about a trip through a bakery by a group of school children. There is a teacher's guide.

3. Association of American Railroads
   Transportation Building
   Washington 6, D. C.

   Many posters, pamphlets, pictures, and units can be obtained free of charge from this address. "Railroad Transportation" includes pictures of all the railroad cards, the railroad men and how they perform their duties in relation to the train.

4. Borden Company
   Consumer Services Department
   350 Madison Avenue
   New York 17, New York

   "Milk Goes to Town" is the story of milk from the farm to market told in simple rhyme and illustrations.

5. Continental Baking Company
   Home Economics Department
   630 Fifth Avenue
   New York, New York

   "Bread to Help Build Strong Bodies" is a reprint from the Grade Teacher. "Enriched White Bread" is background information for teachers. There is a chart entitled "Structural Composition of a Grain of Wheat."

6. General Mills, Education Section
   Department of Public Service
   Minneapolis 15, Minnesota

   "The Basic Seven," is a novel poster of the basic seven foods in Mother Hubbard's cupboard. Also available are: a handbook for the teacher, series of wall posters, pupil booklets for the elementary grades, parent leaflet, a nutrition guide, and "The Story of the Cereal Grains," sample tests and survey forms, and other materials including filmstrips, booklets, and leaflets. (Free)

7. Hayden Planetarium
   Junior Astronomy Club
   New York 24, New York

   Inexpensive charts show the location of the stars in the sky. Write for information.

8. Ideal School Supply Company
   8324 South Burkholf
   Chicago 20, Illinois

   "30 Arithmetic Aids" is available.

9. Kellogg Company
   Home Economics Service, Department GT257
   Darien, Connecticut

   Available is a breakfast game: Kindergarten-3, order "Early Bird Game"; grades 4-6, order "Wild Bill Hickok Game." List the number of students in grade. They also have full color wall poster, individual score cards, prize badges, and special merit seals.

10. Kimberly-Clark Corporation
    Cellucotton Division, Educational Department
    910 N. Michigan Avenue
    Chicago 11, Illinois

    Available is "How to Catch a Cold," large colored posters.

11. Lincoln National Life Insurance Company
    Fort Wayne, Indiana

    Considerable material about Lincoln is available: Lincoln National Life Foundation, Little Known Lincoln Episodes, Little Known Facts About the Gettysburg Address, Little Known Lincoln Humor, Little Lincoln Interprets the Constitution, Little Known Boyhood Adventures of Abraham Lincoln, Abraham Lincoln -- a Concise Biography, Little Known Facts about Thanksgiving and Lincoln Proclamation.

12. National Wild Life Federation, Servicing Division
    232 Carrole Street N. W.
    Washington 12, D. C.

    Seventeen of the most common songbirds are described and illustrated in a leaflet.

13. Oak Ridge Institute of Nuclear Studies, Inc.
    P. O. Box 117
    Oak Ridge, Tennessee

    A teacher's kit on atomic energy is available.

14. Pendleton Woolen Mills
    218 S. W. Jefferson Street
    Portland 4, Oregon

    "Story of Wool" is available pamphlet. Also available is free color movie, "Romantic Story of Man and Sheep."

15. Pepperell Manufacturing Company
    160 State Street
    Boston 2, Mass.

    Available are samples of cotton: raw, combed, carded and spun; also "The Magic of Textiles."

16. Proctor and Gamble
    Education Department Y
    P. O. Box 599
    Cincinnati 1, Ohio

    Included in "Cleanliness Game" are a colored wall chart and stickers in the form of miniature cakes of Ivory Soap for perfect scores. Yellow ones indicate caution, red ones indicate stop, and merit badge stickers indicate good week's record. Indicate number of pupils.

17. 'Ranger 'Rithmetic
    U. S. Department of Agriculture
    Forest Service
    Washington 25, D. C.

    'Range 'Rithmetic has different booklets for different grades.

18. Revere Copper and Brass, Inc.
    New York Central Building
    230 Park Avenue
    New York 17, New York

    "Paul Revere" is a poem, stories and pictures. Four colored pictures are reproduced Beale paintings suitable for framing.

19. Sinclair Oil and Gas Company
    Sinclair Oil Building
    Box 521
    Tulsa 2, Oklahoma

    Book of Dinosaurs is available.

20. Trans-World Air Lines
    380 Madison Avenue
    New York 17, New York

    There is a folder of information sheets, Air World Education, Study Series Instructor, Units I, II, III. One folder is Flight Ten, story of early development of air

322

transportation. Second folder is Flight Now, air transportation today. Third folder is Flight When, air transportation of the future.

21. United Air Lines, School and College Service
    35 East Monroe Street
    Chicago 3, Illinois

    "History of Mail" is a set of 16 pictures to show the progress of mail delivery. Booklets and leaflets include: DC-1 Mainliner, a study of its important parts; "Mike and Nancy Learn About Jets," "Mike and Nancy at the Airport," "Mike and Nancy Take a Flight," and others. Second grade level, quantities of 40 are free.

22. U.S. Steel Corporation
    71 Broadway
    New York 6, New York

    Good, colorful material on the history of steel is available for every grade level. A list of publications is available.

23. Wards National Science Establishment, Inc.
    Box 24, Beachwood Station
    Rochester 9, New York

    Material is free to teachers: "Outline of Classification of Animal Kingdom," 8-1/2" x 12-1/2" chart; "Tree of Animal Life, 8-1/2" x 11" chart.

24. Watchmakers of Switzerland, Education Service Department
    Information Center, Inc.
    730 Fifth Avenue
    New York 19, New York

    "Learning to Tell Time," is primary teaching material, consisting of one large clock (tagboard) with moveable hands, individual small clocks for the children and a message to the parents.

MEANINGS TO BE DEVELOPED

There are many facets of language which the teacher can isolate for directed study, drill, and testing. As already mentioned, one of the very difficult problems in learning English well is that of the prevalence of idiomatic expressions in common use. The teacher can prepare exercises to teach children many of the idiomatic expressions used in everyday speech. Other types of exercises to be prepared for directed lessons include: multiple meanings of common words, opposites, homonyms, synonyms, and heteronyms, prepositions, contractions, roots, prefixes, suffixes and deriving compound words, recognizing figures of speech, and learning to interpret wise sayings and proverbs.

Idiomatic Speech

   Idiomatic expressions occur in all the everyday conversation of native English speakers and have extensive usage in the readers and literature used in textbooks in the schools. "Don't let the cat out of the bag," "You'd better make hay while the sun shines," "Don't bite my head off," "I think you have a sweet tooth," "He's a Jack-of-all-trades," "to piece out the supper," "He's not worth his salt," "He stood rooted to the spot," "He was pulling my leg," or "His jokes brought down the house" are part of many people's everyday conversational pattern and, of course, occur also in print. Children for whom English is a second language must be taught the specific colloquial meanings.

   By searching through the workbooks that accompany readers, teachers will be able to find selected exercises for specific lessons with their students. The following exercises are found in the workbook, Practice for High Roads.[27]

> In each numbered sentence below, a figure of speech is printed in heavy black letters. One of the three groups of words below each sentence gives the right meaning of that figure of speech as it is used in that sentence. Use the context to help you decide which meaning is correct, and put an X on the line before it.
>
> 1. The boys knew they could count on Joe, for he never <u>lost his head</u>.
>
>   _____ got behind
>
>   _____ lost the lead
>
>   ___X___ became confused
>
> 2. Everytime Mary opens her mouth to talk, she <u>puts her foot in it</u>.
>
>   ___X___ says things that cause trouble
>
>   _____ shows how clever she is
>
>   _____ does a good trick
>
> 6. Sam said, "<u>Don't get your back up</u> just because he doubted your word."
>
>   _____ stretch
>
>   ___X___ get angry
>
>   _____ go backwards

7. When we reached the top of the hill, Jack said, "Let's drop anchor here."

    _____ hold the ship

    _____ dig a hole

    __X__ stop

Practice material of the type illustrated above may be found in the following workbooks that accompany readers in graded series:

1. Paul McKee, et al., Reading for Meaning (Boston: Houghton Mifflin Company).

    Practice for Looking Ahead, Third Reader, Level I, 1950, pp. 65-66.

    Practice for Climbing Higher, Third Reader, Level II, 1957, p. 83.

    Practice for High Roads, Fourth Reader, 1954, pp. 39, 47, 70, 86.

    Practice for Sky Lines, Fifth Reader, 1955, pp. 58, 72.

    Practice for Bright Peaks, Sixth Reader, 1955, pp. 30, 59.

2. Mabel O'Donnell and Margaret L. White, Workbook for If I Were Going, Third Reader, Alice and Jerry Basic Reading Program (Evanston, Illinois: Row, Peterson and Company, 1957), p. 115.

3. William S. Gray, Marion Monroe, and A. Sterl Artley, The New Basic Readers -- Curriculum Foundation Series (Chicago: Scott, Foresman and Company).

    Think and Do Book to Accompany the New Times and Places, Fourth Grade, Level I, 1954, pp. 17, 21, 38.

    Think and Do Book to Accompany More Times and Places, Fourth Grade, Level II, 1955, pp. 68.

Multiple Meanings

A widely used elementary school dictionary shows seventy-five different uses of the word run, e. g., "to run a race; to run a garage; a run on a bank; a run in a stocking; not the common run of persons."[28]

The illustrative exercise on the following page shows how one teacher encouraged her class to think of many meanings of the same word.[29]

The word track was being discussed in the classroom in connection with a story regarding streetcars. Some of the children had never seen a streetcar, and so Bill, a city boy, said that they were cars that ran by electricity on tracks. When asked to describe what a track looked like, he said that it was a long steel thing that ran in two lines down the middle of the street. John, the "desert rat," with a puzzled look on his face, wanted to know what kind of tracks the car made. We got to talking about the words that looked the same, but meant different things, and it was suggested that each child tell what the word track meant to him.

Sharon said that many times her mother told her not to track up the clean kitchen floor. To her it meant to get something dirty. Melinda mentioned that she had heard her father discuss the sound track of his tape recorder. Steve contributed the fact that his father tracked a missile on a tracking board. Peter mentioned the new race track outside El Paso. Joe told of riding on a train which ran on tracks and how the wheels make a clicking sound as they went over the joints in the tracks. John told of the time he had found them to the boundary lines of the Post. Bruce, the slowpoke of the class, said that his mother had told him to make tracks for school that morning. "She meant me to hurry up," he said by way of explanation.

By the time we were through, we had collected quite a few meanings for the word track and had learned a lesson in word comprehension. For, as one child expressed it, "You have to know what you are reading about to know what the word means."

A second teacher developed a sample series of exercises for teaching multiple meanings of words.[30]

All of the following exercises require the use of the word record or the word with a prefix or suffix added. Sometimes the word will be the name of something, sometimes it will be an action word, and in a few cases, it will be used as a descriptive modifier. Write the correct word in the blank provided in each sentence and be prepared to tell whether it is used as a noun, a verb, or an adjective:

1. His academic   (record)   was poor.
2. His score was a new   (record) .
3. The invention of writing led to   (recorded)   history.
4. New films   (record)   color accurately.
5. She wanted a new   (recording) .
6. This has been a   (record)   vote.

7. He plays a ___(recorder)___ .
8. A seismograph ___(records)___ earth tremors.
9. Every word was taken down by the tape ___(recorder)___ .
10. The voice was ___(prerecorded)___ .
11. The ___(record)___ was ___(recorded)___ in ___(record)___ time.

Teaching uses of the word record. Underline the word which means the same as record.

1. He read the minutes of the last meeting.
2. The man had a criminal history.
3. He set a new distance in the shot put.
4. They kept a weekly sales inventory.
5. He bought a phonograph disc.
6. They checked the court proceedings.
7. He tried to preserve the sounds.
8. One should register legal documents.
9. Newspapers are chronicles of the times.

These are merely examples. Teachers can expand and develop similar exercises around word meanings giving trouble in their own classes.

Pictures can be very useful in developing understanding of the multiple meanings of many common words. The teacher may be able to draw upon a master vertical picture file in her school; the children may draw pictures to illustrate meanings; or many usable pictures can be cut from magazines. The words show and track are depicted on page 328 in series of pictures to show how this activity may be carried out. Notebooks, prepared as either individual or group projects, might provide motivation for such an activity.

Exercises Which Require Boys and Girls to Think About Words That Express Precise Meanings in Different Contexts

When an author writes a story, he wants to make it interesting to read. If he keeps using "he said," "they said," over and over again, his story will sound dull and boring. Instead, he will use many different words that mean said, but these words add life and color.to the story. For example, if a sentence says:

The king roared, "Stop that noise! "

You know that the king said, "Stop that noise! " in a very loud, rough voice.

The teacher will show which story it is.

The show began with a Mickey Mouse cartoon.

The clown will show us some tricks.

He pointed to show us the way.

Multiple Meanings of SHOW.

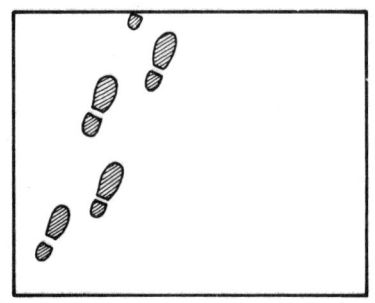

The man made tracks in the snow.

Don't track up the clean kitchen floor.

The horses ran around the track.

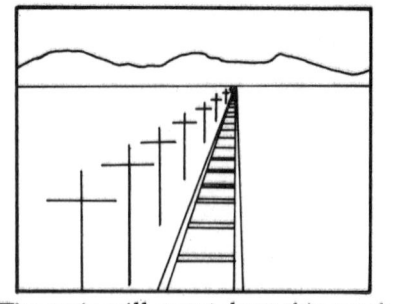

The train will come down this track.

Multiple Meanings of TRACK.

A. Here are some sentences from "Fritz the Master-Fiddler." Each sentence has an underlined word that means said, but each of these words adds some special meaning as well. From the list below the sentences, pick out the meaning of the word. Write the letter of the correct answer in the space. The same answer in the space. The same answer may be used more than once.

1. "Dear me!" cried His Majesty, surprised.

    Cried means _____.

2. "This fiddle does not play by notes," mumbled Fritz.

    Mumbled means _____.

3. "I do not care to play," he replied.

    Replied means _____.

4. "Ah," whispered the king to the queen.

    Whispered means _____.

a. to give a glad, excited shout
b. to make a deep sound showing
c. to speak in a low, soft voice
d. to answer
e. to make a loud sound with the voice
f. to speak out suddenly and with strong feeling[31]

---

rich, 1. having wealth, owning much money or property; wealthy. 2. having much of something, well supplied. 3. worth much; valuable. 4. full of fats, or fats and sugar. 5. full, deep, and brilliant. 6. producing much.

tongue, 1. the movable muscle attached to the floor of the mouth. It is used in tasting, eating, and speaking. 2. An animal's tongue used as food. 3. the act or power of speaking. 4. a manner of speaking. 5. a language.

A. One of the most important steps in understanding what you read is understanding the meaning of each word. Many words have more than a single meaning. In such cases, you must choose the definition that makes sense in the context. Several meanings or definitions for the words rich and tongue are listed above. Choose the number of the definition that makes sense in each question below. Write the number of the definition on the line after the question.

1. Which definition for the word tongue makes sense in the title of this exercise? _____

2. Which definition for the word rich makes sense in the title, "Striking It Rich"? _____

3. Which definition for the word rich makes sense in this sentence, "English is a very rich language?"[32] _____

Reading workbooks also include exercises fostering the recognition of multiple meanings of a single word:

Skill: Deriving word meanings from context.[32]

1. It was <u>hard</u> for the farmer to get his cow on the roof.
2. He made a bridge out of a wide, <u>hard</u> board.

    ____ It was surely hard for him to keep the cow on the roof.

1. One cold day a man went to the village to buy a <u>stamp</u>.
2. In the store he began to <u>stamp</u> his cold feet.

    ____ Then he bought a stamp and hurried home.

1. A farmer's wife said, "I <u>mean</u> to have chicken for dinner tonight."
2. I'll eat that <u>mean</u> old rooster who makes such a terrible noise.

    <u>(2)</u> It's a mean thing to do, but I want to get some sleep tonight.

1. The day before Christmas everyone in school was <u>present</u>.
2. The children grew very quiet as they waited for their <u>presents</u>.

    <u>(2)</u> Some presents were small, but others were great big ones.

Skill: Comprehending simple definitions of meaning in the light of a given context.[34]

Find the meaning that the underlined word has in each sentence and put the number of the sentence before it.

1. The prince was <u>satisfied</u> that there was nothing fit to eat in the castle.
2. None of the delicious foods the cooks knew how to prepare <u>satisfied</u> him.
3. The excellent ice cream with the hot chocolate sauce satisfied his hunger.

<u>(2)</u> pleased
<u>(3)</u> ended
<u>(1)</u> sure
__ paid

. . .

1. The prince said, "I want something <u>new</u> and delicious to eat."
2. The cook was frightened. A food that was both hot and cold was <u>new</u> to him.
3. The boy who had peeled potatoes took off his dirty apron and put on a <u>new</u> one.

<u>(3)</u> fresh, unused
<u>(1)</u> different
__ later
<u>(2)</u> unknown

. . .

Practice lessons directing children to choose the correct meanings of words in sentences or to choose correct meanings given in the dictionary may be found in the following workbooks:

1. Paul McKee, M. Lucille Harrison, Annie McCowen, and Elizabeth Lehr, Reading for Meaning (Boston: Houghton-Mifflin Co.).

    Practice for Looking Ahead, Third Reader, Level I, 1950, p. 42.

    Practice for High Roads, Fourth Reader, 1954, p. 42.

    Practice for Sky Lines, Fifth Reader, 1955, pp. 11, 24, 34, 48.

    Practice for Bright Peaks, Sixth Reader, 1955, p. 20.

2. Mabel O'Donnel, et al., The Alice and Jerry Reading Program (Evanston: Row, Peterson, and Company).

    Workbook for If I Were Going, Third Reader, 1957, p. 30, 77, 91.

    Workbook for Singing Wheels, Fourth Reader, 1957, p. 12, 35, 48, 60, 71, 78, 103.

    Workbook for Engine Whistles, Fifth Reader, 1955, p. 22, 26, 56.

    Workbook for Runaway Home, Sixth Reader, 1956, p. 17, 34, 50, 108.

3. William S. Gray, Marion Monroe, and A. Sterl Artley, The New Basic Readers, Curriculum Foundation Series (Chicago: Scott, Foresman and Company).

    Think and Do Book to Accompany The New Streets and Roads, Third Grade, Level I, 1956, pp. 3, 19, 64.

    Think and Do Book to Accompany the New Times and Places, Fourth Grade, Level I, 1954, pp. 2, 9, 50.

    Think and Do Book to Accompany More Times and Places, 1955, pp. 22, 55.

    Think and Do Book to Accompany Just Imagine, 1953, pp. 30, 52, 71.

    Think and Do Book to Accompany More Days and Deeds, 1956, pp. 18, 53, 68.

Synonyms, Antonyms, Homonyms, and Heteronyms

Students learning English as a second language need to master the necessary vocabulary in recognizing the similar meanings in words; the words that are opposites in meaning; words that are spelled different, pronounced the same, but have different meanings; and the words that are spelled the same, pronounced the same, but have entirely different meanings in different contexts.

Antonyms are practiced in several different types of exercises, including the following:

1. Either -- or [35]

    Write the word that you think belongs on the blank in each sentence:

    1. Elevators may go either down or _____.
    2. Automobiles may turn either to the right or to the _____.
    3. A bicycle may go either slow or _____.
    4. An hour may seem either long or _____.
    5. The wind can bring either cool air or _____ air.

2. Directions: On each part of this page are two paragraphs. Read the first paragraph and notice the underlined word. Then read the second paragraph and draw a line from the word that means just the opposite from the underlined word.[36]

    Mrs. Jackson told Streak to take all the rocks out of his room.

    She said, "The paper hangers are coming tomorrow. None of the rocks must be here then."

    . . . .

    "Remember what I told you," Mother said. "Take all the rocks out and put them in the tool house."

    "I won't forget," grumbled Streak. "But I don't want to do it."

    . . . .

    Streak held his favorite rock in his hand for a long time.

    Then suddenly he dropped it and darted out of the room after his mother.

    . . . .

3. Directions: In each sentence you will find two words with opposite meanings. On the lines below the sentence write the two words. The first one is done for you.[37]

    a. If you commence your work on time, you will finish before noon.

    _____ _____

    b. Most of the boys departed for home this morning, but a few remained at camp.

    _____ _____

    c. The Mouse is a tiny animal, but the lion is enormous.

    _____ _____

Many antonyms can be illustrated with pictures. Others can be demonstrated through activity. The following list constitutes more than one hundred pairs of opposites which elementary school children need to know.

TABLE XXIII

Antonyms Used in Elementary School Textbooks

1. above -- below
2. full -- empty
3. on -- off
4. tall -- short
5. up -- down

6. large -- small
7. left -- right
8. out -- in
9. man -- woman
10. boy -- girl

11. black -- white
12. red -- green
13. stop -- go
14. little -- big
15. sick -- well

16. cold -- hot
17. fast -- slow
18. push -- pull
19. dark -- light
20. happy -- sad

21. loud -- soft
22. shut -- open
23. noisy -- quiet
24. forget -- remember
25. summer -- winter

26. bad -- good
27. before -- after
28. full -- empty
29. open -- closed
30. front -- back

31. clean -- dirty
32. buy -- sell
33. slowly -- quickly
34. hit -- miss
35. early -- late

36. small -- huge
37. bright -- dark
38. softly -- loudly
39. young -- old
40. walk -- ride

41. happy -- cross
42. ripe -- green
43. wide -- narrow
44. save -- spend
45. first -- last

46. hard -- easy
47. north -- south
48. east -- west
49. smooth -- rough
50. sour -- sweet

51. common -- rare
52. sunny -- cloudy
53. capture -- free
54. remain -- leave
55. afterwards -- before

56. halt -- advance
57. gain -- lose
58. deny -- confess
59. bold -- timid
60. afraid -- unafraid

TABLE XXIII (Cont.)

Antonyms Used in Elementary School Textbooks

61. simple -- complicated
62. crooked -- straight
63. strength -- weakness
64. opposite -- alike
65. bright -- dim

66. frequently -- seldom
67. none -- all
68. few -- many
69. held -- dropped
70. bottom -- top

71. asked -- answered
72. lazy -- ambitious
73. overjoyed -- unhappy
74. vast -- small
75. slyly -- openly

76. revealed -- concealed
77. mercy -- cruelty
78. hazy -- clear
79. hero -- coward
80. straight -- curly

81. determined -- undecided
82. commence -- finish
83. depart -- remain
84. tiny -- enormous
85. elder -- younger

86. cheap -- expensive
87. salesman -- customer
88. sharp -- dull
89. divided -- united
90. praise -- blame

91. vacant -- occupied
92. borrow -- lend
93. confident -- distrustful
94. obey -- disobey
95. modern -- antique

96. foreign -- domestic
97. customary -- unusual
98. ancestors -- descendants
99. presence -- absence
100. reprove -- commend

101. friend -- enemy
102. retreat -- advance
103. accept -- reject
104. smoldered -- blazed
105. curious -- uninterested
106. charge -- donate
107. clever -- stupid
108. give -- take

The same types of exercises may be used to provide practice with homonyms. Some of the common homonyms used in children's texts in the elementary school are the following:

TABLE XXIV

Homonyms Used in Elementary School Textbooks

1. to -- two -- too
2. knew -- new
3. our -- hour
4. tale -- tail
5. rode -- road

6. wood -- would
7. blew -- blue
8. pail -- pale
9. bare -- bear
10. deer -- dear

11. sale -- sail
12. cents -- sense -- scents
13. their -- there -- they're
14. praise -- preys -- prays
15. by -- buy

16. beet -- beat
17. lone -- loan
18. mail -- male
19. right -- write
20. dual -- duel

21. wait -- weight
22. foul -- fowl
23. seem -- seam
24. knot -- not
25. no -- know

26. wear -- ware
27. four -- for
28. I -- eye
29. bee -- be
30. sea -- see

31. ate -- eight
32. hole -- whole
33. meat -- meet
34. one -- won
35. son -- sun

36. week -- weak
37. your -- you're
38. red -- read
39. read -- reed
40. due -- dew

41. creek -- creak
42. tide -- tied
43. heir -- air
44. seller -- cellar
45. root -- route

46. taut -- taught
47. flow -- floe
48. sew -- so -- sow
49. piece -- peace
50. rose -- rows

51. vane -- vain
52. through -- threw
53. soar -- sore
54. shown -- shone
55. thrown -- throne

56. cheap -- cheep
57. sighed -- side
58. heard -- herd
59. oar -- ore
60. oh -- owe

61. in -- inn
62. maid -- made
63. waist -- waste
64. rains -- reins
65. dye -- die

66. lye -- lie
67. heel -- he'll
68. steel -- steal
69. fare -- fair
70. sight -- site

71. hoes -- hose
72. peer -- pier
73. stairs -- stares
74. main -- mane
75. bury -- berry

76. strait -- straight
77. cell -- sell
78. stile -- style
79. gait -- gate
80. beech -- beach

Heteronyms are pairs of words spelled alike, accented differently when pronounced, with entirely different meanings. A few of the heteronyms encountered in elementary texts are:

record	survey´
rec´ord	sur´vey
excuse´ ("s" ending)	permit´
excuse´ ("z" ending)	per´mit
prog´ress	insult´
progress´	in´sult
protest´	conflict´
pro´test	con´flict

A search through the workbooks which are used by children in language arts work -- reading, English, spelling -- has revealed that most of these workbooks do provide one or two exercises useful to students learning English vocabulary. Most teachers will recognize that the few exercises found in any one book are insufficient; however, they can serve as models for the teacher to build additional practice, and if many workbooks are available in the Learning Materials Center in the school, the teacher will be able to locate many pages of practice by studying the indexes of skills being developed.

Prepositions

The preposition in English must be used accurately to convey meaning. The difficulty which second language speakers have with prepositions makes it appropriate to suggest that teachers have specifically planned lessons to give practice in the use of prepositions. While the correct preposition is needed in the usual prepositional phrase, prepositions are also used a great deal in idiomatic speech in both figurative and abstract sentence structure. In writing about the English language problems of the Spanish-speaking teacher teaching English, Burris says:

> Analysis of the Spanish student's difficulty with English idiom points to the fact that his greatest trouble occurs where prepositions are concerned. The trouble is accentuated by the fact that English prepositions outnumber Spanish prepositions, and prepositions are the home of idiom. In simple spatial relations the difficulty is considerable; when abstract relations are involved, or when the idiomatic use of the preposition is figurative as it often is, the student of a foreign tongue who tries to learn English is at a great loss.[38]

In addition to the preposition used singly, there is the use of two or more prepositions together, as shown in the following list of prepositions used with about.

of about	for about	in about
on about	at about	after about
by about	to about	within about
from about	since about	until about
with about		

The combination of verbs with prepositions in idiomatic usage must also be understood. The following list of prepositional combinations with the verb "get" illustrates the problem:

get about	get after	get along
get at	get before	get between
get among	get around	get with
get by	get for	get from
get in	get inside	get into
get near	get off	get on
get onto	get out	get outside
get over	get through	get to
get under	get up	get upon

Using the multiple meanings provided in an elementary dictionary, children are asked in the exercise below to select the appropriate meaning for "get" used with different prepositions.

> The mother otter had forbidden her baby to get out on the ledge.
>
> It did not take long for the otter to get over his fright.
>
> Otters sleep when they are tired and get up when they are hungry.
>
> Young otters are often foolish, but as they get on in years, they become very wise.[39]

As previously mentioned, Condie has illustrated the use of the hollow log as a device for teaching many different prepositions. The device can be used over and over, the only precaution being that beginners need to hear, practice, and habituate one of these meanings at a time so that they will be sure to know the precise meanings when they have practiced all of them.

Richard's diagram, using a water tank with fish and other objects, should be useful in teaching twenty prepositions that have to do with position or direction in space. It is reproduced on the following page.[40]

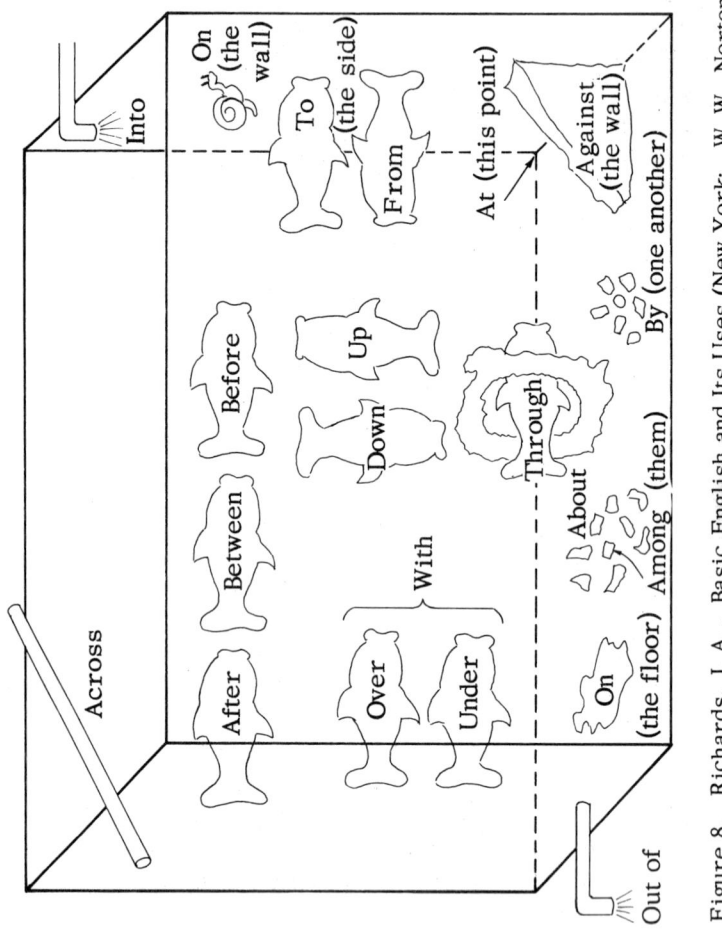

Figure 8. Richards, I. A., Basic English and Its Uses (New York: W. W. Norton and Company, Inc., 1943), page 35. Twenty prepositions that have to do with position or direction in space -- illustrated in this diagram.

Below are listed some of the prepositions which students of English as a second language will hear in everyday conversation.

TABLE XXV
Prepositions in the English Language

1. about
2. across
3. after
4. against

5. along
6. among
7. around
8. at

9. before
10. beneath
11. beside
12. besides

13. by
14. beyond
15. but
16. concerning

17. down
18. during
19. except
20. for

21. from
22. in
23. inside
24. into

25. like
26. near
27. of
28. off

29. on
30. onto
31. out
32. outside

33. over
34. providing
35. regarding
36. since

37. through
38. throughout
39. till
40. to

41. towards, toward
42. under
43. until
44. up

45. upon
46. with
47. within
48. without

Exercises similar to the one provided using the verb "get" followed by prepositions can be devised to practice idiomatic usage. A few of the many common idiomatic expressions in which the meaning of the preposition is determined by its usage with a verb are listed below for purposes of illustration.

set about (begin; start work upon)
set back (stop; hinder; check)
set forth (make known; declare; start to go)
set in (begin)
set off (explode)

set up (build; begin; start)
put by (save for future use)
put forth (grow; sprout)
put off (lay aside; go away)
put on (pretend)

put out (extinguish; destroy; be provoked)
put through (carry out successfully)
put to it (put in difficulty)
put up (lay aside, preserve; build)
put up with (endure)

run down (stop going; tired or ill)
run out (come to an end)
run out of (used up)
run through (spend rapidly; pierce)
run about (from place to place)

Words Associated in Pairs

The teacher should use every opportunity throughout the child's day to emphasize needed vocabulary. One of the devices not to be overlooked is that of words associated in pairs -- things that go together. Many of these can be illustrated with real objects which is always the best means of learning. They can also be illustrated with pictures, and the activity of matching pairs of pictures can be constructive seatwork for children in subgroups while the teacher works with others in the room. The following list will illustrate things that are associated together in pairs.

cup -- saucer	paint -- paint brush
pen -- pencil	dog -- bone
baby -- buggy	nose -- face
broom -- dustpan	moon -- sun
shirt -- tie	cake -- baker
ball -- bat	tree -- leaf
ring -- finger	doll -- dress
lamp light bulb	milk -- milkman
desk -- chair	horse -- colt
fork -- knife	sow -- pigs
pan -- lid	sheep -- lamb
hair -- comb	cow -- calf
behind -- in front of	goat -- kid
hammer -- nails	hen -- chicken
football -- football players	goose -- gosling
fireman -- fire engine	dog -- puppy
girl -- boy	duck -- duckling
parents -- children	cat -- kitten
man -- woman	frog -- tadpole
mail -- postman	bear -- cubs
lion -- cubs	

340

Other Aspects of Concept Development

Contractions, deriving meanings of roots, prefixes, and suffixes, recognizing figures of speech and interpreting proverbs need more than the casual attention directed toward them in children's textbooks. Teachers will find exercises in texts and workbooks used in teaching English and reading by perusing the contents for indexes of skills developed.

The following exercise is designed to help the child put two words used separately together to build a compound word: [41]

Identifying as meaning units the root words in compounds.

Directions: You will find two words underlined in each box. These words may be put together to make a compound word that fits the meaning in the blank space. Decide how to put the two words together and write the compound word on the line below the paragraph.

Father said, "I can't <u>work</u> in any <u>room</u> in this house. I need a _____ of my own."

The <u>bed</u> was <u>spread</u> with a fine old woolen cover. "I'm proud of this _____," said Mrs. Page.

The <u>side</u> of the <u>hill</u> was covered with beautiful purple flowers. They made the whole _____ look blue.

"A <u>crow</u> eats my seeds when I'm not around to <u>scare</u> it off," said Woody. "I'll make a _____."

The simile expresses a comparison between two persons or things. The simile uses "like" or "as" to make the comparison. For people who use English as their vernacular, these comparisons become everyday expressions through usage. For the child learning English as a second language, however, these need to be specifically taught. "Brave as a lion," "Cross as a bear," "Sharp as a tack," or "Clean as a whistle," are commonly used. Other examples found in the <u>Think and Do Workbooks</u> to accompany Scott, Foresman graded readers include: [42]

1. The bad old shoemaker was <u>as sly as a fox</u>.
2. A fox hid behind a log and kept <u>as still as a mouse</u>.
3. The dog scampered off <u>as quick as a wink</u>.
4. In her new dress, Judy looked <u>as pretty as a picture</u>.
5. The cook's roast lamb was <u>as tough as shoe leather</u>.
6. Sojo, the Strong Man, was <u>as strong as an ox</u>.

7. The children made the classroom as neat as a pin.

8. The dancer was as graceful as a fairy.

9. The bottom of the pit was as dry as a bone.

10. The baby's eyes were as blue as the sky.

Arranging sequences of ideas in the sentence, interpreting other figures of speech, interpreting meanings of proverbs and stilted or affected or unfamiliar ways of saying things, and discussing connotations of sentences where different emphases are given to the five senses are other aspects of enriching vocabulary in learning English as a second language.

Literature is filled with figures of speech based upon an understanding of biblical characters. The Indian student who has no familiarity with the Bible as literature needs to be directed to the kind of reference dictionary that will interpret for him such expressions as:

"Don't be a Lot's wife . . . ."

"She was a Jezebel leading him on . . . ."

"He's a doubting Thomas . . . ."

"Another Daniel in the lion's den . . . ."

"A voice crying in the wilderness."

"The land of milk and honey."

"The wisdom of Solomon."

"It was a David and Johnathan friendship."

The faith of Abraham, the burning bush, greedy as Judas, the wailing wall, as old as Methuselah, as patient as Job, back to the fig leaf, "Wither thou goest," the golden rule, the seven plagues.

"Don't let yourself get crucified."

"Vanity, vanity, all is vanity, saith the preacher."

Or, sometimes when one observes that the outer forms are being properly kept, but the inside is corrupt, he speaks of the "whited sepulchre."

SUMMARY

Empirical data has been presented to substantiate the hypothesis that one of the most pressing problems in education of minority ethnic groups is that of teaching English as a second language.

Results of an exploratory test of common English idiomatic expressions reveal that Anglo sixth graders performed statistically significantly better than did Navajo, Pueblo, and Apache Indian and Spanish-American pupils. In the sample populations tested, the median scores for Navajos, Pueblos, and Spanish-Americans were at the first, second, and fifth percentiles respectively for an Anglo norming group.[42]

A fourth-grade Anglo norming group performed statistically significantly better on exploratory tests of multiple meanings of commonly used words, analogies, and antonyms, than did either fourth- or sixth-grade Navajos, Apaches, Pueblo Indians, and Spanish-Americans. All critical ratios were significant in this testing.[43,44,45]

Research of this nature is needed to develop awareness on the part of public school personnel of the extent of the problem. Teachers who have not experienced bilingual problems themselves often fail to grasp the significance of the language handicap of others.

Practical aids for teachers have been given, including the following: descriptions of devices and booklets for teaching English; a list of sources for free and inexpensive materials; sample exercises and workbook sources for exercises showing the use of idioms, multiple meanings, synonyms, antonyms, homonyms, heteronyms, prepositions, pairs of words and similes.

The hope is expressed that teachers will use such examples as a beginning, adding to them with exercises developed to illuminate the problem-meanings of words discovered in their own classrooms.

FOOTNOTES

[1] Pauline M. Rojas, "A Critical Analysis of the Vocabulary of Three Standard Series of Pre-primers and Primers in Terms of How the Words Are Used" (with Special Reference to the Language Problems of the Spanish-Speaking Children of Puerto Rico) (Unpublished Doctoral dissertation, University of Michigan, Ann Arbor, 1945).

[2] Ibid., p. 54.

[3] Ibid., p. 55-56.

[4] Ibid., p. 68.

[5] Le Roy Condie, "An Experiment in Second-Language Instruction of Beginning Indian Children in New Mexico Public Schools" (unpublished Doctoral dissertation, The University of New Mexico, Albuquerque, 1961).

[6] A. L. Davis, Diagnostic Test for Students of English as a Second Language (Washington: Educational Services, 1956).

[7] Richard Scott, "Acculturation Among Mescalero Apache High School Students" (Unpublished Master's thesis, University of New Mexico, Albuquerque, 1959).

[8] Test results were provided in April, 1958, by Margaret Knight, Home Economics Instructor, Practical Nurse Training School, Albuquerque Indian School, Albuquerque, New Mexico.

[9] Navajo Orientation Program, 1960 (Albuquerque: The University of New Mexico Press, 1960), p. 32. (Mimeographed.)

[10] Florence Hawley Ellis supports this thesis. See The Indian Problem in New Mexico (Albuquerque: Division of Research, Department of Government, University of New Mexico, 1948), p. 39.

[11] This is a well-known tale in the Southwest. It is recorded in J. Breed, "Better Days for the Navajo," National Geographic Magazine, 114-809-847, December, 1958.

[12] Maurine Dunn Yandell, "Some Difficulties Which Indian Children Encounter with Idioms in Reading" (Unpublished Master's thesis, University of New Mexico, Albuquerque, 1959).

[13] Orpha McPherson, "Problems of the Bilingual Child," Indian Education, November 1, 1956.

[14] Yandell, op. cit.

[15] David H. Russell, et al., Ginn Basic Readers (Boston: Ginn and Company, 1956).

[16] Mabel O'Donnell, The Alice and Jerry Basic Readers (Evanston: Row, Peterson and Company, 1954 and 1956).

[17] William S. Gray, et al., Curriculum Foundation Series (Chicago: Scott, Foresman and Company, 1954 and 1955).

[18] O'Donnell, op. cit., Singing Wheels, Fourth Reader.

[19] Yandell, op. cit., p. 31.

[20] Jewel Baker, "A Comparative Study of Three Cultures, Anglo, Spanish American, and Indian, with Idioms, Proverbs, and Figures of Speech" (Unpublished research paper, University of New Mexico, College of Education, Albuquerque, May, 1959).

[21] Yandell, op. cit., p. 34.

[22] Ibid., p. 32-33.

[23] Stephen G. Hess, "A Comparative Study of the Understanding Which Bilingual Students have of the Multiple Meanings of English Words" (Unpublished Masters Thesis, University of New Mexico, College of Education, Albuquerque, 1963).

[24] Christine Dudding, "An Investigation into the Bilingual Child's Comprehension of Antonyms" (Unpublished Master's thesis, The University of New Mexico, Albuquerque, 1961).

[25] Veta W. Mercer, "The Efficiency of Bilingual Children in Understanding Analogies in the English Language" (Unpublished Master's thesis, The University of New Mexico, Albuquerque, 1960).

[26] Clara Jett Cox, "An Experimental Study in the Teaching of Certain Facets of the English Language to Navajo Pupils in the Sixth Grade," unpublished paper, College of Education, University of New Mexico, July, 1963.

[27] Paul McKee, et al., Practice for High Roads, Fourth Reader (Boston: Houghton Mifflin Company, 1954), p. 70.

[28] E. L. Thorndike and Clarence L. Barnhart, Thorndike-Barnhart Advanced Junior Dictionary (Chicago: Scott, Foresman and Company, 1957), pp. 703-704.

[29] Marjorie F. Day, primary teacher, White Sands Missile Range, New Mexico.

[30] Charles C. White, elementary teacher, Albuquerque, New Mexico.

[31] Harris, Albert J., Marion Gartler, and Caryl Roman, A Discovery Book to Accompany The Magic Word, (New York: The Macmilliam Company, 1967), p. 38.

[32] Harris, Albert J., Marion Gartler, and Caryl Roman, A Discovery Book to Accompany Bold Journeys, (New York: The Macmillian Co., 1967), p. 42.

[33] William Gray, et al., Think-And-Do Book to accompany The New More Friends and Neighbors, Second Reader, Level II (Chicago: Scott, Foresman and Co.), p. 71.

[34] Ibid., Think-And-Do Book to accompany The New More Streets and Roads, Third Reader, Level II, 1956, p. 35.

[35] Ibid., Think and Do Book to Accompany The New Streets and Roads, p. 9.

[36] Ibid., Think and Do Book to Accompany Just Imagine, p. 13.

[37] O'Donnell, et al., op. cit., Workbook for Singing Wheels, p. 79.

[38] Quincy Guy Burris, English for Rural New Mexico, Summer Workshop, 1945 (Las Vegas, New Mexico: New Mexico Highlands University, 1945), p. 4.

[39] Gray, Monroe, Artley, op. cit., Think and Do Book to Accompany More Times and Places, p. 38.

[40] I. A. Richards, Basic English and Its Usage (New York: W. W. Norton and Company, Inc., 1943), p. 35.

[41] Gray, Monroe, and Artley, op. cit., Think and Do Book to Accompany Just Imagine, p. 11.

[42] Ibid., Think and Do Book to Accompany the New Streets and Roads, p. 56; To Accompany Just Imagine, p. 68; and To Accompany New Times and Places, p. 74.

[43] Yandell, loc. cit.

[44] Hess, loc. cit.

[45] Dudding, loc. cit.

[46] Mercer, loc. cit.

CHAPTER 11

Counseling the Indian Student

INTRODUCTION

In terms of academic performance, one may conclude from the evidence already presented, that most Indian students are not succeeding. As long as the norms for what is acceptable are based on the work of the typical, unilingual middle-class Anglo, the culturally different, language-handicapped student is almost sure to fail. As long as the schools do not distinguish the teaching of English to native speakers of English from the teaching of English to speakers of other languages, many of these students will never feel comfortable in the spontaneous use of English.

It is understandable that many of these students set very low levels of aspiration of themselves and protect themselves from the uncomfortable experiences of never measuring up by not even trying where failure is practically guaranteed.

What is counseling?

Counseling is a problem-solving relationship between a counselor and one person or a small group of people. The counseling effort is an attempt to restructure the environment of the person so that he can more clearly analyze his problem and select alternate solutions. The effort of the counseling process is to arrive at decisions that can be tested. Out of the counselor-client relationship, the process of evolving a decision is based upon analyzing present knowledge and arriving at plans for future behaviors.

In his personal relationship with the client, the counselor attempts:

1. To evaluate the strengths and weaknesses of the individual and help the client to emphasize his strengths.
2. To the client select out of his verbalizing those things that have most meaning for him now.
3. With the client, eventually to begin arriving at possible hypotheses. What are some of the possible solutions to the situation?

Counselors, as contrasted to teachers, parents, or others, try to minimize the "authority" figure and to maximize the point of view that the client must arrive at his decision and be ready to accept the consequences of that decision.

If the counselee makes the decision, tries it out and finds that it doesn't work, he may be willing to come back to the counselor to evaluate the reasons why it failed. However, if the counselee felt that he was "told" by the counselor what to do and then it failed, he might either feel he had failed the counselor or that he need not return for further counseling.

Counselors as judges of human behavior.

Every mature adult, counselor or otherwise, has his own personal set of values, personal standards for his own behavior, and feelings about behavior of other people. It behooves the counselor at work, however, to begin with the premise that any behavior that human beings exhibit is human behavior. Each one has his personal values, standards, and feelings.

The counselor can be much more effective, then, if he understands the ethnic background of the person he counsels. As evidenced in the reports of Spang and Bryde which follow, understanding the cultural values of any individual from another ethnic group may be essential if the counselor is to understand why the student does or does not respond in the counseling session.

It is important to minimize the extent of emotional involvement with the client since the counselor may accept too much responsibility in the counseling relationship and then have guilt feelings when things do not work out.

Behavior is a function of the total situation.

The counselee may need time to grow in his thinking; time to adjust to the counselor; and time to think through old ways of behaving and replace them with new ways.

The parent, the grandparent, or the confidante that has been the counselee's primary support up to this time may have had a set of values and future aspirations of what is good and desirable far removed from an emerging set of values of a young person who is interested in an academic education. Especially among the Indian people, parents may not be interested in formal education if it leads to taking them away from home and causing them to forget the ways of the old people.

Smith writes about this resistant attitude on the part of one of the Rio Grande Pueblo Councils:[1]

> .... many drop out of high school .... This fact, plus the unwillingness of the Council to support or approve higher education (a matter on which parents consult the council) have

resulted in a very small number of students obtaining education beyond high school. The council has opposed higher education on the grounds that it will encourage the young to leave the Pueblo, or will change the old order of things at the pueblo, and "there might be women doing men's jobs, or even wanting to sit on the council."

Intelligence Tests in the Counseling Situation

The testing of students with serious language handicaps with group intelligence tests predicated upon a middle-class Anglo culture and the language of that culture, has probably been more damaging than it has been helpful. Students are apt to internalize for themselves the value that they come to understand the teacher holds for them. If little is expected; often, only little is forthcoming. The literature about intelligence testing among the Indian and the Spanish-speaking in the southwest was summarized briefly in chapter five.

The performance of a typical Navajo adult on the Wechsler Adult Intelligence Scale is reproduced here. This adult was employed by his tribe in a responsible position in which he spoke Navajo most of the time. The result of the verbal test must be interpreted in terms of: (1) The limited ability of the individual to understand and verbalize the English language; (2) The cultural bias of some of the questions in the test, for example:

a. Why must two people be married in order to live together?

For the traditional Navajo in a matrilineal society, marriage and divorce did not function as they do in our present day society. In a matrilineal society the mother has protection and support for her children if she owns all the property and livestock. Marriage in the Navajo way was not recorded in courts of law nor were violations of the marriage bonds settled there.

b. Why must everyone who owns land pay taxes?

For Indians on reservations, this question may not have the same meaning that it has for the typical, lower-middle-class tax payer.

Respect for Personality

The so-called "normal" individual feels that he is an accepted member of a social group, that he is at least resonably well-liked by the majority of the people in that group, and that he likes and respects them as important people.

The individual from a minority ethnic group may have had many negative experiences: discrimination, school failure, social rejection by the dominant "Anglo" group, or in many other, perhaps subtle, ways felt unaccepted.

Hopefully, the well-integrated personality eventually arrives at satisfactory answers for himself to these philosophical questions: Who am I? Why am I here? and Where am I going?

Menninger expressed this need for Indian high school students at an Indian Education Conference in this way:

> . . . . the most important thing in all children's lives is to establish with a kind of certainty what their own identity is -- just who they really are . . . the American Indians, or at least many of them, have trouble with this. They don't know whether they are Arizonans or Hualapais or Republicans or Democrats or something else. This becomes more confusing for them if they have had more outside contact.[2]

The transcripts of 146 Southwest Indians were examined in the summer of 1967.

The names of these 149 students were taken from the annual commencement bulletins of the University of New Mexico between the years 1960 and 1965 which, during those years, included a list of all awards and scholarships for the academic year. These scholarships were offered by such organizations as: United Pueblos Agency, Laguna Tribe, Jicarilla Apache Tribe, Navajo Tribe, North American Indian Club, Kiva Club, and the Foundation for American Indian Education. The list does not include Indians who may have been awarded other scholarships not designated for Indian students and it does not include many Indians enrolled in the University. One hundred forty-six transcripts were located and xeroxed for the research. The three students who had no permanent record probably withdrew from school in the early weeks of their first enrollment.

The following table gives the Tribal breakdown of the students whose records were examined:

Tribe	Number	Tribe	Number
Isleta	17	Zuni	2
Laguna	17	Hopi	2
Navajo	65	Santa Clara	2
San Juan	4	San Felipe	2
Taos	6	Jemez	1
Santo Domingo	4	San Ildefonso	1
Cochiti	3	Zia	1
Jicarilla Apache	3	Tribe not determined	16
		TOTAL	146

When the sixteen whose tribal affiliation was not known are discounted, one sees that sixty-five Navajos constitute one half of the 130 remaining students. In terms of total population of Navajos in New Mexico, this is very reasonable since their number is approximately equal to all other Indians combined.

Three of the students were enrolled as non-degree only or as graduate students after earning a degree elsewhere. When their records are discounted, 143 transcripts remain. These 143 were examined to determine how many students at the time were suspended, ineligible to return, placed on probation at the end of one semester for very low scholarship, or placed on probation in a degree granting college for low scholarship. Ninety of the 143 students were in these categories. This is 63% of the total. Sixty-three per cent of a student body making failing grades is significantly higher than usually found in university populations.

Because of the very small numbers of other tribes, only the Navajo population was analyzed as to success in college. The students were categorized as having unsatisfactory scholarship records, eligible to continue in school, or earned a degree. Forty-eight fit category one, six, category two, and eleven, category three as is seen in the following table:

Success/Failure Records of Sixty-five Navajo Students at The University of New Mexico, 1960-1967

I.	Unsatisfactory Scholarship (Probation/Suspension; Used up eligibility in University, College; Probation in degree granting college)	48	74%
II.	Undergraduate record satisfactory to continue in school	6	9%
III.	Granted B.A. or B.S. degrees . . .	11	17%
		65	100%

Two of these Navajos have continued into the graduate school where they have satisfactory records.

Indian students who earned degrees, 1960 - 1967. Twenty-nine of the 146 students in this study earned degrees at The University of New Mexico. Three were not identified by tribe, but the other twenty-six represented nine different tribes. Of the twenty-nine, seventeen did all their work at UNM and twelve transferred work to The University of New Mexico. Usually the work transferred was equivalent to one or two years earned before enrolling at UNM.

Of the twenty-nine degree winners, fourteen were on probation at some time. One was continued on probation seven semesters; one, six semesters; two, three semesters; one, two semesters; and nine, one semester each. One of the students who earned a degree was suspended at the end of the freshman year and stayed out an academic year before re-enrolling. Two of the graduates were graduated by special administrative council approval in their respective colleges because they were a fraction of a grade point average short of the minimum requirement. For example, 2.0000 is required; one student had only 1.9806 GPA for about 150 semester hours of work.)

Among those earning degrees, one finds that several students attended through ten semesters, eleven, or in one case, twelve semesters. It is not unusual for good non-Indian students to attend one or two summer sessions in addition to eight semesters in academic years, but ten or more semesters is excessive. Students may have withdrawn from courses, neglected to withdraw and been given failing grades in courses not attended, or failed to make satisfactory grades.

A tutoring-counseling program, sponsored by the Lilly Foundation, was offered at the University of New Mexico during the years 1960-63. One of the most frustrating aspects of the tutoring program was that each student who was scheduled for individual or small group help brought course assignments with him that were "imminently" pressing and required most of the tutoring time in editing, discussing, or preparing outlines for. Even though the tutor realized that the student's primary need was improvement of reading and study skills, this need had to take a secondary role since assignments continued to come due as made.[3] The tutors tried to offer help to students in small group instruction in taking notes, using reference materials, taking examinations, and how to study. Making out weekly study schedules and attempting to follow them was also emphasized. (See Figure 9).

During 1960-61, fifteen students asked for assistance. Of these, twelve attended tutoring sessions on a regular basis, though for varying lengths of time. The second year, fifteen students worked in the program, again for varying lengths of time. Some of the latter fifteen were enrolled both years. Sufficient records were obtained on twenty-six students over the two-year period that fifteen were judged to be successful in their university work and eleven were unsuccessful and needed much more tutoring if they were to re-enroll in college. Success was based upon passing the English Proficiency Examination required for entering a degree granting college and upon obtaining the minimum grade point average required by the college in which the student was enrolled.

Most of these Indian students who failed in college, failed because they lacked communication skills in English. Whether they

Hours	Monday	Tuesday	Wednesday	Thursday	Friday	Saturday
7-8	Breakfast	Breakfast	Breakfast	Breakfast	Breakfast	Breakfast
8-9	Study Psychology	Study Speech	Study Psychology	Study Speech	Study Psychology	
9-10	Psychology Lecture	Study Speech	Psychology Lecture	Study Speech	Psychology Lecture	
10-11	Study Ch. Gr. D.	Speech Class	Study Ch. Gr. D.	Speech Class	Study Ch. Gr. D.	
11-12	Lecture Ch. Gr. D.		Lecture Ch. Gr. D.		Lecture Ch. Gr. D.	
12-1	Lunch	Lunch	Lunch	Lunch	Lunch	Lunch
1-2	Study Eng. Lit.	Study Math.	Study Eng. Lit.	Study Math.	Study Eng. Lit.	
2-3	Eng. Lit. Lecture	TUTORING	Eng. Lit. Lecture	TUTORING	Eng. Lit. Lecture	Study Mathematics
3-4	TUTORING	Math. Class.	Study Eng. Lit.	Math. Class	TUTORING	Study Mathematics
4-5						
5-6						
6-7	Dinner	Dinner	Dinner	Dinner	Dinner	Dinner
7-8	GROUP TUTORING	Study Psychology	Study Ch. Gr. D.	Study Eng. Lit.		
8-9	GROUP TUTORING	Study Psychology	Study Ch. Gr. D.	Study Eng. Lit.		

Name: Alfred Begay　　　　　　　　　　　　　　　　Semester: II, 1962.

This schedule provides for approximately two hours out of class study for each hour in class lecture. It is arranged to provide for study the hour before class. It is also flexible and will permit using some additional time not scheduled for special assignments.

Figure 9. Time expenditure schedule for Alfred Begay.

attended schools supervised by the Bureau of Indian Affairs, public schools, or mission schools, they were never given intensive systematic, sequenced instruction in English as a second language. They were taught English by teachers whose only preparation was directed toward teaching English to native speakers of English. These differences are pointed out in the chapter on TESOL.* Before one is ready to undergo formal study based on the mastery of the reading and writing of the language, he must feel comfortably at home in easily and clearly understanding and speaking the language.

Advisors to Indian students who do not recognize some of the cultural differences and who wish to counsel students wisely are not generally knowledgeable in either the teaching of English as a second language or in the teaching of developmental reading skills in a remedial reading situation. Without these two basic needs being

---
* Teaching English to Speakers of Other Languages.

in a rehabilitation process for the Indian student, his possible success in the academic world is slight.

Before these students are to profit from instruction in developmental reading, they must have acquired proficiency in understanding and using the spoken language.

Intensive reading and study skill instruction will be an "absolute must" if these students are to be given an opportunity to succeed in college. Developmental skills, word study and vocabulary development, and phonetic and structural analysis skills taught at whatever level the student needs is absolutely necessary if he is to become an independent reader. Abilities of student reported here ranged all the way from those who needed instructional help beginning at about the fourth grade level to those who needed only reading-counseling help with college courses.

One freshman who asked for tutoring help, but who was later suspended for low grades, described his difficulties with English in this way:[4]

> I regret that during my high school years I didn't take English seriously. Now that I'm in college my poor vocabulary has been an obstacle to understanding many of my academic subjects, one of them is literature. What's more is that my knowledge of grammar is so restricted that when I try to write in formal English, the issue, to me is ashame (sic). To me formal English is unsurmountable (sic), but I think sometimes intensive studying and efficient work on meanings of words will improve my comprehension.

A junior student described his reading and language problem in this manner:[5]

> Looking back to my high school days, I find that the ACADEMIC course that caused the UTMOST agony was English. It was my belief that English was an insurmountable obstacle; but after a lengthy discussion with my English tutor, Mr. Charles, who is also a philosopher, I was enlightened (sic) that my belief was false. He said that English can be mastered if a student is willing to persistently and diligently works (sic) at it. . . .

During the tutoring-counseling program, it became quite evident that some beginning students:

1. expect that just graduating from high school entitles them to college attendance;
2. have extremely limited ability in the use of English;
3. have no study habits, no independence in planning ahead through the semester;

4. feel some rejection by the other college students;
5. give up easily and accept failure;
6. cannot be involved in group counseling situations until a minimum adjustment to campus life, study routines, and reading and writing skills have been cultivated first.

The Tempe Report of Success and Failure of College Students shows that Indian students are more successful in some of the other institutions of higher education than at the University of New Mexico but the overall results are in accord.

The Tempe study of success and failure of Southwestern Indians showed financial reasons (48 per cent), lack of encouragement of tribal leaders and family members (38 per cent), and inadequate preparation (38 per cent) as major reasons for college drop-outs.[6]

Thirty-five per cent of the Indians in school had less than a "C" average.

Facility with the English language seems to be of even greater importance for success in college among Indians than it is among non-Indians.

Thirty-two per cent of the Indians in school and two percent of the non-Indians had been on academic probation.[7]

Bryde found that Indians were more anxious, compulsive, and alienated than non-Indian students; but he also found that twelfth graders were better adjusted than eighth and ninth graders. Part of this latter finding may be because of the attrition of students between ninth and twelfth grades.[8]

Spang writes about his problems in counseling Indian students in Arizona State University. He describes their level of aspiration, he expresses concern about the type of counseling relationship to be established, and finally, he raises questions in counseling "across cultures:"

> . . . . the majority of these people have no initiative or desire to change their plight . . . . the vocational aspirational level of these reservation-oriented Indians is very low - at best, they aspire to seasonal type of employment - very rarely does one find a "far-sighted" youth who expresses a desire to become a member of a professional occupational group.
>
> . . . . the value system of the Indian is so different from that of the non-Indian that to do an effective job of counseling one must become conversant with it.

Now, a counselor of Indian students cannot, in general, apply the same philosophy of counseling that he has for non-Indians. If one is non-directive, ... the counselor would be ineffective because the Indian student is extremely non-verbal and passive. He will speak only when asked a question. Too, he will answer the question as briefly as possible without elaborating or qualifying his answer. Thus, a non-directive counselor would certainly have to adjust to either becoming an eclectic or directive type counselor if he is to be effective as a counselor of Indian students.[10]

Spang raises pertinent questions about counseling students with such different value systems from typical western mind of the counselor:[11]

> How does one encourage an Indian student to become competitive when it is not in his value system to be so?
>
> How does the counselor approach the problem of an Indian student who is failing because he does not compete but has the ability to do better?
>
> What does a counselor do to instill in the minds of Indian students to want to aspire to higher level occupations?
>
> How does one encourage a student to seek medical help when he believes in "medicine men?"

General suggestions that may help:

Counseling for Indian students either in high school or college must do several things:

1. Help the student work out a time expenditure schedule such as the one on page 353 and discuss it in considerable detail so that the student will be conscious of making efficient use of his time.

2. Through tests, determine the level of oral language ability of the student and make sure, first, that he gets instruction which is not English for Native speakers of English but English for Speakers of Other Languages if he needs it.

3. Determine just how well he can read and how extensive his vocabulary is. Then provide remedial reading instruction in developmental reading at the level at which the student is ready to begin.

4. Offer to discuss with the student, personal, as well as academic, problems. The counselor must be very "direct" in insisting on adherence to time schedules, building morale, and emphasizing the positive attributes of the student.

5. Help the student obtain services auxiliary to his school attendance. For example, medical services not available through the student health service on campus are likely available through the Indian Division of the United States Public Health Service.

6. Maintain a cumulative record for each counselee:[12]

.... a good cumulative record can facilitate both acceptance and understanding. It will often help with the initial ice-breaking stage by suggesting topics in which the client is likely to be interested. It may furnish warnings as to areas to be avoided at the beginning.

An Indian student is not apt to share any very personal information with the counselor in the beginning. But as he begins to have confidence and trust in the counselor's desire to be helpful, he will decide what kinds of information he would like to share. The mental notes made while in the counselee's presence need to be recorded immediately following the interview so that they may not be forgotten.

FOOTNOTES

[1] Smith, Anne M., New Mexico Indians: Economic, Educational and Social Problems, (Santa Fe: Museum of New Mexico, 1966), p. 143.

[2] Menninger, Karl, "Who Am I?" Journal of American Indian Education, 4:28, No. 3, May, 1965.

[3] Zintz, Miles V. and Joyce Morris. A Tutoring-Counseling Program For Indian Students in College, 1960 - 1962, (College of Education, University of New Mexico, 1962), p. 16.

[4] Zintz, Miles V and Joyce Morris. A Tutoring-Counseling Program For Indian Students in College, 1960 - 1962, (College of Education, The University of New Mexico, 1962), pp. 13-14.

[5] Ibid.

[6] McGrath, G.D., Robert Roessel, Bruce Meador, G.C. Helmstadter and John Barnes. "Higher Education of Southwestern Indians with Reference to Success and Failure," Journal of American Indian Education, 4:9, No. 2, January, 1965.

[7] McGrath, G.D., Robert Roessel, Bruce Meador, G.C. Helmstadter and John Barnes. "Higher Education of Southwestern Indians with Reference to Success and Failure," Journal of American Indian Education, 4:10, No. 2, January, 1965.

[8] Bryde, John. Doctoral dissertation, University of Denver, 1965.

[9] Spang, Alonzo, "Counseling the Indian," Journal of American Indian Education, 5:11, No. 1, October, 1965.

[10] Spang, Alonzo, "Counseling the Indian," Journal of American Indian Education, 5:13, No. 1, October, 1965.

[11]Spang, Alonzo, "Counseling the Indian," Journal of American Indian Education, 5:14, No. 1, October, 1965.

[12]Tyler, Leona E., The Work of the Counselor, (Appleton-Century-Crofts, Inc., New York, 1953), p. 63.

CHAPTER 12

Adjusting the Curriculum

When asked what curricular changes she felt necessary in order that the school might meet the needs of her first-grade children more adequately, one teacher wrote:

Thirty per cent of the children in my first grade are Navajo. I would not be too concerned about radical changes in the curriculum if I had the freedom to shift emphasis where it is desirable and if there were funds to implement the program.

I would like: A room large enough for various areas to be set up instead of having the children crowded to the walls; storage facilities convenient to the children; means for experiential activities to enrich meager backgrounds, trips by bus to see a train, a supermarket, a post office, a municipal swimming pool; appropriate records and an available record player; good, appropriate films and filmstrips; books with the right kind of pictures, easy-to-read books, books for the teacher to read, beautiful books.

For the first grade, with emphasis on vocabulary development, the program suggested by this list is a radical change from the often-found rigorous emphasis on the teaching of 158 basic sight words to enable the child to read Fun with Dick and Jane.[1]

The volume of material easily available to teachers permits only the selection of a few basic ideas for change to discuss in this chapter. The need for change is highlighted by Tireman and Watson.

The Spanish-speaking children present an exaggerated situation. The curriculum now followed in New Mexico was originally designed for English-speaking children of the Atlantic coast. When the settlers from the East and Middle West came to make their homes in the Southwest, they brought their schools along as naturally as they brought the right to worship as they pleased. The curriculum was based on the accepted principle that all children should go to high school and college. . . all of these accomplishments were useful to the child who would go on to high school and college. But the Spanish-speaking people of New Mexico had no such body of accepted principles. Education has never been the prerogative of the common people in Spanish-speaking countries.2

This chapter will discuss briefly: (1) The place of the course of study in teaching; (2) The classroom as a learning laboratory; (3) The need for a learning materials center in the school; (4) The community school as a needed curricular adjustment; (5) The teaching of remedial reading; and (6) Special problems related to elementary science teaching.

THE PLACE OF THE COURSE OF STUDY IN TEACHING

A perpetually-recurring, erroneous idea voiced in teachers' groups is that the state course of study must be followed in the classroom. This apparently generates a slavish endeavor to force each child through a precisely-cut and well-established pattern as he progresses through any particular grade in school. The curriculum, for these children, has become a Procrustean bed which they will be tailored to fit. Do we send children to school only so that we can administer a program, or does the school really exist for the education of the child?

Every state has produced a course of study for its teachers so that each teacher may have an outline of the materials which the average child may logically be expected to utilize. A state course of study is a very valuable document when used in this frame of reference. It permits children to obtain more or less uniform general educations as they progress through the public school. It makes possible the transfer of children from one part of the country to another with satisfactory school adjustment in the new situation. It insures the transmission of basic knowledges in the cultural heritage, one of the basic purposes of the school.

Beyond this philosophical basis, the course of study is only as useful or as meaningful as the classroom teacher can make it. The "average" child is nothing more than that hypothetical statistical median class performance that establishes the level of achievement above and below which half of an unselected class will perform. Testing has shown that only a relatively small percent of the children in a given grade actually perform at that grade level on any achievement test battery. The overlap between grades in achievement has been liberally demonstrated for decades.

Naturally, then, the course of study is only a suggested guide which a teacher will find helpful for those children who achieve somewhere near the expected "normal range" for a large sample of children in that grade. The teacher must make his adaptations in at least three broad areas:

1. With respect to the language arts and arithmetic skills. No fourth-grade child, as an example, can do the prescribed pattern of listening, speaking, reading, and writing (including spelling) activities outlined in the course of study for the fourth year in elementary school if he has never learned to do those activities outlined for the third year in the course of study. As pointed out later in the teaching of remedial reading, the sequential development of language arts skills must begin each September at the level where the child is able to perform successfully, completely without regard to any arbitrary standard prescribed either by the state course of study or by the teacher.

2. With respect to the appreciations and physical education skills. A flexible teacher can accommodate a very wide range of performances in art, music, literature, rhythms, participation in the folklore of the community, physical sports, games, and dances.

3. With respect to units of work to be covered in the content areas. A problem-solving approach to learning can accommodate an extremely wide range of abilities in reading, initiative, thinking, planning, discussion, problem-solving, and evaluation. No single textbook can ever accommodate the range of interests, experiences, attitudes, apperceptions, intellects, reading abilities, work habits, or perseverance in a heterogenous classroom. With regard to reading ability alone, Horn has written of the single textbook approach:

    A single textbook is commonly provided for a grade, in spite of the incontestable evidence of the wide range of knowledge and ability in that grade. The range of reading ability, expressed in grade norms, is almost invariably at least five years, and often seven. Investigations have repeatedly pointed out that the typical textbook, even within the limits of its potential usefulness, is much too difficult for the median child in the grade for which it is designed, and it is hopelessly difficult for the children in the lowest quarter in reading ability.[3]

Through teacher and pupil planned learning experiences utilizing a range of methods of gaining information, reading, observing, experimenting, demonstrating, viewing pictures, listening to recorded information, group discussion, and conducting interviews, the teacher can not only expand the horizons beyond the textbook, but he can also completely free himself from dependence upon a single one. The section on the Learning Materials Center is offered as a tangible means for teachers who are searching for ways to enrich their teaching.

The request here is merely that teachers recognize the course of study as the useful guide that it is and adapt their teaching to the needs of the children in their classrooms.

THE CLASSROOM AS A LEARNING LABORATORY

The classroom must become a learning laboratory where children can experiment with a wide variety of learning aids that will lead them to make discoveries of meanings and ideas, to work out solutions, and to gain insights. Adequate equipment and materials must be provided if the classroom is to become a learning laboratory.

In a learning laboratory, there are jobs to do for which children see real purposes, jobs that will satisfy some fairly immediate need in solving other problems so that a kind of chain reaction to the solving of problems evolves, jobs that are easy and jobs that are difficult, jobs that individuals can do as well as jobs that groups of children can work together to complete, jobs of cooperation, sharing, and planning, as well as jobs of reading, writing, and answering teacher's questions.

In a learning laboratory, where children are actively participating in the learning process, there will be a great deal of oral communication. Listening to explanations and instructions, asking questions to clarify instructions, reporting, conversing, and discussing should not be hurried. A clear understanding of a purpose before starting work can save unlimited amounts of time after beginning.

Planning time is an activity that needs much more direction and emphasis in the classroom. A detailed, well-structured planning period early in the day should give each child a feeling of his jobs to be done throughout the day. Planning needs to be done during the day with individuals and small groups as it grows out of emerging needs. The teacher may well conduct the planning sessions, but the objectives for getting work done must be defined in terms of the ability of the children to do whatever is being planned. Planning requires a great deal of language communication: conversation, discussion, friendly argument, disagreements and their resolution, exploration of mutual interests, and explanations of ways to solve problems. Then, children need to express clearly in language what their personal objectives are. A child is ready to go to work on a problem when he can state clearly in his own words what he is going to do. This principle applies whether his task is a simple manual one or a fairly technical reporting one to be done in writing.

Strickland discusses three requisites to easy use of language:

1. An atmosphere in which language can flourish. Strickland calls this "legalized talking."
2. A happy, wholesome relationship between the teacher and children and among the children themselves.
3. The presence of many dynamic ongoing interests.[4]

These requisites are basic to an efficient learning laboratory. Strickland also emphasizes the value of informal room arrangement in promoting language growth. She says:

> No development in American education has been more detrimental to good language growth than the traditional pattern of screwed-down seats arranged in rows so that each child lived and worked in a little island of isolation as completely cut off from the fellowship of his group as it was possible to make him. Children, as well as most adults, talk better in informal, face-to-face contacts than they do in highly formalized, impersonal situations. There is nothing inspirational about talking to the backs of heads and nothing more terrifying to many children than to be required to stand before an impersonal mass of faces, dotted at even intervals throughout the length and breadth of a large room.[5]

Strickland suggests room arrangements conducive to workshop environment, group work, and areas for centers of interest. All of these are an integral part of a learning laboratory.

The learning laboratory has another basic criterion: that is, that there is no minimum or maximum level of performance set as a standard for any group for any one year. In this place, where learning is an active, participating process, problem solving, creative thinking, memory work and drill can all be engaged in at all levels from that of readiness to reading, reporting, and discussing problems of interest far above the traditional grade placement to which the child is assigned.

The reader will find the story of "Marion Johnson -- Fourth Grade Teacher" pertinent to this discussion. She takes time to plan with her children, and before setting long-range goals with them, she is able to obtain information about each one to make her planning more realistic.[6]

Free Reading Without Stereotypes

Gast found that recent children's fiction generally portrays American Indians, Chinese, Japanese, Negroes, and Spanish-Americans as having adopted the dominant middle-class American values related to cleanliness, kindness, intelligence, ambition, hard work and success.

Yet, Gast also reports that the parents of the children from most of these minority groups are usually portrayed as having lower-class socio-economic status.

The common sterotypes of the Indian craftsman, the Chinese cook, the Mexican shopkeeper, the Japanese gradener, and the Spanish shepherd are perpetuated in the recent literature.[7]

THE LEARNING MATERIALS CENTER

The solution to the problems of providing materials of instruction in the schools seem to be most feasible through what will be described here as the learning materials center.

A learning materials center housed in one central place within each separate school building is a functional unit of the larger curriculum laboratory of the whole school system. A learning materials center should house a good juvenile library, extensive audio-visual materials, maps, globes and charts for social science teaching, all of the apparatus needed for extensive teaching of general science throughout the elementary and junior high school (geology, mineralogy, astronomy, chemistry, physics, zoology, botany, conservation of resources, safety, aviation science), those art and industrial art materials and equipment to be drawn on loan by classrooms, music listening rooms with audio equipment, film and filmstrip viewing rooms, committee and conference rooms, three-dimensional materials for making arithmetic meaningful. Those expensive materials not to be used often or to be shared by whole school systems should be housed in a central laboratory.

It must be emphasized that schools without libraries place teachers in the same position that any craftsman would be in without tools. There is no way to learn to read except by reading; reading can be made pleasurable to the child only when the choice of materials available fits his needs, interests, and level of reading ability. The school library should contain a minimum of total volumes equal to ten times the enrollment of children.

Ahrens outlines the types of materials to be included in a learning materials center in this way:

1. A wealth of carefully selected printed materials. Children's literature, reference books, pamphlets, magazines.
2. Basic audio-visual materials. Filmstrips, slides, recordings, transcriptions, tapes. (A curriculum laboratory for an entire school system will consist of sound films and other less often used materials.)
3. Maps, globes, and charts used only occasionally.
4. Art objects, pictures, prints, music materials and equipment, and museum pieces and specimens.

5. Puzzles, games, and toys, and other similar teaching aids.
6. As wide as possible a range of published textbooks so that an assortment of text material may be drawn by one teacher for unit teaching and selection of materials at many levels of difficulty.
7. A professional library for teachers.
8. An equipment room, with carts so that the equipment desired in home or industrial arts or elementary science may be wheeled to teachers' rooms.[8]

A detailed list of equipment for elementary science teaching is listed elsewhere in this section as is a suggested list of three-dimensional materials for making arithmetic meaningful. A comprehensive manual for planning materials centers has been prepared by the Florida State Department of Education.[9]

For the selection of materials for a teaching materials center, Bird says:

> The most basic tools used in the selection process include the H. W. Wilson Publications (e. g., Children's Catalog, Standard Catalog for High School Libraries, Filmstrip Guide, etc.), publications issued by the American Library Association, current periodicals, publishers' catalogs and brochures, equipment catalogs, pamphlets listing sources, and what seems to be an unlimited number of lists of sources of free and inexpensive materials.[10]

Bird goes on to say:

> Current periodicals are scanned as they arrive. The vertical file in Teaching Materials Center has a rapidly growing collection of free and inexpensive phamphlets, pictures, posters, maps, and postcards. These materials cannot always be selected in terms of immediate contributions they will make, but they are acquired in light of probable future values.[11]

The Vertical Picture File

The organization of an extensive picture file is a difficult task. However, without efficient organization and meticulous re-filing of pictures after used, the file becomes useless for teachers. The ability to draw upon the file for pictures when they meet an immediate need is the factor that will cause teachers to refer to it again and again. Most such files are organized around subject headings that are subdivided, extended, or cross-referenced as found helpful by those using it. Some general suggestions for starting a flat picture file are given below:[12]

1. Begin with a listing of alphabetical subject headings;

2. Allow room for expansion of headings and for the addition of headings;

3. Some pictures may be mounted on gray or tan neutral shades; others left unmounted and filed in manila envelopes;

4. Put subject classification for pictures on back of each so they can be re-filed conveniently;

5. Be constantly aware of picture possibilities. Some schools have combined paper drives and picture clipping parties. This could supply many pictures for a file.

Subject headings arranged under the letter "A" in a flat picture file used in a twelve-grade school are given below:

"A" ENTRIES IN A VERTICAL PICTURE FILE[13]

Africa
Airforce
Airplanes
    Army and Navy
    Model
Alabama
Alaska
Aluminum

American Colonies
American Defense
    See National Defense
American Education Week
American Revolution
American Way of Life
Animals
    Domestic
    Farm
    And Their Young
    In Winter
    Wild

Animal Reactors
Antarctic
Anthropology and Archaeology
Aquarium
Arabia
Arbor Day
Arctic Regions
Arizona
Arkansas

"A" ENTRIES IN A VERTICAL PICTURE FILE [13] (Cont.)

    Armistice Day
    Army, Navy, and Marine Insignia
    Art
        Pictures
        Classical
        In Classrooms
        Modern

    Asia
    Astronomy
    Atmosphere
    Atoms
    Auroras
    Australia and New Zealand
    Automobiles
        Model
    Autumn
    Aviation

Another version of the "A" entries in a vertical picture file follows:

    Africa
    Airplanes
        See Aviation
    Alaska
    American Flag
        See Flags
    Ancient History
    Animals
        May be subdivided alphabetically by names of animals
    Antarctic Region
    Arctic Regions
    Art
        Crafts
        Crayon Work
        Clay Modeling
    Asia
    Athletics
        See Outdoor Games and Sports
    Australia
    Authors
    Automobiles
    Aviation
        Air Mail Service
        Airplanes
        Airports

"A" ENTRIES IN A VERTICAL PICTURE FILE[12](Cont.)
Aviators
Gliders
Helicopters
Jet Propulsion

Sample lists of equipment and other realia that would be useful to teachers for teaching elementary science and arithmetic and which might be housed in a learning materials center in an elementary school are given on the opposite page. Lists will vary from one school to another according to the choices of materials assigned to individual teacher's rooms.

A. EQUIPMENT AND OTHER REALIA FOR PHYSICAL SCIENCE

Aquarium
Airplane, model
Aluminum
Ammeter
Anemometer
Asbestos
Atomizer
Ball and ring expansion
Ball bearings
Balls -- rubber, tennis, pith
Balloons
Bar, compound metal
Barometer
Basketball
Battery, storage
Beakers, assorted
Bell, door
Bolts and nuts
Bottles -- pyrex, milk
Brush, clothes
Bunsen burner
Camera, simple
* Cans, tin -- assorted
Can opener
Candles
Cardboard -- assorted
Cellophane
Chalk
Charcoal
Charts
   Air pressure
   Atmosphere, cross section
   Atoms

Battery
Chemicals
Climate
Clouds
Elements
Engines
Machines
Moon phases
Radio and Sound Waves
Rock layers
Solar system
Storms -- formation
Weather
Wind belts
Chemicals and related materials
   Alcohol, rubbing
   Ammonia
   Baking powder
   Bleach
   Boric acid
   Carbon tetrachloride
   Copper sulphate
   Hydrochloric acid
   Iodine
   Lithium chloride
   Mercury
   Moth balls
   Potassium chloride
   Salt
   Soda -- baking and washing
   Sodium nitrate
   Soap powder

A. EQUIPMENT AND OTHER REALIA FOR PHYSICAL SCIENCE
(Continued)

Strontium chloride
Strontium nitrate
Sugar
Tetrachloride
Vinegar
Water Softener
Zinc, powdered
Chimney, Lamp
Chisel
Clamps, Burette
Clay
Cloth -- assorted (include wool and silk)
Combs -- rubber and plastic
Compass
Copper, sheet and strip
Cord
Corks -- assorted
Crystal detector
Dishpan
Dry cells (include extra terminal nuts)
Dye
Electric Fan
Electric hot plate
Erasers
Eye droppers
First Aid kit
Flashlight
Flask, pyrex
Flower pots -- assorted
Forceps
Foil aluminum and tin
Fulcrum
Funnels
Fur
Fuses -- good and used
Fuse wire
Galvonometer
Glass -- cylinders, jars, sheet, tubes
Glasses, drinking
Hammer
Head earphones
Hygrometer
Ice pick

Inclined plane (model)
Indian ink
Iron filings
Jar, battery
Jugs
Knife
Lamp board for circuits
Lenses -- plain, concave, convex
Light bulbs -- assorted
Light bulb sockets
Magnets -- all kinds
Magneto (model)
Magnifying glass
Matches
Microphone
Microscope
Mirrors -- plain, concave, convex
Nails and spikes -- assorted
Needles -- plain and knitting
Oil can and oil
Paper -- black, blotting, blueprint, colored, litmus, wax, oak tag
Paper clips
Pans -- assorted
Plaster of Paris
Plastic
Planetarium (model)
Pliers
Plumber's Friend
Prisms
Projection lantern
Pulleys -- assorted
Pumps -- tire, models of filter and pressure pumps
Radio -- old one
Radio tubes
Rocks and mineral samples
Rods -- carbon, metal, rubber, wooden
Rope
Rosin
Rubber -- hose, insulation, strips, pieces and synthetic

A. EQUIPMENT AND OTHER REALIA FOR PHYSICAL SCIENCE
(Continued)

Rubber stoppers -- 1 and 2 hole
Rulers -- metric and English
Sandpaper
Saucers
Sawdust
Scales and balances -- assorted
Screen wire
Screws -- assorted
Screwdriver
Scissors
Spoons -- wooden and assorted
Stands, metal
Steam engine (model)
Soil samples
Spools
Steel wool
Sticks
Straws
Switches, electrical
Tacks
Tape -- insulated and assorted

Teakettle
Telegraph set (model)
Telephone set (model and real)
Test tubes
Thermometers -- assorted
Thread, silk
Tin -- assorted
Tongue depressors
Tuning forks
Volcano (model)
Vacuum, thermos bottle
Wax, bees and parafin
Weather vane
Wedge (model)
Weights
Wheels -- cog, gear, water
Wheel and axle
Wire -- insulated, copper, aluminum, iron
Wood -- assorted pieces
Yardstick
Zinc -- assorted strips and pieces

B. EQUIPMENT AND OTHER REALIA FOR TEACHING ARITHMETIC

Supplies of counters -- buttons, poker chips, shells, etc.
Supply of sticks for fixing bundles of tens -- paste sticks, tongue depressors
Number lines -- 1-100
Pegboards, and pegs -- individual and large ones
Flannel boards and supplies
Calculating blocks or unit number blocks
Abacuses
Large domino cards
Spool rods and spools for counting tens
Tens blocks
Place chart (pocket) for 1's, 10's, 100's, etc.
Rulers
Flash cards -- addition, subtraction, etc.
Clock dials -- old alarm clocks, and cardboard dials
Scales for weighing objects (0-25)
Measures -- cup, pint, quart, egg cartons. Gallon and 1/2 gallon should be included

B. EQUIPMENT AND OTHER REALIA FOR
TEACHING ARITHMETIC (Continued)

Mechanical devices for measuring -- speedometer from car, hourglass, (3 minute type), rain gauge, radio dial
Thermometers (c and F) for showing boiling point, outside and inside
Mail order catalog for price lists, quantities, descriptions, etc.
Road maps
Supplies of 2" x 4", 3" x 5", and 5" x 8" cards
Commercial games -- dominoes, monopoly, lotto, bingo, and race games, such as parcheesi

THE COMMUNITY SCHOOL

Mead discusses two contributions that cultural anthropology has to make to community education programs:

> It helped to break down the image of a great mass of savage, illiterate, superstitious peoples clustered in jungle, mountain, and desert, whose major characteristic was their ignorance of our culture, and establish the fact that each of these peoples of the world had a historical tradition of its own, a cherished way of life, a "cup from which they drank their life," as old as our own.

> It helped establish the importance of differences among peoples and a recognition that methods of education for change must be developed in connection with the special attitudes of the different groups.[14]

Mead summarizes the advice of the anthropologist in helping to effect cultural change: first, to know the culture in detail, to make change slowly, and to recognize and make allowances for equivalence between the new and the intruding culture. She says, for example:

> . . . study the shaman before you introduce a physician, the local midwife before you introduce a public health nurse, provide a pig as a substitute victim before forbidding headhunting.[15]

Two basic principles that emerge from cross-cultural studies are:[16]

1. Cultures all over the world are composed of human beings made of the same basic material. Each social group has evolved a system which provides, as best it can, for their physical, psychological, social, and moral and spiritual needs. Insofar as it has made technical and ethnical ad-

vances, each society provides for its atypical individuals: the blind, the deaf, the cerebral palsied, and mentally retarded. Social outcasts in the historical past, many of these are provided for and habilitated in advanced societies.

2. Rapid change in converting cultural groups to new ways of living is possible. Examples of rapid change are evident the same as examples of slow change. The idea that acculturation processes can take place within a generation, without the often cited social disorganization with resultant delinquency, alcoholism and antisocial behavior, presents a great challenge to all people whose work is humanitarian in nature in order to make cultural change as smooth as possible. One way to ease the transition is the community school.

The component tasks in the successful community school are:

. . . (1) to collect facts concerning the problems and resources of the community; (2) to set up demonstrations and experiments attempting to find answers to various aspects of their problems; (3) participate in group deliberations involving study, reporting, planning, and decision making; (4) observe community situations in regard to recognized problems and consider methods of solving such problems in their own and in other communities; (5) to work on individual and group projects in order to solve problems; and (6) to use different types of instructional materials -- involving such activities as reading, writing, and arithmetic -- in attacking their problems.[17]

Tireman, in the Nambe school experiment, demonstrated a workable community school in the Southwest.[18] Since it operated in the geographical area with which this book is concerned, it will be discussed in further detail. In 1939, Nambé was a small, somewhat isolated Spanish-American community. It was situated about twenty miles north of Santa Fe, New Mexico, where the shallow Nambe River had provided the necessary irrigation water for the growing of the garden crops for generations. The language of the life outside the school was almost exclusively Spanish; there were 160 Spanish-speaking families and eight English-speaking families.

Tireman identified two major areas of living -- health practices and land use -- and recognized the possibilities for improving the total community by giving major emphasis to these two problems in a community school situation. The general philosophy developed by Tireman and his staff is stated as follows:

A school should be the center of the community. It should be sensitive to the needs of the community, and, in cooperation with the parents, plan a program that will make the best use of all available resources. Such an environment should stimulate pupils to engage in many activities. Through participating in planning, executing and evaluating their work they will learn to think and to use the facts and tools of learning. They should find the school a vital place in which it is good to live.[19]

While the objectives started with identifying problems and solving them in the community, utilizing all available resources and service agencies in the community, using planning, thinking, and decision making in organized group work, the objectives also included gaining proficiency in the 3 R's and the English language.

The starting point for every part of the curriculum was to be Nambe with learning spreading outward in concentric circles from this home base until it included, if possible, the total world community. Hanna presents graphically this relationship of the local community to its greater and greater involvement in the world community.[20]

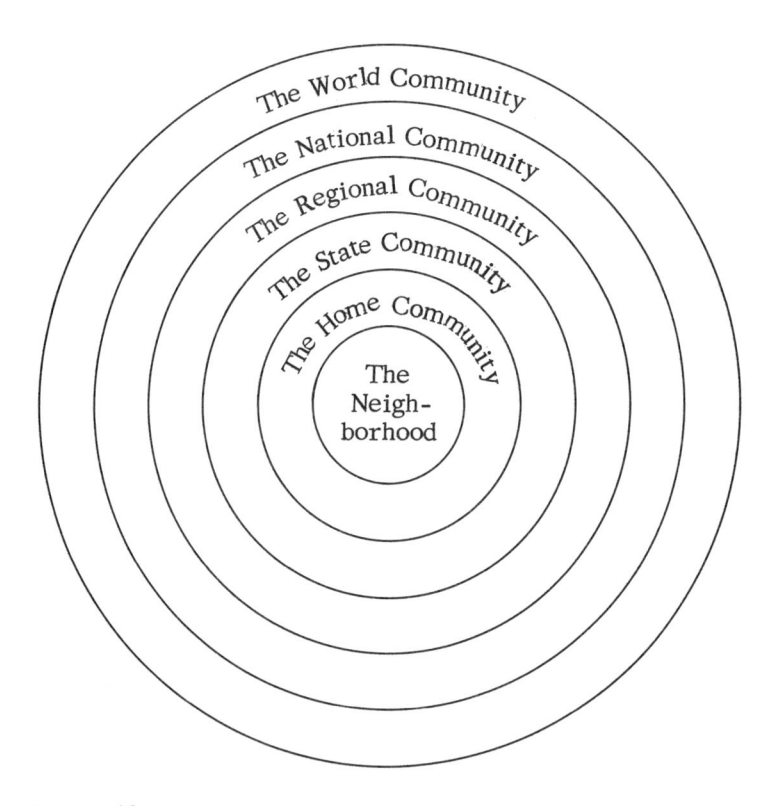

Figure 10. Relationship of local community to world community.

Tireman describes the health situation:

> Traditional ways of sanitation, attitudes toward cleanliness, folk remedies for illnesses, the inadequate diet were evaluated and found wanting. . . people saw no relation between illness and flies as carriers of disease. . . wells were uncovered and drilled without attention to the location of privies. . . babies' illnesses were still attributed to Mal Ojo. . . the loss of a child or two in a family of ten or twelve was accepted as the will of God. . . vegetables, when available, might be boiled until all the food value was lost. . . impetigo and other skin diseases spread easily.[21]

Attitudes towards land use were as follows:

> The tradition of sub-dividing the land for inheritance with each generation had reduced some plots to less than enough for subsistence. . . the tradition was one of mutual aid in planting, irrigating, ditch cleaning, and harvesting. One-third of the land and the climate were not suited. . . arroyos were believed to be the inevitable result of land use. . . overgrazed land was not restored and large gullies were not stabilized.[22]

Poverty caused deterioration of community morale, and outmoded farming practices on the land available led to apathy and resignation.

Tireman's experiment produced significant, tangible results. The community school met needs of the children and their parents with no loss in achievement in the usual academic skills. Those children who began school with the start of the experimental program achieved closer to grade level on standard tests than did the Spanish-American population in the state at large.[23]

The course of the experiment did not continue, but there was indication that if the child could have been taken all the way through the school system, he could have achieved at grade level at the end of the elementary school, on the average, just as Anglo children do. The success of the experiment made possible Tireman's recommendation that all of the rural schools in this state consider modifications of the traditional curricula to teach children to solve their own local problems first.

Teacher selection was a most important ingredient in the process which Tireman used. The teachers lived in the village, had a genuine interest in the people and an academic understanding of their cultural background. Many spoke Spanish; the others had some familiarity with it. They were sophisticated in the comparative phonology between Spanish and English and were able to emphasize good usage, good pronunciation habits, and vocabulary development in English. In fact, the teachers accepted vocabulary development as one of their greatest challenges.

Drummond has described the qualities sought in a teacher in a community school. Two merit inclusion here:

> Faith in people: (a) One must believe in the perfectability of man; (b) One must understand that processes of cultural change move slowly and require much mutual effort and understanding; (c) One must have a faith that he is helping to build a better world for all men everywhere.
>
> An ability to integrate the aspects of living and those of learning, be sensitive to social problems and trends, and to know techniques for studying one's community.[24]

The curriculum of both the elementary and secondary schools needs to be oriented to community life. This is given emphasis and stated concisely in the policy of the Department of Rural Education of the National Education Association:

> The curriculum of the rural school, whether in the open country or town, should be based on the individual and group needs of the pupils, should grow out of the life of the community, and should look to the future welfare of society as a whole. . . In his immediate environment, the child will encounter mathematics as an aspect of his experience with seed time, harvest, temperature, floods, farm machinery, play trips, or communication. His problems of sanitation, hygiene, and safety may be found in the school lunch, the farm well, the disposal of wastes under rural conditions, the share of the dairy farm in urban as well as in rural health, the hazards of farm machinery, the lighting and ventilation of the rural schoolroom, or the heating of the farm or town home. His concept of social and economic relations will be based upon their expression in the standards of living and morality in the rural community.
>
> The curriculum of the secondary school should grow out of the life of the community and be a means of enriching it.[25]

In addition, high schools must meet the individual needs of those who do not wish to stay in the country, those who go to the city, those who go on to higher education, those who get other kinds of jobs, and those who marry.

As indicated in Chapter 2, the school of the future needs to prepare students to use a problem-solving approach to living: how to think, even when they do not know what method to use, about a problem that can yet be formulated.

THE TEACHING OF REMEDIAL READING

Any program that purports to meet the needs of the minority groups described in this text must include personnel and programs

375

for remedial instruction. While all schools have a statistical incidence of reading disability cases, the educational retardation of the minority groups reported here is of much higher incidence.

The progressive retardation reported in the Puerto Rican Study, the Tempe Study of Pseudo Mental Retardation of Mexican-American Children in the Phoenix Area, the Indian Research Study at the University of New Mexico, and the survey testing by Townsend in senior high schools, all emphasize the extent of the problem.

Remedial reading instruction is the instruction needed by those people whose functioning level of reading is distinctly below their capacity level for reading. Capacity for reading is dependent upon level of intelligence and command of the language to be read. Thus, a child who is chronologically eight years old with a mental age of ten, has the capacity to read like an "average" ten-year-old. In dealing with the child for whom English is a second language, only the roughest estimates will be possible concerning capacity for reading. This is because he obviously lacks command of the English language, and there are no intelligence tests available that can validly measure his innate capacity for learning.

A teacher of remedial reading follows the same steps in teaching that he follows in first teaching of reading: build a basic sight vocabulary, teach the word attack skills; build comprehension and evaluation skills; and provide lots of easy practice.

Teaching remedial reading requires additional insights and judgmental abilities, however. Any individual whose level of performance is distinctly inferior to that of his age- or grade-mates will have developed many psychological responses to the reading act which need to be handled in a mature fashion.

The first requisite in teaching remedial reading is to find the level at which the child can read and start from where he is to teach all the developmental reading skills that he lacks. It will be necessary to build security and confidence in the child. Children's books designed to teach "how-to-read" skills have severely controlled vocabularies and provide sufficient repetition to habituate completely the recognition of many, many common words. Consequently, teachers using the current methodology must establish fluency at each half-year level of difficulty before going on to the next level. For example, many children need to read two or three books of second level first grade before they progress to first level second grade.

Starting where the child is in the reading process cannot be overemphasized. Many times teachers have chosen books one, two, or three years below grade level for their poorest readers, but any kind of informal test for reader level would have demonstrated clearly that the book they chose was still a grade level or more too difficult. As long as a child is kept working at his frustration level of reading, he will not grow in independence in reading nor in his everyday life. If he does not develop this independence in use of reading as a tool, the school has failed in one of its primary objectives for him.

Tireman has aptly stated that "where the child is" is exactly that, certainly "not where the child thinks he ought to be, nor where his mother wants him to be, nor where the teacher wishes he were."[26]

The child should start in his remedial program at his instructional level. The instructional level of reading is defined as that level at which the child makes no more than five errors in reading one hundred running words with respect to the mechanics of reading, and at which he comprehends at least 75 percent of the ideas and concepts in the reading material. If the material is too difficult for either the 95 percent accuracy in mechanics or 75 percent accuracy in answering questions over the content, an easier level of material must be found and used.

It is logical that a child cannot learn to read fluently from a higher level book until he can read fluently from one that is easier in the same series. It is further true that most children will make no gain in independent reading power if kept on reading material difficult enough to keep them frustrated. It is preferable in a remedial reading program to assign a child to a book that is easier than his instructional level so that he will gain confidence and overcome some of his anxieties in the reading situation. Acceptance by the teacher of the best work the child is able to do is an integral part of satisfying his psychological relationship with reading.

The teacher will have to build attitudes in the remedial reading situation to help the child accept himself and his problem. The child needs an honest evaluation of his present reading status and what kind of prognosis he may hope for. He should be given praise when it is earned, and he needs to be shown in a tangible way that he is making progress.

In teaching reading to older students from minority ethnic groups, use should be made of teacher-made materials and of reading charts prepared about items of interest in the local environment. Teachers in Indian communities have successfully developed scrapbooks in which children write short articles about current happenings in the community, mount and read newspaper clippings, and incorporate factual information from the social studies with the help of the teacher. For children needing additional help in vocabulary building, reading charts have almost unlimited possibilities. The teacher must be alert to the vocabulary needs of the children, and systematically teach phonetic and structural analysis skills.

There are many excellent textbooks on the market today so that a teacher who feels a need for professional help in the teaching of reading can satisfy that need easily. The following selected references are merely suggestions:

> Hafner, Lawrence, editor, Improved Reading in Secondary Schools, A Book of Readings, (New York: The Macmillan Co., 1967).
>
> Harris, Albert J., How to Increase Reading Ability, Fourth Edition, (New York: Longmans Green, 1961).
>
> Heilman, Arthur, Principles and Practices of Teaching Reading, Second Edition, (Columbus: Charles E. Merrill, 1967).
>
> Karlin, Robert, Reading in the Secondary School, (Indianapolis: The Bobbs Merrill Company, 1964).
>
> Marksheffel, Ned, Better Reading in the Secondary School, (New York: The Ronald Press Co., 1966).
>
> Mazurkiewicz, Albert J., editor, New Prespectives in Reading Instruction, A Book of Readings, (New York: Pitman Publishing Corp., 1964).
>
> Smith, Nila B., Reading Instruction for Today's Children. (Englewood Cliffs, New Jersey: Prentice-Hall, Inc., 1963).
>
> Strang, Ruth, Constance McCullough, and A. E. Traxler, The Improvement of Reading, Fourth Edition, (New York: McGraw-Hill Book Company, 1967).
>
> Strang, Ruth, Editor, Understanding and Helping the Retarded Reader, (Tuscon: University of Arizona Press, 1965).
>
> Zintz, Miles V., Corrective Reading, (Dubuque, Iowa: William C. Brown Co., 1966).

There are many commercially produced series of readers that are particularly well suited for remedial purposes. These books are written with a severely controlled vocabulary but have a high interest level. A bibliography of these books will be found in the Appendix.

A brief outline of topics that may help the teacher answer questions about remedial reading needs of students follows:

A. Remedial reading is reading instruction for those people whose functioning level is below their capacity level for reading. Remedial reading is the same as the first teaching of reading plus the fact that such children usually have concomitant psychological problems that need to be dealt with.

B. Steps in remedial reading.
   1. Start where the child is and build security and confidence.
   2. Follow the same steps necessary in good, first teaching of reading.
      a. Build a basic sight vocabulary.
      b. Teach word attack skills.
         (1) Picture and context clues.
         (2) Word configuration clues.
         (3) Phonetic analysis.
         (4) Structural analysis.
         (5) Dictionary skills.
   3. Build attitudes toward reading that will help the child to accept himself and his problem.
      a. Give a child an honest evaluation of how he now performs.
      b. Give him praise for successes.
      c. Show him in a tangible way that he is making progress.

C. An eclectic approach to teaching beginning reading.
   1. Emphasis on the meaningful nature of reading is always primary.
   2. Reading readiness is continued with a child until he shows he is able to master a sight vocabulary.
   3. The child learns his initial sight vocabulary by a word method. This will be achieved through chart reading, experience stories, labels in the room, blackboard work, workbook lessons, and direct teaching on the part of the teacher toward a specific list of words.
   4. The child reads a series of basic readers to build systematically a larger and larger sight vocabulary, but simultaneously,
   5. He begins a systematic approach to word attack skills by learning:
      a. In the first grade, the initial consonant sounds and a few consonant blend sounds in phonetic analysis and some suffixes in structural analysis.
      b. In the second grade, the consonant blends and some knowledge of long and short vowels.

c. At the third grade reader level, review of previous attack skills and further work needed in phonetics and structural analysis and beginning dictionary skills.
 6. His reading, from the very beginning of preprimers, is supplemented by experience stories, chart reading, labels, following directions.
 7. A "free reading" or supplementary reading program begins as soon as the child has the necessary vocabulary to read other books at the level of difficulty he has finished in his instructional program.

D. The teacher should know the reader level of each child in the room.
 1. Levels of reading in the class.
    a. The "reader level" of a child is the child's instructional reader level as found in a series of readers.
       (1) Choose a series of readers not familiar to the child, if possible.
       (2) Select passages of sufficient length to make it possible to check comprehension (60-75 words at preprimer level; 200 words at grade three).
       (3) The child reads at varying levels of difficulty until the teacher feels that:
          (a) He recognizes at least 19 out of 20 words in context.
          (b) He makes no more than five errors in repetitions, omissions, and substitutions in 100 running words.
          (c) He can answer comprehension questions covering at least 75 percent of the ideas in the material read.
    b. "Reading level" of the class. "Standard norms."
 2. Informal tests for the teacher to use to see if a book is the right level.
    a. Reading from a series of readers.
    b. Test the child on the vocabulary list in the back of the reading book.
    c. Select words at random on selected pages in the reader and ask the child to point to them.
    d. Test the child's knowledge of the 220 Dolch Basic Sight Words.[27]
       (1) Administer as a recall test. The child attempts to pronounce all the words.

(2) Criteria for administering the test:
- (a) If he does not respond in fifteen seconds, encourage him to go on to the next word.
- (b) Mark on a second copy of the test the child's responses.
    - 1' If the word is properly called, draw a line through it.
    - 2' If a child miscalls a word and then corrects it, write above the word what the child said, and make a small "o" or "x" in front of the word.
    - 3' If the word is mispronounced but not corrected, write the child's pronunciation above the word.
    - 4' Write down pertinent comments the child makes as he goes along, for example:
        - -- spelling out each word: "c-a-n, that's can."
        - -- "Oh, I know it but I just can't say it."
        - -- "I had that word in spelling just this week."
        - -- "It's 'on' or 'no' but I don't know which."
        - -- "Am I doing all right? Is that good?"
- (3) The child's score on the test is the total number of words lined through.
- (4) Translate the child's score into a reader level by use of the Scale for Determining Reader Level by McBroom, Sparrow, and Eckstein.[28] The scale follows:

Dolch Words Known	Equivalent Reader Level
0-75	Preprimer
76-120	Primer
121-170	First Reader
171-210	Second Reader or above
211-220	Third Reader or above

3. Levels of difficulty of reading material from the child's viewpoint:
   a. Basal level.
   b. Instructional level.
   c. Frustration level.
   d. Capacity level.

E. Why do so many fail in reading?
  1. These are not the reasons:

a. It is not because we do not teach phonics although there may have been a short period of time in the teaching of reading when phonics were neglected.

b. It is not because teachers are not doing a good job teaching reading. Almost all the children do learn how to read.

c. It is not because schools have become progressive and let children do as they please. Children today read better than comparable groups at any time in the past.

d. It is not because too little time is devoted to the 3 R's. In many places, too much time is spent working on routine, monotonous, unmotivated lessons trying to "make children learn" the 3 R's.

e. It is not because parents are not interested in their children. Teachers need to learn more and better ways of directing parent interest and helping parents to understand their own children's problems.

2. The causes of failure stem from:

   a. The traditional organizational pattern of the school makes it necessary to put children in classes where "standards" have been arbitrarily defined. These standards are achievement centered rather than child centered.

   b. Teachers are habituated to the practice of putting children through textbooks so that we have many children in the wrong book. Children are allowed to read in textbooks at their frustration level.

   c. We do not start where the child is in the process of learning how to read.

   d. Many schools do not have an over-all school policy that gives teachers confidence in what they do in one calendar year as a part of the continuous school program through the grades.

3. These causes will be met by:

   a. Recognizing and meeting individual differences.

   b. Knowing how to obtain and use information about children.

   c. Accepting a school policy that is effective from the first year through senior high school.

   d. Utilizing special services and special personnel in studying about children.

   e. Providing adequate materials of instruction.

   f. Working cooperatively with parents.

   g. Having personal security on the job to do what one knows is best.

h. Having a devotion to one's job to attack the problems conscientiously and comprehensively.

SPECIAL PROBLEMS RELATED TO THE TEACHING OF SCIENCE IN THE ELEMENTARY SCHOOL

The area of elementary science presents a segment of the school curriculum likely to be most in conflict with the child's out-of-school life, that is, with his set of cultural values.

Ellis wrote in 1948:

> There is even the problem of adults assuring the students that scientific theories regarding the world and its people cannot possibly be true because they conflict with the old Pueblo mythology; therefore, the students are to repeat back to the teacher what is told them but they are not to believe it. This, needless to say, does not encourage youthful efforts to understand what they are taught.[29]

Most teachers need to teach more elementary science content than they now do, but it needs to be taught almost entirely from a laboratory point of view. Knowledge that is commonly known by Anglo six-year-olds about personal cleanliness and contagious diseases is almost completely foreign to many Indian and Spanish-speaking six-year-olds entering school. For example, it is not necessary to teach Anglo children not to spit on the floor, but it is necessary to teach some Indian children not to do so. Emphasis could be given in the primary grades to health habits, nutrition, safety, fire prevention, machines and how they work. Older elementary children need to learn about natural resources of the area and their conservation.

The background of experience will be so meager for many Indian and Spanish-American children that they will be unable to understand most of the teacher's concepts unless he is constantly aware of this barrier. "Take nothing for granted" is a good motto to follow when discussing concepts with these children.

The laboratory aspect of the elementary science classroom must make possible active participation on the part of each child. Drills in brushing teeth properly, at the desks and without paste, may be much more profitable than a reading lesson on "How to Brush the Teeth." An abundance of materials, equipment, and apparatus should be housed in a learning materials center in the building so that they may be borrowed by each teacher and used by the children in the classroom.

Charles tested to measure the science achievement status of Indian children in the fifth grade in public elementary schools in New Mexico, and then he explored the relationship between achievement in school and the existence of certain nonscientific cultural beliefs.[30] He constructed a fifty-item culturally biased science test based on traditional beliefs and taboos recorded in anthropological literature. One of the hypotheses stated by Charles was that no relationship exists between science achievement of Indian students and their acceptance of certain nonscientific societal beliefs. Coefficients of correlation obtained between scores on the culturally biased science test and scores on the science achievement test were, respectively, Apache, .47; Navajo, .77; and Pueblos, .62. A high score on the culturally biased test indicated that the child identified the scientific answer in the multiple choice item, and a low score indicated that he identified a nonscientific answer. On this basis, it was concluded that a strong negative relationship exists between the science achievement status of Indian children and the extent of their acceptance of certain nonscientific societal beliefs. Thus, Charles concludes, if desirable learning situations are to be provided, it is necessary that teachers become aware of the factors associated with the learning of elementary science by Indians, and that they learn to deal creatively and tactfully with the many areas of possible conflict.[31]

Additional conclusions made by Charles have significance here:

All three Indian groups tested were three or more years retarded in science achievement as measured by the Elementary Science Test, Grades 4 to 6, Inclusive.

All three Indian groups tested two and one-half to three years retarded in reading ability as measured by the Gates Reading Survey Test.

Indian children, because of their cultural heritage, have a frame of reference which is different, to some extent, from that employed by Anglos in thinking about natural phenomena.[32]

FIRSTHAND EXPERIENCES

The less time that young children must be confined to the four walls of a classroom, the greater are the possibilities of their learning concepts of a lasting value to them. Buses must be made available to haul children for excursions. Hildreth reports that the elementary school children in Hunter College Elementary School are taken as a total group on a planned excursion about every two weeks, on the average.[33]

Teachers can make extensive, but inexpensive, collections of three-dimensional objects by studying their vocabulary lists and being alert in dime stores, drugstores, and department stores. One teacher of first-grade children developed a successful vocabulary-building lesson by bringing a covered market basket to the class. It contained a dozen random articles, some names to be learned new, some reviewed, and some to be learned at that time in English although they were already known in the vernacular. The surprise element, the possibilities for games, and the active participation of the group made this a good teaching device. The child would reach in and draw out a toy bear, for instance. He might say, depending upon the extent of his use of English at the time:

> This is a bear; This is a black bear; This bear is little; This bear is not big; Bears are wild animals; Bears live in the woods; Bears are big animals.

FOOTNOTES

[1] William S. Gray and May Hill Arbuthnot, Fun with Dick and Jane (Chicago: Scott, Foresman and Co., 1947). By the time the child has finished the preprimers and this reader, he has been introduced to 158 sight words.

[2] Loyd S. Tireman and Mary Watson, La Comunidad (Albuquerque: University of New Mexico Press, 1943), pp. 11-12.

[3] Ernest Horn, "Language and Meaning," The Psychology of Learning, The Forty-First Yearbook of the National Society for the Study of Education, Part II (Chicago: The University of Chicago Press, 1942), p. 390.

[4] Ruth G. Strickland, The Language Arts in the Elementary School (Boston: D.C. Heath, 1957), pp. 136-138. Second Edition.

[5] Ibid., p. 132.

[6] Robert Beck, W.W. Cook, and Nolan C. Kearney, The Elementary School Curriculum (Englewood Cliffs, N.J.: Prentice-Hall, 1960), pp. 356-437.

[7] Gast David K., "Minority Americans in Children's Literature," Elementary English, January, 1967, p. 18.

[8] Maurice R. Ahrens, "A Center for Materials," Childhood Education, 33: 118-119, November, 1956.

[9] State Department of Education, Planning Materials Centers, Bulletin 22E, 1958 (Tallahassee, Florida: State Department of Education, 1958).

[10] Thelma Bird, "The Teaching Materials Center: A Case Report," The Teachers College Journal (Terre Haute: Indiana State Teachers College), 30: 16, October, 1958.

[11] Ibid., p. 17.

[12] Bruce Miller, So You Want to Start a Picture File? (Box 369, Riverside, California: The Author).

[13] Headings in the Vertical Picture File in the Curriculum Laboratory, Malcolm Price Laboratory School, State College of Iowa, Cedar Falls, Iowa.

[14] Margaret Mead, "Cultural Factors in Community Education Programs," in Community Education, Principles and Practices from World-Wide Experiences, Nelson B. Henry, editor (Chicago: The University of Chicago Press, 1959), Volume 58, Part I, p. 73.

[15] Ibid., p. 76.

[16] Ibid., pp. 79-93.

[17] Maurice F. Seay, "The Community School: New Meaning for an Old Term," The Community School, Fifty-Second Yearbook of the National Society For the Study of Education, Part II (Chicago: The University of Chicago Press, 1953), p. 233.

[18] Loyd S. Tireman, A Community School in a Spanish-Speaking Village (Albuquerque: University of New Mexico Press, 1948).

[19] Ibid., p. 20.

[20] Paul R. Hanna, "The Community School and Larger Geographic Areas," The Community School, Fifty-Second Yearbook of the National Society for the Study of Education, Part II (Chicago: University of Chicago Press, 1953), p. 233.

[21] Tireman and Watson, pp. 90-101.

[22] Ibid., p. 1-9.

[23] Ibid., p. 145.

[24] Harold D. Drummond, "The Staff of the Community School," The Community School, Fifty-Second Yearbook of the National Society for the Study of Education, Part II (Chicago: The University of Chicago Press, 1953), pp. 106-109.

[25] Shirley Cooper, "Evaluating Rural Education," Education in Rural Communities, Fifty-First Yearbook of the National Society for the Study of Education, Part II (Chicago: The University of Chicago Press, 1952), pp. 253-254, citing Department of Rural Education, A Policy for Rural Education in the United States (Washington: National Education Association, 1940), pp. 19-21.

[26] Loyd S. Tireman, Teaching Spanish-Speaking Children (Albuquerque: The University of New Mexico Press, 1951), p. 166.

[27] E. W. Dolch, Basic Sight Word Test (Champaign: The Garrard Press). The words are arranged on one sheet for testing.

[28] Extension Bulletin, University of Iowa, 1947.

[29] Florence Hawley Ellis, The Indian Problem in New Mexico (Albuquerque: Division of Research, Department of Government, University of New Mexico, 1948), p. 40.

[30] Carol M. Charles, "The Indian Child's Status in New Mexico's Elementary School Science Program" (Unpublished Doctoral dissertation, The University of New Mexico, Albuquerque, 1961).

[31] Ibid., p. 154.

[32] Ibid., p. 148.

[33] Gertrude Hildreth, Educating Gifted Children (New York: Harper and Brothers, 1952).

CHAPTER 13

Unsolved Problems

INTRODUCTION

Margaret Mead has written:

Our future depends. . . on developing, with the help of prophets and poets who have yet to raise their voices, underwritten by the sciences of human behavior, a new conception of the individual in which each seeks fulfillment not in breeding replicas of himself and herself, but in the nurturance of human children, wherever they are, and the realization of what each individual can contribute individually to a world that desperately needs every ounce of creativity we can free for productive thought and social action.[1]

This broad concept of the goal of self-realization in American education may help teachers to place in perspective their appreciation of the universality of man.

Montagu warns us' that, even though we have the repository of the wisdom of the ages to draw upon, we must ever have inquiring minds and rational outlooks if we are to push toward the world view. He says:

If we seem to know more than our ancestors did, it is not because we have brains that are more highly developed, but because we have inherited all that they have bequeathed to us in the form of knowledge and wisdom. We can see farther ahead and over a wider territory not because we have better eyes, but because standing as it were, on their shoulders we can see more -- but if it were not for their shoulders we would be able to see no more than they were able to see. Oftentimes we are not able to see as much, for, casting our vision over so broad an expanse of territory, we often miss the things that are closest to our noses. That is why, every so often, it is a good thing to hang a question mark on the things we take most for granted. Since some of the things men take for granted are likely to be wrong and some right, it is highly desirable that every society encourage the inquiring mind. If we are ever to distinguish between the right and the wrong, we shall most efficiently be able to do so through unimpassioned inquiry. Happily, man is the most inquiring creature in creation, so we needn't worry. We should begin to worry only when obstacles are created to prevent men from pursuing their inquiries in freedom and without restraint.[2]

Frank optimistically posits the future as follows:

The brother hood of man will come. . . through the realization that all men, everywhere, face the same life tasks, share the same anxieties and perplexities, the bereavements and tragedies, seek the same goals in their cultures; to make life meaningful and significant, to find some security, to achieve some social order and to regulate their conduct toward values that make life more than mere organic existence.[3]

Morrison, discussing the problems of teacher education in the Puerto Rican Study, makes several pertinent recommendations. He cites the need for some kind of adjustment in the pre-service program of teachers to acquaint them with the bicultural problems of non-English-speaking pupils; he recommends a fifth-year program for teachers which will constitute a major in the teaching of English as a second language; and he suggests the importance of seminars and workshops.

Morrison also emphasizes the need for the teacher to know and understand the background of the children he teaches. Independent reading or formal graduate courses in the academic disciplines of anthropology, sociology, psychology, and the communication arts should give the teacher sophistication in providing for the social-educational-cultural environment of the child. Moreover, the leadership of the principal is a major factor in the success of teaching bilingual children just as his leadership is a major factor in any area of the school.[4]

Elam reminds us that:

Most of our textbooks are written by middle-class professors for middle-class teachers of middle-class children. Education has not found ways to integrate the findings of anthropology, social psychology, and clinical psychology into the educational and developmental sequence usually taught in the teacher preparation courses.

We must learn to help children move from anxiety, panic, and insecurity through their limbo of no understanding of cultural and language cues to courage, independence, and a positive outlook.[5]

Thompson points out further desirables in teacher attitudes:

> A teacher should have the quality of empathy, of being able to put himself into the place of another and identify with him to the extent that he can begin at least to see the world as an Indian sees it. He should be convinced of the positive values of cultural difference. He respects the unique and persistent patterns of culture found in various parts of the world. He believes that cultural diversity is not only inevitable -- for it is impossible to plan or legislate the differences between peoples entirely out of existence -- but that it also has a dynamic, positive value in the enrichment and vitalization of life in the world of today and tomorrow. [6]

These philosophical admonitions are appropos to the search for adequate educational provisions for children and teachers who may talk with each other, but not understand what they say; who may look at each other, but see only the stereotype they knew before they looked; who may read the same book, but each learn a different story from the context; who may each recognize the chasms which separate them, but not know how to build the bridges that pull them together.

There are immediate needs of the teacher in the Southwest; there are also those not yet defined, but which teachers themselves will define one by one. Tireman said, in his book Teaching Spanish-Speaking Children, "Some reader of this book may well be the one who will advance our knowledge of bilingual education beyond its present stage."[7]

The unsolved problems faced by teachers today can be grouped under three main headings: (1) understanding cultural differences, (2) learning the English language, and (3) remedial education.

UNDERSTANDING CULTURAL DIFFERENCES

Studies rooted in the cultural difference would investigate sociocultural factors in classrooms, adjustments to be made in pre-service education programs for teachers, improved communication between the parent and the school, and problems in motivation of learning.

Studies are needed that will measure the social distance between middle-class teachers and minority group students.

That there is lack of communication between teacher and student is evident from students' achievement test data. Also, Ulibarri demonstrated that there is little awareness of sociocultural factors on the part of teachers.[8] Subtle combinations of empathy and knowledge of sociocultural conditions need to be delineated so that teachers will establish adequate communication in their classrooms. These studies might include:

1. Attempts to sensitize teachers to socioculture differences through in-service education programs, such as workshops, conferences, and case study reports.

2. Extensive use of various sociometric techniques in order to reveal the extent of interaction of children in classrooms (see sample sociogram on following page). Do they accept each other? What behavior characteristics affect acceptance or nonacceptance of an individual? The sociogram illustrated in Figure 10 shows little interaction between ethnic groups in a tri-cultural fifth-grade classroom. How should such a sociogram be interpreted?

Pre-service education programs are needed to make prospective teachers aware of special educational problems in the areas of cultural differences, language barriers, and limitations in life space of children.

Two alternatives exist toward the solution of this problem. College instructors in the academic disciplines of anthropology, sociology, and psychology might make specific provision in their course outlines to teach principles of child growth and development, giving adequate emphasis to the ways in which social, emotional, moral, and spiritual growth and development may be at variance with the dominant culture in the minority groups. Differences in overt behavior patterns and conflicts in social values would need to be stressed. In contrast, or perhaps complementary, to this solution, instructors in courses in methodology might plan their course outlines to help prospective teachers develop specific means of adapting their teaching practices in terms of the expected overt behavior of children with cultural differences, language barriers, and meager life experiences. Either of these two alternatives would require a new sophistication in subject matter background on the part of the instructors.

Improved communication is needed with parents of children from homes where little or no English is understood.

Provision for teachers to visit the homes of children, to understand better the problems of parents in keeping children in school, and to learn ways of interpreting the program of the school to the parents is needed. As a specific example, a project to prepare a Primer for Parents might be undertaken. A booklet, heavily illustrated with drawings, pictures, cartoons, and photographs with captions written in an elementary vocabulary and distributed widely throughout the community, could show parents many of the principles and purposes of present-day education. Such a booklet would probably need to be specifically oriented to the local community served by a particular school district.

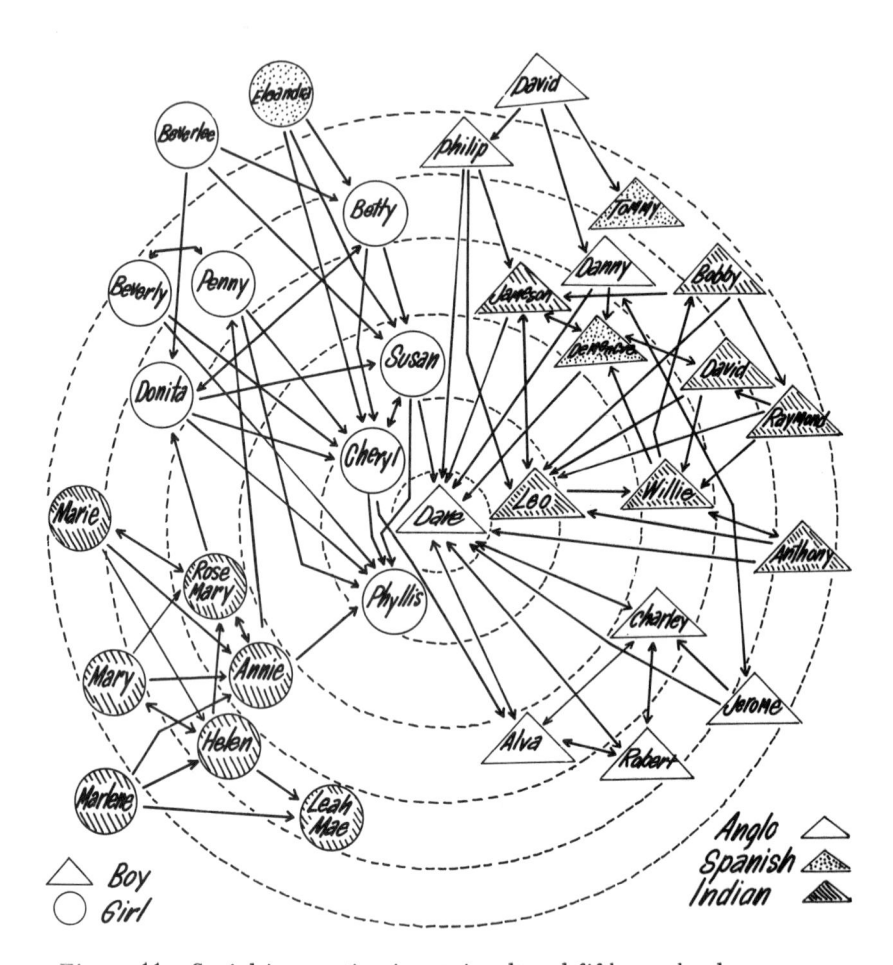

Figure 11. Social interaction in a tri-cultural fifth-grade classroom.

The following two anecdotes illustrate the extent to which parents do not understand simple questionnaires sent to them by teachers and principals. A second-grade teacher sent a questionnaire to the parents of children in her school district seeking information about the local "TV Kindergarten" program. The only question she asked was whether or not parents would like their children to watch the program. Parents were to indicate "Yes" or "No" and then to sign the questionnaire and return it to the school. Two of the reactions that followed are:

> One second-grade pupil brought her five-year-old brother to school the next day, saying that the principal told her mother in the note that he might come to school.

> One parent came to school the next day. He was very much upset by the fact that his son was getting only kindergarten experience. The parent said, "Fred is six years old now, and we want him to do first-grade work. We don't want him to waste his time on kindergarten stuff."9

Studies are needed that will provide better means of motivating learning.

Problems in motivation are mong the most serious of all problems confronting classroom teachers of children who do not place great value on formal education and who do not internalize the long-range goals which the teacher accepts without question. One educational psychologist states that "in school as well as elsewhere, the most important motives are the wants and aspirations of the individual."10

Motivation for learning is largely culturally determined. Shaffer and Shoben define a motive as a "complex, socially learned pattern involving situation, drive, mechanism, and end-result."11 They further describe motives:

> Motives to seek the approval of other people, to get attention, to gain sympathy, to be with others rather than alone, and to be recognized as a person of worth, are among the dominant urges of many cultures.12

> A closely related pattern of social motivation is represented by tendencies to submit to the customs of one's group, to conform, to do the expected thing, and to avoid blame and criticism.13

> Our culture gives many examples of motives to excel, to succeed, to overcome obstructions, to worst a rival, to complete a task once begun, and, in general, to master persons and situations. This is one of the most variable patterns of motivation from one culture to another, and is very weak in some societies.14

The motives of an Indian child are rooted in a deep-seated cultural heritage of which his teacher may be unaware. Some of the child's strongest motives may be those of holding tenaciously to the Indian language, values, and practices which he suspects his non-Indian teacher is working vigorously to eradicate. As an example of the difficulty of motivating Indian students, a high school music teacher reported that he had a Navajo student in the band who showed excellent promise. He told the student that if he would practice more, he could gain first chair. After a few weeks of no noticeable improvement, the music teacher asked the boy if he had been practicing more. The student said that he had not because he did not want first chair. This suggests that excelling, mastering situations, or "worsting a rival" may not be strong motives in Navajo culture.

Another example of difficulties with motivation is that primary school teachers have often found that "Show and Tell" is an excellent medium for motivating oral language expression and furthering the personal satisfaction of the children who participate. However, since young Indian children may have been taught by their families not to reveal family situations to non-Indians, "Show and Tell" may not be a popular activity in schools in which they are enrolled. Some objective, nonpersonal discussion may have to be substituted, such as the "vocabulary basket" cited previously.

Schools need to seek out, to define, and to analyze those motivations which individual teachers find successful and to provide for the necessary exchange of ideas among teachers so that successful motivations will become more widely known and used.

BILINGUAL PROBLEMS

In the Puerto Rican Study, Morrison says that it is necessary to:

> Recognize. . . the teaching of non-English-speaking children as an area of specialization that cuts across many subject areas. . . It recognizes the relations of the child's native vernacular to his social-cultural heritage, the relations of his learning English to his new social-educational-cultural environment. Here is an area of specialization that draws on the communication arts, the modern languages, . . . anthropology, psychology, and sociology.[15]

In view of the evidence presented in this text, the most pressing need in the public schools in the Southwest is that of teaching English as a second language to all those who are deficient in its use. The methodology by which this is to be accomplished must, of necessity, fit each school in its individual way. There are some generalizations that may be made:

1. An established language period in the school day devoted to the development of adequate language patterns for English conversations is recommended. The use of a variety of teaching aids, with the emphasis always on the student's production of the language with appropriate vernacular to imitate, is indicated. Overlearning in the habituation of patterns is stressed.

2. Pronunciation of the phonemes of the language, the intonation, stress, and rhythm need to be habituated.

3. To progress smoothly into extended reading of the language is necessary. To read, to write, and to make use of the language in solving problems is the theoretical end result and will be achieved only if reading and grammar have emphasis after a prescribed level of aural-oral work is completed.

4. Dictionary work in the second language will be necessary to overcome confusions with the idioms, multiple meanings, analogies, slang, and other elements in the semantic use of the language.

Only a beginning has been made in relating the cultural difference and language barrier to problems of methodology. New efforts are indicated to cope with the problem of educational retardation which is resulting from the language, culture, and experience barriers. In New Mexico, where English is a second language for approximately 40 percent of the school children, studies pertaining to the teaching of English as a second language are most strongly indicated. Results of such studies should be applicable wherever bilingual problems exist. Types of studies might include:

1. Tests to give teachers objective measures of the extent to which various facets of the language are obstacles for children in their classes. A battery of such tests should measure the ability to understand idiomatic expressions, slang expressions, multiple meanings, opposites, analogies, figures of speech, and references to mythological and Biblical characters. These tests, standardized on the performance of typical English-speaking, middle-class elementary school pupils, would give teachers comparative results for all school children for whom English is a second language. The need for such testing instruments is accentuated by the lack of awareness on the part of public school personnel of the nature of bilingual difficulties. The stages of bilingualism, as emphasized by Mahlerbe,[16] are not generally understood. Children who function at a "low" stage of English

proficiency are often discriminated against and thought to be lacking in innate ability.

To recapitulate, an exploratory test of common English idiomatic expressions in a sixth-grade population revealed that Anglos performed significantly better than did Navajo, Pueblo, Apache, and Spanish-American pupils.[17] Exploratory tests of multiple meanings, analogies, and antonyms revealed that a fourth-grade Anglo norming group performed significantly better than did sixth-grade Navajo, Pueblo, Apache, and Spanish-American students.[18] Experimental work is needed to find ways to help these severely language-handicapped children.

2. Analytical studies to reveal the nature of language difficulties faced by Indian and Spanish-American children who learn English as a second language. Stevick writes:

We may sort out difficult points fairly satisfactorily into four categories: phonological, grammatical, lexical, and cultural. Phonological difficulties are those relating to the formation and interpretation of the sounds. Grammar has to do with the forms and arrangements of words. Lexical problems are problems of vocabulary. Cultural problems and difficulties arise because speakers of Language A differ from speakers of Language B not only in the way they talk, but also in the way they live and in the way they look at the world.[19]

As an example of the practical value of phonological studies for the primary teacher, studies of the differences in phonemes in the two languages (the child's vernacular and English) could result in specific methodology for primary classroom teachers for the elimination of dialect, keener auditory discrimination of new sounds to be learned, and intensive production of phonemes foreign to the first language.

3. Supplementary lesson plans for teachers' manuals to give teachers specific help in teaching children for whom English is a second language. This type of study would necessitate intensive editorial work on lesson plans of commercially prepared textbooks. The purpose would be to make teachers conscious of such problems as differences in language patterning, language phonemes, vocabulary, and socio-cultural connotations in the semantics of words.

The status of bilingualism in New Mexico, as stated in this text, poses two very important questions.

1. Are the children from the Indian and Spanish-American backgrounds functioning at Mahlerbe's "low" stage of

knowing English and, hence, giving only a superficial appearance of knowing the English language?

2. In their attempts to be bilingual and to use a minimum of vocabulary in two languages without much facility in either of them, do these pupils function on a very low level of equilingualism? In other words, are they more nearly nonlingual than bilingual?[20]

Nursery School Classes for the Teaching of English

The earlier a language is learned, the easier it is assimilated and used, and the more easily is the exact reproduction of the phonemes in the language mastered. The child between the ages of two and four will be able more freely to imitate the speech of the second language teacher. By the time the child is seven, he has already learned to be self-conscious to some degree in speech imitation, and he has also so completely habituated one set of phonemes to represent speech that he finds it very difficult to add "foreign" ones to his repertoire. Nursery school classes for two-year-old children in the villages where they could be assembled in small groups, and continued through the three- and four-year age groups, should send the child to the kindergarten able to communicate with his teacher. This hypothesis might easily be tested in many areas today since there would be ample "controls" who would not have the opportunity for such instruction. If such nursery schools could be financed, it is believed that both the Spanish-speaking and the Indian parents would be interested in having their children attend. Indian parents should be especially interested in any plan that would make it easier for their children to become truly bilingual. This would satisfy both their intense desire that their young people must know the mother tongue and that they learn English well in order to get along in the white man's world. If Indian parents understand that this early introduction to the sounds of the language will help to eliminate confusion of sounds, accent in pronunciation, and misplaced emphasis in sentences, and more important, establish self-confidence in the use of the second language, they will be interested.

BILINGUAL SCHOOLS

A bilingual school is one in which instruction in the school curriculum is offered in more than one language. This requires that content subjects will be taught in both languages. A student might study his mathematics in English and his history in Spanish in a Spanish-English bilingual school. This is to be constrasted with studying Spanish for one period of the day as a foreign language with little attention given to that language except in that class period. Few students who study a foreign language in the high school are able to master the sound system of that language so that they can understand native speakers.

In the Southwest, children are spoken of as bilinguals if they speak an Indian tongue or Spanish as a first language and enroll in public schools where English is the only medium of communication. Naturally, these children are in no sense bilingual. In those schools where they have not been given systematic instruction in the learning of a new language, many students have remained illiterate in Spanish and have achieved barely minimum literacy in English.

Were the school to take advantage of the language that the child already knows and develop literacy in that language, the student would have an excellent chance of becoming a truly bilingual person.

In many schools in the Southwest, Spanish-speaking children have been discouraged, and even punished, for using the Spanish language on the playground or in the classroom even though they may have developed a good understanding of the sound pattern of the spoken language when they first enrolled. Yet, at the high school level, counselors may have encouraged the student to study Spanish as a foreign language since he already understands it! Students must find it difficult to understand the hypocrisy of a school system that operates in this fashion.

It is hoped that the child holds two psychological values about his language and his family that speaks that language. First, he should feel that his language is a good one; that it expresses his ideas and wishes adequately; and that he may be justly proud to use it. Second, all of the people in his extended family use the language which he has learned as his first language and he derives his ego strength and sense of personal worth as a member of that particular ethnic group. If the school teaches, however, that English is the only acceptable language there and that use of another language even during free play on the playground will be punished, the child can only conclude that his school feels that his language is inferior to the one that must be used all the time during the school day.

If the teacher reacts negatively to the child's first language, the child will further conclude that only people that speak English are adequate in his teacher's eyes. In the Southwest for many years, both of these things were done to children. They were denied the use of their own language and subtly taught that their language and their people were inferior.

Bilingual schools taught in Spanish and English would be natural, workable solutions in many schools in the Southwest. Since Spanish is a major language of the world, books, newspapers, and periodicals are readily available in that language. Many nations in the Americas have some 200,000,000 speakers of the language with libraries, government, business, and schools functioning in Spanish.

The question of young Navajo children receiving instruction in school in the Navajo language is an entirely different question—though no less important. Although there are no libraries and there is no indicated future use, the two psychological values are just as valid for the Navajo as for the Spanish child.

Maybe even for him, at age five and at age six, the school should spend up to two-thirds of his day in the Navajo language with planned, sequenced, intensive teaching of English as a spoken means of communication. Learning concepts and reading readiness in Navajo would save the child some time later on. Hopefully, by age seven or eight, he would begin to learn to read in English and use it as his medium of reading and writing instruction. Yet, by the behavior of the adults at school during the first three years, he would know that the school valued his language, and in turn his cultural heritage, and he might well participate in a Navajo conversation class throughout his school life.

What Is a Bilingual School?

Few programs operate in public schools in the United States as bilingual, that is, putting two language to work in the conduct of the school.

The only test results of educational achievement of the bilingual school in operation have been reported by Malherbe concerning Dutch-English bilingualism in South Africa. [21] In statistics released in 1946, he reported that students in the secondary school divided themselves into three groups: those who were educated in English-speaking schools; those who were educated in Afrikaans-speaking schools; and a relatively small number educated in Afrikaans-English bilingual schools.

Malherbe tested about 18,000 students in three types of South African schools: Unilingual Afrikaans, Unilingual English, and Bilingual Schools.

Some of his conclusions are:

The main point . . . is that the figures show a clear advantage in favour of the bilingual school as regards language attainment in both English and Afrikaans at all intelligence levels . . . the gains, though seemingly small, are all statistically significant. [22]

. . . those children with a bilingual home background who attend the bilingual medium school top the list, while right at the bottom of the list come the children with a unilingual home environment who attend a unilingual medium school. [23]

In geography the pupils in the bilingual school were, on an average, about four-fifths of a school year ahead of those in the unilingual school. In arithmetic they were half a year ahead. [24]

Adverse sectional discrimination is from three to four times as great in unilingual as in bilingual schools. The children with bilingual home environment display the least adverse discrimination . . . The consistency of our data on the main issue leaves no doubt about the fact that in bilingual medium schools, where pupils of both sections mix and associate freely, the children display a comparatively low degree of intercultural antagonism.[25]

Davies writes about second language learning and describes one situation in Wales.

The supplementing of second language teaching by the study of another subject through its medium, is the only way in which the second language will ever come to life in unilingual environments, in South Africa or anywhere else . . . The mastery of a language must become subconscious, and this can never be achieved merely by studying that language in the language lesson only . . . World Geography is a possibility.[26]

A pleasing feature of parallel-medium or "two-stream" schools in Wales is their complete lack of separatism. The Primary School, Aberystwyth, reorganized in 1948, has 340 pupils, of whom 225 are English- and 115 Welsh-speaking. The staff is bilingual, and the spirit of the school on the whole is Welsh, with Welsh the language of the staff and staff meetings. English is used as the medium of instruction for the English-speaking section throughout, with Welsh introduced as a subject in the second year and taught in every subsequent year. For the Welsh speaking section, English is introduced during the second half of the first year, the time devoted to it being increased during the second and subsequent years; by the third year, the medium of instruction has become 50% Welsh, 50% English, and by the fourth, equal facility in the use of both languages is aimed at.[27]

Peal and Lambert demonstrated that bilingual children are superior on both verbal and non-verbal intelligence tests when compared with monolinguals. They compared monolingual and bilingual groups of ten-year-old children who were students in six French schools in Montreal, Canada. Their groups were matched on age, sex, and socio-economic status. They concluded that their bilingual subjects had greater mental flexibility than did the monolingual children and in addition demonstrated a superiority in concept formation.[28]

Rojas reported at the end of the 1964-65 school year about a bilingual school in Miami:

The bilingual school has two groups of Spanish-speaking pupils and two of English-speaking pupils in grades one through four with eight native Spanish-speaking teachers and eight native English-speaking teachers. English is the medium of instruction for all pupils for approximately half of each day; and Spanish, the medium of instruction for all pupils during the other half. Next year the fifth grade will be added and the following year the sixth. The expectation is that at the end of the sixth grade both groups of pupils will know the two languages well enough to operate effectively in both.[29]

Modiano did a comparative study of two approaches to the teaching of reading in the national language.

Modiano[30] studied reading achievement of native Indians in the Chiapas highlands in southern Mexico, where some of the Indian children are taught to read first in their native Indian languages while others are immediately taught in Spanish. In each of three tribal areas studied, the researcher found significantly better reading ability among children who were first taught to read in their original language.

Modiano's findings are applicable to all schools, and to test this hypothesis she urges experimental programs to begin in regions in the United States having large linguistic minorities. No school system in the nation now employs the native language first approach.

Materials for Spanish-English Bilingual Schools

Schools interested in finding text materials for elementary school classes in Spanish will be able to find an adequate supply. The following brief bibliography suggests sources from which school administrators may select:

Textbooks:

(1) Laidlaw Brothers, Inc., River Forest, Illinois, Angeles Pastor, et. al., Por el mundo del cuento y la aventura, Serie de textos básicos para Hispanoamérica, 1962.

Mis juegos y cuentos	Apresto
A jugar y a gozar	Precartilla
A la escuela!	Cartilla
Amigos de aquí y de allí	Libro Primero
Pueblo y campo	Libro II, Nivel I
Sorpresas y maravillas	Libro II, Nivel II
Por esos caminos	Libro III
Nuestro mundo maravilloso	Libro IV
Aventuras por mundos desconocidos	Libro V
Una mirada al pasado	Libro VI

Puertas de la Luz, Angeles Pastor, et al., Una serie de libros de
   de lectura para los tres primeros grados, 1959-1962.
   Campanillitas Folkloricas
   Esta era una vez bajo las palmeras
   Esta era una vez bajo los yagrumos

Personal del programa de salud, por Edwina Jones, Paul Landis, Edna Morgan, and Thelma Shaw, six book series for grades I-VI.

A series of arithmetic books with teacher's editions have also been published by Laidlaw.

2. La Serie Meso-América, Regional Office for Central America and Panama, ODECA, El Salvador, San Salvador.
   a. A reading series finished through the fifth grade.
   b. An arithmetic series finished through fourth grade.
   c. A social studies series in preparation.
   d. A language series in preparation.
   e. A science series in preparation.

3. Serie Educativa de Ciencia Básica, por Bertha Morris Parker (Evanston, Illinois: Row, Peterson and Company, 1958).

   24 titles are available, for example:
   La vida a través de las edades

4. Serie de libros de lectura (San Jose, Costa Rica: Editorial Las Américas, 1959).

Flor nueva	I y II grados
Mi pequeño mundo	II grado
Leer y hacer	III grado
Patria grande	IV grado
Madre América	V grado
La tierra y el hombre	VI grado
Nuestro país	III o IV grado

Schools need to be experimenting with the use of the first language for boys and girls who enter school with little knowledge of English. Haarhoff writes convincingly about the need for the bilingual school if we hope to educate children to use two languages well:

> . . . we are not producing bilingual school children and we never shall, as long as the second language is not used as an instrument of expression and not merely as a subject to be learned for an examination. In other words, the second language must be used as a medium in the school.[31]

> . . . There is general agreement all over the educational world that the child should begin his education in his mother tongue or . . . the language he most easily understands.[32]

One of the possible ways of overcoming the educational retardation of boys and girls beyond the third grade might be that of providing for cognitive growth, vocabulary development, expanding concepts with the six- and seven-year old children during the first two years of school by teaching in their vernacular perhaps half of the school day, while they are provided systematic teaching of English as a second language during the remainder of the day. If the vernacular is a language in which much has been written and textbooks are readily available (as, for example, Spanish) the boys and girls might learn to read and write in their vernacular before they began reading and writing in English.

REMEDIAL EDUCATION

Teachers must be prepared to provide remedial instruction for those Indian children making the adjustment into the public schools.[33] Learning in school needs to be rooted in the child's background of experience in order to be meaningful. Schools need to know more about the experiences which the child brings with him, and they need to make adequate provision for the older child who is academically achieving several years below his expected grade placement. Studies such as the two suggested below should be fruitful.

1. Measures of children's concepts in English and in their vernacular at the time of starting school would be useful in assessing their readiness for formal teaching in English. Possible uses to be made of the Common Concepts Foreign Language Test with young children will be investigated.[34] Another example might be that of number readiness. Research is available to show which number concepts are possessed by "average" English-speaking kindergarten children. A check list could be built and translated into the child's language. It would then be possible to determine whether or not the child possesses certain number readiness knowledges in his first language. It would be helpful to the teacher to know to what extent he must teach only the English translation of a concept or whether he must develop the concept and teach the language.

2. More adequate methods for meeting problems of remedial teaching and school dropouts are needed. The presence of many adolescents in junior high schools who possess extremely limited English language power poses many administrative and guidance problems. Different programs should be evaluated experimentally. Should emphasis be given to special tutoring in use of oral English, to tutoring in sequential reading skills in usual remedial reading instruction, to partial segregation in grouping for special instruc-

tion, to efforts to assign special language teachers to small groups of bilingual children?

Different methods of helping nonreaders in various school grades certainly need to be evaluated.

CROSS-CULTURAL RESEARCH IN PROGRESS

During the past decade there has been an awakening among educators to the many problems inherent in education across cultures. Specializations in ever narrower and narrower academic fields have caused many short-sighted people to see sociology, anthropology, psychology, linguistics and other related fields as tightly walled-in compartments of isolated disciplines. Short-sighted people in those disciplines saw educators largely as people steeped in superficial methodology but unable to understand much of their respective "academic" discipline. The last decade has evolved a much greater awareness of the dependence of the school on the educational psychologist, the educational sociologist, and the educational anthropologist if the contribution of these disciplines is to be felt in the educational process and the manner in which it is effected. In those areas where children enter school speaking a language other than that used as a medium of instruction, specialists in linguistics and language pedagogy are making a major contribution in teaching teachers that learning a second language quickly for school use differs in many ways from having learned a first language automatically in the process of growing into childhood.

Some of the research now in progress includes:

1. Regional Educational Laboratories, including:

    a. Inter-Laboratory Committee on Indian Education, Claremont Hotel, 1 Garden Court, Berkeley, California 94705.

    b. Southwestern Cooperative Educational Laboratory, 117 Richmond N. E., Albuquerque, New Mexico 87106.

    c. Northern Regional Educational Laboratory, 710 Southwest Second Avenue, Portland, Oregon 97232.

    These laboratories state such purposes as: "Innovate and develop promising curriculum and teaching methods that will improve Indian education but will also serve as models for improving education of all children in similar circumstances." Evaluation of methodology in cross-cultural settings includes such topics as: teaching English to speakers of other languages, linguistic interaction in the classroom, development of culturally based language arts materials, analyzing self-fulfilling expectations, and establishing entry skills.

2. Spindler, George D. and Louise Spindler, Stanford University, Stanford, California. Case Studies in Education and Culture,

Case Studies in Cultural Anthropology, and Studies in Anthropological Method. Titles of finished monographs published by Holt, Rinehart and Winston, Inc., include:

Edward Dozier, The Tewa of Hano.

Margaret Read, Children of Their Fathers, Growing up among the Ngoni of Malawi.

John Gay and Michael Cole, The New Mathematics and an Old Culture, A Study of Learning Among the Kpelle of Liberia.

A. Richard King, The School at Mopass: A Problem of Identity.

John Singleton, Nichu: A Japanese School.

Richard L. Warren, Education in Rebhausen: A German Village.

Harry F. Wolcott, A Kwakiutl Village and School.

3. Demonstration in Navajo Education, Rough Rock Demonstration School, Rough Rock, Arizona. The Major objectives are: (1) active involvement of Navajo leaders and the community in the operation of the school; (2) encouragement of close contact between students in the borading school and their parents; (3) a planned program in cultural identification to make Navajo culture a part of the curriculum; (4) in-service training for staff members; (5) adult education for the people of the community; and (6) availability of school facilities for community use.

4. Bryde, Father John, S.J., Ph. D., The Sioux Indian Student: A Study of Scholastic Failure and Personality Conflict, (St. Louis: J. S. Swift Co., 1966). Father Bryde's doctoral dissertation proposed a new secondary school course designed to give the Indian student a conscious awareness of Indian culture and values and the place of these values as a part of total adjustment to school work and to future careers. Teachers have always been instructed that they must know and understand the behavior of their students before they can teach them. In Indian cross-cultural education teachers of Indian students must: (1) understand the behavior of the Indian and know something of his system of values; (2) utilize these values to motivate Indians to goals of self-fulfillment acceptable to Indian culture; (3) help the Indian to understand that he is accepted as a worthwhile person within his Indian cultural context and not necessarily within the cultural context of the teacher; and (4) avoid alienating the Indian student by giving emphasis to the teacher's goals and norms of acceptability. Bryde has written and recommends a course of high school students in Acculturational Psychology or Understanding the Modern Indian. To teach pride in Indian cultural heritage and adaptability to the modern social and economic world, Bryde suggests the following outline:

1. The psychology of the modern Indian;
2. The concept of culture;
3. Cultural differences;
4. Values and value systems;
5. Establishing values and values that endure;
6. Indian values and motivation;
7. Indian history;
8. Non-Indian values;
9. Conflicts in values;
10. Defense mechanisms: Behavior of adjustment;
11. Behavioral deviations;
12. Psychology of adjustment in the Indian value system;
13. Taking the best from the two cultures;
14. The emerging, contributing citizen.

5. Headstart Programs sponsored by the Office of Economic Opportunity. The language development, the cognitive growth, and the attention to health and nutritional needs of young children has produced excellent results in many areas where children living in cultural deprivation have attended. Smith's report of Headstart Programs sponsored by Indian Community Action Programs in Northern, New Mexico indicates that, even in a relatively short period of time young Pueblo Indian parents have felt personally involved and appreciative of the results.[35]

6. A Language Program for Navajo Children, being prepared for the Navajo Area, Bureau of Indian Affairs by Dr. Robert Wilson, University of California, Los Angeles. The program being written for grade one is attempting to provide the teacher with guides for teaching all day (a six-hour day).

7. An Adaptation of the Fries-Rojas American English Series for use in schools with Navajo Children, being prepared for the Navajo Area, Bureau of Indian Affairs by Dr. Mary Jane Cook, University of Arizona, Tuscon.

8. Cultural Identification Units for the Social Studies Curriculum, being prepared for use in the Navajo Area, Bureau of Indian Affairs, by Dr. Le Roy Condie, University of New Mexico, Albuquerque. One unit at each grade level from kingergarten through twelfth grade is being written, used experimentally, revised, and prepared for distribution.

9. Renaud, Andre, Indian and Northern Curriculum Resources Centre, College of Education, University of Saskatchewan, Saskatoon, Saskatchewan, Canada. The Curriculum Centre evaluates and develops instructional materials for schools in Indian and Northern Areas. The College of Education offers a graduate program in Indian Education. The Resources Centre has two excellent publications: The Northian, a quarterly journal, and The Northian Newsletter.

SUMMARY

Additional research has been suggested as being essential to helping solve the problems of the adjustment of Indian children into the public schools of New Mexico. Research studies in the areas of cultural differences, bilingual problems, and remedial education, the development of language test instruments, and suggestions for improved methodology can be applicable not only to the Southwest, but also for other places where children from minority ethnic groups are being assimilated into public school systems, bringing with them problems of native languages, different cultures, meager experience backgrounds, and educational retardation -- problems which teachers must be prepared to face.

As a concluding note on acculturation of minority groups, the thought expressed by Kennan may well serve as a guideline:

> Wherever the authority of the past is too suddenly and too drastically undermined -- wherever the past ceases to be the great and reliable reference book of human problems -- wherever, above all, the experience of the father becomes irrelevant to the trials and searchings of the son -- there the foundations of man's inner health and stability begin to crumble. Insecurity and panic begin to take over, conduct becomes erratic and aggressive. These, unfortunately, are the marks of an era of rapid technological or social change. A great portion of our globe is today thus affected. And if the price of adjustment to rapid population growth is to cut man's ties to the past and to catapult him violently across centuries of adjustment into some new and unfamiliar technological stratosphere, then I am not sure that the achievement is worth the price. [36]

Teachers can anticipate continuing changes in the lives of the Spanish-speaking families and the Indian families in the Southwest. A few specific examples might be mentioned to emphasize the point.

The improved roads throughout reservation lands and the improved technology which the minority groups are becoming a part of either in home appliances or in industrial jobs causes an increased effect of Anglo society on the minorities. The new attitude about creating "tourism" as an industry - whether on the Navajo Reservation, in the Sangre de Cristo Mountains in northern New Mexico, or beside the new dam in the Rio Grande River on the Cochiti Reservation.

Mass media, and the rapidity with which news is transmitted, affects cultural diffusion and borrowing and, in turn, makes of the borrowers something more nearly like the "mass culture."

Minority groups are, quite obviously inthe Southwest, showing a new awareness of their problems. This is observed in various activities ranging from the rise of vocal, young leadership among the Mexican-Americans appraising their status in labor, economy, and education to the recent plan by the Navajo people to create a Navajo Cultural Center to collect and record their traditions before it is too late.

Finally, the impact of the draft and military service that caused many changes when Indians and Spanish-Americans came home after World War II continues to have a more permeating effect than may be realized. The military experience may be taking its place as a kind of institution along with education, relocation, and politics in broadening the cultural horizons of many young people.

FOOTNOTES

[1] Margaret Mead, "Significance of the Individual," The Liberal Context (Milford, New Hampshire: The Hunter Press, 1961), p. 27.

[2] Ashley Montagu, Man: His First Million Years (New York: The New American Library of World Literature, Inc., 1957), pp. 14-15.

[3] Lawrence K. Frank, "World Order and Cultural Diversity," Free World, June, 1942.

[4] J. Cayce Morrison, Director, The Puerto Rican Study, 1953-1957. (New York City: Board of Education of the City of New York, 1958), pp. 215-226.

[5] Sophie L. Elam, "Acculturation and Learning Problems of Puerto Rican Children," Teachers College Record, February, 1960, p. 261.

[6] Laura Thompson, Culture in Crisis, 1950 (New York: Harper and Brothers, 1950), p. 190.

[7] Loyd S. Tireman, Teaching Spanish-Speaking Children (Albuquerque: The University of New Mexico Press, 1951), p. 20.

[8] Horacio Ulibarri, "Teacher Awareness of Socio-Cultural Differences in Multi-Cultural Classrooms" (Unpublished Doctoral dissertation, The University of New Mexico, Albuquerque, 1959).

[9] Katherine V. McNerney, "Evaluation of TV Kindergarten Program in a Predominantly Spanish American Community" (Unpublished research paper, The University of New Mexico, College of Education, Albuquerque, 1961).

[10] James B. Stroud, Psychology in Education (New York: Longmans, Green and Company, 1946), p. 230.

[11] Laurance F. Shaffer and Edward J. Shoben, Jr., The Psychology of Adjustment (Boston: Houghton Mifflin Company, 1956), p. 85.

[12] Ibid., p. 86.

[13] Ibid., p. 87.

[14] Ibid., p. 88.

[15] Morrison, op. cit., p. 240.

[16] E. G. Mahlerbe, The Bilingual School (London: Longman's, Green and Co., 1946), pp. 17-29.

[17] Maurine Dunn Yandell, "Some Difficulties Which Indian Children Encounter with Idioms in Reading" (Unpublished Master's thesis, The University of New Mexico, Albuquerque, 1959).

[18] Christine Dudding, "An Investigation into the Bilingual Child's Comprehension of Antonyms" (Unpublished Master's thesis, The University of New Mexico, Albuquerque, 1961); Stephen G. Hess, "A Comparative Study of the Understanding Which Bilingual Students Have of the Multiple Meanings of English Words" (Research in Progress, The University of New Mexico, Albuquerque, 1960-1962); and Veta W. Mercer, "The Efficiency of Bilingual Children in Understanding Analogies in the English Language" (unpublished Master's thesis, The University of New Mexico, Albuquerque, 1960).

[19] Earl W. Stevick, Helping People Learn English (Nashville: Abingdon Press, 1957), p. 26.

[20] These questions are also posed by George I. Sanchez, "The Crux of the Dual Language Handicap," New Mexico School Review, 33: 13-15, 38, March, 1954.

[21] E. G. Malherbe, The Bilingual School (Capetown: Juta and Co., Ltd., 1946).

[22] Ibid., p. 62.

[23] Ibid., p. 69.

[24] Ibid., p. 73.

[25] Ibid., p. 84.

[26] R. E. Davies, Bilingualism in Wales (Capetown: Juta and Company, Ltd., 1954), p. 90.

[27] Ibid., p. 17.

[28] Elizabeth Peal and Wallace Lambert, "The Relationship of Bilingualism to Intelligence," Psychological Monographs: General and Applied, No. 76:1-23 (Washington: American Psychological Association, 1962).

[29] Pauline Rojas, "The Miami Experience in Bilingual Education," Carol J. Dreidler, Editor, On Teaching English to Speakers of Other Languages, Series II (Champaign, Illinois 61820: National Council of Teachers of English, 1966), p. 45.

[30] Nancy Modiano, "A Comparative Study to Two Approaches to the Teaching of Reading in the National Language," New York University School of Education, 1966.

[31] T. J. Haarhoff, "Introduction," in E. G. Malherbe, The Bilingual School, (Capetown: Juta and Company, Ltd., 1946), p. 5.

[32] Ibid., p. 8.

[33] Zintz, Miles V., Director, The Indian Research Study: The Adjustment of Indian and Non-Indian Children in the Public Schools of New Mexico, The Final Report (Albuquerque: College of Education, University of New Mexico, Albuquerque, 1961). (Mimeographed) Sponsored under grant-in-aid by the U.S. Office of Education, 1957-1960.

[34] Bela H. Banathy, Miles V. Zintz, W. James Popham, Joseph M. Sadnavitch, Rena Krichbaum, Fred Gannon, Geschrieben van Valdemar Hempel, and Klaus A. Mueller, Common Concepts Foreign Language Test (English, Spanish, French, German), California Test Bureau, Del Monte Research Park, Monterey, California, 1963.

[35] Anne Smith, "Indian Headstart Programs in Northern New Mexico," El Palacio, December, 1968.

[36] George Kenman, Realities of American Foreign Policy (Princeton: University Press, 1954), pp. 34-35.

Part Four

Appendix A -- An Autobiography

Appendix B -- A Spanish Culture in Transition

Appendix C -- Ways of Working with the Navajos Who Have Not Learned the White Man's Ways

Appendix D -- Reading List for Retarded Readers

Appendix E -- Tests

Bibliography

Author Index

Subject Index

APPENDIX A

An Autobiography[1]

Rose Begay was born on the Navajo reservation in northern Arizona. She was one of nine children. There were two older sisters, two brothers, both older than Rose, and four younger sisters. Between Askii, the younger brother, and Rose was a gap of some seven years. The mother often spoke of a boy and a girl who died in infancy and Rose always thought they must have been born, and died, in those seven years.

The family included the Begays, the maternal grandmother, and her two younger daughters and their families. This extended family always lived and moved as one unit except when unusually poor grazing conditions forced them to separate. Each of the aunts had almost as large a family as the Begays.

Rose's father, Hosteen Begay, and mother, Nizhoni Dziil, had married when he was thirty and she was almost sixteen. Hosteen came from a small, respected family of modest means. Nizhoni's family was large and extended, for her father, like other Navajo men of his time, had three wives and many children. His wives were sisters. He was well-to-do, for he had many horses and a large flock of sheep.

Hosteen and Nizhoni had been wedded with an elaborate ceremony in the traditional Navajo way. They had not known each other personally before their marriage. Hosteen's uncle had come to Nizhoni's parents with an offer of marriage between the two, and her parents had accepted. After their marriage, they lived in the camp of her parents until their second child was born. Hosteen then said that they were self-sustaining enough to live independently now. They had acquired a sizeable flock of sheep and goats and a large number of horses and cattle. So they moved away, and Nizhoni's mother and her younger children went along. Nizhoni was the oldest of her mother's children. Hosteen raised corn, beans, squash, and melons at the new location and tended the horses and cattle while grandmother and her children took care of the sheep.

413

Hosteen was easy to get along with. He had an even temperament and a pleasing disposition. He was held in high esteem by those who knew him, and his counsel was often sought. He was known to admonish, but never scold. Although he was permissive with his children, he never allowed them to get out of hand. He was a quiet and soft-spoken man. When he spoke, his family listened. The children sometimes talked back to their mother but never to their father, although it was mother, not father, who was apt to scold or punish. Throughout all her life, Rose stood in awe of her father. To her, he was the kindest and wisest of men. She remembers her father best in her early years for his gentleness and patient instructions. The children would fight to get into his lap so that he could sing to them. Rose, being the oldest of the younger children, sometimes felt foolish to be contending with them, but she too liked to get into her father's lap. When her mother scolded a child, the father would put his arm around that one and say, "Your mother isn't being mean to you; she just wants you to learn things in the right way. She must teach you so that when you get a home of your own you will know how to do these things. Your mother knows everything you need to learn to be a successful homemaker. Watch her and learn from her. When you are grown, your parents will not be there to teach you how to do things. You must learn while you are young and while your mother is here to teach you."

Like most Navajo men of his time, Hosteen was taught the religious and moral precepts of his people. He learned legends and sacred songs. In his tribe, a man proved himself by the number of sacred songs he knew. Many evenings he would give a "lecture" to his family on some legend, stressing its moral teaching. Although by the time Rose was born, Hosteen was a man of considerable means, he was a firm believer in thrift. To him waste was sinful and generosity was a virtue. When there was death in the home of an acquaintance, he would kill a sheep, dress it, and take it to the bereaved family. In Navajo custom, no sheep of the flock is to be killed during the four-day mourning period, and Hosteen would say that was a long time for anyone to go without meat. "Be thankful for everything that comes to you"; "Eat your food with a word of prayer"; "Handle everything you own with reverence"; these were some of his sayings. He told his children that they should never let a visitor depart without feeding him, regardless of who he was. "He may have come a long way, or he may have a long way to travel," he would say.

Nizhoni too, had learned things from her people, both by precept and example. She was a woman of independent spirit, self-confident, and she could stand in her own right; but she subordinated herself to her husband as she had been taught. She could get very impatient with the children, and was often tempted to spank them, although it is doubtful if she ever did. When her daughters were grown, she was able to say to each prospective son-in-law, "We have done our best to rear good, respectable and sensible women. We never laid a finger on them in punishment; we never needed to. I hope you will never feel that you need to, either. They have been children we could be proud of." She was an efficient housekeeper, had learned well the skills of rug-weaving, and knew the many things that a Navajo woman is expected to know by the time she is ready for marriage. These she was diligent to teach to her children.

The family lived alone and isolated on the Navajo reservation. Their nearest neighbors were eight or ten miles away. The nearest "civilized" contact was the Government Agency and boarding school some twenty miles distant. Rose remembers almost nothing of her childhood up to the time she was five years of age. She was living with her grandmother in the same camp as her parents. Her most vivid memory up to this time was the coming of a man from the Agency in a big automobile. The grown-ups called him a policeman. He came frequently, it seemed, to tell Hosteen and Nizhoni that Rose and a cousin of the same age must be placed in school. Nizhoni argued that they were much too small to be away from home. Rose wasn't even five yet, she said, Couldn't the school wait another year? She wasn't refusing, only asking to wait until the children were a little older. Whenever they heard a car, Rose and the cousin hid behind a stack of boxes and luggage in the back of the one-room hogan and sat there very still to hear what the man was saying. Just before Christmas, Hosteen and Nizhoni took the children to the government boarding school to be kept there the rest of that school year. Rose was five years old at the time.

Rose was frightened by the strangeness of the school atmosphere. She had never been inside a house before. She cried when the matron removed her velvet blouse and colorful skirt and put a dress on her. She kept pulling the dress down to cover her knees because it was immodest not to have one's legs covered. She cried even harder when the white woman cut off her long hair. The woman kept talking to her, but Rose did not know what she was saying. She had never heard this kind of talking before. At home they spoke only Navajo. As soon as the haircut was over and the sheet off her shoulders, Rose was out the door and off like a frightened rabbit in the direction in which she had seen her mother go. Two older girls pursued her. Her mother had walked over to the home of a friend while Rose was being bathed and dressed. After much persuasion by the mother and a promise that she would visit her soon, the child allowed herself to be taken back to the dormitory. Such was Rose's introduction to formal education and a different way of life.

Everything was strange to her -- her clothes, the food, the big dormitory in which she frequently lost her way, the hospital with its frightening gadgets and smelly interior, and even the teachers who didn't look at all like people she knew. She thought about what strange color of hair some of these people had and how some of them even had eyes that reminded her of the goats at home, all blue and grey and kind of striped. But after a few weeks, the initial shock passed and she began to like school. There were many children, all of them Navajos with backgrounds similar to her own, to play with. At that time, the school accommodated around 200 children from kindergarten through the sixth grade.

This little school which Rose attended for the first nine grades of her education was a U.S. government boarding school for Navajo children, situated on the Navajo reservation. Dirt roads were the only access to the school. The nearest town was thirty miles distant. The few outside contacts the children had consisted of an occasional trip to the town to see a circus or a movie. These were rare treats and were talked about for many days afterwards. There were also visits from students of other Indian schools to play a game of basketball or baseball. A small public school was also operated for children of the school personnel, but there was almost no mixing between students of the two schools.

The first year of school seemed to be a matter of playing blocks or drop-the-handkerchief, going for walks out into the country (Rose couldn't walk far because she was very small, so older girls took turns carrying her on their backs), or going to sleep on the hard wood floor of the classroom every afternoon. These naps she hated. It seemed, too, that they were always standing in line. They lined up to go to the dining hall, to the movies, to the store, for a walk, just everywhere. This she hated also because, being the smallest of the girls, she was always on the end of the line, usually without a partner, and the boys would make fun of her. Her parents came often to visit, and once in a while her father came alone. The children were not permitted to go home during the school year. Thus, they were away from their homes from September through early June.

The following year Rose went through the first grade. A year later the class started the second grade, but after a few weeks, three of them, including Rose, were put in the third grade. In this class were older and taller boys, and they made great sport of hitting girls. Rose noticed that when the girls fought back the boys would start crying before they were even touched. She discovered that she could render a mean little boy helpless by holding his head down by the hair. Whenever she got hold of one in this fashion, she made a fist and punched away with uppercuts until she saw a chance to get away without getting hit anymore.

Rose's teacher in the first few grades was the wife of the principal of the school. To this dedicated woman, above all others, she gives credit for preparation for all future education she has received. Without this foundation, she would not have been able to undertake all that has followed.

In this third grade class, Rose got to know a pretty little girl named Rachel, who was a year older than she. They became close friends under painful circumstances. One day their matron, Gladys, a young Navajo woman of about 25, announced a new ruling that she had made. Any child found with torn clothes (clothes were supplied by the school) would be punished. Every laundry day Gladys would inspect the clothes and call in the children whose clothes were torn. Once Rose was among those called in. They were ushered into the linen room where Gladys applied a leather strap to bare bottoms. Rachel was there also. Rose and Rachel came out crying, sat down on the steps, and talked about what a mean woman Gladys was and how they hoped she would die that night. Rachel was a quiet and timid girl, but she seemed very smart because she always gave the right answers in class. The two were inseparable for several years until Rachel dropped out of school in the sixth grade.

At the end of each school year, Rose's parents took her home. Most of the summer she spent with her grandmother. Since the grandmother took care of the sheep, she sometimes moved away from the rest of the family, taking Rose and one of the other children with her. Usually the other child was Hago, a son of one of the other aunts and of the same age as Rose. In these summer camps, they lived in temporary brush shelters. They always carried their sheepskin bedding with them. As a little girl, Rose never had a blanket. Her grandmother tanned four goatskins and sewed them together. This big pelt Rose used for a blanket at night. It was very warm, soft, and fluffy and had a homey smell. The grandmother took good care of the children, but she allowed no foolishness and expected immediate obedience. She was quick-tempered and often uttered hard sayings. Once when she was cooking breakfast, she asked Rose to bring in some wood. Rose had just gotten up and wasn't paying much attention to anything. The third time that Grandmother spoke and Rose had not moved, she reached for a stick. Rose was out the door in no time at all, with her grandmother right behind her. She chased the child right to the wood pile and told her not to enter the hogan without wood. Her grandmother had numerous ways of enforcing her orders. Many times she came very near to spanking Rose. Only the child's quick legs allowed her to escape her grandmother's reach, but she couldn't escape her scolding. At these times Rose remembered her father saying, "Your mother does not enjoy scolding you. If you are scolded, it is because you need a scolding. If you do what you are told, and the first time you are told, there will be no need for your mother to scold. She will be happy then, and you will have no reason to cry. It will be the same with your behavior at school, also." Rose thought that maybe it worked that way with her grandmother, too, so she was usually careful to obey before grandmother lost her patience. But Rose loved her grandmother and preferred to live with her. She always called her "Mother."

Nizhoni did much weaving. Whenever Rose was with her parents, she would sit at her mother's loom and try to weave. When she was eight years old, her mother put up a loom for her. She made a rug about eighteen by fourteen inches out of scraps left from her mother's weaving. An experienced weaver can do this in half a day. It took Rose five days and many errors to finish. It was just a lot of colors and stripes, for Rose had picked her own colors and put them together the way she wished. She was very self-conscious about her new product and couldn't decide what to do with it. Her mother said, "Why don't you give it to your brother? He does not have a saddle blanket." (This was too small for a saddle blanket, but Rose didn't know that.) The mother told the brother that his sister wanted him to have the rug. Rose had not wanted to give it to him herself, because she knew that he would laugh, as he did at most things she did. But Askii only said, "Thank you very much. I shall have a saddle blanket." And he actually used it when riding bareback!

When with her grandmother, Rose went out after the sheep with her every day. They rode horseback. Rose liked to sit behind her grandmother with a pile of rags and leaves or sunflowers in her lap and play "doll." These were her playthings and she loved them. She knew no other. She learned a way that she could sit and nap without falling off even when the horse was moving. It seemed that she went along mainly for company, for her grandmother seldom asked her to do anything. When it got hot, the grandmother made wreaths out of leafy twigs of trees to wear on their heads because these were cooler than anything else.

There were no other children to play with when they lived alone. She and cousin Hago or brother Askii could not play together like they would if they were two little girls or two little boys. In Navajo society, girls do not play freely with their brothers. In terms of Navajo kinship, Hago was brother also. Sometimes they would go out into the juniper forest or among the rocks of the desert to look for baby rabbits to use for pets. These summers with her grandmother were happy ones for Rose. Because she was with her most of the time, Rose had little contact with the rest of the family. When they finally rejoined the family, the children were timid with each other for several days.

When Rose was nine years old, her oldest sister, who by then was married and had a baby, asked that Rose come and stay with her to watch the baby when she herself was busy. The sister said, also, that she got very lonesome living with her in-laws whom she didn't know well yet. Every summer after that Rose went to her sister's instead of her grandmother's. She did not always want to go, preferring to go with grandmother, but Nizhoni said that the sister needed her. At the sister's, too, there were no children her age to play with. Besides, a girl of nine was too old to play all the time. She should be learning some simple cooking and household duties by that time. Besides baby tending, she helped her sister with the preparation of wool for spinning and weaving and she also helped with the cooking. If she started to play while there was anything left undone, the sister scolded her. But when everything was finished and the baby asleep, she could play until there was something to do.

Rose's sister was much like the grandmother. She was a hard worker who couldn't tolerate laziness. She would get up before daylight and work late into the night while her family slept. She made beautiful rugs. She did not show affection like the mother or grandmother, but she saw that Rose had all material needs and would often ask if Rose were homesick and whether she'd like to go visit her parents. She tried to teach the child various methods of food preparation and of working designs into rug-weaving. About two weeks before school started, she would make or buy all of Rose's clothes and take her back to her parents.

Like her grandmother, the sister could really scold. When she started scolding, Rose was careful not to listen and to keep her mouth closed. The sister never punished Rose physically, but often she would say, "I could whip you good, but you'll tell mother and father and they might take you back. It is better that I just tell them how stubborn and senseless you are and let them spank you." But she didn't tell, at least not in Rose's presence.

Sometime in this period Rose became aware that she had another older sister and another brother. Whether they had been home before or not, she didn't know. All of a sudden they were just there at her mother's. She didn't know how long they had been there. Mother said they had gone away to a boarding school in California when they were a little older than Rose was at the time she entered school, and that they had been gone a long time -- a number of years. The brother, who was the younger of the two, spoke Navajo with a strange accent. Rose never really got to know this brother. She always felt shy in his presence. He was very reserved, not at all like Askii who was outspoken and often obnoxious, as far as Rose was concerned. She was also somewhat of a stranger to her sisters because she had lived so little with them. Only Virginia, two years younger than herself, was very friendly and affectionate. She followed Rose everywhere and when they were both at home, they were seldom apart.

The boarding school had many restrictions. One regulation Rose remembers distinctly. This was the matter of earning merits or demerits in every activity of school life. Penalties for demerits were well defined. Only children in and above the fifth grade were affected by the regulation. When a student got two to four demerits, he was not allowed to attend movies, parties, and other school functions for a specified length of time. Five or more demerits brought a paddling, the number of contacts being determined by the number of demerits one had. The paddle, about eighteen by four by one inches was known popularly as "The Board of Education." It was always administered by a huge male teacher. Rose had one paddling of seven strokes. It was very painful, but she determined that she wasn't going to cry. She bit her lip while tears blinded her eyes, but she didn't make a sound. This and the strapping by Gladys were the only two spankings Rose received in her life. At this time, Rose was attending the public school which was run for children of the employees, both Indian and white. She and three other girls had, in the middle of the year, been transferred from the fifth grade at the boarding school to the sixth grade at the public school. But in all aspects, they remained students of the boarding school. They attended this school the rest of the year and returned to the boarding school the next fall. They liked the public school because there the boys didn't fight or pick on girls. They even did things for girls without being asked. But it was strange that the employee's children cried easily and as loudly as they could. The Navajo children said that these children were crybabies. One day at a spelling bee Rose outspelled Vivian, who had been spelling champion of the class. Vivian went home crying. When the children went to eat supper that night, Vivian's mother, who was the dining room matron, came over to Rose and slapped her and told her that she had made her girl cry and if she did so again, she would get something worse than a slap. Rose was careful not to outspell Vivian after that, although she competed freely with the other children.

In this year Rose played in the school band, sang in the children's choir at church, and was a member of the Girl Scout troop. The children in different classes gave programs on various occasions. Sometimes there would be a play on the life of some famous American, or there might be just a comedy skit. In one play, Rose had the leading role of an uninhibited tomboy. She enjoyed the part, and the teacher remarked that Rose seemed to be the right one for it.

The only church at the school was a Presbyterian Mission, where all the children went as attendance was compulsory. They heard many stories and learned many verses from the Bible, and they memorized verses to win prizes. Rose liked the Sunday School but hated the worship service which followed. She disliked having to attend twice a week. Aside from vaguely noticing that some of the ideas sounded somewhat like her father's, she wasn't particularly impressed with this religion. Although Hosteen and Nizhoni held to their native religion, they never told their children that they, too, must accept it, or that they should not adopt the white man's religion. There was no religious teaching in the usual sense in the home, although Hosteen frequently used legends to bring out moral precepts. Years later Rose learned that there had once been a mission school close to where the Begays lived. In the early years of his married life, Hosteen had formed a close friendship with the son of the missionary. Rose remembers Tom as a carefree, irresponsible young man. Hosteen and Tom became inseparable in spite of the fact that Hosteen was almost 15 years older and that neither understood the other's language. In recounting his experience, Tom (when an elderly man) wrote that he and Hosteen were like "Damon and Pythias." The Begays wondered who these two people were.

Rose was eleven years old when she attended her first native dance with her parents. It was soon after school was out in the spring. They had been asked to help because the dance was being held for one of Hosteen's relatives. In the evening when the dance began, Aunt Mary, who loved to dance, asked if she could take Rose over to the dance arena. (Nizhoni had never taken her other girls to dances. She waited until they were old enough to be interested and then she let them go. This was not in accord with common practice in which a child was taken to a dance very young.) At the dance Mary suddenly pointed to a man and told Rose to get him for a partner. She was not to turn him loose until he had paid her. Reluctantly she obeyed. Not knowing how to dance, she just walked while he danced. After a while he handed her a nickel and started to leave. Mary had neglected to tell her how much to ask for the dance, but a nickel did not seem very much. She held on to his coat and at last he gave her 20 cents more and left. Rose decided then that she did not care to dance in that manner. As she grew older, she attended other dances and enjoyed them. But always her parents instructed her that she was not to dance with any man who was a clan relative. If she did not know him, she was to ask to what clan he belonged. Also, she was not to dance "for free" because girls who did so were considered not nice. These instructions she tried to follow at native dances. But sometimes boys from school asked her to dance, and they never had any money. She preferred to dance with them rather than with boys she didn't know. She didn't think of asking them to pay her because they did not do so at school dances. At these times she told her mother that they didn't pay her because that wasn't the way they did at school and that they didn't feel the way the older people did about those things.

At school, also, there were dances for the children. Rose danced with any one who asked her. It didn't occur to her to ask about clan memberships. Somehow the taboos and restrictions seemed to lose their validity when she was at school. She felt no inhibitions about dancing with "brother" Hago, and evidently he didn't either for he sometimes asked her for a dance. Other children danced with relatives, too. But at a native dance, they would never have dreamed of dancing with a relative.

Sometimes Rose's father would ask the children what they had learned at school, and they would try to tell him. He would say,

"Listen well to what they teach you and learn all you can. The Washington people took you when you were small. We think that they must be teaching you things that we ourselves would want you to know. They would not teach you things that are bad. But don't be stubborn, because a stubborn mind gets hardened; and a hardened mind is not teachable. Many words cannot penetrate a mind like that. Some day, when you are grown and have learned the white man's ways, you will come back to help your people." Being "grown-up" and helping her people were things Rose hadn't thought about and she failed to grasp the meaning of her father's words.

One summer when Rose was 12, her mother noticed that she was acting strangely. Rose replied, "Nothing," to her mother's questions as to what was the matter with her. But Nizhoni knew that it was time for her daughter's puberty rite. It seemed to Rose that she had always known about the rite. She had seen other girls go through it and heard girls at school talk about it. She knew that her time would come. Nevertheless, coming face-to-face with it was distressing. She was shocked when her mother began talking about which medicine man should be called. Mother said that this was the period of transition from childhood to womanhood and that the rite was performed for all girls to insure them a happy and prosperous adult life. According to tribal tradition, from this time forth, Rose would be considered a woman, meaning first of all, that she could be given in marriage at any time to the man suitable to the parents. But Rose did not want the rite performed for her. To her it was embarrassing to have a public announcement of what was happening to her and she told her mother this. Finally, after much discussion, Hosteen said, "Well, if she doesn't want it, we can't force her into it. If she lives well and uses her common sense, I don't see why she can't live a happy and prosperous life even without the ceremony. School children have ideas of their own. Many times they are not the same as those they learn from the Navajo way. They learn to look lightly on things that are sacred." So for Rose there was no puberty rite.

At school Rose's favorite subject was English. She liked spelling and arithmetic, too, but detested home economics. She doesn't remember having difficulty with any subject.

In the later years at the small boarding school, Rose's friends were mostly girls in her own class. This was a close-knit group. One year they caused some disturbances for the school. Their escapades took the form of running off from the school without permission and taking night hikes to parts of the reservation, or crawling through manholes to "explore" endless tunnels under the sidewalks only to come out filthy at some end of the campus. This was fun and they felt brave and daring. A young teacher eventually took the "gang" and formed a Campfire group.

At graduation from the ninth grade, Rose was chosen to give the valedictory. She did not understand the meaning of graduation;

neither did it occur to her that being a valedictorian was an honor. That same week the class was baptized at the church. This had no real meaning, either. To her there was no distinction between these happenings and the many "have-to's" of the school. It was in high school that Rose finally realized the significance of these things.

Rose had a boy friend the last year at the school. He was older and bigger than most of the boys at the school and had been to a large off-reservation boarding school. This gave him much prestige. Dating was forbidden to students, and girls seen with boys had to stay indoors for a prescribed length of time. Boys and girls got around this by writing notes to each other or sitting together in the dining hall. One summer day Bill came to the Begay home and announced that he had come to see Rose. Rose's mother asked who the boy was, and Rose said that he was one of the boys in her class and a friend of hers. She thought she would die of shame because such things just weren't done in Navajo society without some definite intentions on the part of the parties involved. At school it wouldn't have mattered but at home it was a serious thing. However, her mother didn't make an issue of it other than to ask if Rose was interested in him. Bill came many times after that. He would help haul wood or water or help with the farm. He seemed to enjoy being there. He was an orphan and lived with an uncle who showed little concern about what he did or where he went. Looking back now, Rose is amazed at the flexibility of her parents, particularly in view of their own strict upbringing. She recalls many times when they made remarkable departures from native tradition and practices to keep harmony in the family.

Rose's grandmother had been sick frequently the whole year before. At the end of this summer she died. She had been unconscious for many days before her death. Rose would go in and look at her for a long time. One day she went in again and her grandmother was breathing strangely and at long intervals. Rose stood staring at her until she heard her mother say, "Go out!" She ran out then. She was frightened. A short time later there was loud weeping and her mother and aunt were taking everything out of the temporary shelter where they had been staying with the grandmother since she became critically ill. Hosteen left on horseback to see about a casket at the school. Rose sat where her mother had put the household furnishings, waiting while her mother and aunt were inside preparing the body for burial. They could not eat until the body had been taken away and the temporary shelter burned. But Rose was not hungry for many days. After they moved to a different location, Rose used to take the sheep out every morning before anyone else did. She did not feel like talking to anyone and in this way there wouldn't be anyone around to talk to. Also, she could go up on the hill from where she had a good view of the old place. It seemed to her that any day she would see her grandmother walking around over there. When grandmother was very sick, Rose heard her tell Nizhoni that she would not want any of them to be afraid to go near her grave. She said she had never hurt them in her life and would not do so after she was separated from them. She would want them to visit her without fear. She was buried at the school cemetery where Rose visited her grave several times. Rose knew that her mother would understand, but she wasn't sure what her father's reaction would be, so she never told them of these visits.

For high school, Rose was sent to an off-reservation Boarding School. There were hundreds of students there from many tribes. She was just one of many. She had not wanted to attend this school. The principal of her old school had tried to get her into a school in Lawrence, Kansas, but the school was filled to capacity. Another school in California had been filled for months. She had looked forward to either of these schools. As a third alternative, she had chosen a school in Phoenix, Arizona, but since her old "gang" were going there, the principal thought it unwise to send her along also. Therefore, he discouraged her going as he thought they probably wouldn't stay in school long without someone to show definite interest in them, and he was afraid that Rose would be influenced by whatever they did. She was sent elsewhere. After some weeks of resentment, she settled down to school routine. She encountered no academic difficulty throughout high school. Everything was relatively simple, and she got good grades. In her entire high school life, she felt no compulsion to excel, no real sense of competition. She took courses as they came. If she disliked a course, she dropped it if she could. There was no pressure to study, and courses being quite easy, there was no real motivation. She met requirements and forgot about them. This was not like the other school where she always had a positive and lively attitude about school and where each course meant a challenge. This seemed more like repetition.

During the first year of high school, Rose's oldest sister with whom she had lived many summers died and left four small children. In Navajo tradition, the oldest eligible girl would be in line to replace her sister as wife of the man who had been her brother-in-law. To no one's surprise, the man presented himself that summer and asked that the family provide him a wife. Rose was just short of 14 years of age. He said he wanted the older girl, meaning her. Rose's uncle was all for the marriage. Her father said he'd never force Rose to marry against her will; she wouldn't know how to raise the children, anyway. Her mother said she was too young. Besides, she said, Rose was a "school girl." This expression, in Navajo, carried with it a connotation of ignorance of, and inability to meet, demands of adult life; in a more negative sense, it implied lack of dependability and mature judgment. If the man wanted to wait two years until Rose was sixteen, her mother would not object, provided the girl was willing. Rose, knowing that her uncle had much influence in the family, told her mother that she wasn't marrying anybody and if anyone tried to pressure her, she'd run away to school and not return. The idea of the marriage was abandoned.

In summer during the high school year, Rose worked in town and made only brief visits home at the beginning and the end of the summer. High school was uneventful and she graduated when she was sixteen. There was no one at school to take any real interest in her future. When she left high school, she had only vague ideas about going to college.

The summer after graduation she got a domestic job. She also got to know the man who was at that time principal at the little boarding school where she had gone as a child. He asked if she had ever considered going to college. Through him she learned that she could go if she could get a government loan. She applied for a loan with the idea of studying to become a teacher. But she learned that, because she was a minor, her parents would have to bear responsibility for the loan. She recorded her birthdate as two years earlier, hoping that this would change the picture, but it didn't. So for the time being she abandoned the idea of a loan and continued as a domestic employee for one and one-half years and tried to save enough money to begin college. At the end of this time her father said that it was all right for her to go to college on a loan, and he would make himself liable for it. He had no fears about her success. So at the end of the year and one-half, she got the loan and enrolled in college. Fortunately, she used only eleven dollars of the loan and had no difficulty in repaying it later. She worked for room and board, plus a few dollars a week for incidentals, in the same home where she had been working previously. By this time she was engaged to a young Navajo.

About the middle of the first year in college, a mobile x-ray unit toured the schools of the city. Rose had herself x-rayed and was soon informed that she had tuberculosis. She knew very little about the disease other than that it was communicable to other people. The doctor pointed to a spot on the film and said that was where the trouble was. The spot seemed so small and insignificant that she wondered why there was such a fuss about it. It would probably heal up in no time at all. The longer the doctor talked and urged that she go to a sanatorium, the more dangerous it seemed. By the time she left the doctor, Rose knew her world had ended; all of her hopes and dreams were shattered. She said she would go home first and let her parents know where she was going. The doctor said, "If you go to the hospital right away, you should not have to stay more than eight or nine months; if you wait, in eight or nine months you may be dead." The shock of learning that she had tuberculosis had so stunned her that the idea that she might die didn't register in her mind. Eight months was an eternity!

Rose went home, and then to a hospital from where she was taken to a sanatorium. This wasn't the sanatorium she had anticipated going to, and she didn't like the place. She thought that if she was to be in a sanatorium, it might as well be a place that she liked. She stayed a few weeks and then left to go to a sanatorium of her choice. She spent more than two years there, with numerous ups and downs. Finally, in a very discouraged state of mind, she left without being discharged. Since she didn't feel at all sick, she found herself a job as a missionary's interpreter. Before three months had passed, she was back in another sanatorium in a neighboring state. The missionary had, after much difficulty, succeeded in getting her to go in for a checkup. At this sanatorium the months began to stretch into years. She was given every new medicine that became available, but her condition would not stabilize, much less improve. Often there were months without a sign of progress or change and at times she was very discouraged. Why must so much happen to her? Should she leave the sanatorium and get what enjoyment she could out of life? Even the danger of infecting other people made no impression. She knew how to take care of herself and to protect others as much as was possible. Besides, let others look out for themselves; she had enough problems of her own without worrying about them. Her life was over anyway, and she was barely past twenty! If she was going to die, she might as well live a little while she could. Better to have lived and then die than not to have lived at all and die anyway. What form this "living" was to take didn't occur to her. But there were her parents to consider. They were worried enough already, and her mother sent letters often to say, "Please stay until the doctor says you may go. We are all right. We do not worry when you are under a doctor's care." Rose made the decision: She must stay and try harder to get well.

Despite the advanced stage of her disease, Rose rarely felt ill. She was as active as she was permitted to be, and often more than was permitted. After two years she became contented and began to participate in everything provided for the patients: recreation, occupational therapy, church services, and other activities. She became good at handcrafts. At times she served as interpreter between doctors and Navajo patients, for she spoke both English and Navajo well. She discovered that the Christianity that was so meaningless and burdensome in her childhood was coming back to her. It suddenly took on meaning in her life now that she felt a need for it. She took pleasure in translating the minister's sermons into her native language for patients who didn't understand English. She got so well adjusted to sanatorium life that she seldom gave thought to the world outside other than her own family. Her father died one summer and she couldn't get permission to go home either before or after his death. This seemed very cruel of God and man. But, on the whole, she was contented.

Four years after her admission to this sanatorium she married a young Navajo man. The day began and ended with Tom.

These two years were easily the happiest of her life. Six years after entering this sanatorium, she was finally permitted to go home for a visit. Her sisters, who were children when last she had seen them, were all married now.

One day Tom complained of a severe headache and other discomforts, as he had done several times before. A doctor diagnosed a cardiac condition. In two days Tom was in a coma and in another two and a half days, he died. The shock of seeing big, husky, healthy-looking Tom lying so still was almost too much for her to take. Life seemed to crash about her. For two years her life had been full and she had become oblivious to everything and everyone else. Now she could hardly bear the loneliness. At night she would go to bed hoping somehow God, in His mercy, would decide to take her life. Awakening in the morning was a disappointment. She was to have been discharged this year, but now her health declined so that she had to stay three years more.

Gradually, within those three years she managed to regain her perspective. She became convinced that there must be some purpose to her life. Believing that there is no disorder in God's planning, that He saw the end from the beginning, she began to accept the belief that there must be more to life for her than mere existence in a sanatorium. She pondered various possibilities. She and Tom had had plans, but these she put out of her mind as too painful. She tried helping other patients with their lessons, taught them what she knew of handicraft, went into a small "business" with some of her own products, interpreted for the missionaries that ministered to the patients, and, with the help of a Bible teacher, taught a small Bible class of patients. The doctor tried to prepare her for life outside the sanatorium, for it had been a total of fourteen years since her college education had been interrupted by tuberculosis. She went outdoors for exercises daily, but walked only around the sanatorium. She didn't go near busy streets because she was afraid of traffic; she seemed to lose her sense of balance and direction when she got into traffic and crowds. Everything and everybody moved terribly fast. She'd come in exhausted from just seeing this mad pace. Everything was different from what she remembered. She said to the doctor, "I wonder if this is how Rip Van Winkle felt after he slept twenty years."

There had been many changes. A major war had been fought. Her generation had grown up and was nurturing a succeeding generation. Her family had been broken up to form other families. She would have to find new friends altogether. She'd have to live alone and dependently while people her age were independent. She didn't want to live at home, first because she didn't know how to live out there, and secondly, because her father was gone and her sisters were all married. Life out there would never be as she remembered it. The doctor said that since she would always need to live within certain limitations, she should consider something that was not too physically demanding. Had she ever considered going back to school? "School at my age?" she questioned. But she began to wonder if such a thing was possible. She struggled and struggled with the pros and cons of the idea. Counselors from Vocational Rehabilitation and the University testing services were contacted for her. Her aptitude tests indicated that she showed the qualifications of "the average college freshman," and the University's testing bureau expressed surprise to find her a "fairly well-adjusted" individual in spite of her long hospitalization. Still, she hesitated. She reasoned that these were young people at the University. They were recently out of high school. They had well-formed study habits. What chance would she have, after fourteen years of "hibernation" with seldom a book to read and little opportunity to speak English, in competition with students of this caliber? In the sanatorium most patients were illiterate, and she had had to talk mostly in Navajo. Furthermore, she had lapsed into thinking in Navajo, rather than in English. She would never be able to keep up with the youths at the University. The doctor and the counselor encouraged her to enroll for just one semester. If she didn't think she wanted to continue after that, she didn't need to. But she could at least give it a try. Nothing would be lost, and she would gain experience and regain much of her strength by the end of the semester. She could go several hours a day from the sanatorium. She decided to try for one semester. She thought, "Well, here's where I show them that they're wrong." She submerged her faint hope of success, not daring to bring it to the surface of consciousness for fear of disappointment.

Under the Vocational Rehabilitation program, Rose was enrolled at the University for the second semester. Her mind seemed atrophied from inactivity and paralyzed with fear and uncertainty. It seemed to her that she was literally picking cobwebs off her brain. On the campus, she was timid, actually afraid of people. She spoke only when it was required. She would lose her voice and break out in perspiration if anyone spoke to her. Everyday she came back to the sanatorium exhausted, and with a throbbing headache. Her mind failed to grasp anything she read. She felt the college textbooks were beyond her capacity to handle. Only her English course was understandable. Although she had plenty of time to study, her mind refused to cooperate because it wouldn't grasp or retain anything. She wondered if she had been unwise to enroll at all. Her two professors, upon learning about her plight, made special efforts to help her personally. With their help she got through this second semester. Toward the end of the semester, she realized that things were becoming easier, even enjoyable. Socially she was still a misfit, but she wasn't too concerned about that as long as she had the security of the sanatorium to come back to.

Before the opportunity for college arose, Rose had often thought of working with missionaries or some service group on the Navajo reservation. She had liked helping the missionaries minister to individual patients. Translating from one language to another was a challenge she had enjoyed meeting. She does not recall ever having any ambition to work anywhere else but among the Navajos. She had wanted to be a missionary, but being able to serve in other ways also would be even better. She calculated that she would have over twenty years of productive service ahead of her. This wasn't long. She wasn't deceiving herself about being a humanitarian, for she wasn't, and she wouldn't have time for that anyway. She had no dream of serving humanity at large. The Indian people were the only people she had really known and she loved being with them and helping them. She could spend her twenty years working among them. She knew that nothing would ever be the same for the Navajo. With rapidly changing conditions, old ways were no longer functional for them. Countless numbers were encountering difficulties of transition and assimilation. She was seeing that happen right here in the sanatorium.

Was there a role for her that but few others could perform? She had interpreted the white man's tongue to the Navajo -- could she now interpret his culture as well? Could she stand between the "old" and the "new," and help ease the pains and stresses of transition? If so, this would be her life work. So, her decision made, she structured her college work in that direction. She chose, carefully, all her courses in accordance with this plan.

Rose more or less "shifted for herself" through the four years of college. She asked little help because she still had difficulty phrasing questions that would bring the desired assistance. All through school she was just the average student. She met at least minimum requirements. She took very little part in school activities, partly because of restrictions on physical activities and partly because she did not feel her interests were quite compatible with those of people fifteen to twenty years her junior.

FOOTNOTE

[1] An autobiography by Rose Begay, April 21, 1959.

APPENDIX B

A Spanish Culture in Transition[1]

This is an attempt to describe my family as an example of the New Mexico Spanish American culture in the process of transition towards the Anglo values in our society. I shall begin by conveying, in a general way, the philosophy which guides the traditional rural Spanish culture and compare it to that of the Anglo culture. I shall then give a history of my family and shall try to show the changes in our cultural values that come about with our inter-action with the Anglo culture. This will be followed by a description of our family today and the status it holds in the process of acculturation.

To appreciate a changing culture, one must be aware of the traditional values that were once firmly accepted but which are now being forsaken for those of the host culture, in this case, the Anglo culture. My family seems to be at the end of a cultural transition; that is, we adhere more to the values of the Anglo culture than to the traditional Spanish culture. But even so, my family still has characteristics which stem from the traditional culture. What are the old Spanish values that we are losing to the Anglo culture? What are the new Anglo values we are adopting in place of the old Spanish values? To answer these questions I shall attempt to give a general description of the Spanish culture and then compare it with the Anglo culture.

I. A COMPARISON OF SPANISH AND ANGLO VALUES

A. C. Campa believes that every society has a philosophy to which it adheres.[2] He believes that both the Anglos and the Spanish Americans have a philosophy which guides their way of living. He gives an accurate comparison of both cultures by saying that "both the Anglos and the Mexicanos are romantic, except that American romanticism is based on the future and Spanish romanticism is nourished in the past."[3,4] In other words Campa feels that the Spanish culture is "past" oriented whereas the Anglo is future oriented. Campa states that American children are taught that the present is simply a preparation for the future, "that the past is past and gone and that one must look into the future for a vision."[5]

430

Campa reveals such Anglo expressions as: "Don't cry over spilt milk," "Hitch your wagon to a star," and, "Save for a rainy day," as sayings of a future oriented Anglo culture. In the Anglo culture, therefore, the individual lives for the future; he holds to the belief that the present is just a preparation for the future.

In the Spanish culture the future is too remote for practicability. The future to the traditional Spanish American is just an idea; an unreality. The present is the reality. The emphasis is on the present because the present constitutes the reality. As a result, planning for the future by the Spanish American is superfluous because "they meet their needs when they meet it and not before."[6] Also, the Spanish American seems to be fatalistic in accepting and complying to the conditions of the status quo. If he finds himself in poverty and living in the slums, he tends to accept it as "God's will," or he patiently hopes that God will change the situation: "a ver que Dios nos. . ." -- let us see what God will bring. On the other hand he might not like the conditions under which he lives but again he accepts the status quo because, "no hay mal que por bien no venga. . ." -- from bad there will inevitably be good. Dorothy Pillsbury sums up this philosophy by saying:

> "Time to the Spanish American is an endless panorama unwinding on slowly turning spindles. It has neither beginning nor end. . . The future is in the hands of his saints. For that reason his emphasis is on hoy mismo. . . this very day."[7]

With this philosophy I will attempt to convey the values to which the Spanish American adheres and how they apply within my extended family. In doing so I will attempt to show the differences in cultural values and goal-orientation between the Anglo and the Spanish American.

The traditional rural Spanish American in New Mexico knew little of the Anglo middle-class values. He had no tradition of democracy, competition or of achievement and success. These are values he will have to acquire as his interaction with the Anglo culture becomes more frequent and intense. In this interaction he will, generally speaking, forsake his traditional values which represent the weaker culture, to those of the Anglo, the dominant culture.

Within this time element of living for the present, the rural Spanish American had values that were consistent with his philosophy of living for hoy mismo. The major difference in values between the Anglo and the traditional Spanish American, then, is in time orientation. The values to which the Anglo ascribes will apply to his future-oriented philosophy; and the values to which the Spanish American ascribes will be consistent to his present-oriented philosophy. Parsons conveys some of the major differences between the goals of the Anglo and the traditional Spanish American. Among these differences are:

> The Anglo tends to give status and prestige to achievement and success. The Spanish American tends to give prestige and status on ascription, that is, not for what an individual does, but for what an individual is, especially family lineage. 8

The Anglo, in this outlook, envisions future achievement and success through his own individual efforts. A financially poor Anglo could, through hard work and diligence, change his standard of living and thus increase his importance within the Anglo society. This is not so for the traditional Spanish American. He believed that the individual is born with a certain degree of status and prestige, and he believed that an individual's importance came by birth and not through individual efforts. This whole concept of status and prestige is difficult to understand for my paternal grandparents. In the Spanish rural communities it is hard to define status and prestige because there were no members of a "nobility" as would be the case in the middle ages. 9 Although the Spanish American had feudal ideas, they did not apply economically. As far as my paternal grandparents were concerned, they seemed to find little that was outstanding in order to ascribe prestige and status to any one of their peers when they lived in the rural community. "Todos eran lo mismo. . ." -- "Everybody was the same," they would say. They felt as successful as anyone else in the community. To them no one was less or more successful. Everybody was basically equal in terms of economics because all the people lived on a bare subsistence level in their community. A successful individual, according to my paternal grandparents, was a happy individual. A happy individual was one who devoutly practiced the Catholic faith. According to my grandparents, the faith was a way of life, in which they patterned their living habits to the will of God. A certain degree of status then, was with one at birth because he was a "Child of God." "You can never be more important than what you are at birth." However, one could lose this happiness by not adhering to the precepts of the church. My grandparents also felt that the amount of wealth a person might have would not enhance his importance unless he was a Catholic who devoutly obeyed the laws of the Church.

On the other hand, there has always been great prestige in family lineage. There is a strong loyalty to members of the extended family. For instance, my family trades at a particular grocery store because a cousin of ours owns it and not because bargains are offered at the store. We feel it a duty to patronize him because he is a member of the family. On the other hand, in reciprocation, he manages to add a few pounds of potatoes, or meat to the purchase, and often graciously gives the children some ice cream or candy.

> "The Anglo is universalistic in perspective; the Spanish American is particularistic."[10]

The Anglo, in his universalistic approach, saves money for broad possibilities in the future. In this perspective, the saving of money idealistically affects his whole future. To the Anglo, money provides education, health, a new home, a better living environment, holiday trips, a liquidation of expenses, and many times there is the belief that money will bring social and emotional benefits. Money is an Anglo panacea, a means by which the Anglo gains social recognition and success.

The Spanish American in his particularistic approach looks only to the immediate effects of money. Because of his "present" orientation, saving money for the possibilities of better living conditions becomes futile. The traditional Spanish American would feel that if one does not have money and his living conditions are not too comfortable, these are situations he must accept as being the will of God. Living for the present as he does, the future becomes too remote and impracticable for him to accept. The future benefits which the Anglo believes money can bring, when saved in large quantity, becomes too far-reaching for realization. My paternal grandparents were caught in this situation. In their interaction with the Anglo culture, they have seen the need of saving money and the possibility of change in their living conditions, but how can they save, they wonder, or even plan for the future, when they are caught living on a bare subsistence level? As a result, they look to money for more immediate effects: the purchasing of food, clothing, and a 24" console TV set.

> The Anglo is affectively neutral, that is to say that the role of the individual is looked upon first as a professional one. . . . The Spanish American tends to be affective in that he looks at himself as a friend, a father, a relative or the like while at the same time looks at the individual in the professional capacity that the role demands.[11]

This is a value which is highly interrelated with the other values just mentioned. This is closely related to the value of prestige in family lineage. In voting, for instance, the traditional Spanish American would choose, in this order; a relative, a friend, a Spanish American, and last, the unknown Anglo. My older relatives (55 years of age and above) vote in terms of their own needs, or possibly for the needs of the candidate, but never in terms of a broader perspective, such as the community, the city, or the state. Party affiliation has nothing to do with determining their vote. Senator Chavez, for instance, is certain to get their vote because he used to be a childhood neighbor and, secondly, because he is Spanish American. In most cases, other reasons become incidental.

Ulibarri gives other differences between the Anglo culture and the Spanish American culture.[12] There is, for instance, a language difference which presents a barrier. Personality frustrations are concomitant with a language barrier. Feelings of inferiority and shyness are aroused when the English language is spoken by a Spanish American person. There is a feeling of complete dependence on others for translation when a traditional Spanish American person has to meet an Anglo. Such situations might occur when a doctor or lawyer would need to be consulted. On such occasions, for instance, my paternal grandparents use their children as interpreters. At other times, meeting Anglo friends becomes a dreaded social situation for them because of the language barrier. For instance, if my grandparents were visiting in my home when Anglo friends arrived, they would prefer that my parents let them dash off into the bedroom rather than be introduced. This social escape, I feel, is just as well because not only is there no communication of ideas or formation of friendship, but even worse, the cordialities by both parties seem to be superficialities, which convey an interest that is not there.

Ulibarri identifies other values to which the Spanish American adheres. These other values are in relation to his attitude toward change, to his attitude toward acceptance and resignation, and to his attitude toward dependence and independence. That values are inter-related in a culture is suggested. The Spanish American's attitude toward change can be related to his religious belief in accepting the status quo. His attitude toward dependence and independence can be related to the mutual responsibilities the individual has as a friend, brother or Spanish American. One can see however, that the Spanish American individual and his values are guided by his "present" oriented philosophy and by the precepts of the Catholic Church to which he adheres, and which constitutes a happiness. From his basic philosophy, one can determine the opposition to the future-oriented Anglo whose goal is the attainment of happiness through material wealth.

II. MY PATERNAL FAMILY HISTORY

My father was born fifty-four years ago in a small rural village named Jarales, a few miles south of Belen. The entire village was Spanish-speaking, so that during his childhood and youth his only contact with the English language occurred during his brief period of schooling. As a boy and as a young man he worked in "la juerta" (the garden), where he would take care of the chile and the corn, onions, tomatoes, cucumbers, and other vegetables. There were also a few farm animals, including pigs, cows, chickens, and horses. The diet of my father's family never consisted of only chile and beans contrary to the stereotype. Although his family was poor in terms of Anglo standards, it still had a well-balanced diet, with plenty of meat, vegetables, and fruit.

When my father reached the age of twenty, he married my mother who was then sixteen. My mother had been a resident in Jarales, but moved to Albuquerque a few years before her marriage. Because of this, my father made many frequent visits to the city to see her during their courtship.

After his marriage, my father moved to Albuquerque and began married life in the Albuquerque Spanish slum district called Barelas. Soon after, my father's parents moved from Jarales and they, too, set up housekeeping in the Barelas district. This movement of both families took place during the early part of the depression of the 1930's, and was made for economic reasons. [13]

III. MY MATERNAL FAMILY HISTORY

My maternal grandfather, who was orphaned at an early age, spent his childhood living with different relatives for short periods of time. At times he lived with relatives in Jarales, and at other times with relatives in Albuquerque. Anxious for self-employment and economic independence, he broke away from his extended family ties and, through apprenticeship, learned the trade of welding. While working in Albuquerque, he lived in the Spanish slum area of Barelas, which he says he did not enjoy. Through experiences with the Anglo environment, he felt that he, too, should enjoy a standard of living comparable to that of Anglos. However, when he married, he moved back to Jarales where he became an unsuccessful farmer. Remaining there only a few years, he returned to Albuquerque, bringing his family with him. He was re-hired at the same place where he had acquired his apprenticeship and where he has worked for over forty years. When he brought his family to Albuquerque, however, he had definite plans about where he was going to live. One thing he decided upon was that his family was not going to be brought up in the slum area of Albuquerque. My maternal grandfather saw the need for a new and liveable environment in terms of Anglo middle-class standards. The Barelas slum district did not appeal to him. Having lived in the urban slums of Albuquerque, he wanted to provide a better environment where conditions would be more conducive for his children to "get ahead."

IV. MATERNAL AND PATERNAL COMPARISON OF URBAN ADJUSTMENT

A. <u>The Paternal Grandparents' Adjustment</u>. My father's family has had a very difficult time adjusting to the Anglo middle-class culture. The family has always lived in the Barelas slum district since it moved from Jarales many years ago. Grandfather, for instance, has never been able to acquire a trade to maintain Anglo-middle-class standards. Economically, then, his family has always lived below such standards. This fact limits their living possibilities to the slum area in which they presently live. In this environment, the family is surrounded by neighbors who are Spanish American and who have comparable rural backgrounds and comparable living standards. Socially, then, my paternal grandparents are limited to the Spanish American lower-class. They have no personal social connections with the Anglo; all their social relationships are centered around the immediate family or other Spanish people living in the same area.

The field of education seems to have been unrewarding. For instance, none of my paternal grandparents' children has a high school education; none of the children has a trade, and all are, therefore, classified as unskilled labor. As a result, the children, with little useful education, have a difficult time succeeding in the urban Anglo culture. Such things as a limited education and a strong language barrier have made them feel very inadequate because, with these limitations, the Anglo middle-class standards are very hard to obtain.

B. The Maternal Grandparents' Adjustment. When my mother's father moved to Albuquerque and brought his family with him, he wanted to provide a better environment where conditions would be more conducive for his children. Because he had a trade and a steady income, he was able to purchase materials to have a home built in a middle-class urban community which happened to be predominantly Anglo. His children were, then, brought up in a Anglo middle-class environment.

What are some of the things that make a person "Anglo"? As a child, I was aware of differences between my maternal and paternal grandparents. My maternal grandfather, for instance, was the first of my relatives to plant grass in the front yard; he was the first to acquire a water hose, a rake and other garden tools which my paternal grandparents did not possess, for such tools are not needed in a rural or urban slum area. These things, however, do not necessarily reveal Anglo acculturation, but they do represent middle-class possessions in an urban community.

Another great difference was the variety of food available to the maternal grandparents. White, whole wheat, and French breads were something new in foods. My paternal grandparents preferred making their own bread in an oven in the backyard, or baking their own tortillas. Asparagus, artichokes, celery, salads, and salad dressing, were used by maternal grandparents.

Interest in the education of their children was, for my maternal grandparents, a blind faith. Grandfather's interest was grounded on the sincere belief that an educated man is a successful man, that education was concomitant to success. Although the interest in education for his children was intense, there was little participation in school affairs or in the guidance of the children's activities in school. The reason for this is that there was complete trust in the teacher and the things she would be doing for the child. What the teacher did was considered right and good. The teacher could never be wrong. She was considered all-powerful and all-knowing when it came to matters concerning the classroom. If there was trouble, grandfather firmly believed it stemmed from the child. For this reason the teacher had every right to spank his children.

The interest in education was not very strong in my paternal grandparents. Educationally, there was little motivation by the paternal grandparents for their children to attend school. The future benefits of education were too remote; the children were needed at home to help with the present-day chores. Also, Anglo education seemed superfluous since the children had little practical use for it in the home. In the first place, my paternal grandparents could not understand the English language, so their children had little occasion to use it at home. In the second place, they could not help, guide nor even encourage them to go to school since they saw little need for it themselves. The children were expected to speak the Spanish language at home because their parents did not understand English. Within this environment, my father's family had little opportunity to attain middle-class values.

Education for my maternal grandparents, however, had more favorable results. The children were encouraged to go to school; they were encouraged to make good grades and to obey the teacher. My maternal grandfather encouraged his children to speak English. The children, on the other hand, were forced to speak English because most of their peers in school and in the neighborhood were Anglo. Of eight children, seven graduated from Albuquerque High School. The one who did not graduate was my mother who married before she finished junior high school. She was the oldest female child. Grandfather's oldest child, a son, holds a Master's degree in Economics from the University of New Mexico and a Doctor's degree from Cornell University. As evidence of middle-class Anglo success, this son is president of the National Labor Relations Board in Puerto Rico and Professor of Economics at Puerto Rico University. Another of the sons holds a degree in Engineering from the University of New Mexico, and one of the daughters holds a degree in Government and Sociology. Educationally, then, my maternal grandfather's family has been successful. Socially, they live within the Anglo culture. They all possess middle-class homes, and, their friends are both Anglo and Spanish American.

V. THE NUCLEAR FAMILY

The family into which I was born is a blend of both my mother's family and my father's family. As previously mentioned, my parents set up housekeeping in the slum area of the Barelas district in Albuquerque after their marriage. My father, an unskilled laborer during the early 1930's, could not afford a better place to live. Their living conditions were typical of those in the district. There was an outside toilet; and in the house, there was a cold water tap and a single unshaded bulb which hung from a long cord fastened in the center of the high ceiling. The floor was covered with old worn out linoleum. The most important room in the house was the kitchen with a wood-burning stove; this room was our combined living and dining room. In winter it was noted as the coziest room, and during the day, it was the place where the aroma of cooking food would water our mouths. We had an icebox in the kitchen but it seldom had ice in it, only on pay days when we could afford it. Father would insist on buying ice on pay day, never worrying that the money could be better used for some other necessity. When the icebox was not in use we would store our food in the back porch or on the window ledge, the coolest places in the house.

My mother gave birth to four children in four years. The children included two girls and one boy, and a younger boy who died at six months. We were all delivered at home by midwives. My father found intermittent employment as a laborer, but the income was not enough to support a family of five. As a result, my family depended on our relatives for assistance. Both the maternal and paternal grandparents helped as much as they could. They made or purchased clothes for the children. Many times, they would bring a box of groceries, including such staples as flour for tortillas, beans, cans of tomatoes, rice, onions, and, of course, chile, red or green. However, during the economic depression, their assistance dwindled down to almost nothing. When my father became unemployed, we lived with both maternal and paternal grandparents. We also received financial assistance from the welfare department which enabled us to move out again and live semi-independently. My father finally got a permanent job at the railroad where he became a skilled laborer. He has held this job for over twenty years.

When it was time to eat, we all waited for him to serve himself first. Then the food would be passed on to the children, with my mother usually serving herself last. We never said our prayers before or after meals. In fact, our prayers were never a family affair. The only time we prayed together was in church and that, too, was seldom. Father never insisted on prayers because he never was, after his marriage, a religious man.

Father is a practicing Catholic, but not a devout one. He does not necessarily question particular aspects of the faith, but he is dubious of the people who practice it with intense fervor. He sees many inconsistencies in people's ideal practices and behavior, not only among Anglos, but among Spanish Americans as well. As a result, he attends Sunday masses when he wishes and shows no worry nor concern that missing Sunday mass is a mortal sin and cause for "eternal damnation." As a result my family has never been religious. My father's brother, on the advice of my paternal grandparents, enrolled his children in a Catholic parochial school. My father refused to enroll his children in a parochial school for two reasons: (1) he could not afford the tuition and (2) he felt that the public schools, supported by his taxes, should also educate his children. Besides, he felt that he could use the money for other, more "practical," purposes. To his children, my father was the ultimate leader. But as our education expanded, he began looking to us for consultation, advice and for "making out the tax form." He is still the leader, however, in terms of sentimental respect and financial security.

My father has had a difficult time adjusting to the Anglo culture. He has felt inadequate for many reasons. First, he had a language barrier which hindered his chances for getting a job. With his rural Spanish background, he was not prepared for the competitive society in which he was caught. He did not see the need for developing his individual resources because, within his experience, there was always help within the extended family. Acquiring a job was most difficult because there was little use for rural experience in an urban environment. The language barrier caused frustration because when applying for a job, the Anglos seemed to him to be unsympathetic and totally unconcerned for him as a person. He began to feel that he was not hired merely because he was Spanish. He found many instances where the Anglo was hired in preference to a Spanish American. This could quite possibly be true because the Anglo did not present a language or experience barrier. Father's reaction has been that the Spanish American must work harder to accomplish the same goal which the Anglo is trying to achieve.

My father wanted his children to avoid the hardships he was experiencing. He realized that although education was an important part of success, money made success more tangible and brought success sooner. According to Anglo middle-class values, he might not be entirely wrong. The Anglo middle-class society is materialistically motivated. Success, he found, is measured in terms of wealth, other values being secondary.

Although my father has felt inadequate in terms of education, language, and Anglo social experiences, he has gained through the years some feelings of self-importance. He is not a wealthy man, but he is financially secure. He owns some property from which he receives rent; he has a steady income and no debts; he pays cash for all his purchases and lives comfortably. He enjoys the "respect" he gets when, for instance, he pays for a new car in cash. He enjoys the security his money seems to give him. These possessions compensate, it seems for the inadequacies he feels within himself. He said one day: "I might not be as educated as you are, but it was my money that educated you." He is right. He has a right to feel proud in the respect that he exemplifies the Anglo ideal of working hard and saving.

My father's inadequacies in the Anglo culture motivated him to pressure his children into avoiding those things which he felt had made him a failure. First of all, his living with my mother's family, showed him that our social and living environment was poor. Saving money at this point made social mobility possible. As soon as he was financially able, he built a home in a middle-class environment, the one in which I live today. It was a different home from the one we had previously known. Although our home was made of adobe, it had an inside toilet, hot water, and other livable rooms besides the kitchen. This present home is only one block away from Barelas. We live in a transitional section of town, which is largely Spanish-populated. We children wish my father would move to a better section of town; he certainly can afford it. However, both my parents are happy in this transitional section. My father doesn't want to move because it would be too far from the railroad, in which he works. My mother feels the same way. Also, they do not feel the need for a more luxurious home.

Our house, it seems, grew and expanded as our experiences with the Anglo culture multiplied. Money was the motivating force. It enabled us to compete successfully with our middle-class peers. Before long, each of the children had a bedroom of his own. Our wooden kitchen furniture was replaced by the modern and colorful kitchen sets sold in furniture stores today. We gradually got rid of those things which identified us as lower-class Spanish Americans. The hanging of crosses and saints' pictures throughout the house, so prevalent in my paternal grandfather's house, is not a practice in our house. The use of coffee cans for plants to put in the windows is also discouraged. Two reasons for this change are, first, that we are not very religious, and secondly, that these practices do not fit the physical environment of our home. They look "out of place."

As our house changed toward Anglo standards, I, for one, did not feel uneasy about inviting my Anglo friends over for a visit. As a child, I was ashamed of those things which identified me as a "dirty Mexican." For instance, I never told my friends that for a long time our daily diet consisted of chile and beans and tortillas. I remember when I was in the third grade, my teacher invited our parents to come and see a program which was to be given by our room. My mother came, and much to my embarrassment, she brought with her my great-grandmother, whose complete lack of English and black shawl over her head and shoulders identified her as "Mexican." I was ashamed because it made me feel different. I felt that I was set apart from my peers, because she was there. Her presence made me feel different from my Anglo friends. My teacher was most gracious to her, but I felt even more uneasy when my great-grandmother answered her in Spanish.

Other changes within our family unit have taken place as a result of our social interaction with the Anglo culture. My mother's role, for instance, is not just one of being a housewife and a mother, but she, like father, is a financial contributor. She no longer prepares my father's lunch, nor does he even come home for lunch. Both are actively working and the living pace is much faster than it used to be. We rush to work; we rush home to eat; we rush to meet other commitments. Our whole pace of living has changed since my mother was employed. Even my father now helps with the cooking of food, the cleaning of the house and all those duties that were once considered her's.

There has been a great change in the use of the Spanish language. My parents frequently converse in Spanish; however, they use many English words to convey an Anglo idea. They never converse totally in one language; their conversation is now a mixture of English and Spanish. They speak to me in both languages, but they prefer that I respond in English because my Spanish "es muy quebrado," very broken. However, when speaking to my paternal grandparents, they consider it very rude if we should talk to them in English. Although I understand Spanish, it is very difficult for me to speak it. My parents address their grandchildren in English because the children do not understand Spanish. There is a wide gap between father's grandchildren and his parents. There is no exchange of ideas between them; there is a complete language barrier. They are strangers to one another in the family group. The attitude of the children toward their great-grandparents is ambivalent. They don't know if they should love them or not love them. All they say is "Hello" in English, and then dash off to play. My paternal grandparents try to fondle them but the children squirm away. The children are taught to love their great-grandmother, but how can they love someone when they do not even understand what she says? Besides, they always have to "be still" when great-grandmother is around.

VI. SUMMARY AND CONCLUSION

The process of acculturation is indeed slow. In my extended family, it has taken over fifty years. Not only is it time consuming, but it is also very difficult to change from one culture to another. My paternal grandparents will not change; they are too old to acquire and apply the new Anglo values. They feel that it is of little value at this point to start saving money and working hard. Because of their age, they are physically unable to work hard in order to have money to save. By being faithful to the Catholic Church and guiding their behavior by its rules, they are happy and feel confident that they will be ultimately successful because they are living "con favor en Dios," within God's favor.

My maternal grandparents, however, were helped tremendously by their urban experiences and by my grandfather's ability to acquire a trade. His trade provided the money to build a home of middle-class standards. He acquired Anglo values and because of the influence of the Anglo environment, he pressured his children to acquire and apply the values their Anglo peers were practicing.

My grandparents ventured into the stream of acculturation; my father was caught in it. As a result, my father developed feelings of inadequacy because the Spanish values and practices to which he adhered were characteristics which were not considered successful in an Anglo culture. Many experiences with the Anglo have been unfortunate and unrewarding so that today he feels that the Spanish American must work harder than the Anglo for the same things. However, he has a sense of security in that he has attained an Anglo goal: the accumulation of property. It was through his experiences, in this transitional stage, that our family has profited. He provided the means for his children's success; he was the motivating force and the dividing line between the Anglo and the Spanish culture within our family.

FOOTNOTES

[1] A Spanish Culture in Transition by Elias.

[2] A. C. Campa, "Manana is Today," The New Mexico Quarterly, Vol. 9 (Feb., 1939), 3-11.

[3] Ibid., p. 3.

[4] In using the term, "romantic," Campa was referring to the ideals of a culture as being "sentimental rather than rational." That is, one adheres to and obeys the ideals of a culture because one is a member of that culture, and to forsake or question any of those ideals endangers one's importance and prestige within the culture. A member of a culture is forced to be loyal to the ideals of that culture or suffer the consequences of possible social ostracism. Now, both the Anglo and the Spanish American are romantic in their outlook on their ideals. They are romantic in that both look to their cultural ideals as ideals rather than as specific behavioral practices. These ideals seem to be only guides and goals to their behavioral practices. As a result, there can be found many inconsistencies in the behavioral practices and the cultural ideals.

The difference in the "romantic" outlook between the Spanish and Anglo culture is in their time orientation. The Spaniard finds meaning to his cultural ideas in a present oriented philosophy that is "nourished in the past." The Anglo finds meaning to his cultural ideals in a future oriented philosophy. For instance, one of the romantic ideals held by the Anglo is the belief in the importance and dignity of every individual in its society; a belief in developing the individual to his fullest potential. This is a sentimental ideal, far from actual practice, because behavioral practices and attitudes in the Anglo culture prevent certain minority groups the opportunity to develop individual potential. Here, then, is a behavioral practice inconsistent with their romantic and sentimental ideal. This "development" has future emphasis: the present is a means of future ends.

The Spanish American did not see a need for "future development." The traditional rural Spanish American experienced little in social and financial mobility. If father was a farmer, the other generations would be farmers. There was no need for competition in "getting-ahead" since the future was already mapped out for future generations.

[5] Ibid., p. 4.

[6] Ibid., p. 8.

[7] Dorothy L. Pillsbury, "Adobe Grace," Common Ground, Vol. 5, Summer Edition (1945), pp. 87-91.

[8] Talcott Parsons, The Social System (Glencoe, Illinois: The Free Press, 1951), pp. 198-199.

[9] According to my maternal grandfather, a patron has two meanings: (1) an owner of a large ranch; a wealthy person, and (2) the owner of a store; a leader and boss of his laborers in a corporation. A political patron was a leader or spokesman for the community. In Jarales there was none. Any legal or political matter for the people in Jarales was usually handled in Belen. However, the community looked to the clergy as a source of personal advice and counsel because they were the more easily available and the more educated in the area.

[10] Parsons, Ibid.

[11] Ibid.

[12] Horacio Ulibarri, "The Effect of Cultural Difference in the Education of Spanish Americans," University of New Mexico Research Study, Albuquerque, September, 1958. (Mimeographed.)

[13] The crop yield was becoming increasingly unpredictable. There was little knowledge of soil conservation and, as a result, there was much erosion. Droughts were rather frequent and added to the uncertainty of a plentiful crop. They felt the need of a wage economy to help support the "juerta." When my paternal grandparents moved, grandfather found intermittent employment. In the meantime, there was added support from his small juerta in the backyard, a couple of pigs, many chickens and rabbits.

BIBLIOGRAPHY

Bright, Robert. The Life and Death of Little Jo. Garden City, New York: Doubleday, Doran and Company, Inc., 1944.

Davis, W. W. H. El Gringo, or New Mexico and Her People. Santa Fe: The Rydal Press, 1938.

Jaramillo, Cleofas M. Shadows of the Past. Santa Fe: The Seton Village Press, 1941.

Pillsbury, Dorothy L. "Adobe Grace," Common Ground, 5: 87-91, Summer, 1945.

Reid, J. T. It Happened in Taos. Albuquerque: The University of New Mexico Press, 1946.

Russell, Janet. "Fusing Two Cultures," New Mexico School Review, 28: 8-9, January, 1949.

Sanchez, George I. The Development of Higher Education in New Mexico. New York: Kings Crown Press, 1944.

Sanchez, George I. Forgotten People. Albuquerque: The University of New Mexico Press, 1940.

Saunders, Lyle. "The Spanish-Speaking Population of Texas," Inter-American Educational Occasional Papers V. Austin: The University of Texas Press, December, 1949.

Saunders, Lyle. Cultural Difference and Medical Care. New York: Russell Sage Foundation, 1954.

Ulibarri, Horacio. "The Effect of Cultural Difference in the Education of Spanish-American Children." Unpublished monograph, University of New Mexico, Albuquerque, Indian Research Study, September, 1958. (Mimeographed.)

APPENDIX C

Ways of Working With the Navajos Who Have Not Learned the White Man's Ways[1]

I. INTRODUCTION

Many people come to help the Indians on the Navajo Reservation. Some get along well and are able to help the people. Others become confused, frustrated, and disappointed. Some of these give up and quit. Others plug along by trial and error methods. Many of these people are well trained in their subject matter fields, and have much to offer the Navajo Indians, but something is missing. Something makes their work difficult. This something may be a lack of understanding of certain taboos in the ways and thinking of the people. Such may seem unimportant to the non-Navajo, but these can make a difference in the degree of success or failure achieved, and the happiness of all concerned.

Who are the people who come to work closely with the Navajo's? They are many. Some are land operation personnel, doctors, nurses, telephone operators, salesmen, teachers, traders, missionaries, home economists, social workers, construction workers, and numerous others.

From where do these people come? Some come from large population centers, such as New York, Chicago, and Los Angeles. Others come from small towns, and rural areas, some even from Hawaii. Some know much about the Navajos; others know little.

One by one as each appears, the Navajo feels that, before being accepted, each must be studied. It is like Mr. Paul Jones, Navajo Tribal Chairman, said in a welcoming speech for Mr. Glenn Landbloom, new Navajo Agency Superintendent:

We Navajos will look you over for a couple of years, and then we'll decide whether we are for you or against you.

Dr. Bertha P. Dutton, speaking at the Gallup Public Library, said:

Today, we realize that the Indian is here to stay. . . From the initial entrance of the white men into the New World, the

Indian people have been generous; through three or four centuries they have shared their knowledge and production with the ever-increasing numbers of non-Indians who have encroached more and more upon the native holdings. . . for agriculture and timber lands, for ores and mineral wealth, for water and for game. . . physically, spiritually, and technologically. The Indians have tried to make themselves understood, and have tried to secure treatment as human beings. Were they not a great people, they would have given up long ago and would have ceased to maintain their cultural entity. But they have kept trying and are still trying -- perhaps more today than ever before.[2]

Perhaps this is the reason that Navajos take time to evaluate. One important thing for the person working with them is to realize that they do not like being pushed. No matter how eager one may be to hurry things along, too much pushing may slow down the progress. Projects should be throughly explained, and whenever possible, demonstrated. Then, if the people see that this will benefit them (and they want and need to be in on the planning), then they will be ready to support the project one hundred percent. This takes time, and often repetition, and patience, until everything is understood. Otherwise, a few may go through the motions, because they are told to do so, but there may be little of lasting value accomplished. If time is not given the people, they may be suspicious that something is being sprung on them. Then they will drag their feet all the more. Sometimes, the non-Navajo, in his eager desire to carry out a worthwhile project, isn't aware that he is spinning his own wheels, but often, if he tries, he can learn to be sensitive to the reactions of the people.

This paper has been written because many people who come to work on the reservation do need help in understanding the Navajo people. The Navajo people referred to in this paper are the uneducated ones who do not understand the English language. While a few leaders of the Navajos are becoming acculturated to Anglo society, the great majority do not know or understand the ways of the white man.

Since I am a Navajo-Hopi, and have worked among my people for several years, I sincerely hope that these remarks will help newcomers to understand the uneducated Navajo better.

II. EXPRESSING DIFFERENCE OF OPINION

How can one tell if there is a reluctance to cooperate? Usually no one will come right out and say: "No, we don't believe in this, there is a better way." Instead you may hear Navajo words such as: "doo-ahalyani,"[3] or "diigis."[4] These express disapproval in rather a strong way. Severe ridicule and teasing, perhaps about something entirely different, also indicate that something is wrong. People may leave the room, or they may start paying attention to something else. Someone who is really interested and who perhaps understands the feelings of all concerned, may start to tell a story. Sometimes the story is a true one; often it is a made-up one. In the story, the person will try to show the non-Navajo what the people are thinking and feeling. He may do this for his own people as well. It sometimes takes careful interpreting to get the point. Once a person is aware of this indirect way of expressing an opinion, one can profit well by listening for the message. What should be done if there is discord? Always listen. Sometimes things can be talked out. Other times, it is best to drop the matter, think about it, study it, and then maybe it can be approached in a better way. Maybe it needs changing in only a small way. Often things can be worked out with time and understanding.

III. PROCESSES OF CULTURAL CHANGE WORK SLOWLY

It used to be that uneducated people could be leaders on the Tribal Council, which is the governing body of seventy-four people.[5] There still are some, but more and more stress is being placed on educated tribal delegates. The uneducated often say that the world is going by too fast for them; life is changing too rapidly. For this reason, they feel that having some uneducated leaders on the council will help to slow the others down, so that they can still catch up. They say that they prefer their old ways and slower life. They would like to keep these ways, and sometimes point to the white men's ulcers as proof of the value of their way of life. But, things are changing, not just here, but for people everywhere. We cannot stand still or wait. For this reason, the people need much patience, and understanding and help, to be able to maintain a life that has meaning for themselves.

Dutton, in the speech referred to earlier, stressed the many changes which are taking place in the lives of the Navajo people, including a new social pattern, in which many Indian men are becoming wage earners, while the important traditional role of the woman is decreasing. She says:

> When we see Indians behaving in a manner unbecoming to their dignity. . . let us remember that they are undergoing tremendous and very rapid changes, that old familiar props are being pulled from under them, and that they are often bewildered, insecure, and facing situations entirely new to their long evolved and time-tried ways.[6]

IV. DIFFICULTIES WITH THE ENGLISH LANGUAGE

Some people who come to work with the Navajos, those who speak only one language, often do not realize the tremendous handicap which exists in not being able to understand and to speak English fluently. One time a Navajo driver was asked to back a large truck. His foreman told him, "Back up a shade." The driver didn't understand the meaning of the expression "a shade." One can imagine how many understandings and hazards result from the language problem. One man argued intensely over the word "resign." He insisted that his daughter didn't "resign"; she "quit." He was probably confusing the word "fired" with "resign."

Sometimes misunderstandings come when a person doesn't understand the power of the English words he is using. He may have heard these words used, and not realize that these are not acceptable for all times, places, and people.[7] The person may be saying things which come out differently than is intended. This needs to be thoughtfully considered.

It is important to speak clearly, slowly, and with a vocabulary simple enough to make sure that the individual understands. This is true even when using an interpreter. Many a person has given a speech thinking that it is being communicated to the audience. The interpreter, finding the speech too difficult, politely says whatever he can, and often these piecemeal statements don't make sense, and even sound ridiculous. For this reason, a person who has something important to say and who really wants the people to understand, should take time to go over his speech with the one who is going to interpret for him. This should not be ten minutes before the meeting. Time is needed to arrange the ideas in such a way that the people will understand the message.[8] Experienced interpreters vouch for this. Sometimes it might be more economical, time-wise, for the interpreter to be given the speech. Discuss all of it with him thoroughly. Then, if only Navajo speaking people are present, and if they are a group who do not understand English well, have him present the speech in Navajo only. A little English adds up to a lot of Navajo, and people often are surprised at how much time it takes to interpret a few words of English.[9] The speaker, who doesn't realize how turned around the Navajo language is from the English language, may speak rapidly, using an impressive vocabulary, and never know that the speech, as given, was impossible to interpret on the spur of the moment. One must realize too that different cultures also have different ways of expressing the same things. The illustrations and examples should be within the experience of the people, so that they can understand.[10]

Another point to consider is that the people who have difficulty with a second language often fear to express themselves in that language. Also, if the Navajo speaks good English, he may avoid "showing off" before his own people, who may speak less well than he does. For these reasons, even English-speaking Navajos sometimes prefer to speak in their own language in which they feel at home. It is well that the non-Navajo understand this and does not himself become suspicious! Usually the people are neither

448

discussing him, nor do they intend to be rude. One should not expect every spoken word to be interpreted. Much of what is spoken is not that important!

V. DEROGATORY REMARKS ARE USUALLY UNDERSTOOD!

Derogatory remarks can often lead a person into trouble rather quickly. This is just as true for Navajos as for Anglos. The story is told of a young man trying to impress his officer in military school. He felt that he should lead in the conversation. Since he had nothing else to say, he said: "Who is that awful looking woman sitting across the hall?" The officer answered coldly: "That, sir, is my mother." Then the young man said quickly: "No, not that one. The real ugly one beside her." "The officer gave him another frozen stare. "That, sir," he said, "is my sister." The young man gulped, and said: "Boy, she sure can dance!"[11]

Almost everyone on the Navajo Reservation is somebody's mother, sister, father, brother, aunt, or uncle, either by clan ways, blood relation, or by marriage, even though they may live on another distant part of the reservation. In this way, the reservation is not as large as it seems, and derogatory remarks seem to travel with speed and can hurt someone, including yourself and your work. For here, as elsewhere, people have deep feelings for relatives and friends. Hurt feelings may not be forgotten for a long while, and unkind remarks, coming from a stranger, will not be understood.

VI. DON'T ASK PERSONAL QUESTIONS

The Indian people do not appreciate a stranger asking them questions. Sometimes they do not answer. (What is an interpreter to say then?) Often an answer may be given, but sometimes this is the answer which they think you want to hear, and is given only for the purpose of getting rid of you. An untrue answer may also be felt to be justified, if the question is one which should not have been asked. So, it is good to remember to try not to ask too many questions. This seems very difficult for many non-Indians. It seems to be one of their ways of showing interest in other people. This can be disastrous. Sometimes the person asking the question never realizes that his questions are making others angry. The questions may be in asking a man about his wife, or a mother about her children. "How many children do you have?" etc., etc., etc.! Such simple, well meaning questions may be thought of as being ones of obnoxious curiosity, which are none of your business. And, whereas the stranger may intend to be polite, his interest may not be taken kindly. There is resentment, especially in regard to inquiry about family relationships. The non-Indian seems so accustomed to figuring out who is who, who is so and so's brother, sister, aunt, uncle, cousin, etc., that he doesn't realize that the

Navajos don't do this. They will tell you, if and when they want to, when they know you that well. Until that time, one should be content to know that the person is a member of an extended family. That's all that matters to the Navajos.

The Navajo will tell about himself if and when he trusts and likes you as his friend. When he does this, he feels that he is confiding in you. If you pass along this information carelessly, he will feel that you have betrayed him, and that you cannot be trusted. This applies not only to his family relationships, but also to small daily happenings, which, to the non-Indian seems to be small talk, carrying little weight or importance. But let this get back to him, and you are really "doo ya shoda" (no good), someone who doesn't know any better. When asked how someone else feels about something, often the answer will be: "I don't know, you'll have to ask him." Let each speak for himself!

VII. BE A GOOD LISTENER

One value which the non-Navajo holds which is also valued in Navajo ways is that of being a good listener. For the person to take time to listen is of utmost importance. To be brushed off by a clock-watcher is an insult. Problem solving in old ways was often accomplished by talking it through. The older people still regard this as a valuable way of working through a problem. Often, one by one, each will give his views. This takes time, sometimes hours, but taking time to listen, having patience, is valued, appreciated, and held important.

VIII. USE OF MAYBE

The English word and concept "maybe" is a difficult one for the Navajo people to understand. "May we will do this or that. . . maybe we will go," is often not understood. For this reason, it is better not to make "maybe promises," but wait until the maybe becomes a reality. Otherwise you could be made to appear as one whose word cannot be relied upon. "He lied to us," might be said of you, not because you did, but because you didn't realize how difficult and foreign this concept and word are to the people.

IX. IS HE NEGATIVE?

The non-Navajo is sometimes disturbed by what he calls Navajo negativity. This feeling comes from words expressed in English like "But you shouldn't have," or "We should have done it this way," etc. One must learn that this is considered a form of evaluation. It is used to improve future performances. Only if the non-Navajo can realize the value the Navajo places upon this can he tolerate this constant habit of review. This is not intended to be critical in the same way that many other people look at things.

X. YOUR GOOD WORK WILL BE APPRECIATED

It is said that an Indian never forgets. Sometimes this seems true. One good thing about it is that this applies not only to mistakes (stock reduction misunderstandings, number one example), but it also happily applies to achievements of general good. People and activities are remembered for the good accomplished. (You may not feel appreciated while you are here, but the good you do will be spoken about after you have gone!)

XI. VISITING THE HOGAN

A word about entering a hogan. You'll hear "Hago," which means "come in." On entering, don't stand there. If there's a chair, don't wait until someone asks you to sit down; sit on it. If there's no chair, sit on a box; no box, sit on a sheep skin; no sheep skin, then squat on your legs.

Sometimes when going into a hogan, or when receiving visitors, it is best to skip the introduction of strangers. Introductions, so important in another culture, aren't understood by most of the old people. Perhaps some of this comes from the idea that overuse of a person's name is bad. (And if a person says his own name too much, they say his ears will dry up.) So, the rule seems to be to act friendly, and forget that so and so may or may not know someone else who is present. It doesn't seem to matter. The people will get acquainted and shake hands if they decide that they want to. Children are taught to shake hands, and often do this easily and confidently with their own people, and if not shy and afraid, with others too.

The people may live close to the land of the Morman handshake, but unless they are converts, theirs could hardly be called that. It's more of a passing of the hands, not a vigorous, exuberant pumping!

XII. DON'T FUSS OVER THE BABIES AND VERY YOUNG CHILDREN

About the small ones in the family, in some cultures, one makes over and plays with the babies and small children. It is different in Navajo ways. They do not like to have a stranger close to their babies. This is especially true when the baby still has the soft spot on his head. A stranger, by his attention (it is said) may witch the child, and the result will be that the child will stutter or be unable to talk all of his life. Some other cultures avoid what they believe to be early traumatic experiences for their young children. They say that these may have a harmful psychological effect on the person's life. So it is best to save your "itchie, gitchie, goo" baby talk for your own children. It is especially awkward for a non-Navajo man to be making over an Indian baby. This makes an uncomfortable feeling for all concerned, except perhaps for the man, who thinks he's doing the right thing!

XIII. WHAT ABOUT COMPLIMENTS?

Why does the Navajo appear to be embarrassed and ashamed when complimented? "That's a pretty skirt," "What lovely jewelry," may be all right for elsewhere, but uneducated people here don't understand such compliments. They feel that if it is pretty, they know about it. You need not tell them. That's why they may say, when told something is pretty: "Oh, yes, I know it," instead of "Thank you." If a well-meaning person says some imitation or cheap article is pretty, though he may be sincere, this may be considered an insult to the wearer. For to say, for example, that a poor string of turquoise is pretty would only be considered ridicule. Perhaps it is all that the person can afford, but he knows that it is not genuine. To make over it seems as though you are merely "rubbing it in," and teasing him.

XIV. SOME WISE SAYINGS

Speaking of the admiration of lovely things does not mean that one must always be dressed in his Sunday best, though there are occasions when this will make them proud of you. But the old folks have a saying which many of us remember being handed to us from our parents. The saying goes: "Silks and satins will put out the kitchen fire." (This probably came when we wanted to wear our best clothes at home.) So, the people recognize that there are different requirements for different occasions.

Another old saying is that two articles are of utmost importance. For material comfort, a person must have a good pair of shoes and a comfortable bed, for you are either in one or the other all of the time. Sturdy shoes can still be purchased at every trading post on the reservation, and on a cold night, a sheep skin "bed" is still about as soft and warm and comfortable as any man-made layers of nylon blankets.

XV. TEASING

Some say that the Navajos are cruel in their teasing. This is true to a certain extent. Teasing is used as a means of control. Other cultures may use equally cruel methods of control (paddling a child, threats, for example). The Navajos also say: "What will people say," or "People will laugh at you if," and the action of which they are speaking is understood to be unacceptable, and must be avoided (another method of control). Rules of conduct for the individual as well as the group are quickly learned and complied with so as to avoid hard teasing, and being talked about.[12]

XVI. NAVAJOS HOPE YOU LIKE THEIR ARTS AND CRAFTS

The Navajos appreciate seeing their own arts and crafts. Ruth Polacca, the writer's mother, herself a weaver, says: "To wear turquoise and silver, to have Navajo rugs in your home, makes the people feel that others appreciate the work of their hands. It somehow makes you feel closer to them."

Then, too, turquoise is worn for its religious value. It brings good fortune and blessings to the person who wears it and to the person who sees it being worn.

Even as the Navajos appreciate seeing others with their arts and crafts, so it goes with the language. Whereas a few may not want you to understand everything they say, most do appreciate people who care enough to learn a few words in their language. "Hello" -- "ya'ateeh," "pretty" -- "nizoni," "my friends" -- (when addressing a group) -- "kwa' asini," "goodby" -- "hagoonee," all are indications that you'd like to communicate.

To be able to address an old man with respect, by calling him "my grandfather," "shicheii," and an older woman as "my grandmother," "shimasani," brings light into the eyes and a warm feeling to the heart. It takes a little effort to learn a few words, but it pays off in big dividends to those who try. It is easy to see how the old folks, who may not speak a word of English, appreciate this. It makes them want to know you, and to want their children, who can speak your language, to know you.

Don't be surprised if you are given a Navajo name by the people. One well-liked agricultural expert was fondly called "Beegashii Likish." It means "spotted cow," and it had a good meaning and was associated with someone and something the people liked and appreciated!

XVII. BE NATURAL AND CONSERVATIVE IN YOUR DRESS

A little has been said about fine clothes and dressing for the occasion, but nothing has been said about acting or dressing in beatnik fashion. Both are taboo. If you want to act or dress this way, a Halloween party with your own people would be a better place than on the Navajo Reservation! It seems strange that some people wear and do things here that they would be afraid or ashamed of wearing or doing back where they come from. To fit in, to conform, not to stick out like a sore thumb, is considered important to the people. "What would people say" is again probably one of the controlling forces in social custom.

XVIII. WHITE MAN'S TIME ORIENTATION

If you say that you'll be at a certain place, at a certain time, every effort should be made to be there. (The Navajos do not set the same standard for themselves. This, they feel can be forgiven. After all it is you who are educated, not they, and it is your culture that lives by the clock, not theirs. It is said that in old ways if a man said he would arrive when the sun is high in the sky, it would probably be sunset time when he actually arrives. This has been called "Indian time." But, remember, you are expected to be on "bilaganna" (white man's) time. You will be respected for this.

Another thing along this line is the concept the Navajo has of not planning ahead. This is considered "bahazid," i.e., dangerous. To talk about something too far in advance (a few days is all right; a year is too long) just is not done, not outloud anyway. This statement does not apply, of course, to tribal leaders who are now planning well into the future in industry, business, land operation, and education. For this reason, it should be re-emphasized that this discussion is dealing with not the progressive, advanced people of the tribe, but with the uneducated who have not experienced much of the white man's activity in today's world.

XIX. SHARING IS BETTER THAN SAVING FOR THE FUTURE

In regard to savings in the bank, some would question what good the money could be doing anyone there, when it could be used to help someone. This brings us to the Navajo's idea of sharing. To be able to help members of one's clan and family when in need has always been held in esteem. Favors are not expected to be returned person for person, but there is the expectation that in the time of need, help will be provided. If you are good to others, people will remember you when you are in need.

How can one explain how the people feel about food? It is not thought of only in terms of money or even taste, but also in terms of kinship and friendship. To share food at mealtimes, even if it is only a bowl of stew or pinto beans, and a cup of coffee, this is friendship and acceptance. The same goes for accepting food offered. To refuse to share or to refuse to accept food is taboo spelled with a capital T. "Chineago" (eating together) at home, or in the community, or at a religious ceremonial, is a pleasure to be enjoyed.

XX. THE NAVAJO SENSE OF HUMOR

The writer's father, Howella Pollaca, Sr. (a Hopi Indian, married to a Navajo), learned to speak the language of the Navajo. He lived with his family on the Navajo Reservation, and had many dealings with them. Although he is now deceased, tales are still told of how he would be seen surrounded by a group of Navajos, laughing and telling them stories. He often said that in order for an outsider to get along with them, he needs a good sense of humor. He himself had a way of making everyone laugh.13 Navajos do appreciate lighthearted laughter and fun. A long face, to be too serious, and most of all to be sad is something uncomfortable. It can be "bahadzid" -- i.e., dangerous, or evil. (Laugh and we Navajos laugh with you, cry and you may witch us with your tears!)

So to be able to laugh with the people (even at yourself) is another way of bringing about a good feeling. Many Navajos who are poor in what they call "hard and soft goods" may be rich in their ability to share and enjoy life with other human beings.

When they can relax and laugh, they feel more free to share a part of their life with you. They will enjoy working with you and will want to learn from you. Story telling is an art they understand and in which they excel.14

XXI. NAVAJO RELIGIOUS CEREMONIES

On attending religious ceremonies, the curiosity of the non-Navajo regarding something so personal as religion is not easily understood. However, visitors are accepted at some ceremonies. But, before attending, it would be well to know what is expected. For example, when one visits a church, it is helpful to know if you must cover your head, if the communion service is for all, or for members only, whether or not you are expected to sit, stand, or kneel. The same thing goes for a Navajo ceremony. The collection plate may be passed at a church, but the Navajos do it another way. They help pay the medicine man with such things as a bag of flour, groceries, cloth, etc. (It is felt that the medicine man's service, to have value, must be paid for.) Other people would hesitate or question a doctor's qualifications were his services free. The same is true of the medicine man. He will have spent long hours getting the herbs and precious sands ready for the ceremony. He will have spent years learning by heart the sacred chants. It has cost him time and effort, so it is necessary for his services to be rewarded.15

It is well to know the kind of a ceremony to which you are invited. There is a ceremony when a young girl becomes a woman, to which you may be invited to participate. It is believed that an article brought to the girl (loaned) during the ceremony by a non-Navajo may bring special blessings. The person bringing the article brings with him his superior qualities of intelligence, wealth, health, etc. So, if you are asked to participate in this ceremony, you will know that you are well thought of. Someone will tell you what to do.

For those who would criticize the religion of the Navajo, I would like to make this observation. When an Anglo is severely disturbed in mind, costly consultations and treatments with a psychiatrist often take place. When the Navajo is out of harmony with himself, his world, and others, his family also become concerned. They seek the Navajo medicine man and the therapy is a religious sing. Both ways are costly, but the results, if successful, are the same: the restoration of peace of mind.

It is helpful if people can respect the things which others find sacred and helpful. No one likes to have his religion torn to shreds by outsiders. Today, public health doctors and Navajo medicine men work side by side to help their patients regain mental and physical health.

XXII. AT TIME OF DEATH

It is well for the non-Navajo to realize that many things about death and a dead person are considered "bahadzid" (dangerous).[16] There are many religious rules and customs which accompany such an occasion, even as there are in other cultures. A person working with one who has lost a member of his family may profit by understanding that this person may have certain obligations which will demand his attention for a few days at this time. Soon things will be back to normal.

XXIII. HOW DOES AN EXPERT PERFORM?

The Navajos expect those who are experts in their field, those who have come to help them, to be almost perfect. This includes among other things the keeping of your word. If you make a promise, keep that promise.

My mother, when a young girl, worked in the home of Dr. Albert Wigglesworth, a well-loved and remembered Anglo doctor at Fort Defiance. One thing told of him is that he was a man who kept his word to the people.

Other ways in which the Navajo expects those who come to work with them to be almost perfect are in personal appearance, the clothes you wear, the car you drive, the house you live in, in other words, in what you have. The Navajos feel that if a person is good and worthy, and not lazy, he will be blessed with material wealth. If you, who have come to help him, appear poor, you can imagine what his first impressions will be! An old pair of shoes, or a ragged piece of clothing, worn at a meeting, for example, can lower the image of yourself in his eyes rather quickly. He has been taught that a well-educated person and a good person is clean, neat, well dressed, and well off. If you cannot show him something better than he has, then he wonders what you have to offer him. Even an older car that is paid for, and money in the bank, cannot be greatly valued in his "live for today" world. The shiny new cars seen on the reservation tell us how these are admired, treasured, and turned in for a newer model whenever possible.

Navajos don't like to be considered museum pieces. Too many "ah's" and "oh's" on the part of the newcomer are not appreciated.

XXIV. SUMMARY

Some may say that the things recorded here are not true anymore. Maybe it has not been made clear enough that this paper deals with the uneducated Navajo, not with those who speak and understand English, and who have a knowledge of the white man's world and ways. And, again, it could be that things are changing more rapidly than I have recognized. But are these changes not on the outside, rather than on the inside -- what people want and have, rather than what they feel and believe and do? Of course, there is a relationship between these two.

Perhaps it seems that the opinions expressed in this paper emphasize too much the responsibility of the non-Navajo to bridge the cultural differences. Some might say that telling people about the things discussed here does not guarantee that they will be able to adjust to the ways of the Navajos. Others may say that one cannot expect them to adjust. Or, that too much adjusting will not help the people grow, but keep them where they are. Some may feel that these things are not a problem. Let it be said that for some, this is true. Some people who come to work here seem to know and feel and understand the people. It is for those who feel that they don't that these suggestions are given.

This paper was written to tell how the non-Indian can better understand the uneducated Navajo. Perhaps the problem should have been broader, to include how the uneducated Navajo can be helped to understand better and appreciate those who come to help him.

Many other things could have been included which were not, but the writer tried to mention those things, which from experience, have proved most helpful.

XXV. CONCLUSION

Manuelito, an old leader of the people, spoke of education as being the bridge which would help the people find a better life. It is the writer's feeling that this bridge must not, can not, be made for the people, nor only by the people, but that it can only be built with the people.

This involves understanding. We must all try to begin where we find ourselves. It seems like more and more people are realizing the need of understanding and are trying to do something about it. The task force committee which has been studying the Indian problems and projects in our country has reported:

> The aid of the tribe or. . . the Indian community is crucial to the achievement of objectives and this support should be secured

before projects are commenced. The Bureau of Indian Affairs should aim for maximum Indian economic self sufficiency, full participation of Indians in American life and equal citizenship privileges and responsibilities for Indians. Indians should be encouraged to help themselves. Membership in a society imposes obligations as well as bestows privileges. Assisting Indians to recognize and fulfill their obligations is as important as helping them to take advantage of their privileges. . . . The Indian role must be "contributory rather than passive" in any federal program if it is to benefit both other Indians and the United States.[17]

We have another "Long Walk" ahead of us before the paths of our cultures merge. There are still rough paths. But, as more of us take time to study, observe, give, and share, and try to know each other, perhaps our inter-cultural relations will improve. It is like someone said, "We need to walk a few miles in the other fellow's moccasins. Then we will know how they feel." This would help us to understand each other better.

FOOTNOTES

[1] Written by Kathyrn Polacca (Navajo Hopi), Adult Education Specialist, Bureau of Indian Affairs, Twin Lakes Trading Post, Gallup, New Mexico. Reprinted with permission from the Journal of American Indian Education, November, 1962, (College of Education, University of Arizona, Tempe, Arizona).

[2] Dr. Bertha Dutton, Address given at the Third Annual Dorothy Canfield Fisher Library Award, Gallup Public Library, April 16, 1961.

[3] Wall-Morgan, Navajo-English Dictionary, p. 30. "doo ahalyani": "blockhead," "stupid person."

[4] Ibid., "diigis": "insane." P. 29.

[5] Bureau of Ethnic Research, Indians of the Southwest (Tempe: University of Arizona, Department of Anthropology, 1953), p. 82.

[6] Dr. Bertha Dutton, Address given at the Third Annual Dorothy Canfield Fisher Library Award, Gallup Public Library, April 16, 1961.

[7] A tape recording explains the importance of this: "A Word in Your Ear," Department of Anthropology, University of California. A discourse on "language."

[8] Dr. Orpha McPherson, Director, Workshop "We Look at Indian Education," Arizona State College, Tempe, 1959. Workshop notes.

[9] Laura Thompson, Culture in Crisis (New York: Harper, 1950), p. 194.

[10] For an excellent, concise discussion of the problem of translating and interpreting, see Kluckhohn and Leighton, The Navajo (Cambridge: Harvard University Press, 1956), pp. 210-223.

[11] Arlene Frances, That Certain Something (New York: Dell Publishing Company, 1960), pp. 10-11.

[12] Robert Havighurst and Bernice Neugarten, The American Indian and White Children (Chicago: University of Chicago Press, 1957), p. 82.

[13] Deric Nusbaum, Deric in Mesa Verde (New York: G. P. Putnam's Sons, 1926), pp. 119-122. "Two summers ago a Hopi Indian came to Camp. He said 'My name is Howella Polacca. I come from the Hopi Indian Reservation. My father belongs to Little Corn Clan. My mother belongs to Butterfly Clan, so I am Little Corn Butterfly.'" Here the young author said: "I had to beat it, as the old fellow weighed nearly 200 pounds, and was a far cry from a 'Little Butterfly.'" He continued: "Mother and Dad took him out on the porch, and when I stopped laughing, I joined them. Howella explained that he had been brought up to be a medicine man, and had learned many of the old stories." Then, he proceeded to tell the family about an old Hopi myth about the Cliff Ruins at Mesa Verde. This was so like my father, always telling stories, and making people laugh. He enjoyed it as much as they.

[14] John Ladd, The Structure of a Moral Code (Cambridge: Harvard University Press, 1957), p. 232. Ladd tells that certain folk stories are told only in winter months and may not be told in the summertime, for fear of being struck by lightning.

[15] S. H. Babington, Navajo Gods (Greenberg Publishing Company, 1950), pp. 186-207.

[16] Ladd, op. cit., p. 233.

[17] Helene Monberg, columnist, Gallup Independent News, Wednesday, July 12, 1961, p. 4.

BIBLIOGRAPHY

A. Books

Babington, S. H. Navajo Gods. Greenberg Publishing Company, 1950.

Bureau of Ethnic Research. Indians of the Southwest. Department of Anthropology, University of Arizona, 1953.

Frances, Arlene. That Certain Something. Dell Publishing Company, 1960.

Golden, Gertrude. The American Indian, Then and Now. San Antonio, Texas, Naylor Company, 1957.

Havighurst, Robert, and Neugarten, Bernice. American Indian and White Children. Chicago: University of Chicago Press, 1957.

Ladd, John. The Structure of a Moral Code. Cambridge: Harvard University Press, 1957.

McPherson, Orpha. We Look at Indian Education. Summer Workshop report, University of Arizona, Tempe, 1957.

Nusbaum, Deric. Deric in Mesa Verde. New York: G. P. Putnam's Sons, 1926.

Thompson, Laura. Culture in Crisis. Harper, 1950.

Wall-Morgan. Navajo-English Dictionary. Phoenix: Phoenix Press, 1958.

Waters, Frank. Masked Gods. Albuquerque: University of New Mexico Press.

Young, Robert. Navajo Yearbook. Window Rock, Arizona: Navajo Agency, 1958.

Zintz, Miles V. Final Report of the Indian Research Study, "The Adjustment of Indian and Non-Indian Children in the Public Schools of New Mexico, sponsored under grant-in-aid from U. S. Office of Education, 1957-1960, University of New Mexico, Albuquerque.

B. Periodicals

Gallup Independent News, "Ceremonial Edition," August 12, 1958.

Gallup Independent News, Wednesday, July 12, 1961.

The American Anthropologist, "The Navajo and Christianity," January-March, 1949.

C. Consultants

Bratton, Mae, Educational Specialist, United Pueblos Agency.

Condie, Dr. LeRoy, Associate Professor, Education, University of New Mexico.

Henry, Dr. Burton. Professor of Education, Los Angles State College, visiting professor, University of New Mexico, Summer Inter-Cultural Relations Workshop, 1961.

Morelock, Mrs. Winifred, Teacher, Gallup High School.

Polacca, Mrs. Ruth A. (The writer's Navajo mother.). Crystal Trading Post, Fort Defiance, Arizona.

Porterfield, Dr. James C., Assistant Superintendent of Schools, Gallup-McKinley County Schools, Gallup, New Mexico.

Young, Robert, Assistant Superintendent, Navajo Agency, Bureau of Indian Affairs, Window Rock, Arizona.

Zintz, Dr. Miles V., Professor of Education, University of New Mexico, Albuquerque.

D. Speech

Dutton, Dr. Bertha, Director, Hall of Ethnology, Santa Fe, New Mexico.

E. Tape Recording

"A Word in Your Ear," Anthropology Department, University of California.

APPENDIX D

Reading List for Retarded Readers

1. Our Animal Story Books

   D. C. Heath & Co., 1815 Prairie Ave., Chicago 16, Illinois. 40¢ each. Available from the Follett Library Book Co., 1018 W. Washington Blvd., Chicago 7, Illinois, in Duro-tuff binding.

   Pre-Primers
   > My Dog Laddie
   > Biddy and the Ducks
   > Friskey and the Goats
   > Little White Rabbit
   > Peanuts the Pony
   > Hundreds of Turkeys
   > The Little Crow
   > Shadow the Cat
   > Fun for Fidelia
   > Maybelle the Donkey

2. Follett Beginning-to-Read Series

   Follett Publishing Company, 1010 West Washington Blvd., Chicago 7, Illinois. Cloth-bound, reinforced edition of each book is available for school and libraries. (Each 32 pages).

   Level One: For First-Grade Readers
   > Beginning to Read Picture Dictionary
   > Big New School
   > The Curious Cow
   > Gertie the Duck
   > The Hill That Grew
   > In John's Backyard
   > Just Follow Me
   > My Own Little House
   > Nobody Listens to Andrew
   > Something New at the Zoo
   > Too Many Dogs

Level Two: For Second-Grade Readers
- The Four Friends
- The Boy Who Would Not Say His Name
- The Hole in the Wall
- Mabel the Whale
- Miss Hattie and the Donkey

Level Three: For Third-Grade Readers
- Benny and the Bear
- Christopher Columbus
- Peter's Policeman

3. Beginner Books, Inc.

   Random House, 457 Madison Ave., New York 22, New York.

   About First Grade Level

The Cat in the Hat	Dr. Seuss
The Cat in the Hat Comes Back	Dr. Seuss
A Fly Went By	Mike McClintock
The Big Jump	Benjamin Elkin
A Big Ball of String	Marion Holland
Sam and the Firefly	Philip Eastman
Are You My Mother?	

4. Children's Press, Jackson Blvd., and Racine Avenue, Chicago 7, Illinois. 1958.

Mystery of the Gate Sign	Margaret Friskey, 1958
Six Foolish Fishermen	Benjamin Elkin, 1958
Learn to Read by Seeing Sound (No. 1 of a series)	Thomas Chandler

5. The Button Books

   Beckley-Cardy Company, 1900 N. Narrangansett, Chicago 39, Illinois. By Edith McCall.

Pre-Primer	The Buttons at the Zoo	(30 words, 48 pages)
	Bucky Buttons	(55 words, 48 pages)
Primer	Buttons and the Pet Parade	(80 words, 64 pages)
First reader	Buttons at the Farm	(147 words, 64 pages)

6. The Jim Forest Reading Series

Harr Wagner Publishing Company, 707 Browder Street, Dallas, Texas, 1960.

Grade Level	Title	Pages	Different Words
1.7	Jim Forest and Ranger Don, Book I	64	103
1.9	Jim Forest and the Bandits, Book II	80	230
2.2	Jim Forest and the Mystery Hunter, II	96	309
2.6	Jim Forest and Dead Man's Peak, IV	96	419
2.8	Jim Forest and the Flood, V	96	498
3.1	Jim Forest and Lone Wolf Gulch, VI	96	535
	Teacher's Manual, 75 cents	48	

7. The Deep-Sea Adventure Series

Harr Wagner Publishing Co., 707 Browder Street, Dallas, Texas, 1960.

Reading Level	Title	Pages	Different Words
First Grade	The Sea Hunt, Book I	72	159
Low Second	Treasure Under the Sea, Book II	80	227
High Second	Submarine Rescue, Book III	80	306
Low Third	The Pearl Divers, Book IV	96	
High Third	Frogmen in Action, Book V	96	
	Teacher's Manual,		

8. The Jerry Books

Beckley-Cardy Co., 1632 Indiana Ave., Chicago 16, Illinois. By Florence Battle.

Grade Level	Title	Words	Pages
Pre-Primer	Jerry	35	48
Primer	Jerry Goes Riding	86	64
First	Jerry Goes Fishing	214	64
Second	Jerry Goes on a Picnic	235	96
Third	Jerry Goes to the Circus		

9. The Cowboy Sam Series

Beckley-Cardy Co., 1630 Indiana Ave., Chicago, Illinois. By Edna Walker Chandler.

Primer	Cowboy Sam		
Primer	Cowboy Sam and Porky	Second	Cowboy Sam and the Rodeo
Primer	Cowboy Sam and Miss Lilly	Second	Cowboy Sam at the Fair
Primer	Cowboy Sam and Dandy	Third	Cowboy Sam and the Rustle
Primer	Cowboy Sam and Flop	Third	Cowboy Sam and the Indian
First	Cowboy Sam and Freddy		
First	Cowboy Sam and Shorty		

10. The Wonder Story Books

    Row Peterson and Co., Evanston, Illinois. Although planned for primary grades, these books of old folk tales have considerable appeal for older children.

First Reader	I Know A Story
Second Reader	It Happened One Day
Third Reader	After the Sun Sets

11. Core Vocabulary Readers

    The Macmillan Co., 2459 Prairie Ave., Chicago 16, Illinois. By Huber and others, 1943. These books were first of this type to be published. They have been widely used.

Primer	The Ranch Book
First	Rusty Wants a Dog
Second	Smoky the Crow
Third	Planes for Bob and Andy

12. The Aviation Series

    The Macmillian Co., 2459 Prairie Ave., Chicago 16, Illinois.

First	Straight Up	$ .96
Second	Straight Down	$ .96
Third	Planes for Bob and Andy	$1.52
Fourth	Airplanes at Work	$1.24
Fifth	The Men Who Gave Us Wings	$1.32
Sixth	Aviation Science for Boys and Girls	$1.40

13. The Pioneer Series

    Benefic Press (Beckley-Cardy Co.), 1900 N. Narragansett, Chicago 39, Illinois. By Irene Estep.

    Third Grade Level

    Pioneer Tenderfoot
    Pioneer Buckaroo

　　　　Pioneer Sodbuster
　　　　Pioneer Engineer
　　　　Pioneer Pilgrim

14. The Clyde Bulla Books

　　Thomas Y. Crowell Co., 432 Fourth Ave., New York 16, N.Y.

　　About Third Grade Level

A Surprise for A Cowboy	Johnny Hong of Chinatown
A Ranch for Danny	Riding the Pony Express
Star of Wild Horse Canyon	The Secret Valley
The Donkey Cart	Song of St. Francis
Down the Mississippi	Squanto, Friend of the White Men
Eagle Feather	White Sails to China

15. Dolch Materials

　　The Garrard Press, Champaign, Illinois.

　　Basic Vocabulary Series.

Folk Stories	Navaho Stories
Animal Stories	Dog Stories
"Why" Stories	Elephant Stories
Pueblo Stories	Bear Stories
Tepee Stories	Lion and Tiger Stories
Wigwam Stories	Circus Stories
Lodge Stories	

　　Pleasure Reading Series.

Fairy Stories	Old World Stories
Anderson Stories	Far East Stories
Aesop's Stories	Greek Stories
Famous Stories	Gospel Stories
Robin Hood Stories	Bible Stories

　　The First Reading Books. Sturdy cloth bindings, 64 pages, 1958.

In the Woods	Tommy's Pets
Monkey Friends	Zoo is Home
On the Farm	

16. The American Adventure Series

　　These books are noted for a combination of high interest levels with low readability levels.

Level	Title
A Second Grade	Squanto and the Pilgrims Friday, the Arapaho Indian Portugee Phillips
B Third Grade	Alex Major Chief Black Hawk Pilot Jack Knight Grant Marsh, Steamboat Captain Sabre Jet Ace
C Fourth Grade	Cowboys and Cattle Trails Kit Carson Dan Morgan, Rifleman
D Fifth Grade	Buffalo Bill Wild Bill Hickok Davy Crockett
E Sixth Grade	Daniel Boone Fur Trappers of the Old West The Rush for Gold John Paul Jones

17. Scott, Foresman and Company, 433 E. Erie St., Chicago, Illinois.

    Third Grade Level Vocabulary

    Boxcar Children
    Surprise Island
    The Yellow House Mystery
    The Six Robbens
    The Flying Trunk
    Mystery Trunk

18. The Childhood of Famous Americans Series

    Bobbs-Merrill Co., Inc., 730 N. Meridian St., Indianapolis 7, Indiana. Reader level for all books is fourth grade. There are more than one hundred titles in the series. Some illustrative titles are:

    Abe Lincoln: Frontier Boy
    Alex Hamilton: The Little Lion
    Booker T. Washington: Ambitious Boy
    George Rogers Clark: Boy of the Old Northwest
    Kate Doublas Wiggin: The Little Schoolteacher
    Walter Reed: Boy Who Wanted to Know

Will and Charlie Mayo: Doctor's Boys
Bird Girl: Sacagawea
Clara Barton: Girl Nurse
Dolly Madison: Quaker Girl

19. The Landmark Books

Random House, 457 Madison Ave., New York 22, N.Y. There are more than a hundred titles in this series. Illustrative are:

Abe Lincoln: Log Cabin to White House	North	R5	I 4-8
Coming of the Mormons	Kjelgaard	R6	I 6-9
The Early Days of Automobiles in America	Janeway	R4	I 4-9
John Paul Jones, Fighting Sailor	Sperry	R6	I 5-9
Mr. Bell Invents the Telephone	Shippen	R6	I 4-10
Thirty Seconds Over Tokyo	Lawson	R7	I 7-10
Martin Luther	Fosdick		Junior High School

20. The Everyreader Series

Webster Publishing Co., 1808 Washington Ave., St. Louis 3, Missouri. By William Kottmeyer and others. Fourth Grade level of reading difficulty, with interest level for ages 10 through 18.

The Gold Bug and Other Stories	Men of Iron
Cases of Sherlock Holmes	Ben Hur
Ivanhoe	Count of Monte Cristo
A Tale of Two Cities	Juarez, Hero of Mexico
Simon Bolivar	To Have and to Hold
Flamingo Feather	

The Junior Everyreader Series

Third grade level, with interest level for ages 9 through 16.

Robin Hood Stories	Old Testament Stories
King Arthur and His Knights	Greek and Roman Myths
The Trojan War	

21. The Morgan Bay Mysteries

Harr Wagner Publishing Co., 707 Browder St., Dallas, Texas, 1962.

Grade Level	Title
2.3	The Mystery of Morgan Castle
2.6	The Mystery of the Marble Angel
3.2	The Mystery of the Midnight Visitor
3.5	The Mystery of the Missing Marlin

22. The Signal Books

    Doubleday and Co., Inc., Garden City, New York, 1961.

    About fourth grade reader level. There are many books in the series.

    Interest: Senior high school level.

    Sample titles: Carol Heiss: Olympic Queen;
    Pony of the Sioux;
    Bonnie;
    North Pole: The Story of Robert E. Peary; and
    The Jungle Secret

23. The Dan Frontier Series

    The Benefic Press, 1900 North Narragansett, Chicago 39, Illinois, 1962.

Title	Reading Level	Interest Level	Pages	Price
Dan Frontier and the New House	PP	pp-2	48	$1.35
Dan Frontier	PP	PP-2	48	1.35
Dan Frontier Goes Hunting	P	P-2	64	1.47
Dan Frontier with the Indians	1	1-4	96	1.65
Dan Frontier and the Wagon Train	2	2-5	128	1.74
Dan Frontier, Sheriff	3	3-6	128	1.74
Teachers Manual for the Series				.75

24. The Sailor Jack Series

    The Benefic Press, 1900 North Narragansett, Chicago 39, Illinois,

	Reading Level	Interest Level	Pages	Price
Sailor Jack and Eddy	PP	PP-2	48	$1.20
Sailor Jack	PP	PP-2	48	1.20
Sailor Jack and Homer Pots	PP	PP-2	48	1.20
Sailor Jack and Bluebell	P	P-3	64	1.26
Sailor Jack's New Friend	1	1-4	64	1.26
Sailor Jack and the Target Ship	2	2-5	96	1.35
Sailor Jack Goes North	3	3-6	96	1.35

25. Tom's America and Tom Travels the Trail

Cascade Pacific Books, 5448 Forty-Seventh, S. W., Seattle 16, Washington.

Each book is published at three reading levels: 2.5; 4.0; and 6.0.

Might be used as a core outline of fifth-grade social studies. Authors: Upton, Durfee, Tucker, Doak, and Bennett.

APPENDIX E

Tests

TESTS

1. A Reading Test - Page 473
2. Multiple Meanings Test - Page 485

A READING TEST

(Idioms, proverbs, and figures of speech used in elementary school readers.)

prepared by

Maurine Dunn Yandell, Sixth Grade Teacher
Gallup-McKinley County Schools

and

Miles V. Zintz, Director
Indian Research Study
College of Education
The University of New Mexico

DIRECTIONS

This is a test to find out if you know the correct meanings of many unusual expressions you find in your reading. For each test item, select the best answer and look at the letter in front of it. Find that number on the separate answer sheet and make a circle around it.

Read the sample item silently while your teacher reads aloud:

A. <u>If your heart is still set on</u> a fleece, I'll bring you a few in the morning.

"<u>If your heart is still set on</u> means:

a. If your heart is quiet;
b. If you want a fleece very badly;
c. If you have a fleece on your heart;
d. A heart is a place on a fleece.

Since the expression means that the person wants a fleece very much, letter <u>b</u> is circled on the answer sheet.

A. a (b) c d

Do all of the items in this way. Think what the part of the sentence that is underlined means. Be sure your letters on the answer sheet correspond to the items in the test booklet.

PART ONE

___ 1. "<u>Saved by a hair!</u> Just by a hair!" yelled Tom.
    a. by using his head
    b. just barely made it
    c. safe and secure
    d. by sticking his head out

___ 2. Then, as if he were <u>rooted to the spot</u>, Tom stood still, overcome with surprise.
    a. touching the ground
    b. right on the spot
    c. unable to move
    d. with his foot in a hole

___ 3. "Tom was <u>tired enough to drop in his tracks</u>, as his grandpa used to say."
    a. to drop his load
    b. to follow the tracks
    c. stop where he was without moving
    d. to follow in his footsteps

___ 4. "<u>Mark my words</u>, you'll spoil that girl."
    a. take my advice
    b. words are important
    c. what I say is always right
    d. place a mark on the words

___ 5. "Go no faster than a trot, and <u>keep your head about you</u>."
    a. keep your head with you
    b. hold your head still
    c. stay awake
    d. be sensible and act wisely

___ 6. "When you are boarding around doing a little of this kind of work and a little of that, you grow sick and tired of being a <u>Jack-of-all-Trades</u>."
    a. being good at all trades
    b. doing a little of all kinds of work
    c. restless like a Jack-in-the-box
    d. not doing any work well

___ 7. "Because Ma had <u>a warm spot in her heart</u> for Sam, she talked to Tom after Sally was in bed."
    a. was sick because of Sam
    b. Sam made her angry
    c. special liking for Sam
    d. liked everyone

___ 8. "<u>My mouth is watering</u>, he said to Ma."
    a. wanting something badly
    b. is very sick
    c. needed a drink
    d. has water in his mouth

___ 9. "He won't be worth his salt for a long time to come."
   a. worth very much
   b. worth as much as salt
   c. worth what he eats
   d. uses too much salt

___ 10. "I leave it to you to break him in."
   a. break his habits
   b. to get him inside
   c. to hurt him
   d. get him used to things

___ 11. "Before another year comes round, the cabins will begin to climb the hill."
   a. cabins will be built higher
   b. climb the hill to get to the cabins
   c. cabins will be built farther up the hill
   d. cabins will have to be moved

___ 12. "There is a sight of hauling still to be done."
   a. too much to see
   b. hauling too much
   c. seeing what is hauled
   d. a lot of hauling

___ 13. "You are a better man than I am; it takes you to bring home the bacon."
   a. to feed the children
   b. to get things done
   c. to bring home food
   d. to be good

___ 14. "Ma had to piece out the supper with sausage, ham, and headcheese."
   a. to serve small pieces
   b. serve the supper
   c. leave out the extra food
   d. add more food to have enough

___ 15. "Don't bite my head off."
   a. don't be so cross
   b. don't get so close
   c. don't bite my head
   d. don't be so loud

___ 16. "During the gold rush, many people were staking a claim."
   a. taking a stake on the claim
   b. driving stakes in the ground to mark boundaries
   c. claiming land that wasn't theirs
   d. making claim to a stake

___17. "A miner spent much of his time panning out."
   a. taking the pan out of the water
   b. washing earth and gravel in a pan in search of gold
   c. digging for gold
   d. putting the pan in and out of water

___18. "And the captain always saw through everyone."
   a. saw everyone in view
   b. looked through everyone
   c. understood everyone
   d. saw everyone's faults

___19. "When pioneers blazed a trail, they chipped the tree trunks at a certain height."
   a. set the trail afire
   b. followed a trail
   c. made a new trail
   d. hurried down the trail

___20. "The man felt heavy at heart, for he thought it was better to share the last bite with the children."
   a. big hearted
   b. sad and worried
   c. his heart was a load
   d. thought he had gained some weight

___21. "Then it's all set, said Toto happily."
   a. it's all gone
   b. it's all ready
   c. it's all there
   d. it's all still

___22. "When I give a dog, I give him for good."
   a. I treat him good
   b. give him for keeps
   c. a good way to give him
   d. give him to stay awhile

___23. "Travel on the magic carpet of printed words" means
   a. to go many different places in stories
   b. to go on a carpet in a book
   c. to sit on a carpet while we travel
   d. to sit on a magic carpet and read

___24. "This California weather changes quickly in the orange belt."
   a. place where oranges are grown
   b. the color of something we wear
   c. place where oranges are sold
   d. a belt made of oranges

___ 25. "What will Barnum do next, was on everybody's tongue."
   a. everyone is talking at the same time
   b. something is on everybody's tongue
   c. everyone is discussing it
   d. on the tongue of everybody

___ 26. "Killing the goose that laid the golden egg" means
   a. Things worth having are worth waiting for.
   b. Be kind to others.
   c. Don't count your chickens before they are hatched.
   d. Something valuable may be lost by being greedy.

___ 27. "The lad took to his heels as if bewitched."
   a. to take his heels to the witch
   b. flew away
   c. to run behind someone's heels
   d. ran as fast as he could

___ 28. "Thanks for the tip, Chief," replied the reporter."
   a. keep your hands to yourself
   b. thanks for the sharp object
   c. thanks for the money
   d. thanks for the information

___ 29. "Got cold feet, did you" teased one of the boys."
   a. became afraid
   b. became very cold
   c. got cold and went home
   d. feet were cold

___ 30. "Now I have let the cat out of the bag," chuckled Mr. Burd."
   a. let the cat jump out of the bag
   b. forgot to tie the string
   c. told the secret
   d. let the cat make too much noise

PART TWO

___ 31. "Big Bill Turner, crack engineer of the Prairie Flyer, was bringing this "puffing billy" home to roost!"
   a. returning to its starting place
   b. roosting like a bird
   c. perching in the roundhouse
   d. starting back home

___ 32. "But see to it that you keep your hands to yourself."
   a. do not help with the work
   b. my business is not yet your business
   c. keep your own hands
   d. leave things alone

477

___33. "It would <u>suit me to a T</u>," grinned Pierre."
    a. his suit fit him
    b. I'd agree to the T
    c. I'd like it fine
    d. not in agreement with

___34. "I tell you <u>those were the days</u>."
    a. more difficult days
    b. longer days
    c. easier days
    d. days to remember

___35. "You can see for yourself he's learning all there is to know about railroading <u>from the ground up</u>."
    a. all the different kinds of railroading jobs
    b. from the rails to the cars
    c. groundwork and engines
    d. the dirty jobs

___36. "What kind of <u>monkeyshines</u> do you call this, Tom?"
    a. acting like a monkey
    b. a shining face
    c. a trick or a prank
    d. acting in a strange way

___37. "So that's the reason for this <u>Sunday-go-to-meeting</u> attire."
    a. finest clothes
    b. clothes worn to meet someone on Sunday
    c. clothes that are tiring
    d. everyday clothes

___38. "I'd be the <u>laughing stock</u> of the town."
    a. laughing with the town
    b. laughingly taking stock of the town
    c. the town clown
    d. made fun of

___39. "He did a splendid job of <u>locking the barn door after the horse was stolen</u>."
    a. looking for the horse
    b. being careful after it's too late
    c. locking the door to protect the horse
    d. being careful before danger comes

___40. "We have always insisted that Tom Fuller was <u>worth his weight in gold</u>."
    a. worth as much as gold
    b. weighs as much as gold
    c. very valuable
    d. very important

___41. "Gave him his walking papers not ten minutes ago," announced Mrs. Gray."
　a. gave him papers to leave
　b. told him to walk away
　c. fired him
　d. replaced him with someone else

___42. "I've talked to the man who owns it, and we can get it for a song."
　a. if we sing him a song
　b. for a small amount
　c. for nothing
　d. for a little music

___43. "By and by an idea began to dawn upon them."
　a. the sun came up
　b. it became brighter
　c. began to understand
　d. began to see them

___44. "I'll be beat if you ever saw a town with as much spunk for pulling itself out by the bootstraps."
　a. pulling off its boots
　b. getting along without help
　c. using bootstraps to pull itself up
　d. becoming better

___45. "So you've definitely decided to let Hastings go to the dogs."
　a. go from bad to worse
　b. to do what is right
　c. play with the dogs
　d. go with the dogs

___46. "Automobile riding lost some of its edge for Tom."
　a. he didn't like it any more
　b. lost its beauty
　c. lost its thrill
　d. became tiring for him

___47. "Once you set your eyes on that car, I can call from now until kingdom come."
　a. from now on
　b. from here to heaven
　c. until the other kingdom
　d. until you come with us

___48. "You're a chip off the old block," laughed Captain Joe."
　a. the part that's good
　b. just like your father
　c. solid like a block
　d. a small part

___49. "But I'll show ye a bit of old time fiddlin', just <u>to start the judges off on the right track</u>."
    a. to start the judges down the track
    b. to get the judges started
    c. it's hard to find the right track
    d. to track the judges down

___50. "In this story Betsy <u>turned the tables</u> on several people."
    a. made the people move over
    b. changed her mind
    c. surprised everyone
    d. turned the tables around

___51. "The black clouds let fall <u>sheets of rain</u>."
    a. squares of rain
    b. solid rain
    c. heavy downpour of rain
    d. white rain

___52. "I am <u>empty as a gourd</u>," he sighed."
    a. had seeds inside himself
    b. shaped like a gourd
    c. hollow inside
    d. made a strange noise inside

___53. "<u>With a sweep of his arm</u>, he took in the countryside."
    a. with a broom in his hand
    b. with his arm above his eyes
    c. a movement of his arm
    d. moving himself around

___54. "<u>Actions speak louder than words</u>" means
    a. actions mean more than words
    b. words mean more than what we do
    c. words are not important
    d. actions always come before words

___55. "Think I'll call him '<u>Greased Lightning</u>'," Zeke replied."
    a. as bright as lightning
    b. as fast as lightning
    c. hot and dangerous
    d. stormy and loud

___56. "The cowboys were going to <u>cut the herd</u>."
    a. to drive part one place and part to another
    b. to brand the cattle
    c. to butcher or cut up part of the herd
    d. to make the cattle run

___57. "<u>Pike's Peak or bust</u>" means
    a. I'll get there or die trying
    b. the trip is too hard
    c. want to see Pike's Peak
    d. Pike's Peak is the place to burst

___58. "He talked for some time, but he couldn't convince Uncle Lem, who was as stubborn as a mule."
   a. as agreeable as a mule
   b. as difficult to manage as a mule
   c. as yielding as a mule
   d. gave in too easily

___59. "Uncle started in a beeline for the river."
   a. following an imaginary line
   b. straight and fast
   c. busy like a bee
   d. with a bee after him

___60. "Most of these were given to blind flying."
   a. a blind man flying
   b. too dark to see
   c. flying with a blindfold
   d. flying only with instruments

PART THREE

___61. "She wants him to come and live with her, and he is planning to pull stakes this summer."
   a. to pull up sticks
   b. to go to live in another place
   c. to pull stakes to earn money
   d. to go back to his home town

___62. "But I'm getting on, and you're my nearest relatives."
   a. going on
   b. getting along fine
   c. going strong
   d. getting older

___63. "He says bloods' thicker than any bank roll."
   a. relatives are more important than money
   b. blood is worth more than money
   c. blood can be spilled over a bank roll
   d. there is more blood than money

___64. "But Mother, who understood thoroughly how Lucy was feeling, tried to turn the matter off lightly."
   a. to turn away
   b. to turn off the lights
   c. to dismiss the matter without seriousness
   d. to turn the matter off quietly

___65. "The old lady was kindhearted, but a bit sharp-tongued."
   a. her tongue was too long
   b. she talked too much
   c. her tongue was too sharp
   d. she spoke harshly

___66. "The Hardings went to bed in <u>a pleasant glow of anticipation</u>."
   a. glowing and happy
   b. happy with remembrance
   c. to anticipate a glow
   d. expecting something pleasant

___67. "Uncle John doesn't expect us for five or six months, and we've <u>burned our bridges behind us</u>."
   a. already crossed the bridge
   b. burned everything we don't need
   c. made our decisions and can't change our minds now
   d. set fire to the bridge after we crossed it

___68. "May I <u>give you a lift</u>, sir?" he asked."
   a. lift you up
   b. give you a ride
   c. help you left something
   d. give you something light

___69. "They're a little scared of me maybe, but they ought to know <u>a barking dog never bites</u>."
   a. a barking dog isn't dangerous
   b. a dog that bites doesn't bark
   c. someone who talks mean may not really be mean
   d. someone who acts mean usually doesn't talk

___70. "You're new at this business," said Monty Green. "<u>Breaking the ice is what's hard</u>."
   a. ice is hard to break
   b. beginning something new
   c. to begin to break ice
   d. breaking a new record

___71. "I've lost a man who <u>got a touch of sun</u> and got sick."
   a. touched sunshine
   b. got too much sun at one time
   c. was out of the sun too long
   d. the sun burned him

___72. "Then he <u>sat bolt upright</u>, as though a charge of electricity had gone through him."
   a. sat on the right side of a bolt
   b. sat up on the right bolt
   c. sat up very straight, immediately
   d. had been told to sit uprightly

___73. "<u>He who steals a good name is not made richer</u>."
   a. honest effort is required to earn a good reputation
   b. stealing a good name is not a good way to get rich
   c. stealing a good name is not the easiest way to get it
   d. a good name is not as valuable as gold

___ 74. "I'd <u>work like a steer</u>, I swear I would."
   a. in a straight line
   b. very hard
   c. like a good driver
   d. as often as a steer

___ 75. "She moved <u>from pillar to post</u>."
   a. from a soft place to a hard one
   b. moving in order to get a new job
   c. from one place to another
   d. from a big house to a small one

___ 76. "A <u>tall tale</u>" means
   a. a long story
   b. a story about a tall man
   c. a story told as if it were true
   d. a tale told over and over

___ 77. "A tornado <u>headed for</u> his cattle."
   a. came toward
   b. wanted the heads
   c. followed
   d. was ahead of

___ 78. "He was <u>yanked up</u> into the middle of the ugly green cloud."
   a. pushed upward
   b. jerked up quickly
   c. moved slowly
   d. floated up

___ 79. "He was <u>mooning around</u> like a love-sick puppy."
   a. dreamy
   b. excited
   c. lonesome
   d. studying the stars

___ 80. "She accepted before he could <u>back out</u>."
   a. go backwards
   b. decide it was a good idea
   c. change his mind
   d. go out the back way

___ 81. "The bray <u>shattered the stillness</u>."
   a. stopped the noise
   b. broke the silence
   c. made a soft sound
   d. added to the stillness

___ 82. "He was <u>shedding crocodile tears</u>."
   a. large tears
   b. crying like a crocodile
   c. the tears of a crocodile
   d. crying easily without being very sorry

___83. "I know a certain young fellow who's gettin' too big for his breeches.
  a. outgrowing his clothes
  b. smart and sassy
  c. too big to play with children
  d. his pants are too tight

___84. "He was fourteen, skinny, and badly spoiled."
  a. in bad health
  b. had a bad smell about him
  c. used to having his own way
  d. did what others told him to do

___85. "Skip it," said Jimmy briefly. "You wouldn't understand."
  a. forget it
  b. pretend it didn't happen
  c. jump over it
  d. wait till later

___86. "I think I'll call it a day."
  a. I'll stop now
  b. stop at the end of the day
  c. call it today
  d. name it "day"

___87. "Martha Daniels was the star diver of the club, and all eyes were on her as she stood ready at the edge of the platform."
  a. all eyes were open
  b. she was watching them
  c. she was not seen by all
  d. everyone watched her

___88. "She's coming around now," Bob announced after he had worked with her for a few minutes."
  a. she's coming over now
  b. she's waking up
  c. coming with us
  d. she's coming in a little while

___89. "They were carrying only a skeleton crew - a mechanic and a radioman.
  a. the bones of the crew
  b. a little crew
  c. the necessary members of the crew
  d. a crew's skeleton

___90. "Once more Bolivar must leave South America, now with a price put upon his head by Spain."
  a. a number on his forehead
  b. a reward for his capture
  c. his head was in demand
  d. he was for sale

MULTIPLE MEANINGS TEST

FORM I

Clara Jett Cox, Graduate Student

The University of New Mexico

Name_____ Age_____ Grade_____

Sex____Teacher_____ School_____

Town_____ Date_____

DIRECTIONS: This is a test to find out if you know the right meaning of the underlined word in each sentence. Look at the group of words above the sentences. These words tell the meanings of the underlined words. Read the sentences and decide which of the meanings is the best to use for each of the underlined words. Place the letter of that meaning beside the sentence in which the underlined word has that meaning. The sample is done for you. Read the sample item silently while your teacher reads it aloud.

SAMPLE: a. endure b. animal c. loaf d. produce e. relate

    _a_ 1. Kathy cannot bear the sight of snakes.
    _d_ 2. The trees did not bear fruit this year.
    _e_ 3. These are the facts which bear upon your question.
    _b_ 4. The hunters shot the bear.

Do the remainder of the items in the same way.

1. a. symbols b. scratches c. grades d. targets e. buffalo

    ____ 1. Paul's boots made marks on the floor.
    ____ 2. Eddie's marks in school are always high.
    ____ 3. There are question marks after the words.
    ____ 4. The men shot their rifles but missed the marks completely.

2. a. give b. display c. prove d. accept e. guide

    ____ 1. Did Jane show her new dress?
    ____ 2. John planned to show the boys that he was good enough to play on the team.
    ____ 3. The cruel king did not show mercy to the prisoners.
    ____ 4. "Tom, will you show Mrs. Farr to the attic?"

3. a. tool b. row c. class d. folder e. lay away orderly

   ____1. He kept a <u>file</u> of his best work.
   ____2. <u>File</u> the pictures so they may be used next year.
   ____3. Mary used a <u>file</u> to shape her fingernails.
   ____4. The pupils followed the teacher in single <u>file</u>.

4. a. long howls b. reddish brown c. part of the sea d. tree e. building

   ____1. The <u>bay</u> horse galloped up the dusty road.
   ____2. The <u>bay</u> of the dog awakened the baby.
   ____3. The boat sailed across the <u>bay</u>.
   ____4. He made a crown from the branches of the <u>bay</u>.

5. a. defeat b. struck c. throb d. flee e. sound

   ____1. The angry man <u>beat</u> the dog.
   ____2. His heart <u>beat</u> is regular and normal.
   ____3. The <u>beat</u> of the drum could be heard in the distance.
   ____4. Do you think their team will <u>beat</u> our team?

6. a. platter b. write c. recorder d. copy e. best yet

   ____1. Bob kept a <u>record</u> of his earnings.
   ____2. Mary bought a <u>record</u> by Elvis Presley.
   ____3. He finished the race in <u>record</u> time.
   ____4. <u>Record</u> your spelling score each week.

7. a. most unlikely b. only one left c. most recent d. endure d. fire

   ____1. This paint will <u>last</u> forever.
   ____2. John was the <u>last</u> person I expected to win.
   ____3. Have you read Augusta Stevenson's <u>last</u> book?
   ____4. He won the <u>last</u> award.

8. a. collect b. sew by drawing together c. conclude d. meet e. increase

   ____1. Mother will <u>gather</u> my skirt for me.
   ____2. Would you like to help me <u>gather</u> the eggs?
   ____3. The members of the club will <u>gather</u> in the clubhouse.
   ____4. I <u>gather</u> that Tom will not be here.

9. a. satisfactorily b. fully c. with reason d. intimately e. healthy

   ____1. I knew him <u>well</u>.
   ____2. Mary did quite <u>well</u> on the test.
   ____3. I cannot <u>well</u> refuse.
   ____4. He was <u>well</u> out of sight.

10. a. older by a generation b. long continued c. superior d. favored e. full

  _____ 1. Robert E. Lee was a <u>great</u> general.
  _____ 2. John hasn't seen his grandmother in a <u>great</u> while.
  _____ 3. He described the village in <u>great</u> detail.
  _____ 4. Jim visited his <u>great</u>-grandmother.

11. a. in the act of b. rotation c. near d. away e. concerning

  _____ 1. She received some sad news <u>about</u> her son.
  _____ 2. Marie was <u>about</u> to enter the cave when her mother called her.
  _____ 3. Turn <u>about</u> is fair play.
  _____ 4. He was here yesterday <u>about</u> this time.

12. a. brief visit b. talk with by telephone c. summon d. name e. yell

  _____ 1. What shall we <u>call</u> the baby?
  _____ 2. The judge will <u>call</u> the court to order.
  _____ 3. Mother plans to <u>call</u> Mrs. Horn and invite her to dinner.
  _____ 4. Mrs. Begay made a <u>call</u> on her new neighbor.

13. a. abstain from food b. sound c. permanently dyed d. firm e. long

  _____ 1. The contestants got a <u>fast</u> grip on the rope.
  _____ 2. Do you <u>fast</u> during Lent?
  _____ 3. The baby was <u>fast</u> asleep.
  _____ 4. Her dress is <u>fast</u> color.

14. a. harvest b. entertain c. keep bound d. accept e. carry on

  _____ 1. We <u>hold</u> these truths to be proof of the equality of man.
  _____ 2. They <u>hold</u> no prejudice against anyone.
  _____ 3. The judge will <u>hold</u> him to his word.
  _____ 4. The class will <u>hold</u> a meeting in Room 9.

15. a. correct b. outward c. degree d. directly e. just

  _____ 1. He placed the tree <u>right</u> in front of the window.
  _____ 2. You did not give the <u>right</u> answer.
  _____ 3. The criminal received the <u>right</u> punishment.
  _____ 4. She turned the <u>right</u> side of the rug inward so the sun would not fade it.

16. a. week b. direction c. method d. determined course e. passage

  _____ 1. The astronauts followed a set <u>way</u> of performing.
  _____ 2. That is not the correct <u>way</u> to work that problem.
  _____ 3. Which <u>way</u> shall we go?
  _____ 4. She made her <u>way</u> through the crowd.

17. a. refrain   b. preserve   c. last   d. maintain   e. stay

   _____ 1. Milk will not <u>keep</u> in such heat.
   _____ 2. The sign read, "<u>Keep</u> to the right."
   _____ 3. She was unable to <u>keep</u> from talking.
   _____ 4. During the air raid they had to <u>keep</u> silence.

18. a. class   b. room   c. mark   d. hill   e. level

   _____ 1. The car went up a steep <u>grade</u>.
   _____ 2. What <u>grade</u> are you in this year?
   _____ 3. I will <u>grade</u> your paper now.
   _____ 4. The workmen will need to <u>grade</u> the road after this rain.

19. a. place where liquor is sold   b. fasten   c. ale   d. barrier   e. the court

   _____ 1. Don't <u>bar</u> the door.
   _____ 2. The men had a drink in the <u>bar</u>.
   _____ 3. The class constructed a sand <u>bar</u>.
   _____ 4. The lawyer pleaded the man's case at the <u>bar</u>.

20. a. courage   b. feelings   c. important part   d. memory   e. toy

   _____ 1. Children are the <u>heart</u> of the school.
   _____ 2. How could he have the <u>heart</u> to do such a terrible thing?
   _____ 3. The class learned the poem by <u>heart</u>.
   _____ 4. The <u>heart</u> and head often disagree.

21. a. bake   b. severe trail   c. burning   d. shooting   e. place

   _____ 1. The general was under <u>fire</u> for his decision to attack.
   _____ 2. The men were ordered to cease <u>fire</u>.
   _____ 3. We shall <u>fire</u> the pottery in the kiln.
   _____ 4. The house is on <u>fire</u>.

22. a. snouts   b. chests   c. axle   d. shorts   e. bases

   _____ 1. The athletes wore white <u>trunks</u>.
   _____ 2. They bore holes in the <u>trunks</u> of the trees.
   _____ 3. The elephants picked up the sugar with their <u>trunks</u>.
   _____ 4. <u>Trunks</u> of gold were found in the cave.

23. a. square designs   b. figures   c. ticket showing price   d. mark   e. control

   _____ 1. She placed a red <u>check</u> on the best papers.
   _____ 2. The matron had to keep <u>check</u> of the girls.
   _____ 3. She prefers <u>checks</u> to stripes.
   _____ 4. The man waited until the waitress gave him his dinner <u>check</u>.

24. a. lower   b. remove   c. weapon   d. knotted ribbon
    e. front of a ship

    _____ 1. They have learned to use a <u>bow</u> and arrow.
    _____ 2. Janet always wears a <u>bow</u> in her hair.
    _____ 3. The minister asked them to <u>bow</u> their heads as he prayed.
    _____ 4. Water seeped into the <u>bow</u>.

25. a. church   b. festival or exhibition   c. just   d. average
    e. light

    _____ 1. The judge asked the jurors to be <u>fair</u>.
    _____ 2. His mother is very <u>fair</u> and dainty.
    _____ 3. The children had fun at the <u>fair</u> in Window Rock.
    _____ 4. Timothy makes <u>fair</u> grades in school.

Bibliography

1. Ablon, Joan, "Relocated American Indians in the San Francisco Bay Area," Human Organization, 24:296-304.

2. Abraham, Willard, Research Coordinator, Investigation of Mental Retardation and Pseudo Mental Retardation in Relation to Bilingual and Sub-cultural Factors, (College of Education, Arizona State University, Tempe, Arizona, 1960), 363 pp.

3. Adair, John J. "A Study of Culture Resistance: The Veterans of World War II at Zuni Pueblo," Unpublished Doctors Dissertation, UNM, Albuquerque, 1948.

4. Adair, John, "Patterns of Health and Disease Among the Navajos," The Annual of AAPSS, 311:89, May, 1957.

5. Adair, John, and Kurt Dueschle, "Some Problems of the Physicians on the Navajo Reservation," Human Organization, 16:19-23, Winter, 1958.

6. Agard, Frederick, B. and Dunkel, Harold B., An Investigation of Second Language Teaching, (Boston: Ginn and Co., 1948). 344 pp.

7. Ahrens, Maurice R., "A Center for Materials," Childhood Education, 33:118-119, November 1956.

8. Albert, Ethel M., "The Classification of Values: A Method and Illustration," American Anthropologist, 58:221-248, April, 1956.

9. Alexander, Louis, "Texas Helps Her Little Latins" Saturday Evening Post, 234:30-31 pp., Aug 5, 1961.

10. Allen, Virginia French, (Editor), On Teaching English to Speakers of Other Languages, (508 South Sixth Street, Champaign, Illinois 61820: National Council of Teachers of English, 1965).

11. Allen, Virginia French, People in Fact and 'fiction, New York: Thomas Y. Crowell, 1957.

12. Allen, Virginia French, People in Livington, A Reader for Adults Learning English, New York, Thomas Y. Crowell Co., 1953.

13. Allport, Gordon W., "Reading the Nature of Prejudice," 17th Yearbook, Claremont College Reading Conference, Claremont, Claifornia, 1952.

14. The Ameridian, A Current Review of Happenings Among American Indian, Chicago, The Americitia (27 East Monroe St.)

15. Amsden, Charles Avery, Navajo Weaving: Its Technic and History, (Santa Ana, California: The Fine Arts Press, 1934).

16. Anderson, James G. and Dwight Safar, "The Influence of Differential Community Perceptions on the Provision of Equal Educational Opportunities," unpublished paper, Research Center, New Mexico State University, March 1967.

17. Anderson, Kenneth E., et al, The Educational Achievement of India Children, Washington: Government Printing Office, 1953.

18. Angel, Frank Jr., "Wheel of Fortune," National Education Ass'n Journal, 38:585, November, 1949.

19. Annal of the Academy of Political and Social Science, "American Indians and American Life," 311:266 pp., May, 1957.

20. Annals of the American Academy of Political and Social Science, Volume 311, May, 1957. The entire issue is devoted to the Status of American Indians Today, Articles are written by many "specialists" in the total field of acculturation of Indians.

21. Antonovsky, Aaron, "Toward a Refinement of the Marginal Man Concept," Social Forces, 35:57-62, October, 1956.

22. Arlitt, Ada Hart, "On the Need for Caution in Establishing Race Norms" Journal of Applied Psychology, 5:188-195, April, 1921.

23. Arsenian, Seth, Bilingualism and Mental Development, (New York City: Bureau of Publications, Teachers College, Columbia University, 1937), 164 pp.

24. Arthur Point Scale of Performance Tests, Chicago: C. H. Stoelting, 424 North Homan Ave.

25. Atencio, Tomas C., "The Human Dimensions in Land Use and Displacement in Northern New Mexico Villages, in Clark Knowlton, editor, Indian and Spanish-American Adjustments to Arid and Semiarid Environments, (Lubbock, Texas: Texas Technological College, 1964), pp. 44-53.

26. Baker, Jewell, "A Comparative Study of those Cultures Anglo, Spanish-American, and Indian, with Idioms, Proverbs, and Figures of Speech, Unpublished research paper, UNM, Albuquerque, May, 1959.

27. Basehart, Harry and Tom Sasaki, "Changing Political Organization in the Jicarilla Apache Reservation Community, "Human Organization, 23:283-9, Winter, 1964.

28. Bass, Willard and Henry G. Burger, American Indians and Educational Laboratories, Publication No. 1 - 1167, (117 Richmond Drive, N. E., Albuquerque, New Mexico, 87106: Southwestern Cooperative Educational Laboratory, Inc., 1967).

29. Beatty, Willard, W., Education for Action, (Chilocco, Oklahoma: Chilocco Agricultural School Printing Department, 1944) for education division of the United States Indian Service, 347 pp.

30. Beatty, Willard W., Education for Cultural Change, (Chilocco, Oklahoma: Chilocco, Indian Agricultural School, for Bureau of Indian Affairs, U.S. Department of the Interior, 1953), 512 pp.

31. Beer, David F., "The Trouble with the," Journal of American Indian Education, 4:13-15, No. 3, May 1965.

32. Bell, Paul W., "A Beginning Reading Program for the Linguistically Handicapped," Vistas in Reading, Proceedings of the Eleventh Annual Convention, IRA, 1966, pp. 361-366.

33. Benedict, Ruth, Patterns of Culture, New York: Penguin Books, Inc., 1937, p. 144, 1947.

34. Bennett, Robert L., and Madison Coombs, "Effective Education to Meet Special Needs of Native Children" Journal of American Idnian Education, 3:21-25, No. 3, May, 1964.

35. Bernardoni, Louis C., "Apache Parents and Vocational Choice," Journal of American Indian Education, 2:1-8, January, 1963.

36. Bernardoni, Louis, C., "Results of the TOGA with First Grade Indian Children," Journal of American Indian Education, 1:24-28, June, 1961.

37. Bigelow, Gordon E., and David P. Harris, The United States of America, Readings in English as a Second Language, New York: Holt, Rinehart & Winston, Inc., 1960.

38. Billows, F. L., The Techniques of Language Teaching., London: Longmans Green, Inc., 1961.

39. Bird, Thelma, "The Teaching Materials Center: A Case Report," The Teachers College Journal, Terre Haute, Indiana, St. T.C., 30:16, October, 1958.

40. Blackhorse, Mitchel Emerson, Miracle Hill, The Story of a Navajo Boy, (Norman: University of Oklahoma Press, 1967).

41. Blough, Glenn O. & Allan, Dodd, "Children and Their Own Resources," Childhood Education, 34:21-24, September, 1957.

42. Boas, Franz, "Introduction, Handbook of American Indian Languages, Part I, Washington, 1911, p. 93; cited by Harry Hoijer, editor, Language in Culture, Volume 56, No. 6, Part 2, Memoir No. 79. Chicago: University of Chicago Press, 1954.

43. Boyce, George, "Why Do Indians Quit School?" Indian Education, No. 344, (Lawrence, Kansas; Haskell Institute, May 1, 1960), 8 pp.

44. Boyd, Dorothy L., "Bilingualism as an Educational Objective," The Educational Forum, 32:309-313.

45. Boyer, Ruth M., "The Matrifocal Family among the Mescalero." American Anthropologist, 66:593-602, No. 3, part 1, 1964.

46. Brault, G. J., "Some Misconceptions about Teaching American Ethnic Children Their Mother Tongue," Modern Language Journal, 48:67-71, February, 1964.

47. Breathitt, Edward T., et. al. The People Left Behind, A Report of the President's National Advisory Commission on Rural Poverty, (Washington, D.C.: Government Printing Office, 1967).

48. Breed, J., "Better Days for the Navajo," National Geographic Magazine, 114:809-847, December, 1958.

49. Brett, Sue M., "A New Measure of Language Maturity," Elementary English, October, 1965.

50. Brooks, Nelson, Language and Language Learning: Theory and Practice, (New York: Harcourt, Brace and World, 1960).

51. Brophy, William A. and Sophie Aberle, The Indian: America's Unfinished Business, (Norman, Oklahoma: University of Oklahoma Press, 1966). Report of the Commission on the rights, liberties and responsibilities of the American Indian.

52. Brown, Francis, J., Educational Sociology, (New York: Prentice-Hall Inc., 1947), 626 pp.

53. Brown, Ina Corrine, Understanding Other Cultures, (Englewood Cliffs, New Jersey: Prentice-Hall, 1963).

54. Bryan, Miriam M., & Janet G. Afflerbach, New Standard Vocabulary Test, Forms A and B, (230 Park Avenue, New York, New York: Educational Measurement Service, 1956).

55. Bryde, J.F., "The Sioux Indian Student: A Study of Scholastic Failure and Personality Conflict," PhD Dessertation, 1965, University of Denver.

56. Bryde, Father John, S.J., Ph.D., The Sioux Indian Student; A Study of Scholastic Failure and Personality Conflict, (St. Louis: J.S. Swift Co., 1966).

57. Bumpass, Faye L., Teaching Young Students English as a Foreign Language, New York: American Book Company, 1963. 198 pp.

58. Bunker, Robert, Other Men's Skies, (Bloomington: Indiana University Press, 1956), 256 pp.

59. Bunker, Robert & John Adair, The First Look at Strangers, (New Brunswick, Putgers, University Press, 1959), 151 pp.

60. Bunzel, Ruth, "Introduction to Zuni Ceremonialism," Forty-Seventh Annual Report of the Bureau of American Ethnology, (Washington, D.C.: U.S. Government Printing Office, 1932).

61. Bureau of Indian Affairs, (Washington, D.C. 20402: U.S. Government Printing Office:

    Indians of Montana/Wyoming, 1966, 20 pp.
    Indians of California, 1966, 20 pp.
    Indians of Central Plains, 1966, 20 pp.
    Indians of the Gulf Coast States, 1966, 20 pp.
    Indians of North Carolina, 1966, 12 pp.

62. Burger, Henry G., Ethno-Pedagogy, A Manual in Cultural Sensitivity, with Techniques for Improving Cross-Cultural Teaching by Fitting Ethnic Patterns, Publication No. 2-0768, (117 Richmond Drive, N.E., Albuquerque, New Mexico, 87106: Southwestern Cooperative Educational Laboratory, Inc., 1968).

63. Burma, John, The Burma Report concerning recommendations for El Rito Normal School, 1960.

64. Burma, John, Spanish-Speaking Groups in the United States, (Durham, N.C.: Duke University Press, 1954).

65. Burma, John H., "The Present Status of Spanish Americans in New Mexico," Social Forces, 28:133-138, December, 1949.

66. Burris, Quincy Guy, English for Rural New Mexico, Summer Workshop, 1945, Las Vegas, New Mexico Highlands University, 1945.

67. California State Department of Education, Generalizations Relating to Anthropology, Report of the State Central Committee on Social Studies, (Sacramento: State Department of Education, 1959).

68. California State Department of Education, Teaching English to Spanish Speaking Children, (Sacramento: State Department of Education, 1954).

69. California State Department of Education, Teachers Guide to the Education of Spanish Speaking Children, (Sacramento: State Department of Education, October, 1952), Volume 21, No. 14, 84 pp.

70. Calverton, V.F., (editor), The Making of Man, (New York: Random House, 1931), New York: Modern Library, 879 pp.

71. Caplan, Stanley W. & Ronald A. Ruble, "A Study of Culturally Imposed Factors on School Achievement in a Metropolitan Area," Journal of Educational Research, 58:16-21, No. 1, September, 1964.

72. Carroll, Herbert A., Mental Hygiene, The Dynamics of Adjustment, (Englewood Cliffs, New Jersey: Prentice-Hall Inc., 4th edition, 1964).

73. Carroll, John B., Language and Thought, (Englewood Cliffs, New Jersey: Prentice-Hall, 1964).

74. Cassel, John, Health, Culture, and Community, Benjamin David Paul, editor, New York Russell Sage Foundation, 1955.

75. Cather, Willa, Death Comes for the Archbishop, (New York: Alfred A. Knopf, 1927, 1955, 1959), Chapter 3, "The Mass at Acoma," pp. 81-114.

76. Center for Applied Linguistics, The Study of the Problems of Teaching English to American Indians, Reports and Recommendations, (1717 Massachusetts Avenue, N.W., Washington, D.C., 20036: Center for Applied Linguistics, 1967).

77. Charles, C.M., "A Science-Mythology Relationship among Indian Children, The Journal of Educational Research, 37:261-264, January, 1964.

78. Charles, Carol M., "A Tutoring-Counseling Program for Indian Children in College, "Journal of American Indian Education 1:10-12, No. 3, May, 1962.

79. Charles, Carol M., "The Indian Child's Status in New Mexico's Public Elementary School Science Program, Unpublished Doctoral dissertation, University of New Mexico, 1961), 214 pp.

80. Chavez, Fray Angelico, From An Altar Screen, (New York: Farrar, Straus, and Cudahy, 1957), 119 pp.

81. "Children of No-Place, U.S.A.," What's New, Part I, No. 221, January, 1961,; Part II., No. 222, February-March, 1961, (North Chicago, Illinois: Abbott Laboratories, Inc., 1961).

82. Ching, Doris Camvone, "Effects of a Six Months Remedial English Program on Oral, Writing and Reading Skills of Third Grade Hawaiian Bilingual Children," Journal of Exceptional Children, 32:133-145, Winter, 1963.

83. Ching, Doris Camvone, "Methods for the Bilingual Child," Elementary English, 42:22-27, January, 1965.

84. Clark, Margaret, Health in the Mexican-American Culture, A Community Study, (Berkeley: University of California Press, 1959).

85. Clements, Forrest, "Notes on the Construction of Mental Tests for American Indians," Journal of Social Psychology, 1:542-548, November, 1930.

86. Cochran, Anne, Modern Methods of Teaching English as a Second Language, (Washington, D.C.: Educational Services, 1954).

87. Cohen, Felix S., Handbook of Federal Law, Washington, D.C.: Government Printing Office, 1942.

88. Cohen, Y.A., (editor), Social Structure and Personality, New York: Holt, Rinehart & Winston, 1961.

89. Coleman, James S., et al. Equality of Educational Opportunity, U.S. Office of Health, Education, and Welfare, Office of Education, Washington D.C.,: Government Printing Office, 1966.

90. Collier, John, On the Gleaming Way, (2679 South York Street, Denver 10, Colorado: Sage Books, 1962)   163 pp.

91. Condie, Le Roy, The Effect of Cultural Difference and the Education of Navajo Indians, (unpublished, college of Education University of New Mexico, 1958).

92. Condie, Le Roy, "An Experiment in Second-Language Instruction of Beginning Indian Children," Bulletin of the New Mexico Society for the Study of Education, 1:8-11, 1962.

93. Condie, Le Roy, "My Name is Hope Martine," New Mexico Quarterly, 34:179-184, No. 2, Summer, 1964.

94. Condie, Le Roy, Social Studies Units to Teach Cultural Identification for Navajo Indians, College of Education, University of New Mexico, 1967-1969.

95. Congressional Hearings: Hearings before General Subcommittee on Education of the Committee on Education and Labor, House of Representatives, Ninetieth Congress, on Bills to Amend the Elementary and Secondary Education Act of 1965 in order to Assist Bilingual Education Programs, (Washington, U.S. Government Printing Office, 1965).

96. Congressional Hearings: Hearings before the special subcommittee on Indian Education of the Committee on Labor and Public Welfare, U.S. Senate, Ninetieth Congress, First and Second Sessions, The Study of the Education of Indian Children, Parts I and II, 1969.

97. Conklin, Paul, "A Good Day at Rough Rock," American Education, February, 1967, 4 pp.

98. Cook, Mary Jane and Margaret Amy Sharp, "Problems of Navajo Speakers in Learning English," Language Learning: A Journal of Applied Linguistics, 16:21-29, Nos. 1 and 2, 1966.

99. Coolidge, Dane and Mary Roberts Coolidge, The Navajo Indians, (Boston: Houghton Mifflin Co., 1930).

100. Coombs, Madison L., Doorway Toward the Light, Bureau of Indian Affairs, U.S. Department of the Interior, 1962. The story of the special five-year Navajo educational program.

101. Coombs, L. Madison, et al., The Indian Child Goes to School, (Washington, D.C.: Government Printing Office, 1958).

102. Cooper, Shirley, "Evaluating Rural Education," Education in Rural Communities, 51st publication of NSSE, Part II, Chicago: University of Chicago Press, 1952.

103. Cowen, Phillip A., "Testing Indian School Pupils in the State of New York," Mental Hygiene, 27:80-82, January, 1943.

104. Coze, Paul, "Twenty-four Hours of Magic: The Zuni Shalako," Arizona Highways, 30:10-27, November, 1954.

105. Crane, Leo, Desert Drums: Pueblo Indians of New Mexico, 1540-1928, (Boston: Little, Brown, & Company, 1928), 383 pp.

106. Crosno, Maude Davis, and Charlie Scott Master, Discovering New Mexico, (Austin, Texas: The Steck Company, 1950), 354 pp.

107. Davies, R.E., BILINGUALISM IN WALES, Capetown, South Africa, Juta and Company, 1954.

108. A. L. Davis, Diagnostic Test for Students of English as a Second Language, (1730 Eye Street, N.W., Washington 6, D.C.: Educational Services, 1953).

109. Davis, Allison, Social Class Influences Upon Learning, (Cambridge: Harvard University Press, 1952).

110. Davis, Allison, and Robert J. Havighurst, Father of the Man, (Boston: Houghton Mifflin Company, 1947), 245 pp.

111. Deutsch, Martin, Minority Group and Class Status as Related to Social and Personality Factors in Scholastic Achievement, Monograph No. 2, (Ithaca, The Society for Applies Anthropology, Cornell University, 1960), 32 pp;.

112. Devlin, Joseph, A Dictionary of Synonyms and Antonyms, (New York: Popular-Library, Inc., 1961).

113. Dexter, Earle F., Doors to the Sunrise, (New York: Friendship Press, 1955), 116 pp.

114. Dixson, Robert J., Practical Guide to the Teaching of English as a Foreign Language, (New York: Regents Publishing Company, 1960).

115. Dolch, E.W., "How to Diagnose Children's Reading Difficulty by Informal Classroom Techniques," The Reading Teacher, 6:10-14, January, 1953.

116. Dolch, E.W., Basic Sight-Word Test, Champaign: The Garrard Press.

117. Dozier, Edward P., "A Brief Description of Southwestern Indian Speech Sounds," in Greenberg and Greenberg, Education of the American Indian in Today's World, (Dubuque, Iowa: William C. Brown Book Company, 1964).

118. Dozier, Edward P., Hano: A Tewa Indian Community in Arizona, Case Studies in Cultural Anthropology edited by George and Louise Apindler), (New York: Holt, Rinehart & Winston, 1966).

119. Dozier, Edward P., "The Pueblo Indians of the Southwest," Current Anthropology, 5:79-97, No. 2, 1964.

120. Dozier, Edward P., "Rio Grande Pueblos," in Spicer (editor), Perspectives in American Indian Cultural Change, (Chicago: University of Chicago Press, 1961), pp. 94-186.

121. Drummond Harold D., "The Staff of the Community School," The Community School, 52 Publication of NSSE, Part II, Chicago: University of Chicago Press, 1953.

122. Du Bois, Cora A., "The Dominant Value Profile of American Culture," American Anthropologist, 57:1232-1239, December, 1955.

123. Dudding, Christine, An Investigation into the Bilingual Child's Comprehension of Antonyms, unpublished Masters thesis, University of New Mexico, 1960, 89 pp.

124. Dutton, Bertha P., Handbook of Southwestern Indians, (Santa Fe: Museum of New Mexico, 1965).

125. Dutton, Bertha, Address given at third annual Dorothy Caufield Library Award, Gallup Public Library, April 16, 1961.

126. Dworkin, Anthony Gary, "Stereotypes and Self-Images held by Native-born and Foreign-born Mexican-Americans," Sociology and Social Research 49:214-224, No. 2, January, 1965.

127. Eggan, Dorothy, "The General Problem of Hopi Adjustment from Personality in Nature," Society and Culture, (New York: Alfred Knopf, 1948).

128. Eggan, Fred, Social Organization of the Western Pueblos, (Chicago: University of Chicago Press, 1950), 373 pp.

129. Elam, Sophie, "Acculturation and Learning Problems of Puerto Rican Children," Teachers College Record, pp. 258-264, February, 1960.

130. Electronic Teaching Laboratories, Everyday American English, A Modern Intensive Course of Study Employing Prerecorded Plastic Magnetic Tutorial Tapes Expressly Prepared

for Use in the Language Laboratory, (5034 Wisconsin Ave., N.W., Washington 16 D.C., 1954), 191 pp.

131. Ellis, Florence Hawley, The Indian Problem in New Mexico, Albuquerque Department of Government, UNM, 1948.

132. El Paso Public Schools, A Manual of Aids and Devices for Teaching Bilingual Children in the El Paso Public Schools, Grades I, II, III, IV, and V, El Paso, Texas: Public Schools, 1948.

133. Embree, E.R., Indians of the Americas, (Boston: Houghton Mifflin Co., 1939).

134. English Language Services, English This Way, Twelve books for six years, (New York: The Macmillan Co., 1963).

135. English Language services, English 900, Six books in a series for adults learning English as a second language, (New York: The Macmillan Company, 1963).

136. English Vocabulary Cards, (2017 South Perry Street, Dayton 2, Ohio, Visual Education Association, Inc.).

137. Evvard, Evelyn, and George C. Mitchell, "Sally, Dick and Jane at Lukachukai," Journal of American Indian Education, 5:2-10, No. 3, May, 1966.

138. Evvard, Evelyn and Robert R. Weaver, Jr., "Testing Some Implications of Counselors and Teachers," Journal of American Indian Education 5:15-17, No. 3, May, 1966.

139. Fergusson, Erna, Dancing Gods, (Albuquerque,: The University of New Mexico Press, 1957).

140. Fife, Robert H., and H.T. Manuel, The Teaching of English in Puerto Rico, (San Juan Puerto, Rico: Department of Education Press, 1951), 410 pp.

141. Finocchiaro, Mary, English as a Second Language: From Theory to Practice, (200 Park Avenue South, New York, New York 10002: Regents Publishing Co., Inc., 1964).

142. Finocchiaro, Mary, Teaching Children Foreign Languages, (New York: McGraw-Hill Book Company, 1964).

143. Finocchiaro, Mary, Teaching English as a Second Language in Elementary and Secondary School, 1958.

144. Fisher, John, "Status Symbols and Status Roles in America," Explaining the Ways of Mankind, Goldsmith, etc., pp. 349-356. Also in receipt for a fast million, Harpers Magazine, July, 1958.

145. Fishman, Joshua, "The Implications of Bilingualism for Language Teaching and Language Learning," in Albert Valdam, editor, Trends in Language Teaching, (New York: McGraw-Hill Book Company, 1966).

146. Fitzgerald, J.A., and W.W. Dudeman, "The Intelligence of Indian Children," Journal of Comparative Psychology, 6:319-328, June, 1926.

147. Fitzpatrick, Goerge and Mildred Fitzpatrick, New Mexico for Young People, (Lincoln, Nebraska: The University Publishing Company, 1965).

148. Flint, Kathleen Dush, English for New Americans, Teaching Procedures and Story Text, (Philadelphia: Book Division, Chilton Company, 1960).

149. Florida State Department of Education, Planning Materials Centers, Bulletin 22E, 1958, (Tallahassee, Florida: The State Department of Education, 1958), 49 pp.

150. Fonaroff, Leonard S., "The Trouble with the Navajo. . .," The John Hopkins Magazine, 13:14-18, 30-31, December, 1961, His land and his culture are disintergrating; yet he has resisted the kindly efforts of Uncle Sam to help him "get ahead," Why?

151. Foster, George M., Traditional Culture: The Impact of Technological Change, New York: Harper & Row, 1962.

152. Frank, Lawrence K., "World Order and Cultural Diversity," Free World, June, 1942.

153. Frank, Lawrence K., The School as Agent for Cultural Renewal, (Cambridge: Harvard University Press, 1960), 55 pp.

154. Fries, Charles C., Teaching and Learning English as a Foreign Language, (Ann Arbor: University of Michigan Press, 1947), pp. 300.

155. Fuchs, Estelle, "Innovation at Rough Rock: Learning to Be Navajo Americans," Saturday Review, September 16, 1967.

156. Gaarder, A. Bruce, "Education of American Indian Children," Indian Education, Hearings before the Special Subcommittee on Indian Education of the Committee on Labor and Public Welfare, U.S. Senate, 90th Congress, 1969.

157. Gaarder, A. Bruce, "Organization of the Bilingual School," The Journal of Social Issues, 23: No 2, April, 1967.

158. Galarza, Ernesto, Merchants of Labor: The Mexican Bracero Story, (McNally and Loftin, Santa Barbara, California, 1964).

159. Garth, Thomas E., "The Intelligence of Mixed Blood Indians," Journal of Applied Psychology, 11:268-276, 1927.

160. Garth, Thomas R., "The Intelligence and Achievement of Mixed Blood Indians," Journal of Social Psychology, 4:134-137, February, 1933.

161. Garth, Thomas R., and James E. Garrett, "A Comparative Study of the Intelligence of Indians in the U.S. Indian Schools and in the Public or Common Schools," School and Society, 27:178-184, February 11, 1928.

162. Garth, Thomas R., "The Performance of Full Blood Indians on Language and Non-language Intelligence Tests," Journal of Abnormal and Social Psychology, 32:376-381, October, 1937.

163. Garth, Thomas R., Hale W. Smith, and Wendell Abell, "A Study of the Intelligence and Achievement of Full-Blooded Indians," Journal of Applied Psychology, 12:511-516, 1928.

164. Gast, David K., "Minority Americans in Children's Literature," Elementary English, January, 1967, pp. 12-23.

165. Gates, Arthur I., Yates Reading Survey Test, Form 3, New York Teacher's College, University, 1958.

166. Gilmore, John, Gilmore Oral Reading Test, From A. Yonkers-on-Hudson; (World Book Co., 1952).

167. Gleason, Henry A., An Introduction to Descriptive Linguistics, (New York: Holt, Rinehart and Winston, 1955).

168. Goldfrank, Esther, "Socialization, Personality, and the Structure of a Pueblo Society," American Anthropologist, 47: 516-539.

169. Goldschmidt, Walter, editor, Exploring the Ways of Mankind, (New York: Holt, Rinehart, and Winston, Inc., 1960), 700 pp. for Ch. VI, use pp. 508-520.

170. Goldschmidt, Walter, "Language and Culture, A Reply," Quarterly Journal of Speech, 41:279-283, October, 1955.

171. Gonzales, Clara, "The Shalakos are Coming," El Palacio, A Quarterly Journal of the Museum of New Mexico, Autumn, 1966, pp. 5-17.

172. Goodenough, Florence L., Draw-A-Man Test, Measurement of Intelligence by Drawing, New York: World Book Co., 1926.

173. Goodfriend, Arthur, Rice Roots, New York, (Simon and Schuster), 1958.

174. Goossen, Irvy W., Navajo Made Easier, A Course in Conversational Navajo, (Flagstaff: Northland Press, 1967) (A audio tape of 64 practice lessons accompanies the tape.)

175. Gray, William, et al, Curriculum Foundation Series, Chicago: Scott, Foresman and Co., 1954-1955.

176. Gray, William S., On Their Own In Reading, Revised, Chicago, Scott, Foresman and Co., 1960.

177. Gray, W.S., and Eleanor Holmes, The Development of Meaning Vocabularies in Reading, Publication of the Laboratory School of the University of Chicago: No. 6, University of Chicago Press, 1938.

178. Greenberg, Joseph H., "Concerning Inferences from Linguistic to Non-Linguistic Data," in Harry Hoijer, editor, Language in Culture, Volume 56, No. 6, Part 2, Memoir No. 79. Chicago: University of Chicago Press, 1954, pp. 3-19.

179. Greenberg, Norman and Greenberg, Gilda, Education of the American Indian in Today's World, (Dubuque, Iowa: Wm. C. Brown Book Co., 1964).

180. Greene, Joel E., and Harry L. Saslow, "Psycholsocial Adjustment in an Indian Boarding School" NIMH Grant 00843, Progress Report, November 20, 1964, New Mexico Highlands University.

181. W.S. Guiler and J.H. Coleman, Reading for Meaning, A Program for Improving Reading Habits, Teachers Manual for books 4-8, (Chicago: J.B. Lippincott Company, 1965).

182. Gunsky, Frederic R., "School Problems of Indian Youth," California Education, Volume III, No. 6, 1966.

183. Hammond, George P., and Agapito Rey. Gallegos Relation of the Rodriquez Expedition to New Mexico, Albuquerque, : Historical Society of New Mexico. 1927.

184. Hanna, Paul P., "The Community School and Larger Geographic Areas," the Community School, 52nd NSSL Part II, Chicago: University of Chicago Press, 1953.

185. H.C. Hardwick, Words are Important, Simplified Introductory Book of Vocabulary Improvement, (Maplewood, New Jersey: C.S. Hammond and Co., 1959).

186. Haring, Douglas G., Cultural Content of Thought and Communication," Quarterly Journal of Speech, 37:161-172, April, 1951.

187. Harris, Albert J., How to Increase Reading Ability, (New York: Longmans Green and Company, Inc., 1961, Fourth Edition), 624 pp.

188. Haught, B.F., "Mental Growth of the Southwestern Indian," Journal of Applied Psychology, 18:138-142, 1934.

189. Havighurst, Robert J., "Education Among American Indian: Individual and Cultural Aspects," The American Indian, American Academy of Political and Social Science, 311:105-115, May, 1957.

190. Havighurst, Robert J., "Social-Class Influences on American Education," Social Forces Influencing American Education, Sixtieth Yearbook of the National Society for the Study of Education, Nelson B. Henry, editor, (Chicago: University of Chicago Press, 1961). pp. 120-143.

191. Havighurst, Robert J. and Bernice Neugarten, American Indian and White Children, a sociopsychological interpretation, (Chicago: University of Chicago Press, 1955).

192. Havighurst, Robert J. and Bernice L. Neugarten, Society and Education, Second Edition, (Boston: Allyn and Bacon, Inc., 1962).

193. Hawley, Florence, Some Factors in the Indian Problem in New Mexico, Albuquerque: Department of Government, University of New Mexico, 1948, 48 pp.

194. Hawley, Florence, and Donavon Senter, "Group Designed Behavior Patterns in Two Acculturating Groups," Southwestern Journal of Anthropology, 2:133-151, Summer, 1946.

195. Heilman, Arthur, Principles and Practices of Teaching Reading, 2nd Edition, Charles Merrill, Columbus, Ohio, 1967.

196. Hemphill, Rogerick, J., Background Readings in Language Teaching; PCLS Monograph No. 1, (Pasay City, Philippines: Philippine Center for Language Study, 1961).

197. Hemsing, William Moyer, "History and Trends of Indian Education in New Mexico, Administration of Federal and State Governments," Unpublished, Master's Thesis, UNM, Albuquerque, 1953.

198. Henninger, Daniel and Nancy Esposito, "Non-Education for Indians," The New Republic, 160:18-21, February 15, 1969.

199. Henry, Jules, "Attitudes Organization in Elementary School Classrooms," American Journal of Orthopsychiatry, 27:117-133, January, 1957.

200. Henry, Jules, "A Cross-Cultural Outline of Education," Current Anthropology, 1:267-305.

201. Henry, Jules, Culture Against Man, (New York: Random House, 1963).

202. Henry, Jules, "The Problem of Spontaneity, Initiative, and Creativity in Classrooms," American Journal of Orthopsychiatry. 29:266-279, April, 1959.

203. Henry, Nelson B., Community Education Principles and Practices from World-Wide Experiences, 1959, (Chicago: University of Chicago Press, 1959), 417 pp.

204. Henry, Nelson B., Education in Rural Communities, 51st Yearbook NSSE, (Chicago: University of Chicago Press, 1952), 359 pp.

205. Henry, Nelson B., The Psychology of Learning, 41st Yearbook of the NSSE, (Chicago: University of Chicago Press, 1942), 463 pp.

206. Henry, Nelson B., Editor, the 52nd Yearbook of the National Society for the Study of Education, Part II, The Community School, (Chicago: The University of Chicago Press, 1953), 292 pp.

207. Henry, Nelson B., Editor, Development in and Through Reading, The Sixtieth Yearbook of the NSSE (Chicago: University of Chicago Press, 1961), 406 pp.

208. Henry, Nelson B., Social Forces Influencing American Education, 60th Yearbook NSSE, Part II, (Chicago: University of Chicago Press, 1961), 252 pp.

209. Henry, Nelson B., Editor, The Education of Exceptional Children, 49th Yearbook of the NSSE, Part II, Chicago University of Chicago Press, 1950.

210. Herriott, M.E., "Administrative Responsibility for Minorities," California Journal of Secondary Education, 18:362-364, October, 1943.

211. Hertzler, J.O., "Toward a Sociology of Language," Social Forces, 32:109-119, December, 1953.

212. Hewitt, E.L., and B.P. Dutton, Pueblo Indian World, Albuquerque: University of New Mexico Press, 1945.

213. Hess, Stephen G., "A Comparative Study of the Understandings Which Bilingual Students Have of the Multiple Meanings of English Words," Unpublished Master's Thesis, University of New Mexico, Albuquerque, 1963.

214. Hickerson, Nathaniel, Education for Alienation, (Englewood Cliffs, New Jersey: Prentice-Hall Inc., 1966).

215. Hildeth, Gertrude, Education Gifted Children, New York: Harper and Row, 1952.

216. Hill, W.W., Santa Clara Pueblos, Unpublished manuscript, University of New Mexico, 1958.

217. Hinckley, Edward Charles, "The Need for Student Records in the Counseling of Navajo Students," Journal of American Indian Education, 2:1-6, No. 3, May, 1963.

218. Hoffenbacher, Harold B., Putting Concepts from Anthropology into the Secondary School Program, Dearborn: The Authro, 5757 Nickel Avenue, Dearborn, Michigan, 1959, Mimeographed.

219. Hoijer, Harry, Editor, Language in Culture, Volume 56, No. 6, Part 2, Memoir, No. 76, Chicago: University of Chicago Press, The American Anthropology Association, December, 1954.

220. Hok, Ruth, "Principles and Techniques Characteristic of the Oral Approach," Language Learning, 16:87-92, No. 1 and 2, 1966.

221. Holland, William R., "Language Barrier as an Educational Problem of Spanish-Speaking Children," Exceptional Children, 27:42-50, September, 1960.

222. Holm, Wayne, "Let it Never BE Said," Indian Education No. 416, March 15, 1965, pp. 4-6.

223. Holm, Wayne, "TESOL: The Nature of the Venture," Indian Education, No. 437, October 1, 1966, 4 pp.

224. Horn, Ernest, "Language and Meaning," The Psychology of Learning, The 4th Yearbook of the NSSE, Part II, Chicago: University of Chicago Press, 1942.

225. Horn, Thomas D., "Three Methods of Developing Reading Readiness in Spanish-Speaking Children in First Grade," The Reading Teacher, 20:38-42, October, 1966.

226. Horn, Thomas D., A Study of the Effects of Intensive Oral-Aural English Language Instruction, Oral-Aural Spanish Language Instruction, and Non-Oral-Aural Instruction on Reading Readiness in Grade One, Austin: University of Texas, 1966. 115 pp.

227. Hornby, A.S., The Teaching of Structural Words and Sentence Patterns., London: University of Oxford Press, Stage I, 1959, 1961 Stage II.

228. Horney, Karen, The Neurotic Personality of Our Time, New York: W.W. Norton and Co. Inc., 1937.

229. Hoyt, Elizabeth E., "An Approach to the Mind of the Young Indian," Journal of American Indian Education, 1:17-23, No. 1, June, 1963.

230. Hoyt, Elizabeth E., "Some Light on the Adjustment of Indian Children," Journal of American Indian Education, 4:26-29, January, 1965.

231. Hughes, Marie M., Teaching a Standard English Vocabulary, with Initial Reading Instruction, Santa Fe: State Department of Education, 1932.

232. Hughes, Virgil H., "A Study of the Relationships Among Selected Language Abilities," Journal of Educational Research, 47:97-106, October, 1953, See page 102.

233. Hughes, Virgil H., "A Study of the Relationships Among Selected Language Abilities," Journal of Educational Research, 47:97-106, October, 1953.

234. Hunter, W.S., and E. Sommermier, "The Relations of Degree of Indian Blood to Scores on the Otis Intelligence Test," Journal of Comparative Psychology, 2:257-275, October, 1922.

235. Hunt, Amy Passmore, "The Zuni Shalsko," Desert Magazine, November, 1959.

236. Jacobs, John F. and Marnell L. Pierce, "Bilingualism and Creativity," Elementary English, 43:499-503, May, 1966.

237. James, Preston E., "The Use of Culture Areas as a Frame of Organization for the Social Studies," New Viewpoints in Geography. 26th Yearbook of the National Council for the Social Studies, Washington: NTA, 1959.

238. Jamison, Elmer, and Peter Sandiford, "The Mental Capacity of Southern Ontario Indians," Journal of Educational Phychology, 19:313-328, May, 1928.

239. Jenson, A.R., "Learning Abilities in Mexican-American and Anglo-American Children," California Journal of Educational Research, September, 1961.

240. Johnson, Broderick H., Navajo Education at Rough Rock, (Rough Rock, Arizona: D.I.N.E., 1968).

241. Johnson, Charles, E., Joseph S. Flores, Fred P. Ellison and Miguel A. Riestra, "The Non-Specialist Teacher In FLES," The Modern Language Journal, 51:76-79, February, 1967.

242. Jones, Ann, "The Application of School Administration Competencies in a Spanish American Community," unpublished research paper, UNM, Albuquerque, 1958.

243. Jones, Lewis Wade, "The Social Unreadiness of Negro Youth," The Saturday Review, 45:81-83+, October 20, 1962.

244. Joseph, Alice, B. Rosamond, & Jane Chesky, The Desert People: A Study of the Paperjo Indian, Chicago: University of Chicago Press, 1949.

245. Jung, Carl G., Modern Man in Search of A Soul, New York, Harvard Brown and Co., 1939.

246. Kaulfers, Walter V., "Gift of Tongues or Tower of Babel," The Educational Forum, 19:75-83, November, 1954.

247. Keach, Everett T., Jr., Robert Fulton, and William E. Gardner, Education and Social Crisis: Perspectives on Teaching Disadvantaged Youth, New York: John Wiley and Sons, 1967.

249. Kimball, Solon T., "Anthropology in Education," Educational Leadership, 13:480-483, May, 1956.

250. Klineberg, Otto, "An Experimental Study of Speed and Other Factors in Racial Differences, Archieves of Psychology, 93:109, November, 1930.

251. King, Harold V., The Verb Forms of English, Lessons AND Oral Drills, New York: Longmans, Green and Co., 1957.

252. Kluckhohn, Clyde, Culture and Behavior, edited by Richard Kluckhohn, New York: Macmillian Co., 1962.

253. Kluckhohn, Clyde, Mirror for Man, New York: Whittlesey House, McGraw-Hill Book Co., Inc., 1949.

254. Kluckhohn, Clyde and Dorothea C. Leighton, The Navaho, Cambridge: Harvard University Press, 1946: 1956, 258 pp.

255. Kluckhohn, Florence, "A Method of Eliciting Value Orientations" Anthropological Linguistics, 2:1-23, February, 1960.

256. Kluckhohn, Florence Rockwood, and Fred Strodtbeck, Variations in Value Orientations, Row, Peterson, and Company, 1961.

257. Kneller, George F., Educational Anthropology: An Introduction, New York: John Wiley and Sons, Inc., 1963.

258. Knifke, John J., editor, "'Horned Moon' Navajo Lumber Products," Santa Fe Magazine, 60:4-7, March, 1967.

259. Knifke, John J., editor, "Navajo 'Know-How' Lays the Rail," Santa Fe Magazine, 59:4-6, October, 1966.

260. Knowlton, Clark S., "An Approach to the Economic and Social Problems of Northern New Mexico," New Mexico Business, 17:3, 15-22, No. 9, September, 1964.

261. Knowlton, Clark S., "Causes of Land Loss Among the Spanish Americans in Northern New Mexico," Rocky Mountain Social Science Journal, 1:201-211, April, 1963.

262. Knowlton, Clark S., "Changes in the Structure and Roles of Spanish-American Families of Northern New Mexico," A Paper Prepared for the Annual Meeting of the Southwestern Sociology Association, Dallas, Texas, April 16, 1965.

263. Knowlton, Clark S., Editor, Indian and Spanish-American Adjustments to Arid and Semiarid Environments, Lubbock, Texas: Texas Technological College, 1964, No. 7 or the Committee on Desert and Arid Zone Research.

264. Knowlton, Clark S., "Land Grant Problems Among the State's Spanish-Americans" New Mexico Business, 20:1-13, No. 6, June, 1967.

265. Knowlton, Clark S., "Patron-Peon Pattern Among the Spanish-Americans of New Mexico," Social Forces, 40:12-17, No. 4, October, 1962.

266. Knowlton, Clark S., "Some Present Trends and Prospects Among Indians of the Southwest," Western Review, Prepared for publication in the Western Review, October 19, 1965.

267. Knowlton, Clark S., "The Spanish-Americans in New Mexico," Sociology and Social Research, 45:448-454, July, 1961.

268. Knowlton, Clark S., "Spanish-Speaking People of the Southwest," unpublished paper, March 31, 1967.

269. Kreidler, Carol J., editor, On Teaching English to Speakers of Other Language, Series II, Champaign, Illinois 61820: National Council of Teachers of English, 1966.

270. Kutsche, Paul, "Cherokee High School Dropouts," Journal of American Indian Education, 3:22-30, January, 1964.

271. Lado, Robert, Language Teaching, A Scientific Approach, New York: McGraw-Hill Book Company, 1964.

272. Lado, Linguistics Across Cultures, Applied Linguistics for Language Teachers, Ann Arbor: The University of Michigan Press, 1957.

273. Lado, Robert, and Charles C. Fries, English Pattern Practices, (establishing the patterns as habits), Ann Arbor, Michigan: The University of Michigan Press, 1960.

274. Lado, Robert, and Charles C. Fries, English Pronunciation, exercises in Sound Segments, Intonation, and Rhythm, Ann Arbor: The University of Michigan Press, 1960.

275. Lado, Robert, and Charles C. Fries, English Sentence Patterns, Understanding and producing English grammatical structures, An Oral Approach, Ann Arbor: The University of Michigan Press, 1960.

276. Lado, Robert and Charles C. Fries, Lessons in Vocabulary, English Language Institute Staff, the University of Michigan Press, Ann Arbor, Michigan, 1961.

277. La Farge, "Assimilation, the Indian View," New Mexico Quarterly, 26:12-13, Spring, 1956.

278. La Farge, Oliver, Behind the Mountains, Boston: Houghton Mifflin Co., 1956, 179 pp.

279. La Farge, Oliver, Laughing Boy, Boston: Houghton Mifflin Co., 1929, Published by Poclet Library, 1959.

280. La Farge, Oliver, "Termination of Federal Supervision: Desintegration and the American Indian," The American Indian, the Annal etc., 311:41-46.

281. Laird, Charlton, The Miracle of Language, World Publishing Company, 1953, Fawcett World Library, 67 West 44th St., New York 36, New York, 1957. Premier Book 50¢.
282. Lambert, Wallace, "Psychological Approaches to the Study of Language," Teaching English as a Second Language, (edited by Harold B. Allen), New York: McGraw-Hill Book Co., 1965, Part I, Section 4, pp. 25-50.
283. Lambert, Wallace, "Psychological Approaches to the Study of Language. Part II: On Second Language Learning and Bilingualism" Modern Language Journal, 47:114-121, 1963.
284. Lancaster, Louise, Introducing English, An Oral Pre Reading Program for Spanish-Speaking Primary Pupils, Boston: Houghton Mifflin Co., 1966.
285. Landes, Ruth, Culture in American Education, New York: John Wiley and Sons, Inc., 1965.
286. Language Guide Series, Teaching English to Puerto Rican Children, The Puerto Rican Study, New York: The Board of Education of the City of New York, 1956. Teaching English to Puerto Rican Pupils in Grades 1 and 2; Teaching English to Puerto Rican Pupils in Grades 5 and 6.
287. Ledere, William J., and Eugene Burdick, The Ugly American, New York 36, New York: Fawcett World Library, 1960, (W.W. Norton, 1958, 240 pp.).
288. Lee, Dorothy, "The Cultural Curtain," The Annual of the American Academy of P. & S.S., 323:120-128, May, 1959.
289. Lee, Dorothy, Freedom and Culture, Englewoods Cliffs, New Jersey, Prentice-Hall, Inc., 1959. A Spectrum Book.
290. Leighton, Alexander H., and Dorothea C. Leighton, The Navaho Door, An Introduction to Navaho Life, Cambridge: Harvard University Press, 1944, 149 pp.
291. Leighton, Dorothea C. and Clyde Kluckhohn, Children of the People, The Navajo Individual and his Development, Cambridge: Harvard University Press, 1948, 277 pp.
292. Leighton, Alexander and Dorothea Leighton, "Therapeutic Values in Navajo Religion," Arizona Highways, 43:2-13, No. 8, August, 1967.
293. Leighton, E. Roby, editor, Bicultural Linguistic Concepts in Education, (2934 East Cushman Drive, Tuscon, Arizona: E. Roby Leighton and Associates, 1964).
294. Leonard, Olen, and G.P. Lommis, Culture of a Contemporary Rural Community: El Cerrito, New Mexico, (Department of Agriculture, Bureau of Agricultural Economics Rural Life Studies, No. 1. Washington: Government Printing Office, 1941), 72 pp.

295. Le Roy, W.J. and Cyrene B. Dinsmore, English Speaking (Workbook), Albuquerque: Home Education Livelihood Program, 1967. 104 pp.

296. Lewis, Oscar, Five Families, New York: Basic Books, Inc., 1959.

297. Lewis, Oscar, The Children of Sanchez, New York: Random House, 1961.

298. Lindzey, Gardner, Projective Techniques and Cross-Cultural Research, New York: Appleton-Century-Crofts, Inc., 1961. Chapter 7: "Cross-Cultural Applications of Projective Techniques" pp. 194-305. Chapter 8: "The Contribution of Projective Techniques to Anthropological Research" pp. 306-330.

299. Linton, Ralph, "The Essentials of Family Life," in Walter Goldschmidt, Editor, Exploring the Ways of Mankind, New York: Holt, Rinehart and Winston, Inc., 1960, pp. 227-233.

300. Linton, Ralph, The Study of Man, New York: D. Appleton-Century Co., Inc., 1946, pp. 503.

301. Linton, Ralph and Adelin Linton, Man's Way, from Cave to Skyscraper, New York: Harper and Brothers, 1947, 185 pp.

302. Loomis, Charles, et al. Culture of a Contemporary Rural Community, El Cerrito, New Mexico, Rural Life Studies, No. 1, Washington: Government Printing Office, 1941.

303. Loomis, Charles, "El Cerrito, New Mexico: A Changing Village," New Mexico Historical Review, 33:53-75, January, 1958.

304. Loomis, Charles, Informal Groupings in a Spanish American Village, Washington: U.S. Bureau of Agricultural Economics, 1940.

305. Lynd, Robert S., "Elements of the American Culture," Exploring the Ways of Mankind, Walter Goldschmidt, (editor), New York: Holt, Rinehart and Winston, Inc., 1960, pp. 30-39.

306. MacGregor, Gordon, Warriors Without Weapons, A Study of the Society and Personality of the Pine Ridge Sioux, Chicago: University of Chicago Press, 1946.

307. McCanne, Roy, A Study of Approaches to First Grade English Reading Instruction for Children from Spanish-Speaking Homes, Denver: Colorado State Department of Education, 1966. 270 pp. A summary appears in the Reading Teacher, Volume 19, 1966, pp. 670-675.

308. McCombe, Leonard, Evon S. Vogt., and Clyde Kluckhohn, Navajo Means People, Cambridge: Harvard University Press, 1951.

309. McDermott, Walsh, et al, "Introducing Modern Medicine in a Navajo Community," Science, 131:197-205; 280-287, January 22 and 29, 1960.

310. McGrath, G.D., Robert Roessel, Bruce Measor, G.C. Helmstadter, and John Barnes, Higher Education of Southwestern Indians with Reference to Success and Failure, Tempe, Arizona: Arizona State University, 1962. Cooperative Research Project #938.

311. McGrath, G.D., Robert Roessel, Bruce Meador, G.C. Helmstadter, and John Barnes, "Higher Education of Southwestern Indians with Reference to Success and Failure," Journal of American Indian Education, 4:5-13, No. 2, January, 1965.

312. McIntosh, Louis, Narrator, Learning English Early, a thirty minute sound motion picture, six year olds learning English patterns in a TESOL program during the summer before entering first grade. Academic Communications Facility, Film and Media Library, 405 Hilgard Avenue, Los Angeles, California, 90024.

313. McNerney, Katherine B., "Evaluation of TV Kindergarten Program in a Predominantly Spanish American Community," unpublished research paper, COE: UNM, Albuquerque, New Mexico., 1961.

314. McNickle, D'Arcy, "How to Help Indians Help Themselves," American Indians, Walter Daniels, editor, New York: H.H. Wilson Co., 1957.

315. McNickle, D'Arcy, The Indian Tribes of the United States, New York: Oxford University Press, 1962.

316. McNitt, Frank, Richard Wetherill: Anasazi, Albuquerque: The University of New Mexico Press, 1957, 362 pp.

317. McPherson, Orpha, "Problems of the Bilingual Child," Indian Education, November 1, 1956.

318. McWilliams, Carey, North From Mexico: The Spanish-Speaking People of the United States, Philadelphia: J.B. Lippincott Co., 1949. Although dated, this work represents the closest that any author has come to making a general survey of Mexican-American history and development. New York: Monthly Review Press, 1961.

319. Madsen, William, The Mexican-'Americans of South Texas, New York: Holt, Rinehart, and Winston, 1964.

320. Maestas, Sigfredo, "Life Styles of Lower Class People and Their Motivational Structure," unpublished Graduate paper, UNM, Albuquerque, 1958.

321. Malan, Vernon D., "Factors Associated with Prejudice Toward Indians," Journal of American Indian Education, 2:25-31, No. 1, October, 1962.

322. Malan, Vernon D., "The Value System of the Dakota Indians," Journal of American Indian Education, 3:21-26, No. 1, October, 1963.

323. Malherbe, E. G., The Bilingual School, New York: Longman Green and Co., 1946.

324. Manuel, Herschel T., Inter-American Tests, New Jersey: Educational Testing Service, 1951.

325. Manuel, Herschel T., Spanish-Speaking Children of the Southwest: Their Education and the Public Welfare, Austin: University of Texas, 1965.

326. Marinsek, Edward, The Effect of Cultural Differences in the Education of Apache Indian Children, Mimeographed, College of Education, UNM.

327. Marinsek, Edward, "The Effects of Cultural Differences in the Education of Pueblo Indians," unpublished Monograph, College of Education, University of New Mexico, Albuquerque, 1958. Mimeographed.

328. Marriott, Alice, The Potter of San Ildefonso, Norman, Oklahoma: University of Oklahoma Press, 1948.

329. Marsh, Lucille J., "Health Services for Indian Mothers and Children," Children, November-December, 1957. (Reprints)

330. Martin, Paul S., George I. Quimby, and Donald Collier, Indians before Columbus, Chicago: University of Chicago Press, 1949.

331. Mead, Margartet, "A Redefinition of Education," NEA Journal, 48:15-17, October, 1959.

332. Mead, Margaret, editor, Cultural Patterns and Technical Change, New York: The New American Library of World Literature, Inc., A Mentor Book, 1955, 352 pp.

333. Mead, Margaret and Martha Wolfenstein, Childhood in Contemporary Cultures, Chicago: University of Chicago Press, 1955, 473 pp.

334. Mead, Margaret, "New Inventions for Survival," The NEA Journal, 50:11-13, November, 1961.

335. Mead, Margaret, People and Places, Cleveland, World Publishing Co., 1959.

336. Mead, Margaret, The School in American Culture, Cambridge: Harvard University Press, 1951.

337. Mead, Margaret, "Significance of the Individual," The Liberal Context, Milford, North Hampshire: The Hunter Press, 1961.

338. Meaders, Margaret, "The Indian Situation in New Mexico," New Mexico Business, January, March, July, and August, 1963.

339. Meador, Bruce, "The Pupil as a Person," Journal of American Indian Education, 4:17-22, No. 2, January, 1965.

340. Menninger, Karl, "Who Am I?," Journal of American Indian Education, 4:27-32, No. 3, May, 1965.

341. Mercer, Veta, The Efficiency of Bilingual Children in Understanding Analogies in the English Language, Unpublished M.A. Thesis, 1960, University of New Mexico.

342. Meriam, J.L., Learning English Incidentally: A Study of Bilingual Children, Office of Education, U.S. Department of the Interior, Bulletin, 1937, No. 15, Washington: Government Printing Office, 1938.

343. Meriam, Louis, The Problem of Indian Administration, Baltimore: John Hopkins Press, 1928.

344. Miller, Bruce, So You Want to Start a Picture File? Box 359, Riverside, California, The Author.

345. Mills, George, Navaho Art and Culture, Colorado Springs: The Taylor Museum of the Colorado Spring Fine Arts Center, 1959, 273 pp.

346. Minimum Essential Goals, Revised Edition, For Indian Schools, Beginning Year, Levels One and Two, Bureau of Indian Affairs, Department of the Interior.

347. Minimum Essential Goals, Revised Edition, For Indian Schools, Levels Three and Four, Bureau of Indian Affairs, U.S. Department of the Interior.

348. Minimum Essential Goals, Revised Edition, For Indian Schools, Levels Five and Six, Bureau of Indian Affairs, Department of the Interior.

349. Modiano, Nancy, A Comparative Study of Two Approaches to the Teaching of Reading in the National Language, unpublished dissertation, New York University School of Education, 1966.

350. Montague, Ashley, Man: His First Million Years, New York: The New American Library of World Literature, Inc., 1957.

351. Mosser, Ann and Susan Motylewski, "From Navajo to White Man's Tongue," The Elementary English Review, 16:303-306, No. 8, 1939.

352. Moyers, Robert Arthur, "A History of Education in New Mexico," unpublished doctoral dissertation, George Peabody College for Teachers, Nashville, Tennessee, 1941.

353. Mulligan, Raymond A., "Socioeconomic Background and Minority Attitudes," Sociology and Social Research, 45:289-294, April, 1961.

354. Nader, Ralph, "Lo, the Poor Indian," New Republic, March 30, 1968.

355. Nash, Philleo, "Education - The Chance to Choose," Indian Education, No. 428, February 1, 1966.

356. Nash, Philleo, "The Education Mission of the Bureau of Indian Affairs," Journal of American Indian Education, 3:1-4, No. 3, January, 1964.

357. National Association of Educational Broadcasters, The Ways of Mankind, Radio Programs supervised by Walter Goldschmidt. Titles of the Thirteen Programs in Series I: 1. A Word in Your Ear; a study in language. 2. Stand-in for a Murderer; a study in culture. 3. Desert Soliloquy; a study in education; 4. When Greek Meets Greek; a study in values; 5. The Sea Lion Flippers; a study in ethics; 6. Sticks and Stones; a study in religion; 7. Legend of the Long House; a study in authority; 8. You are not Alone; a study of groups; 9. All the World's A Stage; a study in status and role; 10. Home Sweet Home; a study in family; 11. Survival; a study in technology; 12. I know What I Like; a study in art; 13. Museum of Man; a summary. Each program is a thirty minute long-playing record. The series is a fascinating exploration into the origin and development of cultures, customs and folkways in various parts of the world... an analysis of cultural rather than the biological basis for the variations of behavior between one people and another... an attempt to understand the ways of other peoples so that we can get along with them, live with them, think with them, grow with them. Address: NAEB, 14 Gregory Hall, University of Illinois, Urbana, Illinois. $25.00 per album.

358. National Association of Educational Broadcasters, The Ways of Mankind, Series II. Programs supervised by Walter Goldschmidt, each program is a thirty minute long-playing record. The series is a fascinating exploration into the origin and development of cultures, customs, and folkways in various parts of the world.... an analysis of the cultural rather than the biological basis for the variations of behavior between one people and another... an attempt to understand the ways of other peoples so that we can get along with them, live with them, think with them, grow with them. Titles of the 13 programs in Series II: 1. The Case of the Borrowed Wife;

Wife; Eskimo; 2. The Case of the Bamboo-sized Pigs; Ifugao, p. 1.; 3. The Repentant Horse Thief; Cheyenne. 4. Lion Bites Man; Ba. Ila; 5. The Forbidden Name of Wednesday; Ashanti; 6. Laying Down The Law; Summary; 7. Life of a Yurok; 8. The Reluctant Shaman; 9. The Sea-Monster and His Bride; 10. World Renewal; 11. The Isle Is Full of Voices; 12. The Coming Out; 13. The Fighting Cock Refrain.

359. National Commission on Professional Rights and Responsibilities of NEA and the Executive Committee of the New Mexico Education Association, Report of an Investigation, Rio Arriba County, New Mexico, (1201 Sixteenth St., N.W., Washington, D.C. 20036; NEA, 1964).

360. Navajo Education Conference, Fourth Annual Report, January, 1961, Education Committee, Dillon Platero, Chairman, Navajo Tribe, Window Rock, Arizona.

361. Navajo Orientation Program, Edward Marinsek, Director, 1960, (Albuquerque: The University of New Mexico, College of Education, 1960) 130 pp.

362. Nielsen, Wilhelmina, "Twenty Language Experiences Which Form the Framework of the Experience Approach to the Language Arts," Claremont Reading Conference: On Becoming a Reader, (Claremont, California: Claremont Graduate School, 1965), pp. 168-174.

363. Nine, Carmen Judith, "Experiences in Culture Shock: The NDEA Overseas Institutes on English as a Foreign Language," The Modern Language Journal, 51:89-92, February, 1967.

364. O'Connor, Patricia, and Ernest F. Haden, Oral Drill in Spanish, Boston: Houghton Mifflen Co., 1957.

365. O'Donnell, Mabel, the Alice and Jerry Basic Readers., Evanston: Row, Peterson & Co., 1954 and 1956.

366. Olsen, James, "Instructional Materials for Functionally Illiterate Adults," Adult Leadership, 13:275-276, March, 1965.

367. Olson, Willard C., Child Development, Boston: D.C. Heath, 1949.

368. Olson, Willard, and Bob Hughes, "Growth Pattern of Exceptional Children," The Education of Exceptional Children, 49th Yearbook of the NSSE, Part II, Chicago: University of Chicago Press, 1950.

369. Ortiz, Alfonso, "Project Head Start in an Indian Community," Northern New Mexico - summer, 1966.

370. Packard, Vance, The Status Seekers, (New York: The David McKay Co., Inc.,) 1960, p. 112.

371. Paratore, Angela, English Dialogues for Foreign Students, New York: Rinehart and Co., 1956.

372. Paratore, Angela, English Exercises: English As a Foreign Language, Forms A and B, (New York: 232 Madison Avenue, New York 16, New York: Rinehart and Co., Inc., 1958).

373. Parsons, Elsie, Hopi and Zuni Ceremonalism, The American Anthropoligist Association, 1933.

374. Parsons, Talcott, The Social System, (Glencoe, Illinois, The Free Press, 1951), pp. 198-199.

375. Paschal, Franklin C., and Louis R. Sullivan, "Racial Influences in the Mental and Physical Development of Mexican Children," Comparative Psychology Monographs, 3:1-76, October, 1925.

376. Pascual, Henry W., "What About Non-English Speakers?" New Mexico School Review, 42:17, No. 7, March, 1963.

377. Peal, Elizabeth and Wallace Lambert, The Relation of Bilingualism to Intelligence, Psychological Monographs, General and Applied, Volume 76, No. 27, (Washington, D.C.: American Psychological Association, 1962).

378. Pei, Mario, The Story of Language, (Philadelphia: J.B. Lippincott Co., 1949, New York, The New American Library, 1960.

379. Pei, Mario, Language for Everybody; What It Is and How To Master It, New York: The Devin-Adair Co., 1956.

380. Perrigo, Lynn I., Texas and Our Spanish Southwest, (Dallas: Banks, Upshaw and Co., 1960).

381. Peterson, Shailer, How Well Are Indian Children Educated? Washington: Government Printing Office, 1948.

382. Pettitt, George A., Primitive Education in North America, (Berkeley: University of California Press, 1946), 182 pp.

383. Pettitt, George, "Educational Practices of North American Indian," in Expl. The Ways of Mankind, Walter Goldschmidt, editor, New York: Holt, Rinehart and Winston, 1960, pp. 215-218.

384. Philippine Center for Language Study, Teacher's Guide for Teaching English, Grades I, II, and III, Manila: Bureau of Public Schools, Department of Education, Republic of the Philippines, 1960-1962.

385. Pinkney, Alphonso, "Prejudice Toward Mexican and Negro Americans: A Comparison, Phylon, 24:353-9, Winter, 1963.

386. Pintner, Rudolf, Intelligence Testing, New York, Henry Holt and Co., 1924.

387. Polacca, Kathryn, "Ways of Working with the Navajos Who Have Not Learned the White Man's Ways," Journal of American Indian Education, 2:6-16, No. 1, October, 1962.

388. Jean Praninskas, Rapid Review of English for Foreign Students, (Champaign, Illinois: The Stipes Publishing Co., 1959).

389. Preschool Instructional Program for Non-English Speaking Children, Austin: Texas Education Agency, March, 1964. 137 pp.

390. Puerto Rican Study, Language Guide Series, Teaching English to Puerto Rican Pupils, New York: Board of Education, The City of New York, 1956. Separated guides for each grade level.

391. Ramos, Maximo, Language Policy in Certain Newly Independent States, (Pasay, Philippines, Philippine Center for Language Study, 1961).

392. Rasey, Marie I, (edi), The Nature of Being Human, Detroit: The Wayne University Press, 1958.

393. Ray, Charles K., Joan Ryan, and Seymour Parker, Alaska Native Secondary School Dropouts, (College, Alaska: University of Alaska, 1962).

394. Redfield, Robert, The Primitive World and Its Transformation, Ithaca: Cornell University Press, 1953.

395. Redl, Fritz, and William W. Wattenberg, Mental Hygiene in Teaching, Second Ed., (New York: Harcourt, Brace and Co., 1961.

396. Reed, Allen C., "Ceremony in the Valley," Arizona Highways, 32:26-28, April, 1956.

397. Reichard, Gladys, "The Navajo and Christianity," The American Anthropologist, 51:66-71, January - March, 1949.

398. Reid, J.T., It Happened in Taos, (Albuquerque: UNM Press, 1946).

399. Reifel, Ben, "Cultural Factors in Social Adjustment," Indian Education, No. 298, April 15, 1957.

340. Renaud, Andre, Indian Education Today, Excerpt from Anthropologica, No. 6, reprinted by the Indian and Eskimo Welfare Oblate Commission, Ottawa, Ottawa University, 1958.

341. Reno, Thomas R., "A Demonstration in Navajo Education," Journal of American Indian Education, 6:1-5, No. 3, May, 1967.

342. Resident Populations on Indian Reservations, 1950, Washingtion: Department of the Interior, Bureau of Indian Affairs, 1950.

343. Reuter, Edward B., Race Mixture, New York: McGraw-Hill Book Co., 1931.

344. Richards, I.A., Basic English and Its Uses, (New York: W.W. Norton, Co., Inc., 1943), 143 pp.

345. Richards, I.A. and Christine M. Gibson, English Through Pictures, (New York: Pocket Books, Inc., 1945).

346. Riesman, David, Nathan Glazer, and Reuel Denney, The Lonely Crowd, A Study of the Changing American Character, (Garden City, : Doubleday and Company, Inc., first published New Haven: Yale University Press, 1950), 359 pp.

347. Rivers, Wilma G., The Psychologist and the Foreign-Language Teacher, (Chicago: The University of Chicago Press, 1964).

348. Roberts, Paul, English Sentences, New York: Harcourt, Brace and World, 1962.

349. Roberts, Paul, Understanding English, (New York: Harper and Row, 1958).

350. Robison, Helen, F. and Rose Mukerji, "Cultural Pluralism in the Primary Grades," The Instructor, pp. 34-35, 159, February, 1967.

351. Roessel, Robert A. Jr., Handbook for Indian Education, ERA, Publishers, Inc., 2223 South Olive St., Los Angeles 7, California, 1962.

352. Rohn, Ramona, "Improvement of Oral English in the First Grade in the Santo Domingo School," unpublished Masters Thesis, Graduate School, University of New Mexico, Albuquerque, 1963.

353. Rojas, Pauline M., A Critical Analysis of the Vocabulary of Three Standard Series of Pre-Primers and Primers in Terms of How the Words are Used, with Special Reference to the Language Problems of the Spanish-Speaking Children of Puerto Rico, (Unpublished Doctoral Dissertation, University of Michigan, 1945.).

354. Rojas, Pauline, "Instructional Materials and Aids to Faciltate Teaching the Bilingual Child," The Modern Language Journal, April, 1965, pp. 237-239.

355. Rojas, Pauline M., Director, Fries American English Series, for the study of English as a Second Language, Teachers Guides Books 1-6, (Boston: D.C. Heath and Company, 1957).

356. Roquermore, Lois, "Unfinished Business," New Mexico School Review, 26:8-9, 37, May, 1947. Discusses teaching reading in English to Spanish-American Children before they had English vocabularies and comprehension of meanings in English.

357. Rosenstein, Joseph, "Concept Development and Language Instruction," Exceptional Children, 30:337-343, April, 1964.
358. Ruark, Robert, Something of Value, New York: Doubleday and Co., 1955, p. 245.
359. Rubel, Arthur J., Across the Tracks: Mexican-Americans in a Texas City, (Austin, Texas: University of Texas Press, 1966).
360. Russell, David H., et al, Ginn Basic Readers, Boston: Ginn and Co., 1956.
361. Salisbury, Lee H., "Teaching English to Alaska Natives," Journal of American Indian Education, 6:1-13, No. 2, January, 1967.
362. Samora, Julian, (editor) La Raza: Forgotten Americans, (Notre Dame, 1966). A collection of essays and articles aimed at achieving an understanding of contemporary Mexican-American affairs.
363. Sanchez, George I., The Age - Grade Status of the Rural Child in New Mexico Public Elementary Schools, 1931-32, Educational Research Bulletin, Volume 1, Santa Fe: State Department of Education, November, 1932.
364. Sanchez, George I., "The Crux of the Dual Language Handicap," New Mexico School Review, 33:13-15, 38, March, 1954.
365. Sanchez, George I., Forgotten People, (Albuquerque, UNM Press, 1940).
366. Sapir, Edward, Language, An Introduction to the Study of Speech, (New York: Harcourt, Brace, and Company, 1921).
367. Sapir, Edward, "Conceptual Categories in Primitive Language," Science, 74:578, 1931, cited by Hoyer, Harry, etc., p. 92.
368. Sapir, Edward, "Language and Environment," American Anthropologist, 14:226-242, April-June, 1912.
369. Sasaki, Tom T., Fruitland, New Mexico: A Navajo Community in Transition, Ithaca: Cornell University Press, 1960), 217 pages.
370. Sasaki, Tom and John Adair, "New Land to Farm," in Edward H. Spicer, editor, Human Problems in Technical Change, New York: Russell Sage Foundation, 1952, pp. 97-111.
371. Saslow, Harry L., "Problem Check-List Responses or Adolescents in Three Ethnic Groups," New Mexico Highlands University. A paper based on an NIMH Grant No. MH 843, "Psycho-Social Adjustment in an Indian Boarding School," 1966.

372. Saunders, Lyle, Cultural Differences and Medical Care, (New York: Russell Sage Foundation, 1934), p. 172, ft. 42.

373. Saunders, Lyle, "The Social History of Spanish-Speaking People in Southwestern United States Since 1846," Proceedings of the First Congress of Historians from Mexico and the United States Assembled in Monterrey, Neuvo Leon, Mexico, September 4-9, 1949. (Mexico City: Editorial Culture, T.G., S.A., 1950).

374. Schroeder, Florence Margaret, "An Exploratory Study of Beliefs and Practices of Jemez Pueblo Indians of New Mexico Pertaining to Child Rearing in the Pre-School Years in Relation to the Educational Status of the Mother," Unpublished Doctoral Dissertation, New York University, New York City, 1960.

375. Schulman, Sam, "Rural Health Ways in New Mexico," In Culture, Society, and Health,"Vera Rubin, editor, annals of the New York Academy of Sciences, 84:950-959, December, 1960.

376. Schusky, Ernest L., The Right to Be Indian, Institute of Indian Studies, University of South Dakota and Board of National Missions, United Presbyterian Church.

377. Scott, Richard, "Acculturation Among Mescalero Apache High School Students," Unpublished Masters Thesis, UNM: Albuquerque, 1959.

378. Scott, Richard B., "English Language Skills of the Mescalero Apache Indians," America Indigena, 20:173-182, No. 3, 1960.

379. Seay, Maurice F., "The Community School: New Maning for the old Texas," The Community School, 52nd yearbook of NSSE, Part II, Chicago: University of Chicago Press.

380. Senter, Donavon, and Florence Hawley, "The Grammar School as the Basic Acculturating Influence for Native New Mexicans," Social Forces, 24:398-407, May, 1946.

381. Shaffer, Laurance F. and Edward J. Shoben, Jr., The Psychology of Adjustment, Boston: Hoyt and Muffin Co., 1956.

382. Shapiro, Harry L., editor, Man, Culture, and Society, (New York: Oxford University Press, 1956), 380 pp.

383. Shaw, James R., "Guarding The Health of Our Indian Citizens," Journal of the American Hospital Association, April 16, 1957, p. 8, reprinted by the Public Health Service.

384. Shefter, Harry, Shortcuts to Effective English, (New York: Washington Square Press, 1959), 286 pp.

385. Shipley, Alice M., "I Taught 'Related Subjects' to the Special Navajos," Journal of American Indian Education, 3:19-21, No. 2, January, 1964.

386. Simmons, Leo W., (editor), Sun Chief, the Autobiography of a Hopi Indian, (New Haven: Yale University Press), 1942. (A Yale Western Americana Paperbound, 1966).

387. Simmons, Ozzie, "The Mutual Images and Expectations of Anglo-Americans and Mexican-Americans," Daedalus, (Spring, 1961), pp. 286-299.

388. Simpkins, O. Norman, "Identification and Use of Cultural Patterns by Public Health Workers," Education for Indian Health, Progress Report, 1955-1960, Washington: Division of Indian Health, Public Health Service, June, 1960.

389. Sininger, Harlan, "An Age-Grade Study of the San Jose Training School and Its Two Control Schools, San Jose Training School, UNM, School Series, Volume 1, No. 2, Albuquerque, UNM Press, 1931.

390. Sister Noreen, "A Bilingual Curriculum for Spanish-Americans," Catholic Schools Journal, 66:25-26, January, 1966.

391. Sizemore, Mamie, Teaching Reading to the Bilingual Child, Phoenix: Arizona State Department of Public Instruction, 1963. 57 pp.

392. Smith, Anne, Indian Education in New Mexico, Institute for Social Research and Development, (University of New Mexico, Albuquerque, 1968).

393. Smith, Anne, "Indian Head Start in Northern New Mexico," El Palacio, December, 1968.

394. Smith, Anne M., New Mexico Indians: Economic, Educational, and Social Problems, (Santa Fe: Museum of New Mexico, 1966).

395. Smith, Dora V., Communication, the Miracle of Shared Living, (New York: The Macmillan Company, 1955), 105 pp.

396. Smith, Watson, and John M. Roberts, Zuni Law: A Field of Values, Cambridge: Peabody Museum Papers, 43:64, No. 1, 1954.

397. Spang, Alonzo, "Counseling the Indian," Journal of American Indian Education, 5:10-15, No. 1, October, 1965.

398. Spicer, Edward H., Editor, Perspectives in American Indian Culture Change, Chicago: The University of Chicago Press, 1961, Rio Grande Pueblos, pp. 94-186; Navajo, pp. 278-336.

399. Spindler, George D., "Anthropology in the Social State Curriculum," NEA Journal, 47:626-627, December, 1958.

400. Spindler, George D., (editor), Education and Culture: Anthropological Approaches, (New York: Holt, Rinehart and Winston, 1963).

401. Spindler, George D., The Transmission of American Culture, (Cambridge: Harvard University Press, 1959), 51 pp.

402. Stack, Edward, The Language Laboratory and Modern Language Teaching, New York: Oxford University Press, 1960, 149 pp.

403. Steiner, Stan, The New Indians, (New York: Harper and Row, 1968).

404. Stemmler, Anne O., "An Experimental Approach to the Teaching of Oral Language and Reading," Harvard Educational Review, 36:42-59, Winter, 1966.

405. Stevick, Earl, Helping People Learn English, (New York: Abingdon Press, 1957).

406. Stocker, Joseph, The Invisible Minority - . . . Pero No Vencibles, Washington, D.C.: NEA, Department of Rural Education, 1966, 50 pp.

407. Stockton Unified School District, Teacher Tips to Understanding and Stimulating Mexican-American Youth, Curriculum Bulletin No. 52, (Stockton, California: Stockton Unified School District, August, 1954), 54 pp.

408. Stockwell, Robert P. and J. Donald Bowen, The Sounds of English and Spanish, Contrastive Series, (Chicago: University of Chicago Press, 1965).

409. Stout, Irving W., and Grace Langdon, The Use of Toys in Teaching English to Non-English Speaking Children, Arizona State University and the Ganado Public School, 1963.

410. Strang, Ruth, "The Linguistically Handicapped Child: Learning English as a Second Language -- A Theroetical Model," Expectional Children, 30:14-16, September, 1963.

411. Strang, Ruth, Constance McCullough, and Arther Traxler, The Improvement of Reading, Fourth Edition, New York: McGraw Hill Book Co., 1967.

412. Strickland, Ruth G., The Language Arts in the Elementary School, The Second Edition, (D.C. Heath, Boston, 1957), 464 pp.

413. Strodtbeck, Fred, and Florence Kluckhohn, Variations in Value Orientations, (Evanston, Illinois: Row, Peterson and Company, 1961).

414. Stroud, James B., Psychology in Education, (New York: Longsman Green and Company, 1946), 664 pp.

415. Sutton, Elizabeth, Knowing and Teaching the Migrant Child, (Department of Rural Education, NEA, 1206 16th St., N.W., Washington 6, D.C., 1960), 147 pp., stock no. 45-121. Miss Sutton was project supervisor for studies conducted in 1954-57 in Florida and Virginia by the Migrant Research Fund and the executive board of the National Council on Agricultural life and Labor.

416. Sutton, Elizabeth, "When the Migrant Child Comes to School," The NEA Journal, 50:32-34, October, 1961. Discusses the home backgrounds of migrant children, suggests ways to utilize their wanderings in describing places they have been, and suggests ways to prepare them to move on to the next interim stop.

417. Taba, Hilda, Curriculum Development: Theory and Practice, (New York: Harcourt, Brace and World, Inc., 1962).

418. Taba, Hilda, "Educational Implications in the concepts of Culture and Personality," Educational Leadership, 15:183-186, December, 1957.

419. Talayesva, Don C., Sun Chief, Autobiography of a Hopi Indian, edited by Leo W. Simmons, (New Haven: Yale University Press, 1942), 460 pp. A Yale Western Americana Paperbound, 1966.

420. Teel, D., "Preventing Prejudice Against Spanish-Speaking Children," Educational Leadership, 12:94-98, November, 1954.

421. Telford, C.W., "Test Performance of Full and Mixed-Blood North Dakota Indians," Journal of Camparative Psychology, 14:123-145, August, 1932.

422. Texas Education Agency, Pre-School Instruction Program for Non-English Speaking Children, (Austin: Texas Education Agency, 1961), 62 pp.

423. Texas State Department of Education, A Course in English for Non-English Speaking Pupils, Grades I and II, (Austin: State Department of Education, February, 1930), 126 pp.

424. Thomas, Donald R., and Ralph K. Stueber, "No Desk for Carmen," Teachers College Record, 61:143-150, December, 1959.

425. Thompson, Hildegard, "Culture: The Content of Language," On Teaching English to Speakers of Other Languages, Series II, Carol J. Kreidler, Editor, (Champaign, Illinois: National Council of Teachers of English, 1966), pp. 27-32.

426. Thompson, Hildegard, "Education Among American Indian, Institutional Aspects," The American Indian, AAPSS, 311: 95-104, May, 1957.

427. Thompson, Hildegard, "Experience: Prerequisite to Language," Indian Education, No. 416, March 15, 1965, pp. 1-3.

428. Thompson, Hildegard, "Teaching English to Indian Children," Fourth Annual Conference on Navajo Education, Window Rock Arizona: The Navajo tribe, January, 1961.

429. Thompson, Laura, Culture in Crisis, New York: Harper & Bros. 1950.

430. Thompson, Laura, and Alice Joseph, "The Education of the Hopi Indian Child," The Hopi Way, (Chicago: University of Chicago Press, 1944).

431. Thompson, Laura and Alice Joseph, "The Education of the Hopi Child," in Walter Goldschmidt, editor, Exploring the Ways of Mankind, (New York: Holt, Rinehart, and Winston, Inc., 1960), pp. 187-194.

432. Thompson, Laura and Alice Joseph, "White Pressures on Indian Personality and Culture," American Journal of Sociology, 53:17-22, July, 1947.

433. Tireman, Loyd S., "The Bilingual Child and His Reading Vocabulary," Elementary English, 32:33, January, 1955.

434. Tireman, Loyd S., Children Who Speak Two Languages, Washington: U.S. Department of Health, Education and Welfare, 1953.

435. Tireman, Loyd, Teaching Spanish-Speaking Children, Albuquerque: UNM Press, 1951, p. 151.

436. Tireman, Loyd S. and Mary Watson, La Comunidad, Albuquerque: UNM Press, 1943.

437. Tireman, Loyd, and Mary Watson, The Community School in a Spanish-Speaking Village, Albuquerque: UNM Press, 1948, 169 pp.

438. Tireman, Loyd, and Miles V. Zintz, "Factors Influencing the Learning of a Second Language," Education, 81:310-313, January, 1961.

439. Townsend, Irving D., "Reading Achievement of Eleventh and Twelfth Grade Indian Students," Journal of American Indian Education, 3:9-10, No. 1, October, 1963.

440. Townsend, Irving D., "The Reading Achievement of Eleventh and Twelfth Grade Indian Students and a Survey of Curricular Changes Indicated for the Improved Teaching of Reading in the Public High Schools of New Mexico," Bulletin of the New Mexico Society for the Study of Education.

441. Triggs, Frances O., Chairman, Diagnostic Reading Tests, Survey Section, New York, The Committee on Diagnostic Reading Tests, 1952.

442. Tuck, Ruth D., Not With The Fist, New York: Harcourt, Brace, and Co., 234 pp.

443. Tyler, Leona E., The Work of the Counselor, New York: Appleton, Century, Crofts, Inc., 1953.

444. Ulibarri, Horacio, The Effect of Cultural Difference and the Education of Spanish-American Children, unpublished, College of Education, UNM, 1958.

445. Ulibarri, Horacio, "Social and Attitudinal Characteristics of Spanish-Speaking Migrant and Ex-migrant Workers in the Southwest," Sociology and Social Research, 50:361-370, April, 1966.

446. Ulibarri, Horacio, Teacher Awareness of Socio-Cultural Differences in Multi-Cultural Classrooms, unpublished doctoral dissertation, UNM, 1959, pp. 234.

447. Ulibarri, Horacio, "Teacher Awareness of Socio-Cultural Differences in Multi-cultural Classrooms," Sociology and Social Research, 45:49-55, October, 1960.

448. Ulibarri, Sabine, "Children and a Second Language," The New Mexico School Review, 40:22-23, October, 1960.

449. Underhill, Ruth, First Pent-House Dwellers of America, Santa Fe: Laboratory of Anthropology, Second Edition, 1945.

450. Underhill, Ruth, Here Comes the Navajo, Indian Life and Customs, No. 8, W.W. Beatty, Editor, Lawrence Kansas: Haskell Institute Printing Shop, January, 1954.

451. Underhill, Ruth M., The Navajos, Norman, Oklahoma: University of Oklahoma Press, 1956, 229 pp.

452. Valdman, Albert, Trends in Language Teaching, A book of Readings, New York: McGraw-Hill Book Company, 1966.

453. Van Dresser, Peter, "The Bio-Economic Community: Reflections on a Development Philosophy for a Semiarid Environment," in Clark Knowlton, editor, Indian and Spanish-American Adjustments in Arid and Semiarid Environments, Lubbock, Texas: Texas Technological College, 1964, pp. 53-74.

454. Varner, Carl L., English as a Second Language, Course of Study, Operation Head Start Project, 0162, Calexico, California: Imperial County Education Center, 1965. 57 pp.

455. Vaughn, W.F., Personal and Social Adjustments, New York: The Odyssey Press, 1953.

456. Vogt, Evon S., "The Acculturation of American Indian," The American Indian, Annuals of AAPSS, 311:137-146, May, 1957.

457. Voget, Fred, American Indians and Their Economic Development, Human Organization, 20:157-248, No. 4, Winter, 1961-62.

458. Vogt, Evon Z., Modern Homsteaders, Cambridge: Harvard University Press, 1955, 232 pp.

459. Vogt, Evon, The People of Rimrock, New Haven: Yale University Press, 1966.

460. Vogt, Evon Z., "Navajo," in Spicer, editor, Perspectives in American Indian Culture Change, Chicago: The University of Chicago Press, 1961, pp. 278-336.

461. Vogt and John M. Roberts, "A Study of Values," Scientific American, 195:25-31, July, 1956.

462. Wagner, Guy, "Toward Democratic Teacher Leadership," Midland Schools, 71:10-11, pp. September, 1956.

463. Walter, Paul A. Jr., "Spanish Speaking Americans," Race and Cultural Relations, New York: McGraw-Hill Book Co., 1952.

464. Warner, W. Lloyd, and Leo Srole, The Social System of American Ethnic Groups, Volume III, New Haven: Yale University Press, 1945.

465. Warner, W. Lloyd, Robert J. Havighurst, Martin B. Loeb, Who Shall Be Educated? New York: Harper and Brothers, 1944, 190 pp.

466. Washburn, Wilcomb E., "A Moral History of Indian White Relations, Needs and Opportunities for study," Ethnohistory, 4:47-61, Winter, 1957.

467. Waters, Frank, Book of the Hopi, New York: The Viking Press, 1963.

468. Waters, Frank, The Man Who Killed the Deer, (2679 So. York St., Denver 10, Colorado: Alan Swallow, 1942), 311 pp.

469. Wauneka, Annie D., "Helping a People to Understand," The American Journal of Nursing, 62:88-90, July, 1962.

470. Wax, Murray, "American Indian Education as a Cross-cultural Transaction,: Teachers College Record, 64:693-704, May, 1963.

471. Wax, Murray and Rosalie Wax, "Cultural Deprivation as an Education Ideology," Journal of American Indian Education, 3:15-18, No. 2, 1964.

472. Wax, Murray and Rosalie Wax, "Formal Education in An A-American Indian Community, "Supplement to Social Problems, Spring, 1964, 126 pp. Volume 11, No. 4.

473. Wax, Murray and Rosalie Wax, "Indian Education for What," Midcontinent American Studies Journal, 6:164-170, 1965.

474. Wax, Rosalie H., "The Warrior Dropouts," Transaction, Washington University, St. Louis, Missouri, May, 1967, pp. 40-46.

475. Wax, Rosalie, "The Warrior Dropouts," Transaction, Washington University, St. Louis, 1967, 4:40-46.

476. Wax, Rosalie H. and Robert K. Thomas, "American Indians and White People," Phylon, 22:305-317.

477. Weaver, Yvonne, "A Closer Look at TESL on the Reservation," Journal of American Indian Education, 6:26-31, No. 2, January, 1967.

478. Weaver, Yvonne J. and Evelyn C. Evvard, "Helping Navajo Children Change Pronunciation Habits," Journal of American Indian Education, 5:10-14, No. 3, May, 1966.

479. Weiss, Lawrence, "Kids with the Odds Against Them," Denver Post, November 29, 1958.

480. Werner, Ruth E., "An Oral English Experiment with Navajo Children," Elementary English, 43:777-784, November, 1966.

481. White, Elizabeth, No Turning Back, Albuquerque: University of New Mexico Press, 1964.

482. White, John K., "On the Revival of Printing in the Cherokee Language," Current Anthropology, 3:511-514, No. 5, December, 1962.

483. Whorf, Benjamin, Collected Papers on Metalinguistics, Washington: Department of State, Foreign Service Institute, 1952, p. 5; cited Harry Hoijer, Language in Culture, Volume 56, No. 5, Part 2, Memoir No. 79. Chicago: University of Chicago Press, 1954.

484. Whyte, William H. Jr., The Organization Man, New York: Anchor Books, 1957.

485. Wiggin, Gladys A., Education and Nationalism, An Historical Interpretation of American Education, New York: McGraw-Hill Book Co., Inc., 1962. pp. 428-463 contain Chapter 13: Establishing Schools for Spanish Americans in New Mexico.

486. Wight, Edgar, David Weston, and Clyde Hobbs, Indian Land and Its Care, Lawrence, Kansas: The Haskell Press, 1953, 91 pp.

487. Williams, Robin M., American Society, New York: Alfred A. Knopf, 1951.

488. Williams, Robin Jr., "Generic American Values," in Walter Goldschmidt, Editor, Exploring the Ways of Mankind, New York: Holt, Rinehart and Winston, Inc., 1960.

489. Wilson, Edmund, Red, Black, Blond, and Olive, New York: Oxford University Press, 1956, pp. 23-42.

490. Wilson, Edmund, "Reporter in New Mexico," The New Yorker, 25:78, April 9, 1949, and 25:80-94, April 15, 1949.

491. Wissler, Clark, The American Indian, New York: Peter Smith, 1950.

492. Wolcott, Harry F., "Anthropology and Education," Review of Educational Research, 37:82-95, 1967, Current research in the field of anthropology and education, including references to studies among other ethnic groups for whom the school is an agent of acculturation.

493. Wolcott, Harry, F., A Kwakiult Village and School," New York: Holt, Rinehart and Winston, 1967.

494. Woods, Sister Frances Jerone, Cultural Values of American Ethnic Groups, New York: Harper and Brothers, 1956, 402 pp.

495. Yandell, Maurine, and Miles Zintz, "Some Difficulties Which Indian Children Encounter with Idioms in Reading," The Reading Teacher, 14:256-259, March 1961.

496. Young, Robert W., English as a Second Language for Navajos, An Overview of Certain Cultural and Linguistic Factors, (Window Rock, Arizona: Navajo Area Office, Bureau of Indian Affairs, 1967).

497. Young, Robert, The Navajo Yearbook VIII, A Decade of Progress, 1951-1961, Window Rock, Arizona: The Navajo Agency, 1962.

498. Zintz, Miles, Corrective Reading, Dubuque: William C. Brown Co., Publishers, 1966.

499. Zintz, Miles V., "Cultural Aspects of Bilingualism, Vistas in Reading, Proceedings of the Eleventh Annual Convention, IRA, 1966, pp. 353-361.

500. Zintz, Miles V., (editor), Final Report of the 4th Annual Conference on Navajo Education, unpublished monograph, the Navajo Agency, Window Rock: Arizona, 1961.

501. Zintz, Miles V., Indian Research Study: The Adjustment of Indian and Non-Indian Children in the Public Schools of New Mexico, U.S. Office of Education, Cooperative Research

Branch, 1957. Albuquerque: College of Education, University of New Mexico 1961, 279 pp.

502. Zintz, Miles V., "Indian Children Are Different," The New Mexico School Review, 40:26-27, October, 1960.

503. Zintz, Miles V., "Indian Children in Public School Classrooms in New Mexico--Next Steps in Research," New Mexico Society for the Study of Education, Educational Research Bulletin, March, 1963.

504. Zintz, Miles V., "Problems of Classroom Adjustment of Indian Children in Public Elementary Schools in the Southwest," Science Education, 46:261-269, April, 1962.

505. Zintz, Miles V., "Reading Success of High School Students who are Speakers of Other Languages," Reading and Inquiry, Proceedings of the Tenth Annual Convention, IRA, 1965, pp. 277-281.

506. Zintz, Miles V. and Joyce Morris, "Tutoring-Counseling Program for Indian Students, 1960-1962, unpublished Report, College of Education, UNM, 1962, Mimeographed.

Author Index

Abell, Wendell, 154
Aberle, Sophie, 7, 18, 32, 33, 142, 157, 493
Ablon, Joan, 471
Abraham, Willard, 247, 490
Adair, John, 12, 32, 63, 67, 77, 78, 116, 129, 160, 163, 490
Afflerbach, Janet, 156
Agard, Frederick, 255, 295, 490
Ahrens, Maurice, 385, 490
Albert, Ethel, 171, 172, 185, 490
Alexander, Louis, 490
Allen, Claryce, 295
Allen, Harold, 291
Allen, Roach Van, 268, 295
Allen, Virginia French, 295, 490, 491
Allport, Gordon, 60, 77, 491
Amsden, Charles A., 169, 185, 491
Anderson, James G., 15, 33, 491
Anderson, Kenneth, 32, 491
Angel, Frank, 229, 491
Antonovsky, Aaron, 124, 130, 491
Arlitt, Ada Hart, 154, 491
Arsenian, Seth, 491
Atencio, Tomas, 491

Babington, S.H., 459
Baker, Jewel, 344, 491
Banathy, Bela, 410
Barnes, John, 357
Basehart, Harry, 492
Bass, Willard, 492
Beatty, Willard, 163, 492
Beck, Robert, 385
Beer, David, F., 492
Beggs, Vernon, 129
Bell, Paul W., 492
Benedict, Ruth, 37, 201, 218, 492
Benham, William J., 156, 296
Bennett, Robert L., 33, 492
Bernardoni, Louis C., 492
Berry, Brewton, 74
Billows, F.L., 492
Bird, Thelma, 365, 385, 492
Blackhorse, Mitchell E., 492
Blough, Glenn O., 77, 492
Boaz, Franz, 147, 493
Boggs, Ralph, 292
Bond, Guy, 291
Bowen, Donald 292
Boyce, George, 134, 156, 493

Boyd, Dorothy, 493
Boyer, Ruth M., 493
Bratton, Mae, 460
Breed, J., 344, 493
Breedlove, Caroline, 319
Brooks, Nelson, 292, 493
Brophy, William A., 7, 18, 32, 33, 142, 157, 493
Brown, Francis, 46, 74, 75, 493
Brown, Ina C., 44, 74, 493
Bryan, Miriam, 156, 493
Bryde, Fr. John, 355, 357, 405, 493
Bryngelson, Bryng, 290
Bumpass, Faye, 292, 494
Bunker, Robert, 63, 77, 160, 163, 494
Bunzel, Ruth, 196, 204, 218, 494
Burger, Henry, 494
Burma, John, 494
Burris, Guy, 336, 345, 494

Campbell, R., 290
Caplan, Stanley, 495
Carlson, Vada F., 219
Charles, C.M., 156, 383, 384, 387, 495
Chesky, Jane, 30, 155
Church, Joseph, 104
Clark, Margaret, 69, 78, 122, 130, 234, 248, 495
Clements, Forrest, 154, 496
Clymer, Theodore, 291
Cochran, Anne, 496
Cohen, Felix, 195, 217
Coleman, James S., 496
Cole, Michael, 405
Cole, Stewart G., 75
Collier, Donald, 185
Condie, Le Roy, 109, 165, 166, 181, 184, 186, 188, 301, 317, 337, 343, 406, 460, 496
Conkin, Paul, 33, 496
Cook, Mary Jane, 406, 496
Coolidge, Dane, 206, 219, 497
Coombs, L. Madison, 32, 33, 133, 134, 155, 156, 496
Cooper, Shirley, 386, 497
Cowen, Phillip A., 154, 497
Cox, Clara Jett, 314, 345
Crane, Leo, 497
Cutts, J. Madison, 12

Dacanay, F.R., 292
Danfelser, Maryanne, 219
Daniels, Walter, 32
Davies, R.E., 47, 75, 400, 409, 497
Davis, Allison, 64, 78, 88, 103, 497
Davis, A.L., 343, 497
Day, Marjorie F., 345
Day, Sam, 9, 32, 248
Deuschle, Kurt, 12, 32
Deutsch, Martin, 57, 58, 59, 77, 497
Dexter, Earle, 74, 497
Dixson, Robert, 292, 497
Dodd, Allan L., 77
Dolch, E.W., 31, 386, 497
Dorry, Gertrude Nye, 292
Dozier, Edward, 97, 104, 193, 204, 217, 218, 405, 498
Drummond, H.D., 375, 386, 498
DuBois, Cora, 79, 83, 103, 498
Dudding, Christine, 345, 409, 498
Dunkel, Harold, 255, 295, 490
Durrell, D.D., 291
Dutton, Bertha, 18, 33, 177, 186, 195, 217, 458, 498
Dworkin, Anthony Gary, 498

Edshammar, Claes, 9, 32, 248
Eggan, Fred, 218, 498
Elam, Sophie, 59, 77, 389, 408, 498
Ellis, Florence Hawley, 45, 75, 344, 383, 387, 499
Ellwood, Charles A., 75
Embree, Edwin, 219, 499
Evvard, Evelyn, 21, 499

Finocchiaro, Mary, 292, 499
Fisher, Mary S., 82, 103
Fishman, Joshua, 499
Fitzgerald, J.A., 154, 500
Fonaroff, Leonard, 183, 186, 500
Frances, Arlene, 459
Frank, Lawrence, 389, 408, 500
Fries, C.C., 292, 293, 296, 500

Gaarder, Bruce, 500
Gandhi, Mahatma, 92
Garrett, James E., 74, 154
Garth, Thomas, 74, 154, 155, 500, 501
Gast, David, 16, 33, 364, 385, 501
Gates, A.I., 156
Gay, John, 405
Gilmore, John V., 156, 501
Gladston, Lago, 78
Glaspey, Esther, 290
Golden, Gertrude, 460
Goldschmidt, Walter, 147, 157, 218, 501
Gonzales, Clara, 150, 501
Goodenough, F.L., 155

Goossen, Irvy, W., 501
Gray, Wm S., 325, 331, 344, 345, 385, 501
Greenberg, Joseph, 147, 502
Greenberg, Norman, 502
Guzman, Ralph, 248

Haarhoff, T.J., 402, 410
Haden, Ernest F., 263, 295
Hafner, Lawrence, 378
Hall, Eugene J., 292
Hanna, Lavonne A., 75
Hanna, Paul, 386, 502
Haring, Douglas, 157, 502
Harris, A.J., 137, 156, 378, 502
Haught, B.F., 133, 155, 502
Havighurst, Robert, 56, 60, 77, 85, 88, 103, 104, 132, 155, 459, 502, 503
Heilman, Arthur, 378
Helmstadter, G.C., 357
Hemsing, William M., 47, 76, 503
Henry, Burton, 460
Henry, Jules, 39, 64, 65, 74, 78, 503
Henry, Nelson B., 34, 503, 504
Hertzler, J.O., 157, 504
Hess, Stephen, 344, 504
Hildreth, Gertrude, 267, 295, 384, 387, 504
Hill, W.W., 219, 504
Hoffenbacher, Harold B., 76, 504
Hoijer, Harry, 157, 505
Holm, Wayne, 284, 296, 319, 505
Holton, James S., 295
Hood, Flora, 33
Horn, Ernest, 385, 505
Horn, Thomas D., 505
Hornby, A.S., 281, 505
Horney, Karen, 80, 81, 82, 103, 505
Hoyt, Cyril, 291
Hughes, B.O., 55, 77
Hunter, W.S., 154, 506
Hunt, Amy Passmore, 506

Jackson, Virginia, 319
James, Preston E., 51, 76, 506
Jamison, Elmer, 154, 506
Johnson, Broderick, 506
Johnston, A. Montgomery, 74, 75
Jones, Ann, 243, 248, 506
Jones, Lewis Wade, 286, 296, 506
Joseph, Alice, 30, 132, 155, 506
Jung, Carl G., 110, 128, 506

Kane, John, 293
Karlin, Robert, 378
Kaulfers, Walter, 146, 157, 506
Keach, Everett, 506

Keelty, Gladys, 293
Keleher, William A., 226, 247
Kelley, Earl, 16, 33
Kennan, George, 407, 410
Kimball, Solon T., 507
King, A. Richard, 405
King, Harold V., 290, 507
Kinsey, A. C., 104
Klineberg, Otto, 155, 507
Kluckhohn, Clyde, 30, 75, 95, 104, 128, 132, 152, 155, 157, 185, 260, 295, 507
Kluckhohn, Florence, 25, 33, 107, 128, 507
Kneller, George, 74, 219, 507
Knifke, John J., 186, 507
Knight, Margaret, 344
Knowlton, Clark, 246, 247, 248, 507

Ladd, John, 459
Lado, Robert, 157, 290, 293, 296, 508
La Farge, Oliver, 122, 129, 508
Lamar, Howard Roberts, 246
Lambert, Wallace, 400, 409, 509
Lampman, Evelyn, 33
Lancaster, Louise, 292, 509
Landes, Ruth, 509
Landis, Paul H., 74
Lee, Dorothy, 48, 76, 112, 129, 509
Legant, Jean, 126, 130
Leighton, Alexander, 128, 172, 185, 509
Leighton, Dorothea, 30, 104, 128, 132, 155, 172, 185, 260, 295, 509
Lewis, Oscar, 491
Linton, Ralph, 66, 510
Loeb, Martin B., 60, 77, 104
Loomis, Charles, 221, 246, 247, 510
Ludeman, W. W., 154

MacGregor, Gordon, 30, 155, 510
McCanne, Roy, 491
McCombe, Leonard, 185, 510
McDermott, Walsh, 129, 511
McGrath, G. D., 357, 511
McIntosh, Lois, 511
McKee, Paul, 325, 331, 345
McNerney, Katherine, 408, 511
McNickle, D'Arcy, 32
McNitt, Frank, 511
McPherson, Orpha, 306, 344, 458, 511
McWilliams, Carey, 511

Madsen, William, 492
Maestas, Sigfredo, 68, 78, 511
Malan, V. D., 218, 512
Malherbe, E. G., 144, 157, 395, 399, 409, 512

Manuel, H. T., 232, 247, 512
Marinsek, E. A., 196, 198, 199, 217, 512
Marksheffel, Ned, 378
Marsh, Lucille, 120, 129
Martin, Paul S., 185, 512
Mazurkiewicz, A. J., 378
Mead, Margaret, 48, 76, 83, 103, 160, 163, 229, 247, 371, 386, 388, 408, 512
Meador, Bruce, 357, 513
Menninger, Karl, 350, 357, 513
Mercer, Veta, 345, 513
Meriam, J. L., 32, 232, 247, 513
Michaelis, John U., 74, 75
Miller, Bruce, 385, 513
Mitchell, George C., 21
Modiano, Nancy, 401, 410, 513
Moehlman, Arthur, 78, 164
Momaday, Natachee Scott, 33
Monberg, Helene, 459
Montagu, Ashley, 388, 408, 513
Moore, Harry E., 124, 130
Morelock, Winifred, 460
Morgan, William, 259
Morris, Joyce, 18, 33, 280, 295, 296, 357, 529
Morrison J. Cayce, 31, 34, 389, 394, 408
Mulligan, Raymond, 84, 103, 514

Nader, Ralph, 514
Nash, Philleo, 162
Neugarten, Bernice, 56, 77, 85, 103, 459, 514
Nusbaum, Deric, 459

O'Connor, Patricia, 263, 295
O'Donnell, Mabel, 325, 331, 344
Olson, James, 515
Olson, Willard C., 55, 76, 77
Ortiz, Alfonso, 515

Packard, Vance, 515
Paratore, Angela, 516
Parker, Don H., 291
Parsons, Elsie Clews, 190, 197, 217, 516
Parsons, Talcott, 248, 516
Paschal, Franklin C., 154, 516
Pascual, Henry, 516
Patrick, Kenneth, 186
Peal, Elizabeth, 400, 409, 516
Pei, Mario, 11, 32, 152, 153, 158, 516
Perrigo, Lynn I., 225, 516
Peterson, Len, 218
Peterson, Shailer, 32, 516
Pettit, George A., 49, 76, 202, 218, 516

Phillips, Nina, 293
Pinkney, Alphonso, 516
Pintner, Rudolf, 74, 516
Polacca, Kathryn, 186, 517
Polacca, Ruth, 460
Porterfield, James, 460

Quillen, I. James, 75
Quimby, George, 185
Qoyawayma, Polingaysi, 211

Ramos, Maximo, 498
Rasey, Marie I., 72, 78, 517
Ray, Charles K., 517
Read, Margaret, 405
Redfield, Robert, 219
Redl, Fritz, 51, 76, 78
Reed, Allen C., 517
Reichard, Gladys, 69, 78, 95, 104, 517
Reid, J. T., 517
Reifel, Ben, 32, 517
Renaud, Andre, 406, 517
Reno, Thomas, 517
Reuter, Edward B., 154, 518
Richards, I. A., 337, 338, 345, 518
Riesman, David, 518
Rivers, Wilga, 296, 518
Roberts, Paul, 518
Roberts, John M., 205, 219
Roessel, Robert, 357, 518
Rohn, Ramona, 296, 518
Rojas, Pauline, 293, 300, 343, 400, 409, 518
Rosamond, B., 155
Rosenstein, Joseph, 519
Rosentheil, Annette, 74
Roucek, Joseph, 74
Ruark, Robert, 219
Ruble, Arthur J., 519
Russell, David, 344

Safar, Dwight, 15, 33
Sahai, Prem, 104
Salisbury, Lee, 20, 33, 519
Sanchez, George I., 134, 136, 220, 231, 246, 247, 409, 519
Sandiford, Peter, 154
Sapir, Edward, 147, 157, 519
Sasaki, Tom T., 78, 519
Saslow, Harry L., 519
Saunders, Lyle, 148, 157, 244, 248
Scannell, Genevieve, 291
Schermerhorn, R. A., 248
Scholes, William E., 9, 32, 248
Schroeder, Florence, 202, 218, 520
Schulman, Sam, 520
Schusky, Ernest, 74, 520
Scott, Richard, 344, 520

Seay, Maurice, 386, 520
Segale, Sister Blandina, 246
Shaffer, Laurance, 408, 520
Shaw, James, 129
Shoben, Edward, 408, 520
Simmons, Leo, 102, 218, 521
Simpkins, O. Norman, 46, 75, 521
Singleton, John, 405
Sininger, Harlan, 136, 155, 246, 521
Slager, William R., 293, 294
Smith, Anne M., 186, 348, 357, 410, 521
Smith, Dora, V., 521
Smith, Hale W., 154
Smith, Owen D., 155
Smith, Nila B., 378
Smith, Watson, 205, 219, 521
Sommermier, E., 154
Spang, Alonzo, 355, 357, 521
Spicer, Edward, 521
Spicer, Rosamond, 30
Spindler, George, 81, 90, 91, 103, 404, 522
Spindler, Louis, 404
Srole, Leo, 84, 85, 103, 526
Stevick, Earl, 409, 522
Stone, L. Joseph, 104
Stockwell, Robert, 522
Stout, Irving, 522
Strang, Ruth, 378, 522
Strickland, Ruth, 38, 74, 146, 157, 363, 385, 522
Strodtbeck, Fred, 33, 522
Stroud, J. B., 75, 408, 523
Stueber, Ralph K., 236, 248
Sullivan, H. B., 291
Sullivan, Louis, 154
Sutton, Elizabeth, 523

Taba, Hilda, 50, 74, 76, 523
Talayesva, Don, 197, 523
Talley, Kathryn, 296
Taylor, Grant, 294
Telford, C. W., 155, 523
Thomas, Donald R., 236, 248, 523
Thomas, Hadley, 294
Thomas, Robert K., 19, 33
Thompson, Hildegard, 182, 186, 523
Thompson, Laura, 30, 132, 155, 390, 408, 458, 524
Tireman, Loyd, 29, 34, 75, 133, 136, 155, 157, 220, 226, 231, 246, 247, 359, 372, 274, 377, 385, 386, 408, 524
Townsend, I. D., 156, 524
Triggs, Francis O., 156, 525
Tuck, Ruth D., 130, 525
Tyler, Leona, 358, 525

Ulibarri, Horacio, 98, 105, 109, 114, 244, 246, 390, 408, 525
Ulibarri, Sabine, 525
Underhill, Ruth, 178, 186, 217, 246, 526

Valdman, Albert, 525
Van Dresser, Peter, 525
Vaughan, W.F., 102, 104, 525
Vickery, William E., 75
Voget, Fred, 526
Vogt, Evon Z., 185, 209, 219, 526

Wagner, Guy, 35, 74, 526
Warner, Lloyd, 60, 77, 84, 85, 88, 103, 104, 526
Warren, Richard L., 405
Washburn, Wilcomb, 32, 526
Waters, Frank, 200, 218, 219, 460, 526
Watson, Mary, 35, 246, 359, 385
Wattenberg, W.W., 51, 76, 78
Wauneka, Annie, 184, 186, 526
Wax, Murray, 526
Wax, Rosalie, 19, 33, 526
Weaver, Yvonne, 527

Weiss, Lawrence, 247, 527
Werner, Ruth, 527
Wesley, Clarence, 32
Wheeler, Gonzalez, 294
White, C.C., 345
White, Elizabeth, 219, 527
White, John, 186, 527
Whorf, Benjamin, 147, 527
Wiggin, Gladys A., 527
Williams, Robin M., 87, 103, 528
Wilson, Edmund, 528
Wilson, Robert, 406
Wolcott, Harry F., 405, 528
Woods, Sister Frances, 234, 248, 528
Woodward, Dorothy, 246
Wright, Audrey, 294

Yandell, 290, 308, 344, 409, 528
Young, Robert, 32, 104, 128, 156, 167, 171, 174, 184, 185, 186, 258, 259, 295, 460, 528

Zintz, Miles V., 34, 105, 155, 157, 357, 378, 410, 460, 528

Subject Index

acculturation, 112
Accultural Psychology, 405
acquisition of language, 266
adaptability of Navajos, 178
administrator needs, 287
Adult Basic Learning Examination, 288
affective life, 16
Anaconda Uranium Mills, 101
Anayah Dineh, 62
analogies, 312
animism, 196
anonymity, 52, 208
antonyms, 313, 332, 333
anxiety situations, 19
arithmetic equipment, 370-371
Arthur Point Performance Scale, 132
attitudes
    toward death, 96
attrition, 142ff
aural-oral approach, 254

backward buildup, 274
basic institutions in society, 108
Basketmakers, the, 190
behavior in society, 109
behavior
    individual responses, 71
    role in social group, 71
    rooted in culture, 71
belief-directed change, 214
Biblical characters in figures of speech, 342
Bilingual material, 401
bilingual school, 397
bilingualism, 144
    defined, 397
    stages of, 144
    values in the Southwest, 398
    in South Africa, 399
    in Wales, 400
    in Canada, 400
    in Mexico, 401
Billy Black Lamb, 319
birth rate, for Indians, 117
Blessing Way, the, 173
bogey-man, the, 52, 202, 204
Bosque Redondo, 169
brother's keeper, my, 19
brujeria, 122
cacique, 206

cacique, describes religion, 92
Canyoncito, 166
case reports,
    Tulto, 211
    Polingaysi, 211
    Martiniano, 212
    Lilly, 212 ff
    Frank, 235
causes of reading failure, 382
cautions to the teacher, 279
cedar tea, in hospitals, 120
census,
    Indian, 1960, 7
    Indian, 1966, 8
    Mexican, 1960, 7
ceremonials, Navajo, 173
changing values, 245
checkerboard area, 166
Chihuahua Trail, 222
child rearing, 202
Children of the People, The, 30
ch'indii, 96, 175
classroom,
    as a learning laboratory, 362
Committee on Human Development, 30
Common Concepts Foreign Language Test, 288
Common elements,
    and second language learning, 152
community school, 371ff
comparative phonology,
    Navajo-English, 258
competitive achievement, 28
compliments,
    the Navajo way, 452
compound words, 341
concept of culture, 36
conflicts,
    child vs teacher, 27
conformity, 52, 80
conformity, emphasis on, 55
conjugal relationship, 65
conquistadores, 7
consanguinal relationship, 65
conservatism,
    among the Pueblo, 207
consonant contrasts, 257
content of culture, 41
Coronado expedition, 222

counseling, defined, 347
counselor functions, 347-349
course of study, place of, 360
Coyote and His Name, 319
creation myth,
    Navajo, 167
    Pueblo, 190
cross-cultural understanding, 29
culturally biased tests, 5
culture barrier, 126
culture change, 42
culture content, 41
culture, contrasting values, 43
culture, defined, 36
culture, generalizations, 42
culture, learned behavior, 36
culture, in middle class, 50
culture, process of change, 44
culture, shock, 42, 59
cultural behavior, described by
    psychologist, 46
    sociologist, 46
    educator, 47
    anthropologist, 48
cultural borrowing, 160
cultural diffusion, 45
cultural diversity, 39
cultural factors,
    in social adjustment, 12
cultural identification, 406
cultural pluralism, 40
cultural shock, 226
cumulative record, 357
curanderas, 120
curandero, 23
custom, defined, 37

derived forms, 259
derogatory remarks, 449
Desert People, The, 30
desire, for second language, 149
Developmental Pueblo Period, 191
Diagnostic Reading Test, 137
Diagnostic Test for Students of English as a Second Language, 289, 302
Diagnostician, 173
Dick and Jane, 20
difference of opinion,
    The Navajo way, 447
differences in values,
    Navajo, 183
    Pueblo, 210
    Spanish-speaking, 241
Dineh, 178
discipline at home, 146
dissimilar values, 29
divorce, in Zuni, 66
Dolch word list, 380-381

Draw-a-man test, 132
dress conservatively, 453
drouth prolonged, 191
Durrell Reading Capacity Test, 291

earth, as benovolent mother, 18
economic base, 125
economy, 113
education, as process, 65
education, as state function, 15
"Education is the ladder," 181
educational adjuncts, 152
educational level,
    of Navajos, 182
educational retardation, 132
effecting change, 286
ego needs, 53
ejido, 225
El Sanctuario, 121
empacho, 122
empathy, 63, 390
encomienda system, 193
enculturation, 82
English Reading Test, 290
English-Spanish contrasts, 269-270
enlightened self-interest, 72
equality of opportunity, 60
errors of Spanish-speaking children, 268
Ethiopian airlines, 37
ethnocentrism, 39
excellence rejected, 394
exceptional children, defined, 26
expansion drills, 275
experience charts, 267
experiences, 280
exposure, to second language, 151
extended family, 68
eye contact, 53

false cognates, 153
"father,"
    in two cultures, 145
feelings, sensitive, 62
fertility,
    theme of religion, 196
fetishism, 198
field trips, 384
figures of speech, 342
films, language teaching, 294
first hand experiences, 384
first vs second language learning, 265
folk curers, 122
folkways, defined, 37
foreign language,
    speakers in U.S., 11
four mountains, the, 167

free materials, 319
fully developing personality, 16

germ theory, 21
germs, in Navajo, 184
G. I. bill, 233
Gilmore Oral Reading Test, 137
goals of life, 109
good and evil, 171
Great Pueblo Period, 191
gringos, 228
growth and development principles, 53
Guadalupe Hidalgo, Treaty of, 169, 195

hand trembling, 174
harmony with nature, 12, 107, 170
head start, 406
health, Indian, 116
Henley, William Ernest, 247
herding sheep, 418
heteronyms, 336
historical period, 191
homonyms, 335
Hopi language, 192
Hopi Way, the, 30
Hopi Sun Trail, 198
humor, 454

idiomatic speech, 324
idioms test, 305
idioms test, 1967, 308
    scores by ethnic groups, 311
    results, 1967, 310
illegitimacy, 93
illegitimate children, 66
imitation, in learning language, 281
impact of World War II, 175
incompetent savage, 11
Indian and Northern Canada Curriculum Rosources Centre, 406
Indian census, 1966, 8
Indian Education Research Project, 30
Indians in college, 350-356
Indian Mythology, 52
Indian Reorganization Act, 41, 195
Indianness, 46
inexpensive materials, 319
infant mortality, 127
inflected forms, 259
influence of leaders, in second language learning, 151
informal tests, 290
institutions in societies, 108
instructional aids, 317
intelligence of Spanish Americans, 133
intelligence testing, 131

intelligence testing in counseling, 349
interdependence, religion and health, 127
inter-disciplinary approach, 63

Judeo-Christian influences, 91
judging behavior in the classroom, 70
judging pupil behavior, 71

kachinas, 49, 198
Keres, 192
kindergartens, 233

la familia, 229
language acquisition, 266
language families, 192
language laboratory, 284
language, principles, 263
language programs for Navajo children, 406
languages, map of New Mexico pueblos, 192
law, defined, 38
lazy, 111
learning materials center, 364
life goals, 109
life space, 56
linguistic principles, 263
Long Walk, The, 169
lost generation, 174
Luminario for Antonio, A, 16

mal ojo, 121
Man Who Killed the Deer, The, 212
Manuelito, 181
Manyfarms, 101
map, migrant, 9
marginality, 123
marriage custom, 424
mastery-over-nature, 107
materials for teaching, 291
matrilineal society, 66
"maybe", 450
meanings, 323
medicine man, 120
mentally retarded, 144
Mesa Verde, 191
methodology, 264
Michigan Test of English Language Proficiency, 290
middle class bias in textbooks, 389
middle class values, 88
migrant children, 236
migrant labor, 9
migrant, Spanish-speaking, the, 238
migrant workers, 9
minimal pairs, 278, 281, 282
missionaries, 97

missionaries, present day, 171
Modified Basketmakers, 191
mores, defined, 37
morphology, 259
mother visits school, 440-441
motivation for learning, 57
motives, defined, 393
multiple meanings, 313, 314, 325

Nambe,
    community school, 372
    teacher selection, 372
Nataska, the bogey man, 204
Navajo adaptability, 178
Navajo, changing family life, 181
Navajo, Cornell Medical Clinic, 101
Navajo, cultural borrowings, 167-168
Navajo, differences in values, 183
Navajo discipline 414, 417
Navajo-English contrasts, 258
Navajo family pattern, 176
Navajo Forest Products, 178
Navajo language, description of, 260
Navajo legends, 414
Navajo, map of reservation, 166
Navajo, New Mexico, 178
Navajo, number of school children, 165
Navajo people, migration of, 165
Navajo religion, 95, 172, 175
Navajo Sister, 16
Navajo, story of creation, 167
Navajo, values, 179
Negative self-image, 58
New Mexico State University Extension Service, 179
New Practice Readers, 289
New Standard Vocabulary Test, 140
No Turning Back, 211
Noble savage, 11
normalcy, 56
norming, idioms test, 307
Norms, Diagnostic test for Students of English as a Second Language, 303
Northian, The, 406
Northian Newsletter, The, 406
Nouns, countable and uncountable, 277
nuclear family, 68
nursery school classes, 397
nursing homes, 69

objectives for BIA programs, 160, 161
Oñate expeditions, 222
organismic age, 55
original sin, 93
Our Family, 319
overageness, 135

overlearning, 255
Owl in the Cedar Tree, 16

pairs, words associated in, 340
parent involvement, 14, 21
partera, 23, 120
patrilineal society, 67
patrones, 223
peones, 223
Perceiving, Behaving, Becoming, 17
percentile norms, idioms test, 309
personal questions, 449
personality, respect for, 349
pets, 21
Phonics Survey Test, 291
phonology, 255
picture file, 315, 365-368
pictures, for language teaching, 271-272
pilgrimages, 121
"pillars of society", 85
planning time, importance of, 362
post war educational opportunity, 233
prejudice, 60
pre-marital sex experience, 204-5
prepositions, 336-340
present time orientation, 17
preserving harmony, 18
Primer for Parents, 391
principles of growth and development, 53ff
professional books, for TESOL, 291
progressive retardation, 132-134
Poor Family, The, 35
Protestant Ethic, The, 64, 85
puberty rite, 422
pueblo, 193
Pueblo Bonito, 187
Pueblo, cultural values in conflict, 210
Pueblo Indian,
    Creation Myth, 190
Pueblo Indian population, 187
Pueblo Lands Act, 194
Pueblo personality, 193
Pueblos, Map of villages, 188
Public Law 815, 10
Public Law 874, 10
Puerto Rican Study, 31
Purposes of education questioned, 22

quick class survey, 5

Rapid Test: Vocabulary Game, 288
reading and writing, in second language learning, 281
reading levels, 381
reading readiness, 301

Regional Educational Laboratories, 404
Regressive Renaissance, 191
religion,
    Navajo, 175
    the old cacique explains, 92
    Pueblo theme, 196
religions, separation of, 199
religious ceremonies, 455
religious crimes code, 195
remedial education, 403
remedial reading instruction, 375
research in progress, 404
respect for elders, 229
Revolt of 1680, 168, 193
River Men Ritual, 203
Rough Rock Demonstration School, 405
royalties, Navajo tribal, 182

Saints days, 199
San Gabriel, 7
Sangre de Cristo, 101
Santa Fe Ring, 225
scale of acculturation, 114
scale for determining reader level, 381
school attendance, and second language learning, 151
school program in TESOL, 280
school pushouts, 20
schools, perpetuate stereotypes, 15
science equipment, 368-370
science teaching, 383
second language teaching, 261
second vs first language learning, 265
self-awareness, 72
self-concept, 58
sentence patterns, 280
Shalako, 67, 194
shaman, 199
shame, as discipline, 202
sharing,
    food, 69
    the Navajo way, 454
Silent Reading Diagnostic Test, 291
similes, 341
Singer, education of a, 173
situational language, 285
slave trade, 168
snake, as sacred, 197
sobadores, 120
social class, defined, 84
social disorganization, 126
social distance,
    measuring, 390
    between teacher and pupil, 209
social mobility, 90

socio-cultural differences, 98
sociogram, 392
socio-economics, in second language learning, 151
Soyoku, bogey-man, 204
Spanish-English contrasts, 269-270
Spanish Jurisprudence, 224
Spanish-speaking migrant, 238
specific practices in behavior, 109
Spirit World, The, 92
Stanford, studies in education and culture, 404
status, in Pueblo life, 201
stealing, 172
stereotypes, 111, 363
stock reduction, 107, 170
story of creation,
    Navajo, 167
    Pueblo, 190
structured language, 285
Study of Scholastic Failure and Personality Conflict, 405
subjugation to nature, 107
substitution drill, 272
Sun Chief, 79, 102
susto, 123

taboos, defined, 38
taboos, Navajo, 175
Talayesva, 79, 197
TESOL materials, 292
teacher selection at Nambe, 374
teaching aids, 315
Teaching Films Custodians, 294
teaching science, 383
Teaching Spanish Speaking Children, 390
teasing, 452
Test of Aural Comprehension, 290
testing level of understanding, 287
tests, culturally biased, 5
Tewa, 192
time orientation, 12, 28, 453-454
time orientation,
    Navajo, 183
    Pueblo, 210
    Spanish-speaking, 241
Tiwa, 192
tourists, on the reservation, 180
Towa, 192
transformations, 275-277
translation, 146
transmit the cultural heritage, 15
Treacherous Savage, 11
tribal council, 178
trust, in White Man, 176
tuberculosis, cause of, 184
twins, attitude toward, 206

underworlds, the, 171, 190
unsolved problems, 388
untranslatable words, 153
upper class, 85
upward mobility, 87
uranium, 175

value - directed change 215
values, compared, 430
values, middle class, 87
values, Navajo, 179
verbal symbols conditioned by culture, 148
vernacular of child, 281
visiting the hogan, 451
vocabulary, 280

vocabulary deficit, 297-298
vocabulary load of textbooks, 300
vocabulary sizes,
   listening, 24
   speaking, 24
vowel contrasts, 256

wage economy, 177
Warriors Without Weapons, 30
Wechsler Adult Intelligence Scale, 349
Witchcraft, 121, 173
words, associated in pairs, 340
World View, 216
World War II, impact of, 175
Zunian language, 192